Jürgen Deters

Analytics and Intuition in the Process of Selecting Talent

Jürgen Deters

Analytics and Intuition in the Process of Selecting Talent

A Holistic Approach

DE GRUYTER

This publication was funded by the Open Access Publication Fund of the Leuphana University Lüneburg.

Jürgen Deters is Professor for Human Resource Management and Leadership at the Institute for Management and Organization, Leuphana University, Lüneburg, Germany.

ISBN 978-3-11-099273-1
e-ISBN (PDF) 978-3-11-098096-7
e-ISBN (EPUB) 978-3-11-098117-9
DOI https://doi.org/10.1515/9783110980967

Library of Congress Control Number: 2022942662

Bibliographic information published by the Deutsche Nationalbibliothek
The Deutsche Nationalbibliothek lists this publication in the Deutsche Nationalbibliografie; detailed bibliographic data are available on the internet at http://dnb.dnb.de.

Cover image: Kenishirotie/iStock/Getty Images Plus
Typesetting: Integra Software Services Pvt. Ltd.
Printing and binding: CPI books GmbH, Leck

www.degruyter.com

Content overview

Contents

List of abbreviations

AC	Assessment center
ADM	Automated decision-making
AI	Artificial intelligence
AIM	Agor Intuitive Management Survey
CEO	Chief executive officer
CEST	Cognitive-experiential self-theory
CoSI	Cognitive Style Indicator
CPI	Corruption (perception) index
CSI	Cognitive Style Index
CV	Curriculum vitae
DIN	Deutsche Industrie Norm (German Institute for Standardization)
DISC	Dominance, Influence, Steadiness, Conscientiousness
ed.; eds	Editor; editors
e.g.,	Exempli gratia (meaning: for example)
et al.	et alii (masculine), et aliae (feminine) or et alia (neuter), in all cases meaning "and others"
EPI	Eysenck Personality Inventory
EU-DSGVO	European Union Data Protection Regulation; Datenschutz Grundverordnung
GDMS	General decision-making style
GMAT	Graduate Management Admission Test
HBDI	Herrmann Brain Dominance Instrument
HR	Human resource(s)
HRM	Human resource management/people management
Ibid.	ibidem (in the same place)
i.e.	id est (that is)
I/O	Industrial/organizational
ISI	International Survey on Intuition
ISO	International Organization for Standardization
IT	Information technology
IQ	Intelligence quotient
IQ 2	Intuition Quotient Test or CPI Cappon intuition profile
KSAOs	Knowledge, skills, abilities, and other characteristics
LNTSP	Linear–Nonlinear Thinking Style Profile
MBTI	Myers-Briggs Type Indicator
M&A	Mergers and acquisitions
MNE	Multinational enterprise
NEO-PI-R	NEO Personality Inventory Revised
PID	Preference for intuition and deliberation
R & D	Research and development
REI	Rational Experiential Inventory
sic	Sic erat scriptum (thus written)
SHRM	Society for Human Resource Management
SME	Small and medium enterprises
SMS	Short Message Service
UK	United Kingdom
VUCA	Volatile Uncertain Complex Ambiguous

https://doi.org/10.1515/9783110980967-204

List of figures

https://doi.org/10.1515/9783110980967-205

1 Introduction

It is not enough to know; we must apply. It is not enough to will, we must act. (Goethe)

1.1 Intuition and analytics in the process of identifying suitable talent

1.1.1 The significance of selecting suitable talent

A company's success is significantly influenced by the professionalism and quality of decision-making, especially selecting decisions to hire suitable talent. The term "talent" can be taken to mean as someone who has talent (talent as the sum of one's abilities) and someone who is a talent. Leadership talent makes a difference in organizational success, has the potential to succeed as a leader, and thus will hold corresponding pivotal positions. In this book, we focus on the selection and acquisition of leadership talent, since such talent is more difficult to find in the market and, at the same time, more challenging to select.

Selecting these talented individuals is one of the most critical components of effective organizations (Church et al., 2015, p. 17). Hardly any other corporate decision has such significant effects on corporate success as talent selection. Recruiting and personnel selection are also the first steps in promoting capability building and creating successful teams. For example, Warren Buffet, renowned for his investing prowess, says, "I have only two jobs. One is to attract and keep outstanding managers to run our various operations" (Schwantes, 2019). This highlights the need for an effective and efficient personnel selection process and to improve the diagnostic performance of such procedures (Isson & Harriott, 2016, pp. 179–180). In addition, the increasing diversity of applicants, global competitiveness, and the lack of qualified personnel in specific labor and job markets also increase the importance of high-quality personnel selection processes.

The Covid-19 pandemic has profoundly changed recruiting and especially personnel selection. Due to flexible working policies such as mobile and remote working, location no longer limits the talent pool, and thus, many recruiters have access to a broader pool of applicants. At the same time, virtual or video-based job interviews, digitally performed test procedures, case studies, or assessment centers have become the new normal. As shown in Chapter 8, digital instruments and methods, algorithms, and increasingly, AI, are used to support recruiting and selecting personnel. In many countries, candidates have several options in the labor market, and thus, companies are increasingly becoming applicants for well-suited candidates and have to sell and present themselves as attractive employers. The company's

https://doi.org/10.1515/9783110980967-001

reputation is essential to attract the right talent, and recruiters and selection managers must build a positive relationship with candidates, using their intuitions and emotions.

Organizations are increasingly moving away from traditional post-and-pray recruiting and using active sourcing to attract the right talent via various recruiting channels. Related tasks such as recruiting analytics are becoming more critical. It is becoming increasingly essential to compile data about potential candidates, make it available at the push of a button, analyze it regularly, and draw the correct conclusion to act as effectively as possible, in the company's interests. Recruiting analytics could be used to analyze and optimize the process steps continuously in applicant tracking systems. For example, key figures such as time-to-hire or cost per qualified applicant can be collected to draw appropriate conclusions and create added value for the business.

As an example, global companies face the challenge of examining high-quality personnel selection procedures regarding their suitability for attracting (international) talent as well as considering the acceptance of such practices worldwide (König et al., 2010, p. 23). Therefore, in Chapter 7, the correlations between country cultures and the acceptance and use of rational-analytical and intuitive elements in personnel selection are discussed, in more detail.

Selection decisions are based on judgments. According to Gerrig (2015, p. 322), judging is how people form opinions, reach conclusions, and critically evaluate events and people. Deciding is choosing between alternatives, selecting, and rejecting existing possibilities. Suppose these two terms are now related to personnel diagnostics. In that case, it can be seen that decision-makers form a personal opinion about the candidates and assess them analytically and intuitively during the application process – they make a judgment. The hiring managers then select one of the applicants for a role among several alternative candidates – they make a hiring decision.

Every day, managers make countless judgments and selection decisions about personnel. Selection gathers information to assess, evaluate, judge, and pick individuals with job-relevant competencies and decide who should be employed in particular jobs. And hiring means offering candidates a contract of employment and employing them, based on the selection process results.

An applicant is someone who has applied for a job, and a candidate is a person who is – after some filtering processes – being considered for a position by the organization. Thus, not every applicant is a candidate. Furthermore, this definition of a candidate may differ from the one when talking about "candidate experience." In "candidate experience," a candidate is anyone with even a nominal interest in working for an organization, who clicks and reads job ads, or social media feeds of the organization, visits the company's website, etc., but does not necessarily have to apply for a job. Thus, candidate experience can be defined as that which all interested persons and job seekers, applicants, and candidates experience and the resulting perceptions about the organization, which develop from the processes, practices (including using AI such as chatbots, robots, etc.), and interaction with the organization during any stages of the recruitment process.

The hiring decision comes at the end of the selection process. Since in practice, the selection and hiring managers are usually the same, the terms "hiring managers" and "personnel selection managers" are used interchangeably. Since judging and deciding cannot always be clearly separated, in this book, the terms "selection decision" and "hiring decision" are also used interchangeably.

On an analytical level, the process of recruiting the right employees can be divided into: 1) sourcing and attracting (potential) applicants with the appropriate KSAOs and bringing together those with jobs to fill and those seeking jobs (Kumari & Malhotra, 2013, p. 34); 2) assessing and selecting applicants; and 3) hiring and employing (acceptance of job offer) applicants. But, in practice and on the phenomenological level, personnel sourcing and attraction, selection, hiring, and employing cannot be viewed independently because they interact – especially in interviews – with one another. And, even if HR Managers or personnel consultants carry out tests (e.g., cognitive ability or personality test) for applicants and only communicate the test results to the selecting companies or line managers, they will be asked what the results mean for personnel selection and what recommendations they make, in this regard.

Especially in labor markets with a shortage of qualified applicants, companies often lower their job requirements to hire reasonably suitable applicants. In Germany, for example, the Federal Police have reduced the requirements for applicants because they would otherwise not be able to recruit the required number of staff. In this context, the Federal Police speaks of "adapting to the social changes of young people in terms of the mental and physical requirements for the police profession" (Sanches, 2020). Likewise, companies tend to raise their requirements in labor markets with a surplus of qualified personnel.

Thus, a mixture of attracting, selecting, and hiring processes occurs, in practice. Moreover, evaluating candidates in a recruitment process and deciding for or against hiring them are intertwined and influence each other. Thus, evaluation and decision-making processes are very difficult to distinguish, in practice.

In scientific literature, the concept, and thus, the definition of decision is often understood as a "more or less deliberate, conscious, pondering and goal-oriented action" in the sense of the preferential advantage of one or more options over others (Pfister et al., 2017, pp. 2–3).

But human decisions are not always made in a conscious, balanced, and well-considered manner. Instead, decision-making is often an automatic or semi-automatic process, e.g., based on habits and activities practiced repeatedly. For example, many people know the experience of arriving at a destination in a car without any awareness of actually having made conscious decisions while driving. According to Svensson (1996, p. 263), such semi-automatic actions of humans are – besides the creative-problem-solving aspect – a particular form of intuitive decisions.

Thus, even if someone consciously chooses a person when selecting personnel, the decision-making processes are also influenced by intuitive judgments, emotions, and subjective perceptions.

1.1.2 The significance of intuition in selecting talent

Intuition is the ability to understand something immediately, without conscious reasoning and noticeable cognitive effort. Children build an intuitive model of how the world works through socialization at a young age. Through their experiences in interacting with the world where they grow up, they implicitly learn various situational patterns and develop intuitive expertise (Patterson & Eggleston, 2017, p. 18). Thus, intuition is more than a gut feeling; it's a source of knowledge and pattern recognition that is often emotionally charged. And, intuitive processes in judgment and decision-making are responsible for associative information integration and output formation, e.g., specific preferences or decisions (Betsch & Glöckner, 2010, p. 279). Intuition is an "experience of knowing without knowing the reasons" (Salas et al., 2010, p. 944); it is a kind of felt knowledge that one cannot, or can only, with difficulty, justify with words (Gigerenzer & Gaissmair, 2015, p. 20; for a more differentiated discussion of the concept and content of intuition, see Sections 4.1 and 4.2).

Hiring managers know the situation. "On paper, the candidate seems perfect: excellent qualifications, the experience that is relevant to the job, good letters of reference, and so on. The candidate also answers your questions well. However, you sense something about the candidate during the interview that makes you uneasy. Although you cannot identify its source, you have a distinct sensation that hiring this person would be a mistake. What do you do? Do you ignore your feelings and try to analyze the hiring decision in a strictly 'rational' manner? Or do you trust your feelings and use these as a way of identifying a 'reason' not to hire the candidate" (Hogarth, 2003, p. 2)?

In particular, the final decisions in personnel diagnostics are often not scientifically or analytically guided. Instead, practitioners rely on their intuition and regard it as a suitable basis, or even, essential guidance for their decision-making.

Candidates also have similar experiences. The salary is correct, the tasks are exciting, and the new city is also appealing. And yet, the job offer feels wrong. While the rational mind lists the facts and the advantages on the plus side, intuition says something is not right and gives an uncomfortable feeling. Half (2019) shows that 43% of employees, who started a job despite bad gut feelings, quit. And 35% remained in the position, unhappily. In four out of five cases, to have accepted a job offer that applicants were intuitively unconvinced about turned out to be a mistake. Ignoring intuition, thus, does not seem to be a good idea. Candidates are well-advised to listen to their intuition and follow the motto: "The head thinks the gut steers." Flaherty & Pappas (2004) use the example of salespeople to show that they do not act purely rationally when choosing their employer. Instead, job selection is rather based on a bounded rationality perspective. Thus, subjective impressions of the job and the associated intuitive evidence of the organization have a decisive influence on their decision to choose an employer and accept a job offer.

Neuroscientific research on intuition shows that the influence of intuition on human decisions cannot be eliminated entirely (Roth, 2009, pp. 301 and 549). Moreover, the research of Kahneman (2012, p. 33) confirms that the intuitive system is permanently active. Psychological research on decision-making also confirms the finding of neuroscience that intuition cannot wholly be switched off (Pfister et al., 2017, p. 347).

Intuition is considered a part of every decision and an integral part of the decision-making process (Salas et al., 2010, p. 966). The neuroscientist, Daniel Levitin, states in his book on "Successful aging" (2020, pp. XI–XII): "Yes, older minds might process information more slowly than younger ones, but they can intuitively synthesize a lifetime of information and make smarter decisions, based on decades of learning from their mistakes."

Intuitions are part of human judgments, and they are ever-present and real phenomena. And, what's present and real must be taken seriously. Practice and research show that intuitive assessments are also the rule in personnel selection (Highhouse, 2008, p. 33; Lèvy-Leboyer, 1994, p. 173). Personnel managers and executives attribute a high degree of influence in personnel selection to intuition (Malewska, 2015; Malewska & Sajdak, 2014, p. 44.; Van der Zee et al., 2002, p. 176). In addition, even when using a scientifically based personnel selection procedure, an intuitive decision is usually made at the end (Lohaus & Habermann, 2013, p. 225).

This regularly involves an integrative interaction of different types of intuition described in Section 4.1.3: the expert, moral, creative, and social type of intuition.

Unconscious and preconscious processes are constantly active and influence our current decisions by processing early cognitive and emotional experiences (Roth, 2010, pp. 16–18). Neuroscience shows that decisions are unconsciously prepared in the limbic system and can be located there, even a few milliseconds before the decision is made (Soon et al., 2008; Roth, 2010).

"If it is accepted that intuition cannot be completely avoided and that it can be helpful, then it represents a way of knowing that is, on its face, mysterious. It is, by its nature, not easy to grasp. At the same time, it exists, and hence is known, albeit intuitively, through experience, and deserves our attention in the interests of professional competence and effectiveness. Focus and effort are required to advance beyond an 'intuitive' understanding of intuition" (Alred, G., 2012, p. 2).

Steve Jobs, the legendary founder of Apple, is credited with the following quote (Medeiros, 2018):

> Intuition counts! Intuition is a very powerful thing, more powerful than intellect . . . that's had a big impact on my work.

Richard Branson (2021), an English entrepreneur and investor, and founder of the Virgin Group, is reported to have said:

> In the same way that I tend to make up my mind about people within
> thirty seconds of meeting them, I also make up my mind about whether
> a business proposal excites me within about thirty seconds of looking
> at it. I rely far more on gut instinct than researching huge amounts of statistics.

Albert Einstein said:

> The intuitive mind is a sacred gift, and the rational mind is a faithful servant.
> We have created a society that honors the servant and has forgotten the gift (Quoted in Gigerenzer & Gaissmaier, 2015, p. 19).

Ralph Waldo Emerson is quoted with the sentence (Paprika, 2008, p. 20):

> The primary wisdom is intuition.

Rita Levi Montalcini (1909–2012), an Italian Nobel Laureate in Medicine (1986), said:

> I don´t believe there would be any science without intuition. (Quoted in Fröse et al., 2015b, p. 1)

The personnel and management consultant, Reinhard Sprenger, well known in Germany, writes that he wouldn't know how to decide between various applicants without using his intuition; deciding based on intuition is his experience and competence. Having the right intuition is the crucial part of the expertise of selection managers and what sets them apart and distinguishes them from others. Thus, trust your gut feelings in selection decisions (2012, p. 247).

We all know the advice given to people when they have to decide between two jobs, to listen to their gut.

For the psychologically oriented intuition researcher, Gigerenzer, the real question is not whether, but when, we can rely on our intuition (Gigerenzer, 2007, p. 25).

Although intuition has its positive aspects, it can fail, primarily because it can be based on unconscious biases, stereotypes, prejudices, or other learned unquestioned thought patterns.

1.1.3 The significance of rational-analytical procedures in selecting talent

Rationality has been regarded as a desirable goal, since the Enlightenment. Humans have the competence to be rational-analytical in principle. To decide based on analytics means to examine information in a conscious, logical, and systematic process, breaking a problem down into smaller elements (see the Greek verb "*analyein*" – to break up), weighing the pros and cons, and so on. To judge and behave rationally means to use knowledge and decide based on clear and objective reason, on a well-grounded, transparent, understandable, and verifiable justification; and these reasons should support attainment of one's goals.

Thus, many people would like always to know how to make the right decision by behaving in the most rational-analytical way possible. They assume that the higher the rational-analytical effort they put into a decision-making process, the better the output quality. Likewise is the assumption that analytical thinking and calculating is the only true path to knowledge. However, it neglects emotional aspects that are concealed behind reason. Logical and abstract thinking is glorified. This devaluation of intuitions and emotions is partly due to the fact that in science and practice, conscious and constructive reflection on intuitions are neglected and may have led many people to not really understand and interpret their intuitions (Fröse et al., 2015b, p. 4).

Based on psychometric thinking, rational-analytical selection methods are developed to improve selection decisions, in practice. The US National Council on Measurement in Education (2017) defines psychometrics as the objective assessment and measurement of competencies such as skills and knowledge, abilities, attitudes, personality traits, and educational achievement.

In the field of personnel selection, psychometrics is about the construction and validation of assessment instruments such as questionnaires and interview guidelines, behavioral anchors and scales, tests (e.g., cognitive ability or personality tests, including the development of test theories such as classical test theory or item response theory), construction of assessment centers, etc.

The psychometric approach demands rational, analytically oriented selection procedures, which are usually based on research findings and lead to rules, standards, and guidelines for personnel selection, such as ISO 10667 (ISO 2020) or guidelines for tests and assessment centers (ISO, 2011; International Taskforce on Assessment Center Guidelines, 2015). For example, a standard for personnel selection in Germany is called DIN 33430 (Ackerschott et al., 2016). This psychometric or rational-analytical approach suggests a systematic and consciously considered procedure to ensure objective, reliable, and valid selection decisions (e.g., Kanning 1999, Kanning et al., 2008, 2015). In a rational-analytical approach, the results of the applied personnel selection method are evaluated according to a rule-based deployment, so that the decision is comprehensible and transparent (Lohaus & Habermann, 2013, pp. 225–226; Scherm et al., 2016, p. 308).

Quality standards such as the DIN 33430 or ISO 10667 are "process norms." They describe how to implement a high-quality selection process, in practice. In addition, they make statements about the competencies, qualifications, and expected behaviors of selection managers. At the same time, these standards also concede that the expert judgment of the manager is highly relevant (Ackerschott et al., 2016). This leaves room for managers to use their intuition as an expression of their expertise.

The psychometric personnel diagnostic approach focuses on the objective measurement of the personal job fit, measuring relevant competencies and characteristics objectively and optimizing the instruments used to predict performance on the job. Psychometric selection procedures allow making differences between individuals, observable and measurable (Palmer & Kersting, 2017, p. 36). However, suppose personnel selection decisions are made to pursue non-job-related objectives such as nepotism or promote specific groups of persons (e.g., specific ethnic groups and female applicants), this can only rudimentarily be understood as rational-analytical personnel diagnostics (Ackerschott et al., 2016, p. 6).

From this psychometric perspective, personnel diagnostics consciously and systematically collect and process information to justify, monitor, and optimize selection decisions. The aim is to assess the competencies of the candidate (predictors) and criteria of professional success at the job and compare these two variables. Thus, a high-quality selection procedure describes developing, testing, and implementing comprehensible methods to provide requirement-related success prognoses in an occupational context (Schuler, 2014, p. 3; Deters, 2017, p. 67). However, this very general definition of personnel selection does not say anything about the concrete contents and procedures in personnel selection, in practice.

> Generally, the goal of personnel selection is to identify whether candidates have the knowledge, skills, abilities, and other characteristics (KSAOs) needed to perform effectively in particular jobs. . . . Personality traits are among these KSAOs. To reach their goal, personnel selectors use prespecified procedures to assess whether a focal person has the required KSAOs and to assess whether this person's standings on these KSAOs will be satisfactory to perform the job (Lievens, 2017, p. 425).

While specific competencies and personality traits are objectively measurable, intuitions and feelings are difficult to be measured objectively. Kanning (2015, p. 138) speaks of nebulous concepts, integrating "gut feeling" or "visceral feeling" as well as intuition, becoming the most crucial weapon in the fight against professional personnel selection. Thus, the prevailing opinion is that personnel selection should not be based on intuition and that feelings should be minimized (Kanning, 2015, p.138; Krings, 2017, p. 1). Scientifically validated selection methods claim to exclude personal sympathies, unconscious bias, stereotypes, prejudices, etc., and thus, aim to eliminate or, at least, reduce intuitions and feelings in selection processes (Apelojg, 2010, pp. 45–48; Reimann, 2010, p. 25; Riedel, 2015, p. 7).

There is a discrepancy between scientific recommendations and practical implementation. In practice, psychometric methods are a bundle of theoretical principles, questions, and techniques; thus, the rational-analytical procedures are only rudimentarily implemented. "People tend to place substantial weight on intuitive judgment, despite a preponderance of the evidence that shows that the performance of statistical formulas far exceeds the performance of intuition for predicting job performance" (Slaughter & Kausel 2013, p. 57). Interestingly, the psychometric, rational-analytical approach is equated with a "scientifically proven approach." Although one of the most well-established findings in behavioral science is that the rational-analytical approach outperforms intuition in predicting human behavior, intuition remains very appealing, in practice. For example, instead of implementing scientifically proven selection methods, there is a stubborn reliance on intuition and subjectivity, in employee selection (Highhouse, 2008, pp. 333 and 336–337).

1.1.4 Shortcomings of rational-analytical procedures in selecting talent: why practitioners rely on their intuition

Despite overwhelming evidence demonstrating the greater efficacy of rational-analytical approaches, recruiters rely on their intuitions, emotions, and subjectivity and believe they can intuitively predict the future behavior of candidates. The problem with the general preference for less standardization is that it is in direct conflict with the preponderance of evidence, showing that more standardized selection procedures improve objectivity, reliability, and validity, and thus, outperform – as Schmidt and Hunter (1998) have shown – less standardized procedures (Lodato et al. 2011, pp. 352–353; Nachtwei et al., 2013, p. 34).

Betsch (2008) shows that in science, the influence of intuition on decision-making is often neglected, and reliance on intuition in selection processes is often equated with dubious, untrustworthy, and poorly made decisions (Kanning 2015, p. 138; Julmi et al., 2016, p. 195). Critics recognize that "personnel selection is still too much based on appearance, tradition or self-proclaimed experts" (Kanning, 2015, p. 150). And when selection decisions are not based on scientifically proven methods, considerable costs such as lack of performance, demotivation, frustration, as well as costs for renewed candidate search, etc., threaten. "Good hiring decisions can result in substantial increases in performance levels and productivity. Consequences of unwise decisions can range from inconvenience to disaster" (Highhouse et al., 2016, p. 4).

A significant cause of costly mistakes is that many selection managers (HR specialists, line managers, professional recruiters, etc.) rely on their gut feelings rather than on well-founded psychometric diagnostics (Nachtwei et al., 2017, p. 34). Studies show that the influence of intuition on personnel decisions, in general, is rated very high by both HR managers and executives (Nachtwei et al., 2013, S. 39).

Conversely, psychometric-based rational-analytical selection procedures alone are insufficient to make excellent and promising hiring decisions (Julmi et al., 2016, pp. 195–199). Hiring managers see the selection process also as a social situation and a "candidate-attraction-process" in which they have to win over candidates for their organization. They know that candidates have feelings and want to be courted and won over emotionally. Thus hiring managers use personal branding and "sell themselves" to applicants to recruit personnel. In their meta-analysis, Uggerslev et al. (2012) explored predictors of applicant attraction and found that the perceived person–organization-fit is the strongest predictor of applicant attraction to the organization (Potočnik, 2021, p. 167).

In interviews conducted in our empirical research, we were told that candidates particularly value personal contact or a direct approach – in addition to contacts via Active Sourcing or social media. For them, personal contact reflects respect, attention, and individuality. Even digital natives, who have grown up with digital communication, value interpersonal exchange. And intuition, emotion, empathy, and other things are needed to establish trust, understand people's feelings, build positive relationships with applicants, and create a positive applicant experience.

Thus, the performance and success of a hiring manager are measured on two levels: First, they must win the candidate for the organization (acquisition), and secondly, they must select the right one. Success on these two levels is most likely, when situations allow hiring managers to integrate rational-analytical procedures and intuitive competencies.

Gigerenzer (2007, p. 3), a scientific representative of the position that gut feelings should be taken seriously and are useful for decision-making, also shows that rational analytics is preached but, in reality, is not consistently used in decision-making processes.

One reason for this gap between science and practice is that the psychometric approach does not sufficiently acknowledge the fact that hiring managers as humans cannot (and, in most cases, don't want to) act as neutral measuring instruments, because they are influenced in many ways through their imprints, socialization, and previous experience (Riedel, 2015, p. 17).

According to the Dutch social psychologist, Dijksterhuis, people who claim to be able to ignore their emotions and intuitions and think to decide only based on conscious and rational considerations commit self-deception (Treufetter, 2009, p. 22). Neuroscience research shows that unconscious intuitive signals come to our conscious mind by processing, especially, earlier emotional experiences. Before decisions can be made rationally, they have already gone through intuitive-rational processes and evaluations (Roth, 2010, p. 18), and humans can't do anything against it.

A theoretical concept of the psychometric approach, which demands purely rational-analytical decision-making behavior by selection managers, does not match practical experience. Thus, this approach is a barrier to a holistic concept of personnel selection (Apelojg, 2010, p. 45).

Historically, intuition plays an essential role in religions and is regarded as a truth that surpasses the power of the intellect (Langan-Fox & Shirley, 2003). One of the first scientists to investigate this concept was Thomas Reid (1710–1796). The Scottish philosopher was one of the founders of the "common sense" philosophy, which refers to a select set of intuitive judgments. As an inborn ability, he regarded intuition as responsible for regulating the conscious experience of every individual (Reid, 1764).

In the literature on personnel diagnostics, opportunities to handle intuition constructively and discussions on the contribution of intuition to the quality of personnel selection are rarely mentioned (Riedel, 2015, p. 32). This is understandable, because it is challenging to conceptualize, operationalize, and measure intuition from a scientific perspective and evaluate its influence on the success of personnel selection decisions.

In addition, research findings clearly show that attempts are made to rationalize intuitive decisions in retrospect, since intuition is considered unprofessional in science and often, in practice, and is difficult to justify and comprehend. Thus, as a researcher, one could get the impression that dealing with intuition borders on charlatanry and – since intuition is difficult to operationalize and measure – can be interpreted as an escape from the world of science.

Psychologists, economists, and neuroscientists have been working on how human decisions can be described and improved. However, in this context, the role of intuition has often been neglected in mainstream research on decision-making. As a result, one could gain the impression that intuition borders on parapsychology and that you are entering a social science minefield, if you are scientifically interested in the topic of intuition (Claxton, 2000).

Western culture, in particular, is replete with cognitive maxims like "look before you leap" and "think before you act." Intuition is distrusted. More weight is attributed to careful, conscious thought than intuition, perhaps from a wish that decisions should be based on verbalizable reasons and not feelings (Dijksterhuis & Nordgren, 2006, p. 105).

One reason for this comprehensible skepticism about intuitive judgments is that the concept of intuition is often used too broadly, as an umbrella term for many kinds of different processes.

There are likely several qualitatively different cognitive processes that unconsciously influence peoples' choices and produce feelings, leading them to decide without knowing why (Claxton, 1998). Thus, the challenge is how to study "this evasive and mostly non-conscious phenomenon objectively using scientific methods" (Sinclair & Ashkanasy, 2005, p. 355).

Studying intuition objectively using scientific methods has several limitations and significant difficulties to overcome. First, the exact processes that produce intuitions and feelings are difficult to specify, and therefore predictions may remain imprecise. Second, intuition research in decision-making is not sufficiently connected to work in cognitive psychology that aims to specify processes underlying intuition. Third, since, psychometric selection procedures were constructed under the assumption that intuitions and heuristics lead to deviations from rationality, intuition is doomed to lead to wrong decisions. This has hindered the detection of intuition's merits. Thus, Lopes (1991, pp. 78–79) states: "The idea that people are irrational and science has proved it is useful propaganda for anyone who has rationality to sell. . . . In claiming that most people make foolish errors, . . . authors suggest that they have superior knowledge or insight into difficult decision situations."

But in recent decades, the analysis of intuition has emerged as a legitimate subject of social science and aims to overcome limitations such as lack of operationalization and measure it with scientifically proven methods (Jekel et al., 2012, p. 147; Sadler-Smith & Burke-Smalley, 2015, p. 52). Furthermore, Samba et al. (2019) stated that the concept of intuition has increasingly been recognized as a hot topic in decision-making research over the past few decades and that it is a central feature in several top journal publications, paper sessions, professional development workshops, and practitioner-oriented articles.

More and more research results support the idea that decision-making involves cognition, emotion, and intuition.

> Intuition was once considered a vague and hard-to-define phenomenon, in the domains of the paranormal and transcendentalism . . ., beyond scientific investigation and not something that could be trained, developed, or cultivated. Developments in intuition research in management and other fields, such as educational studies . . . have challenged these claims: intuition can be defined and theorized, intuition is open to scientific methods of inquiry, and training, developing, and cultivating managers' intuition is eminently achievable (Sadler-Smith, 2019, p. 22).

The importance of intuition in decision-making processes is increasingly being addressed: "The study of intuition and its relation to thoughtful reasoning is a burgeoning research topic in psychology and beyond. (This) area has the potential to radically transform our conception of the mind and decision-making . . ." (Glöckner & Witteman, 2010, preface).

Hogarth (2010, p. 338) states that the

> study of decision-making has attracted considerable scientific attention from many disciplines including psychology, economics, sociology, political science, biology, neuroscience, and different areas of business administration. There are at least two reasons. First, decision-making provides an intrinsically interesting set of phenomena. Second, a good description can lead to a good prescription. If we know how people make decisions, we may be able to help them make better decisions.

In times of digitization, big data, and radical transformation, making quick decisions is becoming increasingly essential. Although it was never easier to collect comprehensive data on which to base a decision, there are situations where not all the background information needed is available; in other situations, far more information is available than people could hope to process. These are the situations in which their intuition plays a central role.

Both the person and the situation influence human behavior and especially human decision-making. Specific organizational contexts with limited resources, for example, may require that a relatively elaborate analytical selection process with all the scientific requirements is not implemented (see Section 3.2).

Viktor Frankl says that every situation contains a call people must obey. First, people must always ask themselves: what does the specific situation require regarding decisions and behavior? Secondly, besides the situation, the person comes into play: what kind of personality am I, how do I usually react in such situations, or how do I deal with the demands of the specific situation? But Frankl also considers human freedom and that people can choose what to do in any given set of circumstances (Frankl, 2002, p. 75; see also Frankl, 2006).

Cronbach (1957, p. 671) maintained that researchers on human (decision-making) behavior should value and emphasize both – a perspective known as interactionism. The various influencing factors of a situation and the individual characteristics of a hiring manager (e.g., is the hiring manager more of the rational-analytical or more of the intuitive type; see Section 4.2.9 and cognitive style index in Allinson & Hayes, 1996) and the interplay of both should be considered, in more detail.

The acceptance of intuitive judgments is not only a question of the personality of the hiring manager but also of the decision context. Situational factors, e.g., problem characteristics or acceptance of intuition in a specific culture or working area (e.g., finance and controlling or HR/People management and marketing), as moderators of using intuition, are described in Section 5.6. Research shows that personnel decisions, in particular, are made more intuitively, whereas major investment decisions, e.g., the acquiring process of an organization or a machine, are more based on rational analysis (Allinson & Hayes, 1996, p. 129).

Miles & Sadler-Smith (2014, p. 624) summarize their research findings on intuition in personnel selection as follows:

> Intuition was perceived as being hard to explain, based on experience and manifested as a physical feeling which emerged rapidly and involuntarily.Some participants were more convinced of its benefits than others however we did not seek to embark on any quantitative analysis of individual differencesin this regard as a basis for generalizations (though this could be an area for further investigation). The reasons for the use of intuition included personal preferences, resource constraints, and recognition of the limitations of more structured approaches. Intuition was used an indicator for performance, personality and person-environment fit. Intuition tended to be used with requisite caution. Participants were aware of its limits, the potential for bias and the difficulties in justifying its use. Several participants used their intuitions in concert with more structured, non-intuition-based approaches.

The increasing importance of intuition in management decisions can also be seen in the scientific publications of the Academy of Management, which dealt with the subject in detail, at a symposium in 2017 (Academy of Management Proceedings, Vol. 2017, No. 1). There are various articles in the Academy of Management Executive such as Behling & Eckel 1991; Burke & Miller 1999; in the Academy of Management Review such as Dane & Pratt, 2007, or Sadler-Smith & Shefy, 2004, in Academy of Management Learning and Education. Modern conceptions and strategies of marketing don't follow a rational choice model of consumer decision-making, especially when consumer choices are emotionally driven and many consumer decisions are based on intuition (Patterson et al., 2012).

Research shows clearly that intuitive judgments can have unwanted effects (e.g., discrimination against specific candidates) but also can lead to excellent results (Kahneman & Klein, 2009). Thus, human intuition is not always worth eliminating from a decision-making process. Consequently, research on intuition in personnel diagnostics should be promoted and expanded due to the gap between psychometric requirements and the implementation of these requirements, in practice.

1.2 Balancing intuition and analytics

The importance of intuition in personnel selection can also be seen in how selection managers deal with contradictions between the results of analytical methods and their intuitions and emotions. Although there are different ways of dealing with this, empirical research shows that practitioners do not put their intuition aside and exclusively follow analytical results. This reflects the conviction of HR practitioners that they can predict candidates' future performance better by intuition than any analytics (Colarelli & Thomson, 2008, p. 347; Kanning, 2012, p. 20; Brauner, 2019, p. 86).

From this perspective, it seems necessary to create a more realistic picture of how selection decisions emerge and reimagine the concept of intuition in personnel diagnostics. If the concept of intuition is appropriately used, it can be recognized as something useful and valuable for personnel selection processes.

Advocates of the psychometric approach, such as Kanning, consistently oppose intuition in personnel selection. He argues that there will be no more critical inquiry, if someone refers to nebulous concepts such as gut feeling or his own experience in personnel selection. Thus, gut feelings, intuitions, and emotions become the most crucial factors in the fight against professional personnel selection and immunize the decision-makers against any criticism (Kanning, 2015, p. 138).

Even though Kanning is correct in asserting a critical attitude towards one's intuitions and emotions, the solution cannot regard intuitions and emotions only as negative, with no room in personnel selection.

A question that arises is: How can intuition be accommodated within a psychometric endeavor and, especially, within the tradition of "technical rationality"? Bringing science and practice together is far from straightforward and calls for a creative synthesis that addresses critical issues about the thinking of each perspective. And this "marriage" should create a place for intuition, emotions, creativity, and improvisation and provide a framework for their systematic use (Alred, 2012).

The experiences of HR managers with intuition should be reflected, extended, and described by our empirical data and reflexive accounts. From this empirical analysis, according to Alred (2012), different processes to re-conceptualize intuition can be used:

1) Recognizing and claiming intuition
2) Developing social support to share intuition with trusted others
3) Recognizing ways of responding to intuition
4) Raising consciousness of the value and potential disadvantages of intuition and its implications for personnel selection5) Showing how intuition can be developed and how it can be used constructively

By using both analytics and intuition in personnel selection processes and by recognizing and accepting their specific limitations, HR managers may drop the mask of managerial control and strength. More than seeing intuition as something to be avoided at all costs, recognizing the power and value of intuition creates the opportunity to open up to holistic methods in personnel decision-making processes.

On the one hand, a more scientific approach is required in intuition research, if the construct wants to achieve scientific credibility. The search for the most objective possible knowledge is, and remains, the core task of science. On the other hand, the reality to be studied in science is not what we desire, but what is. And intuitions and emotions are real. Salas et al. (2010, p. 966) state that the time for a science of intuition in organizations capable of guiding practice and improving effectiveness has come. Although intuition is frequently ascribed to intangible or transcendental quality, the phenomenon is real. Therefore, it is vital to organizational effectiveness and the management sciences to contribute to the practice, through more rigorous research into the nature and development of intuitive decision-making skills.

Miles and Sadler-Smith (2014, p. 624) note that "to the best of our knowledge, there are no qualitative studies that have investigated the use of intuition in employee hiring decisions."

By analyzing interviews with middle and senior managers, global line leaders, and HR managers and presenting our own reflexive insights, a lack of empirical research on intuition in HR/People Management can be addressed. This approach intends to impact and improve personnel selection processes by integrating analytics and intuition, professionally.

Intuitions and emotions cannot and should not be avoided because they give humans essential clues. Thus, it's not about reducing or even avoiding one's intuitions as much as possible, as required by the rational-analytical approach. Instead, it is essential to recognize intuitions, perceive them, and reflect on them critically and constructively, because intuitions and emotions can be helpful and valuable advisors. But, they can also be misleading. Thus, it is essential to recognize the value of intuitions and the emotions associated with them, consider them, and anchor them conceptually in personnel diagnostics.

It is necessary to re-conceptualize and demystify the concept of intuition and not regard it as something to be minimized. The rational-analytical approach of psychometrics has a quasi-paradigmatic effect and defines and postulates how to proceed in personnel selection and which questions can and should be asked and answered in a meaningful way. However, suppose this psychometric paradigm of thinking and deciding is no longer sufficient for explaining and solving existing challenges. In that case, it should not continue to serve as a dogma for decision-making in personnel selection. This equals a paradigm shift, since the psychometric approach is based on features and assumptions that hiring managers as humans cannot and will not guarantee. Therefore, the psychometric, rational-analytical approach needs to be replaced by a holistic, transdisciplinary approach and framework that takes into account actual human decision-making behavior and integrates knowledge from psychometric and other fields of research (e.g., intuition research, decision and emotion psychology, neurosciences, behavior-oriented economics, etc.).

The scientifically proven psychometric approach pays too little attention to actual human decision-making behavior and, thus, neglects important insights and proven knowledge from other areas of science. Intuitions and related feelings are regarded as sources of error. The psychometric approach, thus, declares intuitions and emotions as something to avoid. Starting from this limited mechanistic conception of man that wants to turn people into rationally acting hiring managers, always and everywhere, see them as determinable objects and deny their ability to act independently and responsibly. However, the practice of personnel selection clearly shows that in selection interviews, for example, people do not act as data-recording devices that are free of emotions and intuitions. However, if the scientific approach is that intuitions should be avoided, the focus is exclusively on the negative sides of intuitions and feelings. This negative view can lead to neglecting essential questions, e.g., about the benefits of intuitions and emotions or how decision-makers should deal with the problem when objective test results differ from their individual intuitions and emotions. The psychometric approach, by itself, does not meet the requirements of a holistic view in personnel selection. Instead, it requires a reflected and critical-constructive integration of psychometrics with intuitions and emotions in the personnel selection process.

1.3 Intuition and theory formation in personnel selection

Research shows that intuition plays a significant role not only in decision-making but also in promoting creativity, generating ideas, and gaining new insights. Thus, intuition can be seen as an inexhaustible source of knowledge (Ruthenbeck, 2004, p. 74). Scientific progress and the discovery of new knowledge are regularly based not only on rational analysis and evaluation of data but are also driven by intuition.

French mathematician and physicist, Henri Poincaré, is credited with the insight that by logic, we prove, but by intuition, we discover. “With logic, one can lead proofs, but not gain new insights. This requires intuition” (Kaudela-Baum & Brasser, 2015, p. 130).

In earlier centuries, especially before the Enlightenment, which focused on rational reason, intuition was considered a recognized principle of gaining knowledge; for example, the influential Dutch philosopher, Baruch de Spinoza (1632–1677), rated it the highest of three types of knowledge development. He describes intuition as the "greatest virtue of mind" and superior to reason (Soyarslan, 2013). According to Spinoza, intuition (scientia intuitive) would help get direct access to the essence of things (essentiae rerum). The French philosopher Rene Descartes (1596–1650) and the German philosophers Immanuel Kant (1724–1804), and Arthur Schopenhauer (1788–1860) also see intuition – besides reason – as an important way to gain new knowledge (Mamin, 2020).

Research on decision-making in marketing (Patterson et al., 2012, p. 42) shows a big gap between the theory of decision models and how decisions are made in practice.

> Our empirical findings dispute the commonly held contention that intuition should be strenuously avoided if "good" strategic marketing decisions are to be taken. On the contrary, this research shows how intuition is widely practiced by marketing managers striving to make better decisions. . . . intuition becomes a particularly powerful tool in instances where there is a paucity of data, when options are manifold, when the future is uncertain, and when the logic of strategic choice needs to be confirmed. Moreover, since people in business are generally rewarded for displaying logic and supporting strategic choices with facts, we would estimate that the use of intuitive processes actually runs much deeper than this empirical study suggests.

While logic, rational-analytical, and data-driven marketing are still essential for effective marketing decisions (and their evaluation), theory building in mainstream marketing undervalues intuition (and inspiration and imagination). Therefore, a holistic theoretical concept integrating analytical and intuitive approaches is needed.

For Julius Kuhl (1990), the founder of the "Theory of Personality-System-Interactions (PSI), science is the old play between intuition and analytical thinking. He emphasizes that scientific research has to do with analytical thinking. Progress in science and the "Logic of Research" (Carl Popper) differ from everyday thinking, precisely in that diffuse concepts such as intuition in everyday thinking should be deliberately left out.

Nevertheless, Kuhl is convinced that scientific progress and further developments are not conceivable without scientists' implicit knowledge representations and intuitions. Therefore, the dialogue between intuition and rationality is also necessary for science. Kuhl attributes the resistance to intuition, which still exists in large areas of science, to three main reasons (Kuhl, 1990, pp. 46–48):

1. Fear of ambiguity and the associated timidity in dealing with vague, speculative, and not entirely explicable concepts. However, as Kaplan (1964, p. 71) explains, tolerance of ambiguity is as essential in science as anywhere else in

human life. Kaplan sees the risk that the purely analytical logic of research has become disconnected from the tacit knowledge base of people.
2. Involuntary introspection. In essence, this means that people, especially scientists, attribute successful problem-solving to what they have consciously experienced and remembered. However, this overlooks the fact that processing stimuli and other information happens unconsciously and intuitively.
3. Explicability illusion. When scientists apply certain theoretical concepts or models to deal with problems, they pretend that things are as simple as the few consciously accessible parts of knowledge suggest. Such theoretical models or concepts are used, for example, when scientific quality criteria are determined in personnel selection (e.g., in connection with the determination of validity). However, if theoretical concepts, such as a specific motivational approach, are used in reality, other complex tacit knowledge systems are unconsciously used.

Kuhl, therefore, criticizes the purely rational scientific concepts of psychology as lacking intuitive empiricism.

This involves a paradigm shift that also addresses the tacit knowledge representations and thus, intuitions of scientists. This means not to see intuitions as something to be avoided but to understand them as implicit knowledge, perceive them, talk about them with others, and enter into a reflected resonance process. He, therefore, calls for a theory-based increase in complexity, which would improve the generalizability and practicability of psychological theories (Kuhl, 1990, p. 48).

In their book *Intuition and Science*, Bachhiesl et al. (Eds., 2015) give many examples of the role of intuition in the scientific discovery process. They show that intuitions, when they play a role in academia, are at the beginning and not at the end of scientific knowledge-producing. The various contributions in that book also show how intuitions have driven the development of individual scientific disciplines (Bachhiesl, 2018a, p. 15).

One problem is that intuition does not appear rationally precise, unambiguously graspable, or even measurable. Also, it has not yet been clarified how intuition concretely comes about, how intuition can be methodically induced, and how these unmediated and introspectively gained insights can be concretely developed. Science is supposed to create knowledge by methodically guided rational-analytical and comprehensible cognition. If people like scientists develop new knowledge by intuition, this cognition process is not methodically and rationally comprehensible for third parties. However, comprehensibility and verifiability of findings are seen as fundamental prerequisites of scientific knowledge. In addition, scientific statements must be verifiable for their accuracy and truthfulness. And, scientists should check how other scientists have arrived at their findings. Thus, science is bound to procedures and methods that operate beyond subjective conviction and express their credibility precisely, by being transparent and verifiable.

Intuition is challenging to grasp and make accessible to scientific analysis. It is intangible and mixes with other mental and spiritual impulses like feelings, sensations, fantasies, or moods. Intuition, thus, merges into an experiential unity that is difficult to differentiate analytically. Thus, intuition becomes contourless and is difficult to explore in a rational-analytical way. The rational-analytical approach gives people and scientists security and support. It meets the requirements for controllability and verifiability by third parties. Those who trust their intuition surrender to their subjectivity and arbitrariness and, ultimately, build their thinking and decision-making on the sand. Only rational-analytical methodology can claim general validity in science. Applying corresponding scientific methodologies can make people unsure of perceiving or even trusting their immediate impulses, such as intuitions and emotions (Eggenberger, 1994).

There is seemingly no room for intuitions in this process, among others, because they are not meant to stand merely as placeholders for decisions made unconsciously.

Bachhiesl (2018b) draws the following conclusion: intuition plays a role in science and the process of producing new scientific knowledge. It has a cognitive and a shaping dimension and can bring new insights. The scientist can make an effort to enter a state of heightened receptivity (for example, through mindfulness training, etc.) but cannot, however, intentionally and consciously, bring about intuitive insights, since they are processed at an unconscious level. Intuitively gained insights are, by nature, subjective and can hardly be objectified. However, objectification and rationalization can be attempted, subsequently, by applying the usual methodological means of science. The intuitively gained insights should, thus, be checked and evaluated, according to the scientific criteria of rational comprehensibility.

According to Tokarski (2008, p. 458) or Staub-Bernasconi (2007, p. 237), scientific realism allows talking about intuition but rejects equating individual intuitions and emotions with valid scientific knowledge.

However, it must be doubted whether the image of man aimed by psychometrics is based on valid findings. While neoclassical economics is based on the unrealistic model of homo economicus, the psychometric approach aims for a human being (selection manager) who should turn off his intuitions and emotions, as much as possible (Schuler, 1996, p. 86). People are not seen as and should not be as they are but should act as reduced rational beings. But, this is also a theoretical human being and reminds us of the idea of humans as machines and reducing man and seeing humans not as a whole. But humans, as selection managers have free will, are sometimes idiosyncratic, and have intuitions and emotions. This rational-analytical way of thinking demanded by psychometrics is based on rational idealisms but is constantly refuted in practice, and can, therefore be considered untenable. Instead of taking up and reflecting on the supposed contradictions, ambiguities, and paradoxes of personnel selection in practice, the psychometric approach emphasizes scientific reason and quality. Thus, the psychometric approach does not see the strength and advantages of intuitions and feelings. This is neither respectful nor appreciative of HR professionals as holistic human beings.

The psychometric view of the human being only considers "true," what can be empirically recorded with the help of rational-analytical methods and can thus be measured and controlled. However, this measurement of people overlooks that successful managers and entrepreneurs also base their decisions on their intuition. Especially in human resource management, which is about working with people, essentials remain unseen, if intuitions and emotions are not included. This applies equally to theory building and training personnel managers and executives. It cannot be denied that scientists and selection managers also arrive at new findings intuitively. As much as a rational-analytical approach is a valuable and efficient method of gaining knowledge, awareness of its limitations should not be lost (Eggenberger, 1994, 1998).

Even the scientific, theoretical conception of critical rationalism can be seen as a criticism of the assumption of the rationality of human beings.

The impression that intuition and rationality are opposed or even mutually exclusive can arise. But this is not the case. Instead, it is crucial to integrate the rational-analytical approach with the intuitive one, to complement each other.

Therefore, the idealistic conceptions based only on man's rationality should be skeptically questioned. It is a matter of taking a realistic view of the role of reason in human decision-making and what it is, and is not, capable of achieving (Schurz, 2013, pp. 1–3). Therefore, a theoretical concept for personnel selection should not be based on the idea of an ideal human being but on real ones. Thus, theory formation should be about a realistic view of hiring managers and the role of reason in human decision-making. Instead of just asking how selection managers should decide, science should also answer the second question: "How do selection managers really decide, in practice?"

What becomes so readily apparent is that intuitions and emotions should not be excluded from theory building in the area of Human Resource Management, leadership, and especially personnel selection. Therefore, holistic theoretical conceptions that consider people's intuitions and emotions can explain human decision-making behavior better than idealistic rational concepts (Schurz, 2013). However, suppose we continue to operate with an illusory reality in personnel management or, in particular, personnel selection, we should not be surprised if we fail to get to grips with the problems. Thus, we should engage with the reality in which everything is in flux.

This is explicitly not a matter of discrediting rational-analytical approaches but, instead, recognizing the complementarity of these methodologies, by integrating intuitions and related emotions in theory formation.

"Nothing is as practical as a good theory" was the advice given by Kurt Lewin, one of the founders of modern social and organizational psychology, to scientists and practitioners in the 1940s. Thus, this study aims to bridge the psychometric requirements of rational-analytics and the practical use of intuition. The aim is to integrate analytics and intuition into synthesis and use their respective strengths. In this way, we will try to go beyond an intuitive understanding of intuition. For example, suppose we include in theory building how people decide in reality, the personnel selection process can be better understood and the gap between theory and practice can be reduced.

1.4 Goals of this book

In science, the power of argumentation is always linked to the question of methodology and how specific research results are collected and evaluated. Therefore, it is essential to develop competencies to classify and use knowledge sources and methods of generating knowledge correctly, and critically reflect on research results and their methodical origin.

To reflect on intuition not only in practice but also in the scientific community, a clear definition and dissociation of the term and the use of scientifically recognized research methods are required to make the construct of intuition tangible, comprehensible, and measurable.

But just as the emotional impact of music can hardly be put into words or understood with abstract rational analyses, so too the effects of people on other people, and thus, intuition and related feelings cannot be easily operationalized.

From the prevailing scientific perspective, the problem of measuring and operationalizing intuition can only be solved, if the construct of "intuition" – besides a precise definition – is made verifiable and thus, comprehensible by measurable criteria. This requires a clear distinction between intuitive and rational-analytical decisions to reliably and comprehensively determine when a decision was made intuitively and when it was made rational-analytically. Another question is how intuitions and emotions are related, whether they can be distinguished from each other, and how people can be sure whether their decisions were made intuitively or rational-analytically. Then, the question is whether intuition and analytics can be conceptualized and measured separately and independently of each other or if they are different poles on a continuum.

It is also important to clarify which decision situations are advisable for more intuitive or more rational-analytical judgments or a mixture of both. A further question is: What methods can be used to validly investigate an intuitively-driven judgment and decision-making processes of personnel managers and applicants, and how can the credibility of (individual and team/collective) intuition be evaluated?

These questions will be examined in more detail, and ideas for solutions will be developed.

With the gap between science and practice as a starting point, a review of the current state of research on intuition and analytics in personnel diagnostics as well as qualitative interviews will be carried out to find out how science and practice can work together effectively, and how selection processes in organizations can be qualitatively improved and professionalized.

Based on Simon (1987, p. 59) and Sadler-Smith (2019b, p. 6), perhaps the fundamental question for management intuition research is how intuition is used in management practice.

Intuition as a construct cannot be measured directly. Researchers try to determine what processes occur in the brain when certain emotions or intuitions arise. As social scientists, we can try to measure results, based on intuitive decisions. For this reason, the concept of intuition will be explored, and various approaches to understanding intuition will be presented. The importance of intuition in different fields of professional activity is discussed, and the differences between decisions based on an analytical, rational approach and decisions based on intuition in personnel selection are presented.

This book answers the following questions:

- How can the concept of intuition be explored in processes of personnel selection and hiring be explored?
- What are the possible advantages and risks of intuitive decisions in personnel diagnostics?
- How can the concept of intuition be reconceptualized and used as something valuable in theory and practice of personnel selection?

Findings available in the research literature are reviewed, and the results are presented. In addition, new empirical studies and expert interviews were conducted to answer these questions from a practical perspective.

As this research field is relatively unexplored, we used an explorative, qualitative approach in our empirical studies.

We have developed theory-based interview guidelines based on the research results published in the literature. Using these guidelines, interviews with selecting and hiring managers from HR departments, selecting and hiring line managers, and recruitment and selection consultants/headhunters from different hierarchy levels and countries were conducted and transcribed. A qualitative content analysis was carried out, based on (deductive and inductive developed) category systems and followed by presenting results.

Nachtwei et al. (2013, p. 40) note that empirically collected attitudes of personnel managers towards intuitive judgments can be only rudimentarily derived from subjective self-assessment. More decisive is to know which and how hiring managers actually use selection instruments and methods, in practice.

Thus, some further questions are answered:

- What distinguishes rational-analytical personnel selection processes, how should they be designed from a scientific perspective; what are the shortcomings, and how are they implemented in practice?

In addition, it is essential to show how evidence-based scientific research findings and related methods and instruments for selecting personnel can be implemented more successfully, in practice. Therefore, the following research questions will also be addressed:

- How is it possible to integrate analytics and intuition into synthesis and use their respective strengths in selection and hiring procedures?
- In which ways can the gap between science and practice be bridged to improve the impact of scientific research results (and vice versa)?

From a practical perspective, this book gives professionals (especially recruitment and hiring managers, talent acquisition managers, line managers involved in personnel selection, and other HR managers and readers), insight into improving their decision-making skills and making better decisions. The book can be used in courses and lectures on “decision-making” (decision-making in management, entrepreneurial decision-making, etc.), I/O-psychology, and Human Resource Management, especially personnel selection. In addition, undergraduate and postgraduate students can learn to explore intuition and analytics in decision-making and develop and improve their skills in these areas.

From a scientific perspective, a further important goal of this book is to develop a conceptual framework and approach to integrate rational-analytical and intuitive-emotional procedures in theory and in the practice of personnel selection (see Section 10.6).

1.5 The need for a more valid approach to decision-making processes in personnel selection

It is not only a knowledge gap or a gap between knowledge and action (knowledge-behavior gap), but also the fact that intuition in psychometric personnel diagnostics is seen as something to be criticized and to be avoided, that increases this gap (Kanning, 2015, pp. 138–149). According to the psychometric approach, intuitive and emotional influences on judgments in personnel selection should be reduced, as much as possible (Schuler, 1996, p. 86).

A conclusion of behavioral research is that managers frequently fail to meet standards of theoretical rationality (Smith & Kosslyn, 2014, p. 401). Thus, an accurate description of everyday decision-making behaviors is more needed than the demands of a rational-analytical approach. The research approach of “how decisions should be made” should be complemented by “how they are, in fact, made.” A holistic approach that considers the practice of decision-making and integrates knowledge of different sciences is appropriate.

Knowledge acquisition and theory formation in personnel diagnostics should always include complex realities and social constructions of decision-makers. Data and facts of rational-analytical processes should not be understood as "the reality," but should also be critically reflected on their origins and limits. And, it's about critically questioning prevailing patterns of interpretation, frames of reference, and approaches in personnel selection on their effectiveness and implementation possibilities.

To gain a more realistic understanding of decision-making, theory formation must reflect the complex reality and the systemic connections between analytics, intuitions, and emotions, as accurately as possible. Theory building based on illusory realities helps neither science nor practice. Thus, an interdisciplinary approach is needed, using research results from behavioral economics, psychology, neuroscience, philosophy, etc.

Thus, scientists and practitioners should get involved in this reality, in which everything is in flux and not stable.

As explained below, a holistic approach to personnel selection is less about measuring intuition. Instead, it is about the perception of what influences people in their decisions. For example, why does a hiring manager have a better feeling for candidate A than for candidate B, although both are equally technically qualified? Or, why does a recruiter have a bad feeling about candidate B? Therefore, hiring managers must reflect on these topics and question their impressions.

This more constructionist approach to selection helps focus on existing research results, especially normative approaches to selection.

The idea of individual construction of reality must not be confused with any relativity of truth, because constructivism is not the same as relativism. Instead, adopting a constructive perspective means consistently dealing with the different individually constructed perspectives and asking, for example, what criteria – personal experiences such as educational, work, or social backgrounds, cultural imprints, goals or situational implications, etc. – influence these different perspectives. Behind this, is the question: what are the differences that make up perspectives? What are essential distinctions, and what differentiation should be made in science and practice? Then, based on such reflections, a differentiated view of reality can be taken.

Psychometrics claim to consider the aspect of social acceptance in their approach. But, because it demands minimizing consideration of social factors such as intuitions, emotions, etc. (which means nothing else than to avoid them, as far as possible), they assume an ideal conception of selecting and hiring practices that cannot be realized. Adopting a constructive perspective does not mean that constructivism as a scientific approach is being advocated here, because it is a matter of critically questioning subjective constructions of reality and carrying out personnel selection in a legally secure manner and from an ethical stance, and implementing evidenced research results, as far as possible.

Decisions are not only made by rational-analytical processes. Psychometrics is based on a simplified model of decision-makers and, thus, does not really succeed in integrating psychometric and social aspects of selection processes. A focus only on the psychometric approach in selection processes is an important reason for the science-practice gap, preventing practitioners from using their (reflected) intuition and rational-analytical (logic) thinking.

This topic is reminiscent of the discussion that has been going on in economics for many years about the underlying image of man in the managerial decision-making process. An ideal conception of man as being rational, always and everywhere, has long been assumed, here. Behavioral economics studies the effects of, for instance, social, psychological, cognitive, emotional, cultural, intuitive, psychophysical, or neurological factors on the economic decisions of individuals and institutions, and how those decisions vary from those implied by classical theory. As scholars in economics have to consider that observed human behavior deviates very strongly from the model assumptions, science should recognize how selection managers actually make their selection decisions in personnel diagnostics.

This indicates the need to do a more realistic analysis of decision-making processes in personnel selection and to overcome the limitations of disciplinary approaches by recognizing the need for inter- and transdisciplinary collaboration in practice and research, integrating knowledge across disciplines and between research and practice (the value of transdisciplinary collaboration is shown in Laasch et al., 2019).

2 Research-practice gap in personnel selection: the current state of implementation of scientific findings

The great aim of education is not knowledge, but action. (Herbert Spencer)

Research results show significant discrepancies between research findings and practitioners` beliefs concerning successful selection procedures (Sanders et al., 2008; Rynes et al., 2002; Johns, 1993). As Highhouse notes: "Perhaps the greatest technological achievement in industrial and organizational (I-O) psychology over the past 100 years is the development of decision aids (e.g., paper-and-pencil tests, structured interviews, a mechanical combination of predictors) that substantially reduce error in the prediction of employee performance . . . . Arguably, the greatest failure of I–O psychology has been the inability to convince employers to use them" (Highhouse, 2008, p. 333). And Anderson (2017, p. 11) states that research often fails to influence practice and vice versa.

However, scientists and practitioners are increasingly no longer accepting this practitioner-researcher gap in personnel diagnostics (Anderson 2017, p. 2).

Neil Anderson therefore proposes to make the gap and relationship between sciences and practice, an independent research area of personnel and organizational psychology. He notes that a strictly scientific, rational, and economic way of thinking is not necessarily the best approach for transferring scientific results into the general practice of personnel selection. However, before anything else can be done in this regard, researchers in the field of personnel selection must themselves be convinced that this subject area is worth taking seriously as a field of scientific research (Anderson, 2017, p. 10; see also Anderson et al., 2001; Van de Ven & Johnson, 2006; Guion, 2011, p. 47).

With these observations by Highhouse and Anderson, the gap between scientifically founded, high-quality research results and implementation in practice on personnel selection becomes quite clear. So, why do hiring managers initially choose and persist in using intuition over more scientifically based decision-making methods?

A meta-analysis by Anderson et al. (2010) shows that work samples, mainly interviews, are the most preferred and favorably perceived selection methods. And Levashina et al. (2014) observed that candidates' reactions to structured interviews were more negative than reactions to unstructured interviews, although there seemed to be moderator variables in this relationship, such as the age of applicants (Potočnik, 2021, p. 166).

Research shows that practitioners mainly use non-standardized selection methods (Miles & Sadler-Smith, 2014; Terpstra & Rozell, 1997; Van der Zee et al., 2002). For example, Van der Zee et al. (2002, p. 176) identified five main reasons for the

https://doi.org/10.1515/9783110980967-002

lack of structuration in practice: (1) Not being aware of the academic literature supporting structuration; not taking it seriously; or not perceiving it as relevant; (2) Important interviewer needs (e.g., autonomy) are frustrated through structuration; (3) Structured interviews may harm the attraction of applicants, e.g., through less personal communication; (4) Social pressures, e.g., through organizational philosophy; (5) Budgetary and time constraints of interviewers that hinder the adoption of structured interviews.

The following are identified as the main reasons for this gap between science and practice:

2.1 Lack of dialogue between researchers and practitioners about research results

2.1.1 Lack of dialogue between science and practice

Science is accused of being too little practice-oriented and conducting too few field studies in companies, especially about actual decision-making in practice. For example, Rasmussen & Ulrich (2015, p. 237) complain that academics often lack a deep enough understanding of the issues of practitioners, and waste time and resources on developing academic models, instead of practical models.

Proponents of rational-analytical approaches are often based in academic departments and tend to favor well-controlled research conditions. Proponents who focus on the success of expert intuition are typically operating in real-world organizations. They use methods such as field observation to investigate judgments and decision-making under complex conditions (Kahneman & Klein, 2009, pp. 515–518).

In the view of many practitioners, scientists often have a reputation of lacking awareness of the real problems and questions in practice. In addition, there is a perception that scientists do not develop their research questions by having an open dialogue with practitioners and that these questions are not aligned with the needs of practitioners (Bellmann 2013, p. 1041). As a result, many practitioners do not see their relevant questions, such as using their emotions and intuitions, constructively answered by scientific research (Funk et al., 2015, p. 27).

On the contrary, open exchange and cooperation between science and practice partners could provide information on the usefulness of the research findings, apart from working constructively together.

In a study on how recruiter characteristics affect the adoption of new selection technologies, Oostrom et al. (2013) found that perceptions of usefulness and ease of use were better predictors of intentions to use new technology in personnel selection than perceptions of face validity (the extent to which applicants perceive a selection procedure to be related to the content of the job and it appears to measure what it purports to measure), predictive validity (see Section 3.7.7), and fairness (see Section 3.7.9).

Another critical factor in the lack of dialogue between practice and science is the scientific publication behavior. Researchers are evaluated according to the journals in which they publish or how often they are cited. In addition, discussions on objectives with university professors almost exclusively refer to corresponding publications. The status and reputation of a researcher are enhanced in the scientific community if a scientist's research results are published more in English and in high-ranked A-journals. However, only a few of these journals are read by practitioners.

Thus, the information sources and reading behavior of practitioners also play a role. According to Bellmann (2013, p. 1040), practitioners spend little time reading research findings and prefer popular science books that are free of complexity, are concise, simple, and use straightforward language without the academic jargon, but with concrete examples. Research by Slaughter and Kaudel (2013, p. 61) found very little coverage of the efficacy of cognitive ability or personality in employee selection in *Harvard Review* and *HR Magazine*, two publications with large readerships that are meant to bridge science and practice. They found that several articles in these publications presented findings that are either inconsistent with published scientific HR findings or made claims beyond those findings (e.g., suggesting that personality can be assessed by evaluating interviewee behavior during a meal at a restaurant). Practitioners want prepared (solution-oriented and realizable) knowledge, best practice examples, and guidelines. They are interested in success factors and concrete recommendations for action that can be implemented directly to practical problems.

2.1.2 Lack of knowledge and competencies

Although evidence-based personnel diagnostics tools and methods exist, they are not adequately used in practice. And according to Kanning (2012, p. 20), practitioners use scientifically dubious procedures and their intuition because they are not aware of the scientific findings.

Research suggests that Human Resource managers often lack knowledge about the state of the science or have little incentive to implement such knowledge. And, often, they believe the selection process should be social and informal (Lodato et al. 2011, p. 353).

From a scientific perspective, rational-analytical or psychometric personnel selection procedures should be based on a high level of diagnostic expertise. However, many personnel recruiters have no psychological background (Palmer & Kersting, 2017, pp. 37–38). Often, the quality criteria are unknown or can only be inadequately described in terms of their meaning. This professional deficit is also described in a study by Varelmann and Kanning (2018, p. 44). They found that personnel managers considerably overestimate the predictive validity of their selection methods (e.g., unstructured interviews), compared to validity studies.

The study also took into account the educational background of the interviewed personnel. As a result, the used selection methods are overestimated concerning their validity, but the psychology graduates overestimate the validities less than the non-specialists. For Kannig (2002, p. 74), this indicates how important it is for selection managers to have the psychological know-how to apply the psychometric selection methods correctly. The companies can then adapt the science-based selection procedures to requirements that are relevant to their company. And this becomes difficult if the necessary skills are unavailable.

The lack of professional competence, both among selecting HR managers and line managers, leads to the fact that, in many cases, not all quality criteria (see Section 3.2, where quality in a selection process is defined from three main perspectives) are taken into account when selecting or purchasing suitable methods (Kanning, 2015, p. 147). One consequence of this approach can be that applicants may find themselves exposed to dubious, discriminatory, or even personality-violating questions in selection interviews.

Providers of test procedures can take advantage of the lack of specialist competence, as the technical content or, e.g., the validity of specific tests or other selection procedures may not be comprehensible to the companies, in their role as buyers (Kanning, 2015, p. 110). There are no binding regulations; only recommended guidelines. Therefore, it is questionable whether the so-called laypersons can adequately check the quality of the tests before the purchase (Schuler et al., 2014, p. 189). A study by König et al. (2010, p. 23) supports the concern that the costs, the possible applicant reactions, and thus, the face validity, and the distribution of selection procedures in practice play a crucial role in such a purchase. The consideration of technical quality criteria seems to be less critical.

Apelojg (2010, pp. 178–179) has found in his empirical research that in larger companies, line managers tend to feel more responsible for checking professional and technical competencies and whether a candidate fits into the team. But the expertise for checking the personality, values, social skills, etc., is with the HR managers.

Unfortunately, from a scientific perspective, too many questionable methods and procedures are still used in personnel selection. Whether these are commercially successful procedures, such as the MBTI or DISC or involve graphology, enneagrams, completely unstructured interviews, etc., all these procedures are highly questionable from a scientific perspective and have little to do with high-quality psychometric selection procedures.

Science, in turn, is criticized by practitioners for having developed less practical methods and for failing to take actual complexity into account, especially in small and medium-sized companies (SMEs).

According to Kanning (2016a, p. 29), 47% of the interviewed companies do not use any transparent job requirements to evaluate the application documents. For

52% of the companies, the selection decision is based on the overall impression, and objectivity is not given much importance in practice – on the contrary, it is more a matter of subjective fit with the company (Schuler et al., 2007, p. 63).

Although Schuler et al. (2007) found an increase in the use of valid selection methods, the current international state of affairs is that scientists continue to explore issues that can best be described as “content areas” in personnel selection (e.g., criterion validity, adverse impact, candidate reactions, etc.), while practitioners continue to work with commercially popular approaches, methods, and decision guidance.

Analytically oriented personnel diagnostic procedures developed in science are, on the one hand, little known and often too little oriented to practice, particularly in SMEs (Kanning, 2015, p. 144).

DIN 33430, a German recommendation for a rational-analytical selection process (for a detailed description of this selection standard, see Section 3.2.4), is based on scientific findings and psychometric quality criteria, but is only partially implemented in practice. And, knowledge of this guideline is often incomplete among personnel managers (Reimann et al., 2008, p. 178).

According to a study by Kleebaur (2007), the DIN 33430 is only partially implemented in practice.

1. I do not know the DIN 33430: 74%
2. My personnel selection is based on the DIN 33430 standard: 4%
3. I orient myself relatively strictly to the DIN 33430: 0%.
4. I would like to orient myself to the DIN 33430, but lack time: 9%
5. I would like to orient myself to the DIN 33430, but I cannot convince my colleagues: 9%

In another study by Nachtwei et al. (2013), 78.08% of the 187 HR managers surveyed did not even know the DIN 33430, and only 26.83% of those who knew it at all rated it as beneficial for their work. They also found in their survey that only 6% of the respondents would choose someone against their gut feeling if the applicant demonstrated the required competencies. In addition, only 24% stated that their selection interviews were consistently based on an interview guideline; only 9% operationalized their behavioral descriptions with behavioral anchors and the corresponding numerical scores; and 47% said that they asked their questions intuitively (Nachtwei et al., 2013; Riedel, 2015, pp. 32–33).

Lodato et al. (2011, p. 357) state that practitioners often make decisions based on their experiences and experiential thinking style; and this is strongly associated with a preference for intuitively driven decisions. In the absence of knowledge and awareness of the evidence-based superiority of standardized selection procedures and training regarding human perception distortion, bias, etc., HR employees prefer intuitive approaches. If employees are trained in using standardized methods, they are more inclined to use them (Lievens & Paepe, 2004, pp. 41–42).

When people lack specific knowledge, they also like to fall back on explanatory principles that they are personally familiar. Therefore, it is unsurprising that they base their decisions on intuitions and feelings. The more experienced the recruiters, the more they rely on their intuition (Walter, 2016, p. 109).

According to a study by Rahe Management Consultants (Rahe & Rahe, 2017), in cooperation with the Federal Association of German Management Consultants (Bundesverband Deutscher Unternehmensberater e.V.), only 25% of 192 German companies of different sizes surveyed use rational-analytical selection tools to select managers. The larger the company, the more specialized the recruiters and the more structured the selection process.

Research results also show that the predictive power of scientifically based test procedures, e g., cognitive ability tests, is often underestimated. And if, for example, personality tests are used, these are often scientifically not well-founded, e.g., the MBTI (Myers Briggs Type Indicator) or DISC (Dominant- Inspiring – Cautious – Supportive- Personality test). For example, Hossiep et al. (2000) have examined numerous personality tests from both the scientific field and commercial providers –the result is that not one of the 15 German-language personality tests and questionnaires analyzed has been scientifically proven to make a noteworthy contribution to improving selection decisions. This also applies to such respected and well-known tests as the German versions of the 16-PF (16 Personality Factors), the California Psychological Inventory (CPI), the NEO-PI-R, the EPI (Eysenck Personality Inventory), and the MBTI.

However, tests such as the MBTI or DISC are easy to understand and have high face validity. Low face validity was rated the most significant potential reason for scientifically proven psychological tests not finding their way into corporate practice (Benit & Söllner, 2013; Cohen, 2007; Deller & Albrecht, 2007; Albrecht & Deller, 2011).

In a meta-analysis, Schilling et al. (2021) show that candidates with higher cognitive abilities score higher on personality tests (but only in selection situations), providing evidence that applicants with higher cognitive ability are more likely to fake in personality assessment (Potočnik et al., 2021, p. 164).

Hossiep et al. (2015, p. 128) show in a study with 120 of the 580 largest German companies that 66% use personality-based methods, but these methods are questionable concerning their scientific validity. Among the reasons for the non-use of valid diagnostic procedures could be the lack of awareness of such procedures. This study shows that the DISC model and the MBTI test are the most frequently used methods. However, the DISC procedure is not valid for personnel selection and, therefore, not recommendable for talent diagnostics (König & Marcus, 2013, p. 191). Hossiep et al. (2015, p. 128) state that the well-known NEO-PI-R, despite its high validity, is still used relatively little (Costa, McCrae & Kay, 1995, p. 126).

Companies (and also applicants) seem to orient themselves less on scientific quality criteria than on other aspects, such as positive relationship building, costs, ease of use, or face validity when evaluating selection procedures (Walter, 2016, p. 107).

Highhouse (2008, p. 333) adds that although some practitioners know of these research findings, they are not aware of their usefulness in their particular situation: “Although one might argue that these data merely reflect a lack of knowledge about effective practice, there is considerable evidence that employers simply do not believe that the research is relevant to their own situation.”

As these studies show, it is not enough to know the rational-analytical standards in selecting people; applying them is much more essential.

2.1.3 Lack of (globally) recognized standards and guidelines in selection processes

Although there are approved standards, such as the DIN 33430/ISO 10667, to design personnel selection processes or guidelines for implementing assessment centers (e.g., International Taskforce on Assessment Center Guidelines, 2015), these standards have not yet been established in practice worldwide. However, working groups of the International Organization for Standardization (ISO), composed of representatives from various national standard organizations (practitioners, employer, and employee representatives, academics, etc.), develop voluntary international standards for HR/People Management and improve its quality worldwide. Nevertheless, the lack of knowledge, acceptance and implementation of selection standards in practice can be traced back to cultural peculiarities (see Chapter 7).

2.2 Lack of practicability of psychometric selection procedures and limited resources in organizations

2.2.1 Limited resources in organizations

Knowledge is only beneficial if someone is willing and able to take effective action and implement the necessary procedures in practice. For this reason, the following paragraphs show what prevents practitioners from using their knowledge of rational-analytical quality standards, such as the DIN 33430 or ISO 10667, or why they rely on their personal beliefs and impressions and less on scientifically proven, rational-analytical selection procedures.

New scientific results and recommendations, primarily science-based selection procedures, are not implemented because of insufficient resources, e.g., time, money, and people.

Practitioners often have problems, e.g., keeping up with current research findings, e.g., for reasons of time. They are criticized for not considering relevant research results, while considering their practical procedures as best practices, which are not sufficiently supported by evidence of scientific findings (Bellmann, 2013, pp. 1041–1042).

And to do a job of organizational requirements analysis, develop interview guidelines, or implement an assessment center according to psychometric rules need a lot of time, personnel, and monetary resources, especially for each position to be filled. Thus, it is comprehensible that the top management rarely supports corresponding psychometric procedures, especially when positions have to be filled rarely, e.g., only every five years. Therefore, especially in most SMEs, practicability plays a crucial role in the choice of personnel selection procedures.

The human resources managers are often under high time-and-cost pressure. They, therefore, scan applications in a matter of seconds. However, as long as personnel selection is seen rather as an administrative act that should be carried out as quickly and cost-effectively as possible, the resources required for a structured rational-analytical personnel selection are not provided. Additionally, HR managers often lack the necessary power to place the topic of high-quality personnel procedures more prominently in the company (Kanning, 2015, p. 149), where managing directors may not consider these procedures necessary and believe that the prevalent selection methods have worked well in the past.

Companies, as economic institutions, pay attention to the profitability of investments, and quality standards and the related selection procedures should be scalable in companies. More frequently used selection systems and procedures are practicable from a cost and time perspective. Thus from an economic perspective, it is understandable that if certain jobs have to be filled only relatively rarely, then the expenditure for requirement analysis, interview guidelines, behaviorally anchored rating scales, etc., is perceived as too high.

On the contrary, companies often prefer in-house tools for personnel selection rather than scientifically proven instruments (Berthel & Becker, 2017, p. 365) because the scientifically validated personnel selection procedures are considered very time-consuming, cost-intensive, and complex.

2.2.2 Lack of practicability of psychometric selection procedures

For many practitioners, the complexity of scientific findings and theories represents a barrier to implementing appropriate procedures (Lindemann, 2020, p. 48). Practitioners especially criticize the lack of practicability of scientifically proven selection procedures. In this context, practicability means the ease of use, the difficulty, complexity, and resources (time, money, workforce, etc.) required to implement a psychometric selection procedure.

The clues uncovered in scientific studies are often perceived as too abstract and unspecific. For example, the DIN 33430 selection standard, also in the new, revised version, is perceived as insufficiently concrete and less implementation-oriented, especially for SMEs without large personnel departments and related resources. In a study by LinkedIn (2019), almost 9 out of 10 small business owners report being directly involved in searching for, vetting, and interviewing potential staffers. These business owners, in particular, rely on their intuition and related experience, and are very critical of standardized selection tools.

Thus, these rational-analytical instruments' practicability and economic value are perceived to be lower than less valid ones (Kohn & Saar, 2006, p. 61). In addition, standards are often associated with additional bureaucratic work, less flexibility (Deters, 2017, p. 53), and high implementation costs (Braun et al., 2015, p. 101).

Therefore, research well-meant by science is far from being well implemented in practice, or, as an English saying goes: "The proof of the pudding is in the eating."

2.2.3 Lack of systematic and independent evaluation of the selection decision

One potential reason for the persistence in relying on their intuitive judgment is that hiring managers do not often use critical evaluations of their selection decisions (Kanning, 2016a, p. 29), and the main reasons are the lack of resources and knowledge.

And, if there is no systematic evaluation of the selection decisions made, hiring managers develop a subjective opinion of the success of the procedures they used. As a result, they favorably evaluate information that supports their decision while disregarding or reacting negatively to subjectively unsupportive information.

They seek self-serving information and want to reduce or avoid cognitive dissonance. According to the Festinger`s Theory of Cognitive Dissonance (1957), human beings strive for internal psychological consistency by avoiding information that does not confirm to their own opinion or perspective.

> In a selection decision-making situation, what this means is that, when a manager decides to extend a job offer to an applicant, he or she becomes more likely to evaluate that person as a successful hire in the future. To justify the initial decision, managers may attend only to the employee's successful performance outcomes and overlook the unsuccessful ones. Moreover, because the manager expects the employee to perform well, the manager may also provide opportunities and assignments that actually encourage the employee to perform successfully . . . Such behaviors would lend managers continued confidence in the efficacy of their current selection methods (Slaughter & Kausel, 2013, p. 62).

2.3 Hiring managers want control, flexibility, and autonomy

One main goal of rational-analytical processes and thus the standards is to achieve uniformity of a product or a process to satisfy specific requirements, while uniformity is what many practitioners, especially in SMEs, fear. They do not want to be restricted in their flexibility and freedom in designing selection processes. For them, standardization often seems to be a form of unification and bureaucracy, while, being successful and competitive in the market means being special, different, and unique.

Organizations' structures and processes are not an end by themselves but should reach specific user goals. Thus, procedures should meet users' specific and individual wishes and needs, for example, their desire for uniqueness or flexibility.

This striving for flexibility, uniqueness, and distinctiveness, to stand out from others, not to be standard, and to place increasing emphasis on the singular and the individual, is described in a very differentiated way by the sociologist Reckwitz in his book *The Society of Singularities* (2020). And, this striving for uniqueness also applies to applicants as customers in the job market. Standardization of processes – even if it may be helpful for economic reasons – is therefore viewed critically, especially in SMEs.

Managers fear that by adopting standardization, they may no longer be able to distinguish their organizations from competitors, which use the same procedures. They fear losing their main advantages as an SME, such as

- Flexibility (Because of their size and simpler structure, they have a greater capacity to adapt to changes and be closer to their customers, employees, etc.)
- Faster decision-making (Normally, they are much more agile than large companies, where decisions often require formal and complex decision-making mechanisms involving many people, etc.)
- Familiarity (Fewer staff members and smaller departments and more chances of getting to know co-workers and managers personally. It`s easier to know the competencies of others, the requirements of the jobs, etc.)
- Clear communication (Being closer to each other makes communication easier).

The desire to be special and unique and have the freedom and flexibility manifests in unstructured interviews and subjectively reasonable and non-standardized selection procedures.

And, hiring managers, especially in SMEs, are often convinced that standardized processes do not lead to better selection decisions.

In decision-making, rational analysis is often perceived as too time-consuming, slow, and paralyzing (Patterson et al., 2012, p. 39). Benit et al. (2014, p. 258) state that

> one reason for the frequent use of unstructured interviews may be that developing a structured interview is time and cost-intensive. To ensure the validity of structured interviews, interviewers usually have to participate in a workshop before conducting the interviews . . . A further explanation of the preference for unstructured interviews may be the interviewers' unwillingness to relinquish decision-making power. After unstructured interviews, interviewers can evaluate candidates' performance regarding their own nomination preferences. Unstructured interviews also allow interviewers to explore unexpected statements that arise during the interview

Lievens and de Paepe (2004, p. 41) attribute the preference for unstructured interviews to the need for autonomy and more control over the selection process. Many selection managers, especially line managers (e.g., managing directors in SMEs), do not want to be told what to do or how to conduct an interview. Investigating their resistance to standardized decision-making practices is critical to understanding why psychometric and evidence-based selection procedures are not implemented in practice. The theoretical contributions of this study are that it empirically identifies autonomy needs as a user-related factor, and it demonstrates that individual differences in perceptions of autonomy are related to people's general causality orientation. The practical contributions of this study are that it demonstrates that written descriptions of employee selection practices are capable of influencing people's beliefs about autonomy potential and that modifications to standardized practices can be made to enhance people's perceptions of autonomy potential and the subsequent use intentions (Nolan & Highhouse 2014, pp. 343–344).

As shown, there are many unintended risks associated with using standards. For example, standards can lead to more formalization and bureaucracy, thus restricting flexibility, autonomy, and freedom.

If the risk of wrong or lousy staffing is reduced by using standards, hiring managers are constantly faced with other threats. Therefore, weighing the advantages and possible disadvantages of such selection procedures is always a matter of weighing the advantages and disadvantages.

And, hiring managers may find it difficult to change something if there is no pressure to do so. For example, if HR managers feel no pressure from their management directors, applicants, and other stakeholders to change their selection procedures, they don't tend to do so.

2.4 Felt lack of recognition for practical-intuitive competence and experience

Especially in SMEs, managers rely heavily on their entrepreneurial intuition and consider their business acumen very important when making decisions. And in this way, patterns of thought and behavior in organizations are developed and consolidated.

Patterns, frames, or schemes as mental structures shape the way humans see and interpret the world and their specific perspectives and their ways of thinking, deciding, and behaving. Patterns can limit perception and judgment because they exclude some contextual factors, ideas, views, etc., and pattern recognition describes mental processes that match information from a stimulus with information retrieved from memory. Intuitions, as a kind of pattern recognition, are based on experiences. They are directly connected to the emotional or limbic brain (see Section 4.2.4), meaning that lack of agreement on psychometric issues is not just rooted in ignorance. Experienced hiring managers especially want to rely on their intuition. They consider their intuitions and related emotions as valuable signals for selecting personnel; they will not change their minds and selection behavior simply because they have more knowledge. "Simply delivering scientific facts to an audience is not convincing to most people. You need to frame issues in ways that resonate with your audiences" (Robertson, 2019, p. 21).

People develop into experts in specific areas over their lives. And, people also develop this expertise concerning whether another person is a good match for them or not. What applies to their choice of a partner in private life also develops at the professional level. Therefore, selection managers develop an intuition and a related feeling that they have learned to rely on (Kas, 2007, p. 84).

For Gary A. Klein (2019 and 2020, see also Klein et al., 2019), expertise and intuition are not opposites but are closely related. Not only are scientific researchers in a specific research area true experts, but so are many experienced, highly skilled practitioners who know when to rely on their intuitions.

Most managing directors of SMEs interviewed in our empirical research say, "We rely on our experience and our knowledge of human nature in our decisions, especially in personnel selection" (Röbe-Oltmanns, 2020, p. 31).

Personnel managers, recruiters for personnel consultants, or other hiring managers are responsible for selecting suitable candidates. If the entire process is standardized, they often no longer feel personally involved and accountable for selection decisions. Some feel that not acting autonomously has devalued their role as experts, despite having experience and intuitive knowledge, especially when the scientific requirements for the selection process are perceived as over-standardized and restrictive of their freedom and flexibility (Weuster, 2012, pp. 212–213).

Even if Highhouse calls the personnel selection experience of practitioners a myth (Highhouse, 2008, p. 337), many practitioners see these experiences as meaningful and helpful skills. Unfortunately, recruiters often feel devalued and not recognized and appreciated for their practical experiences by the scientific community. The desire for self-enhancement is, therefore, understandable.

2.5 Selection as a social exchange and acquisition process: the meaning of emotions, social validity, and a positive applicant experience

A further significant reason for the science-practitioner gap is that the scientific rational-analytical approach to personnel selection does not accept, recognize, and value that personnel selection actually is a social exchange and acquisition process.

Personnel selection procedures, for example, interviews, are processes of mutual influence. Darwin wrote almost 150 years ago:

> The movements of expression in the face and body, whatever their origin may have been, are in themselves of much importance . . . They serve as the first means of communication between (people). . . . We readily perceive sympathy in others by their expression; . . . and mutual good feeling is thus strengthened. The movements of expression give vividness and energy to our spoken word. They reveal the thoughts and intentions of others more truly than do words (Darwin, 1872, pp. 365–366).

The rational-analytical approach demands the hiring manager to be a more or less uninvolved data recording observer who should exert as little social influence as possible on the applicant. And this also means reducing the impact of intuitions and emotions. But this is not how the practice of personnel selection works, especially in interviews or assessment centers.

Hiring managers and candidates actively influence each other's perceptions and behaviors in the interview. Thus, communication in selection interviews is accompanied by constant feedback loops through which the hiring managers and candidates constantly influence the behaviors of their counterparts.

Many practitioners know that expressing perceptions of candidates in words or even operationalizing and scaling observations in an assessment center with numbers does not come close to the reality of their experience. In practice, hiring managers have great difficulties in verbalizing their impressions and observed behaviors of other people and what they find good or bad about them; quantifying them purely rational-analytical and criterion-oriented. Instead, they take a holistic approach and use both their unconscious and conscious knowledge (see System 1 and System 2, Section 4.2.2.4).

In rational-analytically oriented science, everything expressed in language or numbers dominates. On the one hand, this is understandable; on the other hand, many practitioners find it challenging to put their intuitions and emotions into the format of rational language. And even more, many practitioners feel cut off from the messages of their intuitions and feelings if they are not allowed to consider them in making decisions. And unlike Kant, who believed that people are only truly free when they follow their reason and not their feelings (Kast, 2007, p. 32), many practitioners see this entirely differently. Intuitively, selection managers sense and feel whether a candidate fits them, their organization, or their team. And they don't want to make their selection decisions without these sources of insight. The conscious mind is closely coupled to human language and therefore primarily puts forward arguments that can be verbalized. However, what can be put into words is not necessarily what is considered essential when selecting personnel (Kast, 2007, pp. 76–77).

Aldous Huxley (n.d.) expresses these relationships as follows: "We must learn how to handle words effectively; but at the same time, we must preserve and, if necessary, intensify our ability to look at the world directly and not through that half opaque medium of concepts, which distorts every given fact into the all too familiar likeness of some generic label or explanatory abstraction."

In addition, assessment centers, in practice, often have significant shortcomings, such as poor planning, inadequate job analysis, weakly defined dimensions, insufficient exercises, lack of pretest evaluation, unqualified assessors, inadequate assessor training and candidate preparation, not multiple assessors evaluating each candidate in each exercise, lack of behavioral checklists or poorly designed checklists, sloppy behavior documentation and scoring, and misuse of results (Lievens, 2016, pp. 6 and 11; Caldwell et al., 2003).

Hiring managers and candidates interact not only through verbal expression (the content of spoken words, choice of words, etc.), but also through the emotions shown on the nonverbal level. In this way, spoken words and physically expressed emotions (e.g., facial expressions, gestures, postures, paralinguistics (such as tone of voice, loudness, inflection, or pitch), eye gaze/contact, or proxemics (personal space, physical distance, etc.) create interpretative thoughts in both the candidate and the hiring manager. And these, in turn, lead to new behaviors so that an interview is always an interactive, transpersonal interaction of mutual influence (Sinclair, 2011b, p. 11).

In all human relationships, there are explicit and implicit communications. For example, in a selection process, an applicant's professional experiences are regularly discussed concretely. But then there are hidden messages that resonate simultaneously. And these hidden messages are often about recognition, appreciation, respect, relationships, and power or control. The processes of perception on the emotional level run primarily intuitively and are not consciously controlled (Plassmann, 2019, p. 50). Thus, human intuition and emotions help perceive and interpret these hidden messages.

Emotions and the associated feelings are sources of information and assessments in the complex processes of human communication.

Intuitions and emotions can be considered evolutionary heritage and part of human nature. But the rational-analytically oriented process of personnel diagnostics tries to leave no room for intuitions and emotions, and demands personnel selection free of them.

Recruiting, as a process of sourcing, attracting, assessing, and employing applicants for an existing or new position within the organization, should create a positive applicant experience. Companies seek to give applicants an experience that gives a positive overall impression throughout the entire recruiting process. This positive applicant experience plays a decisive role in whether a candidate decides for or against a position. Research shows that organizations that focus on this positive "candidate experience" during the recruitment process strengthen the employer brand while improving recruitment and business outcomes (Miles & McCamey, 2018).

The competition for the best talents is about recruiting in an applicant-oriented way. And this goes beyond the mere selection process and attempts to integrate the applicant's perspective.

A core success factor for a positive candidate experience is a positive relationship and the associated emotional bond between the candidate and the selection manager.

Research results show very clearly that, among other factors, personal contact, respectful communication, warm behaviors of hiring managers (Farago et al., 2013, p. 224), and a relationship that is perceived as pleasant, authentic, appreciative, and generally positive plays a decisive role for the candidate in the application process. Psychological research on emotions shows that the connection between people begins with emotional resonance and understanding in an ongoing conversation (Plassmann, 2019, p. 45).

Hiring managers show emotions and use their intuition to win candidates for a company. Thus, they try to create positive relationships by showing positive emotions. Emotions provide a sense of belonging, attachment, and solidarity in organizations (Miller et al., 2007).

Here, SMEs often have a particular advantage since they usually manage better than large companies to present the soft factors in the choice of work very well. In addition, they provide positive experiences for applicants because the future colleagues are often introduced to the candidate during the first interview, and the applicant can get an impression of the company and the team (Verhoeven, 2016, pp. 134–135).

The acceptance of the selection procedures by applicants also plays a decisive role in the positive candidate experience. Research results show that scientifically confirmed and valid methods do not always meet with acceptance among applicants. Suppose a personnel selection procedure is not accepted, no matter how valid, it will still not contribute to the company's success because it will deter too many qualified applicants in advance (Funk et al., 2015, p. 29).

Applicants must perceive a selection process as fair and just, and they want personal contact with their interviewer. Therefore, selection managers should personally meet applicants (Schuler et al., 2007, p. 64).

2.6 Self-confidence and overconfidence in one's abilities, striving for decision-making power, and "belief systems" of decision-makers

Our comforting conviction that the world makes sense rests on a secure foundation: our almost unlimited ability to ignore our ignorance. (Daniel Kahneman, 2011, p. 201)

From the perspective of Kanning, one of the most important reasons for not applying rational-analytical selection procedures lies in the almost blind self-confidence of many decision-makers in their selection competence.

Many practitioners are convinced of having an excellent knowledge of human nature, enabling them, from their perspective, to select personnel competently (Kanning, 2004, p. 58).

Kahneman (2011, pp. 14–15) describes that people are prone to overestimate how much they understand their world and underestimate the role of chance in events. Reasons for this belief are the unwillingness to make a cognitive effort and that recent memories rise up more quickly than older ones. Thus, people rely on their intuition.

For example, the renunciation of written requirement profiles or interview guidelines is not only justified by a lack of resources but also by the experiences and professionalization of the selection managers and thus by intuitions as judgment-forming instruments. "Due to the experiences from their daily practice and the associated necessity of forming judgments based on their intuition, they also apply this behavioral pattern, which is considered successful, in personnel selection and do selection procedures without supporting and standardizing procedures" (Bastian, 2018, p. 121).

Kahneman (2011, p. 212) considers this aspect of self-confidence very critically:

> Subjective confidence in a judgment is not a reasoned evaluation of the probability that this judgment is correct. Confidence is a feeling that reflects the information's coherence and the cognitive ease of processing it. It is wise to take admissions of uncertainty seriously. Still, declarations of high confidence mainly tell you that an individual has constructed a coherent story in his mind, not necessarily that the story is true.

And Kahneman is convinced that neither the quantity nor the evidence counts for much in subjective confidence that results from intuitive system thinking. If the story is coherent for the manager, confidence is high. This is disastrous in some ways because people can make a very coherent story out of very little information and information that is unreliable. The quality of the story depends very little on the quality and quantity of the data. So, people can be very confident – with very little reason. Therefore, self-confidence should be questioned critically in diagnostics for whether you can trust yourself or somebody else. And, if you are to evaluate whether you can trust somebody with a lot of confidence, that's not the way to do it. The way to do it is to ask what environment they have been in and have had an opportunity to learn its regularities. Subjective confidence is not a good adviser (Kahneman, 2011b).

Nachtwei et al. (2013, p. 39) show that HR and line managers assume that their intuition plays a significant role in decision-making. A study by van der Zee et al. (2002) shows that HR managers prefer intuitive, unstructured interviews to structured ones. The authors cite general attitudes, subjective norms, and "belief-based" attitudes of HR managers that significantly influence their intention to conduct one or the other type of interview as reasons for preferring unstructured interviews to more valid ones (Krause 2017, p. 247).

For example, Lievens et al. (2005, p. 464) show that Belgian retail managers attach much more importance to skills and characteristics from an unstructured interview than to the same abilities and characteristics measured by tests. This applies regardless of the perceived relevance of the skills or characteristics to the job.

Headhunters report that they intuitively know who`s the best fit for the company because of their experience and good knowledge of the culture of the client companies. They feel threatened by young, inexperienced people (such as psychologists who have not yet seen a company from the inside) and their approach of using psychometric tests and assessment centers (Gigerenzer & Gaissmaier, 2012, p. 2). As a result, they do not feel valued in their competence, and sometimes even feel devalued. And, that builds resistance.

Highhouse is very critical of practitioners` belief in their abilities as personnel selection decision-makers solely based on experience and a supposedly good understanding of human beings:

> I have argued that one of the reasons that people have an inherent resistance to analytical approaches to hiring is that they fail to view selection in probabilistic terms. A related but different reason for employer resistance to use selection decision aids is that most people believe in the myth of selection expertise. By this I mean the belief that one can become skilled in making intuitive judgments about a candidate's likelihood of success. This is reflected in the survey responses of the HR professionals who believed in `reading between the lines` to size up job candidates. It is also evidenced in the phenomenal growth of the professional recruiter or 'headhunter` profession (Finlay & Coverdill, 1999) and the perseverance of the holistic approach to managerial assessment (Highhouse, 2008, p. 337).

Our empirical research shows that managing directors in smaller companies sometimes have specific personnel selection practices. For example, an advertising agency managing director asks applicants to play table tennis with him. When asked about this, he said that he wants to see how someone reacts spontaneously to unforeseen events, whether they get involved or run themselves down (e.g., by saying: "I can't do that."), or whether they take up the new challenge, remain open and make positive contact with the managing director. Another example: A managing director said he invites applicants to a trial workday and conducts a small test with the shortlisted candidates: "We have a corridor in our warehouse where you can only walk one after the other. And if I then run behind the applicant and the speed gets on my nerves, and they slow me down too much, it won't work. So if someone sneaks along in this aisle like that, then that is not a person for us" (Röbe-Oltmanns, 2020, p. 36).

For example, research by Shelley E. Taylor (Taylor & Brown, 1988; Taylor & Gollwitzer, 1995) shows that human perception and decision-making are often positively biased by the "positive illusion" that leads to overestimating oneself, one's health, professional abilities, leadership skills, etc., or to the illusion of having control over situations.

Understandably, people look for competence and control beliefs from a psychological perspective. But, overconfidence in one's abilities can lead to self-enhancement (see Section 3.5.2). Self-enhancement refers to the observation that people strive to feel good about themselves. Such a positive self-observation can lead to specific information-processing biases, such as hiring managers who cast themselves in an unrealistically flattering light. Overconfident and insufficiently self-critical managers can tend to believe themselves to be experts in human nature and exaggerate their ability to bring about the desired outcomes (Brown & Kobayashi, 2003). Kahneman & Klein (2009, pp. 517–519) described such managers as overconfident pseudo-experts. Based on the fact that intuitive expert decisions can be highly accurate and extremely faulty, and off the mark, the authors explain that a skeptical attitude towards expertise and expert judgment is needed. "True experts . . . know when they don't know. However, nonexperts (whether or not they think they are) certainly do not know when they don't know. Subjective confidence is, therefore, an unreliable indication of the validity of intuitive judgments and decisions" (Kahneman & Klein, 2009, p. 524).

Overconfidence leads to judgment processes based on a high subjective validity (Larrick et al., 2007, p. 76), mainly where managers have been in business for several years and rely on their experience and gut feelings. If they defend decisions with their "knowledge of human nature," "experience," or "intuition," no one will ask critical questions anymore. Knowledge of human nature and claimed experience thus become the most crucial weapon in the fight against psychometric personnel selection and immunizing decision-makers against criticism. From the perspective of psychology, blind faith is an understandable human illusion. Numerous studies in the past decades have uncovered the causes and effects of erroneous judgment formation (Kanning 2015, p. 138; see also Kanning, 1999; Kanning et al., 2004; Werth, 2004).

Managers at higher hierarchical levels, managing directors or even independent entrepreneurs, see themselves responsible for selecting the right employees. They see themselves as competent decision-makers who can rely on themselves; they often do not want to give up decision-making power to systems and tools. Instead, they count on their knowledge of human nature, previous experience, and intuitive competencies in personnel selection.

For the final say, hiring managers want to use their subjective judgment. Hiring managers rely on their subjective judgment for collecting predictor information because they believe in developing expertise in predicting job performance. Accounts suggest that experienced managers believe that years of interviewing experience and the richness of the information exchanged between interviewer and interviewee can lead to improved accuracy (Slaughter & Kausel 2013, pp. 57–60).

For Apelojg (2010, p. 180), one of the main reasons for relying on intuitions and emotions is structurally based decision-making power, such as hiring executives or entrepreneurs. This decision-making power enables them to follow their intuitions and not hire employees against their feelings.

Even if personnel recruiters apply proper methods correctly due to their professional competence, it can still happen that (skilled) superiors and managing directors make the final recruitment decision without having the necessary professional competence (Kanning, 2012, p. 109; Kanning, 2015, p. 149). Executives in their position of authority influence the judgments of the personnel managers if they are involved in the process. For example, they signal their preferences without psychometric diagnostic knowledge (e.g., possible distortion effects), and the personnel practitioners follow their judgment for integrity reasons (Kanning, 2015, p. 145). Wald et al. (2018, p. 10) reveal that around 44% of those surveyed did not involve HR managers in the final selection decision. Guion (2011, p. 24) also addresses this issue. He writes that managers, without the necessary know-how, are either skeptical about the test procedures and their results or overestimate the test results and overlook the actual implications. In some cases, the selection manager alone decides whether or not to take the test results into account for the final decision.

Frequently, the lack of professional competence is overshadowed by the wealth of experience of personnel decision-makers (Kanning, 2012, p. 108; Kanning, 2015, p. 145). Confidence in one's own experience and intuition is often very dominant, and the awareness of the lack of specialist competence does not exist; thus, the need for further training options is not perceived (Kanning, 2015, pp. 146, 149). This can lead personnel selection managers and decision-makers to resist scientifically proven selection methods or new technologies (Highhouse, 2008, p. 333). In addition, selection processes and procedures are rarely systematically reviewed and evaluated retrospectively so that possible errors may not be revealed. Hiring decisions are seldom reflected in the selection process, even in the early termination of the newly hired employee (Kanning, 2012, p. 108).

Selection decisions are very complex. And the more complex the environment, the tasks, and the associated demands on selection managers, the more pronounced the need for simplicity. According to the constructivist view, human beings construct their realities subjectively based on their experience, knowledge, social and situational factors, etc. Consequently, they tend to choose explanatory principles for their own actions and events in their environment that are personally familiar to them.

Suppose scientific findings and psychometric knowledge about statistical correlations, validities, reliabilities, or quality standards such as the DIN 33430 are not part of the intellectual toolbox of many personnel managers. In that case, it is understandable that they use the intuitions and feelings they experience in themselves, their existing knowledge, and their own experience in personnel selection as a basis for successful personnel selection.

Although such bases have easily identifiable shortcomings from a psychometric perspective, and although this dangerous cocktail of competence illusion and complacency may have a narcotic effect, these hiring managers and their self and competence perception should not be devalued and dismissed as unsuitable. Instead, practitioners should evaluate their experiences with critical-constructive openness, curiosity, and respect. Only by acknowledging the "existing situation and current status" (which always has its positive sides and its benefits) can sustainable changes be brought about in these personnel managers (Kegan & Laskow Lahey, 2009, pp. 31–32).

3 Rational-analytical quality in selecting and hiring candidates

Neither the best personnel selection procedures nor the most experienced decision-makers can guarantee the right personnel selection. Consequently, miscasts cannot be avoided entirely. However, avoiding them would be desirable for economic and social reasons. On the company side, poor selection decisions are associated with early turnover and fluctuation costs, and on the employee side, with being under- or over-challenged, not feeling well, stressed, and so on (Melchers, 2017, p. 1). A right decision regarding the position to be filled is key to the success of the organization and the employees. Consequently, the quality of personnel diagnostics is of central importance (Kersting & Püttner, 2018, p. 3).

To define what is meant by quality in personnel selection, it is necessary to have a uniform concept of quality and, thus, a consistent definition.

But what is understood by "quality," and how the term is defined varies not only in theory and practice but also in different cultures, and possibly from person to person and situation to situation. Quality means different things to different people; indeed, the same person may adopt different conceptualizations, at different moments. This raises the issue of "whose quality?" (Harvey & Green, 1993, p. 9).

In principle, quality can be understood as the degree to which a procedure satisfies specific requirement criteria. Therefore, in science, requirement criteria of the quality of personnel selection have been developed; these criteria correspond to the psychometric paradigm and, thus, to the rational-analytical procedures.

> Many researchers view rational-analytical decision-making as the contrast to intuitive decision-making. For example, Dane & Pratt (2012) state that "analytical decision making is highly dissimilar to intuition in that analytical approaches involve the use of systematic procedures designed to thoroughly assess all pertinent information, evaluate costs and benefits, and invoke conscious deliberation" (p. 4). But Dörfler & Ackermann (2012, p. 559) note critically using non-intuitive as opposed to intuitive rather than analytical, to avoid misunderstandings and contradictions.

Rational-analytical decision-making is conscious, slow, and systematic information processing by making logical connections that result in a reasoned judgment (Soffner, 2021, p. 19). Rational-analytical selection procedures are based on research and try to exclude intuitions and emotions as sources of error. An increase in the quality of personnel selection is to be achieved by adhering to scientific standards such as validity, reliability, or objectivity.

The rational-analytical procedures of judgment and decision-making in personnel diagnostics and hiring candidates are primarily oriented towards the use of reasoned, thoughtful, and structured reflection. These decision-making procedures are systematically and consciously reflected upon and controlled by mental activities. They are based on collecting, analyzing, and interpreting information, consciously

https://doi.org/10.1515/9783110980967-003

calculating the pros and cons, and choosing what appears to be the best outcome. Particularly in selection processes, a rational-analytical approach is oriented to clear rules, standards, and/or guidelines. As Sadler-Smith (2010, p. 11) writes: "The analytical mind is the rule maker and rule follower."

How practitioners define quality in selection varies from manager to manager and company to company and is, often, very subjective. Practitioners define quality differently, based on varying experiences, resources, needs, contexts, and objectives. On the one hand, there is a scientifically oriented definition of quality in personnel diagnostics, in practice. On the other hand, our empirical research shows that quality in personnel selection is not clearly defined for most interviewed managers and companies.

However, research suggests that our interview partners agree that quality in selection and hiring processes should not be defined subjectively. The ISO 8402–1986 standard defines quality as "the totality of features and characteristics of a product or service that bear upon its ability to satisfy stated or implied needs."

Like the quality of products, the quality of a selection procedure can be determined not only by the results but also by the process. Quality begins with the creation of a product, the manufacturing process. Therefore, errors or defects in the personnel diagnostic process inevitably lead to defects in the product or result (Schmidt-Atzert & Amelang, 2012, p. 130). But it should also be noted that "unfortunately, no matter how good a selection system is, it cannot correct problems of poor supervision, inadequate training, lack of proper equipment, or inconsistent performance management" (Ryan & Tippins, 2009, p. 33).

The primary need or goal of selection and hiring processes is selecting and hiring the most suitable candidates. To determine and hire (or promote) the most qualified candidates, it is helpful to differentiate between quality in selection (process) and quality in hiring or promotion (result). Thus, the criteria for quality in hiring or promotion (result) and quality selection (process) should be clearly defined.

3.1 Quality of hire

The rational-analytical or psychometric perspective on quality in selection processes meets scientific quality criteria such as objectivity, reliability, and validity. A selection decision should be based on evident selection results.

The quality of hire can be defined and evaluated by the new hire's performance and the fulfillment of the required competencies for the job specification. Thus, the quality of hire can be seen in the effectiveness of the hiring process; this means that from the available candidates, the most suitable candidate, who, most likely, would make the best contribution to the organizational success, is selected. In addition, this quality of hire or promotion can be measured by metrics such as early fluctuation rate, productivity, and other performance criteria.

The quality of hire can also be measured by the satisfaction of the employee's manager with the new employee or the job satisfaction of the new employee, the support of his colleagues and manager, the retention rate, career development, and so on. Quality, in this perspective, means fulfilling the specific customer or user requirements. In essence, this is what is meant by predictive validity. Predictive or criterion validity describes how a selection process effectively estimates a candidate's performance, based on a few outcome measures; for instance, the outcome measure, or criterion, the performance of the candidate, is the primary variable of interest in this analysis, because the score in the selection process (construct) is correlated to the role success (criterion).

The main goal of personnel selection is to predict who will be successful and perform well on the job. Measurable and operationalizable success factors are required to determine success or good performance. Therefore, HR professionals or hiring managers need to answer the following questions:

1. What are the success criteria and performance outcomes for the job/specific position or a global leader? In the literature and organizations, different criteria for success are mentioned. However, success criteria are not uniform, consistent, or standardized: possible examples are results of performance appraisals (by executives, supervisors, customers, peers, etc.), performance measurements, for example, reaching goals, career or salary developments, and personal satisfaction.
2. What are the predictors of success, for example, adaptability or good performance on the job, and in that organization? Which competencies/behaviors are necessary to perform that job? Are there further predictors, for example, support by a spouse?
   - There are different predictors for success as a global leader. Mesmer-Magnus & Viswesvaran (2008) distinguish in their research on expatriate selection between
   - Person-related predictors (competencies, expectations, maturity, willingness to move, etc.) Job-related predictors (technical knowledge, qualifications, work, leadership and international experience, language skills, availability, etc.)
   - Non-work-related predictors (support by family, health status, country-specific and cultural requirements, such as standard of living, environment, safety, social security, medical care, cultural offerings, and religion)

3. How can the predictors of interest be measured in the selection process? What are the best selection techniques and methods to measure the predictors?
4. How will the information collected be analyzed, combined, and interpreted to make the selection decision? Must scaled behavioral anchors and numerical evaluation sheets be used?

Some of our interviewed HR managers made it clear that the quality of a selection procedure depends only on the quality of the hire or promotion. Practitioners told us in this context that in the end, it does not matter how the candidate was selected, as long as the results are positive (performance on the role). Here, the concept of quality of selection is only seen from a result-oriented perspective; this leaves room for intuition in the process of selection.

An interviewed HR manager from a global organization said:

> In the end, it's the result that counts. Quality is shown in the fact that we've hired the right people. This is particularly evident in whether they perform or not. How the selection process was designed is rather irrelevant. But, of course, we must evaluate whether someone is successful. And if not, we have to check why. This may be because the selection process went badly. But, poor performance can also be due to something completely different.

In a similar vein, the head of a large personnel consultancy in England argues:

> As long as I`m successful and get positive feedback from my clients, I don't need the confirmation of science that I have done everything right from a scientific point of view. I need confirmation from my clients. The customer determines good quality in personnel selection, not the science. Quality is what the clients want. And if they are happy with the selected candidates and the candidates perform, I know I did a good job.

Defining quality from the customer's perspective is a widespread practice and, at the same time, an expression of a certain kind of rationality. Moreover, it reflects agreement on quality in selection between the customer and the hiring manager.

3.2 Quality of personnel selection

The quality of the hiring decision is measured, in particular, by the later performance of the new hire. However, employee performance is influenced by various factors, on which the selection process cannot have any influence, for example, leadership by the supervisor and feeling comfortable in the team. Thus, the hire's performance and the fulfillment of the required competencies cannot be the only quality criteria. Since we cannot predict what will happen after hiring and employing a candidate, it is essential to raise the quality of the selection decision to the best possible level, before the influence of everything else affects the candidate's subsequent performance. Thus, the quality of the selection decision must also be assessed at the time of the decision process. This is why the quality of the selection process is so important. In this way, a good starting position should be created, on which the onboarding process and making the newly hired employee successful can then be built.

A rational-analytical decision-making style is based on precise, structured, and systematic analysis and encompasses conscious and well-calculated judgments. The rational-analytical selection decision should be based on specific steps of selection, comprehensible facts, and transparent assessment criteria. In this way, a selection decision can be understood by others. Rational decision-making presumes that available information enables the decision-maker to settle for the best possible alternative.

Research clearly shows a close connection between the quality of selection (from a scientific perspective) and the quality of the hire (represented, for example, as predictive validity).

From a scientific perspective, good quality personnel selection should include a mixture of selection methods, be requirement- and evidence-oriented, and be based on explicit decision-making rules (Kersting & Wottawa, 2014, p. 39).

To realize these quality requirements, standards for selecting suitable applicants, such as the ISO 10667 or (in Germany) the DIN 33430 (Kersting & Püttner, 2018, p. 2), have been developed. In addition, science expressly demands implementing selection instruments according to science-based quality criteria (Kanning, 2004, pp. 164–165.).

The Industrial and Organizational Psychology (I-O-psychology) area particularly

> emphasized the empirical evaluation of the value of employee selection methods that were based on principles of scientific research methodology being developed in experimental psychology and on standardized measurement of individual differences. . . . The basic cornerstone of employee selection from the perspective of I-O psychology is that measures of the abilities, knowledge, skills and other characteristics of job applicants can be used to predict which individuals will be (more) effective employees. Such measures are developed systematically, based on job requirements, to maximize accuracy and minimize error in the assessment of these individual differences among applicants (Farr & Tippins, 2010, p. 2).

Quality criteria in a selection process can be defined from three main perspectives:

1. Psychometric quality criteria (objectivity, reliability, validity, etc.)
2. Reciprocal quality criteria
   2.1 Social acceptance, fairness, justice, and ethics (social validity, maintaining the psychological contract, accepting a procedure by selecting managers and applicants, building a positive relationship, ensuring a positive candidate experience, and so on; and the acceptance of selection procedures is also influenced by cultural factors, the labor market situation, etc.)
   2.2 Legal and ethical criteria (general personality rights, data protection, labor law, ethics of IT-based, for example, artificial intelligence procedures)
3. Economical quality criteria: Organizational effectiveness and efficiency, including cost-effectiveness, cost–benefit ratio, practicability (i.e., resources required, feasibility, and ease of use), and the availability of a candidate (Deters 2017, pp. 62–63).

Looking at the quality in personnel selection from these different perspectives shows that the quality of personnel selection processes is inevitably related to the specific context of this process and the interacting parties. Thus, the information process in selecting candidates, what data and information are included, how they are processed, and so on, is directly tied to the situational context. As shown in Chapter 7, what constitutes quality of selection also differs between and within cultures.

3.2.1 Psychometric quality criteria

Psychometric quality criteria refer to the systematic collection of job requirements, the objective measurement of these job requirements such as skills and knowledge, abilities, attitudes, personality traits, and educational achievement, and the statistical underpinning of quality criteria, for example, objectivity, reliability, and/or validity. This is not the place to describe these various quality criteria in detail, and how they can be observed in designing selection procedures (a detailed description can be found in Deters, 2017, pp. 65–70). Instead, the aim is to briefly describe how selection procedures should be designed, so that consistency with scientific quality criteria is guaranteed, as far as possible.

Psychometric selection procedures aim to provide measurable, objective data and reduce reasons for low validity, for example, unstructured selection interviews. Psychometric personnel diagnostics is characterized by a conscious procedure by which results are converted into signs (language, scores, etc.), translating observations in CV screenings or application forms, interviews, or assessment centers into verbal scales or numbers. Therefore, in an interview or assessment center, for example, scaled behavioral anchors and evaluation sheets are required to evaluate the observed behaviors of the candidates, numerically. Thus, to get consistent observations and scorings of an applicant from a psychometric point of view, it is necessary to define behavioral anchors and to have clear rules for converting observations into scores.

Research clearly shows that a combination of selection procedures (e.g., general cognitive ability tests and structured interviews) based on scientifically proven research findings leads to better selection decisions (Schmidt et al., 2016). Thus, the psychometric selection procedures are based on evident research results and help HR managers secure a high-quality selection process and high-quality hiring.

In order to benefit all concerned (especially candidates and hiring managers), the decision-making process in personnel selection should be free of personal interests, biases, or arbitrariness. In addition, a rational-analytical approach in personnel selection requires that selection decisions should be based on the best available evidence and, thus, on sound research and not opinion.

3.2.2 Evidence as a prerequisite for high-quality selection decisions

Evidence has validity beyond subjective opinions and experiences. Therefore, evidence-based selection procedures should use theory-derived, research-based information and reflect the current state of empirical knowledge, that is, the best available "evidence" from systematic research. Evidence-based selection procedures, thus, require scientific, that is, methodologically determined proof. Furthermore, such a proposed procedure must be understandable, transparent, and explicitly justified.

Evidence-based hiring decisions should rely on empirically collected and evaluated scientific findings and be made based on empirically proven effectiveness of procedures. Empirical data is obtained, when the collection is conducted in a methodologically validated, systematic, and transparent process. Selection managers should use concrete and explicitly stated criteria and methods to interpret a procedure, based on evidence, ensure objectivity, validity, and reliability.

The everyday experience of human beings can lead to conclusions that contradict scientific findings. This is not only true in personnel selection but also, for example, in medicine. Here, people may rely on homeopathy or alternative therapies, whose benefit is not proven from a scientific perspective but have helped these people. This subjective evidence is based on the motto: One who heals is right.

A central question is defining and proving the effectiveness of a (selection) procedure. The classic answer to this question is: Effectiveness is equivalent to achieving the objectives of a procedure; and the reliable determination of effectiveness is done in validity studies. These are based on several methodological premises (paradigms). Proof of effectiveness requires specific study designs and settings, for example, in medical research:

- a study (= experimental conditions)
- on a cohort (= repeated observations on many participants)
- with one control cohort (= comparison)
- that is randomly generated (= randomization)

Different levels of evidence can be distinguished (based on OCEBM, 2011):

Ia Systematic reviews; availability of at least one systematic review (meta-analysis), based on methodologically high-quality randomized and controlled studies.

Systematically collected data that verifiably meet scientific quality criteria and are subject to a review process by experts before the results are published in a (high-ranked) scientific journal.

Ib Individualized randomized controlled trials; availability of at least one high-quality randomized and controlled study with sufficient sample size.

IIa Availability of at least one high-quality controlled study (non-randomized control).

IIb Availability of at least one high-quality quasi-experimental study.

IIc Systematic reviews (with homogeneity) of cohort studies.

III Availability of more than one high-quality non-experimental study (e.g., several high-quality descriptive studies).

IV Individual case-control study; case-series. This level of evidence can also be achieved in research by using qualitative research methods and the interpretation of interview results with a variety of experts (to ensure interrater-reliability).

V Intersubjectivity: Experts agree on a given set of meanings or definitions of the situation. In selection processes: Hiring managers share and integrate their subjective impressions about an applicant in an open, transparent discussion and reflection process. As a result, they reach a consensus or an agreement on an applicant's suitability for a vacant position.

Thus, the demand for evidence can be seen as a strategy to ensure quality and credibility, recognizing valid and reliable knowledge and proven procedures.

It is possible to reach evidence levels IV and V without a systematically performed scientific validity study, if there has been a corresponding exchange between the hiring managers and a systematic evaluation of the selection decisions. But, intersubjectivity, in particular, and thus, the agreement of selection experts on a candidate to be selected, is the weakest form of evidence. The claim of selection managers that even their professional experience can count as evidence cannot be accepted from a scientific point of view. The subjective belief that a specific selection procedure is of high quality cannot be described as credible, as evidence must be objective, from a scientific perspective.

Although subjective selection decisions based solely on intuition can be understood and even justified, they do not meet the quality criteria of evidence-based procedures.

Thus, from a scientific perspective, evaluating the effectiveness of selection procedures should not be based on individual or subjective personal experiences or observations.

The requirement that selection procedures and decisions should be evidence-based excludes specific selection procedures, especially those with very low objectivity, reliability, and validity (e.g., personnel selection based on graphology, astrology, or unstructured types of interviews). Therefore, in practice, scientifically proven methods and the corresponding acquired knowledge should be applied in personnel selection.

Nevertheless, several practitioners that were interviewed do not accept that the sole authority to interpret the evidence and determine the quality of personnel selection procedures should lie with science. This may be due to the imposition of a standard devaluing knowledge and practices that are not evidence-based, from a scientific perspective. For example, if practitioners feel that their competence, expert knowledge, experience, and intersubjective evidence of selection procedures are not taken seriously, their resistance and their criticism of science as too theoretical and not realizable in practice, is understandable (see Section 2.4).

The rational-analytical procedures in personnel selection, based on evident research results, for example, the DIN 33430 or ISO 10 667, are guidelines that will only be applied in practice, if the potential users are convinced of their value and benefit for their success (Kleebaur, 2007). To put evident and scientifically proven research results into practice, one should not make the mistake of thinking that these research results or DIN and ISO norms speak for themselves. Many practitioners fear that these norms and standards do not meet organizational context-specific requirements and restrict their autonomy and flexibility. Moreover, their competence in personnel selection is mainly based on their experience and expert knowledge of selecting appropriate candidates.

Moreover, the research results must be clearly formulated and available, if they are to be applied. Indeed, their implementation can measure the usefulness of research results, in practice. And, evidence-based findings from the research are only implemented in practice, if they are known and tailored to the users and their contextual environments. In addition, the individual attitudes, expertise, and related experience of the decision-makers should also be considered.

Evidence-based research findings in personnel selection are of little value, if they are not implemented.

3.2.3 Psychometric selection procedures

3.2.3.1 Standardized design of selection processes and instruments

One aim of standards is to describe a common understanding of quality and, at the same time, to create a common language for quality. Therefore, a standard is "a required level of quality" (Deters, 2017, p. 62). Standards are (usually) consensually developed, tested, and agreed-upon requirements and rules that should be followed in specific processes. They promote the comparability, similarity, and homogeneity of processes across organizations and can, thus, increase confidence in the quality of these processes and the quality of the products. Standards, as a guideline, give orientation and can lead to greater clarity and security about how to behave, how applicants are to be treated, and which processes they have to go through. In addition, they foster transparency, equal treatment, and comparability of candidates.

On the other hand, standards limit flexibility and individual adaptation to specific circumstances. As a result, they can lead to higher costs and time expenditure, for example, for developing job descriptions and interview guidelines. Complex and abstractly formulated quality requirements can also be challenging to understand and may meet skepticism and, even, rejection (Deters, 2017, p. 51).

The more standardized the selection processes are, the more likely they will meet psychometric quality criteria (Deters, 2017, pp. 61–121).

In a study by Mc Daniel et al. (1994) (see also Levashina et al., 2014), unstructured means no predefined questions, no grading on rating scales, and in the end, a global judgment is made. Structured or standardized means that predefined, job-related questions are used consistently for all applicants, without asking further questions. In addition, rating scales are used, and an overall evaluation expressed in numbers is made at the end of the interview.

A meta-analysis conducted by Schmidt and Hunter (1998, pp. 265, 272; see also Schmidt et al., 2016) shows which selection methods and instruments (and combination of methods) have a high degree of validity, and which, due to their low values, resemble a random selection. For example, tests for measuring "general cognitive abilities and general intelligence" (Schmidt & Hunter, 1998, p. 264) achieve a validity of 0.51 and work samples of 0.54, thus advocating their use in practice (Schmidt & Hunter, 1998, p. 272).

Employment interviews are the most frequently used technique in personnel selection, and applicants and selection managers accept them very well. Many studies have shown that interviews can validly predict job performance (Oostrom et al., 2016). However, the validity of interviews differs according to how they are structured. While the validity of structured interviews is relatively high (0.51), unstructured interviews reach only $r = 0.38$. Thus, structured interviews are preferable. If tests and structured interviews are combined in the selection process, a validity of 0.63 can be achieved (Schmidt & Hunter, 1998, p. 265).

Related to unstructured interviews, Weuster (2012, p. 205) states that the selection decision is made in the form of an intuitive, impressionistic global assessment, sometimes as a random decision or as an ad hoc decision, according to the "matching chemistry" or "from the gut." From a scientific perspective, the disadvantages of unstructured interviews outweigh the advantages (Kanning et al., 2008, p. 123), and highly structured interviews are superior to less structured or unstructured interviews (Levashina et al., 2014; Kanning, 2019, p. 580). Huffcut & Culbertson (2011) discuss "The Paramount Role of Structure." "If a sample of researchers and practitioners in the field were asked what was the single most important influence on the interview process and its outcome, a majority would no doubt say it is structure" (Huffcut & Culbertson, 2011, p. 194).

Oostrom et al. (2016) show that structured, situational interviews predict candidates' work-related performance because "participants' ability to decipher situational demands correctly was related to performance in both the interview and work-related situations. Furthermore, the relationship between the interview and performance in work-related situations was partially explained by this ability to decipher situational demands. Implications: Assessing interviewees' ability to identify criteria might be of additional value for making selection decisions, particularly for jobs where it is essential to assess situational demands."

The research of Schmidt & Hunter (1998) and Schmidt et al. (2016) confirm that selection procedures with a higher level of standardization are superior to those with a lower level of standardization (Schmidt & Hunter, 1998; p. 272; Lodato et al., 2011, p. 353). Also, to ensure that all candidates are asked the same questions, it is advisable to standardize them, using interview guidelines (Kanning, 2004, pp. 411–412). Standardization of questions and structured interviews increases candidates' comparability and helps decision-makers make better decisions (Conway et al., 1995, p. 575).

> The research evidence . . . shows that different methods and combinations of methods have very different validities for predicting future job performance. Some, such as person-job fit, person-organization fit, and amount of education, have low validity. Others, such as graphology, have essentially no validity; they are equivalent to hiring randomly. Still others, such as GMA (General Mental Ability, J. D.) tests and integrity tests, have high validity. Of
>
> the combinations of predictors examined, two stand out as being both practical to use for most hiring and as having high composite validity: the combination of a GMA test and an integrity test (composite validity of .78); and the combination of a GMA test and a structured interview (composite validity of .76). Both of these combinations can be used with applicants with no previous experience on the job (entry level applicants), as well as with experienced applicants. Both combinations predict performance in job training programs quite well (.78 and .72, respectively), as well as performance on the job. . . . The validity of the personnel measure (or combination of measures) used in hiring is directly proportional to the practical value of the method – whether measured in dollar value of increased output or percentage increase in output. In economic terms, the gains from increasing the validity of hiring methods can amount over time to literally millions of dollars. However, this can be viewed from the opposite point: By using selection methods with low validity, an organization can lose millions of dollars in reduced production, reducing revenue and profits (Schmidt et al., 2016, pp. 48–50).

Based on meta-analyses of data, more recent research shows that unstructured interviews may possess greater validity than previously recognized. In other words, it may be the case that unstructured interviews are as valid as structured interviews (Oh et al., 2013, pp. 298 and 323).

In their study from 2016, Schmidt, Oh, and Shaffer included new data from research conducted over the last 20 years, taking into account progress in research methodology and, therefore, providing more accurate results; in addition, new selection methods and criteria, such as telephone interviews and school grades, which were not considered in 1998, were included. Furthermore, corrections were made about possible distortions of validity coefficients by range restrictions and publication bias. As regards the validity of interviews, they came to surprising results. While structured interviews in the 1998 study had a validity of 0.51, unstructured interviews only had a validity of 0.38. But the study of 2016 shows that structured and unstructured interviews can very well have the same high validity (0.58).

According to Oh et al. (2013), an explanation of why unstructured interviews can also be of relatively high validity is that interview validity is determined more by content (the constructs being measured) than structure (the mode of measurement). Likewise, unstructured interviews may be conducted by skilled human resource professionals or managers with significant interviewing experience. Such interviewers may possess a repertoire of effective interview techniques applied rather consistently across candidates. In addition, the free-flowing structure of the informal interview puts the subject at ease and perhaps "off guard" and allows more diagnostic cues relevant to factors that predict job performance. They, therefore, conclude that just as it is possible to conduct poorly structured interviews, it may also be possible to conduct good unstructured interviews.

These results of Oh et al. (2013) and Schmidt et al. (2016) show that skilled and experienced hiring managers can be successful even without complete standardization of interviews.

Eisenkraft (2013) shows in a study that people can make accurate judgments about the personalities of applicants, even based on small behavioral excerpts. In particular, when the judgments of several assessors are evaluated, measurement errors are reduced, and, thus, validity, that is, predictive validity concerning performance and success in the job, is increased. This means that intuition is particularly risky, if assessors do not critically question their conclusions and do not reflect on their judgments with other hiring managers (Nachtwei et al., 2013, p. 36).

However, the more specific and narrowly defined the job requirements to be measured, the more structured the interview. Thus, high-quality selection interviews shouldn't completely lack structure. Semi-structured interviews with behavioral anchors and rating scales are an excellent way of assessing an applicant's personality, values, motives, and fit with the company, corporate culture, team, and job.

Therefore, only the core elements of a rational-analytical selection interview are presented here (Schuler, 1996, p. 87; Ackerschott et al., 2016, p. 103; Krause, 2017, p. 248).

Core elements of a selection interview (from a psychometric perspective)

1. Requirement-related interview design using a job description: This should be based on a systematic requirements and job analysis. For the requirements analysis, Kanning (2015, p. 85) recommends distinguishing between competence dimensions, which use consistent criteria and a scale to show the extent of competence to create a comparable assessment standard for all applicants.
2. Ensure that all candidates are assessed against the developed job requirements and selection criteria, at every stage.
3. Restrict the interview to those requirements and questions that cannot be identified more reliably by other personnel selection procedures, such as analyses of CVs and tests.
4. Structure the interview: Develop, at least, a semi-structured interview guideline based on the job requirements and use tested and anchored behavioral scales (the empirical verification of individual questions). Use these anchored scales to score every candidate.
5. Several questions should be asked for each requirement and selection criterion.
6. Make sure that the recruitment process meets ethical and legal requirements.
7. Appoint multiple (at least two) interviewers.

8. Integrate components/exercises from different selection methods, for example, from an assessment center (a critical situation in the position to be filled), and use tests, for example, cognitive ability tests.
9. Separate observation and collection of information from decision-making.
10. Use structuring tools to observe and evaluate the interview and document the results.
11. Train all interviewers.

Figure 1 given an example of a standardized evaluation of interview questions.

Questions:
Have you taken any leadership roles during your studies, for example, at university or in a club? Have you been, for example, a class representative or youth group leader? Have you organized an activity, for example, a theatrical performance or a youth camp for a larger group, on your own? (Further question: How long did you do that?)

Evaluation of the answer	
– (3 points)	Management responsibilities with a specific action designator (class representative, management of youth groups in the club, etc.) for at least 2 years
– (2 points)	(Other) management tasks with a concrete action designator for at least 3 months
– (1 point)	Management tasks without formal function (e.g., field trip or youth recreational organization)
– (0 points)	No or only insignificant management tasks (e.g., organized group orders)
. . . . .Total points	

Figure 1: Standardized evaluation of a selection interview (referring to Schmidt-Atzert & Amelang, 2012, p. 324).

An excellent way to conduct interviews with high validity is the Multimodal Interview, developed by Schuler (2014) (see Section 10.3.5).

3.2.3.2 Psychometric tests as part of rational-analytical procedures

Psychometric testing aims to assess how a candidate's specific characteristics and abilities will relate to the requirements of a particular role by identifying and measuring a candidate's abilities, for example, cognitive abilities, personality (traits) and behavioral characteristics, integrity, attitudes, motivation, skills, knowledge, leadership potential, and intercultural competencies. They identify the extent to which a candidate's personality or cognitive abilities match those required to perform the function. The information collected from the psychometric test can identify hidden aspects of candidates that are difficult to get from a CV or an interview. Thus, tests can help determine which candidates are most likely to succeed in a particular job.

A psychometric test that meets the scientific quality criteria is developed using statistically examined methods. And, a test should not care about a candidate's looks, name, gender, race, sexual orientation, height, weight, and so on.

Setting up a psychometric test as a filter for a flood of candidates can effectively reduce the number of people the hiring manager spends time and energy with. Thus, psychometric tests can improve selection decisions and reduce recruitment time and costs.

A good psychometric test meets scientific quality criteria such as objectivity, reliability, and validity. Also, it should be perceived as fair and unbiased against any particular candidate and administered and interpreted by someone qualified to do so, competently.

Many psychometric tests are valid and reliable in predicting the performances of candidates and success in a specific job. Met analyses have shown that a valid psychometric test, for example, cognitive ability, integrity, or personality tests (one valid personality test is the NEO-PI-R), can improve recruitment outcomes (Schmidt et al., 2016).

Personality and personality traits manifest themselves in thinking, feeling, and behaving. The personality of human beings is more or less stable, and enduring characteristics influence their thinking, feeling, experiences, perceptions, and behaviors (Eysenck, 1953, p. 2).

Personality tests confirm relatively high stability of personality, and especially personality traits. This assumption, which characterizes many concepts of personality (e.g., Big Five personality traits by Costa &McCrae, 1988), is that people's behavior remains relatively constant, regardless of the social context or situation. Researchers have conceptualized personality in various approaches, but among all personality characteristics, five factors are widely accepted and most commonly used by researchers and practitioners to describe and evaluate individual personality. These five factors are extraversion, agreeableness, conscientiousness, emotional stability, and openness or intellect. Researchers labeled these five factors the "Big Five" (Costa & McCrae, 1988).

But, human behavior is also influenced by the context; behavior can be explained as a reaction to the behavior of others, for example, the behaviors of applicants in response to the behaviors of an interviewer (and vice versa). Thus, it is necessary to look at the interaction of personality and situation (interactionism). In some contexts, the influence of the situation is overpowering, whereas in others, it is minimal, and all variations in behavior are due to personality characteristics. Therefore, it is essential to recognize the influencing personality and situational factors on human behavior.

Research shows that there is a dynamic in the process of personality development. Many twin studies show that there is always interplay between genes and the environment. For example, in a large-scale twin study in Germany, 300 pairs of same-sex twins aged 18–70 were investigated. The study shows that differences (total variance) across all personality traits could be explained by genetic influences in

42% of cases, by effects through the environment shared by the twins in 18% of cases, and by the impact of the environment specific to the individual twin in 35% of cases (Spinath et al., 2002). In a study by Assary et al. (2020), 2800 pairs of identical uni- and dizygotic twins were interviewed . Their analysis led them to assume that 47% of the different sensitivities of the respondents were due to their genes, the other 53% due to environmental factors. The results also show that the genetic basis of a person's sensitivity determines the extent of positive or negative experiences and their effects on behavior.

For many researchers, human personality is much more than personality traits. Personality is also determined by a person's motives, values, attitudes, or habits. Using this broad definition of personality, our "personality is constantly developing" (Specht, 2018, p. 14). Personality development is not only a question of human maturation but also depends on taking on social roles and responsibilities, for example, in the transition from school to working life or the founding of a family. Personality characteristics such as attitudes, values, or motives are more accessible to change than intelligence or personality traits (Asendorpf, 2018, p. 217). High stability in social-emotional personality characteristics is only achieved in old age. The Big Five personality traits (Costa & McCrae, 1988) are relatively stable until the age of 55 and then become more unstable (Asendorpf & Neyer, 2012, p. 271).

Personality development takes place based on our genes and environmental influences; conversely, from a dynamic-interactional perspective, people can also influence their genes (e.g., epigenetic change by DNA methylation or histone modification) and the environment through their personality and related ways of thinking and acting. Thus, shown behavior is not only a consequence of personality characteristics but also of situational factors (Asendorpf & Neyer, 2012, pp. 304–308).

What does this mean for selection decisions? First, the behavior shown in a selection process should not automatically be attributed to stable personality factors but also situational context reactions.

For example, a target personality profile is required when using personality tests. This ideal-typical picture of the desired job holder is compared with the applicant's actual profile. This reveals specific personality and associated behavioral tendencies. The more the existing profile of a candidate meets the target profile, the less "energy" the candidate needs to invest to meet the requirements of the job or the environment's expectations.

In addition, scientifically-based personality tests, usually based on self-assessment, should be supplemented by external assessment, for example, by peers or superiors (Oh et al., 2011; Poropat, 2014).

However, results of psychometric tests are often challenging to understand for people without psychological education or training. Companies using psychometric test procedures, thus, often consider procedures and processing results that require no psychological training or degree to understand them. Nowadays, many psychometric test reports, for example, on personality or integrity, are less complex and easy to understand. Usually, test providers use simplified, real-world language and graphics that tell the hiring managers and candidates precisely what they need to know.

Using modern, for example, AI-based test procedures can create a powerful initial impression of an employer's brand, since applicants may be attracted to new recruitment and selection processes. Applicants often name the objective approach to assessing their capability as a key reason behind their satisfaction with the recruitment process (see Section 2.5).

To select (global) leadership talents, it is essential to assess the potential of candidates.. Psychometric assessment is about future-proofing. In the age of digitalization and fast change, it is not enough to look at someone's CV and do a traditional interview, from a psychometric perspective. Identifying and developing the potential to handle challenging situations, having the right mindsets, attitudes and attributes such as situational awareness, openness, flexibility and adaptability, and other personality characteristics will be crucial to the future workplace.

Specific tests of cognitive ability, personality, or integrity can help analyze an individual's more "hidden" traits and potential because formal education and past experience will not always provide a clear, up-to-date assessment of these personal competencies and potential.

Psychometric tests can increase the scope of information. IT-supported data analysis methods can also help recognize patterns, interrelationships, and correlations and improve personnel selection decisions. The human mind has clear processing limits and is subject to effects such as distortions of perception. For this reason, analytically oriented personnel selection can be further optimized using IT-supported psychometric data analysis methods (e.g., artificial intelligence; see Chapter 8).

Psychometric results, for example, results of a high valid cognitive ability or personality test, can be used for pre-selection. The results of a personality test, in particular, can also be used to provide valuable information of the applicant in the further selection process.

Personality tests, in general, are controversial in personnel selection because many of them show relatively low validity; Funk et al. (2015, p. 27) have calculated the validity of 0.12 as the mean across different scientific studies. However, a meta-analysis by Barrick et al. (2001) shows that conscientiousness is the most valid personality trait for predicting professional performance (.27), and the second most valid personality trait is emotional stability (.13). "Results support the previous findings that conscientiousness is a valid predictor across performance measures in all occupations studied. Emotional stability was also found to be a generalizable predictor when overall work performance was the criterion, but its relationship to specific performance criteria and occupations was less consistent than was conscientiousness" (Barrick et al., 2001, p. 9).

Since the significance and validity of many personality tests used in practice (e.g., MBTI) for predicting career success as (global) leaders are relatively low, and because in many countries, managers and applicants are critical of tests as methods of personnel selection, these test results should be handled very carefully. They could be used to reflect on and analyze possible reasons for deviations and as a basis for more in-depth or clarifying questions in the selection interview.

Additionally, using language analysis software and personality tests based on social media data can also be criticized, mainly because the scientific quality of such methods has not been clearly proven (see Sections 8.6–8.12).

As a result, it can be stated that valid psychometric tests can help filter the candidates (especially for "high volume recruitment") and make selection decisions much better informed, but they can't make a decision perfect.

3.2.3.3 Development and application of selection decision rules

Personnel selection decisions are usually complex, because they have to consider various contextual factors. To cope with this complexity, rules can be helpful in giving orientation to selection decisions.

From a rational-analytical perspective, selection decisions should not be based on subjective convictions and intuitions but on rules previously developed and agreed upon by selection experts. Therefore, according to psychometric requirements, a necessary step is developing, documenting, and applying explicit and verifiable decision-making rules. In addition, some selection standards, including the ISO 10667, the DIN 33430, Standards for Assessment Center or Interviews, Standards for Educational and Psychological Testing, International Guidelines for Test Use, and Principles for the validation and use of personnel selection procedures, also point to such rules. (Many examples for standards are given in Kersting & Püttner (2018, p. 16). For decision rules in selection processes, see Kanning (2004, pp. 268–285).)

A decision rule is a "sequence of information-processing operations" to form – based on the information available – a preference, judgment, and decision (Pfister et al., 2017, p. 96).

With the implementation of decision rules, the selection process is more standardized, and in particular, the following goals and associated advantages should be achieved:

- Objectivity and transparency are promoted when the decision rules and job requirements are clear to all selection managers. Therefore, they do not proceed according to subjective rules or requirements but according to those implemented in a systematic survey process. In this way, the subjective influence of the individual hiring manager can be reduced, and scientific quality criteria can be applied more efficiently.
- The scientifically proven quality of personnel selection increases. Through the exchange between managers and the agreement on rules, on the one hand, the knowledge gained from experience is used, and on the other hand, a practical

approach to learning with and from each other is encouraged (Wottawa, 2013, pp. 914–916).
- The legal position is strengthened if concrete, objectively understandable reasons for the rejection of an applicant can be given (Wottawa, 2013, pp. 914–916).
- Equal treatment and fairness are fostered, because all candidates are assessed according to the same rules, which are decided upon before starting the selection process. With precise procedures and decision-making rules, every candidate is treated more equally, and discrimination and biases can be reduced.

Acceptances and rejections of candidates are perceived as fair, as they can be justified with previously defined selection criteria and decision-making rules.
- A personnel selection process based on clear rules and requirements can be evaluated more systematically, afterward. At the same time, it is possible to see whether the selection process and the associated decision rules need to be adapted and changed.

A question to be answered is how decision-making rules are developed. From a rational-analytical perspective, these rules should be set, as far as possible, based on scientifically proven evidence (Westhoff & Flehmig, 2013, p. 906).

In theory and practice, very different decision rules for personnel selection have been developed so far, depending on the corporate context, corporate goals, or even requirements of specific stakeholders (e.g., concerning diversity and prevention of discrimination). In addition, the particular labor market situation, such as the availability of specific skills, also plays a significant role in determining which rule is used. Thus, no generally valid decision-making rules for personnel selection have yet been developed.

In many companies, especially SMEs, selection managers often have implicit decision-making rules in mind, without explicitly knowing or formulating them or making them transparent. For example, such rules could be that no one will be hired without at least a grade of "good" (B) on their math degree or an IQ score of 100. Or that they do not employ anyone they personally dislike or who they feel does not fit into the team.

A distinction can be made between a) scientifically guided and b) subjective individual decision rules. However, it becomes clear that this distinction cannot always be maintained in practice, since even scientifically guided procedures can incorporate subjective and individual experiences.

3.2.3.3.1 Scientifically guided and systematically developed decision rules

Job requirements and competency models often do not provide concrete cut-off scores, such as how distinctive an applicant's cognitive ability or achievement motivation should be (Montel, 2006, p. 129).

To develop the decision rules, selecting and evaluating criteria and ratings of aspects of the job, in this case, predictors for job success are needed. To get these predictors, a correlation should be established between selection results (e.g., test results or scores in an interview or assessment center) and various criterion measures or scores, which should be based on reliable and valid performance measurement systems, for example, objective performance data or objective assessments by superiors.

In this context, a few questions must first be clarified. What makes successful job holders different from others? What scores and rater judgments do they achieve in quantitative procedures such as tests, questionnaires, interviews, assessment center evaluations, or analysis of application documents?

In addition, it must be clarified how the selection criteria (required KSAOs) should be weighted, for example, personal characteristics and predictors such as cognitive ability, language skills, technical knowledge, or other required competencies. For example, the weighting of the criteria measured can be based on evaluating which KSAOs are particularly decisive for success on the job or when the lack of a particular KSAO might indicate the likelihood of trouble.

Often, practitioners weigh up the measured selection criteria against each other and make a distinction between "must have" (e.g., define minimum KSAOs, Deters 2017, p. 155), "should have," and "nice-to-have" qualities. Not only scores of selection criteria (predictors) should be measured, but also the gut feelings of hiring managers can be included in this weighing up, for example, positive feelings toward a candidate on a scale from 1 to 5 (Montgomery, 1983, p. 343). Then, based on this information, one or more rules can be developed and used for decision-making. One rule in practice can be: "We don`t hire a candidate we have a bad gut feeling about."

The decision rules apply the same way to the specific job to be filled as for analyzing all job-specific data sets. Decision rules may include the following aspects: Interpretation examples, cut-off scores, profiles, tolerance scores, the weighting of KSAOs and specific competency dimensions, critical differences, norms, and mathematical allocation rules (Kanning, 2019, p. 346; in this book, Kanning gives several different examples for decision rules in personnel selection; see also Schmidt-Atzert et al., 2018, pp. 199–200 or Wottawa, 2013).

Montgomery (1983, p. 345) gives some examples of decision rules:

- **DOM (dominance rule):** An option is chosen if it "dominates" the others (candidate A is better than candidate B on at least one criterion measured and not worse on all other criteria). Using a complete pair comparison can be very time-consuming if you have many applicants (unless you use IT-supported procedures).
- **CON (conjunctive rule):** In this case, cut-off scores are defined for every selection criterion. Only candidates whose scores exceed or are equal to predefined baselines are selected. These could be cut-off scores, for example, at least 100 on the IQ standard classification scale, minimum scores in knowledge or ability

tests (e.g., 80% correct solutions in a concentration test or other performance tests), or specific physical fitness criteria in selection of police officers.

Cognitive ability, conceptualized as a mental or intellectual capability for abstract reasoning, problem-solving, thinking abstractly, comprehending complex ideas, learning quickly and from experience, and adapting to new tasks and environments, strongly predicts learning and overall job performance, leadership effectiveness, and career success (Ones et al., 2012; Deters, 2017, p. 166). An IQ test score is calculated, based on a norm group with an average score of 100 and a standard deviation of 15. The standard deviation is a measure of spread, in this case, IQ scores. An IQ score of 100 means that the test-takers performance is at the median level of performance in the sample of test-takers of about the same age used to norm the test. An IQ score of 115 means performance one standard deviation above the median, a score of 85 performance one standard deviation below the median, and so on.

A standard deviation of 15 means 68% of the norm group has scored between 85 (100 − 15 = 85) and 115 (100 + 15 = 115). In other words, 68% of the norm group scored within one standard deviation of the average (100).

Also, 95% of the norm group has an IQ score within two standard deviations of the average. So, 95% of the norm group scored between 70 (100 − 30 = 70) and 130 (100 + 30 = 130). This means scores of over 130 only occur in 2.5% of cases.

In employment testing, cut-off scores can filter out job candidates who did not score high enough on a pre-selection test or assessment. Candidates who fail to obtain the required scores in the pre-selection test can be excluded from further selection procedures and receive a rejection. Conversely, the applicants who have exceeded the required scores remain in the selection process.

Cut-off scores are only as good as the test and the outcome measures used to "validate" them. Cut-off scores can be determined using different methods. Classical test theory assumes that each person has a "true score" (T), which would be obtained if there were no errors in measurement. A person's true score is the expected number-correct score over an infinite number of independent test administrations. Unfortunately, test users never observe a person's true score, only an observed score (X). It is assumed that the observed score corresponds to the true score plus some error:

For cognitive ability or IQ, a cut-off score could be (depending on the job and job requirements)

- one standard deviation above the average score
- two standard deviations above the average score

As a rule, no single IQ score is recommended as a cut-off, but an IQ in the range of 85–115 might be established as a requirement for specific jobs or applicants (see Figure 2).

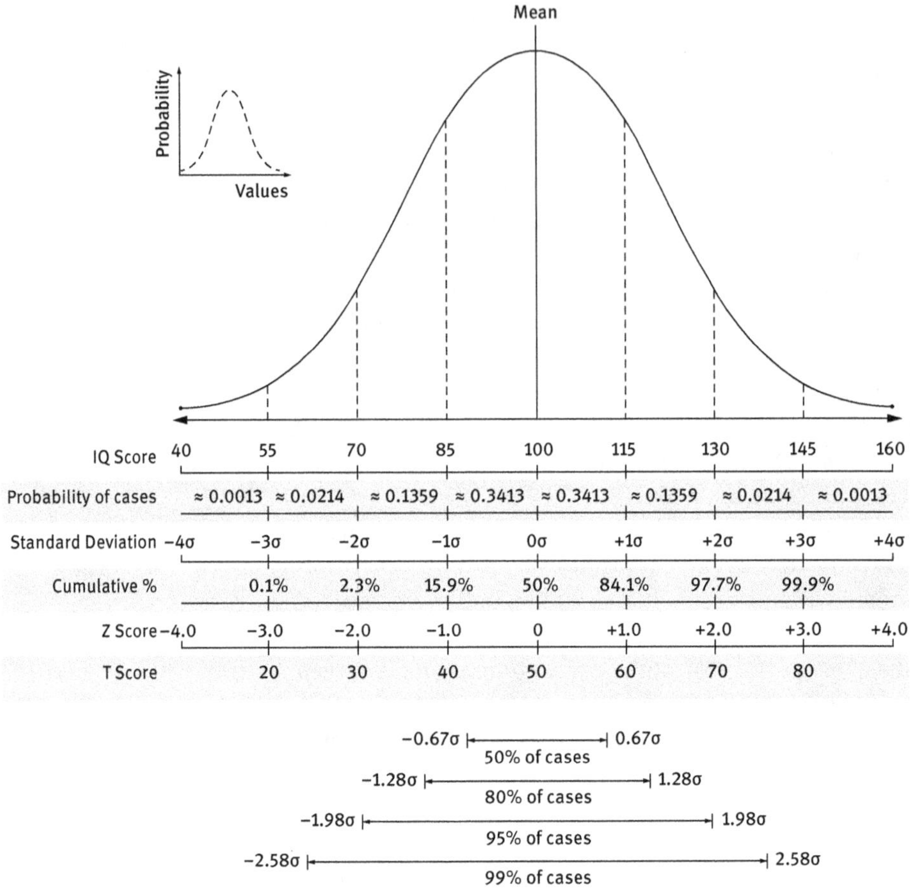

IQ Range ("deviation IQ")	IQ Classification
130 and above	Very superior
120–129	Superior
110–119	High Average
90–109	Average
80–89	Low Average
70–79	Borderline
69 and below	Extremely Low

Figure 2: Wechsler (WAIS–IV, WPPSI–IV) IQ classification (data provided by 123test, 2022).

Research shows that traits such as conscientiousness and emotional stability are valid predictors of job performance (Salgado, 1997; Deters, 2017, p. 166). However, decision rules for personality tests, integrity tests, intercultural adaptability, or global leadership tests may also be helpful (Deters, 2017, pp. 167–171). Therefore, apart from the fact that the test results can be used as information for further interviews with the applicant, companies and selecting managers can also formulate minimum scores or specifications for specific items such as emotional stability or cultural adaptability. This can be done by taking the test results of successful managers as a benchmark for comparison with the test results achieved by applicants.

The following decision rules should be discussed for appraisals and performance reviews by superiors of (internal) candidates.

- **DIS** (Disjunctive Rule): Only candidates with at least one score exceeding or equal to a predefined baseline are selected. This can be useful in pre-selection, for example, concerning a degree or score in a specific subject or a final or exam grade.
- **LEX** (lexicographic rule): Candidate A is chosen over candidate B if s/he is better on the most critical criterion measured (KSAOs). If this is not possible, the choice is based on the next most vital measured criteria. The most important attributes should be defined in advance, in order of importance for the job, and it must specify by which criteria the importance of an attribute is determined. Then, a profile comparison can be made between the applicant's and target profiles.
- **EBA** (elimination-by-aspects rule): This method first identifies a single most important attribute to the decision-maker. Exclude all candidates who do not fulfill the most critical attributes. If a candidate doesn't meet the cutoff score for these attributes, then s/he is eliminated from consideration. Repeat this procedure with new criteria measured in the order of importance.
- **MAU** (Multiattribute utility rule): Each scored attribute is multiplied by its percentage of importance (the weighting factor for all criteria measured together is 1,0 = 100%). The overall score of a candidate is determined by the weighted total (sum) of the attribute scores. A psychometric procedure requires these numerical (quantitative) data (Görlich & Schuler, 2014, p. 1151). This decision rule is widespread in personnel selection (see Figures 3.1–3.3).
- **Multiple cutoff rule:** A minimum cutoff score for several criteria measured can be formulated. Only those whose scores are above the minimum cutoff for every attribute are selected. A ranking procedure can be used if several applicants score above this cutoff.
- **Ranking rule:** Rather than using an absolute score, applicants are ranked according to their performance compared to other candidates. Then, depending on the number of vacancies to be filled, the person or persons ranking highest are selected.

In Figures 3.1–3.3, rules to analyze and evaluate candidates are shown, example evaluation of a curricculum vitae (see Deters, 2017, p. 158; according to Mueller, 2012, p. XXVII).

It is also possible to weigh the different job requirements as follows; the result is to choose candidate B:

Selection criteria (KSAOs)/job requirements	Weighting		Candidate A		Candidate B	
	Rank	(max.) score *x*	Individual judging points *y*	Individual judging sum: *x* multiplied by *y*	Individual judging points *y*	Individual judging sum: *x* multiplied by *y*
Study degree in engineering	1	10	8	80	4	40
Foreign language skills	2	9	7	63	6	54
Foreign experience	3	8	2	16	8	64
Work experience (at least 3 years in a company)	4	6	6	36	6	36
Leadership experience	5	5	4	20	5	25
Shown flexibility and mobility	6	4	2	8	4	16
Total amount				223		235

Figure 3.1: Choose the candidate with the highest sum (weighted): candidate B.

Job requirements	Weighting factor (sum = 1,0)	Score of candidate B (0–10)	Score × weighting factor
A (e.g., study degree in engineering)	0.3	7	2.1
B (e.g., technical knowledge)	0.3	8	2.4
C (e.g., foreign language skills)	0.2	6	1.2
D (e.g., leadership experience)	0.2	4	0.8
			Sum 6.5

Figure 3.2: Weighted score for candidate B (decision – choose candidate B).

Job requirements	Weighting factor (sum = 1.0)	Score of candidate A (0–10)	Score × weighing factor
A	0.3	8	2.4
B	0.3	5	1.5
C	0.2	5	1.0
D	0.2	5	1.0
			Sum 5.9

Figure 3.3: Weighted score for candidate A.

The rational-analytical approach demands a standardized evaluation of questions asked in a selection interview (see Figure 4).

On the subject of leadership experience, for example, the following questions could be conceivable: "Did you take on any leadership tasks during your studies or school days, for example, in sports or as a student representative? Have you perhaps organized an activity for a larger group on your own, for example, a theater performance or a trip with a sports team? If so, for how long did you do this?" (Schmidt-Atzert & Amelang, 2012, pp. 324–325).

Evaluation of the answer	Score	Description of "leadership motivation in the past"(0–10)
–	10 points	Leadership tasks with a concrete job description (student representative, leading youth groups, etc.) for at least 2 years
–	5 points	Leadership tasks with concrete job description (student representative, leading youth groups, etc.) for at least 1 year
–	2 point	Leadership tasks with concrete job descriptions (student representative, leading youth groups, etc.) for at least three months; organizing a school/class trip, youth leisure time, theater performance, and so on
–	0 points	No or only insignificant leadership task

Figure 4: Evaluation and scoring of answers in a job interview (Schmidt-Atzert & Amelang, 2012, p. 324–325).

At the end of an interview, every selection manager's scores are added up, and an average is taken. Then, the results/scores of the different applicants are compared, discussed, and placed in ranked order (DIN 2016, p. 14).

The described decision rules by Montgomery are non-compensatory (Montgomery, 1983, p. 346). This means that an organization decides that every potential candidate should at least perform on specific attributes with a particular score, for example, 5 in leadership experience, and a candidate should be sorted out when their score in "leadership experience" is below 5. The non-compensatory rules do not allow a low score on one criterion to be compensated by another criterion.

Compensatory decision rules: It can be decided that a specific attribute or job requirement can be compensated by another one. When applying a compensation strategy, the organization and hiring managers consciously accept that strengths can compensate for weaknesses in a job requirement. In any case, it should be carefully considered whether such a compensation decision rule makes sense.

For example, a candidate's low score in working in a team can be compensated by a high score in another critical attribute. Finally, the candidate who achieves the highest multi-attribute score is selected.

Conversely, a company can decide that low performance in one job requirement (for example, eyesight for pilots or ability to concentrate for flight controllers) cannot be compensated by high performance in another. Therefore, which job requirements or predictors are used and whether it should be possible for other criteria to compensate for a poor score in a specific attribute should be decided based on the results of a job and requirements analysis and evaluated data (Schmidt-Atzert et al., 2018, pp. 199, 411–412).

Digitally supported methods are increasingly being used systematically to evaluate correlations between competencies and success on the job. In particular, using data mining, big data, or people analytics can support this process (see Sections 8.1–8.4).

3.2.3.3.2 Implicit decision-making rules

If the selection process is systematically planned, the selection managers are committed to decision rules and the required KSAOs (Kanning et al., 2008, pp. 64–65). In practice, personnel managers often decide by using the decision rules that have been most successful in the past. When considering how to decide, the trade-off between accuracy and effort must be taken into account: The more closely taken into account and calculated the various influencing factors are the more accurate, but also complex, the decision rules (Pfister et al., 2017, p. 248). It depends on the management's willingness and resources (time, money, etc.) and how systematically developed and agreed-upon decision rules in personnel selection are used.

In practice, these decision-making rules can also be carried out implicitly by individual judgments of hiring managers. The selection managers make a holistic, intuitive, overall assessment of the applicant. They evaluate a candidate, for example, on the whole as "good," without being able to define precisely whether the applicant is good in all attributes or very good on some and satisfactory on others (Pfister et al., 2017, p. 97).

According to Montgomery (1983, p. 343), a decision is made, not based on statistical results but produced by a "click experience" or feeling of confidence in knowing what's most important. In this scenario, the feeling of making the right decision is triggered when a subjective dominance rule is fulfilled or not. Then, candidates may be rejected because they have not shown the appropriate level of proficiency in that subjectively essential job requirement of a decision-maker.

According to Pfister et al. (2017, p. 247), a decision is considered "good" if as much information as possible has been taken into account and if this information has been integrated in a way that is consistent with the generally accepted theories of rational decision-making, for example, decision-rules.

Such implicit and usually non-transparent subjective decision rules must be identified, made transparent, and integrated into general organizational decision rules.

3.2.3.3.3 Legal or diversity influences

Specific selection rules may eliminate candidates who do not meet the specified selection criteria, but some possibly rejected candidates could still be of great interest to the company. Therefore, the decision-making rules should always be reflected critically. A further risk in fixed rules is that you may end up with a relatively homogeneous workforce, reducing diversity and, thus, innovative strength and competitiveness.

Another reason to favor diversity is when based on legal or voluntary agreements, companies give exceptional support to specific groups of people (e.g., ethnic groups or minorities, people with physical challenges, women, and older people). This can result in particular decision-making rules, for example, a physically challenged applicant or a woman is hired if qualifications are otherwise equal to other applicants. Or, to comply with the law, a specific position must be filled by a woman, a member of a minority group, and so on.

3.2.4 Norms, standards, and guidelines for rational-analytical selection procedures

Unfortunately, many "black sheep" still exist among selection managers who use bizarre and questionable tests or interview methods. Applicants want fairness and transparency in selection processes, based on scientifically proven methods. Therefore, rational-analytical procedures, supplemented by ethical standards, can protect candidates from improper or abusive selection procedures and guarantee each applicant, a comparable and fair process.

3.2.4.1 The DIN 33430, DIN Spec 91426, or ISO 10667 as examples of selection norms and standards

There are various quality standards and organizations developing standards in personnel selection worldwide. Kersting & Püttner (2018, p. 16) list some examples: ISO 10667 (International Organization for Standardization: Assessment service delivery: 1. Assessment service delivery – Procedures and methods to assess people in work and organizational settings – Part 1: Requirements for the client. ISO 10667–2. Assessment service delivery – Procedures and methods to assess people in work and organizational settings – Part 2: Requirements for service providers); AKAC-I (Standards for Interviews): APA (American Psychological Association: Standards for Psychological Testing); EFPA (European Federation of Psychologists Associations: Assessment system for tests); ITC-CB (International Guidelines on Computer-Based and Internet-Delivered Testing); ITC-TA (International Guidelines for Translating and Adapting Tests); SIOP (Society for Industrial and Organizational Psychology: Principles for the validation and use of personnel selection procedures); TF-AC (International Taskforce on AC Guidelines). In addition, there are other standards; for example, specifications for certain countries, for example, in Germany, the DIN 33430, or the DIN Spec 91426 (standards for video-based methods of personnel selection) or AC-Standards: Standards of Assessment Center Method, developed by the Working Group Assessment Center (Arbeitskreis Assessment Center, 2016).

For instance, companies and selection managers in Germany can obtain a license for job-related aptitude testing according to DIN 33430 and, thus, stand out from other selection managers or companies in the labor market, by guaranteeing minimum qualitative standards.

By formulating requirements for personnel diagnostics, the DIN 33430 serves:
(1) as a guideline to plan and carry out selection processes
(2) as a yardstick to evaluate selection procedures
(3) as an instrument for securing and optimizing the quality of personnel decisions
(4) to protect candidates from personnel diagnostic procedures that are improperly applied (DIN, 2016, p. 13)

With the DIN 33430, a quality standard for selection procedures can be implemented to reduce poor decisions and the resulting individual, economic, or social consequences and costs (DIN, 2016, p. 13).

This procedure entails analyzing application documents and evaluating applicants in interviews, assessment centers, or tests, based on verbal operationalized selection criteria (e.g., What does giving constructive feedback mean in behaviors?) or KSAOs linked to numbers. Clearly formulated and delineated behavioral anchors with a distinctive scaling form are the basis for a rational-analytical selection process. This means, for example, rating operationalized behavioral characteristics with different numerical scores. Then, the concrete selection decision is based on a numerical comparison of the applicants, where the applicant with the highest numerical score should be selected.

Specifically, the DIN 33430 demands defined and documented rules as a basis for results leading to a judgment and selection decision (DIN e.V., 2002, p. 8).

From the perspective of the DIN 33430, the interpretation of the results should leave no room for subjective or intuitive elements but calls for a clear operationalization of required competencies in behavioral anchors and explicit decision-making rules.

In addition, all hiring managers involved in conducting and evaluating selection procedures should have a profound knowledge of the following topics (DIN e.V., 2002, p. 11):

- Systematic observation in selection procedures (e.g., how to separate observation and evaluation of behaviors)
- Operationalization of required competencies (KSAOs)
- Definition and differentiation of observation units
- Observation, registration, documentation and scoring/evaluation
- Reference standards
- Rating/scaling methods
- Judgment-making forms (statistical and non-statistical)
- Distortion of perception and possible errors of observation (e.g., biases and selective perception)
- Quality criteria/test criteria such as objectivity, reliability, and validity, and how to ensure and implement these scientifically proven quality criteria, including knowledge of the results of relevant evaluation studies
- Interview classifications
- How to conduct interviews and use interview guidelines and questioning techniques
- Assessment areas
- Legal admissibility

The DIN 33430, therefore, demands an explicit, rule-guided selection procedure based on a carefully validated job and requirements analysis.

The DIN Spec 91426 for video selection systems refers explicitly to the DIN 33430, for example, transparency and fairness, behavioral observations, or document analysis. However, in essential details, it also goes beyond the DIN 33430; for example, it is stricter concerning the use of AI. The DIN Spec 91426 also prescribes a mandatory separation between information collection (observation) and assessment and requires the selection process to be rule-based. According to the DIN Spec, a purely intuitive assessment of applicants is, therefore, excluded when using video interviews. Furthermore, two independently proceeding assessors are also prescribed to assess all participants for each required criterion. The only exception is when two independent valid selection methods are used: for example, a well-developed interview and another psychometric procedure, for example, a valid test, both of which independently assess the same requirement criteria. Only then can it be sufficient, if only one assessor evaluates and assesses the information collected in the interview. However, this exception must be justified.

Furthermore, it is the first German standard that also refers to the international standard on assessment services, ISO 10667, parts one and two. These two international standards provide guidance, in particular, on the rights and obligations that should apply between client and contractor. After all, good aptitude diagnostics is only possible if the contractor and client work hand in hand (Ackerschott, 2020).

3.2.4.2 Separation of observation and recording of applicants from scoring and interpretation

In a systematic and controlled approach, behaviors of applicants should be observed and recorded descriptively and not in an evaluative or scoring manner. This means the first step is only for trained assessors to observe and note behaviors of applicants according to pre-defined rules (Höft & Kersting, 2018, pp. 33–35). This separation of observation and scoring is because scoring, interpretation, and evaluation influence our perceptions. Therefore, there is a risk that selection managers only perceive what supports their scoring. Thus, separating observation, scoring, and interpretation aims to reduce confirmation bias and self-fulfilling prophecies (see Section 3.5.2).

Observation is the systematic process of collecting data by perceiving, recording, documenting observed behaviors, and so on, during an interview or exercise, in an assessment center. An observation should be descriptive and linked to just observable facts. For example, in an interview or assessment center, specific behavioral observations should be noted accurately while observing (The applicant said ". . . .," or "During the first ten minutes, the applicant only looked at the table and made no eye contact," etc.).

A neutral, unbiased, non-judgmental, pure observation can only be achieved through slow thinking (see System 2 of Kahneman, Section 4.2.2.4). This act of scoring and evaluating people`s behaviors engages the human mind in interpreting what they are observing and is very exhausting, at least initially. Moreover, because usually fast and associative thinking (System 1) works reliably and automatically, people are usually not wholly aware of their judgments and interpretations, during the process of observation.

Suppose this procedure includes descriptive note-taking and behavioral checklists. Then, directly after the exercise, interview, and so on, the assessors must evaluate and score the perceived behaviors, using behaviorally anchored rating scales. Therefore, during the process of observation and recording, there should not be any interpretation, evaluation, or scoring of observed behaviors.

Thus, each assessor (selection manager) should interpret and rate his/her observations with number scores and draw a conclusion only after the interview or exercise in an assessment center.

3.2.4.3 Data integration

In an integration discussion among assessors (also known as "consensus discussion"), assessors consider the behavioral construct-relevant information collected from the assessment components (recorded observations). This should be an open and deliberative discourse among all hiring managers or assessors.

The individual ratings, scorings, and interpretations by each hiring manager involved are integrated into an overall statistical result. For example, the integration may – in an assessment center, where assessors (hiring managers) observe behavior in exercises simulating critical job situations – result in exercise-specific dimension scores (scores of a specific criterion), exercise scores (the applicant's overall performance in one particular exercise will be evaluated), across-exercise dimension scores, and/or an overall assessment rating (the applicant's overall performance in all exercises will be reviewed in summary).

They should not consider information obtained outside the documented processes of the assessment center (International Taskforce on Assessment Center Guidelines, 2015, p. 1251). From a psychometric perspective, it should be a rule to evaluate only behaviors demonstrated in the exercises. For example, behaviors outside the exercises, at meals, or during small talk at the bar should not be assessed. However, whether this is realistic and whether humans can free themselves from impressions made outside the exercise situation are questionable (see Sections 3.7.3–3.7.5).

3.2.5 Reciprocal quality standards

3.2.5.1 Social acceptance and ethics in selection procedures

Research shows that the quality of a selection process should not be evaluated only by "hard" economic criteria such as costs or scientific criteria like objectivity or validity, but also include more "soft" criteria such as social acceptance, fairness, respect, and judgment by the stakeholders (Deters, 2017, pp. 122–133). If the selection procedures are not accepted, adverse effects on the company's reputation are possible.

Social acceptance and judgments usually reflect the subjective perception of the selection process. Therefore, an organization should translate this system into understandable terms to win the acceptance of a selection system, especially for applicants, executives, and HR professionals. In addition, it should be perceived as fair, respectful, and non-discriminating (Ryan & Tippins, 2009, pp. 58–59).

Research on justice and fairness in selection processes and applicants' reactions to employment-selection systems demonstrate the importance of considering applicants' subjective reactions. Gilliland (1993, pp. 694–695) argues "that psychometrically fair selection procedures are important from business, ethical, and legal perspectives; applicants' perceptions of test fairness are also important from these perspectives. From a business perspective, reactions to selection procedures may influence the ability of the organization to attract and hire highly qualified applicants, which, in turn, can influence the overall utility of selection procedures. From an ethical perspective, organizations should be concerned with the effects of selection procedures on applicants' psychological well-being. For example, the perceived fairness of selection testing may influence the efficacy and self-esteem of rejected applicants . . . Finally, from a legal perspective, the perceived fairness of the selection procedure may influence applicants' decisions to pursue discrimination cases."

Steiner and Gilliland (2001) show that the perceived fairness of different selection techniques varies from culture to culture. "In some cultures, emphasizing how the valid technique is job-related may be important; in others, it may be more useful to focus on the opportunity to perform, the consistency of treatment, the possibility of applying again later, or on interpersonal treatment. That is, the arguments for justifying a particular selection procedure may not be the same everywhere" (Steiner & Gilliland, 2001, p. 135).

Schuler (1993) developed the concept of social validity. He suggests that four components make selection situations socially acceptable: 1. Information: relevant information about critical task requirements and characteristics of the organization (including social-psychological characteristics, culture, and goals). 2. Participation: direct or representative participation in the development and the execution of assessment programs exert control over the situation or one`s own behavior or relevant others. 3. Transparency: of the selection situation, the assessment tools, acting persons and their roles, behavioral expectations, the evaluation process and principles, for example, judgmental criteria. 4. Feedback: the content and the methods of communicating the results, that is, feedback in an honest, considerate, and understandable manner (Schuler, 1993, p. 12; see also Schuler & Stehle, 1985).

Research on selection as an acquisition process shows, and most of our interviewed HR professionals agree, that a high-quality selection process should lead to a positive candidate experience. This includes the candidate's feeling of being treated with fairness, trust, honesty, respect, and appreciation.

3.2.5.2 Legal and ethical criteria in the selection process

Since the employment of people distributes life opportunities and supports economic, social, or cultural participation, it is essential to implement selection procedures that do not discriminate and exclude certain groups (Knobloch & Hustedt,

2019, p. 10). Therefore, the recruiting process must be designed to be legally and ethically correct. Keeping up with rules and taking steps to comply with relevant country-specific laws and ethical standards, governance guidelines, company policies, or other regulations are an expression of quality. Ryan & Tippins (2009, pp. 91–92.) distinguish between three legally related domains: a) discrimination against protected groups, b) regulations on hiring foreign workers, and c) privacy laws (See also Dunleavy et al., 2008; Myors et al., 2008 or – with a particular focus on India – Premarajan et al., 2008, or with a focus on Russia, Praslova, 2008).

3.2.6 Economics of quality criteria

Practical requirements demand that a selection procedure be easy to understand and implement, flexible in use and – especially in SMEs – consider organizational resources. SMEs that do not very often select and hire people and may not have the resources to meet all the requirements of a rational-analytical process pay particular attention to economic factors in using quality criteria. Therefore, the managers we interviewed from SMEs justify their approach that is often not scientifically proven with cost–benefit considerations.

3.2.7 Evaluation of selection processes – measuring the success of selection decisions

Evaluating the selection and hiring procedures and results is recommended to know whether personnel selection methods are successful.

The entire evaluation process should be planned carefully, and all aspects of the selection procedures should be examined. Approaches to evaluation exist at pre-selection, predictor selection (determination of job requirements and operationalization of predictors), selection decision rules and decision-making stages, and so on. Furthermore, the construct validity of the criteria should be assessed by reviewing what is generally defined as "success as a global leader." From a psychometric perspective, it is also necessary to assess predictive validity, and, thus, the success of a candidate in the role, for example, after one year, should be evaluated (see predictive validity, Sections 3.2.1; 3.7.7). Furthermore, the evaluation should consider the predetermined job requirements, decision rules, and other regulations (see Sections 3.2.3 and 3.2.7). Finally, the selection process costs and the potential economic benefits should be evaluated. Based on these findings, practical implications can be derived.

However, an evaluation should not only be conducted for psychometric or economic reasons but also to question and assess the quality of managers' intuitions (Kahneman & Klein, 2009).

Evaluating personnel diagnostic decisions and, thus, developing selection expertise in practice is also to be questioned, because selection managers rarely evaluate the success of their selection decisions and their experiences, systematically. In addition, it is problematic that possible feedback on the outcomes (especially performance on the job) can only ever cover those who have been selected. Rejected applicants, who might have done the job well, are not considered in validity and evaluation studies (Koppers, 2013, p. 48; Kanning, 2004, p. 75).

3.3 Implementation of rational-analytical selection methods

As research indicates that a rational-analytical selection procedure is more appropriate and successful than others, normative recommendations concerning selection procedures may be warranted (Allinson & Hayes, 1996, p. 119).

To secure scientifically proven quality in personnel selection, actions should address two areas: 1) optimization of personnel selection processes (instruments, tools, procedures, etc.) and 2) improvement of the competencies of recruiters and, especially, selection managers.

To be successful in these two areas, the introduction of psychometrically guided selection procedures requires taking a closer look at four different components, according to Rogers' conceptual framework (Rogers, 2003; Deters et al., 2020):

1. Characteristics and specifics of the social system (e.g., specifics of large enterprises and SMEs, and environmental factors such as culture)
2. Characteristics of the innovation to be introduced (e.g., psychometric procedures such as DIN 33,430, the ISO 10,665, cost–benefit considerations, and perceived complexity)
3. Support measures for implementing the innovation (develop competencies of selection managers, because these may substantially influence the perception of rational-analytical procedures, familiarity with these procedures, perceived urgency, and pressure of the introduction, e.g., by stakeholders)
4. Communication of psychometric or rational-analytical selection procedures

Since components 1–3 have already been discussed on the previous pages, the following focuses on component 4 (communication).

Communication of scientific research findings: The aim is to clarify the advantages and benefits of rational-analytical methods for companies and hiring managers. Science has to prove that companies that adhere to the psychometric standards make fewer misjudgments, reduce early turnover, get a higher level of commitment from their employees and, overall and in the long term, reduce their costs for successful personnel selection, become more competitive, and increase their economic success.

In cooperation with practitioners, scientists should develop instruments that support the evaluation of selection procedures. Also, easy-to-understand and practical guidelines that explain the techniques and the benefits of high-quality selection processes to a broad public, including how initial costs can lead to significant long-term gains, should be offered (Reimann et al., 2009, p. 157).

Through increased face validity, practitioners could be convinced, for example, that cognitive ability tests have good prognostic validity (Schmidt & Hunter, 1998; Schmidt et al., 2016). And that a combination of different psychometric procedures, such as a valid and reliable cognitive ability test and a structured interview, have very high predictive validity and will give the most reliable prognoses for future professional success (Schmidt et al., 2016).

Where science is viewed rather suspiciously, there is need for advocates who are trusted, in practice. What are needed are examples of successful companies, including SMEs, that transparently and openly publish their experiences with psychometric procedures and communicate the benefits they have experienced. Kersting (2009, pp. 154–155) describes the DIN 33430 as established and mentions various companies that already base their personnel selection on that standard. These organizations can serve as role models and radiate a signal effect. The increasing mention of the added value of psychometric selection procedures in practitioner literature, specialized fairs, social media, and so on, can lead to a growing acceptance of these procedures, in practice (Deters et al., 2020).

3.4 Rational-analytical requirements for the hiring managers

3.4.1 Requirements of the DIN 33430 for selection managers

Our research confirms that specific knowledge of psychometric research results and, thus, of the possible added value of these rational-analytical procedures is little known, in practice.

Since intuition and rational-analytics interact and complement each other and create synergies, practitioners must be aware of how intuition, emotions, and rational-analytical procedures can be used constructively.

Since the competencies of selection managers affect the design and success of a personnel selection process, the core requirements exemplified by the DIN 33430 are described.

The DIN 33430 strives to increase the transparency of science-based personnel selection procedures and their adequate use, in practice (DIN 2016, p. 6). The requirements of the DIN 33430 are based on the three pillars: (1) process, (2) procedure, and (3) qualifications.

Although the DIN 33430 is primarily a process standard relating to the design of selection procedures, it also guides determining desired qualifications and competencies for hiring managers. According to Kersting (2016), the process and procedure are necessary elements but not sufficient for a high-quality selection process. In fact, people and their qualifications are the core elements of a high-quality personnel selection, because they determine whether and how professional the corresponding methods and personnel selection procedures are designed.

The DIN 33430 distinguishes between qualification profiles of responsible personnel diagnosticians, observers for behavioral observation and assessment, and observers for direct oral interviewing (DIN 2016, pp. 22–23). Thus, it places the most comprehensive demands on the selection manager who designs, and is responsible for, the entire personnel selection process. Here, the DIN 33430 standard requires proof of defined knowledge and experience but does not specify the required level of proficiency, weighting, or compensability (Kersting, 2016).

Quality assurance requires transparent and verifiable criteria that prove selection managers' skills, experience, and thus expertise. A selection manager may demonstrate appropriate competencies through an independent examination and a related certification. However, since this cannot be introduced on a mandatory basis in practice, the DIN standard lists 45 qualification elements (Ackerschott et al., 2016; DIN 2016, pp. 22–24).

According to psychometric research results, qualified hiring managers should know a selection procedure thoroughly. Also, they should have supervised experience in the development, planning, construction, and controlled administration of selection procedures and their evaluation.

Based on the recommended process of personnel selection and the tasks and responsibilities involved, the following competencies, in particular, are required:

a) For the professional development of requirements analyses, knowledge of the following is necessary:
   - job and requirement analysis, including analysis methods;
   - methods for integrating the results of the analysis in a requirements profile;
   - methods for the operationalization of requirement criteria;
   - the influence of biases, stereotypes, and so on on a requirements analysis and vice versa;
   - the culture dependency of requirements (to avoid that only members of a particular culture can meet the requirements).

b) For the professional use of selection processes, hiring managers should know of
   - procedures, instruments, and methods of selection and their opportunities and limits;
   - statistical and methodological principles (for the selection and interpretation of procedures and evaluation);
   - classical test and item-response theories, measurement theories (types of tests and measures, e.g., cognitive ability, personality, and motives);

- design and construction fundamentals (e.g., how to construct high-quality interviews, assessment centers, and interpret applicants' behaviors);
- how to conduct a selection procedure in conformity with the law and ethical standards (legal and ethical constraints on personnel selection such as data protection);
- conditions and contexts of the implementation of specific selection procedures;
- quality criteria, for example, what do objectivity, validity, reliability, fairness, and so on mean? Knowledge of research results and relevant evaluation, for example, the predictive validity of specific selection procedures;
- writing a report on the results of the personnel selection;
- accurate cost estimation for the different selection methods and instruments;
- evaluation methods, including cost–benefit aspects or performance review.

c) For the professional application of behavioral observations and assessments, knowledge of the following is necessary:
   - the term "observation" (and the difference between observation, interpretation, and evaluation);
   - how to observe systematically;
   - operationalization of the job requirements (e.g., behavioral anchors);
   - definition and delimitation of observation units;
   - documentation of observations;
   - evaluation and assessment of the observations;
   - reference standard for the assessment of scales (e.g., behavioral anchors);
   - the cultural influence on human behavior and job requirements;
   - the influence of stereotypes, prejudices, bias (e.g., gender, age, confirmation, and religion);
   - rating and scaling procedures;
   - types of judgment formation (statistical and non-statistical).

d) For the professional application of selection interviews, knowledge of the following is necessary:
   - interview classification;
   - handling and application of interview guidelines;
   - interview techniques and how to formulate questions effectively and legally, and ethical compliance;
   - interview-related assessment criteria;
   - distortions of perception, stereotypes, bias, and so on;
   - dealing with self-representation and impressions management strategies of applicants;
   - interpretation of observed behaviors.

3.4.2 Further requirements for hiring managers beyond the DIN 33430

The DIN 33430 more or less formulates functional skills and does not specify other criteria, which see personnel selection as an acquisition process. A hiring manager should understand how and why individuals enter and move within an organization.

Thus, they need:

- **Communication skills:** If hiring managers can't communicate clearly and effectively (orally, nonverbally, in writing, by phone, video, email, etc.), if they are not versed in active listening and showing empathy, expressing appreciation and respect, building trust, and so on, they will not be successful. They must be able to communicate unambiguously and interact with every candidate, regardless of the position to be filled, the hierarchical position, or the applicant's personal background.
- **Marketing and relationship-building skills:** The hiring manager is a crucial link between a company and a candidate. Depending on their impression, they can either attract or discourage the candidate. Thus, hiring managers think of selection processes as creating a relationship between a candidate and a company (represented by the hiring manager). They know how to sell the position and the company, create a positive candidate experience, and act to the benefit of both parties.

Hiring managers are also expected to have:

- **Technological skills:** With the whole world going increasingly digital, HR managers need the ability to adapt to new technology such as AI, using algorithms.
- **Learning skills** (e.g., a commitment to ongoing learning): This includes the ability to reflect on oneself, again and again, to obtain feedback, and educate oneself continually. In particular, HR managers must understand and implement new HR research findings connected to the current trends in the HR field, selection procedures, and so on.

3.5 Situational factors and perception distortions as reasons for rational-analytical selection procedures

Research shows that personnel selection decisions can be colored by context-specific factors, such as time pressure or unconscious bias that distorts perception and may, subsequently, lead to discrimination and unfairly hurting people's life chances. These possible negative consequences are significant reasons for a rational-analytical approach, which mitigates the dark side of biases, stereotypes, intuitions, and emotions. In addition, rational-analytical methods promise more objectivity and, thus, reduce arbitrariness and discrimination in personnel selection.

The risk of discrimination against applicants exists in all phases of the selection process, particularly in the first phase, that is, before someone is invited for a personal interview; therefore, it is recommended to anonymize application documents (Antidiskrimierungsstelle des Bundes, 2012, p. 3).

Which situational factors influence the subjective perception of hiring managers and, thus, the selection judgments and decisions, and which distortions of perception can occur in the selection process are described below (Figure 5; for a detailed summary, see Kanning, 2019, pp. 57–85).

Situational circumstances of selection processes
- Time pressure, information overload, social influence by third parties, labor market situation, selection as a political and power game

Biases and other perceptual distortions in selection processes (examples)
- Limited human cognitive capacity (e.g. information overload), pattern recognition, and selective perception
- Contrast or anchor effect and order of the candidates
- Emotional state and mood, including "noise" (see Section 3.5.2.4)
- Conformity pressure and social influence by third parties
- Fear and conflict aversion in hiring managers
- Poor or no evaluation of the selection process and its results
- Stereotyps and prejudices
- Primacy effect and first impression
- Halo effect
- Attractiveness bias or lookism
- Similarity effects, in-group favoritism and homophily
- Confirmation bias
- Self-serving bias
- Recency effect
- Correspondence bias or fundamental attribution error
- Cultural bias, ethnic biases
- Hindsight bias
- Gender bias, sexual orientation bias, age bias, disabilities bias, overweight bias
- Rating scale bias
- Psychological projection
- Overconfidence bias
- Technologically induced bias
- Etc.

Possible misjudgments
- Individual over -or underconfidence in one's one selection competencies
- Preferential or disadvantageous treatment of certain applicants, due to for example
  - Weight
  - Appearance (attractiveness)
  - Accent/dialect
  - Name (e.g. foreign sounding name)
- Discrimination against
  - gender
  - age
  - ethnic groups (up to racism)
  - religion
  - etc.
- Etc.

Figure 5: Problems of judgment formation in decision-making in selection procedures (based on Kanning, 2015, p. 139).

3.5.1 Situational circumstances of selection processes

Time pressure: Many selection managers have a heavy workload and act under time pressure. As a result, application processes are not carried out with the necessary care and intensity, and, for example, requirement profiles are not – for example, for time reasons – developed and used in a written form (for every role), although they may be present as inner lists or guidelines in the minds of involved selection managers.

Thus, clearly defined and transparent selection criteria are often missed. Or interviews are unstructured, lacking interview guidelines. This makes it more challenging to compare applicants, and the quality of personnel selection can suffer (Kanning, 2015, p. 142).

Information overload: Selection managers have to process a lot of information, for example, in an assessment center, observing two or more candidates simultaneously in a group discussion on five or more competence dimensions while documenting their observations. In that case, this will inevitably lead to automated processes of information processing. However, studies show that the validity of such procedures decreases (Lievens, 2001; Lievens & Conway, 2002).

This problem lies not only with the observers but also with the assessment center developers or HR managers responsible for the process, who put too much pressure on the assessors. The principle "less is more" applies in an assessment center and an interview. It is diagnostically more meaningful to observe fewer competencies than too many (Kanning, 2015, p. 142).

Social influence by third parties: Often, selection managers are influenced by social context and pressure from colleagues or superiors to align their judgments with colleagues/superiors, even if they do not correspond to their selection results (Kanning, 1999, p. 249).

Especially in less structured and non-standardized selection procedures, where, perhaps, no clear requirement profile is used, it is relatively easy for selecting managers to exert social influence on each other. This happens, for example, before an interview, by exchanging information about which candidate is favored or by exchanging information about observed candidates, during an assessment. A bit more subtle but equally inappropriate is the social pressure some HR professionals face when they know that influential, higher-ranked executives or groups prefer a particular candidate. This is particularly problematic in selection procedures with internal applicants (Kanning, 2015, p. 142; see Section 3.7.5).

Therefore, it is essential that each selection manager makes his/her observations and evaluations independently and that the observations and evaluations are recorded in writing.

Labor market situation: Empirical studies of people's decisions show that human preferences for alternative options in choice situations depend very strongly on the number and type of options. If there are many options to choose from, the decision situation is different from one where there are hardly any options (Tversky & Simonson, 1993).

Depending on the situation, particularly the labor market or individual circumstances (e.g., applicants urgently looking for a job because they have been unemployed for an extended period), an applicant may feel dependent on the company's goodwill or hiring manager. Such situations, also known as employers' markets, can lead to a loss of confidence in the applicant, such as accepting procedures and answering questions that are not appropriate or not requirement-oriented.

If specific competencies and professional qualifications are in short supply in the labor market, the situation is reversed for applicants with these sought-after competencies. In the case of an employee or applicant market, the applicant has the market power. This causes companies to make more intensive efforts to recruit these people and hiring managers to appreciate the recruiting process. In such situations, selection procedures are increasingly adapted to the wishes and needs of the target groups; this can mean that requirement standards are reduced, and a classic selection situation becomes more of an application situation for companies.

Selection as a political and power game: Power and politics can also be factors in self-serving bias and anxiety about possible competitors for the hiring managers. Certain personnel selection decisions, for example, rejection of promotions or outstanding applicants, can be influenced by individual political motives of the selection manager. For example, suppose selection managers are consciously or unconsciously afraid that outstanding applicants could threaten or even oust them from their position, there is a risk that these applicants will be met with great skepticism.

Lee et al. (2015, p. 790) show that decision-makers prefer applicants who are considered more helpful to them personally and are less likely to hire applicants they expect might compete with them, or even endanger their job or career. They might even use the opportunity to make the candidates look bad in the selection process and to argue against them by asking tough questions and using inappropriate arguments (Bozionelos, 2005, pp. 1606–1625; Apelojg, 2010, pp. 42–43; see also Marlowe et al., 1996).

From an evolutionary biology perspective, fear of competition also plays a role. For example, a laboratory study by Luxen & van de Vijver (2006, p. 3) shows that women reject more attractive female applicants than men and suggests that women give priority to supposedly unattractive women. However, a further study with corresponding HRM professionals could not confirm these findings.

If such factors influence personnel selection decisions, even the knowledge of high-quality personnel selection and psychometric procedures is of little help, because they are, consciously or unconsciously, undermined.

3.5.2 Biases and other perceptual distortions in selection processes

The distance from others, where this awareness moves us, becomes even greater when we realize that our outside form doesn't appear to others as to our own eyes. Humans are not seen like houses, trees, and stars. They are seen with the expectation of being able to encounter them in a specific way and thus making them a part of our own inside. Imagination trims them to suit our own wishes and hopes, but also to confirm our own fears and prejudices. We don't even get safely

> *and impartially to the outside contours of another. On the way, the eye is diverted and blurred by all the wishes and fantasies that make us the special, unmistakable human beings we are. Even the outside world of an inside world is still a piece of our inside world, not to mention the thoughts we make about the inside world of strangers and that are so uncertain and unstable that they say more about ourselves than about others. How does the man with the cigarette see an exaggeratedly upright man with a gaunt face, full lips and gold-framed eyeglasses on the sharp, straight nose that seems to me to be too long and too dominant? How does this figure fit into the framework of the pleasure and displeasure and into the remaining architecture of his soul? What does his look exaggerate and stress in my appearance, and what does it leave out as if it didn't even exist? It will inevitably be a caricature the smoking stranger forms of my reflection, and his notion of my notional world will pile up caricature on caricature. And so we are doubly strangers, for between us there is not only the deceptive outside world, but also the delusion that exists of it in every inside world.* (Excerpt from *Night Train to Lisbon* by Pascal Mercier, transl. Barbara Harshav, pp. 79–80)

What people perceive and sense is shaped by their needs, desires, intuitions, and associated emotions. And, what is important to one personally is recognized better and more quickly. To exaggerate, people perceive the world as they themselves are. The American artist David Lynch (2007, p. 21) says: "The world is as you are."

In addition, concrete judgments are influenced by how specific information is prepared and presented. Thus, decisions turn out differently, although the facts and data, for example, the factual content of the information in an interview, does not change, for example, the presentation of professional experience by the applicant.

One of the aims of the rational-analytical approach in personnel selection is to reduce the influence of hiring managers' intuitions and emotions. The primary reason is that intuitions and feelings can lead to bias, prejudices, and discrimination. Although, on the one hand, this is because intuitions and emotions are primarily based on individual experiences, on the other hand, they can also be attributed to the limited processing capacity of the human brain or evolutionary developments (e.g., xenophobia).

The critical reflection on corresponding biases, stereotypes, and so on, serves not only to reduce discrimination or promote fairness and justice but also to improve the economic success of organizations. For example, a study by Hardy et al. (2021), which specifically addresses the issue of gender discrimination, highlights that if the hiring process is not conducted as fairly and objectively as possible, even a small amount of gender bias in hiring can be costly to employers and produce significant rates of hiring discrimination and productivity loss.

It must be emphasized that the phenomenon explicitly addressed in the following is not a conclusive enumeration of possible unconscious distortions of perception. Without claiming to be complete, important distortions of perception and their bases are presented below.

3.5.2.1 Limited human cognitive capacity, pattern recognition, and selective perception

The cognitive processing of information, the evaluation of a situation or a person, and the process of decision-making are not only based on a rational analysis of the objective information available to an individual, but are also influenced, filtered, and distorted by various perceptions of these data (Tversky & Kahneman, 1981, p. 453; Tversky & Kahneman, 1973, p. 207).

Human perception is selective, and people would be overwhelmed if they were aware of everything around them. Selective attention filters information and directs awareness to (subjective) relevant stimuli, while ignoring irrelevant environmental stimuli. This is an essential process, as there is a limit to how much data can be processed at a given time. Selective attention allows us to tune out insignificant details and focus on essential information.

Selective perceptions occur in every human being as a necessary mechanism to cope with the complexity of the environment (Kanning, 1999, pp. 254 and 257).

Research shows that human brains fill in missing information with creative guesses based on experience and pattern matching. Our memory system strives to be efficient in not cluttering our minds with unnecessary detail. For example, the Russian neuropsychologist Alexander Luria studied a patient with a superior and supercharged memory: he could repeat word-for-word speeches that he had heard only once, complex mathematical formulas, or long sequences of numbers. But, he could not form abstractions because he remembered every detail as distinct. Moreover, he had trouble recognizing people because his brain could not generalize and abstract. Also, when he saw the same faces, he saw different faces because human faces change with other expressions. Thus, the ability to generalize, see patterns, and abstract from detail is beneficial to our survival. And as humans age, their brains become better at seeing patterns, extracting generalized common points from prior experience, and seeing the big picture (Levitin, 2020, pp. 33–45).

What a person perceives depends on the processing of incoming stimuli. Only after a stimulus has been perceived can it be evaluated. Which incoming stimuli are perceived depends on the viewer's attention to different stimuli. Salience and, thus, the subjective consciousness and meaning of a stimulus and the accessibility of the stimuli influence human attention.

Thus, selective perception means to perceive only particular competencies or characteristics from a set of total impressions, more or less ignoring other stimuli. Thus, people tend to see what seems essential or true for them but may overlook contradicting perspectives.

In addition, the human ability to interpret and give meaning to perceived objects is also selective. Therefore, the same information about an applicant can be evaluated very differently, depending on the hiring manager's experience, knowledge, socialization, age, gender, cultural background, interests, goals, and so on.

Most cognitive, social, and organizational psychology theories support the idea that individuals use different information processing networks (i.e., schemas), motivations, demographic and experience backgrounds, values, personalities, and attitudes to bear on their interpretations and reactions to social stimuli and perceptions (Nishii & Wright, 2007, p. 9). According to the theory of social cognition (Fiske & Taylor, 2021), it can be assumed that the perception and interpretation of experiences vary from person to person, depending on individual cognitive models, schemas, values, and emotions. "People attach different meanings to social stimuli based on differences in the cognitive frameworks that they use to make sense of social information" (Nishii & Wright, 2007, p. 8).

A person's perception differs from object perception, because it involves more complex psychological mechanisms and cognitive processes. For example, people look at others and attribute-specific characteristics, intentions, emotions, values, and dispositions. These inferences, in turn, influence the relationship and interaction with that person.

What humans perceive and how they perceive is also influenced by the cognitive capacity of the human brain. Unfortunately, the human brain has limited reception-, memory- and information-processing capacity and is also subject to fatigue and attention or concentration difficulties. This limited capacity is like a bottleneck, restricting the flow of information.

Because of these limited mental resources and to save energy, the human brain tends to categorize perceptions. At any given time, the human brain is bombarded with infinite stimuli. Thus, people tend to categorize and encode all perceptual stimuli and finally assign them to known cognitive schemas (Pendry, 2007, p. 120). Assigning and translating stimuli into known structures and schemas enables the individual to deal with the many stimuli that affect them and not be overwhelmed by their complexity. However, it also carries the risk of information and experiences being assigned to situationally inappropriate categories and schemas, thereby distorting the perception and interpretation of what has been experienced (Pendry, 2007, p. 120).

Thus, the assignment and categorization of the same perceived stimuli into different underlying cognitive structures and schemas is the reason for the divergent and subjective interpretations of and reactions to experiences and moments (Fiske & Taylor, 2021). Without an efficient method of processing and making sense of this information, our brains would become overloaded. Although generalizations about people will not accurately consider the characteristics of a particular group member, humans can navigate their social life more efficiently by sorting stimuli into categories. Thus, this categorization frees up mental resources for other tasks.

Two processes occur during perception and candidate assessments by observers: an automated and a controlled process. Since a person's cognitive capacity is too limited to grasp a situation as a whole and assess it comprehensively, automated processes and shortcuts are needed to think and act quickly. These automated assessment processes are subconscious and require only a few cognitive resources; they occur without intention or effort and do not impair other cognitive processes (Fiske & Taylor, 2021).

On the other hand, a controlled process occurs when the observer consciously influences the assessment process. Conscious processes require effort, constant attention, and time. In addition, conscious processes have a clear intention (Fiske & Taylor, 2021).

Intuitive judgments are formed by pattern and similarity recognition. People perceive a specific constellation of impressions and search unconsciously for similar constellations in their life experiences. Previous decisions will be activated, which to some extent, proved valid. People then continue working with these judgments. Depending on the similarity and pattern recognition type, these intuitive judgments, more or less, fit the new situation.

These intuitive cognitive processes in which individuals' thoughts, feelings, and actions are subject to a certain automatism, make it possible for previous life experiences, internalized thinking, and behavior patterns to be applied to new situations, without further processing effort.

On the other hand, rational-analytical cognitive processes are activated when new or more complex contexts require a higher degree of attention. Thus, although both intuitive and rational-analytical information processing systems are continuously active, the intuitive system is usually dominant. As a result, unconscious bias occurs through this unconscious form of information processing (Kahneman et al., 2011, p. 52).

All bias and perception distortions are a kind of selective perception.

Since the human brain wants to save energy and avoid effort, human information processing in everyday life is primarily based on unconscious and automatic pattern recognition, schemas, and other categorizations. In personnel diagnostics, this is a possible source of errors (Höft & Kersting, 2018, p. 51) and distortions of judgment stemming from the hiring manager's unconscious stereotypes, prejudices, or biases (Kanning, 1999, p. 257).

3.5.2.2 Contrast or anchor effect and order of the candidates

The contrast effect is an unconscious bias, when candidates are judged compared to one another instead of being assessed individually and independently. The perception of hiring managers is altered once they compare candidates; they tend to judge them relative to each other rather than on their own merit. CV screening is prone to the contrast effect, since it's natural for selection managers to assess candidates relative to the CV. Thus, hiring managers may perceive greater or lesser differences between candidates than actually exist. A previously assessed (in a CV or interview) or simultaneously observed candidate (in an assessment center) is seen as an anchor for hiring managers to contrast other candidates with this "anchor candidate." For example, a hiring manager might grade a mediocre candidate more harshly after interviewing an excellent candidate. Similarly, weaker candidates may be made to look strong, and a good fit may be overlooked in a more substantial candidate pool. This effect can also occur if several applicants are interviewed on the same day; the first and the last are remembered better and usually more favorable (Höft & Kersting, 2018, p. 57).

3.5.2.3 Emotional state and mood of the selection manager and applicant

The human brain may interpret the same stimuli in one way or another. This has to do with the emotional state. Attention varies, depending on the current state of mind, and specific characteristics are considered more important than others.

Thus, the emotional state and, subsequently, the mood, influence the judgment and decision-making process. If the decision-makers are in a positive mood, they will use this – unconsciously – as additional information and evaluate candidates more positively than when they feel unhappy (Werth, 2004, p. 28).

In specific situations, for example, under time pressure or stress, people will enter into a conversation differently and focus on aspects other than while being in a good mood. Hiring managers will behave differently as interviewers if they have had a relaxing and stress-free day or something they were pleased about. But, if they have just had some trouble or conflicts, they may behave in a less friendly manner. Or if someone has received very positive information shortly beforehand, they will go into a conversation differently than if they had received very negative information. Someone sad will be blind to sunshine and focus on aspects of the environment that reflect their own misery (Pfister et al., 2017, pp. 301–315).

> It is a common belief that the way people perceive the world, process information, and solve problems is influenced by emotions and moods. For example, probably all of us have experienced that when we are in a depressed mood, our attention appears to be focused rigidly and narrowly, whereas when we are in a happy mood, our minds seem to bubble over with ideas and sometimes far-fetched associations. Such everyday impressions are supported by a growing body of empirical evidence showing that positive and negative moods are accompanied by qualitatively different information processing modes . . . For instance, individuals in a positive mood, compared with those in a negative mood, produce more unusual associations (Isen, Johnson, Mertz, & Robinson, 1985), show improved performance on tests of creative problem solving (Isen, Daubman, & Nowicki, 1987), prefer heuristic over exhaustive decision-making strategies (Isen & Means, 1983) (Bolte et al., 2003, p. 416).

A short-lived emotional state can trigger a mood. However, it must not relate only to a particular situation, because it can be a longer-lasting feeling that colors the experience more positively or negatively. While a positive mood leads to optimism, a sunnier outlook, or risk-taking, a bad mood leads to rejection, pessimism, or negative relationship-building. While a specific stimulus triggers emotions, moods can often occur without an apparent cause (Scherer, 2015, p. 705).

Emotional states, moods, and thus, the perception of others can also be triggered by particular substances such as alcohol or other drugs.

A theoretical approach to explaining the relationship between emotional state and mood is the "Affect-infusion theory" of Forgas (1995, 2000). According to this theory, emotions cause certain moods. "Affect infusion" means that affectively loaded information (e.g., positive information from the CV) becomes incorporated into the judgmental process of hiring managers, influences their thinking, feeling, and behavior, and thus colors their judgments.

Also, the emotional state of the applicant influences the mood and, thus, behaviors of hiring managers and vice versa.

In less stressful situations, applicants who are nervous and under pressure may not act as confidently as they might. In addition, applicants in an observation situation, for example, in a role-play within an assessment center, may behave differently than they would in a relaxed situation (Kolominski, 2009, p. 75). When candidates behave in the selection situation as they think they should act – use so-called impression management techniques or behave according to supposed social desirability – it is challenging to draw predictively valid conclusions from this behavior (Höft & Kersting, 2018, p. 54. But see "Validity and Job Performance" in Section 3.7.7. Ingold et al., 2015a, show that impression management in interviews did not negatively affect job performance).

3.5.2.4 "Noise" and decision-making

In their book *Noise – A Flaw in Human Judgment*, Kahneman, Sibony, and Sunstein (2021) show how human judgment and decision-making are influenced and distorted by various invisible factors and wherever there is judgment, there is noise (Kahneman et al., 2021, p. 12). Judgment noise means that when judgments should be identical, people judge the same object differently at different times. Noise, as being hungry, whether Monday morning or Friday afternoon, rainy or sunny outside, clouds objective judgment and leads to variability or errors in judgments. Also, Loewenstein (1996) shows that people decide and behave as "other persons" when influenced by visceral factors such as hunger, thirst, and pain. Many decision-makers are not aware of these influences that may distort their judgments. And, people are susceptible to noise in many decision-making fields, including performance reviews or personnel selection, but commonly ignore its role in their judgments. For example, judges in the United States tend to be significantly more likely to suspend a sentence immediately after breakfast or lunch.

In contrast, they tend to rule more harshly when hungry. Therefore, it is essential to detect noise and be aware of these influences as a decision-maker. Furthermore, if different colleagues come to very divergent judgments, these should be openly addressed and reflected upon. If many people come to widely differing results in the same situation, it can be assumed that there is much "noise." In addition, the influence of noise can be reduced by having several people participate in decisions and aggregating individual decisions in this way. Thus, decisions can be improved if managers identify and reduce the "noise" influencing them. Using that approach, people can reach "decision hygiene" and increase the reliability of decisions.

3.5.2.5 Salience and decision-making

Salience is an essential human cognitive ability to detect things of possible importance in a stream of sensory information; thus, it supports situational awareness. If specific information is highly emotional to an individual, it gets more salience. This ability has significant advantages (e.g., people can tune their salience to achieve specific goals) but can also lead to invalid perceptions and judgments. Thus, people often do not decide "rationally" when their attention is distracted or even misdirected. Bordalo et al. (2012, 2021) show that salient stimuli attract human attention "bottom-up" automatically and involuntarily, due to their high contrast with surroundings. Bottom-up attention is critical for survival, but bottom-up attention can distort rational-analytical perceptions and, thus, decisions, by distracting decision-makers from their immediate goals or specific choice attributes. Human decision-making beyond the rational- analytical can, thus, often also be explained by attention deficits and, thus, misdirected "salience."

3.5.2.6 Conformity pressure

Judgments of hiring managers can be influenced by social contexts, for example, through pressure from colleagues, superiors, or the majority of assessors (Kanning, 1999, p. 249). Conformity is the act of matching attitudes, beliefs, and behaviors to those of others or societal norms. In selection processes, pressure to conform can lead lower-ranking selection managers or recruiters with less experience to adjust their selection judgment to a higher-ranking manager or the majority of the hiring managers (Höft & Kersting, 2018, pp. 57–58). Sometimes, this pressure is called the "bandwagon effect," the tendency to follow the mass instead of standing by an individual point of view, or even the results of rational-analytical selection procedures.

Thus, conformity pressure can lead to poor selection results. To counteract this, instructions for the hiring managers or assessors (e.g., for preparation, implementation, and evaluation, of hiring decisions) should be carefully prepared and continuously evaluated (Höft & Kersting, 2018, p. 58). In addition, a professional moderation of integrating individual appraisals and scorings into an overall result can support the benefits assigned to assessments made by individual selection managers. But these procedures may be useless, if hiring managers are conflict-averse and do not dare to take a clear position.

3.5.2.7 Fear and conflict aversion in hiring managers

The reluctance to acknowledge one's impressions, giving in to real or perceived pressure from higher-ranked supervisors or line managers, or subordinating oneself to the views of the majority of assessors may be attributable to a fear of conflict and a limited ability to deal with conflict.

When evaluating and selecting internal candidates, in particular, fear and conflict aversion can play a decisive role. Conflict-averse selection managers may fear exhaustive and controversial discussions or be confronted with other views, shy away from precise positioning, and so on. To avoid conflicts for reasons of harmony and to be accepted and recognized by others, these conflict-averse managers hold back their own impressions and judgments and subordinate themselves to others.

3.5.2.8 Little or no evaluation of the selection process and its results

As Kanning (2015, p. 143) states, the validity of selection decisions is only rarely evaluated systematically, in practice. As a result, HR managers, often, do not receive detailed feedback on the possibilities to optimize selection processes and their decision-making behavior.

Suppose the prospective candidate's superior, who makes the final decision to employ the candidate, participates in the selection process and positively assesses a candidate. An HR manager`s tendency may be to positively evaluate this candidate, since otherwise, the superior could critically question their decision-making and selection competence.

Another aspect of an imperfect evaluation process is the "reinvention" of memory. If it turns out in practice that an applicant is not as successful as was hoped for, there is a risk that hiring managers will "revise" their memory of the selection process. For example, they may say they were actually opposed to the hiring but decided in favor of the applicant to give them a chance, or because other managers saw this applicant positively. Due to this denial of what took place in the hiring process, the manager is deprived of the chance to learn something (Kanning, 2015, p. 144).

Possible errors in selection processes are often only reluctantly admitted, if they do not match the infallible self-image of those who claim to have an excellent knowledge of human nature. Or, if these selection managers are convinced, always make the right choice, or if the error culture in that organization is poorly developed, employees feel the need to hide their mistakes. Thus, hiring managers who question themselves, ask for feedback, carry out systematic evaluations of their decisions, and reflect critically on their decisions are needed (see Section 2.6).

3.5.2.9 Stereotypes and prejudices

Social categorization and generalization provide a sense of order and predictability that people can rely on, to guide their interactions with others. For example, the stereotype that the elderly are deaf causes people to speak loudly in their presence; the stereotype that Germans are reliable, follow the rules, have little humor, and plan very systematically influences expected behaviors and how they are met. Stereotypes are based on the belief that specific attributes, personality characteristics, and behavioral tendencies are typical of particular social group members. Categorizing people this way, often encompasses visible features such as skin color, gender, age, and nationality.

Stereotypes are socially constructed and, sometimes, may be based on personal experience. They arise from other people's remarks, the media, or reading about different cultures. Reducing the complexity and diversity of a culture to a few characteristics or dimensions (e.g., Hofstede dimensions; see Section 7.2.4.1) represents a criticism of the cultural models or theories. This reduction of complexity promotes stereotypical thinking and may lead to distortions in the perception of a culture (Büter, 2010, p. 263; Schroll-Machl, 2007, p. 152).

Stereotypes are developed and integrated automatically and unconsciously into a person's thought patterns. They can be positive or negative, influencing what people perceive, how they perceive something, and how they decide and behave, treat specific people, and so on.

Stereotypes can be implicit and explicit. Implicit stereotypes are unconsciously activated in judgment and decision-making, without a person being aware of them.

While stereotypes are the cognitive components of attitudes toward a social group, prejudices are the affective components and value-laden feelings associated with these attitudes. These feelings can be positive or negative. Thus, stereotypes can often lead to negative prejudices and antipathy toward a person, based on perceived group affiliation, for example, with a specific religion, gender, sexual orientation, social class, nationality, ethnicity, education, sports team, and age (Derous & Ryan, 2019, p. 114).

Stereotypes can lead to biases, such as gender bias, age bias, or ethnic origin bias. Bias is a (positive or negative) inclination for or against one person or a group, for example, bias against foreign applicants. Biases such as cognitive shortcuts are regularly learned and highly dependent on variables such as socioeconomic status, ethnicity, educational background, and nationality.

Even at a young age, people learn to distinguish between those who are like them, their "in-group," and those who are not like them, their "out-group." This can provide a sense of identity and safety on the plus side. However, on the negative side, bias can result in prejudgments that lead to discriminatory practices. Thus, discrimination is the behavioral consequence of stereotypes, prejudices, or biases, for example, disability discrimination, age discrimination, gender discrimination.

When an applicant is assessed, categorizations are triggered, enabling impressions to be processed quickly and judgments made, without significant effort (Cocchiara et al., 2016, p. 467). In this case, a person is perceived as representing a specific social group. Consequently, the properties attributed to this group are projected on this person, and related stereotypes and prejudices are activated (Kanning, 2015, pp. 140–141).

Experiments with anonymous applications and many other studies have shown that applicants are discriminated against, based on their name, gender, age, and so on. For example, in Germany, applicants with a German-sounding name are more likely to be invited to interviews than applicants with a Turkish- or Arabian-sounding name; similar experiences have been made in many other countries with the corresponding results (Segrest Purkis, 2006; Böschen et al., 2012; Rayasam, 2012; Rubenstein, 2013; Skrzypinski, 2013). Research results by Buijsrogge et al. (2016) show that interviewer (over)confidence in biased judgments is driven by the initial effects of, and reactions to, the stigmatized applicant. But there is no such stigmatized effect when the partially blind interview technique is used (i.e., when the interviewers and the applicants do not see each other during the rapport building, but this visibility is present during the interview stage). Their findings show that in traditional interviews, the stigma, formed during the rapport-building stage, influences the interviewers' decision-making process, and hence, leading to biased applicant ratings. Using a partially blind interview technique, for example, when applicants for an orchestra play behind a curtain, the biased initial impression of otherwise stigmatized applicants may be prevented. This leads to less stigmatized impressions of applicants in the interview stage, ultimately resulting in less biased interview ratings for stigmatized applicants (Potočnik, 2021, p. 171).

For example, in many cultures, typical gender stereotypes hold that women are nurturing. This association is stored unconsciously and will be called up automatically in a selection situation, for example, when women apply for leadership positions. Thus, cultural knowledge is passed on within a society, including learning about stereotypes for specific groups. For this reason, any individual within a society may be able to describe the content of the stereotype. Simply knowing the content of certain stereotypes immediately activates assumptions about a human being, upon first contact (Reskin, 2005, p. 34).

Besides implicit stereotypes and prejudices, there are explicit ones. These stereotypes are conscious and, often, a result of one`s experiences; they result from intentional and controllable thinking and can, thus, be consciously applied.

Stereotypes and related automatic categorizations (pigeonhole thinking) may facilitate decision-making, but they also can lead to biases, generalizations, devaluations, offenses, discrimination, and injustice, and thus, poor selection decisions.

As a result, organizations may operate with sub-optimal human resource utilization and neglect the potential of labor markets.

In the following, different biases are presented. It has become apparent that these biases cannot always be clearly distinguished from one another and interact in integrative fashion, in some cases.

3.5.2.10 Initial impression and primacy effect

It is very common for people to form opinions about the characteristics of others from single samples, for example, the appearance and clothing. Many managers are convinced to make a correct judgment of a person within the first 30 s or first five minutes; they see quickly in an interview what kind of personality the applicant has when he walks in, how he behaves, shakes hands, dresses, and so on. Thus, "first impressions matter" (Kinnunen & Parviainen, 2016, p. 5).

Besides the initial impression, the primacy effect as a cognitive bias plays a decisive role in judging people. Primacy effect in selection processes refers to the tendency to remember information presented at the beginning of a selection process, for example, in an interview, better, and weighing on this information more heavily.

A Dutch selection manager interviewed in our research says:

> If I meet somebody for a job interview, I will never decide to hire somebody in the first five minutes, but if things go really wrong in five minutes, you can be already disqualified in my head. Never a final yes in the first five minutes, but it does happen that already after five minutes, I know, with this man or this woman, it's never going to work. I have in the past, [. . .] also told people already after 15 min in an interview: "Sorry, we're just wasting our time here, [. . .], but there's just not going to be a connection between us" (Bublitz, 2021, p. 76).

Since humans try to conserve their energy, they are more likely to pay more attention to information that comes first and less likely to attend to later data. In fact, when people read a series of statements about someone, the amount of time they spend reading the items declines with each new piece of information (Belmore & Hubbard, 1987). Research shows that hiring managers are distracted and more likely to show the primacy effect when tired than wide awake (Webster et al., 1996). People regularly develop an initial expectation about a person, based on their first impression. Once that expectation is formed, they tend to process information in ways that confirm that expectation (see confirmation bias). Once selection managers have created a positive impression, new negative information doesn't seem as bad as it might have been, had they got them first (Asch, 1946; Belmore & Hubbard, 1987; Gilbert et al., 1990; Ambady & Rosenthal, 1993; Ambady & Skoronski, 2008; Bar et al., 2006).

Olivola & Todorov (2010) examined whether appearance-based inferences are valid forms of social judgment. They found that judges are generally less accurate at predicting characteristics than if they ignore appearance cues; instead, they regularly rely on their knowledge of characteristic base-rate frequencies and an underlying distribution of characteristics. In most real-world contexts, where various social signals are available, reliance on appearances may actually make people worse at predicting the characteristics of others. Their research also shows remarkable overconfidence in inferring characteristics from appearances. The findings suggest that appearances are overweighed in judgments and can have detrimental effects on accuracy. Thus, they introduce their publication with the warning "not to judge a book by its cover" and quoted Jean de La Fontaine: "Beware, as long as you live, of judging people by appearances" (Olivola & Todorov, 2010, pp. 315, 322–323). Therefore, hiring managers should always give applicants a chance to make a second impression.

3.5.2.11 Recency effect

While the tendency to recall earlier information is called the primacy effect, the tendency to recall the later information is called the recency effect. Information received most recently is perceived as more important and is more likely to be recalled. Therefore, special attention is paid to the most recently acquired information in a selection interview. Along with the initial impression, the information recorded just before the end of a selection situation (interview, exercise in the assessment center) is more likely to be remembered and valued more highly. The recency effect is a result of short-term memory. This memory holds a relatively small amount of information in mind for a brief period and can be retrieved quickly (Jones & Goethals, 1972).

What humans remember is a construction of their mind and has much to do with emotions, less with what is objectively essential. One remembers better what goes to one's heart, what makes one angry and happy, or what is of personal interest. From an evolutionary perspective, people remember what moves them, because emotionally charged events often have survival value. Thus, emotions influence what and how something is remembered.

If the observations in an interview or assessment center are only recorded subsequently, or if information needs to be supplemented later by remembering the situation, errors in the record can occur when only the later information can be recalled.

3.5.2.12 Halo effect

Halo effect means that a positive or negative impression of a person in one area leads to a positive or negative opinion, feeling, or judgment of this person in other areas. One or a few perceived characteristics of the candidate "outshine" all the others. The halo effect can occur when selection managers first perceive external features of applicants (e.g., appearance, clothing, glasses, jewelry, smell, handshake, and facial expressions) and assign specific attributes to that applicant. This can be a positive or negative feature that distorts the overall picture of the candidate, in a given direction (Kanning, 2015, pp. 139–140).

Example: A particular attribute, for example, an applicant holds a degree from a renowned university such as Harvard or Stanford, or looks very attractive or friendly, influences the overall impression of that candidate without any rational-analytical evidence (Kanning, 2015, p. 138). People considered attractive or likable tend to be rated higher on other positive traits such as qualification, competence, or intelligence. The halo effect can also affect internal selection processes in performance appraisals and reviews. Supervisors may rate subordinates based on the perception of a single characteristic rather than the whole of their performance and contribution. For example, an employee's enthusiasm or positive attitude may overshadow a lack of knowledge or skills.

Empirical evidence for the halo effect was first provided by E.L. Thorndike (1920) when he noted a high cross-relation in military officers' ratings of their soldiers' physiques, intelligence, leadership skills, and character. For example, soldiers who were taller and found to be more attractive were also rated as more intelligent and as better soldiers. Thorndike determined from this observation that people generalize based on one outstanding trait to form a favorable view of a person's whole personality.

The halo effect leads to selective perception and affects how hiring managers interpret an applicant's information. The initial impression and the halo effect can influence all other perceptions. Positive or negative expectations are confirmed through selective, hypothesis-filtered perception and information evaluation (Höft & Kersting, 2018, p. 56; Kanning, 2015, p. 141).

3.5.2.13 Attractiveness bias or lookism

A widespread form of the halo effect is the so-called attractiveness bias. The first thing that catches the eye when looking through application documents or profiles on social media is often the photo. As a result, many selection managers attach great importance to a photo, according to the motto: "If I want to get a picture of an applicant, I need a picture."

In the literature, one also finds the term lookism, which stands for positive or negative discrimination, based on appearance (Hammer, 2017, Vedder, 2019, p. 104).

People approach attractively perceived people more benevolently than unattractive people and meet them in a more friendly manner and warm-heartedly. The person approached in a friendly manner also tends to respond in a friendly manner, resulting in a self-fulfilling prophecy that attractive people will be received more favorably, overall.

From the subjectively evaluated attractiveness of the applicant, other characteristics of the applicant are automatically and unconsciously inferred (Kanning, 2015, pp. 139–141). People tend to attribute positive qualities to attractive people and negative attributes to less attractive people. Therefore, job applicants who appear more attractive are more likely to be hired than less attractive candidates (Messner et al., 2011, p. 700; Dipboye et al., 1977).

Ruffle and Shtudiner (2015) found that applications with photos of attractive men receive significantly more positive feedback, even twice as much as average-looking men. Conversely, women receive more positive feedback when they apply without a picture. In particular, applications with photos of attractive women are followed by invitations to an interview significantly less frequently. In addition, studies have identified resentment of female recruiters and prejudices against specific visual characteristics (e.g., blond hair), or fear of sending negative signals by hiring an attractive applicant (Ruffle & Shtudiner, 2015, pp. 1763–1765).

In addition, attractive persons are rated lower in assessments by persons of the same sex than the opposite sex. Here, self-esteem acts as a moderator in decision-making processes. Persons with high self-esteem evaluate attractive same-sex persons significantly more positively than persons with low self-esteem (Agthe et al., 2011, pp. 1043–1044.). While both sexes prefer attractive individuals of the opposite sex in their assessment, women prefer less attractive female applicants in personnel selection. These effects could be found among professional recruiters as well as among students (Luxen & Van De Vijver, 2006, p. 241).

Another study by Desrumaux et al. (2009) shows that in typically male jobs (engineer), when a very high level of professional competence is needed and offered by an applicant, attractiveness had no influence on the assessment, and applicants were assessed equally, regardless of appearance. However, applicants with only average competence were judged more favorably if assessed as more attractive than the unattractive applicants. A different picture emerged for the classic female jobs; here, female applicants with a high level of competence and female applicants with an average level of competence were judged better if they had an attractive appearance (Desrumaux et al., 2009, pp. 33–34).

The entire judgment of candidates can be distorted due to the idea of a candidate created by the application photo. Thus, there are repeated calls to omit photos from applications and selection processes.

To evaluate who and what appears attractive in an interview, candidates and selection managers read their counterparts' faces and body language, equally. The visual impressions made by the facial expressions, gestures, and so on, play a decisive role in assessing attractiveness. For example, research by Imada & Hakel (1977, pp. 296–297) shows that candidates are judged more favorably the more they smile, maintain eye contact, and suggest attention with their body posture.

Further studies confirm systematic judgment bias in personnel selection, such as overestimating physically attractive persons' intelligence and social competence, when reviewing application documents (Schuler & Berger, 1977, p. 67; Watkins & Johnston, 2000, p. 82; Ekman & Friesen, 1974).

Thus, the old clichés like "clothes make the man" or "dress for success" are confirmed by research. Oh et al. (2020) show that economic status cues from clothes affect perceived competence from faces. The researchers ran nine studies in which participants rated the perceived competence of people wearing different clothing. The clothes of applicants bias interviewers. Those wearing clothes seen as "richer" were rated as more competent than people wearing similar clothes that appeared "poorer," although they were not necessarily perceived as such, when explicitly described. When seen with "richer" clothes, the same person was judged to be significantly more competent than with "poorer" clothes. The effect persisted even when perceivers were exposed to the stimuli briefly (129 ms), warned that clothing cues are non-informative, and instructed to ignore the clothes (in one study, with considerable incentives). These findings demonstrate the more or less uncontrollable effect of economic status cues on person perception and show another hurdle to getting a job by less wealthy individuals.

A study by Marlow et al. (1996, pp. 11–17) shows that hiring managers with more experience in selection decisions select more rigorously and pay less attention to applicants' attractiveness than decision-makers with less experience.

Hiring managers should consider that attractiveness bias or lookism can also include aspects of, for example, racism, sexism, and agism.

That hiring managers should be cautious about inferring applicants' personality traits from non-verbal perceptions is also shown by Breil & Back (2019; see also Breil et al., 2020). But they also state that only a few specific non-verbal cues lead to personality impressions, and only a few non-verbal cues are good indicators for the accuracy of personality judgments. And good judges, for example, "socially highly curious judges generally used more available cues and were thus more likely to detect valid cues for visible traits (in this case extraversion and openness)" (Breil et al., 2020, p. 29; see also Hall et al., 2017. For possible universals in facial expressions see Ekman, 1994; critically see Gendron et al., 2014).

However, these research results should be critically questioned regarding their applicability to current times, as socio-economic factors are subject to constant change.

3.5.2.14 Similarity effects, in-group favoritism, and homophily

According to Weuster (2004, p. 265), Condon & Crano (1988, p. 792), or Anderson & Shackleton (1990, pp. 64–65), similarity is one of the most critical determinants of interpersonal attraction that leads to having a liking for someone, and a certain amount of sympathy for somebody. According to the similarity-attraction-paradigm, people like and are attracted to others similar to themselves and share similar attitudes, interests, and/or other characteristics, for example, personality traits, similar social, ethnic, and cultural backgrounds, education, socioeconomic status, hobbies, values, beliefs, attitudes, religion (Berscheid & Walster, 1969; Byrne, 1971).

Similarity can be recognized in an interview or when looking at application documents. For example, research shows that personalized cover letters, a friendly and positively perceived appearance in the application photo, or friendly relationship building by applicants in the interview significantly reduce the social distance between manager and applicant and lead to more positive judgments (Trope & Liberman, 2010; Trope et al., 2007).

Humans develop positive emotions and like people with whom they find similarities; they know from their experience that these positive emotions could positively affect possible cooperation. Therefore, people perceived as similar to themselves are evaluated more positively (Anderson & Shackleton (1990, pp. 64–65). Thus, people's intuitions and emotions may tell them to surround themselves with similar people. In addition, people prefer what they know and are familiar with.

Thus, people with whom we have something in common are assessed more positively than others.

In Germany, there is a saying: "Smith is looking for little Smith"; or "John is looking for Johnny" (See Figure 6). This means that people are intuitively drawn to people they perceive to be like them (Sadler-Smith, 2019, p. 16).

Figure 6: Smith is looking for little Smith (illustration by Ninon Kolacz).

An error in assessment may occur because candidates who are similar to the selection manager tend to be rated higher. These distortions of perception or errors of judgment can arise from sympathy or antipathy, which are usually reactions to qualities people like or dislike in themselves. Applicants are likewise attracted to companies where people are similar to them (Orpen, 1984, p. 116; Kolominski, 2009, pp. 72–73).

3.5.2.15 In-group favoritism

In-group favoritism is a subtype of the similarity effect. It is also known as in-group-out-group bias, in-group bias, or intergroup bias. In-group-favoritism is the tendency to respond more positively to people from in-groups (a social group to which one psychologically identifies as a member) than to members of out-groups. People also make trait attributions in ways that benefit their in-groups, just as they make trait attributions that benefit themselves.

For example, in processes of employee referrals, there is a risk of in-group favoritism, similarity attraction, and homophily, the tendency to bond with similar others, as the well-known proverb says: "Birds of a feather flock together." One of the principles that family businesses are persistently said to adhere to is: "Blood is thicker than water"; as far as filling management positions is concerned, this means: The family or clan comes first, always.

This kind of favoritism, called nepotism, means that members of a family or clan use their power in various fields, including business, politics, entertainment, sports, religion, and other activities, to get good jobs or other advantages for the family/clan members.

Research results show that people, and thus, also selection managers, who are deeply embedded in collectivist or family/clan structures are subject to very great social pressure to select personnel not according to job requirements but according to supposed expectations of the collective (Hotho et al., 2020, p. 676). In addition, hiring managers can also be subject to social pressure, such as if their superiors require them to hire children of friends or executives, and customers or business partners.

Since our ancestors settled and lived in small social groups and were frequently in competition and conflict with other groups, it was evolutionarily functional for them to view members of other groups as different and potentially dangerous (Brewer & Caporael, 2006; Navarrete et al., 2004). Differentiating between "us" and "them" probably helped keep humans safe and free from disease, and as a result, the human brain became very efficient in making these distinctions (Van Vugt & Schaller, 2008; Zárate et al., 2008). The problem is that these deep-seated reflexes may lead hiring managers to prefer people like them and, in some cases, even decide unfairly and reject people from out-groups.

Research shows that people who can be assigned to the social or ethnic group of the decision-maker are given preferential employment (Åslund et al., 2014, p. 406). Suppose the decision-makers fear that the performance of a group member could shed a negative light on the whole group (e.g., damages the evaluation of the in-group). In that case, they could consider the risk and decide to the detriment of a candidate of the own in-group, for example, to avoid costly errors. "By considering the cost of errors, we can predict selective in-group favoritism and denigration as a function of the self-esteem implications of the judgments. Selective in-group favoritism emerges when it has social identity advantages but reverses when such favoritism would have a negative impact on social identity" (Lewis & Sherman, 2003, p. 273).

Employee referrals may also be subject to in-group favoritism, as employees often address people from their social environment. Since referred candidates are more likely to be hired and less likely to leave the company, and because the recruiting costs are regularly lower (Burks et al., 2015, pp. 807–816), hiring managers should be aware of the possible risk of in-group favoritism.

In-group favoritism can also mean filling management positions abroad with parent company employees (ethnocentric approach).

In-group favoritism can also be a consequence of cultural imprint. We know that human decision-making and behavior are not really objective; people construct the world in which they live and act according to different cultural preconditions and related, partly normative reference frameworks and associated patterns of thought and behavior. Moreover, intercultural research shows that national or group culture strongly influences human perceptions and what is (or is not) particularly perceived and observed in specific situations. For example, it can be seen that people from low-context cultures recognize and emphasize other things than people from high-context cultures, when perceiving the same situation (Masuda & Nisbett, 2001; for more details, see Section 7.2.4.2.1).

Since maintaining harmony among group members and voluntary cooperation toward group goals are essential characteristics of collectivist culture, in-group favoritism is a social expectation. It is confirmed in practice that in collectivist cultures, in-group favoritism (for example, preference for members of the family, extended family, or clan) is relatively widespread in the selection of personnel (Yamagishi et al., 2002; for the relationship between *Guanxi* and HR/People Management in China see Jones & Law, 2009). Moreover, due to the rapid professionalization of HR/People management, scientific research, global standards, legal and ethical requirements, and so on, hiring managers in these societies are, nowadays, commonly expected to base recruitment decisions exclusively on candidates' qualifications and merit (Stahl et al., 2012). Thus, in-group favoritism, as a kind of nepotism in recruitment and selection, remains a persistent challenge in these cultures, especially for European or American organizations (Horak, 2017; Hotho et al., 2020).

3.5.2.16 Confirmation bias

When filtering and processing information and solving problems, people tend to focus on information that confirms previous perceptions, attitudes, beliefs, and convictions and ignore information that does not. Humans are wired to see what they expect to see, which means they have selective attention. Thus, confirmation bias means that people tend to seek out and pay attention to information that confirms their beliefs and hypotheses, ignoring data that do not. In addition, they tend to surround themselves with people or read information, books, newspapers, internet sources, and so on, that confirm their opinions. This is how people consolidate their worldview and, of course, their prejudices.

From everyday life, everyone probably knows that sports team fans are likely to perceive unfair behavior more often in the opposing team than in their own. The principle is the same, when it comes to personnel selection. HR managers use their previous knowledge to interpret events and behavior. Perceptions are unconsciously influenced, so that information is interpreted to confirm previously formulated opinions. The cognitive process of receiving, storing, and intuitively processing information is also affected by applying mental abbreviations (heuristics), leading to many distortions of perception (Lee, 2005, p. 482).

As a result, they may fail to notice objects or events around them, a behavior known as inattention blindness. This pattern of seeing what we expect to see and discounting evidence to the contrary is known as confirmation bias. A result of confirmation bias can be that we may not change our ideas about an issue, just because we get new facts (Robertson, 2019, p. 7; Myers, 2008, p. 434).

Inattention blindness arises because humans want coherent overall impressions. As a result, many people find it challenging to accept ambiguities or even affirm them and see them as something positive (tolerance of ambiguity).

Since mismatched cognitions and, thus, inconsistencies between cognitions create dissonance, humans attempt to reduce this emotional state of tension. Therefore, information is sought that reduces the cognitive dissonance or prevents it from arising, in the first place. At the same time, an attempt is made not to perceive information that leads to cognitive dissonance. In this way, information or cognitions that create dissonance are eliminated.

Humans do not want to recognize the limits of their own perceptions and are confident in their positions. Thus, they need and want information that is as consistent as possible. In addition, they want to avoid ambiguities and contradictions and reduce cognitive dissonance.

Confirmation biases are, thus, an expression of reducing dissonance or preventing it from arising, in the first place.

People tend to make things easy for themselves and their brains. They often do not want to differentiate but to generalize. These generalizations lead to simplifications and distortions. When the perceived information matches their beliefs, their brain is more likely to evaluate it as correct and valid.

Macan & Dipboye (1990) show that the interviewers` pre-interview impressions positively relate to post-interview impressions. Selection managers form hypotheses about the suitability of an applicant. Whether it is specific references in the application documents like studying at particular universities or the handshake, eye contact, or walk of applicants, the risk of self-deception exists. The hypothesis is then tested in the interview.

Research shows that "expectation shapes reality" (Rock & Schwartz, 2006). The social construction of reality can be seen in hiring managers' behavior and how they perceive and evaluate candidates' observed behaviors. When applicants seem particularly likable, hiring managers search for information that supports the applicant's suitability. Thus, selection managers can overlook candidates' weaknesses by minimizing their relevance to the job, or by devaluation or suppression of conflicting information.

The confirmation bias can also be associated with Antonovsky's concept of "sense of coherence" (Antonovsky, 1979, 1993). According to this, people have an adaptive dispositional orientation to cope with adverse experiences and strive to use understandable, meaningful, and manageable information individually, in a specific situation. The coherence effect describes the phenomenon that information is not objectively incorporated into decisions. Instead, data is unconsciously reassessed when deciding to match a preferred interpretation. As a result, the selective perception of attributes or characteristics of an applicant and the evaluation of these attributes shift to cohere with the information that substantiates the assumptions made in advance (Höft & Kersting, 2018, p. 56).

Suppose we understand the brain as a neuronal network of interconnected information units. In that case, human perception never only activates and recalls isolated information in the brain but also activates associated information units. For example, if we hear the word fire brigade, the associated color red is automatically activated. This activation is bidirectional, that is, there is mutual and parallel activation of information processing in the brain. This way, meaning is formed that best explains and confirms the available information. For example, this mechanism may result in information about an applicant being automatically and unconsciously sorted to support an interpretation as coherently as possible for selection decisions.

In contrast, any existing counterevidence or contradictory information is hidden or devalued. Processing extraneous, for example, information that is not job-relevant (e.g., gender, attractiveness, ethnic group, and social background) requires cognitive resources that compete with resources needed for a requirement-oriented personnel selection. One result of these unconscious processes is, often, at first, a "feeling" that tends in a particular direction, without knowing exactly how this feeling was created. This phenomenon is also called intuition. Furthermore, these processes deliver a feeling regarding the degree of coherence of the current interpretation. This allows interpretations to be accepted or rejected (Glöckner & Towfigh, 2015, p. 272).

3.5.2.17 Self-serving bias

Self-serving bias means that perceptual processes and judgments can be unconsciously biased, due to the hiring manager's self-interest. For example, Berne (1949) states that the assumption of satisfying needs influences human behavior; people take an interest in others, when they serve them to achieve vital needs and interests.

Hiring managers – like all humans – need to maintain strong self-esteem and evaluate themselves positively: I'm worthy, I believe I'm a competent selection manager, and so on.

This can also be a status quo bias, considering the current selection procedures as optimal and anything different as a loss. This leads to a continuation of status quo in selection procedures (Terpstra & Rozzell (1997, p. 483).

Self-serving bias can also mean attributing negative results and failures to external factors and internalizing and attributing positive outcomes and success to one's efforts and competencies. For example, when presented with identical information, individuals tend to view information supporting their position and serving their individual interests as more convincing than those supporting the other side (Bazerman et al., 1997, p. 91; Campbell & Sedikides, 1999; Myers, 2015). Thus, hiring managers might tend to attribute every successful selection decision to their individual competencies and knowledge of human nature and less to the methods and instruments used. Or being hired for a job is attributed by candidates to their competencies and characteristics, whereas failure to obtain a job is attributed to external factors.

Hiring managers convinced of their particular personnel diagnostic competencies have little interest in questioning themselves, and negative aspects or outcomes of their selection decision are ignored. If, for example, a hiring manager gets feedback that a new employee has performed very well two weeks after a vacancy has been filled, this strengthens the belief in the manager's professionalism. However, should the new employee's supervisor express skepticism, the hiring manager may explain that it takes time to integrate the new hire into the company and for him/her toperform (Kanning, 2015, p. 144).

Or hiring managers might perceive a candidate very positively, because they are convinced this candidate can improve their own positive reputation and standing within the company, or promote a candidate as a favor to an important customer or a senior executive. On the other hand, other hiring managers may perceive this applicant as a competitor, who could challenge them for their current position; this candidate would, then, be perceived critically.

Thus, hiring managers should reflect to which extent other people (e.g., specific candidates) can support or threaten the hiring managers in reaching their individual needs and goals, including those of getting benefits, influence, and power (Schmid & Gèrad, 2008, pp. 35–38).

3.5.2.18 Correspondence bias or fundamental attribution error

Humans seek reasons in their judgment processes (Bierhoff & Frey, 2006, p. 332), but attributing false causes can result in decision errors. Correspondence bias or attribution effect describes the phenomenon that the influence of the current situation or circumstances is underestimated in analyzing and assessing behavior. In contrast, the impact of a personal predisposition (personality or traits) is overestimated (Myers, 2008, p. 637).

Thus, correspondence bias or fundamental attribution error is the human tendency to believe that applicants' behavior necessarily reflects who they are and, thus, overattributes behavior to an applicant's traits, values, or motives. As a result, hiring managers may see applicants behaving in a certain way and assume that this behavior expresses their personality. As a result, they neglect the influence of the situation, even when there is a perfectly logical external factor motivating the applicant's behavior. Even when hiring managers are aware of the particular circumstances, they often overlook them and instead infer that this applicant always behaves this way (Miyamoto & Kitayama, 2002, p. 1239).

An example is that a formal error in a CV can be interpreted as low motivation to get the job. Or gaps in the CV will be anchored to the lack of conscientiousness and, thus, in the applicant's personality; or being late to the interview is seen as an expression of the candidate's personality and not a consequence of an hour-long traffic jam on the highway (Kanning, 2015, p. 141).

Similarly, selection managers can make self-esteem-serving attributions (Greenberg et al., 1982). For example, to protect against threats to their self-esteem, they may attribute their successes (e.g., selecting successful candidates) to their own competencies, and failures (hiring an employee who later does not perform) to circumstances or poor leadership of the supervisor of the new employee.

3.5.2.19 Cultural bias

Cultural bias is the phenomenon of interpreting and judging behaviors of others in terms of one's own cultural standards and assumptions; for example, specific cultural values, beliefs, mindsets, and behaviors. Cultural biases occur when people of a specific culture make – without examining the evidence – assumptions about people of other cultures concerning their personalities, attitudes, values, behaviors, conventions, and so on (see prejudices and stereotypes). For example, many cultural biases exist concerning skin color, religious beliefs or rules, and ethnic concepts of right and wrong behaviors. Example: Specific greetings, hand gestures, or prolonged eye contact can be seen in some cultures as a sign of disrespect.

Cultural bias can lead selection managers to form opinions and judge applicants, before any actual experience with them. Since these cultural biases can significantly affect selection processes involving global leaders or expatriates, every hiring manager should reflect upon them, differently.

3.5.2.20 Ethnic biases

Ethnic biases, as a particular cultural bias, consist of attitudes and beliefs about people of specific social groups and can be attributed to stereotypes and prejudices.

The basis of ethnicity can be appearances such as skin tone, cultural origins, behavior, language, ancestry or religion, or connection to a specific area.

Ethnic bias leads to prejudices, anti-foreign sentiments, and discrimination against entire groups, such as Latinos, Afro-Americans, Indians, Scots, Turks, Arabs, Muslims, and Jews. (Brief et al., 2000; Bertrand & Mullainathan, 2004). People with these prejudices prefer not to interact with members of "disliked" groups and try not to hire them. In addition, these ethnic biases can lead to people being excluded from the application process because of their skin color, a particular headgear, or even a foreign-sounding name.

A very extreme form of ethnic bias is racism; racism is the belief in human races and, in particular, in the superiority of one race over another. The term race and its use can be seen critically; current research largely agrees that human races are a social construction without a biological basis. Therefore, it is argued not to use the term "race" when speaking of human beings, but instead of ethnicity. A person who is biased against people of other ethnic groups is prejudiced. Bias or prejudices lead to discriminatory treatment, and no one should be discriminated against, based on ethnic background.

One way to reduce discrimination based on cultural or ethnic biases or physical appearance would be to hide names or photographs from resumes (making them anonymous), whether through government legislation or by simply changing the current convention (Ruffle & Shtudiner, 2015, p. 1775).

3.5.2.21 Hindsight bias

Hindsight bias (or knew-it-all effect) is a retrospective error of judgment and memory distortion in which a person believes, in retrospect, that s/he knew the outcome of a decision that only later proved to be true (Fischhoff, 1975). Thus, hindsight bias causes one to view the success or failure of a hired candidate as more predictable than it`s really possible. If, for example, after hiring a candidate, a hiring manager gets the feedback that the candidate did not perform as expected, s/he may then "remember" not being entirely sure about this particular selection decision from the outset, or to have hired the candidate because there was no one better, or to give the candidate a chance. The hiring manager then may say: "I always thought that!" or "I knew from the beginning that it would go wrong" (Kanning, 2015, p. 144; Höft & Kersting, 2018, p. 56).

Hindsight bias can thus lead to the assumption that hiring managers acted absolutely correctly and did everything right, where they were perhaps simply lucky. Of course, the selection managers are subject to this possible bias, as are superiors or line managers.

The hindsight bias or the illusion of having known (in advance) and done everything right can lead to the illusion that one will continue to be successful in the future, based on one's previous selection behaviors and procedures. Managers experience this illusion as reassuring, because they feel secure having proceeded absolutely correctly.

If hiring managers look back at their past decisions and conclude that their consequences were, indeed, known to them at the time (when they weren't), then they overestimate their ability to foresee the future implications of their selection decisions (Fischhoff & Beyth, 1975; Roese & Vos, 2013; Danz et al., 2015; Hermann & Mayer, 2020, p. 33).

Thus, hindsight bias supports managers to become less accountable for their decisions, less critical of themselves, and overconfident in their decision-making ability.

Two heuristics identified as "mental shortcuts" by Tversky and Kahneman are of immediate importance, in developing the hindsight bias. These are the availability heuristic (the tendency to use information that comes to mind quickly and easily, when making decisions about the future) and the representativeness heuristic (making judgments by comparing results to concepts, for example, selection procedures, people already have in their mind). These heuristics activate hindsight information and, thus, hindsight bias, for example, the knew-it-all-along-effect as a specific hindsight bias and, thus, the risk of overestimating one`s ability to predict the consequences of a past decision.

Selection managers should consider that "wrong" past judgments and making mistakes are not useless, but learning opportunities. It is better to admit mistakes and reflect on them critically than to pretend they did not occur. Of course, the past cannot be changed, but this does not mean that the analysis of past decisions is not helpful for future decisions.

3.5.2.22 Gender bias

The gender of job applicants can also be an object of bias in hiring decisions, generally favoring male over female applicants, for example, for higher leadership positions or some gender-stereotyped jobs (e.g., nursing and geriatric care). Indeed, numerous studies indicate that males are commonly preferred over females in many hiring contexts, regardless of their qualifications (Messner et al., 2011, p. 700). Bowen et al. (2000) found significant pro-male biases in performance appraisals, when only men served as raters; but they also found that feminine measures produced pro-female bias.

Female pilots or skilled female workers such as car mechanics may face distrust in their service provision; women also remain underrepresented in high leadership positions. Studies show that

> (s)o long as . . . recruiters were unaware of applicant gender, women were accurately identified as qualified talent and selected for a job interview. Once recruiters knew applicants' gender, women faced significantly worsened chances of being selected than in a gender-blind setting. Women's personal and functional competencies are regularly overlooked once they

are identified as women. In these cases, highly qualified women are disadvantaged to less-qualified males. Women are held back by stereotypes and socialization and often do not assert themselves enough in the workplace. Women are discriminated against, if not explicitly at least implicitly, as their talent and suitability are overlooked due to gender bias (Keinert-Kisin, 2016, pp. V–VI).

Correspondence bias or the fundamental attribution error may also contribute to gender bias, as more men work in higher positions than women, and successful managers are associated with characteristics, attitudes, and competencies that are more commonly ascribed to men than to women (Eagly & Karau, 2002; Biswas et al., 2109). Both factors may contribute to the stereotype that males are better qualified for managerial positions, often referred to as the "think-manager-think-male" bias.

Conversely, a preference for women is found in low-status domains, where more women than men are employed (Messner et al., 2011, p. 700). In recent years, it has become apparent that more and more women are being selected for management positions, especially in Western countries. Yet, gender bias still significantly impacts selection decisions, especially for management positions.

3.5.2.23 Sexual orientation bias

This usually refers to a predisposition towards heterosexual people and is based on stereotypes about people, based on their sexual orientation and behaviors. These stereotypes and prejudices lead to discrimination against LGBTQ + people (LGBTQ+ is an acronym for lesbian, gay, bisexual, transgender, queer, or questioning; and the + means "or other gender identities"), especially in the labor market and personnel selection processes.

3.5.2.24 Age bias/ageism

Age bias (also called ageism) is stereotyping and discrimination against individuals or groups based on their age, especially older people. These prejudices are often based on the deficit model of aging, for example, that more senior employees are resistant to change and learning new things, are not creative, have reduced physical capacity (Bal et al., 2011; Karpinska et al., 2013).

The consequence is that older applicants have fewer chances in the labor market, are less likely to be invited for interviews, and have fewer chances of getting a job.

3.5.2.25 Disabilities bias/ableism

Disabilities bias (also called ableism) is based on stereotypes and prejudices against people, especially against physical or mental disabilities. For example, hiring managers with this bias think that persons with disabilities are generally less able to perform, are more often ill, want to be cured, and are subject to special protective regulations. The result is that these people have fewer chances in the labor market, are less likely to be invited for interviews, and have fewer chances of getting a job.

3.5.2.26 (Over)weight bias

People with this bias often see overweight persons as indolent, lazy rather than dynamic and efficient, undisciplined, overly sensitive, using humor to be liked, and so on (Finkelstein et al., 2007). "Well, I admit, if someone is really, really fat, he has no chance" (Bastian, 2018, p. 165). The result is that overweight, especially obese people, have fewer chances of getting a job.

3.5.2.27 Rating scale bias

Even if specific behavior anchors and scaled requirement criteria are implemented, many hiring managers have a subjective assessment system and measure candidates, based on their individual aspirations and requirements. This can lead to rating scale errors. Rating scale biases can be influenced by the similarity or difference of the selection manager to the candidate, experience with other applicants, or the tendency of an assessor towards average, mildness, or rigor (Kanning, 2015, p. 140). Via training, supervision, or reflection with other hiring managers, the personal reference or rating scale system could be adapted to a predefined evaluation standard.

An example of these distortions of perception is the so-called mild-hardness effect. In a mild effect, erroneous assessments are made, based on leniency with the corresponding applicants. This effect can be justified, for example, by bad personal experiences with negatively evaluated persons or by the overestimation of emotional components in professional life. The opposite phenomenon is the hardness or severity effect (Fallgatter, 2013, p. 178).

The propensity for giving average ratings is called the tendency towards the middle. If too little information is available for an accurate evaluation, or if the data is contradictory and cannot be precisely evaluated, or if assessors are conflict-averse, they often choose a medium scoring (Fallgatter, 2013, p. 178). In personnel selection, this can lead to a situation in which competencies that cannot be assessed unambiguously are unconsciously and automatically assessed as mediocre, without further search for indications of competencies.

3.5.2.28 Psychological projection

Psychological projection can occur in selection processes. It is a defense mechanism by which hiring managers defend themselves unconsciously against impulses (both positive and negative) or traits, by denying their existence in themselves and attributing them to others. The projection includes the transfer of an inner-psychic content, for example, being aggressive or lazy, to others because these characteristics conflict with one's self-image, values, or social norms and, thus, not acceptable to have it in oneself. Then, these feelings, desires, impulses, or characteristics are projected onto the applicant, rather than admitting, reflecting, or coping with that unwanted or unacceptable feeling, desire, trait, and so on, in oneself. The concept was introduced by the Austrian psychoanalyst, Sigmund Freud (Baumeister et al., 2002).

The psychological projection consists of avoiding dealing with impulses in oneself, for example, negative emotions towards an applicant, and projecting these negative emotions onto the applicant. This process then convinces a hiring manager of a candidate's negative or aggressive emotions. Thus, the selection manager, for example, blames the applicant for an unfriendly attitude, resulting in a negative evaluation.

3.5.2.29 Overconfidence bias

The quality of a decision depends on the self-confidence of the decision-makers and to what extent they trust their judgment.

However, many people tend to overestimate their competence and the accuracy of their judgments. Thus, many managers and human resource professionals overestimate their abilities and the quality of selection procedures used in practice.

They, often, cannot imagine having made suboptimal or poor decisions, and the memory is sometimes distorted, in retrospect. If, however, it is recognized that a wrong decision has been made, then, it may be argued that the candidate has misrepresented himself in the selection procedure, rather than an error having been made in the selection (see self-serving attribution). The decision is perceived as uncertain from the beginning (Kanning, 2015, pp. 143–144).

Daniel Kahneman and Amos Tversky (1973, 1996) summarize this as the overconfidence bias. Plous (1993, pp. 217–218) has called overconfidence the most pervasive and potentially catastrophic of all the cognitive biases human beings could have. Berthet (2022) reviewed the research on the impact of cognitive biases on professionals` decisions and found that overconfidence is the most recurrent bias. Kahneman said in a 2016 interview: "What would I eliminate if I had a magic wand? Overconfidence" (Shariatmadari, 2021).

Thus, any human, especially hiring managers, should recognize the limits of their competencies (Kausel et al., 2016).

A specific kind of overestimation is the "bias blind spot," the tendency of people to see themselves as less susceptible to biases than others. Thus, hiring managers may deny or fail to see the impact of biases on their judgments (see Section 3.5.2).

Overconfidence can also follow from hindsight mistakes, leading to overestimating one's ability to make correct judgments. Retrospectively claiming that hiring managers had predicted a "wrong" outcome makes them immune to criticism. They present their decisions as better than they actually were and avoid critical reflection and evaluation.

The overconfidence phenomenon occurs, above all, with less experienced persons, where a less good decision is judged better than it actually is. However, with more experience, decisions improve and are more accurately assessed (Pfister et al., 2017, pp. 157–158).

Overconfident decision-makers are problematic, because they have an illusion of understanding. In particular, they overestimate the validity of unstructured interviews and often do not know how accurate their selection decisions are. As a result, they are willing to take more risks and may terminate a selection process before finding the (actual) best candidate. Furthermore, they fail to acknowledge the role of uncertainty in personnel selection and that decisions are subject to error (Kausel et al., pp. 34–35).

3.5.2.30 Technologically induced bias

A study by the universities of Magdeburg (Germany) and Sønderborg (Denmark) shows that due to the high data volume, video conferencing systems such as Zoom, Skype, or Teams thin out high frequencies of female voices, to save data volume. The study showed that signal compression codecs used in remote meetings and mobile communications adversely affect perceived speaker charisma, and substantially. The researchers conclude that in the case of female voices participating in videoconferences (and comparable then also applies to video interviews), essential emotional components were not perceived by the test listeners, compared to male participants. The female voices were perceived as less expressive, competent, and charismatic. This can lead to discrimination against women. They also found that the perceived clarity of the pronunciation determines the speaker`s charisma.

The researchers recommend that when developing codes for a digital meeting or interview tool, attention should be paid not only to pure voice quality, word intelligibility, and suppression of background noise, but also to the transmission of characteristics, such as expressiveness, emotionality, and charisma (Siegert & Niebuhr, 2021).

3.5.2.31 Sample (selection) bias

This bias occurs when some population members are systematically more likely to be selected in a sample than others. Sample bias is often caused by choosing non-random data for statistical analysis. The bias exists due to a flaw in the sample selection process, where a subset of the data is systematically excluded, due to a particular attribute. An example is when using algorithms or AI in selection processes. One of the critical challenges in implementing algorithms and AI in selection processes is to provide a large amount of high-quality training data. This training data can be selected by people but also by self-learning AI systems. However, there is a risk that AI could learn human bias and amplify it. Thus, errors such as discrimination might occur in the selection process. If, for example, men were selected predominantly for certain positions in the past, the algorithm might recognize this as a pattern and favor men, accordingly, in future selection processes. The underlying training data would then not adequately represent the actual population in the application area. The creation and preparation of a high-quality and, at the same time, non-discriminatory data set are, therefore, a central challenge for companies that want to use AI and avoid "sample (selection) bias" in the selection process. If, among other factors, this is provided, the use of AI can help reduce other biases as well.

3.5.2.32 Conclusion

The formation of judgment depends on many factors. Bias and distortions of perception are influence factors that must be considered, but there are individual differences in cognitive biases. How selection managers perceive depends partly on their position in the organization. Line managers may have a different view of job requirements than their colleagues from the HR department, the job holders themselves, or other stakeholders, such as customers (Guion, 1998, p. 581). Hiring managers differ in their personality and education, and personal characteristics and experiences influence each individual's limited and selected attention. The competent handling of "cognitive complexity" or "cognitive simplicity" also affects the strength of a hiring manager's judgment, significantly. The better a manager can conceptualize complex situations, requirements, or relationships, the more accurate the judgments. A further parameter of a hiring manager`s success lies in their motivation. They should be aware of the importance of filling the vacancy in a high-quality process and should not see selection as a task that can be done on the side; thus, they should not do their job with the attitude to move on, as quickly as possible, to other tasks (Guion, 1998, pp. 581–582).

It is well known that people find it challenging to admit misconceptions and change their own views and perspectives. Therefore, it is helpful to make iterative or dynamic adjustments to one's decision-making behavior through constant feedback and continuous comparison of the expected and actual consequences of one's decisions.

By knowing about selective perception and biases, especially through feedback, and a critical reflection of their imprints (e.g., in awareness training), hiring managers learn about their assumptions, prejudices, and biases and try to reduce them. Nevertheless, there is always a risk of being unconsciously influenced by them. Thus, selection decision-makers should know what stimuli activate their prejudices and other biases. Furthermore, to overcome a bias, one needs to be mindful of it and have the time, attention, and motivation to counteract it, through rational reflection (Kulik et al., 2007, p. 529).

3.6 Benefits of rational-analytical selection procedures

3.6.1 Reduce perceptual distortions and bias

People are people and, thus, imperfect. Mistakes are bound to happen. However, errors in selection processes can be reduced. Research clearly shows that rational-analytical procedures in personnel selection can reduce perceptual distortions and biases. It is, thus, essential to acquire knowledge about rational-analytical selection procedures and their advantages and disadvantages. This includes, as described in Section 3.5, learning about (unconscious) stereotypes, prejudices, and biases and how they are likely to affect their judgments and decisions.

From a rational-analytical perspective, it is most important to base selection decisions and procedures on evident research results and not only on subjective impressions, feelings, or intuitions.

Several international selection managers interviewed in our empirical research express that, although specific standards of personnel selection are demanded in a global company, the understanding of quality varies significantly, from culture to culture.

At the same time, selection managers report their experience that even within one culture, the understanding of quality in personnel selection is very different and, thus, highly subjective. Most of the interviewed hiring managers agree that using a rational-analytical procedure and implementing science-based quality standards make it possible to reduce biases, discrimination, and law violations.

A large proportion of those we interviewed confirm that the quality of personnel selection is ultimately determined by the result (quality of hiring). However, high quality in the process is required to achieve good results; and the quality of the selection process is most likely to be ensured, when taking a rational-analytical approach.

Even though our interviewees define “analytics in personnel selection” differently, they broadly agree that rational-analytics refers to a systematic and structured personnel selection procedure that is coordinated and standardized, within the company.

The primary goal of the analytical approach should be to establish objectivity and, thus, fairness, legal certainty, and comparability of applicants in personnel selection.

Several interviewees emphasize that it is essential to switch off emotions and intuitive impressions to be able to select people objectively, to assess applicants based on evidence, consistent requirements, and without the risk of subjective unconscious bias.

The selection process, from the analysis of the application documents to the final decision, should be carried out, based on a clear job description and previously defined job requirements; and the selection process, as a whole, should be as standardized as possible. Most interviewees agree that this should include an interview guideline, including evaluating candidates' behaviors, based on behavioral anchors. Almost all interviewed hiring managers agree that at least two selection managers should be involved in a selection process, e g., interviews, to reduce the influence of individual biases such as confirmation bias, and to reflect together upon individual perceptions, intuitions, emotions, and, thus, judgments (Deters, 2019, pp. 112–114).

Effective personnel selection aims to avoid the so-called type I and type II errors (Weuster, 2012, p. 1). In the case of a type I error, an objectively suitable applicant is considered unsuitable. An objectively unsuitable candidate is assessed as appropriate and hired with the type II error.

Research by Höft & Kersting (2017, pp. 59–61) shows that to avoid these type I and type II errors by reducing stereotypes, prejudices, bias, and discrimination and to hire the best suited and qualified applicants, a rational-analytical approach is recommended. In addition, selection training for personnel managers can reduce both types of errors (see Section 9.1).

From a holistic perspective, it is not enough to train selection managers to recognize possible distortions, biases, and so on, and reduce them, individually. It is also essential to act at the process level and, thus, at selection procedures, instruments, and tools.

The tendency to be subject to these effects should be accepted as a hypothesis to understand the consequences and counteract them. For example, one measure to reduce the primacy and recency effects is to write detailed notes, for example, during interviews or exercises at an assessment center; or only accept applications without photos.

The more complex the job to be filled, the greater the differences in individual performance (Alon & Higgins, 2005, p. 501). Since leadership tasks, especially on an intercultural level, require acting in diverse and complex environments, the importance of a high-quality hiring approach increases.

There is positive correlation between implementing scientifically based rational-analytical personnel selection processes and business success (Harter et al., 2002, p. 268; Terpstra & Rozell, 1997).

A meta-analysis comprising 61 primary studies shows that more the effort a company invests in selecting new employees, greater the business success. In addition, poor personnel selection can only be compensated to a limited extent by personnel development measures (Gmür & Schwerdt, 2005, pp. 228 and 237).

In a meta-analysis, Kuncel et al. (2013, p. 1064) clarified that

> across multiple criteria in work and academic settings, when people combined hard data with their judgments, and those of others, their predictions were always less valid, and less predictive of real outcomes, than those generated by hard data alone. This was true even when the judgments were made by experts knowledgeable about the jobs and organizations in question. In predicting job performance, for instance, hard data predictions outperformed a combination

> of data and expert judgment by 50 percent. In evaluating candidates applying to jobs (and no matter what the job was), the team of researchers found that a simple algorithm outperformed human judgment by over 25 percent. What this research suggests is that relying on the most objective data available and using algorithms to interpret it to make selection decisions beats our intuition. By far. (Gino, 2014)

"About 60% of the studies have shown significantly better accuracy for the algorithm. . . . In every case, the accuracy of experts was matched or exceeded by a simple algorithm" (Kahneman, 2011, p. 223). "The research suggests a surprising conclusion: to maximize predictive accuracy final decisions should be left to formulas. . . . Conducting an interview is likely to diminish the accuracy of a selection procedure, if the interviewers also make the final admission decisions" (Kahneman, 2011, p. 225; see also Grove et al., 2000).

In another study, Schlegel et al. (2017) state that algorithms achieve similar results in the pre-selection process, as human experts. The authors assume that the significant differences between human judgments point to the limited objectivity of the human acting like a judge.

Our empirical studies also show that implementing a specific selection procedure depends on situational factors, for example, the position to fill, the acceptance of selection procedures by the applicants, or how often a role has to be filled. The more frequently a job is to be filled, and the more pivotal the position is for the company's success, the more systematic and analytical, the selection procedure.

At the same time, the selection managers widely emphasize that analytics should not lead to unpleasant feelings among applicants and a negative candidate experience.

Ackerschott et al. (2016, p. 13) show that by applying rational-analytical selection procedures, wrong or poor decisions and resulting negative economic, social, or individual consequences for the organization can be avoided.

3.6.2 Advantages of systematic requirement analysis and interview guidelines

A rational-analytical selection process should start with a systematic requirement analysis. First, the requirement profile must describe the requirements relevant for completing the position to fill. The more concrete, behavior-related, and job-specific the requirement profile, the more valid the basis for personnel selection decisions. Ackerschott et al. (2016), also emphasize the behavioral reference and the concreteness of the requirement profile as an essential prerequisite for valid recruitment interviews and hiring decisions.

Using a job and requirements analysis alone leads to doubling the forecast quality (Kanning, 2015, p. 105). In this context, it was also empirically confirmed that a differentiated requirement profile leads to higher interrater reliability (e.g., $r = 0.87$ compared to $r = 0.35$ according to Langdale & Weitz, 1973, pp. 24–25; see also

Hahn & Dipboye, 1988). Furthermore, results from meta-analyses (Wiesner & Cronshaw, 1988, p. 287) additionally confirm the positive influence of a differentiated requirement profile on the validity of a hiring decision.

Structured interviews based on thorough job analyses and job requirements, thus, achieved an average corrected validity of $r = 0.87$, and structured interviews based on superficial digit analysis, only $r = 0.59$.

McDaniel et al. (1994, p. 606) could also prove that the corrected validity coefficient for structured interviews with situational questions was $r = 0.50$ in comparison to structured interviews without reference to requirements ($r = 0.44$) and unstructured interviews ($r = 0.33$) (Koppers, 2013, pp. 19–20).

Without diminishing the importance of a requirement profile for a high-quality personnel selection, a requirement profile primarily shows the company's needs at a given time. However, requirements change over time and are sometimes difficult to predict. Therefore, personnel diagnostics should function more as a potential analysis, since future requirements should also be considered in the profile, due to a dynamic and constantly changing working environment. For this reason, recording a person's potential is of decisive importance (Schuler, 2000, p. 13).

3.6.2.1 Requirement-oriented analysis of application documents

The analysis of application documents should also be strictly oriented to the job requirements. However, in practice, several softer and subjective criteria are regularly used in assessing application documents, which do not possess any prognostic quality. For example, in a study by Kersting (2016), 83.6% of all personnel selection managers stated that they pay attention to gaps in the CV. However, gaps in a CV alone do not provide a valid prediction about the applicants' personality or their later success on the job to be filled (Frank & Kanning, 2014).

According to Kersting (2016), other less valid assessment criteria are a clear formatting of the CV, typographical errors, stains in the cover letter (in paper applications), consideration of the reasons for an application in the cover letter, references, the age, or hobbies of candidates (Frank & Kanning, 2014, Kanning 2016a; Quinones et al., 1995; Watkins & Johnston, 2000).

Thus, from a rational-analytical perspective, the analysis of application documents should be based on a requirement-related evaluation of facts and valid data.

3.6.2.2 Systematic selection interviews based on interview guidelines

In selection processes, a lack of standardization, for example, no precise requirement profiles or interview guidelines, can lead to different evaluation standards by the involved selection managers. A binding selection framework can minimize these negative consequences (Kanning, 2015, p. 140). Parts of this "binding selection framework" or standards are requirement profiles with behavioral anchors and interview guidelines. Thus, behavioral requirement profiles and structured interviews lead to more valid selection results. Above all, structured interviews based on interview guidelines reduce subjective errors of judgment during the decision-making process, which leads to more valid decisions.

3.6.3 Better justification and communication of the selection results

In addition, rational-analytical selection procedures can provide more objective and fact-based documentation of decisions for third parties. The executives and personnel managers surveyed in our empirical studies emphasized this and clarified that rational-analytics also includes detailed documentation of the results, based on the requirement criteria. This also ensures traceability by third parties; for example, candidates can be given structured and systematic feedback (Deters, 2019, p. 113).

3.6.4 Higher intellectual diversity

"(G)reater diversity, in terms of both gender and ethnicity, is correlated with significantly greater likelihood of outperformance. More than that, fostering a diverse and inclusive culture is a critical success factor: it enables individuals both to shine in their own right and to pull together as a team" (McKinsey & Company, 2020, p. 47). From this perspective, there is a business imperative for diversity (Tsusaka et al., 2019; for the value of board diversity see Hagendorff & Keasey, 2012 or Hafsi & Turgut, 2013). In an increasingly complex world, intellectual diversity can foster creativity and is, thus, a critical success factor for organizations. Intellectual diversity must be explicitly distinguished from diversity in terms of demographic characteristics, such as age or gender. "Just because people look different doesn't mean they'll have divergent points of view" (Hill et al., 2014, p. 139). A broad spectrum of thinking and a variety of ideas, skills, expertise, and experience is crucial to stimulate the exchange of ideas and individual explorative activities (Dahlander et al., 2016, p. 282; Hargadon & Sutton, 2000, p. 159; Taylor & Greve, 2006, p. 735). Intellectual diversity generates diverse and sometimes conflicting perspectives and, thus, causes ambiguity, but this can favor innovative solutions (Garud et al., 2013, p. 793). In addition, the breadth and depth of knowledge of the diverse people involved are considered significant for creativity (Andriopoulos & Lewis, 2010, p. 105; Taylor & Greve, 2006, p. 726). To promote this intellectual discourse, a diverse workforce is required. The most likely way to get this is by reducing biases.

3.6.5 More sense of fairness and positive candidate experience

According to Kersting (2008, p. 421), a proponent of the psychometric approach, fairness and acceptance of selection instruments become especially relevant, if several selection procedures appear to be broadly equivalent from a psychometric perspective. Thus, he pleads for selection procedures that, on the one hand, have a high psychometric quality and, on the other hand, meet with high social acceptance. However, for the dilemma between social acceptance and scientific quality criteria, he strongly argues for prioritizing psychometric quality that meets predictive validity, objectivity, and reliability standards (see Sections 3.7.3 and 3.7.7).

If selection procedures are carried out related to the specific job requirements and according to a generally recognized rational-analytical quality standard, the acceptance and sense of fairness will increase among applicants and, so will the trust in the selection managers and the selecting company (Hausknecht et al., 2004, p. 656; Strobel et al., 2010, p. 30; for the limits of acceptance of rational-analytical procedures, see Section 3.7). When candidates feel they are treated fairly, it increases the positive candidate experience.

3.7 Limits of rational-analytical personnel diagnostics

Even rational-analytically reasoned management decisions could lead to mistakes, especially in fast-changing environments. We see it in many company failures, financial crises, and poorly selected personnel. This can be due to missing information, insufficient data, perception errors, and so on.

Decision-makers can be blinded by supposed facts and numbers, ignoring that these are also subject to individual representations, constructions, and evaluations. Also, intuitions may produce vague feelings of doubt, warning people that although all facts speak for option A, something feels wrong with this fact-based option A (Glöckner & Witteman, 2010, p. 1).

Thus, a question arises: To what extent can a rational-analytical selection procedure guarantee good decisions? Are the scientific quality criteria a justified fortress against the inner experiences of practitioners?

3.7.1 Criticism of rationality as the guiding principle of (post-)modernity

In the course of the Enlightenment and industrialization, belief in human reason and, thus, in rationality became the guiding principle of human thought and action.

This change in numerous areas of life, also known as "modernity," experienced its boom between the European Enlightenment and the First World War.

Modernity refers to the conviction that societies and sciences can be advanced, almost exclusively, with the help of human reason and rationality. Rationality assumes that human behaviors and decisions should be based on agreeable, transparent, understandable, verifiable, and thus, objective reason. Only with methods and instruments of rational-analytical procedures, human problems and challenges can be brought under control and solved.

Connected to these assumptions, scientists believe in the superiority and supremacy of human reason over human emotion, intuition, or spirituality. Also, the insight that knowledge is constructed and must be critically reflected does not mean that any knowledge construction is of equal value, from a scientific point of view. Different from subjective opinions or convictions, emotions, or spiritual-religious insight, decisions should be based on scientific quality criteria and rationality claims.

Therefore, it is not surprising that modernity and rationality have promoted thinking about universally valid patterns of thought and solutions, and, thus, also about related concepts of society or even concepts of science and research.

Postmodernism expressed doubts about the possibilities of human rationality and reason. In addition, postmodernism accuses modernity of having an unrealistic view of man. On the contrary, modernity has humanistic ideals about how man is or should be (e.g., see the image of man in communism) and, thus, misjudged science and politics with idealistic impositions. From this perspective, modernity can be perceived as a utopia and a nightmare (Bolz, 1997). This is one reason why people developed an ambivalent attitude towards modernity.

It is increasingly recognized that human beings have the potential and competence to be rational, but they are not always "masters in their own house"; and many experiences of human decisions and behaviors or feedback from psychotherapists and psychiatrists (see the publications of Sigmund Freud), underpin this strongly. There may also be the assumption of free will, mainly because humans have a strong sense of freedom and responsibility. Still, neuroscientific studies on the topic of "free will," show, for example, that brain activity correlated with a decision to move can be observed before a person reports being consciously aware of having made that decision (e.g., Libet et al., 1983; Soon et al., 2008; Heisenberg, 2009). But current research findings in free will, particularly from a neuroscientific perspective, are not always clear and must be critically questioned, and further research is needed.

The fact remains: Rationally is not the sole influence in human thinking, deciding, and behavior.

Postmodernism can be seen as an emancipatory movement and a rebellion against the power and objectivity claim of established systems of knowledge and science and, at the same time, a turn to the individual and the particular. Postmodernism is accompanied by a plurality of thought patterns, behaviors, and lifestyles. As a political-artistic-scientific direction, it turns against specific basic assumptions, methods, and modernity concepts. In this way, postmodernism claims to overcome the arrogance, narrow-mindedness, and self-overestimation of modernity and, thus, the absolute belief in man's rationality.

Apart from the possible risk of relativism, all justified criticism of modernity should not be about declaring reason to be the enemy in general, but about recognizing and taking into account its advantages and, at the same time, its limitations, especially when it comes to explaining human (decision-making) behavior.

3.7.2 Limits of rationality – failure of the concept of unlimited rationality

Kanning (2015, p. 138) states that human decisions are subject to several effects that systematically distort judgments. However, it is not only intuitive and emotionally charged judgments that may lead to distortions of perception, but also supposed rational-analytical procedures.

Errors in the process of rational-analytical decision-making are possible, because the information is often incomplete and inaccurate. And, the rational mind can be lazy and is also very limited. Kahneman (2011, p. 411) states that "the definition of rationality . . . is impossibly restrictive; it demands adherence to rules of logic that a finite mind is not able to implement. . . . in fact our research . . . showed that humans are not well described by the rational-agent model."

Thaler (2016) also uses numerous examples to show that people are pretty lousy at being rational. He believes "mental illusions should be considered the rule rather than the exception" (Thaler, 1991, p. 4). The idea that people, and, thus, hiring managers, could always and everywhere behave rationally fails to capture all the details and variability that characterize human behavior (Ceschi et al., 2014). And it should also be considered that "the human mind does not work on information, but on representations of information" (Gigerenzer et al., 2008, p. 1018).

The concept of unlimited rationality or – in economics – the "homo economicus" model or – in psychology – the assumptions of the rational "homo psychologicus" are based on highly simplified assumptions such as omniscience (all relevant information is known) and optimization (unlimited information processing capabilities) in decision-making.

Therefore, the model of rationality is not a meaningful basis in science oriented toward implementation. It was Herbert Simon, in particular, who changed economic thinking by using the concept of "limited rationality." He calls for more realism in research, because the rational choice theory is an unrealistic description of human decision-making (Simon, 1955, 1957, 1959).

Simon put forward ideas of bounded rationality and heuristics. He found that in practice, rationality can't be bound by logic. Real thinking and feeling, and, thus, human behavior, do not follow the assumptions of logical rationality. Humans have a limited working memory system and limited attention. Due to these cognitive limitations, humans develop adaptive strategies that make trade-offs between the cognitive effort of searching for and processing information and choosing the best alternative. Human decision-making is an adaptive process in which, depending on the context, a balance is sought between the costs of searching and processing information and the quality of the decision. In the real world, such a strategy is a satisfactory alternative, though not necessarily the optimal solution (in decision theory, the term "satisficing" is used). But a satisfying decision is regularly good enough for the decision-maker (Simon, 1955). Thus, Simon proposed replacing rationality and utility maximization with a more realistic view of economic behavior involving satisficing and adapting aspiration levels to success and failure.

Later, the primary concern of Cyert and March (1963) was to deconstruct the fiction of rationality. In doing so, they point to the self-reference of organizational decisions. They show that decision-making is based not solely on rational considerations, but rather on past choices and related experiences.

Evidence from many studies indicates that satisficing strategies provide a more valid description of everyday decision-making behaviors than the expected utility model (Smith & Kosslyn, 2014, p. 400).

Satisficing, as a decision-making strategy, has also been taken up in economic research. For example, Sauermann and Selten (1962) developed the aspiration adaptation theory of the firm. Later, Reinhard Selten investigated the relationship and interaction between rational decision-makers (game theory) and real human beings with bounded rationality. He insists that the assumption of rational decision-making does not capture actually observed human behavior, and that it is necessary to develop a descriptive theory of economic behavior based on bounded rationality and empirical evidence. For his outstanding achievements in economic research, he received the Nobel Prize in economic sciences in 1994 (Selten 1999; Gigerenzer & Selten, 2001).

Management and business research in Germany also integrated the ideas of Simon and Cyert & March (1963) into related concepts of business decision-making and problem-solving behavior (e.g., Kahle, 1973, 2018). On the one hand, this research refers to the use of the term aspiration level in experimental psychological research by Kurt Lewin and, on the other hand, to Simon (1955, 1957, 1959).

In Germany, for example, Edmund Heinen (1962, 1966, 1969) made decisions in companies as the starting point of his research in business administration and management. This was an intensive and thorough review of the American management literature at that time and particularly of Cyert & March (and Simon), associated with a conceptual reorientation of business administration towards behavioral science research results and thought patterns. Decision-oriented business administration said goodbye to rational decision models and turned to practical decision-making problems. Practical decision problems are complex multi-context problems requiring an interdisciplinary approach; and "saying goodbye" to the assumption that managers and other employees always and everywhere act rationally (Deters, 1990, pp. 303–315).

Research on personnel selection shows that human observation in interviews or assessment centers and the perception of correlations between observed behavior and competencies or personality traits are influenced by the design of the selection process (e.g., use of observation sheets). From a rational-analytical perspective, selection managers should describe the observed facts. But the use, meaning, and purpose of terms used to describe the observations are not independent of the observer. What selection managers in an interview observe and make notes of is not only the image of something; it is also a subjective construction in which individual meanings of words or subjective importance of specific observations play a role (Kappler, 1995, p. 129). When hiring managers think they have an objectively correct view of situations, that is, "naïve realism" (Ross & Ward, 1996).

Insights of the research of Damasio and his colleagues show that judgments in the face of uncertainty and complexity are influenced by "somatic markers" as emotional signals (see Section 4.2.5). For example, these emotional signals are established by conditioning or learned processes that warn human beings about threats and opportunities or that something important is about to occur. They show that, in practice, rational-analytical procedures are often supplemented or replaced by a more automatic, emotional, and intuitive process (Damasio, 1995; Smith & Kosslyn, 2014, p. 418). Emotions and intuitions interfere with rational decision-making and may play adaptive and dysfunctional roles in decision-making processes. In personnel selection processes, these emotional signals send information, such as whether the "chemistry" between people is perceived as good and whether someone fits into the team or seems authentic or not. If the chemistry between people is good, they trust and like each other, act like each other, act and react successfully with and to each other, and are convinced to rely on each other (Bastian, 2018, p. 152).

Specific feelings can be warning signals that a possibly important criterion for personnel selection has not yet been considered when making a judgment. For example, emotions guide human behavior and lead people to choose immediate gratification; humans, very often, do what provides satisfaction now and today, and not what would be better for them, in the long run. This particular feeling must be identified, named, and reflected upon as a criterion for selecting people.

Laske and Weiskopf (1996, pp. 310–312) argue that hiring managers are not like blank sheets in the selection process, unaffected by the experiences of yesterday, as if their perceptive skills were independent of previous experience, opinions, or judgments. Hiring managers are not passive individuals. Instead, they act in a social and cultural context of values and beliefs, political considerations, coalitions of roles, interests, and power, shaped by history, geopolitics, culture, economic situation, and so on.

The rational-analytical procedure recommends that selection managers operationalize their decisions by listing and comparing selection criteria and requirements, in a table. This procedure should – from a psychometric perspective – be based on a framework that allows reliable measurements of the different facets of an applicant's competencies, personality, and other attributes. Based on this rational analysis, there is a clear first choice, but, often, some of the selection managers nevertheless feel uneasy. They sense that something does not feel right or some critical selection criteria are missing, which are not easy to formulate and operationalize. These criteria often relate to a feeling that people will fit together on the human-emotional level, that someone reflects the company's values, and that people can rely on each other, find each other likable, or enjoy working together. Although these feelings and intuitions are complicated to operationalize, they cannot be denied; they are there and influence people's judgments and decisions.

In order to reduce these individual influences, training is required. "Training programs are conducted to minimize the effects of interviewers' implicit personality theories upon their judgment" (Herriot 1989, p. 171).

> Experience . . . leads to the development of 'blueprints', 'interpretation schemes', 'patterns', 'templates' and 'theories' which make bracketing easier. In imposing these on the world, one completes the first stage of enactment, limiting the variety of stimuli to make sense of. There is a paradoxical aspect to the use of all kinds of schemes: that much as they facilitate life in general and organizing in particular, they also act as blinders; the more successful they are used, the more resistance they create when the attempt is made to dispose of them (Czarniawska-Joerges, 1994, p. 9; quoted in Laske & Weiskopf, 1996, p. 310).

Suppose practitioners have adequately implemented a psychometric selection procedure, a possible restricted view and narrowed perspective of hiring managers should be considered (Laske & Weiskopf, 1996, p. 300). The psychometric approach assumes a distinction between the subject and the object. What is "out there" (objective) is presumed to be independent of the subject (the hiring manager), and knowledge is achieved when a selection manager correctly mirrors or represents objective reality.

With reference to Barlow (1989, p. 502), Laske & Weiskopf state that selection managers and applicants influence each other. Personnel selection is a social process in which different actors define, negotiate, or modify their interests, interpretations of situations, and expectations and act or react, based on their constructed realities. The image of the hiring manager adopted in psychometrics is that of an ideal individual, which differs significantly from empirical hiring managers (Laske & Weiskopf, 1996, p. 306). There is no independence between assessors and applicants; instead, they are mutually related. Together, they constitute a social situation.

The rational-analytical selection approach does not acknowledge this appropriately. Instead, organizations, selection methods, and theory building in the psychometric approach are conceptualized as rational-analytical (Laske & Weiskopf, 1996, pp. 310–311).

According to Laske and Weiskopf (1996, p. 312), the independently existing, empirically with the help of psychometrics, clearly ascertainable individual can only be described as an invention of poetic freedom. Therefore, it is necessary to carry this assumption to the grave.

Reasoning and rational-analytical procedures in personnel selection have their limits. These limits should be recognized and reflected upon, critically and constructively. Thus, the concept of rationality is not suitable for explaining or predicting human decision-making behaviors, and, thus, it`s not a suitable basis for theory building in management and, especially, personnel selection.

3.7.3 Limits of objectivity

Objectivity is considered a fundamental quality feature in personnel diagnostics. Objectivity means that the results of a personnel diagnostic procedure are free from situational influences such as time, noise (see 3.5.2.4), or room (Schmidt-Atzert & Amelang, 2012, p. 132). The objectivity of personnel selection is considered high, if the individual influence of the selection manager on the decision and, thus, on the results, is as low as possible (Kanning, 2004, p. 165). In an objective process, it does not matter whether the personnel selection is carried out by manager A or manager B. The procedure should be designed so that both selection managers reach the same result, independently (Kanning, 2004, pp. 164–165). Thus, objectivity means that the results of a selection process should be independent of environmental factors, especially selection circumstances and the recruiters (Amelang & Zielinski, 2002, p. 13). Thus, it can be seen as an expression of quality in personnel selection that the outcome of the selection process should not depend on who is, coincidentally, the interviewer or assessor in an assessment center (Schuler, 2014, pp. 52–53). Objectivity means freedom from bias, discrimination, arbitrariness, and subjectivity.

The psychometric approach requires selection managers to use or be replaced by psychometric methods, as much as possible, mainly to prevent selection managers from being disturbing factors with their intuitions, emotions, moods, and so on.

Also, selection managers should be aware of their possible biases, prejudices, and so on, and try to eliminate or reduce them; and they should observe applicants' behaviors independently; the registration and scoring of behavior observed should be done, without the knowledge of the observations of the other hiring managers (Bühner, 2010, p. 78). Thus, the candidate's performance should be evaluated and interpreted independently (Kanning, 2004, p. 165).

An essential question for evaluating the quality of personnel selection is: Are there objective criteria for the "correct" understanding, interpretation, and evaluation of application documents and verbal and non-verbal messages, and so on of applicants? And are these criteria superior to subjective assessments, from a rational point of view? These topics, discussed in hermeneutics, aim to avoid (subjective) arbitrariness in evaluating applications, candidates, and so on, as far as possible (Hösle, 2018).

The psychometric approach is based on the idea that an objectively identifiable reality exists and can be described according to, at least, "intersubjectively" agreed criteria; and this "objective reality" can be measured by scientific methods: Within the long tradition of employee selection based on individual differences, one of the main assumptions concerns the idea that human beings can be reduced to relatively independent traits, attributes, skills, and abilities, which can then be reliably and validly measured (Dachler 1989, p. 53). The assumption is that psychometric selection procedures can carry out an objective selection process.

As described in Section 3.5.2.10, a common mistake in the selection process is that the interviewers quickly form an opinion regarding the interviewee. In addition, hiring managers strive to eliminate contradictions and ambiguity and try to achieve consistency in their perceptions. As a result, unstructured interviews can lead to a self-fulfilling prophecy by primarily addressing topics that are particularly important to the manager personally, or that stand out subjectively in the application documents, while other relevant aspects are overlooked.

These subjective impressions influence the interviewer's behavior, which, in turn, affects the answers and the behaviors of the interviewee. In a fully structure d and standardized interview, both the selection manager and the applicant may feel emotionally uncomfortable and insecure in this tightly regulated situation. In this very regulated form of interviewing, both interviewer and applicant may miss the individual approach to each other, and hence, this selection method may be judged negatively. If the process is unstructured, applicants can only be compared to a limited extent, and even more effects such as the focus on irrelevant information may impact the interviewer. For this reason, a semi-structured interview is recommended: the candidate can be approached, while a guideline ensures comparability (Müllerschön, 2005, pp. 79–81).

Implementing guidelines (e.g., DIN 33430 or ISO 10667) for assessing and interpreting the collected information can promote the objectivity of a selection situation (Schuler, 2004, p. 41). A careful and prompt recording of observations and answers is a reasonable basis for later scorings. However, logging afterward is disadvantageous, since the memory can be distorted (Strobel et al., 2010, p. 28).

Nevertheless, even the most methodical care and practical experience cannot always prevent hiring managers from behaving contrary to the principles of psychometric theory.

Apart from individual differences in information processing, experience shows that selection managers gradually modify how they conduct their interviews over time, adapting them to their individual needs and no longer adhering to predefined interview modes. These so-called destructuring processes (Dipboye, 1994) can be observed in all selection instruments, over time: The longer practitioners use a selection instrument, the more independent and detached from the prescriptions and guidelines they feel (Strobel et al., 2010, p. 27).

Evaluations of assessment centers show that they have an excellent predictive, but often, a deficient construct validity, if they are created based on psychometric recommendations. Halo effects often cause this. Additionally, ratings in assessment centers are situation-specific, and the assessors can often not distinguish clearly between the most diverse requirements or observation dimensions (Sackett and Dreher (1982, p. 406). Klimoski and Strickland (1977, p. 355) speak of "indirect criteria contamination," which states that observers do not objectively refer to the requirement dimensions relevant for assessment, but that they intuitively contaminate their assessments with their own "implicit criteria" without being aware of it. In addition, specific behaviors in assessment centers are challenging to observe, making it difficult to compare applicants objectively (e.g., in a group discussion).

Höft & Kersting (2018), or International Taskforce on Assessment Center Guidelines (2015), have developed standards and guidelines for specific procedures in assessment centers or other selection processes. However, Höft & Kersting show that many large German companies employ poor practices in assessment centers: The observers may receive preliminary information about the applicants and, in some cases, can already get to know each other before the assessment process starts. This favors, for example, the bias of confirming the initial impression (confirmation bias). In addition, during breaks or meals, the assessors talk about individual applicants or even directly with applicants, forming impressions about them. These informal contacts lead to the risk of assessors being guided by personal critical selection criteria rather than the requested and agreed upon selection criteria.

While trained selection managers may be able to reduce their prejudices, biases, and so on, coming to the same result, regardless of the assessor, is very difficult. This demand for objectivity may work when using tests, for example, for reading the result of cognitive ability or personality tests. But a critical issue in recruiting objectively is how HR managers agree on what behaviors they perceive in applicants, and how they evaluate these observed behaviors.

To reach objectivity, the rational-analytical approach of psychometrics requires evaluation templates or rating scales; an applicant's observed behaviors and answers should, therefore, be scored by numbers accordingly, to express how well the applicant meets the requirements. It may be possible that interviewers or assessors can independently make their observations and evaluations. However, if they present their evaluations to each other and discuss them, they do not come to the same result independently of each other. Instead, they influence each other, through discussion. The same problem applies to the evaluation of observations in assessment centers. Thus, they don`t reach objectivity but intersubjectivity (see the end of this chapter and Section 9.6).

Therefore, it is recommended not to discuss the individual interviewers` or assessors` results from a psychometric perspective. Instead, the quantified results of the interviewers/assessors should be added, an average should be taken, and the applicant with the highest overall score should be selected.

Certainly, objectivity can be increased this way, but how individual recruiting managers assess concrete answers or applicants' verbal and non-verbal behaviors is always influenced by their individual and subjective perceptions. If managers find applicants likable and particularly suitable from their subjective perspective, there is a risk that they will, accordingly, rate them high. Thus, although hiring managers are instructed to leave their subjectivity away, at the end of the day, when they review the collected data and have to evaluate and score them, it's their feeling and intuition that is their counselor in decision-making (Koppers, 2013, pp. 6 and 10). The evaluation of behavior in numbers, then, only reflects a pseudo-objectivity.

Even if personnel selection processes are rationally-analytical and psychometric, it cannot be excluded that recruiters who see their assessment results expressed in numbers will receive "inner signals" of intuition telling them: That's not right, we shouldn't hire this candidate. For example, an interviewed manager states: "If I find something positive from my feeling, I interpret the facts accordingly. And if I have a negative feeling about an applicant, I interpret and score the facts so that they correspond to my impression" (Soffner, 2021, p. 83).

In a rational-analytical procedure, subjectivity is seen as a distorting factor in searching for a candidate's "true nature." In its purest sense, this idea of objectivity assumes that truth or independent reality exists outside of any social investigation or observation. Objectivity attempts to uncover truths about the natural world by eliminating personal biases or emotions. The task of a selection manager is to uncover this reality, without contaminating it in any way. However, in a selection interview, this notion that a human being can observe or uncover phenomena without affecting them is illusory.

The objectivist assumption and search for a true and stable nature may exist in the natural sciences or certain scientific laboratory situations. However, there is no immutability in social environments, where people deal with people who have gone through specific socialization and always decide and act in certain changeable contexts. Nor do such stable and unchanging contexts exist for organizations that compete.

According to Klopprogge (Klopprogge et al., 2019, pp. 222–224; Klopprogge, 2022, pp. 305–311), there is a risk that the objectification of personnel selection can jeopardize necessary changes in organizations, because tasks and job requirements are already defined in advance, and all new employees are only expected to fit into them as precisely as possible. The requirement of matching applicants to a specific job presupposes a static understanding of organizations, environments, tasks, and people. Jobs and, thus, requirements change over time, however. People also fill their jobs individually and continue to develop.

Sherman, Nave, & Funder (2009) state that it is often presumed that objective measures of behavior (e.g., counts of the number of smiles in an interview or assessment center) are more scientific than more subjective measures of behavior (e.g., ratings of the degree to which a person behaved cheerfully). However, they show that the apparent objectivity of any behavioral measure is illusory.

It is possible to reduce biases, but "pure reason will never win," says Treufetter (2009, pp. 21–23). Even if pro-contra-lists or other supposedly rational decision-making aids are used, human judgments will always be distorted to a certain degree. Whether in the reviewing of documents, in interviews, or assessment centers: When people are involved in observation, implementation, and the evaluation process, they will inevitably be influenced by perceptional distortions, bias, and other effects such as likability, since the human psyche wants to avoid contradictions in the formation of judgment and strives for consistency.

Since absolute objectivity is impossible in personnel selection when people are involved, Laske and Weisskopf advocate striving for intersubjectivity (1996, pp. 312–315). They suggest that the various subjective impressions of hiring managers should be brought together and integrated into intersubjectivity. Thus, they propose to speak of intersubjectivity instead of objectivity, since this is achievable.

Personnel selection should be as objective as possible to avoid bias, arbitrariness, and discrimination. Psychometrics offers various procedures to increase objectivity. However, it is also important to name the limits of objectivity and reflect upon them critically and constructively. This is especially necessary for selection managers.

In the psychometric construction of objectivity, feelings are equated with critical biases. But that's not always the case; intuitions and feelings can be valuable sources of information. Hence, apart from whether managers can actually succeed in turning off emotions and intuitions, there is also the question of whether intuitions and emotions can provide valuable and essential clues for the right selection of personnel.

3.7.4 Limits to separating observation and evaluation/scoring

Confirmation bias involves favoring information that confirms previously existing beliefs, for example, an applicant's suitability for a job. Rational-analytical personnel diagnostic processes require separating observation and evaluation in interviews or assessment centers, to reduce confirmation bias.

In an interview or assessment center, recruiters are expected only to "observe and record candidate behavior, classify these behaviors in dimensional terms, and provide dimensional ratings. Afterward, the assessors should gather to assign an overall assessment rating to each candidate (e.g., select, reject, promote, develop, etc.) by discussing behavioral observations and discrepancies in ratings" (Lievens &

Goemaere 1999, p. 215). But, in practice, recruiters – although they may have attended appropriate training and try to record only what they observe (behaviors, words/phrases spoken by applicants, and so on; the facts and no interpretations) – have difficulty making distinctions between observation and the interpreting and rating process. "(A)ssessors (especially line/staff managers) often made no distinction between observation and evaluation processes and gave global judgments" (Lievens & Goemaere 1999, p. 217).

Although a "Realistic Accuracy Model" (RAM) to clarify success-critical aspects of monitoring and assessing candidates is scientifically developed (Funder, 2003, 2012; see Höft & Kersting, 2018, pp. 36–37), and although selection criteria are operationalized, and training in selection procedures is conducted, human beings have a lot of difficulties in clearly separating observation, assessment, interpretation, and evaluation. Humans are not passive observing beings. They are actively participating social beings. What they observe and how they observe, is always influenced subjectively, and this subjectivity cannot be eliminated entirely. Even if only the observations are to be written down in an assessment center, subjective unconscious evaluations are included and determine what is perceived and what is written down as an observation.

The coherence effect also plays a role. The coherence effect represents a distortion caused by bidirectional activation and describes the phenomenon that information is not objectively incorporated into decisions. Instead, it is unconsciously revalued when decisions are made to fit the preferred interpretation (see confirmation bias). Subconsciously running cognitive processes enhance coherent information and devalue opposing information (Glöckner & Towfigh 2015, pp. 272–273).

The difficulty in separating observations and evaluations of candidates is also understandable from a neuroscientific perspective; the human limbic system sends positive or negative assessment and judgment impulses much faster than the conscious mind. These impulses can be described as intuitions. Therefore, intuitions and, thus, former experiences and associated emotions influence how people observe, what they observe, and what is reported. Hence, separate observation and evaluation in practice is challenging, if not almost impossible, since what people observe is already influenced by evaluations.

3.7.5 Social influence of the other selection managers

Even if each selection manager makes his/her observations and, in particular, evaluations independently of the other selection managers and the observations and evaluation results are recorded in writing, social influence by discussion cannot be excluded. For example, at an assessor conference at the end of an assessment center or in a discussion after a job interview, selection managers/assessors exchange their observations, impressions, and evaluations. During this exchange, communication and persuasion skills play a significant role. In addition, hierarchy effects or possible feelings of competition between selection managers can also influence the judgments.

Therefore, a selection procedure may meet the highest psychometric requirements; however, when people discuss their impressions of an applicant, they cannot exclude the influences of the hiring managers' communication and social skills, hierarchical power, personality, and so on.

3.7.6 Limits of selection decision rules – no rule without an exception

Decision rules for selection are not simply learned or observed but are interpreted subjectively and implemented context-specifically. Particularly, in more individualistic cultures, people want autonomy and the freedom to understand the meaning and benefits of rules for themselves and in their specific context. Thus, decision rules are broken, in practice, when it seems reasonable in a company-specific or personal sense.

Kanning (2019, pp. 345–346) states that decision-making rules often meet with little acceptance and approval, in practice. For example, he refers to studies showing that fewer than 50% of medium-sized companies use formalized decision-making rules. Only 18% of companies compare the results of an applicant assessment with a detailed requirement profile. He attributes it to that HR managers probably feel restricted in their freedom by such rules. Thus, Kanning states that decision-making rules should not be perceived as control but as a helpful instrument to reduce poor selection decisions. Those responsible for selection should not stubbornly follow the rules. Instead, they should be trained in using decision-making rules and regularly reflect and review them regarding their fit and benefit for the company, and even in the individual case of a specific applicant.

Decision rules and cut-off scores are based on value judgments. From a scientific perspective, there is no clear solution for setting correct cut-off scores. Cut-off scores are not always scientifically justifiable but are regularly based on personal, social, and economic values and practical considerations. This is particularly the case, if the personnel selection decisions consider not only later professional success but also take into account economic conditions such as the labor market situation, or social or legal considerations such as promoting diversity or ethnic minorities, and avoiding discrimination (Schmidt-Atzert & Amelang, 2012, pp. 422–423).

The example of job analysis can illustrate further limitations of psychometric methods. According to Reimann (2010), a proponent of the psychometric-oriented DIN 33430, three methodological approaches can create a requirements profile. One of these is the experience-based intuitive method. A prerequisite for using this method is that the person carrying out the analysis has the necessary knowledge and experience. This procedure is expressly regarded as compatible with the DIN

33430. Here, it becomes clear that the intuitive experience of experts should be used (Reimann, 2010, p. 103). The DIN 33430 as a process norm virtually demands the use of expert judgments in selection processes. Intuition is, therefore, required in the experience-based intuitive method of job analysis.

A fundamental rule is that personnel selection should meet the job requirements. But often, the job market does not provide correspondingly qualified applicants. For example, police or army vacancies in Germany cannot be filled with people who meet the required qualifications. Thus, the requirements are lowered (Sanches, 2020). This means that minimum job requirements and the use of decision rules are not only determined by the demands to be met but also by labor market conditions.

As shown in Section 3.7.3, hiring managers know how an applicant should score in an interview or an assessment center to be shortlisted, in practice. If a candidate is likable from the subjective impression of selection managers, the score on their observed behavior is likely to be high. Rules agreed upon will, therefore, not preclude subjectivity.

3.7.7 Limits of validity

One of the factors determining the economic value of a selection procedure is the variability between the output of employees selected by a specific process and those selected randomly (Hunter & Schmidt, 1990, p. 28). The term validity is defined as the degree of appropriateness, significance, meaningfulness, and usefulness of inferences drawn from tests and other selection scores. Predictive or criterion-related validity is the extent to which the results of an implemented selection procedure can predict future outcomes and performance on the job.

High validity is shown when low predictor scores (e.g., scores in an interview or assessment center) correlate with low scores on the specific external criteria (e.g., performance on the job) and when high predictor scores translate into high scores on these criteria (Jackson et al., 2012, p. 236).

This (predictive) validity is the central quality criterion, as, without it, the scores in selection would not be interpretable (Tippins et al., 2018, p. 4).

The importance of validity for the success of personnel selection is emphasized by Schmidt et al. (2016, p. 48):

> The validity of the personnel measure (or combination of measures) used in hiring processes is directly proportional to the practical value of the method – whether measured in dollar value of increased output or percentage increase in output. In economic terms, the gains from increasing the validity of hiring methods can amount, over time, to literally millions of dollars. However, this can be seen from the opposite point of view: By using selection methods with low validity, an organization can lose millions of dollars in reduced production, reducing revenue and profits.

But many employers throughout the world are currently using suboptimal selection methods such as handwriting analyses (graphology with a validity of 0.02) or using age as a basis for hiring, although the age of job applicants shows no validity for predicting job performance (Schmidt et al., 2016, pp. 33 and 37). Also, personality traits such as extraversion (0.09), openness (0.04), or agreeableness (0.08) have relatively low validity. Schmidt et al. (2016, p. 33) write that these results are counterintuitive findings for many people.

As shown in Section 3.2.3.1, structured and unstructured interviews can have the same high validity (0.58); thus, it is possible to conduct unstructured interviews with high validity. An explanation is that these unstructured interviews are conducted by skilled hiring managers with significant interviewing experience and a repertoire of effective interview skills (Oh et al., 2013).

Since Schmidt et al. (2016) show that valid selection interviews can be conducted based on experience, this indirectly speaks for the importance of intuitions, known to be based on experience.

Koppers (2013, p. 50, with reference to Ryan & Sackett, 1989) states that experienced hiring managers come to more accurate personnel decisions than novices. Due to their years of experience, they may be capable of fast and differentiated pattern recognition. However, this assumption has not yet been clearly confirmed. In fact, research in psychodiagnostics shows that experienced and novice clinical psychologists do not differ in diagnostic accuracy (Skvortsova et al., 2016). Thus, these researchers conclude that decision-making accuracy may not be primarily a question of extensive experience but of conscious deliberation about the task.

Kanning (2012, pp. 11–12) reflects critically on whether professional experience – operationalized by the length of time the selection manager has been engaged in a specific activity such as personnel selection – is enough to ensure the future professional performance of hiring managers.

Simple repetition may increase the subjective certainty in the decision-making process,

but not necessarily the personnel diagnostic objectivity and validity of the decision (Kahneman & Klein, 2009, p. 518). This insight is supported by a meta-analysis by Quinones et al. (1995). They found that the predictive validity of the mere duration of the professional activity only reaches a score of $r = .21$. That is better than nothing but hardly justifies relying only on the period of experience of selection managers (for a more detailed description of experiences as an aspect of intuition, see Section 4.2.1).

Experience through practice and education means more than a certain number of years in a particular job. Apart from the fact that the situational conditions in which this experience was gained must be taken into account, it is evident that expertise should also be based on a corresponding broad and deep competence in terms of knowledge and skills in personnel selection, and a critical-constructive reflection and evaluation of the selection decisions made.

Kahneman and Klein point out that the extensive experience of an expert in a regulated environment can reduce the error rate of intuitive decision-making (Kahneman & Klein, 2009, p. 515). Due to the dependence of judgment on the experience and competence of the decision-maker, it is recommended that persons make decisions with high expertise. In addition, the ability to process large amounts of information quickly and efficiently is characteristic of an expert (Kahneman, 2011, p. 457).

Studies on the validity of selection procedures are challenging to evaluate and compare, as the measurements of the required competencies and the outcome or performance measures (external criteria) differ across studies and job profiles (DeNisi & Murphy, 2020, p. 116). For example, the validity of assessment center scores varies from study to study and ranges from 0.37 to 0.71, depending on practical implementation and compliance with psychometric quality criteria (Höft & Funke, 2006, p. 162; Schmidt & Hunter, 1998, p. 265). This variance is due, among other things, to the influence of subjective assessment errors, the degree of standardization, the learning effects on the application side, and the requirement reference of the exercises. This means that reliable statements on the quality of a selection process can only be made, if the concrete implementation of the respective procedure and the requirements of the target position are considered.

Scullen et al. (2000) show the influence of individual rater personality on ratings and how the rating of the same employee can differ depending on the rater. "In light of these findings, we renew the call for research investigating ways to decrease idiosyncratic rater biases while increasing the amount of actual rater performance in performance ratings" (Scullen et al., 2000, p. 969).

The evaluation of validity strongly depends on situational circumstances. On the one hand, the validity level strongly depends on the selection procedure's reliability. Sufficient reliability, in turn, can only be achieved through optimized objectivity. On the other hand, every deviation of the reliability from the value of 1.0 inevitably leads to a decrease in the correlation between the result of the selection procedure (predictor) and the criterion (for example, performance in the job).

The measurement of job performance still proves to be a significant challenge for both practitioners and researchers (Murphy, 2008, p. 148). Thus, a key question is: How can we measure job performance accurately? In general, employee performance is determined by and is the result of successfully using employee competencies, as manifested in the contingency approach: Maximum performance can be achieved when an individual's competencies and "capability or talent is consistent with the needs of the job demands and the organizational environment" (Boyatzis & Boyatzis, 2008, p. 6). Employee performance can be measured against job-specific requirements (Schuler, 2014, pp. 144–145).

Objective measures of employee performance are linked to measurable outcomes and are, therefore, often, backward-looking, for example, sales figures, output rates, and absenteeism rates (Murphy, 2008, p. 149). In practice, objective measures are often difficult to be applied, especially if there is no direct link between employee performance and profitability. This is due to the fact that the performance of most employees is only partially quantifiable or can be depicted in key figures or KPIs. The most common method to measure employees' job performance, in practice, is performance ratings given by the supervisor(s) or other stakeholders in an organization (Wall et al., 2004, p. 97). Compared to objective measures, subjective performance measures capture qualitative job dimensions, such as openness to effectively acquiring new knowledge and skills and sharing them with others, supporting the team, communicating behaviors, and employee commitment and loyalty to the company.

Moreover, they are based on the supervisor's individual perception of an employee's performance (Fehrenbacher, 2019, p. 31).

Regularly, performance is measured at the individual level in organizations, but this individual performance depends, to a large degree, on the context (e.g., the effectiveness of processes, technology used), the team performance (e.g., the shared understanding of goals, mutual support, and interpersonal interactions), leadership (e.g., managers with poor emotional competencies such as in empathy, emotional regulation, and social skills regulation will be more likely to use bullying tactics, demotivate employees, not create effective relationships with their fellow workers), and so on.

Here, it must be seen that performance appraisals by supervisors can also be influenced by the goal of motivating employees; as a result, the performance can be evaluated higher. For example, in some organizations, performance ratings in a team or department are based on the assumed Gaussian normal distribution or bell curve (O`Boyle J. & Aguinis, 2012, p. 79), although the performance of the employees may not be normally distributed. Or the performance measure is influenced by prejudices, stereotypes, and other biases such as recency bias or by the rater`s motivation to give accurate ratings. In practice, supervisors, sometimes, must adhere to a fixed monetary budget in their performance ratings; these budget constraints can trigger conscious rater biases, such as underrating an employee's performance to avoid pay rises or bonus payments.

However, primarily objective measures alone cannot perfectly capture all performance dimensions, such as creativity, and often neglect contextual and team performance factors and are not applicable in all organizational settings (Kalefeld, 2021, pp. 9–11).

Consequently, many performance measures are not valid indicators of individual employee performance (Webber et al., 2020, pp. 98–99). Therefore, for psychometrically valid correlations between scores in a selection process and performance on the job, subjective performance evaluations must be seen critically, and limits of objective performance measures should be considered.

A study by König et al. (2012, p. 249) shows that Chinese candidates use self-presentation tactics and lie as much as American candidates in the job interview, but significantly more than their European counterparts. Thus, it happens repeatedly that interviewers can be influenced by "good faking" by applicants. In a study, Buehl et al. (2019) found that 90% of all applicants in job interviews (in Germany) try to present themselves favorably and give untruthful answers to create a better impression. Even trained and experienced selection managers find it very difficult to recognize whether an applicant is really honest in the interview. This study shows that honest applicants were rated lower than dishonest ones.

Research by Ingold et al. (2015a) shows that the self-presentation tactics of candidates, such as faking (e.g., on personality inventories), were positively related to supervisors' job performance ratings. Still, impression management in interviews did not relate negatively to job performance, although also not positively. Also, candidates who dissimulate are more likely to use impression management in selection processes. Thus, the question arises: What value do procedures such as personality inventories have, if faking may positively correlate with performance?

Researchers often do not use similar approaches and methods when comparing validities of assessment centers, structured interviews, cognitive-ability tests, or personality tests. Thus, we must know more about the constructs measured within specific evaluation procedures. Without such information, comparative evaluation of validity is almost meaningless (Robertson & Smith, 2001).

In concrete terms, a selection procedure with a predictive validity of $r = 0.30$ can ultimately be more valid than a selection procedure with a validity of $r = 0.50$ (Schmidt-Atzert & Amelang, 2012, p. 153).

The better a criterion can be expressed in numbers or scores, the higher the reliability. Thus, Viswesvaran and Ones (2017) state that a general definition of the construct of job performance reflects scalable behaviors that can be evaluated.

Also, because success on the job is often not directly observable and scalable, measurable indicators such as salary progress, promotion on the career ladder, achieved sales, training grades, job knowledge test scores, or supervisor ratings are used.

This raises the question: After what period of employment should the success on the job be measured (after six months, one year, or two years)? For example, research on the validity of assessment center scores in Germany shows that predictive validity is most meaningful after approximately two years between the selection procedure and the analysis of success criteria (Holzenkamp et al., 2010, pp. 17–25). However, this is not the case in many validity studies. Therefore, the problem of comparability of results from validity studies also arises, here.

However, it is also essential to question whether the scores of a specific selection method (e.g., assessment center scores) are valid for the performance outcomes on the job. Also, the extent or cut-off of a predictor score, for example, the scoring in an assessment center, to predict future job performance successfully, should be evaluated regularly.

Threats to the validity of any criterion measure and, thus, criterion contamination and criterion deficiency can result from external circumstances such as (in-)

competent leadership (e.g., uncaring leaders who do not ensure their employees feel valued and supported), economic situation, and the idiosyncratic rater effect. Or a flawed onboarding process can lead to lower levels of employee engagement, lower employee confidence, a lack of trust within the team, and, thus, negative impacts on the performance. This has nothing to do with how the personnel selection is carried out.

Criterion contamination also occurs when the criterion measure includes aspects that are not part of the specific job or is affected by construct-irrelevant factors (e.g., age, attractiveness, and gender). Finally, criterion deficiency occurs, when the criterion measure fails to include or underrepresents essential aspects of the criterion construct; it is the degree to which the used criterion fails to overlap with the conceptual criterion, in practice. Criterion contamination is most profound when construct-irrelevant factors that influence the criterion measure are correlated with the predictors. Similarly, criterion deficiency is a problem when the criterion measure fails to include elements of job performance related to the predictor constructs (National Research Council, 1991). While these errors can be reduced by good operationalization of the criterion and the predictor constructs, they can never be eliminated entirely.

Thus, an important question is, for example, whether the superiors' rating of employees' performance on scales is a reliable and valid criterion. The content of the selection method (e.g., exercises in an assessment center) should match the tasks, responsibilities, and requirements of the specific job. In particular, content validity requires that predictor and criterion are symmetrical. This means that the predictor covers the same aspects and is measured on the same level of abstraction as the criterion. Here, the problem that the performance criteria used by the supervisor and the criteria for selecting an applicant do not necessarily coincide arises. There is also the risk that the scales used for the predictor and criterion are nominally the same but that the same designations conceal different content-related ideas (e.g., what is meant by the ability to work successfully in a team or by assertiveness). In addition, sample size and individual characteristics of the sample influence the validity (Schmidt-Atzert & Amelang, 2012, pp. 156–161).

The "Idiosyncratic Rater Effect" states that people are pretty bad at evaluating others objectively and reliably. Thus, evaluations and ratings by superiors often generate insufficient data. It is not that some managers misevaluate employees on purpose, but that unconscious biases, selective perceptions, individual experiences, and so on, can lead to very subjective evaluations. Thus, the assessment of employees has a lot to do with the rater. Buckingham (2015) refers to studies that found that more than half of the variation in a manager's ratings could be explained by the unique rating patterns of the individual doing the rating: In the first study from 1998, it was 71%, in the second from 2000 it was 58%, and in the third from 2010 it was 55% (Mount et al., 1998; Scullen et al., 2000; Hoffman et al., 2010). Hiring managers are human and, thus, prone to subjectivity – there's no way around it.

Further sources of criterion contamination are, for example, that assessors are not only guided in their assessments by the job requirements but also by implicit subjective selection criteria such as habitus, personal liking (e.g., if the applicant suits me and my values), behavior during breaks, clothes, attractiveness, small-talk competence, bias, noise, and so on.

Criterion contamination can also result from a self-fulfilling prophecy (Klimoski & Strickland, 1977). Successful participants in an interview or AC are strengthened and supported in their self-confidence and are more motivated and goal-oriented concerning their career development. Supervisors or other personnel managers who selected and hired these candidates may treat these new employees, preferentially.

Or dissimulation of supposedly desired behavior can lead to criterion contamination. Candidates know the rules and structure of the AC and may have prepared themselves with a trainer or consultant to behave accordingly. They show practical intelligence, competencies, adaptability, and a "feeling for socially recognized behavior." Impression management can also lead to criterion contamination. But the connections, here, should be investigated by further research.

Personnel economics (Lazear, 1995, 1998, 199; Backes-Gellner et al., 2001, pp. 395–396; Backes-Gellner, 2004) and the principal-agent theory (Jensen & Meckling, 1976) can also give fascinating insights into the process of "objective" performance evaluation. For example, a significant problem in measuring employee performance is setting a standard to judge the performance. In practice, setting an absolute objective performance standard is rarely used, because it is costly and only appropriate for simple repetitive tasks or activities, where employees' output can be clearly operationalized and measured. However, this is difficult for many activities and complex jobs, such as how someone interacts in a team and communicates with colleagues. Therefore, in practice, one often must rely on subjective feedback from supervisors, colleagues, customers, and so on. Often, some form of relative performance evaluation is used by comparing an employee's performance to that of his peers. Thus, performance evaluation is often based on a supervisor's subjective impressions and opinions.

A further problem could be that supervisors may underrate the performance of employees, for example, to avoid having to pay a bonus, or perhaps be rewarded for cost savings; or simply because they don`t like someone. Or employees may focus on the quantifiable goals to be achieved and neglect other important tasks. Employees might also actively attempt to influence the appraisals of the supervisors, for example, by influencing the performance information going to the supervisor.

In recent years, many companies, especially in Germany, have abandoned individual goal-setting systems and quantifiable performance measurement systems, because managers fear that these objective performance measuring systems could demotivate employees (e.g., because they do not see themselves as holistically valued and appreciated by the evaluation that is oriented to purely quantifiable goals), disrupt team spirit, and so on. In addition, managers may shy away from confronting employees if they have not met their goals, and therefore, a bonus may have to be cut. Moreover, agreeing on individual goals is very time-consuming, especially if the goals should be formulated in a SMART way (Specific, measurable, acceptable, realistic). Finally, the holistic performance appraisal of employees cannot only be evaluated by objective data, because subjective impressions will always play a role (Marquardt, 2017).

Performance is socially constructed and determined by each person's subjective perception of, and interaction with, situational characteristics to a certain degree. Performance assessments reflect the individual experiences, the meanings, intentions, and interpretations of individuals involved ("the interpretive community"), and the social structures in the assessment context. Industrial and organizational psychology research findings show that job performance lacks temporal stability, especially in highly complex jobs. Also, situational changes can affect an individual's motivation or opportunity to perform. The result is that the individual works at varying levels of effectiveness at different times during the performance period (Motowidlo & Kell, 2012). Thus, for Holzenkamp et al. (2010), it would be more meaningful to analyze job performance over a more extended period, conceptualize it in episodic terms, and assess it by ratings from different sources.

Furthermore, it must be seen that in the context of selection, scientists and practitioners use constructs, because, for instance, personality cannot be observed directly. Therefore, estimates cannot be excluded. For example, test procedures require many estimation methods already during the development of the test design (parallel test, test retest). Also, determining reliabilities and validities cannot be done without different estimation methods. The estimation ability of test participants also plays a role.

Intra-individual variation in job performance may also result from changes in the individual (e.g., due to motivation, fatigue, changing levels of competence, work engagement, personal or private situation) as well as changes in the job environment (technologies, markets, etc.). In addition, performance on the job can also be influenced by other situational factors such as competent leadership or uncooperative colleagues.

The importance of leadership can be seen in sports, for example. Many examples show that a change of coaches can have the effect that players believe in themselves again and better realize their potential, that teams work together again as a team, and become successful again. Thus, it cannot simply be concluded that poor job performance indicates a poorly designed, implemented, and conducted selection procedure.

Further possible research limitations on the validity of selection procedures may lie in using decision rules. Despite a detailed requirement analysis, the question remains of determining the correct decision rules and cut-off scores for the identified requirement dimensions. For example, suppose the decision rules or algorithm are too narrowly defined, the company may not hire candidates who can think outside the box, use lateral and unconventional thinking approaches, or have creative and colorful personalities.

Companies also cut back on the requirements demanded against the background of the individual labor market situation and change their decision rules, accordingly. In addition, past success behaviors of current job holders do not automatically fit future requirements. Therefore, current decision rules developed by present decision-makers must not automatically work in the future.

To choose the correct cutoff scores, empirically-based decision rules, such as those developed by Montel (2006), with the concept of simultaneous optimization of multiple cutoffs, should be discussed (see Section 3.2.3.3).

A high predictive validity requires high construct validity and high content validity. The predictive or criterion-related validity also depends on the selection and base rate. The selection rate is the proportion of candidates who successfully passed the selection procedure (hired candidates) relative to the number of applicants who applied for the particular job opening. The base rate is the probability of an applicant being successful in the job to be filled without a selection procedure; thus, the base rate is the share of objectively suitable applicants in the total number of applicants ("success without the use of selection procedure"). Also, the lower the job requirements, the higher the base rate. But, organizations can increase the basic rate through excellent pre-selection processes. The higher the base rate (basically appropriate applicants for the job) and the lower the selection rate, the higher the criterion or predictive validity. Thus, using a valid selection procedure is all the more critical, the lower the proportion of suitable candidates among the "unselected" applicants (as the base rate is, then, lower) and the lower the selection rate. The relation between base rate, selection rate, and validity of predictors has further been described by Taylor and Russel. They show that predictive validity changes positively (with a high base rate and a low selection rate) or negatively (with a low base rate and high selection rate).

It would be helpful to know the base rate, but it is challenging to identify a correct base rate, in practice.

Even selection methods with moderate validity (e.g., unstructured interviews) can lead to successful hiring decisions, when the base rate is very high and the selection rate is very low.

Especially in times of a shortage of skilled workers, the question of the availability of suitable applicants and, thus, the topic of the base rate plays a significant role. Therefore, it is the task of companies and politicians to create the conditions for as high a base rate as possible.

These reflections on the base rate show the great importance of a good education system, which usually helps increase the base rate for challenging tasks such as a leadership position. In addition, a high-quality talent acquisition process that generates interest and attracts capable applicants, mobilizing them to maintain their interest in the job also supports achieving a high base rate. Finally, companies need an effective pre-selection process, particularly effective self-selection procedures, to increase the base rate (Deters, 2017, p. 68).

The critical and constructive evaluation of the quality criteria of the psychometric approach shows the limits of this approach. Thus, evidence-based research results can and should be critically questioned, because the results of a personnel selection process need much more interpretation than the psychometric approach suggests.

For correct classification of scientific research results, it should also be considered that scientifically evidenced research results in personnel selection are usually based on a stochastic process. Thus, they provide probability statements but no certainty in individual cases.

However, this does not mean that the psychometric approach should be rejected. On the contrary, although job performance is subject to many interlinked influencing factors, and cause and effect cannot generally be traced back to a single element, rational-analytical procedures in personnel selection represent a recommendable way of making selection decisions. Scientific approaches provide essential information on the design of high-quality personnel selection. Furthermore, a high degree of standardization of the selection process is desirable, to keep the uncertainty of the selection managers as small as possible.

3.7.8 Cultural limits of acceptance of analytical procedures

Although the three quality criteria of validity, reliability, and objectivity are renowned and established in the scientific community, they are rooted in a Western way of thinking and epistemology and, therefore, cannot necessarily be regarded as universally accepted. Moreover, cultural differences between, for instance, East Asian and the Western world, can result in different normative standards of thinking and, thus, understanding quality criteria in selection processes. From a psychometric perspective, the Western approach to high quality reflects an analytical approach to science, but its universal validity can be questioned from a holistic thinking approach (Nisbett et al., 2001, p. 291; see Section 7.2.4). Further criticism comes from radical constructivism, which questions the generalizability of the quality criteria with the cognitive construction of the criteria and, therefore, rejects them (Feyerabend, 1976, p. 45).

Some specific personnel selection methods that prove to be accepted in one culture or country may not be applicable in other cultures and may encounter barriers to acceptance. Against this background, it is essential to reflect on the importance of the country's culture for the design and implementation of personnel selection procedures (Anderson & Witvliet, 2008, p. 2). Culture can influence both the acceptance of intuition or rational-analytical selection procedures and, thus, for example, also the acceptance of artificial intelligence in personnel selection. The relationship between culture and the acceptance, design, and use of selection procedures is discussed in more detail in Chapter 7.

3.7.9 Social acceptance, fairness, and social validity of selection procedures as possible obstacles to rational-analytic selection procedures

3.7.9.1 Social acceptance and positive relationship building

A selection interview conducted by human beings is characterized by interaction, in which both the candidate and the selection manager evaluate each other. This process is an essential source of information to evaluate the personal relationship and whether one wants to work together in the future (Bauer et al., 1998, p. 892).

Some researchers see the personnel selection process only as an examination to objectively, reliably, and validly select the right person for a specific position. For example, for Kanning (2015, p. 117), a job interview is not a dialogue but an examination situation.

But in today's labor market, most companies can no longer post simple job descriptions online and choose from the countless applications that pour in from qualified talent. Instead, recruiters and hiring managers need to do active sourcing to win the candidates.

The required psychometric approach to selection is, thus, more similar to scientific data collection than to a classic job interview, as it is actually practiced in reality (Koppers, 2013, p. 9). In practice, personnel selection is not only an examination; it is – mainly triggered by environmental changes – also an acquisition process and, therefore, conducted as a dialogue.

A managing director of a small enterprise interviewed in our research says that he gave up developing and using a requirement profile because of the lack of qualified applications. "I manage the lack of personnel. . . . At the moment, we are not getting the applications we need, so we hire a not best-suited candidate and try to develop him. . . . Therefore, it does not make sense for us to base our selection process on a specific requirement profile or job description" (Röbe-Oltmanns, 2020, p. 31).

But even independently of the current labor situation, a recruiter has to build a positive relationship to win applicants for himself and the company. Therefore, recruiting should promote a positive candidate experience and make the applicant's selection process a positive experience.

It is not only the applicants who should feel comfortable and accept a selection procedure but also the selection managers. Many of the hiring managers we interviewed emphasize that it is important to them to build a positive relationship with the applicants. In addition, they say that sympathy/likeability plays a decisive role and could, and should, never wholly be disregarded. Therefore, they reject a fully standardized selection procedure, for example, a fully standardized interview.

On the contrary, the managers emphasize how important it is to work with people for whom they have positive feelings. This is because positive feelings are an essential source of human happiness, motivation, performance, and so on. They, therefore, want to surround themselves with people they feel comfortable with. That applies just as much to the managers as it does to the applicants.

Recruiting and especially hiring employees is relationship management. HR and line managers participating in the selection process need to tell their stories to candidates; sharing stories with emotional appeal humanizes the organization and creates a personal connection with candidates. Kouzes & Posner (2017) emphasize that leadership is about relationships, and great leaders inspire employees. Thus, "encouraging the heart" of candidates is one of the most critical roles of hiring managers.

Line managers, in particular, see themselves not only in the role of the "selectors" but also as the candidate's potential future supervisor. Research, particularly on transformational leadership and leader-member exchange, shows that an affective identification enables social exchange and, thus, the quality of relationships leaders share with their followers is a key success factor for the performance of both the leader and the follower (Ng, 2017, p. 386). Managers who are open, honest, and authentic in their behavior ensure that candidates open up accordingly and engage in honest social exchange. In this way, the recruiter and candidate get to know each other much better, build up mutual trust and respect, and, based on this, can make a well-founded selection decision.

Thus, the social acceptance of selection procedures plays a central role in developing a positive relationship between the applicant and the hiring manager. Wrong decisions in personnel selection cost money, but so does broken trust and a damaged relationship.

3.7.9.2 Acceptance of selection procedures and positive candidate experience

Often, advocates of standardized selection methods criticize their limited practical application, although a positive trend has emerged in recent years, and an increasing acceptance of standardized methods is observable. Nevertheless, unstructured interviews show high acceptance, with a usage frequency of 33.6% in personnel departments and 51.2% in specialist departments. In addition, a structured recruitment interview by the HR department was assessed as particularly valid by non-users and users (Schuler et al., 2007, pp. 63–64). Therefore, the use of a procedure does not depend only on the attributed prognostic validity. Elsewhere, it can be seen that a strong argument against the use of psychological test procedures is the low face validity of these procedures (Schmidt & Hunter, 1998, p. 265; Deller & Albrecht, 2007; Benit & Söllner, 2013;). Also, research (e.g., Derous & Born, 2005, or Ekuma, 2012) shows that face validity is essential to perceive a selection process as fair and acceptable, from an applicant's point of view. Therefore, for selection procedures to be effective and implemented into practice, they must possess high predictive and face validity. An especially non-transparent test quality, ethnic concerns, and low applicant acceptance prevent the implementation of standardized and psychometric procedures (Benit & Soellner, 2013, p. 148).

Thus, it is not surprising that Lievens and de Paepe (2004, p. 41) attribute the preference for unstructured interviews to the request that the process should also be sociable, friendly, and informal.

Steiner & Gilliland (2001, p. 127) phrase it as, "interpersonal treatment is largely a function of the interpersonal warmth and sensitivity demonstrated by those administering the selection process."

Schuler et al. (2007, p. 67) also show that in the perspective of companies and hiring managers, the various selection procedures are accepted to varying degrees by applicants. In a study, Kersting (2008, pp. 431–432) states that the assertion that applicants do not accept cognitive ability and achievement tests in Germany does not reflect reality. Applicants' acceptance differs considerably from acceptance by Human Resource managers. For applicants, face validity, in particular, and showing their individual capabilities in the selection process plays a decisive role.

For example, applicant acceptance for unstructured interviews is high in many countries, such as Germany, while it is low for personality tests. The acceptance of selection procedures by applicants must, therefore, be seen against the background of country-specific contexts.

As regards psychometric procedures such as the DIN 33430, research shows that psychometric personnel selection can enhance the employer's image from the applicant's point of view, as applicants are informed about their rights, according to selection standards and the appropriateness of the methods used. One challenge, however, could be that the DIN 33430 requires standardized methods in personnel selection, which restricts the ability of companies to be flexible and present themselves as likable (Klehe, 2008, p. 185). For this reason, both Klehe (2008, p. 186) and Reimann et al. (2009, p. 36) emphasize the importance of providing applicants with comprehensive information about the procedures used and making the selection process as transparent as possible.

Cropanzano and Wright (2003) show that selection procedures with psychometrically high predictive validity, for example, cognitive ability tests, are often perceived by applicants as violating norms of social justice and fairness (see Sections 3.6.5 and 3.7.9); they call this a "justice dilemma." Validity may be of central concern to scientists or personnel managers, but it is only one issue among others, for potential job candidates (Cropanzano & Wright, 2003, p. 24).

From a scientific perspective, a valid cognitive ability test or an extremely formal, fully structured, and standardized interview presents the risk that no pleasant personal contact is established. Also, fully standardized interviews are perceived as impersonal, primarily because the applicant is not addressed individually. Thus, many companies decide to make the application process somewhat unstructured to create a pleasant atmosphere, where the applicant feels comfortable and wants to open up (Weuster 2012, p. 212). And, conducting a semi-structured interview is a good compromise between an open social exchange, the possibility of responding individually to the applicant, and the commensurate standardization of the selection process.

In analytics, however, there is a demand to reduce social influence through personal relationships, as much as possible; one can get the impression that recruiters should function like robots or data-registering devices. In this way, however, personnel selection cannot be successful. It is essential to act empathetically and authentically. The social skills of the recruiters are decisive in attracting the most suitable candidate to the company and bringing about a positive candidate experience.

In addition, selection processes are always reputation management. No matter how strong the corporate image, the positive employer brand crumbles if candidates' negative feedback about impersonal designed selection procedures is repeatedly raised on social media and indicates, for example, a lousy interview atmosphere.

To ensure a positive candidate experience, the social acceptance and the perceived fairness of a recruiting process are essential. The studies of Chan et al. (1997, 1998) illustrate the dynamic interplay of social acceptance of selection procedures and the perceived face validity, fairness, and motivation of applicants to perform in a selection process. The higher the social acceptance of a selection procedure, the higher the motivation of candidates to perform in a selection process.

As shown in Section 3.7.9, the acceptance and perceived fairness of personnel diagnostic procedures can vary from culture to culture (Bartram, 2004) or from labor market to labor market. Thus, it is necessary to look at what applicants from different cultural backgrounds, education, and so on, expect from a selection procedure (see Chapter 7).

However, it can be assumed that it is essential for all applicants to experience interaction with the potential supervisor and teammates in a selection process, to hear how these people think, or how authentic and appreciative they appear. Applicants want to be convinced and won on these personal levels.

Derous & Witte (2001, p. 319) state that a selection process is not only characterized by the specifications of the psychometric paradigm but also by a so-called negotiation perspective. The negotiation perspective pays attention to the social-emotional processes during selection. "The selection activity is not a one-way 'acquisition' facilitated by the use of (psychometric) tools, but a two-way, professional 'learning situation' in which both applicants and selectors can 'win' through negotiation of mutual expectations" (Derous & Witte (2001, p. 338). This social process perspective should be an integral part of a realistic and effective theory and practice of personnel selection.

3.7.9.3 Perceived fairness of a selection process and the concept of social validity

In the "Model of Applicants' Reactions to Employment Selection Systems," Gilliland (1993, p. 700) published a theoretical approach to describing the relationships between the characteristics of a selection process and perceived fairness. It incorporated existing fairness concepts (e.g., Arvey & Renz, 1992; Arvey & Sacket, 1993;

Schuler, 1993) as well as research findings from the field of Organizational Justice Theory (Greenberg, 1990; Lind & Tyler, 1988). Gilliland's model applies organizational justice in terms of procedural, distributive, and interactional justice to personnel selection (Cropanzano et al., 2007, p. 34). By integrating previous research with his findings, Gilliland (1993) established a basis for subsequent research in this area.

Reactions to selection procedures, especially the perception of fairness and procedural justice (1. formal characteristics such as job relatedness; 2. explanation of procedures and decision-making, for example, feedback and selection information; and 3. interpersonal treatment, for example, social skills of selection managers and two-way communication), influence the ability of organizations to attract and hire highly qualified applicants (Gilliland, 1993, pp. 694–697; Gilliland, 1994; Gilliland & Steiner, 2012).

Applicants unconsciously evaluate these rules of justice in the selection situation. Then, depending on whether they feel upheld or violated, different applicant reactions and implications result, for the company (Gilliland & Steiner, 2012, p. 634; Ployhart & Ryan, 1997; Ployhart & Ryan, 1998, p. 9; Ployhart et al., 1999; Truxillo et al., 2001; Truxillo et al., 2002, p. 1020).

Social validity has been conceptualized in many different ways. Schwartz and Baer (1991, p. 231) state that there are numerous meanings and that we know little about the accurate assessment of what is called social validity. German psychologist, Heinz Schuler, developed one concept of social validity. It attempts to balance power differences between applicants and selection managers, non-transparency, and lack of situational control by applicants. Schuler understands this concept of social validity only as a heuristic and not as a falsifiable theoretical model (Schuler, 1993, p. 12).

Studies on the connection between a selection situation perceived positively by candidates and the use of the parameters of social validity show that compliance with the parameters of social validity leads to improved acceptance of selection procedures (Köchling & Körner, 1996, p. 22).

Schuler (1996, p. 182) distinguishes four aspects of social validity:

1. Information: Information for the applicant: for example, about job requirements, organizational characteristics, or development opportunities.
2. Participation and control: Applicants should be allowed to control their behavior and, thus, the selection situation.
3. Transparency: Information about the course of the diagnostic process, the assessment criteria, the persons involved and their roles, and so on.
4. Communication of the selection decision and feedback: Feedback includes accurate and relevant information that enables the candidate to understand the results of the selection process and how these results are to be used. The feedback should be given in a constructive and supportive manner – it should be formulated in an open, understandable, and considerate way, facilitating insight, integration into the applicant's sense of self, development opportunities, and future decisions.

Making the targeted dimensions, the job requirements, and relevant cues or evaluation criteria transparent to assessment center participants helps provide equal chances for all candidates and reduces uncertainty.

Kleinmann et al. (2011, p. 141) show that it is not transparency by the organization but the candidates' subjective assumptions and cognitions about what the selection procedures measure that accounts for the criterion validity. In particular, the "ability to identify evaluation criteria within selection procedures (i.e., the assessment center, interview, or personality inventories) is an important . . . factor that influences performance in these selection procedures as well as in subsequent performance situations on the job."

A study by Ingold et al. (2015b) shows that assessor ratings in an assessment center with non-transparent dimensions for assessees were more criterion valid than ratings from an assessment center with transparent dimensions. Specifically, if transparency reduces error variance by providing equal opportunities for the performance of all assessees, the prediction of job performance should improve. This study indicates that making dimensions transparent may not seem advisable in an assessment center for selection purposes. Also, the data gives no support for the hypothesis that participants' perceptions of their opportunity to perform are higher with transparency.

However, from the perspective of personnel acquisition and to give applicants a positive candidate experience, transparency can be recommended. In addition, questions of fairness play an essential role in accepting selection procedures. The result of a selection procedure is more likely to be accepted if the selection process is perceived as fair (Gilliland, 1993 and 1994; Steiner & Gilliland, 2001; Ryan & Ployhart, 2000; Hausknecht et al., 2004). If the candidate sees a clear link between the selection procedure and the job requirements, it improves the perception and acceptance of selection procedures.

Personal factors such as personal contact, according to Hausknecht's findings, play only a minor role in the perception of fairness of the selection process (Hausknecht et al., 2004, pp. 654 and 669).

However, it must be critically noted that individual studies listed in the meta-analysis cover only small samples and refer mainly to hypothetical situations, rather than to real selection processes, and the time of measurement was not considered as an influencing variable. Due to the experimental character of the study, there is a risk of lack of transferability to practical contexts. In addition, the meta-analysis only covers primary studies published up to 2003, and a follow-up study is needed to reflect the current state of science and practice (Lindemann, 2020, p. 21). This is necessary because recent studies on the acceptance of AI in personnel selection procedures show how important personal contact and personal interviews are, to applicants (Fellner, 2019, p. 12).

3.7.10 Limits of practicability

In practice, massive deficiencies in implementing rational-analytical procedures have been identified (Sarges, 2013, pp. 819–820). A significant reason is seen in the fact that, apart from limited flexibility and the associated bureaucracy, rational-analytical procedures are considered to be less practicable. Practicability comprises the time or financial effort required to carry out selection procedures. For example, suppose specific jobs are filled only relatively rarely. In that case, the needed time and money for a standardized process with requirement analysis, developing an interview guideline, behavioral anchors, and so on, are often perceived as too costly, especially for jobs that are not so pivotal from a business perspective (see Section 2.2).

Moreover, to still meet the requirements of psychometrics, selection procedures often only rudimentarily meet the scientifically desired standards. For example, many selection procedures such as assessment centers fall far short of psychometric standards, but practitioners believe they meet them. However, if selection procedures meet at least some psychometric requirements, the goal of a well-founded personnel selection may be achieved to a certain degree.

3.7.11 Limits of meaningfulness of certificates, references, or school grades

In principle, school, college, or university grades are "valid" measurements of specific abilities. However, in contrast to a test result, these assessments are not based on a flashlight finding but on observations, examinations, and evaluations over an extended period. For this reason, a school grade in mathematics, for example, is usually a relatively valid predictor of vocational or at least vocational training success. Research also shows that specific high-school grades are a relatively good predictor of academic success in certain subjects, such as medicine (Baron-Boldt,1989). Nevertheless, if average final grades of "A" (excellent) are given at specific schools and universities or in particular subjects of study, it is still difficult to classify these grades and compare candidates correctly. Hiring managers should, thus, always pay attention to how someone scored compared to their classmates or fellow students.

However, whether schools or study grades are good predictors of later success at work or as a (global) manager remains questionable.

Furthermore, nearly every country, indeed almost every teacher, school, university, and so on – despite numerous attempts to improve comparability – has different standards for evaluating performance. As a result, the performance levels of university classes or cohorts can be very different. Also, graduates from highly respected universities are often considered more suitable per se than graduates from other universities, although there are very suitable candidates at almost every university.

That's why final grades, school and university certificates, or even (job) references have only very limited significance. To measure all applicants with the same standard, be more objective, and give all applicants the same chances, tests, for example, online cognitive ability tests (GMAT), can select students, apprentices, talents, and so on. Potential candidates with poor grades, who would, otherwise, have had no chance may also be identified. Since a positive correlation between career success and, for example, specific results in a cognitive performance test or also in personality tests could be shown in various studies (e.g., Almlund et al., 2011),, companies are recommended not to be satisfied with the evaluation of school or university certificates, etc., and consider the use of test procedures for the selection of specific employee groups such as talents.

The limits of informative value show that although selection procedures are carried out in a rational-analytical manner, specific evaluated data and supposedly objective and valid information collected from applicants should be seen critically and constructively questioned.

3.7.12 Conclusion

Even if personnel managers assume use of scientific selection procedures, concrete design and implementation methods may not necessarily meet scientific quality criteria.

Moreover, candidates' performance and professional success depend not only on a psychometrically well-done selection procedure but also on the organizational context.

Rational-analytical selection procedures are not automatically accurate and valid, and judgment errors can also occur in these procedures (Kruglanski & Gigerenzer, 2011; Koppers, 2013, p. 60).

Therefore, innovations in the design and implementation of selection methods are necessary to improve effectiveness of selection procedures and match human capabilities, context-specific requirements, and organizational resources. Nevertheless, the aim remains to implement high-quality selection procedures.

4 Intuition and human decision-making

4.1 Intuition in human decisions and definition of intuition

"You know more than you know."

4.1.1 Definition of intuition

Intuition comes from the Latin "intueri" and literally means "to look inside." In lexical works, intuition is the ability to know or understand something, although you have no evident facts; it's a feeling of knowing that results from inspiration. Thus, intuition is colloquially associated with terms such as gut feeling, inner impulse, inner sensing, inner insight, brainwave, hunch, knowledge by inspection, unconscious knowledge, unconscious cognition, subconscious information, impressions, common sense, bone certainty, sudden inclination, spontaneous idea, imagination (e.g., in image form), emotional intelligence, empathy, snap judgment, sure feeling or felt (immediate) knowledge/plain knowing (Gigerenzer, 2007, p. 57).

But intuition is more than a "gut feeling" or instinct. A gut feeling is a specific kind of intuition, and a gut reaction is, for example, hunger or pain (e.g., when because of stress or having eaten something wrong, the stomach reacts with pain).

An instinct is an inherent inclination in a living organism toward a particular behavior; it is an "inherent response tendency that occurs automatically" (Hogarth, 2001, p. 250). Instincts are automatic reactions to environmental stimuli (Sadler-Smith & Shefy, 2004, p. 81); they are innate tendencies toward a particular behavior and not a feeling. The term instinct is often used metaphorically when referring to a manager's judgment; however, it should not be confused with intuition (e.g., "going with one's gut instinct" (Hogarth, 2001, p. 250; see also Sadler-Smith, 2019b, p. 12). "All innate processes, such as reflexes and instinctive behavior patterns, are not considered intuitive because they are not informed by prior knowledge stored in long-term memory" (Betsch, 2008, p. 5).

And for C.G. Jung (1948, pp. 567–569; 1972), intuition is "perception via the unconscious." Intuition enables access to "inner realities" to suspect something or understand the possible and desirable. Thus the intuitive function is valuable and worth cultivating (Berne, 1949).

Although we humans have the capacity for intuition by nature, the question that arises is not about how intuition is defined, but how terms are understood and how which meanings are associated with them, depending on their context. This context is, for example, culturally, historically, politically, linguistically, subjectively, shaped. According to Vogler (2012, p. 77), this means looking closely at the specific context to speak and reflect appropriately on the term intuition.

https://doi.org/10.1515/9783110980967-004

Nevertheless, a uniform definition of the term is needed to properly discuss intuition in a scientific context, empirical research, or practice. However, it has not yet been possible to agree on such a definition, probably due to the context-dependence of terms. And Fields (2000) considered intuition to be one of the least operationalized and defined terms in Human Resource/People management (Malewska, 2015, p. 97).

Therefore, a clarification of the term "intuition" will be attempted further.

In the scientific literature, there are many definitions for intuition (Glöckner & Witteman 2010, p. 2). For definitions of intuition from a more psychological perspective, see Gilovich et al., 2002); from a management perspective, see Sadler-Smith (2019b, p. 6).

Definitions of intuition in the scientific literature

Source	Definition
Barnard (1938, p. 302)	intuitions are ". . . non-logical mental processes . . . not capable of being expressed in words or as reasoning, which are only made known by a judgment, decision or action."
Ben-Zeèv and Krebs (2016, p. 44)	"Intuitive activity is often fast, automatic, and accompanied by little awareness. It is based on readymade patterns that have been set during evolution, social and personal development; in this sense, history and personal development are embodied in these patterns. . . . Since intuitive patterns are part of our psychological makeup, we do not need time to activate them; we simply need appropriate circumstances."
Betsch (2008, p. 4)	"Intuition is a process of thinking. The input to the process is mostly provided by knowledge stored in long-term memory that has been primarily acquired via associative learning. The input is processed automatically and without conscious awareness. The output of the process is a feeling that can serve as a basis for judgments and decisions."
Betsch and Glöckner (2010, p. 280)	"Intuitive processes operate autonomously and automatically, that is, they function without conscious control and cannot easily be assessed by introspection. Moreover, they can process multiple pieces of information in parallel. . . . (I)ntuitive processes are only marginally constrained by cognitive capacity. Second, intuitive processes use all pieces of information that are momentarily activated from memory and salient in the environment. . . . (I)ntuition relies heavily on prior experience. The stronger prior experience has been consolidated in memory, the more likely it will be activated by situational cues and, hence, feed into intuition."

(continued)

Source	Definition
Dane and Pratt (2007, p. 33)	"Affectively charged judgments that arise through rapid, non-conscious, and holistic associations."
Dijksterhuis and Nordgren (2006, p. 105)	"A gut feeling based on unconscious past experience, (that) involves feeling that something is right or wrong, or that A is better than B, while being largely unaware where that feeling came from, or what it is based on."
Haidt (2001, S. 818)	"Intuition . . . can be defined as the sudden appearance in consciousness of a [. . .] judgment, including an affective valence (good-bad, like-dislike), without any conscious awareness of having gone through steps of searching, weighting evidence, of inferring a conclusion."
Hogarth (2001, p. 14)	"The essence of intuition or intuitive responses is that they are reached with little apparent effort, and typically without conscious awareness. They involve little or no conscious deliberation."
Kahneman (2003, p. 697)	"Thoughts and preferences that come to mind quickly and without much reflection."
Khatri and Ng (2000, p.61)	"Intuition is not an irrational process. It is based on a deep understanding of the situation. It is a complex phenomenon that draws from the store of knowledge in our subconscious and is rooted in past experience. It is quick, but not necessarily biased as presumed in previous research on rational decision-making."
Klein (2002, p. 13)	"Intuition is the way we translate our experiences into judgments and decisions. It is the ability to make decisions using patterns to recognize what's going on in a situation and to recognize the typical action scripts with which to react. Once experienced intuitive decision-makers see a pattern, any decision they have to make is usually obvious."
Lieberman (2000, p. 111)	"(I)ntuition is the subjective experience of a mostly nonconscious process that is fast, a-logical, and inaccessible to consciousness, that, dependent on exposure to the domain or problem space, is capable of accurately extracting probabilistic contingencies."

(continued)

Source	Definition
Malewska, K. (2015, p. 98)	"(I)ntuition is a non-sequential process of obtaining and processing information, which takes into account both rational and emotional elements, and the result is direct knowledge without the participation of rational inference. Intuition can be considered a cognitive ability of the human mind that is distinct from traditional forms of objective knowledge. This process is very difficult or sometimes even impossible to reproduce, because it is often unconscious. It differs from the classical rational cognition in that the process itself does not satisfy intersubjective verifiability. In contrast, the result of this process can be logically justified. Therefore, one can conclude that intuition is not an irrational process related to premonitions or revelations, but a process of thinking whose mechanisms differ from the classical rational inference and are difficult to reproduce. However, the results of this process are verifiable and communicable. Therefore, intuition is often referred to as thinking without consciousness or knowledge without consciousness."
Sadler-Smith (2007, p. 31)	"Intuition is an involuntary, difficult-to-articulate, affect-laden recognition or judgment, based upon prior learning and experiences, which is arrived at rapidly, through holistic associations and without deliberative or conscious rational thought."
Sinclair (2011b, pp. 3–4)	"(W)e view the construct of intuition in its broadest sense as 'direct knowing.' . . . 'Direct knowing' implies the absence of conscious information processing. It does not specify how the information was gleaned, which factors influenced it, and how accurate or effective is the outcome . . . we know something without knowing how."
Sinclair & Ashkanasy (2005, p. 357)	"(W)e define intuition as a non-sequential (holistic) information processing mode, which comprises both cognitive and affective elements and results in direct knowing without any use of conscious reasoning."

Intuitive processes are unintentional and automatic, and they are holistic and associative. This means that intuitive judgments process a huge amount of information in parallel by using the entire pattern of information (Betsch & Glöckner, 2010, p. 284).

Intuitions are based on prior (implicit) knowledge and recognition of patterns. But the "processing of prior knowledge is not a sufficient condition to identify a mental activity as intuitive. For example, attempting to recall the names of your friends . . . has nothing to do with intuition; . . . The crucial difference between rehearsal and intuition is that the output of the former is a mental representation of an entity, whereas the latter is a feeling toward it" (Betsch, 2008, p. 6). That means intuition can be an interplay of knowing (intuition as expertise based on experiences) and sensing (intuition as a feeling for the right solution and how to decide).

Intuition is based on the sum of individual experiences, books read, facts and figures learned, feelings associated with specific situations, and the combination of all of these factors; it is a holistic information-processing mode (Sinclair & Ashkanasy, 2005, p. 357), by which implicit knowledge is made available. This knowledge is based on patterns resulting from the past and related personal experiences. However, this knowledge is not produced by conscious considerations but by the situational stimuli and recognizing patterns in these situations (Simon, 1987, p. 63). Therefore, intuition needs experience and expertise; and it is more reliable when more people understand a specific field.

It is important to emphasize that using intuition when making decisions is much more than only heeding one's emotions. Instead, intuition means using the wealth of experience one has built up over the years. Therefore, intuitive decisions must not be equated with selecting personnel according to one's feelings.

Dane and Pratt (2012, pp. 3–4) identified four features to conceptualize intuition. Intuition is
1. a nonconscious information process
2. based on recognizing familiar patterns evolved through learning and experiences
3. (often, but not always) affectively charged by feelings
4. very fast

As we can see, these definitions of intuition show that intuitive decision-making is based on experience and can, therefore, be distinguished from arbitrary decisions.

But at the same time, intuition has two levels: First, it is a mental state or information processing mode, and second, it is the content, information, or message given by this intuitive mode, for example, a specific feeling, inspiration, knowledge, and signal. Deutsch (2015) emphasizes the distinction between intuition referring to a mental state and intuition referring to the content of that state, or between intuit*ings* and intuit*eds*.

Thus, we can add one additional feature. Intuition is a
5. context-specific information or message.
6. not per se irrational or the opposite of rational

In summary, intuition is defined in this publication as follows:

> Intuition is a context-specific automatic and autonomous information processing (mode) and also an inspiration without conscious intervention, awareness, and noticeable effort (content). As a mental ability, it is an enabler for a very fast form of holistic and associative perception of information, judgment, and decision making, whose underlying reasons we are not (fully) aware of and cannot fully describe afterward. Intuition uses unconscious steps and methods based on prior learning, experiences, and empirical knowledge (cognitive part of intuitions). Intuitions are not produced by conscious considerations but by situational stimuli (e.g., verbal or nonverbal behaviors of other people) and pattern recognition in these situations. Pattern recognition

also has emotional aspects, so intuitions are not only expressed in cognitive signals, judgments, and/or interpretations but also in feelings (the emotional part of intuitions). Decision-making, based on intuition, gives one the sure feeling of doing the right thing in a given moment. Intuitive judgments can result in good and correct decisions and lead to the desired results, but some do not.

4.1.2 Intuition in human decisions

The significance of intuition in the practice of human decision-making becomes clear when one considers the frequency with which intuition flows into general decisions at work. For example, 47% of all respondents in a study by Burke and Miller (1999, pp. 93–94) stated that they make intuitive decisions, and 12% answered that they would always do so. In personnel-related decisions, 40% of these decisions were made deliberately and consciously under the influence of intuition. And 66% of the respondents felt that intuition led to better decisions.

People make many decisions every day; the neuroscientist Pöppel speaks of about 20,000 decisions per day (Pöppel, 2008, p. 19). Thus, these decisions cannot all be made in a systematic or analytical-rational way. On the contrary, most human decisions are made based on intuition. And without these intuitions, we humans would not be able to survive at all. Especially in complex situations, where a lot of information must be processed simultaneously, not all can be processed consciously.

Reason, intuitions, and emotions are part of human nature. They serve primarily to ensure our survival. And over the millennia, human survival has been ensured by recognizing at lightning speed, who is a friend and who is a foe. Nothing has changed in this respect to this day. For the survival of humans, it was necessary to recognize the potential danger of other conspecifics quickly. Therefore, throughout evolution, humans have developed intuitive mechanisms to make quick decisions based on the physical attributes of their counterparts (Petrican et al., 2014, p. 259).

The physical attributes of humans can be judged faster than other attributes. For example, not all dimensions of a personality can be observed equally well when assessing people, for example, in job interviews. Suppose one looks at the Big Five personality traits (Costa & McCrae, 1988), above all, the outward-oriented characteristics of extraversion and conscientiousness can be observed with remarkable accuracy. But, for example, Shaffer & Püostlethwaite (2012, 2013) show in a meta-analysis that conscientiousness strongly predicted performance in highly routinized jobs and weakly predicted performance in jobs that require high levels of cognitive ability; and they found higher validities for contextualized measures of personality (Potočnik et al., 2021, pp. 160–161).

On the other hand, emotional stability manifests primarily in internally occurring processes and is more difficult to assess from the outside (Watson, 1989, p. 127). The external assessment of strangers and acquaintances can provide valid results (Mount et al., 1994, p. 272), whereby the validity of the assessments of acquaintances is significantly higher than that of strangers. Personal interaction thus increases the validity of third-party assessments (Colvin & Funder, 1991, p. 888).

Also, neuroscience research shows that most things people do in their lives are intuitive. And human experiences are emotionally coded. Therefore, perceptions are automatically compared and linked with what is already stored in the emotional memory (Roth, 2015, p. 172).

The fact that the term intuition is challenging to define reflects the nature of intuition, which is unconscious, therefore difficult to grasp, and very subjective. Indeed, it is not always clear how to distinguish intuition from other concepts such as emotional intelligence or instinct. Although these terms are often used interchangeably, they differ in meaning. Intuition is learned, not innate. And intuitions are, in most cases, accompanied by or experienced as feelings (Sinclair & Ashkanasy, 2005, p. 356; see Section 4.2.4.3).

4.1.3 Types and functions of intuition

Research on intuition distinguishes different types of intuition. For example, Glöckner and Witteman (2010a) state there is considerable disagreement among researchers about what intuition really is and that at least four different types of intuition can be differentiated:
(a) Associative intuition, which is based on simple learning and retrieval, such as feelings of liking and disliking, affective arousal, and activation of previously successful behaviors.
(b) Matching intuition relies on complex prototype and exemplar storage and retrieval, for example, comparing schemas and images.
(c) Accumulating or evidence intuition is based on evidence-based automatic linear processes and integrating information from memory and currently perceived information.
(d) Constructive intuition is based on the construction of consistent mental representations.

Sadler-Smith (2019, pp. 11–12) summarizes some of the main distinctions of intuition that scholars and researchers have drawn and differentiates between *aesthetic intuition* (perceiving created beauty; conceiving uncreated beauty), *affective intuition* (emotional reactions to decision situations; emotional evaluation of decision alternatives), *holistic intuition* (integrating multiple, diverse cues into a whole), *inferential intuition* (decision making processes that were once analytical but have become intuitive with practice), *intellectual intuition* (immediate solution of a problem not preceded by any connected chain of reasoning), and *religious intuition* (personal experience or knowledge of the divine or absolute experienced as a conviction or revelation of "unity"). He also talks about intuitive insights and intuitive judgments. From the perspective of Sadler-Smith (2019, p. 10 and pp. 11–16), the following four types of intuition are most essential and salient to management.

4.1.3.1 Intuition type 1: expert intuition

Expert intuition refers to analyses that have become a habit to be called up quickly based on recognition (Simon, 1987, p. 63). This type of intuition is based on the bundling of explicit and implicit knowledge in the long-term memory, resulting from learning and experience (Dane & Pratt, 2007, p. 42; Sadler-Smith, 2019, p. 13; Simon, 1987, p. 60). In recalling this knowledge, the new information is unconsciously matched with known patterns (Dane & Pratt, 2009, p. 5; Gore & Sadler-Smith, 2011, p. 307). According to Simon (1992, p. 155), a person quickly recognizes and responds non-consciously to situations that have familiar patterns. These patterns give experts access to their tacit and explicit knowledge (Dane & Pratt, 2007, p. 41; Hogarth, 2001, p. 90). Already Barnard (1938, p. 302) stated that intuition "significantly increases with directed experience, study and education." Based on this information, the expert can answer and solve the problem (Simon, 1992, p. 155). Thus, expert intuition includes inferential and intellectual intuition. Dörfler and Ackermann (2012, p. 550) conclude, based on their literature review and conceptual modeling, that intuition increases with the level of expertise and emerges naturally and it becomes the predominant knowledge form. Hence, senior and more experienced managers tend to make intuitive decisions more often than junior and less experienced managers. Generally, researchers are divided on the definition of this intuition type. Whereas Sadler-Smith and Shefy (2004, p. 81) use intuition as expertise and Kahneman and Klein (2009, p. 515) define it as intuitive expertise, Dane and Pratt (2012, p. 5) describe this intuition type as problem-solving intuition. The authors state that all intuition types are based on expertise, but not all problems are solved by expertise or expert intuition.

According to Kahneman and Klein (2009, p. 524), whether expert and problem-solving intuition can be trusted depends on two factors: the high validity of the environment and the level of experience of the manager. Thus, intuition works best when experience has already been gathered in similar situations (Sadler-Smith, 2019, p. 13). A high degree of validity can be assumed if there is a stable environment and stable relationships between objectively identifiable cues and the subsequent results, as in firefighting or medicine. Long-term forecasts regarding stocks or politics, on the other hand, are not characterized by stable relationships between objectively identifiable cues and the subsequent events, or outcomes; thus, these are examples of low validity (Kahneman & Klein, 2009, p. 524). Prolonged practice and timely and unequivocal feedback in high-validity environments constitute the learning structure necessary for developing intuitive expertise (Sadler-Smith, 2019, p. 14).

4.1.3.2 Intuition type 2: moral intuition

The concept of moral intuition is based on the "social intuitionist model" (SIM) of Haidt (2001, 2012). Moral intuitive judgments happen non-consciously; they are automatic evaluations accompanied by a high level of affective charge. Moral intuition quickly decides what is wrong or right (Dane & Pratt, 2009, p. 4). This decision is more a realization than reason, as often it cannot be explained (Haidt, 2001, p. 814). In contrast to rational models, Haidt's social intuitionist model allows the absence of reasoning. According to Haidt (2001, p. 815), individuals rationalize their behavior post-hoc by explaining and justifying their moral judgment. And also, Gore and Sadler-Smith (2011, p. 238) state that moral intuition is subsequently rationalized. People's judgment is relatively insensitive to refutation as persons believe in their initial intuition (Haidt, 2007, p. 998). As a result, individuals create an illusion of control (Haidt, 2001, p. 815). Haidt (2007, p. 998) developed his Social Intuitionist Model, contrary to traditional rationalist theories of moral judgment. His model emphasizes the strong cultural and social influence on moral judgment. Therefore, moral intuition is expressed differently according to norms and values in a specific culture or subculture (Haidt, 2001, p. 828). Overall, moral intuition can be described as a rapid, automatic, and affect-based judgment by a person responding intuitively to an ethical dilemma in a specific socio-cultural setting.

Accordingly, the moral values of a company can be predetermined to a certain extent, and the top management level plays a decisive role in implementing these morals. Consequently, managers can actively set moral values for their organization and influence corporate culture. In this regard, managers should pay attention as their internalized corporate values can create tensions that conflict with individual norms (Sadler-Smith, 2019, pp. 14–15).

4.1.3.3 Intuition type 3: creative Intuition

Creative intuition is an affectively charged nonconscious judgment that combines divergent associations in a novel way, resulting in a creative outcome (Gore & Sadler-Smith, 2011, p. 308). Thus, this intuition type is contrary to moral and expert intuition, as both imply "a type of convergent categorization (e.g., is this right or wrong . . .)" (Dane & Pratt, 2012, p. 9). This novel combination of knowledge is based on divergent associations. These associations and the subsequent behavior can lead to creative outcomes (Dane & Pratt, 2009, p. 5; Gore & Sadler-Smith, 2011, p. 238). The crucial difference to expert or problem-solving intuition is that creative intuition is based on combined knowledge in holistic and novel ways. In contrast, expert intuition is based on the unconscious recognition of known information. Creative intuition's explorative and transcending function is fundamental for artistic endeavors, new discoveries, business ventures, or technical inventions going beyond previous logic and knowledge (Sadler-Smith, 2019, pp. 11 and 13–14). Thus, creative intuition uses holistic and intellectual intuition and can be regarded as a "key input in the creative process" (Dane & Pratt, 2012, p. 9) because it can foster innovations of all kinds, especially in organizational contexts.

4.1.3.4 Intuition type 4: social intuition

"Social intuition is the ability to detect important attributes, motivations, and intentions of others" (Sadler-Smith, 2019, p. 15). The "rapid and automatic evaluation of another person's cognitive and/or affective state through the perception and nonconscious processing of verbal and/or nonverbal indicators" (Gore & Sadler-Smith, 2011, p. 310) can be defined as social intuition; and social intuition includes affective intuition. Social intuition is used to decide whether another person should be considered a friend, partner, or enemy and is therefore crucial for building interpersonal relationships and trust. In human resource management, this intuition influences selection interviews, negotiations, and preferences in group dynamics. A critical point to consider is that people tend to prefer those who resemble themselves. Therefore, intuition offers room for prejudice and discrimination (Sadler-Smith, 2019, p. 15).

Hänsel et al. (2002, p. 42–43) understand intuition as a bundle of competencies and a specific type of human cognition and knowledge. Intuition is

1. unconsciously applied knowledge of experience and action, and/or
2. an intelligent body feeling (see the somatic markers according to Damasio, Section 4.2.5), which helps people to perceive emotional messages of the body before making decisions, and/or
3. a flash of inspiration, such as the sudden idea to solve complex problems, be creative, and so on.

Functions of intuition, therefore, contribute in particular to:

1. promoting synergies and holistic problem solving and decision making
2. dealing with complexity
3. promoting creativity and new ways, new goals, and new visions
4. shaping human interactions and relationships
5. a sense for considering essential and individually significant aspects in a specific situation

4.2 Approaches to understanding and explaining intuition

In the following, some different aspects of intuition are presented.

Scientific literature has focused on various approaches to explaining intuition. Their functionalities are summarized in the following Figure 7 and are subsequently elaborated on individually.

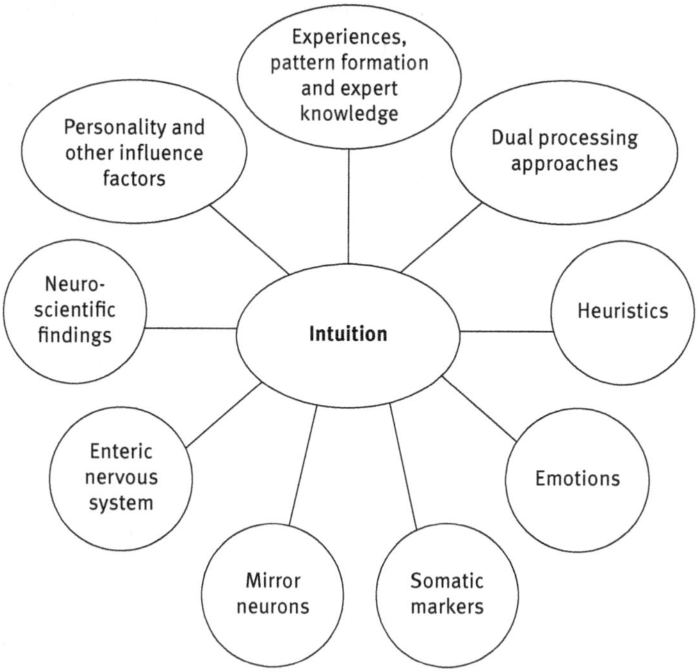

Figure 7: Approaches to explain intuition (based on Holtfort, 2011, p. 507).

4.2.1 Experiences, pattern recognition, and expert knowledge as aspects of intuition

Human judgments and decisions are embedded in individual experiences. Humans learn implicitly and explicitly, and consciously and unconsciously, to draw on their (positive and negative) experiences and the related knowledge for decisions. As shown in Section 4.2.1.1, intuition can be seen as expert knowledge where intuitive competence develops based on collected experiences and pattern formation.

4.2.1.1 Experiences and expert knowledge as (unconscious) cognitive components of intuition

The term expert comes from Latin "expertus" and means tried, proved, and known by experience. People collect different experiences and process them consciously and unconsciously. In principle, a distinction can be made between explicit and implicit knowledge. Knowledge that is based on education and experience and that can be consciously recalled is explicit. The unconscious knowledge that cannot necessarily be articulated, but influences judgments and decisions, is called implicit or tacit knowledge (Section 4.2.2.2 deals with these two forms of knowledge in a differentiated manner).

Implicitly stored knowledge, acquired through experience and associative learning processes, is often described as intuition (Plessner et al., 2008b; Lieberman, 2000). Thus, implicit knowledge can lead to intuitions that make it possible to judge and make decisions faster and more effectively than through rational analysis. Often, experts describe their decision-making processes as intuitive, particularly when facing multiple alternatives with no logical way of choosing between them (Holtfort, 2011, p. 507).

Plassmann (2019, p. 39) states that everyone must have an intuitive knowledge area (in their body or brain). So far, we have not been able to identify a single mental or physical area that produces this ability. We only know for sure, from experience, that this ability exists.

Expertise-based intuitions are neither accidental nor the opposite of rationality but the result of processes that unconsciously occur in the human brain (Hodgkinson et al., 2009, p. 280). Furthermore, intuitive decisions, based on experience, are not automatically irrational because they are based on implicit knowledge accumulated over the years. For example, decision-makers experience, over many years, repeatedly what works and what does not; they learn to ignore irrelevant patterns or pieces of information and concentrate on the critical ones (Prietula & Simon, 1989).

By gathering a lot of experience, experts can make an intuitive decision very competently and quickly, without conscious analytical decomposition and recombination (Dreyfus & Dreyfus, 1980; Dreyfus & Dreyfus, 1991).

Kahneman & Klein (2009, p. 519) determined that intuitive judgments of some professionals are impressively skillful, while the judgments of other professionals are remarkably flawed. Although not contradictory, these core observations suggest conflicting generalizations about the utility of expert judgment.

Experts seem to decide according to the principle of pattern recognition. They have acquired complex cognitive schemes that allow them to generate the right cues to automatically and intuitively make a decision. Klein et al. (1988) show that experienced managers make quick and appropriate decisions by recognizing patterns, and more often than not, the first intuitive chosen option will work.

But a supposed expert scheme can also lead to errors in judgment and wrong decisions if no valid learning environments have been available to acquire expert knowledge, and the decision context has changed (Koppers, 2013, p. 47).

Expertise-based intuitions occur at later stages of experience or development and can become a dominant factor when the decision-maker has developed deep knowledge, based on extensive and accumulated experience in a specific field or domain of activity (Salas et al., 2010, p. 944).

Baylor (2001) similarly suggests that using intuition in the early stages of a job or career is "immature," as it is not supported by domain-specific knowledge. But intuitive skills are not restricted to professionals: Anyone can recognize tension or fatigue in a familiar voice on the phone (Kahneman & Klein, 2009, p. 519). But to use this knowledge-based intuition correctly, expertise is required. Building on Baylor's (2001) U-model, Bangert et al. (2014) developed – oriented on the example of musicians – a spiral model in which people always make decisions based on a mixture of intuitive and conscious processes. By making decisions, people gain experience and develop their expertise. And Bangert et al. (2014) assume that the intuitive processes gradually become more transparent and conscious.

On the other hand, rational-analytical, conscious decision-making processes become increasingly automatic. Depending on the level of expertise, intuition is used to varying degrees. Intuition is used with a low level of experience and expertise as well as with an extremely high level of experience (Ahel, 2020, pp. 82–83).

Existing, stored, and consciously or unconsciously remembered experiences constantly connect with new, current experiences. New implicit knowledge is developed when current and past experiences are linked (Plassmann, 2019, p. 51). And thereby, for example, hiring managers get a feeling for how selection decisions should be made.

Neuroscientific research shows that repeated practice of a specific behavior and repeated experiences lead to a more significant number of neuronal networks, which in turn can merge into a more robust memory representation (Levitin, 2009, p. 249). What is particularly favorable for humans is that our brains remember whether something was good or bad for us and whether it caused good or bad feelings. And this "knowledge" does not have to be consciously activated repeatedly but runs automatically in the background. The experience gained thus leads to an intuitive competence that can be superior to rational decision-making in specific situations.

4.2.1.1.1 How to develop expertise?

Experts develop their expertise through years of experience and different levels of competence (from novice to expert). According to the five-level model of skill acquisition by Dreyfus & Dreyfus (1980), experts know more than novices and no longer rely on rules and guidelines; they grasp situations intuitively, based on deep tacit understanding, and analytic approaches are used only in novel situations or when problems occur. Their knowledge is better organized and integrated, and they have verified strategies for accessing and using knowledge and competencies. They are more self-regulated in using their competencies and know what they do not know (Dreyfus & Dreyfus, 1980).

If one enters a new field of activity, one learns basic knowledge, standards, procedures, and decision rules. For example, in personnel selection, hiring managers can learn from other hiring managers or by reading publications on the topic of selection; they can participate in training on the topic selection, but the most effective is learning by doing, getting feedback, and evaluating the results and outcomes of their decisions, and so on.

Education, such as specific courses of studies (e.g., Human Resource Management, law, or I-O psychology) or special training, also plays a role in developing expertise. For example, Lievens and Klimoski (2001, p. 23) point to a higher discriminant validity for psychologist assessors than for managerial assessors. And assessors receiving frame-of-reference training were better able to use the dimensions in an assessment center differentially. Thus, assessor training and assessor's educational backgrounds (e.g., psychology studies) improve rating accuracy and construct validity of assessment centers. In addition, assessing a limited number of competencies by each assessor leads to higher accuracy of ratings (Lievens, 2016, p. 11).

But many hiring managers are not specifically and systematically trained in personnel selection. Particularly in SMEs, many managing directors, entrepreneurs, and line managers are convinced to have sufficient knowledge of human nature and can carry out competent personnel selection. As a result, they do not deal with scientifically proven research results on personnel selection, do not use job-requirement-related interview guidelines, and do not critically reflect upon selection procedures, their intuitions, judgments, and decision-making. And as a rule, they do not explicitly formulate their selection decision rules and make them transparent (see Section 3.2.3.3).

However, the complexity of decision-making situations is often not reflected in the experiential knowledge of practitioners. This is due, in particular, to selective perception and the associated tendency to simplify. In addition, hiring managers often do not go through an analytical and self-reflective judgment and decision-making process. Their development of expertise does not necessarily start with acquiring knowledge about the psychometric quality standards in personnel selection processes and the application of explicit selection rules.

This is consistent with our interview results. Many interviewees, particularly hiring line managers or managing directors from SMEs, say they have no systematically and consciously developed competencies for selecting personnel. Instead, they rely on their knowledge of human nature and experience.

But most, in our empirical research, interviewed hiring managers from companies with an HR department, especially with systematic training and education in personnel selection, say that they relied more on formal, rational-analytical procedures and decision rules at the beginning of their career. However, as experience grew and information processing became increasingly implicit, formal methods became less critical, and they came to rely on their experience-based intuition.

> At the beginning of my work as a personnel manager, I primarily oriented myself to standards and decision-making rules known from science, which I learned during training and my studies at university. These standards and rules gave me a clear orientation and helped me find my way in these complex decision situations. But with time and increasing experience, I felt more and more secure. Today, I am convinced to use the scientifically required rules unconsciously and intuitively, without always using an interview guideline with operationalized criteria or quantitative rating scales. After more than 20 years as an HR manager, I intuitively know whether an applicant suits us or not (Deters, 2019, p. 126).

4.2.1.1.2 Learning circumstances and expertise

Kahneman (2012) asserts that high-quality decisions can be based on intuition (he talks about System 1; see Section 4.2.2.4), but only if the decision-maker is a true expert.

Kahneman and Klein (2009) affirm that stable and valid environments are best for developing intuitive expertise. Accurate intuitive skills are different from intuitive overconfidence and biased impressions. The authors identified the learning environment as especially crucial for developing expertise.

As long as intuition is based only on subjective experience, it is not a reliable indicator of judgment accuracy. And thus there is a risk that the subjective certainty of being an expert leads to overconfidence if the intuitive decisions are not objectively evaluated by performance measures (Kahneman & Klein, 2009, pp. 515 and 524).

Unconsciously developed intuition can lead to errors of judgment and incorrect decisions, when no stable predictability and appropriate learning environments are available for developing expert knowledge (Hogarth, 2010).

Kahneman (2012, pp. 295–298) defines the conditions necessary for building expertise. First, an expert must have acquired knowledge in a stable and predictable learning environment. In contrast to heuristic intuition (see Section 4.2.3), Kahneman and Klein (2009, pp. 519–524) see valid, and thus stable learning environments with a "causal and statistical structure" as well as opportunities to learn the relevant cues as conditions for the quality of expert-based intuitive decisions. Environments are characterized by high validity if there are stable relationships, objectively identifiable cues (such as scored application behaviors), and clear, measurable outcomes of procedures. And an environment of high validity and sufficient regularity (that does not imply the absence of uncertainty) is – according to Kahneman (2012, pp. 295–298) – a necessary condition for developing skilled and expert intuitions.

Thus, hiring managers should learn in an environment that contains valid cues and offers opportunities to learn, and evaluate these relevant cues by quantitative performance measures.

> True experts . . . know when they don't know. However, nonexperts (whether or not they think they are) certainly do not know when they don't know. Subjective confidence is, therefore, an unreliable indication of the validity of intuitive judgments and decisions.
>
> The determination of whether intuitive judgments can be trusted requires an examination of the environment in which the judgment is made and of the opportunity that the judge has had to learn the regularities of that environment.
>
> We describe task environments as "high-validity" if there are stable relationships between objectively identifiable cues and subsequent events or between cues and the outcomes of possible actions. In contrast, outcomes are effectively unpredictable in zero-validity environments. . . .
>
> An environment of high validity is a necessary condition for the development of skilled intuitions. Other necessary conditions include adequate opportunities for learning the environment (prolonged practice and feedback that is both rapid and unequivocal). If an environment provides valid cues and good feedback, skill and expert intuition will eventually develop in individuals of sufficient talent (Kahneman & Klein, 2009, p. 524; see Koppers, 2013, p. 51).

A stable decision-making environment also requires explicitly formulated, transparent decision-making rules, which should regularly and systematically be evaluated and – if necessary – modified. Therefore, in the perspective of Kahneman and Klein (2009, p. 519), specific criteria for judging expertise are needed. And these criteria should not be based on a history of subjective successful outcomes but on quantitative performance measures.

Kahneman and Klein (2009) also state that developing expert intuition requires consistent analytical judgment and decision-making, and a disciplined self-reflection.

A further common method for defining expertise is to rely on peer judgments. The conditions for determining expertise are the existence of a consensus (e.g., among peers) and evidence that the consensus reflects intersubjective aspects of successful performance even if they are not quantified explicitly. In this way, experts have been recognized within their profession by peers as having the necessary skills and abilities to perform at the highest level.

In sum, the criteria for evaluating expertise in a specific field, such as personnel selection, can be

a) a recognized and in the view of peers, other hiring or line managers, customers, candidates, and so on, high degree of knowledge (psychometric knowledge, knowledge on high-quality standards, etc.), social skills and abilities, personality characteristics, and so on.
b) the stability and thus validity of the environment in which the decisions are made
c) the performance of a hiring manager measured by
   - valid data and a positive correlation between predictors (scored selection results) and criteria such as the success of the selected candidates in their jobs (successful outcomes such as performance)

   A candidate's success on the job can be measured by
   - assessments and feedback of the manager (superior of the hired candidate), peers, customers, and so on.

  – quantitative performance measures of the candidate, for example measurable results such as numbers of products produced.

d) personnel acquisition skills (e.g., social skills and communication skills) and the related ability to arouse interest in applying to the company and accepting job offers.

Hiring managers develop heuristics and intuitions based on their experience and acquired knowledge, enabling them to process information in the personnel selection process quickly. However, these heuristics and intuitions must be based on correct data and the related theoretical models, concepts, and methods. And if the model is correct, their judgments, based on heuristics, may also be correct.

Intuition is based on former experiences. But today, companies are facing significant shifts in technology (e.g., big data and artificial intelligence) and connectivity (e.g., boundless information and instant communication), global competition and dynamic markets, demographic changes (e.g., rapid aging of populations in many countries), climate change, and so on.

Thus, intuitions based on former experiences may have served people well in the past but may become irrelevant in the future. The future may have more discontinuity and volatility, and long-used assumptions may no longer fit the dynamic changes.

Whether experiences and methods of personnel diagnostics used currently will be relevant in the future remains doubtful. Concerning the stability and thus the validity of the recruiter's learning environment and the context of most hiring processes in practice, especially in SMEs, neither objective cues nor stable conditions, or stable relations between cues and outcomes, or explicit decision rules are given.

Therefore, a highly valid environment and a stable learning context for selection managers can be identified as an illusion (Koppers, 2013, p. 47).

4.2.1.1.3 Routine and experience are not automatically expertise

People develop expertise through years of experience, but years of experience do not guarantee that an individual will become an expert. Hiring managers can become experts; but many can be seen as "experienced non-experts."

The reason is that experience can be seen not only as an indicator of expertise but also as an indicator of non-evaluated routine. Routine decisions – such as expert decisions – are characterized only by low use of cognitive resources. The cognitive effort primarily matches the present decision situation with those stored in the memory.

Koppers (2013, pp. 50–51) states that there are many inconsistent findings regarding the effects of experience on the validity of selection interviews, reflecting the difficulty in differentiating between expertise and routine. Some findings show that interview experts, due to their fast and differentiated pattern recognition, as well as years of experience compared to interview novices, come to more accurate personnel decisions. However, this assumption has not yet been clearly confirmed. Indeed, Gehrlein et al. (1993, pp. 462–463) found that experience has a negative effect on the validity of an assessment; the assessments of inexperienced interviewers had a higher overall validity than those of experienced interviewers. Experienced interviewers complained about the given structures and did not consider all rating scales in their assessment.

Betsch et al. (2011, p. 32) show that if judgments are based on integrating remembered behavioral information, expectation-confirming information has a greater weight than information that contradicts expectations. This is because the judgment then tends in the direction of expectations. Thus, there is a risk that decisions based on experience reinforce the tendency toward confirmation (bias) and thus increase the risk of judgment errors.

To become an expert in personnel selection, personnel managers should not only deal with existing quality standards and decision rules of personnel selection but also become aware of their previous procedures, decision rules, and so on, reflect on these with other managers, and systematically evaluate previous selection decisions.

The years of experience and the subjective confidence of hiring managers to do a great job and reach successful outcomes are unreliable indicators for the validity of intuitive judgments and decisions (Kahneman & Klein, 2009, p. 524).

Thus, these findings prove that, in the context of personnel diagnostic decisions, experience can not only function as an indicator of expertise but also as an indicator of non-evaluated routine. Therefore, future research should identify more relevant influencing factors on positive or negative effects of experience.

4.2.1.1.4 Lack of objective evaluations and expert development

Another problem in developing personnel diagnostic expertise is that hiring managers often do not systematically evaluate their learning contexts and selection decisions. But, a systematic evaluation of learning contexts, especially hiring decisions, is essential for developing expert knowledge (Kahneman & Klein, 2009; Einhorn & Hogarth, 1978). Thus, to develop expertise-based intuition, personnel diagnostic experts should learn in a stable environment and evaluate their decision results and learning contexts by critically reflecting, reviewing, and – if necessary – modifying these contexts and their decision-making rules (see Section 10.4).

Suppose there is no explicit, transparent, and systematically implemented decision rule system, the selection managers must build up an individual subjective rule system, under pressure, to make decisions. According to research (Kahneman & Klein, 2009; Koppers, 2013, pp. 45–53), every recruiter should explain and review their subjective decision rules. And these subjective (but also officially implemented) selection decision rules and procedures should be evaluated; this evaluation is part of the learning process to develop expert knowledge.

One particular risk must be seen: If there is no systematic evaluation of the selection procedure and the outcomes, the implicit and subjective rule system will be used as a principle of learning through repetition and this can lead to a consolidation of subjective decision-making rules and illusory confidence in the supposed diagnostic expert knowledge.

Thus, subjective decision rules remain doubtful if they are not evaluated. However, by developing and applying such subjective decision-making rules, an expert can be intuitive and confident for years, but possibly be wrong, objectively (Koppers, 2013, pp. 50–53).

As shown in Section 3.7.7, evaluating decisions remains difficult, because, for example, a candidate's poor performance or even dismissal cannot be clearly traced back to a poor personnel diagnostic process. It must also be taken into account that evaluations can only consider those persons who have been hired and not those who have been rejected. This makes it difficult to draw valid conclusions about whether the hiring manager's selection decision was incorrect (Koppers, 2013, p. 48, with reference to Schuler, 2002, p. 122 and Kanning, 2004, p. 75).

The difficulties in developing genuine (intuitive) expertise (according to Kahneman) thus lie in the fact that practice is far more complex and unpredictable than theory or as scientists assume. The intuitions of HR managers based on previous experience must therefore always be critically questioned.

4.2.1.2 Intuitive pattern recognition and expertise

An intuitive decision is usually based on recognizing available patterns in a person's memory. Situations can unconsciously call up remembered experiences if they are considered equal or unequal, identical or similar, positive or threatening. Recognition can also be linked to strong emotional associations (see somatic markers, Section 4.2.5) with a past positive or negative experience. But recognition often has a positive valence and can thus create a preference: People choose what they know and what causes good feelings (Pfister et al., 2017, p. 351).

Klein states that decision-making based on unconscious situational pattern recognition is called intuitive; and many skilled intuitive decision-making occurs in different domains of expertise, for example, firefighting and diagnosing diseases (Klein, 1998, 2008). Thus, "intuitive decision making involves an unconscious comparison between the current situational pattern and situational patterns stored in memory from previous experiences. A match between the current and the remembered situational patterns generates responses based on previous successes adapted to the current situation" (Patterson & Eggleston, 2017, p. 5).

And from the perspective of Hodgkinson and Sadler-Smith (2018, p. 479, "(t)he effectiveness of decision-makers' initial judgments is affected by the representativeness of the analogies they draw in relation to other, (dis)similar situations."

In a decision-making situation, a perceived cue activates the knowledge stored in the expert's memory and leads to an intuitive recognition. This kind of "(i)ntuition is nothing more and nothing less than recognition" (Simon, 1992; quoted in Kahneman & Klein, 2009, p. 520). Experts recognize a situation or a cue as relevant and can, therefore, quickly find a proper reaction from memory (Koppers, 2013, p. 48).

Recognition is a fundamental operation of intuition and probably evolutionarily that is deeply anchored with elementary adaptive functions (recognition of feeding places, recognition of enemies/friends, etc.). A decision-making process, based on recognition, works fast, effortlessly, and with a high probability of success (Goldstein & Gigerenzer 2002). Recognition has, on the one hand, hedonic consequences because what can easily be recognized is considered familiar, pleasant, harmless, and emotionally positive. On the other hand, recognition can also lead to epistemic consequences because it is experienced as valid and true (Zajonc & Markus 1982; Morewedge & Kahneman 2010; Pfister et al., 2017, p. 351).

Gary A. Klein, Roberta Calderwood and Anne Clinton-Cirocco (Klein, 1993) developed the "**R**ecognition **P**rimed **D**ecision-making model" (RPD model) of how people make quick, effective decisions when faced with complex situations. Especially under time pressure and in situations with incomplete information or changing environments, experts use their unconscious memories, recognize situations and patterns with a similar design, and intuitively make appropriate decisions.

Through various recruitment procedures with different applicants, the recruiter identifies similarities and patterns between individual candidates, their qualifications and behavior, and their performance on the job. Thus, hiring managers implicitly, subjectively, and unconsciously evaluate the validity of their selection decisions in their minds. In addition, hiring managers recognize the behavioral patterns in every new selection process and integrate them into their job- or company-specific cognitive scheme. Finally, they unconsciously integrate their decision-making experiences and rules into new contexts and situations with other applicants (Koppers, 2013, p. 44).

4.2.1.3 Intuitive pattern recognition and emotions

In his book *Psychotherapie der Emotionen* (*Psychotherapy of Emotions*), Plassmann (2019, pp. 17–19) describes emotions as energy sources for human development and human behavior. Emotions lead to patterns in the brain and thus cause certain behavioral and decision tendencies, such as using specific selection procedures or relying on supposed intuitive expertise. And these patterns tend to solidify themselves, especially by the repeating of particular behaviors. Thus, patterns increasingly reduce the potential space for other feelings, mindsets, decisions, and behaviors. This makes changes in learned behaviors, primarily when they are based on unconscious patterns, so difficult.

Suppose hiring managers want to replace dysfunctional patterns or mindsets with new, more positive patterns, it requires not only the recognition of the old pattern but also a creative, change-causing cognitive will and emotional energy. Thus, positive benefits of the new behavior must be felt emotionally.

Modern emotion research has confirmed that the question "What's right for me?" is primarily decided intuitively and based on feelings; not just big life decisions but also an infinite series of small decisions in everyday life. Feelings are the basis for a person's ability to intuitively know what is best for them. Therefore, feelings compass behavioral orientation (Plassmann, 2019, pp. 27–28). In many self-help books and songs, it is therefore emphasized and demanded again and again, as in the case of the German rock musician Udo Lindenberg: "My heart is my compass and shows me the way!"

Research on the connection between emotions and human behaviors shows the difficulties in changing procedures in personnel selection that are subjectively and emotionally perceived as successful. After all, why should "experienced" hiring managers change subjectively successful selection procedures that give them positive feelings?

4.2.2 Dual processing approaches to intuition

Human decision-making and information processing are complex, based on many dynamic and emergent interacting factors. To simplify these complex processes, scientists differentiate these mental processes using two different thought systems (Sadler-Smith, 2019; Sinclair, 2011b, p. 4; Evans, 2008; Stanovich & West, 2000, pp. 658–659).

Dual-process and dual-system theories come in several forms. Still, all share a core assumption that human information processing is accomplished in two different but complementary ways ("analytically" and "intuitively"), utilizing two substantively different types of thinking, one fast and intuitive, the other slow and deliberative. For example, Sadler-Smith (2010, pp. 9–12) talks about the "intuitive and analytical mind" and states that "(s)ometimes the analytical mind and the intuitive mind work together in balance and harmony, at other times they contradict each other and compete for attention and control of our thoughts, feelings, and actions." And he firmly believes humans can benefit by balancing these two sides of nature in their private and professional lives.

Although they simplify the complexity of human decisions, dual-process theories can help explain judgment and decision processes and offer a promising, more comprehensible perspective on how selection managers evaluate candidates (Ingold et al., 2018, p. 1). Thus, the distinction between the two systems should be seen as a theoretical construct and an approach to achieving a better orientation in the complexity of human decisions.

The idea of two mental modes is relatively old. For example, in ancient Greece, the god Apollo stood for order, rationality, and self-discipline, alongside Dionysus, who represented the chaotic, instinctive, and frenzied side of human nature. In ancient as well as modern-day Chinese thought, the mental force of Yin signifies a "front-of-the-mind" intellect that coexists alongside Yang, a "back-of-the-mind" intuition. Although this duality was essential to the ancient Greeks and Chinese, it also recurred throughout history. Humanity has witnessed the light and dark sides of political and business leadership, and the two minds concept is a duality that's reflected in many of our cultural icons, for example, Shakespeare's "thing of darkness" or R.L. Stevenson's Dr. Jekyll and Mr. Hyde (Sadler-Smith, 2010, p. 10). The American psychologist William James (1842–1910) can be seen as a founder of the modern dual-process theory and differentiated it in his book *The Principles of Psychology* (1890) between associative and true reasoning. Later, Peter Wason and Jonathan Evans (1974) described two types of information processing, heuristic and analytic processes. And subsequently, there have been a variety of researchers and authors who distinguish between the two different mental processes.

4.2.2.1 Cognitive-experiential self-theory (CEST)

Epstein (1998) and Sinclair and Ashkanasy (2005, p. 359) state that there are two separate ways of processing information. The first is the experiential system, which is intuitive, emotional, and beyond our conscious awareness. The second system is rational-analytical, intentional, logical, and primarily verbal. People process information using these two parallel and interactive systems, although they operate differently. These processes are anchored in different consciousness levels – the rational in the conscious and the experiential in the nonconscious level; they are independent because they operate by different rules but are, nevertheless, highly interactive. Operating in synchrony, they usually produce compromises, but sometimes conflicts arise, commonly known as "conflicts between the heart and the head" (Epstein, 2003, p. 182).

The experiential system is developed by learning from experience and is additionally characterized by its association with affects and emotions. When a person responds to significant, emotional events, the experiential system automatically compares the new information with existing memories, and the recalled feelings influence further information processing and decision making. If the memories are positive, the individual will act to reproduce the positive emotions. If negative, the avoidance of the feelings will prioritize other behavioral tendencies. In contrast, the rational system is logical, intentional, analytic, primarily verbal, and free of emotions (Epstein et al., 1996).

According to Epstein (2003), neither of the systems is superior to the other – they only constitute different ways of processing external information, such as stimuli and perceptions. From an evolutionary perspective, the experiential system is assumed to be the older one; Epstein (2003) takes this evidence that the experiential system has already proven itself by evolution.

4.2.2.2 Tacit and deliberate system or implicit and explicit knowledge

Robin Hogarth (2001) differentiates – based on research by Seymour Epstein (1994) – between a tacit (implicit) and a deliberate (explicit) system.

Patterson and Eggleston (2017, p. 6) also distinguish between analytical and intuitive cognition and explicit and implicit knowledge (Figure 8).

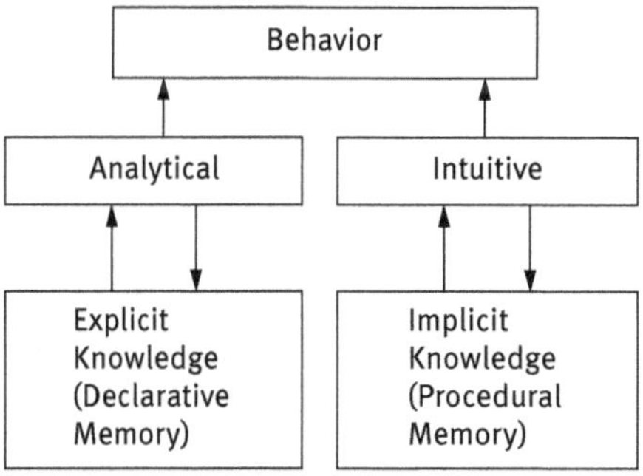

Figure 8: Depiction of two sets of cognitive processes, or two systems (i.e., analytical and intuitive), for human reasoning and decision making (Patterson & Egglestone, 2017, p. 6).

Analytical cognition involves conscious deliberation that draws on limited and slowly declarative memory resources. Intuitive cognition involves unconscious situational pattern synthesis and recognition that is unconstrained by declarative memory limitations. Intuitive cognition is independent of conscious control, large in capacity, and fast; it is particularly linked to emotions.

1. A tacit system (Hogarth, 2001, pp. 21–22; 2003, p. 7) is based on implicit and automatic information processing that is effortless, speedy, and sensitive to context. It is triggered into action by stimuli encountered in the environment. Using the tacit system means accessing implicit knowledge that is not consciously known. This unconscious knowledge can be used, but it is challenging to communicate it to another person. Thus, in many cases, people cannot explain why they know about deciding accurately or deciding in a specific way. Example: A native speaker can immediately tell whether a sentence is grammatically correct or not, but only a few can verbalize the underlying grammatical principles. Ernst (2003, p. 22) summarizes the influence of this "inner knowing" of knowing more than we (consciously) know:

> "That which I know,
> but which I do not know
> that I know,
> affects me more
> than I know."

Tacit knowledge can be equated with implicit knowledge. Implicit knowledge, acquired through experience and associative learning processes, is regularly used intuitively (Plessner et al., 2008a; Lieberman, 2000); thus, the tacit and implicit systems and knowledge are part of the intuitive system (Plessner, 2006, p. 111). Although tacit or implicit knowledge can help make quick decisions in complex and confusing situations with too little, too much, contradictory, incomprehensible, or untrustworthy data, it should be critically noted that misjudgments are still possible if "implicit knowledge and heuristics that are built up in the course of growing professional experience are wrong, but are never explicitly questioned due to a lack of awareness" (Büssing et al., 1999, p. 16).

Betsch et al. (2004) developed the "value-account model of attitude formation" as part of the implicit knowledge system. This model assumes that an individual's "subjective value experiences" are stored in a "value account" procedural memory in every human being. Specific emotional stimuli are especially value-charged; thus, particular stimuli evoke positively or negatively valued feelings or associations. If a decision is to be made, the decision-maker unconsciously uses this value or utility account. It encodes and anticipates the collected value-laden information about the consequences associated with the specific stimuli.

The "value account" represents implicit knowledge and can be retrieved with the help of the intuitive system (Plessner, 2006, p. 113).

It is well known that highly skilled, experienced, and practiced athletes, musicians, or other professionals in test-taking situations and competitions often perform automatically, supported by implicit knowledge of their procedural or implicit memory. Procedural memory is based on procedural learning or repeating an activity repeatedly until it works automatically. Procedural memory operates largely independent of declarative or explicit memory (the conscious, intentional recollection of factual information, experiences, events, etc.). It thus allows people to perform and show their competencies without a deliberate control. Intuitive impulses come from this implicit memory. Therefore, these skills become proceduralized with practice and do not require constant attention. However, highly trained professionals often perform poorly under mental pressure, for example, in a competition, examination, or other stress conditions, for example, penalty shootout or Olympic finals. The term "choking" has been used to describe this phenomenon. Choking can occur within any domain that demands a high level of performance involving complex skills. Regarding the "Self-focus theories"," the subjective feeling of pressure increases anxiety and self-consciousness about performing correctly. This, in turn, can cause increased attention to the processes directly involved in executing the specific skill. This attention to the step-by-step procedure disrupts the well-learned, automatic (proceduralized) performance. Research suggests that the more automated or intuitive a specific skill is used, the more resistant it is to distractions, performance pressure, and subsequent choking. Thus, people should not override their intuition and automated skills with conscious willpower, in specific high-pressure situations. They cannot always turn off their declarative memory, but they can try to distract it, for example, by focusing on their breathing and then performing the task automatically (Beilock, 2011; see the topic of "choking" especially Baumeister, 1984; Beilock & Carr, 2001, 2005; Beilock, 2010 and 2015).

2. The deliberate system processes information through conscious and explicitly controlled cognitive processes and requires mental effort, conscious attention, and more mental resources than the tacit system. It is based on explicit knowledge and can, therefore, be clearly coded, for example, articulated in speech, numbers, or letters, and thus be communicated and transmitted to others. In most cases, explicit knowledge can be stored in media. In addition, conscious decisions usually rely on explicit knowledge and are reflected in deliberative and thoughtful judgments.

4.2.2.3 Unconscious thought theory

Dijksterhuis (2010) developed the unconscious thought theory. This theory applies to decision-making and distinguishes between two modes of thought: unconscious and conscious. Unconscious thought and conscious thought have different characteristics, making each mode preferable under specific circumstances.

For instance, contrary to popular belief, decisions about simple issues can be better tackled by conscious thought, whereas decisions about complex matters can be better approached with unconscious thought (Dijksterhuis & Nordgren, 2006, p. 95). According to the "capacity principle," conscious thought is constrained by the low capacity of consciousness. Unconscious thought does not have this constraint because the unconscious mind has a much higher capacity. Thus, unconscious processes are very economical for our brain because our brain seeks simplicity and consumes as little energy as possible.

It follows that conscious thought, by necessity, often considers only a subset of the information it should take into account. Try to think (consciously!) about where to spend your next summer holiday, the next paper you want to write, and what to eat tonight – all at precisely the same time, please. But, of course, you cannot do this. Conscious capacity is limited; generally, consciousness cannot do more than one thing at a time.

Another example of unconscious decision-making influences is subliminal messages, for example, subliminal commercials in cinemas. We don't consciously see the images or sentences integrated into the film, but they can affect people. Thus, subliminal perception plays an essential role in intuitive processes: we see and hear something below our threshold of consciousness, process this data unconsciously (implicit cognition), and react intuitively, if necessary, for example, by suddenly stepping on the brakes in our car without knowing why, when a child suddenly appears in front of the hood. We are happy to perceive more than we think we perceive (Zeuch, 2003, pp. 42–43; 64–65).

4.2.2.4 Systems 1 and 2 or Type 1 and Type 2 mental processes

In his book *Thinking, Fast and Slow*, Daniel Kahneman summarizes his research, which he has often carried out with Amos Tversky (Kahneman, 2011 and 2012). They also distinguish in a simplified way between two kinds of mental processes. Kahneman (2011) stresses that speaking of two systems is a metaphor that describes these processes that aren't literally true but help explain this idea. Thus, one should not assume that the human cognitive system actually disintegrates into two systems. On the other hand, Pfister et al. (2017, p. 347) speak of modes in which we find ourselves mentally, either in a more automatic and unconscious mode (System 1) or in a more conscious and reflected manner (System 2), in which we think, with some attention and effort, about what is right or wrong and what is the better decision.

System 1: System 1 operates automatically, quickly, associatively, almost effortlessly, and emotionally, with no sense of voluntary control (Kahneman, 2011, p. 20). It spontaneously generates impressions and combines what is perceived from the environment, with remembered categories and previous experiences stored as unconscious or implicit knowledge. These impressions are retrieved without effort, and they are often emotionally charged. They are neither voluntary nor verbally explicit; and they are difficult to control or modify.

John Bargh (2014) points to four components of automatic processes: 1) Unawareness. There are three ways in which people may be unaware of mental processes: To be unaware of the presence of the stimulus (subliminal), how the stimulus is categorized or interpreted (the activation of, e.g., biases, stereotypes, or personality constructs), or how the stimulus effects judgments (misattribution). 2) Unintentionality: The process starts without conscious intent or will. 3) Efficiency: It requires only a few cognitive resources and is very fast. 4) Uncontrollability: The process cannot be stopped.

But Kahneman and other researchers describe the ability to control System 1 consciously by System 2.

System 1 is based on experiences, heuristics, pattern recognition, and other mental shortcuts. The human perceptual system and the intuitive and emotional operations of System 1 generate impressions of the attributes of objects of perception and thought (Kahneman, 2003, p. 699). Thus, the human visual system and associative memory are essential aspects of System 1. In System 1, impressions, associations, feelings, intentions, and preparations for action flow effortlessly and efficiently because it uses implicit knowledge and thus speeds up decision-making. As a result, System 1 helps people act fast and successfully in complex environments with a large amount of partly contradictory information.

This System 1 can be associated with intuition applied to judgments that directly reflect impressions. These intuitions – in the first step – are not modified by System 2 (Kahneman, 2003, p. 698; 2011, pp. 33–34; Riedel, 2015, pp. 52–53).

System 1 produces a constant representation of the world around us, generates continuous judgments and decisions through everyday life, and allows us to do things like walk, avoid obstacles, and contemplate something else at the same time (Kahneman et al., 2011, p. 52; Pfister et al., 2017, p. 347).

System 1 is permanently active and not intentionally activated to solve a specific decision-making problem (Kahneman, 2012, p. 33). As a result, people usually have no conscious power over experiencing certain feelings or having intuitions. After some time has passed, emotions can be relativized by conscious thoughts of System 2 and thus be reduced in their power. But intuitions and feelings cannot be prevented by thoughts. Research in neuroscience and psychological decision-making confirms these results and shows that System 2 can intervene, but it can't completely switch off the continuous working of System 1 (Pfister et al., 2017, p. 347).

Thus, it makes no sense to accuse people or quarrel when they show intuitions and emotions, for example, in selection processes. The limbic system, where emotions are primarily activated, works relatively autonomously and eludes direct cognitive control. Therefore, it is more appropriate to ask what triggered the emotional reaction and what emotional dynamics may be associated with it (Gerrig, 2015, pp. 435–448).

To understand why intuition is activated spontaneously and effortlessly under certain circumstances, Kahneman (2003) takes a look at the concept of accessibility, i.e., the ease with which certain mental contents become conscious. The accessibility of a thought is determined by the characteristics of the cognitive mechanisms that produce it and the characteristics of the stimuli that evoke it. In this respect, the emphasis on a stimulus, selective attention, specific training, associative activation, and priming can play a role (Kahneman, 2003, p. 699). Kahneman refers to a study by Klein (1998) that showed how experienced decision-makers who work under pressure rarely really choose between options since, in most cases, only one option – steered by System 1 – comes to mind.

People often react to the outside world in a way they are unaware of. These reactions are determined by habits or attitudes that are challenging to change (Schrage, 2003, p. 3). An essential part of Kahneman's approach is the so-called **W**hat-**Y**ou-**S**ee-**I**s-**A**ll-**T**here-**I**s rule (WYSIATI rule). This rule states that System 1 often draws premature conclusions from specific stimuli. According to Kahneman, System 1 includes only the already activated or available information for judgment formation and not all information stored in neuronal form. The WYSIATI rule means that only information already available at the beginning of a judgment is used to make a decision. The use of incomplete information (e.g., only emotionally positively valued information) can lead to its merging into a coherent history. Still, it can also be the reason for errors of judgment and decision (Kahneman, 2012, pp. 112–115). Finally, according to Kahneman (2012, p. 33), System 1 can be regarded as the primary problem-solving system.

System 2: System 2 is about reasoning and, thus, the rational or analytic system. It is slower, more reflective, reasonable, and logical. It "encompasses the processes of analytical intelligence" (Stanovich & West, 2000, p. 658) and "draws attention to the strenuous mental activities that rely on it, including complex calculations. The operations of System 2 often go hand in hand with the subjective experience of manual power, freedom of choice, and concentration" (Kahneman, 2011, p. 33). Thus, the logical and sequentially thinking self, the conscious decision-making system, performs complex thinking with energy expenditure, attention, concentration, and conscious control (Kahneman, 2011, p. 33; Riedel, 2015, p. 52). Thinking, in System 2, needs time because pros and cons are weighed, and evidence and alternatives are reflected before making a decision. Thus, System 2 helps people avoid mistakes but requires sustained conscious attention (Kahneman, 2012, p. 35).

Furthermore, controlled and conscious rule-based processes require cognitive effort (attention, memory capacity, willpower, energy, etc.). Thus, using System 2 consciously is exhausting because it requires cognitive resources. And sometimes, people are too sluggish or too lazy to use System 2. From the perspective of reducing effort, only the minimum necessary cognitive effort should be applied to achieve a goal. If System 1 generates a judgment that appears to correspond to the goal, this result is seen as sufficient. For example, based on a quick, automatic, and unconscious evaluation, the initial impression of an unknown person tells people whether the unknown person is trustworthy or hostile (Oosterhof & Todorov 2008), and this immediate evaluation is perceived as (subjectively) valid. Only in the case of emerging contradictory evidence do people make an effort to check their initial impression and, if necessary, correct it. Thus, conscious cognitive processes (System 2) are experienced as exhausting, while automatic and fast processes of System 1 are perceived as fluid and emotionally pleasant (Pfister et al., 2017, p. 348).

System 2 can also be described as an argumentation system (Schrage, 2003, p. 3) that, in comparison to System 1, follows the rules, constructs thoughts in an orderly series of steps, and compares alternatives based on various criteria: thus, it promotes considered, thoughtful, and reasoned decisions (Kahneman, 2012, p. 51). System 2 can also consciously search for decision-relevant information, and think statistically and logically (Kahneman, 2012, pp. 33 and 103).

System 2 focuses on the effortful mental activities that demand it, including complex communications. The operations of System 2 are often associated with the subjective experience of agency, choice, and concentration. "When we think of ourselves, we identify with System 2, the conscious, reasoning self that has beliefs, makes choices, and decides what to think about and what to do. Although System 2 believes itself to be where the action is, the automatic System 1 is the hero" (Kahneman, 2011, p. 21).

System 2 is mobilized when the stakes are high and decisions have a long-lasting and significant impact, such as business, when people detect an obvious error, or when rule-based reasoning is required. System 2 helps keep System 1 in check by preventing "foolish thoughts and inappropriate impulses from overt expression" (Kahneman, 2011, p. 415). But most of the time, System 1 determines our thoughts (Kahneman et al. 2011, p. 52).

Because System 1 operates automatically and cannot be turned off at will, errors of intuitive thought are often difficult to prevent. In addition, stereotypes, prejudices, and biases cannot always be avoided because System 2 may have no clue about the error. Even when cues to likely errors are available, errors can be prevented only by the enhanced monitoring and effortful activity of System 2.

The susceptibility to errors of System 1 becomes clear in this well-known example. A baseball bat and a ball cost $1.10 together, and the bat costs $1.00 more than the ball? How much does the ball cost?

Automatically, most people answer ten cents.

If the ball costs 10 cents and the bat costs $1.00 more than the ball, the bat would cost $1.10 for a total of $1.20. The correct answer to this problem is that the ball costs 5 cents, and the bat costs – at a dollar more – $1.05 for a grand total of $1.10. Only by consciously thinking and switching to System 2, do people get the correct solution.

System 2 is more limited than System 1, for example, the working memory capacity, which can process only a very limited number of items simultaneously, and System 1 can integrate many more items in parallel. Thus, Kahneman points out that System 2 is imperfect, mainly because of its limited capacity or because only a fraction of its capacity is engaged. "Errors are not always due to intrusive and incorrect intuitions. Often, we make mistakes because System 2 does not know any better" (Kahneman, 2011, p. 415).

Stanovich and West (2000) describe the most significant difference between the two systems in addressing a problem. The controlled processes of System 2 serve to decontextualize and depersonalize issues, by representing them in terms of rules and underlying principles. System 1, on the other hand, attempts to embed experiences in a context in a personal way, driven by subjective relevance considerations (Stanovich and West, 2000, pp. 658–659).

Although researchers accept that the distinction between the two systems is a metaphor, there is considerable agreement on the characteristics that distinguish these two types of cognitive processes. For example, Stanovich and West (2000) summarize the characteristics of the two systems in the following Figure 9 scheme (Kahneman, 2003, p. 698).

	System 1	System 2
Dual-Process Theories:		
Sloman (1996)	associative system	rule-based system
Evans (1984; 1989)	heuristic processing	analytic processing
Evans & Over (1996)	tacit thought processes	explicit thought processes
Reber (1993)	implicit cognition	explicit learning
Levinson (1995)	interactional intelligence	analytic intelligence
Epstein (1994)	experiential system	rational system
Pollock (1991)	quick and inflexible modules	intellection
Hammond (1996)	intuitive cognition	analytical cognition
Klein (1998)	recognition-primed decisions	rational choice strategy
Johnson-Laird (1983)	implicit inferences	explicit inferences
Shiffrin & Schneider (1977)	automatic processing	controlled processing
Posner & Snyder (1975)	automatic activation	conscious processing system
Properties:	associative holistic automatic relatively undemanding of cognitive capacity relatively fast acquisition by biology, exposure, and personal experience	rule-based analytic controlled demanding of cognitive capacity relatively slow acquisition by cultural and formal tuition
Task Construal	highly contextualized personalized conversational and socialized	decontextualized depersonalized asocial
Type of Intelligence Indexed:	interactional (conversational implicature)	analytic (psychometric IQ)

Figure 9: The terms for the two systems used by a variety of theorists and the properties of dual-process theories of reasoning (Stanovich & West, 2000, p. 659).

Type 1 and Type 2 processing: Referring to Evans and Stanovich (2013, pp. 224–226; see also Evans, 2010a and 2010b), Hodgkinson and Sadler-Smith (2018, p. 476) reverted from the terminology System 1 and System 2 to the older terminology of Type 1 and Type 2 processing: "These terms indicate qualitatively distinct forms of processing but allow that multiple cognitive or neural systems may underlie them."

Type 1 processing is based on intuitive processes, experienced as fast, automatic, autonomous, heuristic, holistic, or/and independent cognitive abilities.

On the other hand, Type 2 processing is a reflective process; it is limited in its capacity and more demanding in terms of cognitive processing. At the same time, the deliberative process is analytical, controlled, logical, rule-based, and thus slower (Evans & Stanovich, 2013, p. 225; Sadler-Smith, 2019, p. 7; Stanovich, 1999, p. 145).

In Type 2 processes, different modes can be applied, which are cognitively different. For example, the speed of analytical thinking can vary from the processing of rules in working memory. The effort required for this varies, depending on personality traits, and can be determined using scales such as "Need for Cognition" or "Active Open-Minded Thinking" (Evans & Stanovich, 2013, p. 229). Cohen et al. (1955, p. 291) define "Need for Cognition" as a need to structure relevant situations in a meaningful way to understand and rationally classify experiences. Accordingly, this scale measures the extent to which this cognitive processing occurs. The "Actively Open-Minded Thinking Scale" measures individual ways of thinking, such as the tendency towards flexible or open-minded or dogmatic or categorical thinking (Stanovich & West, 1997, p. 350; see also Section 4.2.9).

Two levels of control are assigned to Type 2: the algorithmic and the reflective mind. The difference between these levels is recorded when measuring individual differences in cognitive abilities and ways of thinking. Cognitive abilities are step-by-step algorithmic processes of the mind, influenced by personal differences in cognitive abilities and thinking dispositions. The individual possibilities of the reflective mind can be illustrated using rational ways of thinking. This includes whether the information is collected and whether points of view, consequences, and their advantages and disadvantages are weighed. While Type 2 can be differentiated in terms of two levels of control, Type 1 consists of only one (Figure 10).

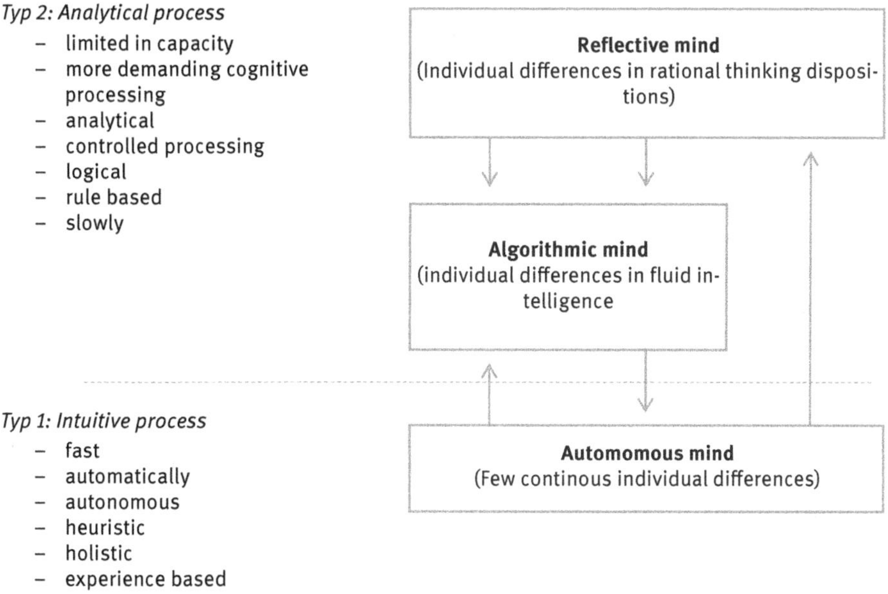

Figure 10: Summary of Type 1 and Type 2 processes (based on Evans & Stanovich, 2013, p. 230).

Nonconscious and conscious information processing: Hodgkinson and Sadler-Smith (2018, p. 476) summarize the different dualistic approaches in 1) nonconscious and 2) conscious information processes (Figure 11):

Nonconscious information processing	Conscious information processing	Source
Automatic processing	Controlled processing	Schneider & Schiffrin (1977); Schiffrin & Schneider (1984)
Heuristic	Systematic	Chaiken (1980)
Implicit inferences	Explicit inferences	Johnson-Laird (1983)
Heuristic processing	Analytical processing	Evans (1984, 1989)
Implicit/tacit	Explicit	Reber (1989, 1993)
Experiential	Rational	Epstein (1994)
Associative	Rule-based	Sloman (1996)
Intuitive cognition	Analytic cognition	Hammond (1996)
Tacit thought processes	Explicit thought processes	Evans & Over (1996)
Automatic	Intentional	Bargh & Chartrand (1999)
System 1 (TASS)	System 2 (analytic)	Stanovich (1999, 2004)
Holistic	Analytic	Nisbett, Peng, Choi, & Norenzayam (2001)
Impulsive	Reflective	Strack & Deutsch (2004)
Reflexive (X-system)	Reflective (C-system)	Lieberman, Jarcho, & Satpute (2004)
Unconscious	Conscious	Dijksterhuis & Nordgren (2006)
Old mind	New mind	Evans & Stanovich (2013)

Figure 11: Alternative Dual-Process/Dual-Systems Information Processing Nomenclatures (selected examples) (Hodgkinson & Sadler-Smith, 2018, p. 476).

4.2.2.5 System X and System C by Lieberman et al.

In social cognitive neuroscience, Lieberman (2000, 2007, 2009) differentiates between System X and System C. Because intuition is a construct that cannot be observed directly, neuroscience tries to examine the neuroanatomical or neural basis, structures, and brain areas of these automatic and controlled processes. Controlled processes (System C, named for the "c" in reflective) score high on dimensions of awareness, analysis, effort, intention, and inefficiency. Automatic processes (System X named for the "x" in reflexive) score low on at least one, preferably most of these dimensions. It's a very complex interaction of different parts of the brain, and working on different tasks are referred to as "systems"; here they are called System X (reflexive, fast, non-reflective consciousness, processes information parallel, sensitive to subliminal presentations, automatic reactions to the circumstances, feels spontaneous and intuitive, typically sensory, etc.) and System C (reflective consciousness, controlled, high arousal; outputs are experienced as self-generated and intentional, typically linguistic).

System X and System C should not be defined as opposing anchors on a number of dimensions.

> The fact that conditions promoting automaticity leads to increased activity in regions not associated with controlled processing indicates that distinct processes are being recruited. Additionally, evidence was presented suggesting that C-system activations can disrupt X-system

> activity. Thus the systems are independent in the sense that they rely on different neural structures, but they are not independent in the sense that only one of these systems is operating at a time. In most everyday experiences, it is likely that both systems are operating and contributing to ongoing thought and behavior, albeit in different ways (Lieberman, in press, p. 21).

Thus, in many cases, System X and System C are not independent and can interact in a competitive or cooperative and supplying way, and regulate behavior productively and simultaneously (Hodgkinson & Sadler-Smith, 2018, p. 482; see Section 4.2.8. for more detailed findings in the area of neuroscience and intuition).

4.2.2.6 Interaction of intuition and rational analytics

Human decision-making is regularly based on an interplay of conscious and unconscious processes and thus, on intuition and rationality. And, both intuitive and analytic processes have their specific powers (Glöckner & Towfigh, 2015, p. 272).

4.2.2.6.1 Cognitive and emotional components of intuition

Research results show that intuition can influence judgments through emotions and (subconscious) cognitions, thus comprising cognitive and emotional elements (Sinclair 2005).

Although both components have a complex interplay, intuition can be conceptualized into these two broad categories (Sinclair & Ashkanasy, 2005, p. 356).

1. **Cognitive components of intuition.** Intuition is primarily based on prior learning and experience and refers to knowledge and pattern recognition in our subconscious. It is immediate cognition without conscious rational processes and can combine various knowledge, experiences, and so on, in a parallel-interactive way.
2. **Emotional components of intuition.** Prior learning and experiences are, in most cases, emotionally charged with feelings, for example, positive or negative feelings. Perception of people, situations, and so on, activates associative networks in the brain and awakens specific memories. These memories are linked to emotions. Emotions can have an information function, such as unconscious evaluations of people, with particular characteristics, skills, or nonverbal signals. Research shows that particularly emotionally charged experiences and self-esteem-serving experiences are often better remembered than others (Sinclair & Ashkanasy, 2005, pp. 357–358; see also Section 4.2.4).

The complex interplay between unconscious cognitive and emotional components of intuition and memory scanning for similar patterns leads to judgments and decisions, which arrive rapidly by subconscious or non-conscious holistic associations (Sadler-Smith, 2008, p. 31).

Although the cognitive and emotional elements of intuition interact and phenomenally belong together, from the dual-process approach, they are conceptualized separately. On the one hand, this is intended to prevent intuition from being an umbrella term for too many different processes. But on the other hand, it should contribute to identifying appropriate tools to explore and measure the construct of intuition.

4.2.2.6.2 The interaction of System 1/Type 1 and System 2/Type 2

The question is whether and when human beings and particularly selection managers use which of the two systems (if there is always a chance to choose) and how fast and slow processes interact.

The interaction of System 1/Type 1 and System2/Type 2 is shown in the research of Kahneman and Tversky, Evans and Stanovich, Lieberman, Sadler-Smith, and so on. As long as information processing is fluid and plausible and all runs smoothly enough, System 1 is the basis for judgments, and System 2 simply accepts what System 1 sends. And often, people are not used to or willing to think intensively and therefore trust in plausible intuitive judgments that quickly come to their mind (Kahneman, 2003, p. 699).

But Kahneman advises putting intuition as far back as possible to avoid sources of error; however, there are exceptions.

The impressions, intuitions, intentions, and feelings of System 1 may be checked by System 2 and thus transformed into deliberately controlled actions. Especially, if information processing is complicated, loses fluidity and plausibility, or if there is a high conscious risk for (potential) errors, such as biases, System 2 can be activated. System 2 can then monitor, overwrite, or undo the intuitive judgments of System 1 if it has been identified as incorrect or inappropriate (Kahneman, 2003, p. 711). This is particularly the case when people know these processes and have the mental capacities, time, and motivation to question the impulses of the intuitive system and undertake deliberate processing.

But even if System 2 opposes System 1, it cannot wholly ignore System 1 because System 1 strives for coherence. If the rational analysis votes for candidate A, but the intuitive impressions say no, it would be difficult to overcome the intuition. Following our intuitions is more natural and pleasant than acting against them (Kahneman, 2011, p. 194). This is why most practitioners say: "For the final selection, the gut feeling must also fit."

System 1 assesses candidates in interview situations automatically, for example, by reading facial expressions and whether the candidate is perceived as likable or not. But if System 1 sends intuitive impulses of inconsistencies, System 2 can be mobilized. Example: In a selection interview, hiring managers "feel" that they like an applicant and that the candidate is a good team fit and emotionally convincing (System 1). But these intuitions don't match the information the selection manager took from the application documents or the personality test results.

And the reverse is also conceivable. For example, System 2 reports that the rational-analytical selection process considers a particular applicant No. 1. And then, System 1 reports discrepancies on the emotional side. Then the hiring managers may have a conflict, and it is questionable whether System 1 or System 2 will prevail. But, on the other hand, conscious thoughts from System 2 can help to understand, check and verify the intuitive impressions and vice versa. Thus, System 2 works as a justification instance, which is influenced by signals of System 1, but usually cannot completely turn off System 1 (Pfister et al., 2017, p. 347). But System 2 can also fail, for example, if it does not know any better than System 1 or take the information from System 1 without verifying it.

Research shows that the probability of correcting System 1 judgments by System 2 decreases when people react quickly or are under stress. However, it increases, for example, when managers are personally responsible for a decision or the decision is personally important to them (Alter et al., 2007, pp. 569–570).

"System 1 is the origin of much of what humans can do wrong, but it is also the origin of most of what they do right. Thus, both systems do some good, and both can fail" (Kahneman, 2011, p. 416). Good decision-making requires recognizing when System 1 or System 2, or both are the best resource in a specific decision situation.

Thus, it is not a general advice to put intuition as far back as possible in personnel selection processes. Both systems have their justification, capabilities, functions, and limitations. And in constructive interaction, both systems can reduce their weaknesses and complement their strengths.

How the analytical and intuitive processes actually operate and might precisely interact has not yet been conclusively clarified. However, according to Sadler-Smith & Hodgkinson (2016), two different ideas concerning the interaction and interrelation of these two systems have crystallized: The "default intervention" and the "parallel (competitive) model" of interaction between intuition and analytics.

4.2.2.6.3 The "parallel (competitive)" and "default-interventionist" approach

The question of how System1/Type 1 and System 2/Type 2 interact in human decisions is not yet a solved problem from a scientific perspective.

According to Evans (2007), the default-interventionist approach tries to explain the conflict between System 1/Type 1 and System 2/Type 2 processes, whereas the parallel-competitive approach addresses fundamental problems in social cognition. Therefore, both approaches offer different insights into judgment and decision-making and thus have their justification and can coexist.

The "parallel-(competitive)" approach assumes that System1/Type 1 processing and System 2/Type 2 processing proceed in parallel and compete to control thinking and behavior. Thus, each has its say, with conflicts resolved, if necessary. Both systems interact bidirectionally, and information can be exchanged in both directions.

Under many circumstances and especially for decisions of individual or organizational importance, their joint operation is synchronous, and the rational and intuitive systems integrate seamlessly, harmoniously, and synergistically (Pacini & Epstein, 1999, p. 972; Hodgkinson & Sadler-Smith (2018, p. 480).

Evans and Stanovich (2013, p. 237) criticize this approach because intuitive reactions are automatic and much faster than analytical approaches; this is consistent with research findings in neurosciences (see Section 4.2.8).

Referring to the Cognitive-experiential self-theory of Epstein, human information processing is a product of an intuitive, experiential system and an analytical-rational system. And both systems are bidirectional interactive and influence human decision-making and behaviors at the same time. The synchronous operation of both systems can lead to holistic information processing. The rational-analytical system and the intuitive system sometimes operate in conflict, manifesting as a "struggle between feelings and thoughts" (Epstein et al., 1996, p. 391; Hodgkinson & Sadler-Smith, 2018, p. 480), but they can also interact cooperatively and collaboratively.

The "default intervention" model: This approach means that intuitive impulses are quickly and effortlessly prompted to generate a default response that may be accepted or intervened upon by analytical reasoning. According to this approach, System1/Type 1 processing generates fast intuitive responses on which subsequent (slow) reflective and voluntary (controlled) Type 2 processing may or may not intervene, depending on the demands and requirements of the situation, the task at hand, and relative to the processing capacity and the knowledge and experience of the decision-maker. Here, the decision-making process takes place sequentially. First, an intuitive impulse of System1/Type 1 is triggered. This intuitive impulse may then be reflected and possibly corrected by a conscious and cognitively controlled System2/Type 2 process. System/Type 2 may intervene on the default System/Type 1 processes, depending on the demands and requirements of the situation or task at hand relative to the processing capacity of the decision-maker. But usually, System 2/Type 2 processes do not intervene to endorse, correct, or override System1/Type 1 processes; hence, errors and biases accrue (Hodgkinson & Sadler-Smith, 2018, pp. 477–478).

Pacini and Epstein (1999, p. 972) state that under most circumstances, the joint operation of System 1 and System 2 is synchronous, and the rational-analytical and intuitive systems integrate seamlessly, harmoniously, and synergistically (Hodgkinson & Sadler-Smith (2018, p. 480).

According to Evans and Stanovich (2013, p. 233), for example, the overwriting of intuitive impressions with logical conclusions becomes visible through the activation of the right prefrontal cortex, which is associated with executive control. This finding reinforces the sequential assumptions of the Default Interventionist model that intuitive decisions are made first, which may then be corrected by the rational-analytical processes, if necessary (Evans & Stanovich, 2013, p. 227; Sadler-Smith, 2019, p. 9).

However, since humans tend to save their cognitive resources, many intuitive impulses are not reflected by analytical System 2/Type 2. But decisions, especially those with a tremendous economic impact on companies or individuals, including personnel selection decisions, tend to belong to this default-interventionist type of decision-making.

Glöckner and Towfigh (2015), reviewing neuroscientific research results, state that the brain is a neuronal network of interconnected information units. Human perception never activates and recalls isolated information from the brain (or other parts of the body, e.g., enteric nervous system) but also activates associated information units. For example, if people hear the word fire brigade, the associated color red is automatically activated. At the same time, there is the principle of bidirectional activation. This is the principle of mutual and parallel activation of information units in the brain.

The interaction of conscious and unconscious processes can be simplified and described with a headlight metaphor: Unconscious processes are activated in every decision situation. One result of these unconsciously occurring processes is often a "feeling" of having to decide in a specific direction without knowing exactly how this feeling has arisen. The best possible interpretation is ad hoc and spontaneity, based on an information network. If this interpretation is sufficiently coherent with the current aspiration level, a decision is made directly. If the "coherence" is too low (or – about for legal reasons – an explicit obligation to conscious reflection), attention is paid to the problem, and in addition, conscious processes are activated. This is comparable to switching on a movable headlamp that can illuminate parts of the network. These conscious processes can be used to explore intuition and find other interpretations to check, obtain relevant information, and so on. Conscious processes (System 2) thus assume a control and correction function to counteract problems of unconscious processes (System 1) and, especially in critical situations, to reduce wrong decisions (Glöckner & Towfigh, 2015, pp. 271–272).

Each approach has its strengths and limitations; thus, Hodgkinson & Sadler-Smith (2018, p. 477) demand that researchers be clear about which particular perspective on the dual-process theory they adopt in a given piece, especially when operationalizing their empirical work.

As shown, for example, in the neuroscientific findings of Lieberman et al. (see Section 4.2.2.5), it can be concluded that both approaches, the parallel (competitive) and default-interventionist approach, have their justification. However, the appropriateness of one or the other approach depends on the respective contextual conditions (task complexity, technical, economic, or legal circumstances, time pressure, etc.) and, in particular, on the individual decision-makers and their competencies, experience, expert status, hierarchical position, cultural imprint, and so on. Thus, it is recommended to follow an integrative and holistic approach that adequately reflects the complexity, dynamic and situational dependence of human decision-making in practice, and the human brain and body.

It needs further research, for example, when do people, especially selection managers, follow more the "default-interventionist" approach" or the "parallel-competitive approach." And maybe researchers will find other approaches.

4.2.2.7 The continuum approach as criticism of the dual-system approach

Some researchers (e.g., Hammond, 1987) see both intuitions and rational-analytics as opposite poles along the same dimension (continuum; see Figure 12), where a relative contribution of each approach is determined by dispositional task factors (autonomy, job/task complexity, degree of certainty, role requirements, time pressure, hierarchical position, etc.), individual factors (personality, education, experiences, age, feelings of rightness/subjective confidence, according to intuition, preferred cognitive style, etc.) and contextual factors (organizational culture, supervisors demands, and support, etc.). Thus, using intuition in employee selection varies according to these factors (Miles & Sadler-Smith, 2014, p. 624).

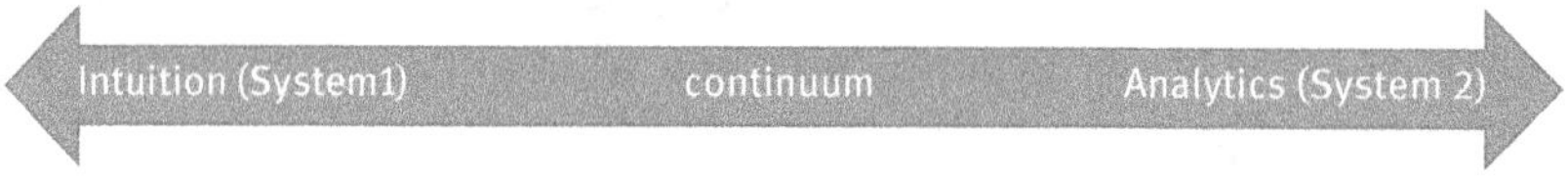

Figure 12: Continuum approach of intuition (System 1) and analytics (System 2).

Hammond et al. (1987, p. 754) or Vance et al. (2004, 2007) reject the dichotomy between intuition and analysis and show that managers need both, intuition and analytics. They need to be able to analyze problems systematically and respond to situations by their intuitions. Thus, effective managers do not have the luxury of choosing between analytic and intuitive approaches to problems.

They see intuition and analysis on a continuum that runs from purely intuitively to purely analytically. Their approach depends on the problem to solve, task characteristics and conditions, environmental contexts, available resources, the managers' knowledge, cognitive style, personality, experiences, and so on., how analysis and intuition interact, and whether people focus more on analytical effort or intuitions. Intuitions can have emotional and cognitive aspects.

Thus, if different people have to solve the same problem (e.g., hiring the best-suited candidate), in one situational context, the decision is possibly made more intuitively and in another, it may be made more analytically.

Therefore, the assumption of a continuum has a certain plausibility, mainly because people rarely decide based on the respective extremes (poles), especially when it comes to decisions that are personally important to them.

Osman (2004) questions the dual-process theory and assumes that there is only a single system of reasoning. Osman's (2004) one-system alternative is an extension of Cleeremans and Jimenez's (2002) dynamic graded continuum (DGC). This one-system approach uses a continuum of reasoning that moves from implicit to explicit (Figure 13);

the single-system framework conjectures that different types of reason arise through the graded properties of the representations utilized while reasoning and the different functional roles that consciousness has in cognition.

Figure 13: Continuum of reasoning from implicit to explicit.

But is it possible to make selection decisions solely guided by intuition or analytics? Yes, and no. It depends on the contexts, the tasks, and the decision-maker.

Betsch and Glöckner (2010) found that deliberate and analytical operations are not always necessary for making specific judgments and reaching decisions. Thus, from their perspective, some decisions could be based primarily on intuitions. "Sometimes, salient information in the environment and accessible information from memory will provide an input sample of information that suffices to reach the necessary level of coherence for a judgment or decision. This may be primarily the case for many routine decision situations that typically do not require additional information search and generation" (Betsch & Glöckner, 2010, p. 290).

But, whether selection managers (and not machines or AI as decision-makers) can make purely rational-analytical decisions, especially when selection managers and candidates have personal contact, should be questioned critically. Moreover, rational-analytical judgments are emotionally charged because humans cannot switch off their intuitive and emotional impulses in such situations (see Sections 4.2.4 and 4.2.8). Therefore, the continuum approach would fit here.

However, this view of Hammond et al. (1987) or Osman (2004) to see intuition (or System 1) and analytics (or System 2) on a continuum can also be reflected critically.

Thus, Hayes developed an integrative model of these two different modes of cognition (Figure 14).

That means, for example, depending on the contextual conditions (task, culture, the personality of the decision-maker, etc.), managers can decide purely intuitive or purely rational-analytically, or they can use a balanced decision-making process by being quasi intuitive, quasi rational-analytical, or adaptive. But Malewska (2015, pp. 101–104) found in her study that most managers adapt to the quasi-rational decision-making approach, which is characterized by the predominance of the rational-analytical approach. The second most used decision-making approach was the adaptive one, but decision-makers rarely used the "pure" analytical or intuitive approach.

But also, this approach should be reflected critically because, especially in personnel selection, it is possible to use purely analytical and additionally purely

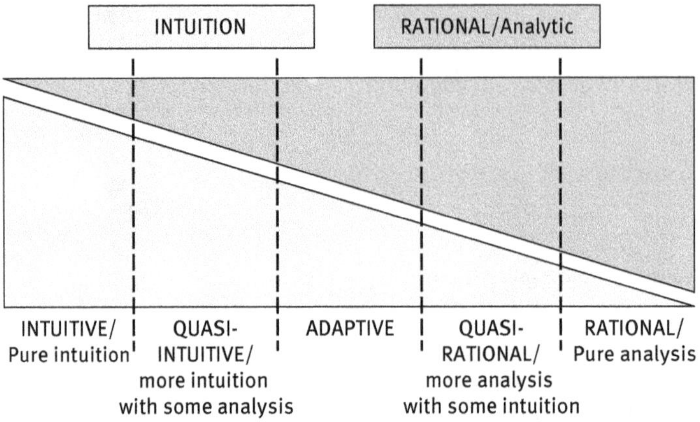

Figure 14: Modes of cognition according to the cognitive continuum theory (Hammond, 2000; Hayes et al., 2003 Malewska, 2015, p. 101).

intuitive decision-making processes. And as a result, the decision is based on a complementary integration of intuition and analytics. The corresponding new theoretical approach for personnel selection is further elaborated in Sections 10.6.1 and 10.6.2.

Sadler-Smith (2019, p. 19) states:

> The ongoing debate regarding whether intuitive and analytical styles should be conceptualized and measured as a single (unitary) bipolar dimension or as two (dual) separate unipolar scales have reached a satisfactory resolution of late. A meta-analytical study by Wang, Highhouse, Lake, Peterson, and Rada (2017) reviewed the evidence relating to the inherent incompatibility of the unitary and dual models. From a database of 80 studies (N = 27,501), Wang et al.'s (2017) analyses showed that intuition and analysis are uncorrelated; their meta-analysis thereby supported the dual model. Thus, based on theoretical arguments and an impressive weight of empirical evidence, it is incontrovertible that intuition and analysis should be viewed conceptually and psychometrically as independent constructs.

In conclusion, personnel selection decisions can be based on high intuition and high analytics. The two processes are explicitly not mutually exclusive. This dichotomy cannot be consistently mapped onto a continuum if only one score may be registered.

Intuitive and analytical styles must not be conceptualized and measured as a single (unitary) bipolar dimension or as two (dual) separate unipolar scales. It is also possible to make decisions, such as personnel selection, by relying on intuitive thinking patterns and simultaneously on analytical results. Thus, decision-making can combine both, high levels of analytics and high levels of intuition in their thinking and judging. Thus, an integrative approach is presented in Section 10.6.2.1, Figure 21, page 483 (overlapping interactions of analytics and intuition).

4.2.3 Heuristics and intuition

Kruglanski and Gigerenzer (2011) criticize the two-system approach and see no clear separation between intuitive and analytical decision-making processes. Instead, they try to overcome these – in their perspective – imprecise dualisms and call for more precise models to describe the decision-making processes. They plea for heuristics, mainly because, due to their research results, deliberate judgments are generally not more accurate than intuitive judgments and because the accuracy of judgments depends on the match between the rule and the environment.

> A popular distinction in cognitive and social psychology has been between *intuitive and deliberate judgments*. This juxtaposition has aligned in dual-process theories of reasoning associative, unconscious, effortless, heuristic, and suboptimal processes (assumed to foster intuitive judgments) versus rule-based, conscious, effortful, analytic, and rational processes (assumed to characterize deliberate judgments). In contrast, we provide convergent arguments and evidence for a unified theoretical approach to both intuitive and deliberative judgments. . . . It is time to move beyond imprecise dualisms and toward specific models of the judgmental process such as models of heuristic inference rules, their building blocks, and their adaptations to task environments that humans confront (Kruglanski & Gigerenzer 2011, pp. 97 and 106).

4.2.3.1 Heuristics as a basis for judgments and decision-making in personnel selection

Since humans do not have unlimited resources, they have developed simple strategies to achieve the best possible result with the limited resources available (Marewski et al., 2010, p. 105). Thus, human judgments are often based on quick, simple rules of thumb, so-called heuristics, and not on formal rational-analytical methods (Gerrig, 2015, p. 322).

Heuristic is a word from the Greek, meaning “serving to find out or discover.” Heuristics are mental shortcuts using straightforward decision-making strategies that are derived from previous experiences with similar problems in similar circumstances. Heuristics are simplifying procedures or rules for information search and decision-making, and rely on a subset of available information. Thus, heuristics is the art of using limited information (e.g., under time pressure) to get practical and pragmatic solutions.

The heuristic approach emphasizes effort reduction and selective information processing. Heuristics substantially reduce cognitive effort because they do not consider all information; instead, they compare alternatives on the most critical dimensions. If they differ, choose the best and terminate further information search (Betsch & Glöckner, 2010, p. 279).

Especially the economist and Nobel Prize winner David Kahneman (together with his colleague Amos Tversky) and the psychologist Gigerenzer have dealt intensively with heuristics in decision-making processes and have developed partly contradictory and also complimentary research results.

Gigerenzer and Gaismaier (2011) define a heuristic as a strategy that ignores part of the information, intending to make decisions more quickly, frugally, and/or accurately than more complex methods. Thus, making decisions based on heuristics is consistent with the human aspiration of effort reduction. The way of thinking and deciding with limited knowledge, incomplete information, and little time to get good, quick solutions through specific rules of thumb is an art. This makes the process of reaching a decision less complex (Gigerenzer & Gaissmaier, 2011, p. 454).

The counter design to the model of Homo Economicus can be called Homo Heuristicus. "Homo heuristicus has a biased mind and ignores part of the available information, yet a biased mind can handle uncertainty more efficiently and robustly than an unbiased mind relying on more resource-intensive and general-purpose processing strategies" (Gigerenzer & Brighton, p. 107). Gigerenzer (2008a, p. 48) writes good intuitions ignore information; thus, intuitions and implicit processes, emotions, and heuristics are not "incidents" in the behavior of otherwise rational individuals but integral components of a functioning human organism.

Heuristics allow focusing on few relevant information and ignoring other data. In a world of limited and selective perception, limited cognitive information processing and reception, as well as limited access to decision-relevant knowledge, it is impossible to make a perfect decision.

These findings by Gigerenzer are comparable to Simon (1955), who assumes limited rationality and that people are happy with satisfactory results. Also, heuristics pursue the goal of satisfaction (Simon, 1955, p. 106) instead of maximization, that is, find a solution that seems just good enough instead of investing a lot of resources to identify the optimal solution to a problem (Gigerenzer & Brighton, 2009, p. 108). Thus, people who use heuristics accept more or less uncertain probability statements.

People who always want to make the best possible choice and strive for the maximum or perfectionism show less life satisfaction and self-esteem than satisficers (Gigerenzer, 2008b, pp. 14–15).

Whether a heuristic works or not depends on the given environment. Because optimal strategies often represent an unattainable ideal in complex realities, simple and fast decision-making rules are necessary. As a practical method, heuristics can speed up finding a satisfactory solution; thus, they do not guarantee optimal or perfect decisions, but they are sufficient in many decision situations to reach the goals (Gigerenzer & Gaissmaier, 2011, p. 456).

Heuristics can never solve all decision problems, but those to which they are adapted. And, crucial is adapting to the specific environment, particularly the informational environment, i.e., what information is available. A valuable heuristic for selecting a doctor will differ from a heuristic used to find a new partner or select a new employee or supplier. The complexity of the environment does not necessarily mean the complexity of the heuristic.

Using heuristics meets people's need to reduce the effort associated with decision-making processes (Shah & Oppenheimer, 2008, p. 207), but this may be at the expense of decision-making accuracy. The search for information for a considered decision takes time and effort, whereas heuristics exchange a specific loss of accuracy for a faster and more economical decision. This happens either because the decision is not significant enough to justify using many resources or because the limitation of existing cognitive capacities prevents rational decision-making (Gigerenzer & Gaissmaier, 2011, p. 457). The phenomenon of using energy expenditure as a function of perceived benefit is evident in every human brain. Only when the brain considers an action as "economical," is it brought about (Spitzer, 2004, p. 262).

Thus, to save energy and make quick decisions, the human mind makes heuristics judgments.

As well as intuitions, heuristics also exploit fundamental capabilities of the human cognitive system. Evolution has endowed humans with perceptual, learning, or memory abilities as fundamentals to survival. And one of these capabilities is to develop and use heuristics. Adapted to specific environments, heuristics often work more effectively and lead to better results than a complex optimization rule or a complex rational analysis (Pfister et al., 2017, pp. 353–355; Gigerenzer & Brighton, 2009).

Although heuristics are not necessarily systematic and orderly, humans develop an adaptive toolbox as a collection of fast and economic heuristics that mostly allow correct but not perfect or optimal judgments in complex situations. Examples of heuristics are "trial and error," "always move to the goal," "random search," "means-end analysis" (a problem is broken into sub-problems), diversification of financial assets, and preference for the familiar in selection processes.

A large body of research shows that many professionals, such as judges (Dhami & Ayton, 2001), physicians, and managers, use heuristics to make decisions. Gilovich & Griffin (2002, p. 1) conclude that the concept of heuristics revolutionized many research fields on judgment and decision-making, for example, in politics, medicine, economics, law, and business administration.

In selection processes, the use of heuristics means to stop searching for information if, for example, selection managers think they already have enough knowledge about an applicant to make a decision; or because they think they have already experienced a similar situation and can draw on their experiential knowledge; or because they do not realize the complexity of the process. Heuristic decisions are mainly made when

- not all information is available at all times, or too much information can be retrieved,
- not all information is cognitively retrievable, or part of the information is ignored,

- there is a high pressure to act, for example, due to lack of resources, such as cognitive capacity, time, and money, or due to uncertainty,
- comprehensive information is not required (e.g., experts base their decisions on their experiences).

Heuristic decisions lead to
- limited absorption of the amount of information,
- a limited perception,
- a selection of information under consideration of individual preferences, attitudes, experiences, and values (Auer, 2016, pp. 139–140).

According to Gigerenzer (2008a, pp. 58–59), rules of thumb or heuristics cannot explain human behavior in the same way as personality traits. This is because heuristics, as rules of thumb, are anchored not only in the brain but also in the environment. He uses an adaptive approach, which tries to explain human decisions and behavior situationally from the respective environmental conditions. The assumption that people's behavior can be explained by stable personality traits alone neglects the adaptive competence of humans. In real life, there is no one strategy for making the best decisions in all circumstances; therefore, certain heuristics are only valid in specific environments.

Heuristics are guidelines that contain specific decision-making rules; thus, many kinds of heuristics can be differentiated. In the following, some examples of heuristics are described (Pfister et al., 2017, p. 356).

Representativeness heuristic: In some cases, people might base judgments mainly on the representativeness of an object for a specific category (Tversky & Kahneman, 1974, p. 1124). The representative heuristic is a judgment rule in which the probability of a specific result is estimated by one of two features. This heuristic guides people to judge outcomes as likely if they represent what is being judged. This means making decisions based on what appears familiar or representative, for example, age, university someone has studied, sports, and math grade. And this can lead to stereotypes, for example, people might assume that someone who plays football or basketball in a team is a good team player, or someone who plays tennis cannot be a good team player; or that all Germans are tidy and plan precisely. Or if an applicant unconsciously looks similar to another successful manager, or if selection managers recognize behavioral and thought patterns in the applicant that correspond to their experiences, the candidate will most likely be assessed positively in terms of competencies.

Availability or fluency heuristic: Availability or fluency heuristics is based on how easy it is to bring something to mind. In other words, we often rely on how easy it is to think of examples when making a decision or judgment. In this heuristic, people estimate the probability or likelihood of a result based on how easily an example can be remembered. It's a mental shortcut that relies on immediate examples from a selection manager's mind when assessing a candidate. These heuristics are based on personal knowledge and experience but can also be shared between different selection managers and made collectively available. Thus, specific experiences can be particularly present in these processes and thus, overestimated or underestimated. There are many situations in which the availability heuristic is valuable and accurate. For example, it's part of what makes us careful in specific situations. Suppose we can think of a similar situation with an applicant with the same background that ended badly for the company and us. In that case, we are more likely to be cautious and protect ourselves better.

The problem with the availability heuristic is that we assume that if several examples are readily available in our minds, the event or subject matter is commonplace. But the underlying assumption is not always correct.

Recognition heuristics: A quick and economical way of choosing between two alternatives; if one of two objects, experiences, patterns, and so on, is recognized and the other is not, then the recognized is valued higher and determines the decision. In this "ignorance-based" decision-making process, people rely on one cue and ignore others, such as contradicting cues (see, e.g., confirmation bias).

Take-the-best heuristic: This decision-making strategy relies on the first helpful information that people find or the best cue available and ignores the rest (e.g., one-reason decision). Thus, it can be seen as a part of the recognition heuristics. For example, an applicant is selected because s/he has the best score on one specific selection criterion, for example, years of leadership experiences, graduation from a well-known university, or because s/he has a higher score on a numerical selection criterion, for example, school grade in mathematics.

Affect heuristics: Affect heuristics as mental shortcuts mean that people base their judgments and decision-making on current and automatic feelings (e.g., intuitive feelings of fear or happiness). Affect heuristic refers to how people let their likes and dislikes or their attitudes determine their beliefs about reality and the accuracy of information and arguments. Affect means a feeling of goodness or badness associated with a specific stimulus from applicants' particular verbal or nonverbal behaviors (Sadler-Smith, 2019, p. 4). Thus, reliance on feelings is an example of affect heuristics.

Cut-off or "killer" heuristics: Based on experience or personal preferences, selection managers formulate, for example, specific cut-off or "killer" heuristics as "must-have" requirements (e.g., final grade in or duration of studies) or certain cut-off grades for specific requirements (see Section 3.2.3.3).

Tit-for-tat heuristic: Behave toward others as they behave toward you.

Tallying heuristic: Count the number of positive cues and choose the alternative with the largest sum.

Imitation heuristic: Decide and behave as the majority do or as an authority figure (e.g., an expert, hierarchically higher ranked persons such as superior, head of HR), and so on does.

Fast and frugal heuristics: These heuristics require little information because a minimum of information (see take-the-best-heuristics or one-reason decision-making) is often sufficient for a good decision (less-is-more effect). According to Gigerenzer (2008a, p. 145), these "fast and frugal" heuristics reveal that simple one-reason decision-making often comes to good results. For selection managers, it may be "ecologically rational" to rely on a fast and frugal heuristic in domains where there is a positive correlation between the used heuristics and the specific criterion, for example, between the use of affect heuristics and the criterion job performance. The higher the validity of a specific heuristic for a given criterion, such as job performance, the more ecologically rational it is to rely on this heuristic, and the more likely hiring managers will rely on it. Gigerenzer and Todd (1999, p. 7) see these fast and frugal heuristics as "good intuitions."

Heuristics, decision trees, and algorithm: Results of heuristics are also found in decision trees where people use a tree as a flowchart structure to go from observations or "tests" about an item to conclusions about the next item. Building a decision tree is quite complex as the volume of data in databases grows. And a further problem is to find the correct splitting criterion to be efficient and get good results.

Usually, heuristics are unconscious and informal, but they can be brought to the level of consciousness (Gigerenzer, 2008a, p. 56). To raise implicit knowledge and thus bring implicit processes to the conscious level, an attempt can be made to reflect on and describe heuristically occurring processes and thus make them explicit and transparent for others. Examples are decision trees or algorithms that support quick decisions in many practical contexts, for example, medical diagnoses or legal regulations.

Using specific heuristics and rules depends on a very individual catalog of subjective preferences, attitudes, values, and experiences. And notably, the heuristic must fit the environment. But to distinguish heuristics from purely subjective guessing, people learn in specific environments to think and approach problems in a particular way. In doing so, they also discover regularities, patterns of success, success rules of decision-making, and so on.

Researchers and practitioners try to develop heuristics based on statistical connections, correlations, or even causalities from existing data and to derive decisions and behavioral recommendations from them, for example, matching processes between specific job requirements of an organization and competencies of applicants on professional networking websites such as LinkedIn.

Building an efficient decision tree is also a tool in Machine Learning (see Section 8.1 and 8.2), for example, developing an algorithm in personnel selection heuristically. Decision trees and algorithms provide systematic and orderly procedures that exemplify how heuristics can be transparent and remediated into awareness and consciousness (Wegwarth et al., 2009). Moreover, they are teachable and trainable and, thus, also can be learned and adopted by others; later, they can be executed unconsciously through frequent repetition.

Heuristics and decision fatigue: People make a multitude of decisions every day. If they have to think about these decisions consciously, this consumes mental resources. Thus, minds are made up sooner than many people think. Far from carefully weighing all possible information, people draw fast conclusions. They categorize people or information quickly as good or bad, suitable or unsuitable, a welcome adaptation that enables action and reduces information overload. Although people think they want as much information as possible for a decision, research shows that although they could get more information, they stop the information process, form a conclusion very soon, and decide quickly. People are less open to comprehensive information than it would be helpful to make holistically considered decisions (Klein & O'Brien, 2018). In a selection process, recruiters may shorten the information process because they have already developed a judgment. As shown in Sections 3.2.4 and 3.6.2, the interview might be shortened or ended quickly without an interview guideline.

The economists Hirshleifer et al. (2019) have discovered something they call "decision fatigue." From their perspective, one could say that our brain functions like a muscle: The more decisions of the same kind that people make, the more exhausted they become and the more they resort to simple solutions. A consequence is that decision quality declines after an extensive session of decision-making. So the more we have to decide, the less we make efforts and increasingly rely on simple rules of thumb. However, the researchers have also made clear that it is not the physical exhaustion of the decision-makers that inevitably occur over the day but the number of decisions taken that causes these results. So, physical fatigue is not crucial, but decision fatigue is. For personnel selection decisions, this means limiting the number of selection decisions per day to a few, if the same care and the same opportunities are to be guaranteed in each selection process.

Criticism of heuristics as a basis for intuitive decisions: Heuristics are neither, per se, good or bad nor rational or irrational; rather, they depend on the context at hand so that they can be valuable decision-making tools in certain situations. With sufficient experience, people learn to select useful heuristics from their adaptive toolbox (Gigerenzer & Gaissmaier, 2011, p. 474). Thus, heuristics are extremely helpful in many cases, especially when a decision needs to be made quickly. Heuristics also allow for simplifying decisions by classifying people and objects, and making generalizations (Tversky, 1977, p. 327).

Heuristics help make quick decisions but can also lead to errors like stereotyping. Kahneman and Tversky (1973) state that heuristics can be based on data of limited validity; thus, representativeness, availability, or affect heuristics can lead to systematic errors and biases or to "cognitive illusions" such as "illusion of correlations" (between a specific heuristic and the criterion such as job performance).

A further problem is reducing complexity by using heuristics, which is inappropriate, for example, in selection processes (Auer, 2016, p. 73). Heuristics are, in many cases, "simplifications of analytic thought. . . . They cope with cognitive limitations by leaving out effortful information process, reducing the amount of information considered or, in short, by reducing complex judgments to simpler ones" (Betsch & Glöckner, 2010, p. 279; see also Tversky & Kahneman, 1973, p. 207).

Intuition and heuristics: How intuitions and heuristics are related and whether intuitions are also heuristics, and vice versa, is viewed very differently in the scientific community. It depends, however, strongly on how heuristics are defined and what is subsumed under the term heuristics.

Kahneman differentiates between two types of intuition: Accurate intuitions are based on practice and internalized experience. Inaccurate intuitions are based on "gut feel." Intuitions that are based on experiences can be effects of using heuristics (Kahneman, 2011, p. 11). Thus, many heuristics have their source in people's experiences and share a basis in experience with "accurate intuitions" (Howard, 2014, p. 63).

But often, some heuristics are employed at conscious awareness (e.g., decision trees as heuristics).

Thus, Gigerenzer and Gaissmaier (2011, pp. 451 and 474) state that heuristics can be conscious or unconscious cognitive processes; usually, the same heuristic can be used, both consciously and unconsciously.

Tabesh and Vera (2020, p. 8) stated that intuition differs from many kinds of heuristics because "intuition involves subconscious processing of verbalized and nonverbalized information, whereas (some kinds of, J. D.) heuristics are grounded in explicitly pre-specified rules . . . Furthermore, heuristics are typically invoked (i.e., deliberately and intentionally applied) in familiar situations."

For Betsch and Glöckner (2010, p. 279), heuristics seem to simplify analytic thoughts, and they doubt whether heuristics actually cover the potential of intuitions. They cope with cognitive limitations by leaving out effortful information processes, reducing the amount of information considered, or reducing complex judgments to simpler ones. Thus, their conviction is that intuition is much more than simply reducing task complexity.

Dane and Pratt (2007, p. 43) explain the difference between intuition and heuristics with the different schemes or patterns used. Intuition is the process of calling up complex and specifically relevant memory patterns for the decision field, which leads to an effective and intuitively made decision. This leads to an experience-based reduction of complexity. Specific memory patterns develop over years of experience from a network of different types of knowledge. On the other hand, heuristics are rather characterized by using simple patterns. Accordingly, a generally and not always valid complexity reduction occurs while using heuristics. Thus, decisions based on heuristics are subject to the risk of losing effectiveness and accuracy.

Since intuition also includes some kinds of heuristics in decision-making processes, these heuristics are not free of unconscious biases (Dane & Pratt, 2007, p. 42).

Heuristics can be correct and simplify a person's everyday life, but they can also be wrong due to unconscious biases or because a specific heuristic does not work in a particular context (Pfister et al., 2017, pp. 132–133, 352).

On the one hand, heuristics can run unconsciously and intuitively by using implicit knowledge (fast and frugal heuristics as intuitive heuristics; see Pfister et al., 2017, p. 351), while on the other hand, they can lead to consciously controlled decisions (conscious heuristics, e.g., decision trees heuristics). Because intuitions are always based on unconscious processes, not every heuristic is an intuition. Thus, heuristic and intuitive decision-making should not be equated.

4.2.4 Emotions and intuition

Since the Enlightenment, rationality and reason have been regarded as the most desirable goal, especially in the working context or in science (of the Western world) (Fröse et al., 2015b, p. 4). The prevailing principle of homo economicus was pursued in economics, representing man as the essence of reason, who oriented his behavior exclusively to reason (Doppler & Voigt, 2018, p. 28). In this thought model, feelings and emotions are "obstructive disruptive factors that impair performance and to which one should not pay too much attention" (Doppler & Voigt, 2018, p. 28). The power of emotions makes humans often throw all reason overboard, leading to behaviors that people regret afterward.

Conscious thought and reason are often blunt and useless weapons against a strong feeling. Therefore, it is essential to look at emotions as factors causing human behaviors.

Emotions are essential aspects of human nature and represent a significant part of evolutionary-biological and cultural heritage; they sensitize people to social life's interesting features that are crucial regulators of human social and interpersonal behavior. They regulate the flow of information and the selection of response processes or outputs on the organism (Izard 2002, pp. 796–797).

According to Davidson (1994, p. 52) or Virlics (2013), human decision-making and behaviors are primarily modulated and influenced by emotions. Virlics (2013) shows the effects of emotions on economic decision-making and that the decision-making process is much more complex than previously thought; thus, she used an interdisciplinary approach by incorporating the research results of many sciences. However, the fact that emotions and reason are inextricably linked and together control a person's behavior and interactions, also in the work context, has been scientifically investigated in greater depth in recent decades (Weiss & Cropanzano, 1996; Ashkanasy & Dorris, 2017, pp. 71–73).

It is striking that emotions as a factor that influence human decision-making are receiving increasing attention in theory and practice. Thus, Barsade et al. (2003, p. 3) talk of the "Affective Revolution." Research shows that in selection processes, emotional judgments influence decision-making (Jenkins, 1986, p. 61; Fox & Spector, 2000, p. 204; Robertson & Smith, 2001, p. 454; Ashkanasy et al., 2017, p. 25).

Although emotions have been a central field of research in various scientific disciplines for many years, there is, so far, no conceptual and substantive agreement on what the term denotes explicitly. According to LeDoux (1996, p. 23), "everyone knows what it is until they are asked to define it." Thus, there is no generally accepted definition of the term emotion. However, without a consensual conceptualization of what exactly constitutes emotion and what phenomenon should be specifically studied and researched, progress in theory and research will be challenging to achieve (Scherer, 2004, p. 695; Scherer, 2015).

4.2.4.1 Emotions as a component of intuition

Intuitions are insights based on implicit knowledge, prior (learning) experiences, pattern recognition, and emotions. Knowledge, experiences, or specific patterns are (primarily) stored in our brains and linked to (positive or negative) emotions.

While intuitions are learned, emotions have both an evolutionary origin and a cultural component, especially as emotions relate to culturally specific expression and evaluation of emotions (see Section 4.2.4.5). While intuitions are often nonspecific and difficult to describe and explain, emotional experiences can be concrete (Engelen, 2010, p. 131).

Hogarth (2010, p. 344) states that the meaning of emotions and feelings is central in intuitive decision-making. Intuitions are regularly, but not always, emotionally charged, and intuition is often experienced as a "feeling of knowing."

There has been a growing appreciation of how emotional states affect judgmental outputs. Thus, many scientists have explicitly discussed the role of emotions in intuitive judgments (Damasio, 1995; LeDoux, 1996; Zajonc, 1980). In some cases, intuitive judgments are simply emotional reactions. In other cases, emotion acts as "intuitive moderators" that partly affect judgments.

Glöckner and Witteman (2010a, p. 13) state "that intuitive processes are closely related to the processing of affective information," and Sinclair & Ashkanasy (2005, p. 356) confirm that "intuitive perceptions are frequently accompanied by emotion." It is emphasized that feelings play an essential role in associative intuition because they are often used as a signal to approach or avoid a stimulus, reflecting (implicit) learning experiences. But in routine models, however, affect regularly plays no role, and learning experiences just activate an option that comes to mind when confronted with a decision task (Glöckner & Witteman, 2010a, p. 13). Thus, not in every decision, but in many decisions that are based on intuition, emotions play a significant role.

Emotions are conceptualized by Frijda (1986) as the experience of a form of biological response to environmental stimulus, resulting in physical and psychological changes and the subsequent readiness for action. Such emotions are characterized by neurophysiological, emotional, and behavioral changes, and serve as signaling mechanisms to adapt human behavior to environmental circumstances (Ashkanasy & Dorris, 2017, p. 68).

Emotions as psychoneural and hormonal processes, as a rule, have a substantial temporary influence on human mental processes, including perception, attention, learning, memory, reasoning, and decision-making. Emotions generate cognitive processes such as emotionally relevant attention and strongly influence the selectivity of attention and what and how something is remembered (Höft & Kersting, 2018, p. 56). They also facilitate encoding information and help in the retrieval of information efficiently. Furthermore, emotion enhances the human ability to form vivid memories (Hu et al., 2007, 160), and humans see things that are emotionally arousing more clearly than those that are more mundane. People are more likely to remember events that arouse their emotions (Robertson, 2019, p. 17). Thus, a key to remembering anything for a long time is to create an intense emotional stimulus. This special significance of feelings becomes very clear in the following quotation by Maya Angelou: "People will forget what you said. But people will never forget how you made them feel."

Human emotions comprise complex interactions of subjective feelings as well as physiological (e.g., neural or hormonal) and behavioral responses that are especially triggered by external stimuli, which are subjectively perceived as personally significant. Thus, from a psychological perspective, emotions can be understood as a brief, stimulus-dependent experience of stimuli (bodily and sensory sensations), accompanied by motivation, expression, and often cognition (Lammers, 2011, p. 29).

While moods can last for hours, emotions last from seconds to minutes. This is why it's typically easier to identify emotional triggers than the triggers for our moods.

Thus, according to Ekman and Davidson (1994), the difference between emotion and mood lies in primarily five factors: Variations in duration, provocation, modulation, facial expression, and awareness of a cause. While a short and intense surge of emotion, for example, a choleric tantrum or acting on an impulse of rage, anger, or wrath (feeling and acting in the heat of the moment), is more of a short affect, joy can be described as a feeling. Gratitude or dejection would then be more of a mood. Moods also don't have unique facial expressions, whereas universal basic emotions do.

There are emotional-cognitive interactions in the various brain regions and other body parts that are intimately involved in emotion and memory systems (Tyng et al., 2017, 1–2).

> Emotion is a complex set of interactions among subjective and objective factors, mediated by neural/hormonal systems, which can (a) give rise to affective experiences such as feelings of arousal, pleasure/displeasure; (b) generate cognitive processes such as emotionally relevant perceptual effects, appraisals, labeling processes; (c) activate widespread physiological adjustments to the arousing conditions; and (d) lead to behaviour that is often, but not always, expressive, goal directed, and adaptive (Kleinginna & Kleinginna, 1981, p. 355).

Emotions have an information function and allow attention to be focused on specific aspects and ignore others. They influence the ability of a human to evaluate and assess other people. Thus, they signal whether a particular situation or person is perceived as pleasant or unpleasant. Humans tend to prefer situations that are subjectively as pleasant as possible (Pfister et al., 2017, pp. 301–302).

The experience and perception of emotions have essential functions for humans. Besides the evolutionary biological perspective, according to which it can be assumed that emotions mainly have an adaptive function that ensures the survival and reproductive success of humans (Brandstätter et al., 2018, p. 170; according to this evolutionary-biological or Darwinian approach, emotions have a survival function), emotions can also be understood as genetically anchored statements about events, persons, or the given environment (Schneider, 2018, p. 408).

Therefore, their function is to evaluate a situation concerning its relevance and consequences for the needs, desires, and values of the experiencing person (Scherer & Moors, 2019, p. 721). As part of this evaluation, the stimulus is first tested for its familiarity and valence in the memory of the experiencer, and then evaluated and categorized according to the result of this test (Weiss & Cropanzano, 1996, p. 33). In a second step, the stimulus is analyzed concerning its significance for the experiencer, interpreted, and transformed into concrete emotional responses (Weiss & Cropanzano, 1996, p. 33). In this way, emotions fulfill both, a behavior-preparing and a behavior-controlling function (Scherer & Moors, 2019, p. 721). Furthermore, emotions have a communicative function and inform other individuals about evaluating a stimulus through expressive reactions (Brandstätter et al., 2018, p. 170).

The words emotion and feeling are often used interchangeably but are they actually the same thing, or what is the difference between emotions and feelings? From the definitions presented, emotions consist of a three-component reaction triad (Frijda, 1996, p. 206; Weiss & Cropanzano, 1996, p. 17; Brandstätter et al., 2018, p. 168; Betsch et al., 2011, p. 124), and one of the three components of emotions are feelings:

1. Physiological and neurological components (at first hormonal and neuronal reactions of the body which lead to and are expressed in bodily reactions, for example, an increased heart rate, changed skin temperature, and sweat production)

2. Subjective experience or feeling component (the affective experience of an emotion and expressed bodily reactions, e.g., positive or negative feelings). Thus, feelings are consciously experienced emotions)
3. Behavioral component (verbal and nonverbal reactions, including mimic expressions such as laughing or crying, fearful facial expression, the motor reaction of the locomotor system, running away as an escape impulse, etc.)

Depending on the individual situation, emotions can be functional or dysfunctional; they can point out dangers or lead to distortions of perception and misjudgments.

Apelojg (2010, p. 186) shows that the success of personnel selection cannot be reduced to matching the job requirements and the candidate's profile. Instead, in the practice of personnel selection, the
- experience of personnel selection as an emotional process,
- the critical-constructive examination and reflection of one's feelings,
- the goal-oriented integration into personnel selection and
- a personal strategy to cope with emotions

play a huge role that should not be underestimated. Thus, there should be an awareness of the emotional and, especially, the feeling dimensions of selecting people.

The managers interviewed in our empirical research emphasize that they can hardly separate intuitions and emotions in their practice. Especially, in personnel selection interviews, where it is a matter of getting to know each other, intuitions and emotions cannot be left out since gestures, facial expressions, and voice underpin what is communicated on the factual level (Reichelt, 2020, p. 61).

The importance of emotions or feelings in the personnel selection process is made very clear by the following quote by a hiring manager who was interviewed:

> It is what I feel, what happens between the applicant and me as the hiring manager, what I cannot put into words, into deeds, but where I believe that something is being triggered or I can move something without being able to measure, justify or explain it. Only my feeling tells me that this judgment and decision I am making right now or this way of acting is the right one (Reichelt, 2020, p. 87).

To deal competently with such topics, hiring managers need emotional skills, which should play a significant role in the selection and development of Human Resources managers.

On the one hand, emotions can hold you captive, force, drive, or unsettle you.

But they can also give support, enrich, support, and direct. They are certainly always an integral part of personnel selection decisions by people. When people choose other people, the emerging emotions should not only be seen as possibly disturbing factors and sources of error but also as possible messages that should be dealt with constructively. Selection decisions are closely linked to one's personality and feelings; personnel selection is a highly complex process in which competent emotions can lead to qualitatively improved results (Apelojg, 2010, pp. 199–202).

Apart from the fact that people cannot simply turn off their feelings, there is the risk that people will build up an inner wall and possibly reduce and even lose contact with their emotional world with a purely rational-analytical procedure. They thus cut themselves off from significant inner sources of knowledge.

As described in Section 4.2.2.4, System 1 also stands for emotional processes because intuitions and the "operations of System 1 are typically . . . often emotionally charged" (Kahneman (2003, p. 698). Thus the concept of intuition is associated with feelings and emotions in decision-making. Or Tilman Betsch (2008, p. 4) in his definition of intuition: "The output of the process is a feeling that can serve as a basis for judgments and decisions." And Dane & Pratt (2007, p. 33) note that intuitions are "affectively charged judgments."

Sadler-Smith (2010, pp. 18–21) states that the intuitive mind speaks in the language of feelings:

> The feelings that come with intuition can be so powerful as to convince us that an intuitive judgment is valid and correct even if we can't explain why ("intuitions are sometimes wrong, but never in doubt"). As a result intuitive judgments usually fall into two groups:
> 1. Compelling and accurate, and it would be very convenient if this were to be the case 100% of the time, sadly life isn't like that.
> 2. Compelling and inaccurate, and therefore an invaluable skill is to be able to weed out inaccurate and feeble intuitions from those intuitions that have something potentially useful to say to us. . . .
>
> (T)he feelings that come with intuition are different from the feelings that come with a "passionate" emotion like anger, love or hate . . . Fast emotionally-driven responses can create intense anger, sadness, happiness, fear or disgust, but fortunately they tend to be short-lived (for example, most people are physically incapable of going around in a rage for days on end – it would simply be emotionally exhausting). Whilst emotions are fleeting, the subtle feelings that come with intuitive judgements are less intense but they can linger on and, once experienced, be called-upon again and re-imagined. Intuitions differ from emotions, and mixing them up can be perilous. For example, if we feel a romantic attraction to another person, or are passionately committed to what we feel is a great business venture our emotions may overwhelm our intuitive, and perhaps better, judgement. Given the fact that intuitions are charged with feelings but aren't emotionally-charged, a vital skill is to be able to disentangle intuition's subtle feelings from intense emotional feelings and the attachment and cravings that strong emotions bring. . . . Intuition arrives in conscious awareness tagged with either a positive feeling or a negative feeling, and this affective "tag" can work in two different ways:
> 1. Negatively-tagged intuitions are a signal for avoidance.
> 2. Positively-tagged intuitions are a signal for attraction. . . .
>
> Like biological reflexes, instincts and emotions, the intuitive mind "kicks-in" on the basis of a snap-shot perception before the analytical mind has the chance to intervene. . . .
>
> Whether we like it or not some of these hangovers from our evolutionary past come into play in personal and professional life, the difference is that in the modern world we don't have to contend with the life-or-death situations that faced our ancestors. Therefore I can't, or don't

> need to, simply "trust my gut" no matter how powerful the feeling is – I have an analytical mind which also may have something useful, if not vital, to say. For example, what does a manager do with two potential job hires – both with equally good résumés, great scores on a battery of psychometric and aptitude tests and work simulations, and excellent track records – one "feels" right, the other doesn't but it's hard to say exactly why?
>
> In this situation ignoring intuition might lead to a bad and very expensive decision, but blindly following it might lead to rejecting a good hire or legal trouble. So what to do? Following-up gut feeling by getting more objective data, for example from written references or making a phone call to a candidate's previous boss can help you to decide if gut-feeling is the basis for a good or bad judgment call. Intuitions are invaluable early warning signals and filtering devices that can be combined with analysis to enable managers, leaders and business venturers to project the future and plan ahead.

Emotions guide attention in a particular direction. Thus, emotions are also critical components of risk perception (Slovic, 1990, pp. 4 and 301). In this context, risk is defined subjectively and influenced by various psychological, social, institutional, or even cultural factors. Emotions help shape subjective reality (Kahle, 1998, p. 354) and assess the individual risk of decisions. Thus, emotions are essential in perceiving and evaluating risks in personnel selection decisions. Seo and Barrett (2007, p. 923) admit that emotions can lead to biases in judgments and decisions, but they can improve decisions if adequately regulated.

Reducing or ignoring your emotions, as recommended in psychometrics, is not the appropriate answer to good decision-making. Research results instead indicate that people who consciously perceive and understand their emotions, who can describe and communicate them in a differentiated way, and who become aware of the role of these emotions in their decision-making, make better decisions (Bublitz, 2021, pp. 15–17).

4.2.4.2 Emotions on the neuro-/psycho-physiological level

According to Roth and Strüber (2020, pp. 148–149), emotion can be defined more broadly from a neuroscientific perspective. According to this, a feeling as a conscious state of experience is a subform of emotions and can have different intensities and forms of expression as well as be experienced positively or negatively.

Emotions are produced in fractions of a second as neuro-psycho-physiological or biochemical and/or electrical reactions to a stimulus, and perceived consciously or unconsciously. For example, there are reactions to perceptions such as a threat, a reward, and everything in between. The bodily reactions can be measured objectively by changes in the body, such as pupil dilation, muscle tension, skin conductance, brain activity, heart rate, blood pressure, breath, and body language, for example, facial expressions such as laughing or crying/weeping.

Emotions are products of human evolutionary development and are helpful and necessary for human survival; they are a heritage of our ancestors and genetic echoes of their experiences. In addition, emotions provide raw data about the world around us that is essential to the functioning of human beings.

Feelings, as consciously experienced emotions, are always linked to the release of certain substances in the brain (Roth & Strüber, 2020, p. 154). Example: The psycho-physiological reactions, for example, the secretion of hormones such as cortisol or adrenaline or endogenous chemicals such as neurotransmitters, are, for example, a result of inborn fight-or-flight stress and vital in helping our body to deal with stressful situations. Without this stress response as a psycho-physiological part of emotion, our mind wouldn't receive the necessary danger signal, and our bodies would be unable to prepare to flee or fight when faced with danger. Thus, our emotion-anchored experiences make humans as unconscious knowledge carriers when it comes to the emotional assessment of a current situation.

Although Plassmann, referring to LeDoux (2001, p. 111), assumes that there is not a single emotional or limbic system in the human brain but several emotional systems (Plassmann, 2019, pp. 64–65), other researchers such as Dijksterhuis and Nordgren (2006) assume that perceptions affect the human hormonal and vegetative systems via the limbic system and lead to the release of certain messenger substances such as neurotransmitters and hormones. In this way, they influence human perception and, therefore, human decisions and behavior.

Especially the amygdala, as part of the human limbic system, plays a vital role in the emotional evaluation and recognition of situations. It "records" – without conscious human control – the sensory impressions such as body language and facial expressions, perceived by our perception apparatus and analyzes these in fractions of a second for their emotional content. It then sends – again in fractions of a second – signals (Brain researchers estimate that information in the limbic system is processed 200 times faster than in the Neo-/prefrontal-cortex; Dijksterhuis & Nordgren, 2006, pp. 96–97).

The powerful "emotional brain" (limbic system) functions, in simple terms, according to the principle of providing maximizing pleasure and minimizing pain. It is the foundation of human everyday life and codes everything we encounter, according to the principle, "pleasant" or "unpleasant."

4.2.4.3 Emotions on the feeling level

While the neuro-/psycho-physiological level of emotions is associated with (primarily physiological) activated reactions, for example, through hormones or neurotransmitters, feelings are the (conscious) experience, perception, and interpretation of emotional reactions, impressions, or other stimuli. Thus, the subjective experience of emotion can be called "feeling" (Holodynski, 2006, p. 12). Originating in the neocortical regions of the brain, feelings are sparked by emotions at the neurophysical level and shaped by personal experiences, beliefs, memories, and thoughts.

Feelings refer to mental experiences that are necessarily valence and accompanied by internal physiological changes in the body. Thus, each emotion has a characteristic "feeling tone." As an essential conscious representation of emotions, feelings are perceivable, even if they cannot be directly described and expressed in words in every individual case (LeDoux, 2012, pp. 653 and 662; Tyng et al., 2017, p. 2).

Feelings are an expression of the human organism to perceive what is happening at the emotional level – long before verbal language is available to humans. Therefore, emotions and feelings, as reactions to stimuli perception, are indispensable and something of a particular character and intelligence (Plassmann, 2019, p. 36).

Emotions, especially feelings, are an essential and automatically running instance of stimuli evaluation, which connects the evaluation of the stimuli with the needs, values, and other concerns of the perceiving individual "in terms of its implications for personal well-being" (Ben-Ze'ev, 2009, p. 46). "Emotions typically arise when one evaluates an event or outcome as relevant for one's concerns or preferences. One does not become emotional over something trivial. Moreover, emotions are 'cognitively impenetrable': One cannot choose to have or not have emotions, given certain events or outcomes that are relevant for one's concern" (Zeelenberg et al., 2008, p. 175).

Emotions at the level of feelings are perceived physically (e.g., heart rate) and mentally (e.g., fear of or happy about something) (Zeelenberg et al. 2008, p. 175; Plassmann, 2019, p. 63). Thus, feelings (How do I feel about it?) can lead to a fear of rejection, a regret of choice, joy about a compliment, and so on (Rolls, 2014, p. 2).

Humans (and also animals) learn to work for rewards and positive feelings, and they try to escape from or avoid punishment or negative feelings (Rolls, 2014, p. 4).

But, such a valence-based two-dimensional approach is at risk of falling short for several reasons. First, some emotions are challenging to place on a positive-negative dimension. Thus, they are often very complex physical and mental systems. Second, a differentiation in positive and negative feelings may perpetuate the worst old stereotype about emotions as simple phenomena (Zeelenberg et al., 2008, p. 178).

Nils Spitzer, who also refers to the classification of emotions into three parts, sees feelings as highly complex mental systems, which serve as an orientation system, and can be created by linking individual experiences and learnings on the one hand, and the innate emotional programs on the other side. In addition, these feelings are linked with individual values, beliefs, and human desires and needs (Spitzer, 2014, pp. 10–13).

While emotions can be seen as essential messages for human decisions, it can be seen more critically as acting on impulses. Thus, acting rather spontaneously based on relatively short-lasting (negative) emotional impulses is different because decisions and behaviors are difficult to control. Example: To act in the heat of the moment. Loewenstein's (1996; 2005) research on "hot-cold empathy gaps" in decision-making shows that people in "hot" affective states (e.g., hunger, thirst, afraid, physical pain, joy, craving for a drug, and sexual arousal) decide as different people. However, even such spontaneous, emotionally driven behavior cannot always be clearly distinguished from other emotionally influenced behaviors.

Emotions and, thus, feelings occur immediately and are mainly independent of cognitions (Betsch et al., 2011, p. 124). So, hiring managers may have a bad feeling regarding an applicant, although all factual arguments or numerical evaluations speak for the candidate. In such a situation, it is recommended to clarify why that applicant triggers negative feelings in the selection manager? Which personal and individual biases or experiences may be associated with this emotionally induced rejection? To what extent do projections, stereotypes, and other things play a role? Are these negative feelings based on critical experiences? And so on.

Cognitive emotion theories assume that cognitive evaluations determine feelings. This is the case, for example, with the rationalization of intuitions. For example, suppose hiring managers are convinced of an applicant, they often do not judge the candidate as a "wonderful person I like," but as a particularly convincing person because of their skills, personality, knowledge, and so on. Thus, it is an interplay of cognition and emotions; the positive feelings lead to positive cognition, and the cognitive evaluation itself supports the positive feeling (Hartmann, 2010, p. 54; Spitzer, 2014, p. 14).

The limbic system and thus System 1 very often overrides the decisions of the prefrontal cortex and counteracts reasonable decisions or System 2 (for example, regarding health-oriented behavior) to satisfy positive emotional needs in the short term or to avoid fear. We know from research on marketing how emotions strongly influence human buying behavior (Naderer & Frank, 2015; see also Section 4.3.8).

In certain situations, hiring managers feel compelled to make a conscious decision against their intuitions and emotions. For example, a low number of applicants and the pressure to fill a position as quickly as possible or only internally (as in the public sector, for example) are reasons for deciding against critical intuitions and emotions (Apelojg, 2010, pp. 181–182).

Feelings can also be influenced by a positive cognitive evaluation of expected or anticipated situations, for example, joyful anticipation of specific situations such as vacation and a concert (Zeelenberg et al., 2008, p. 178).

Unfortunately, many managers are taught: "There's no place for feelings at work." Or "Let's leave emotions out of our discussion." But as shown, ignoring feelings is impossible and unwise, but the notion persists in psychometrics that feelings are bad and no good in personnel selection.

Emotions must be accepted as existing; no one can deny their reality. Thus, taking emotions seriously and reflecting on them is recommended because they are a subjective reality, also in selection processes. Managers, including hiring managers, can learn to pay attention and listen to their feelings, reflect on them critically, and skillfully use them.

4.2.4.4 Emotions and feelings on the behavioral level

Often, certain aspects of what people want to express, need emotional support. For example, when applicants or hiring managers report on something that excites them, it is regularly linked to displaying positive feelings, such as a smile. At the same time, emotions cause priorities in people's behavior (Arvey et al., 1998, p. 106; Seo & Barrett, 2007, p. 936).

Thus, emotions continuously regulate human behavior to adapt to situation-specific requirements, emerging threats, and/or opportunities; they mobilize and give direction to behavior (Zeelenberg et al., 2008, p. 174).

Human face is the epicenter of expressing feelings. The human face is the reflection of emotional life. Our face, in particular, seems to be able to send signals that we cannot articulate with words. Before the complex verbal language system was developed, humans communicated via body language, facial expressions, and gestures. While our body language encoded great emotions such as fear, as in the flight or defense reflex, our face was responsible for expressing subtle reactions and nuances. We humans have learned to develop a fine sense for hidden feelings that accompany our fellow human beings' body language expressions and facial features.

As the saying goes, A glance says more than a thousand words. The importance of body language, gestures, and facial expressions for everyday communication and the associated behavior has been proven by research, for decades. Whoever learns to read the typical emotions and fleeting micro-expressions on other people's faces will gain valuable insights into their emotional world; and they learn, for example, to distinguish between artificial and authentic smiles.

Feelings indicate what is important and valuable to us and what our heart beats for.

Feelings give meaning to perceptions and cause people to pay attention and react to perceived threats or opportunities. Feelings have an informational and a motivational component and can thus serve as basic operators and orientations of cognitive functions. They are responsible for focusing attention and reducing the complexity of perceptual content. In this way, they become an essential component of the individual construction of reality (Holtfort, 2013, pp. 36–37), and people act, to a high degree, on these emotional representations.

In selection interviews, for example, feelings are the communication medium that informs the interviewer and the candidate about the other's state of mind, motivation, or even disposition to act. And, according to this perceived information, the conversation partners regulate their behavior and respond to the perceived feelings (Lammers, 2011, pp. 36–37; Smith, 1989, p. 340). LeDoux & Phelps (2008, p. 160) show that feelings thus have a signaling function and inform about the perceived relevance of a stimulus (e.g., a question or an answer in a selection interview).

The subjective evaluation of a specific stimulus depends on the individual valence and significance that the perceiver ascribes to this stimulus. These evaluations of the personal relevance of a specific stimulus, in turn, give rise to changes at the physiological, neuronal, and, thus, also at the behavioral level (Gross & Thompson, 2007, p. 5; Gross, 2014, p. 5).

To attract candidates to their companies, selection managers show positive feelings at the relationship level to persuade candidates. Furthermore, an appreciative, respectful and trusting relationship allows the applicant to open up. Thus, hiring managers need emotional competencies to achieve an emotional activation of the applicant and to develop a sustainable social relationship (Vössing, 2011, p. 60).

The significance of emotional activation and especially the connection between cognitive performance and emotional activation is described in the *Yerkes-Dodson law*. According to this, an individual's maximum performance is reached at an intermediate level of emotional activation. Conversely, if activation and, thus, emotional involvement are too high or low, performance declines (Easterbrook, 1959, p. 193; Hanoch & Vitouch, 2004, p. 427; Yerkes & Dodson, 1908, pp. 480–481). The activation of emotions, thus, has a significant influence on the behavior and thus also on the performance of applicants in the selection process.

Suppose the interviewer succeeds in ensuring that candidates gain access to their positive emotions, and in this way, both sides feel that an interview went well on the emotional side, the likelihood of applicants gaining a positive impression of the company is increased.

If selection managers can and succeed in showing their (positive) feelings, this activates (positive) feelings in candidates and promotes the perception of a positive relationship. This shows that people have an emotional hunch to decide and behave, reciprocally. Thus, a stimulus (e.g., a friendly behavior of the hiring managers) is recognized and evaluated emotionally by the candidates, and this emotional evaluation is directly connected to their behavior and decisions.

In advertising and marketing, the particular importance of emotions for influencing human behavior is recognized; thus, marketing uses emotionally aligned advertising, and the purchase of certain products is associated with an emotional benefit.

Feelings can cause specific behaviors, but decisions also influence feelings and, thus, behaviors; for example, the emotion of regret can be seen as a feeling when the consequence of the chosen option is worse than the consequence of the unchosen option (Betsch et al., 2011, p. 128). Or, as noted several times, many intuitions are emotionally charged. But "not every kind of emotion or feeling can be attributed to intuition. For example, the sting of a wasp immediately causes feelings of pain. These feelings, however, are not based on prior knowledge but are exclusively driven by the current situation" (Betsch, 2008, p. 5).

Although a select set of basic emotions or feelings are universal and, to a certain degree, innate, neurobiological reactions to specific stimuli and the concrete expression of feelings at the behavioral level are predominantly learned.

Even spoken words are not external to feelings because feelings are expressed in the choice of words and how words are spoken. With sound and the emphasis of words, humans can hear the energy with which people speak, what they want to emphasize, and even how they feel. What people say and how they say also depends on how one assesses the other, how one would like to form a relationship with the other, or how one would like to affect him.

Thus, the interdependencies of emotions, feelings, and behavior, and the high complexity of these physical and mental activities become apparent.

Conclusion: As shown, intuitive decision-making is a complex and simultaneously integrative and holistic process of associations. Emotions are regularly part of this associative, intuitive decision-making process. Human decisions occur in emotional contexts, and emotions shape cognitive functions. Emotions arise when a perceived stimulus (certain situations, people, events, outcomes, etc.) "are relevant for one's concerns or preferences, and they prioritize behavior that acts in the service of these concerns. As such, emotions can be understood as programs for intuitive decision-making" (Zeelenberg et al., 2008, p. 186).

Intuition is – to a certain degree – an unconscious process of feeling and unconsciously knowing how to decide; thus, emotions aid the decision-maker by providing quick intuitive cues on how to behave.

An essential consequence of decision-making is: When people are personally involved in selecting personnel, intuitive impulses are charged by emotional responses of the hiring managers' perception of candidates (and vice versa): What hiring managers feel about candidates depends on how they perceive candidates. What emotions and subsequent impressions does a candidate arouse in the hiring manager? Thus, the construction of the reality in selection processes depends on the hiring managers' (prior, primarily implicit) knowledge, experiences, and associated emotions. In this context, it must also be seen that these processes may bias people's judgments via the selective recall of similarly valenced memories (Zeelenberg et al., 2008, p. 177).

One of the great strengths of emotion-based intuition is that it enables humans to act quickly; secondly, it gives people certainty and orientation when making decisions; thirdly, it can mobilize motivation and enthusiasm. However, the analytical mind is far too slow to evaluate a situation in fractions of a second and take immediate action. Intuitive judgment and decision-making are then vital.

But intuitive decisions are not necessarily optimal. Emotions are inherited and learned. Especially, the inherited part expresses the experience of humankind over thousands of years, while the learned part is more based on the subjective life experiences of certain people. Thus, on the one hand, intuitions based on emotions have the invaluable advantage of reaching beyond the individual life experience. However, on the other hand, they run the risk of misleading us humans at times of change and uncertainty. Today, we live and work under entirely different circumstances than the long chain of our ancestors.

Ciompi (1997) developed the *fractal affect logic theory* to integrate thinking and feeling. He assumes that emotions, human thinking, and human behavior form a functional unity and that emotions and, thus, feelings not only accompany but also guide human decisions.

Ciompi's (1997) findings support the importance of emotions in decision-making processes. Contrary to the traditional Western traditional way of thinking, to control or eliminate emotions as something disturbing, Ciompi (1997) sees emotions as indispensable and essential for holistic human decision-making. Ciompi sees affects (understood as the feeling level of emotions) as part of the individual construction of reality, which cannot be prevented by a targeted concentration on rational action (Ciompi, 1997, p. 124). Feelings are seen as complexity reducers that select, structure, combine, and organize human cognitive structures so that a combination of feelings and cognitions makes human thinking directional and meaningful. His fractal affect logic theory says that feeling and thinking continually interact with the other activities in the cortical network (Ciompi, 1997, p. 130; Holtfort, 2013, p. 36). In human decisions, emotional-cognitive dynamics of interaction are effective (Ciompi, 1997, p. 13). Just as System 1 and System 2 interact, so do emotions and cognitions. It is about recognizing the interaction of cognition and emotion, and their integration.

Küpers and Weibler (2008, pp. 272–273) emphasize the importance of emotions in management: "Seen from an integral perspective, organizations probably become dysfunctional and unhealthy when they refuse to acknowledge and integrate feelings and emotions adequately. . . . On a practical level, organizations increase their chances of becoming more creative, and productive, if their management and members recognize integrally that feelings and emotions play an important role in constituting, shaping, and processing the realities and meanings of working life and corporations."

Those who regularly ignore and pass over their feelings may not only forget to articulate them but also forget to feel them. This certain deafness to one's feelings can also be interpreted as an expression of a lack of emotional competence.

For this reason, selection managers should listen to themselves and what feelings the applicant triggers in them. They can then reflect on where these feelings come from and what these emotional reactions have to do with themselves. Subsequently, all selection managers involved should communicate and discuss the emotions that applicants trigger in them and reflect on these feelings together. They should also discuss whether to make these emotions, a yardstick for selection decisions in this process.

4.2.4.5 Emotions and their cultural construction

Research shows that emotions are universal phenomena. Emotions are not only biologically influenced at the neuro-psycho-physiological level, but especially on the feeling and behavior level, they are influenced by the environment, particularly the specific culture and, thus, by a shared set of customs, beliefs, arts, laws, habits, values, socially expected behaviors, and so on. Hofstede (1980, p. 24) has developed one of the world's best-known definitions of culture and calls it "the collective programming of the mind which distinguishes the members of one human group from another . . . [and] the interactive aggregate of common characteristics that influences a group's response to its environment."

How emotions are experienced, displayed, expressed, perceived, interpreted, and regulated varies from culture to culture. Thus, emotional signals are based not only on our evolutionary heritage (e.g., basic feelings such as fear of strangers) but also on cultural influences.

Culture is a necessary topic for researchers and practitioners to understand variations in emotions, for example, in selecting leadership talent in an intercultural context. Some environmental stimuli are experienced similarly and lead to basic facial expressions. Research comparing facial expressions across different cultures has supported the theory that seven basic and universal emotions are associated with distinct facial expressions. These seven basic emotions are happiness, surprise, sadness, fright, disgust, contempt, and anger (Ekman & Keltner, 1997). "Universal emotions" means that they operate independent of culture and language. But experiencing or expressing emotions show considerable cultural differences. The importance of emotions in personnel selection in different cultures is described in more detail in Section 7.2.4.

Social-construction approach to emotions: Human emotions often occur in social contexts and are therefore influenced by relationships between people. According to the social constructivist approach, emotions cannot be separated from culture because culture essentially constitutes emotions and, especially, the expression of feelings. For this reason, culture provides the context of the evaluations that generate emotions, even if specific processes of emotions have a biological basis. Therefore, emotions are not only adaptive responses to evolutionary demands but are also products of sociocultural processes (Averill, 1990, p. 396; Mesquita, 2007, p. 414). How situations and stimuli are subsequently evaluated is learned from the earliest childhood, and therefore, according to these researchers, emotions are culturally constructed (Levenson et al., 2007, p. 781). Further, regulating emotions is learned in a developmental context, such as family and other social relationships. Thus, emotion regulation norms and how people experience and express their emotions are culturally learned, apart from context-specific display rules.

According to the assumption of Ekman (1994), the basic emotions are revealed through facial expressions and are inborn tendencies that are universal in humans. Ekman (1994; see also Ekman & Keltner, 1997) shows strong evidence for universals in facial expression, but expressions of feeling are also culture-specific (Ekman, 1992, p. 391). Universality was proclaimed based on cross-cultural research that asked people to match pictures showing various facial expressions with a forced-choice list of emotion words. Thus, the participants were not free to name emotions within their language. However, research by Gendron et al. (2014) allowed participants to choose words freely, and the universality of responses was vastly diminished. Moreover, given the opportunity to describe emotions in their terms, for example, the Himba, a tribe in Namibia (who were chosen because of their associated lack of exposure to Western culture), associated emotions with predictions of action rather than with internal mental states (Jurist, 2019, pp. 193–194).

Although there are universals in expressing feelings (e.g., laughing or smiling as an expression and universal marker of joy), how people express emotions varies, depending on the context (Barrett et al., 2019, p. 48). Gendron et al. (2014) and Barrett et al. (2019) show that emotion or feeling perception from facial expressions is not culturally universal. How people express and communicate emotions or feelings varies substantially across cultures, situations, and even among people.

As an alternative and contrary to common sense and people's everyday assumptions (Ekman, 1994), Lisa Feldman Barrett proposes the approach that people construct emotions. And in her book *How Emotions Are Made*, Barrett (2017a) gives insights into that each instance of emotion is constructed through a unique interplay of brain, body, and what is going around a human being, for example, the specific culture. She found evidence that a set of interacting brain regions is commonly involved when emotional and non-emotional processes occur (Lindquist et al., 2012). According to Barrett (2017a, 2017b), emotions are made; and emotions, unlike affects, must be construed in terms of mental representation or concepts.

> A concept is a collection of embodied, whole-brain representations that predict what is about to happen in the sensory environment, what the best action is to deal with impending events, and their consequences for allostasis (the latter is made available to consciousness as affect). Unpredicted information (i.e., prediction error) is encoded and consolidated whenever it is predicted to result in a physiological change in state of perceiver (i.e., whenever it impacts allostasis) (Barrett, 2017b, p. 12).

Researchers like Oatley (1993, p. 342 or Saarni, 2008, p. 333) compare emotions to language. According to them, every culture has its specific vocabulary and associated meanings. Similarly, people in each culture have emotions that result from social practices. These social practices lead to the experience, evaluation, and expression of emotions via learned verbal and non-verbal language.

Gendron et al. (2014) note that there is no consensus among different cultures about the perception of specific emotions and that some cultures have terms and concepts of emotion that do not exist in other cultures. Wierzbicka shows, for example, that in Polish, no word corresponds to the English word of "disgust," so the question arises whether Polish can still name disgust a basic emotion.

Therefore, the crucial role of language in expressing emotions ensures a significant cultural influence on the way emotions are experienced and then named (Levenson et al., 2007, p. 782). The question arises whether people can only recognize emotions in others (facial movements, vocal acoustics, actions, etc.) if they have first developed a corresponding mental concept. Furthermore, words that bundle things or events into a single concept facilitate learning emotional concepts; thus, concepts of emotion are culturally constructed beliefs about emotions.

Barrett (2017a, 2017b) claims that people learn specific concepts of emotions from their parents, society, and so on, from the moment they are born. She admits that babies have and show feelings, but these feelings are tied to (core) affects in her perspective (core affects refer to consciously accessible elemental processes of pleasure and activation; and when people are able to categorize a specific affect, e.g., as good or bad, that's an emotion or feeling). Concepts of emotion or feelings are learned because parents associate demonstrated behaviors with specific words they say to the baby. By this, human beings learn to distinguish between emotions or feelings, how to describe them, and how to perceive them in the behavior of others.

Because the social reality and the specific circumstances under which someone grew up (e.g., upbringing, education, diet, and environmental influences) influence the development of the human brain wiring, the perception of emotions or feelings is not culturally universal. Instead, Barrett states that a specific emotion is the brain's creation of what people's bodily sensation means concerning what is happening around someone in the world. In particular, the individual perceptions of the external situation, the perception of one's inner state (interoception), and the concepts that our fellow human beings often convey to other people through linguistic terms lead to the construction of emotions or feelings. Also, no single brain region is dedicated to any specific emotion/feeling or fixed emotional wirings in the brain that are the same for all people; instead, they vary due to different socialization, individual experiences, and learning circumstances. Thus, every emotion is grounded in a given individual's experience (Barrett, 2017a, 2017b).

Based on these concepts, the brain predicts the right decision for survival and well-being. How people decide depends on the stored emotions/feelings against which the current perceptions of stimuli are evaluated. Thus, for Barrett, interoception is one of the core components of emotion or feeling creation. The brain's interoception system is continuously processing internal and external sensations. Barrett states that when evaluating external stimuli, interoception is more influential on how people decide than how the outside world is. "Emotions are constructions of the world, not reactions to it" (Barrett, 2017b, p. 16). Elfenbein & Ambady (2002, pp. 203–210) found in a meta-study that the emotion recognition rate is relatively stable across different countries. However, recognizing basic emotions in people (e.g., rating emotions or feelings in facial expressions) of one's ethnicity would seem easier to recognize than in people of other origins. The accuracy of recognizing emotions is higher when expressed and recognized by members of the same national, ethnic, or regional group, suggesting an in-group advantage. This advantage was more minor for cultural groups with greater exposure to one another, measured in terms of living in the same nation, physical proximity, and telephone communication. The majority group members were poorer at judging minority group members than the reverse.

Thus, cultural background, experiences, and learnings with different cultures are core success factors for correctly recognizing, naming, and assessing emotions or feelings in other people.

4.2.4.6 Intuition and emotional competencies

For Sadler-Smith (2010, p. 9), "the intuitive mind . . . speaks in the language of feelings."

Therefore, it is necessary to look more closely at the effects of emotions in human decision-making, especially when dealing with personnel selection in science and practice, a critical and constructive analysis of feelings is necessary. This means, for example, dealing with questions such as what feelings certain applicants trigger in the decision-maker, what feelings arise when an applicant proves to be less suitable, but the decision-maker is afraid of not finding a more suitable applicant; or how to deal with a situation where one's feelings about an applicant say yes, but the mind says no (Apelojg, 2010, p. 50)?

Researchers such as Mayer and Salovey (1995, 1997, 2004) engaged intensively with emotional intelligence. According to them, emotional intelligence is primarily a set of abilities to accurately identify and recognize one's own emotions and those of others (emotion recognition), to read, understand and process emotional information accurately and efficiently (emotion understanding). It's about understanding the signals that emotions send, for example, about relationships, and knowing how to use emotional information to guide one's thinking and actions. Thus, it is about using the emotional messages purposefully, in particular, to monitor, regulate, and influence one's own and other people's emotions. Additionally, it's the ability to harness emotional information to enhance thinking; therefore, it's the ability to use emotional information for cognitive tasks (emotion regulating). Finally, emotional competence is about communicating successfully, having empathy for others, and building positive relationships (Mayer & Salovey, 1997). Empathy is an awareness of what other people think and feel, using body language and tone of voice cues. Thus, empathy helps to foster deep connections with other people.

And science journalist Daniel Goleman (2004, p. 83) states that

> emotional intelligence played an increasingly important role at the highest levels of the company, where differences in technical skills are of negligible importance. In other words, the higher the rank of a person considered to be a star performer, the more emotional intelligence capabilities showed up as the reason for his or her effectiveness. When I compared star performers with average ones in senior leadership positions, nearly 90% of the difference in their profiles was attributed to emotional intelligence factors rather than cognitive abilities.

Although the construct of "emotional intelligence" and, especially, the publications of Daniel Goleman have triggered many critical discussions and controversies in science, including their applications to employee selection, there are research results that show a connection between emotional intelligence as defined by Mayer & Salovey and success in organizations (e.g., Libbrecht et al., 2014). Apart from the fact that it depends on the intentions and goals of using emotional intelligence, it should not be neglected that scientific evidence shows a strong correlation between cognitive abilities, conscientiousness, and job performance. Emotional intelligence and interpersonal sensitivity, in particular, promote effective communication.

Since the term intelligence can be seen critically in connection with emotion, it is argued that it is better to speak of emotional competence. Emotional competence helps build positive relationships with employees, especially for leading people. Thus, in leadership, emotional and intuitive competencies complement each other.

Downey et al. (2006, p. 260) investigated the relationship between leadership, emotional intelligence, and intuition and found that intuition and transformational leadership style correlate with a high number of intuitive decisions.

In change management, it is increasingly accepted that recognizing and actively addressing the emotions (e.g., anger, rage, and fear) of affected employees is a critical success factor. Managers and employees often have intuitions and associated feelings but do not dare to address or communicate them actively. To manage these situations successfully, it is not enough to deal with the factual and rational level. People's behavior is often unconsciously influenced by these emotions. Dealing competently with these emotions, both in oneself and in employees, is thus an essential requirement for change managers (Doppler & Vogt, 2018).

Emotional competencies, such as self- and social-awareness, and the ability for self-management and self-regulation help enhance the potential of intuitions, get access to these sources, and reflect on them critically and constructively. Goleman (2004, p. 3) states that self-management and self-regulation control disruptive emotions and impulses and free people from being prisoners of their feelings. Emotional competence does not mean suppressing one's emotions but being aware of them and then controlling them, if necessary.

Experienced managers and practitioners of personnel selection know that they can only inspire people and win them over for the company in the long term, if they succeed in arousing positive emotions. Those who want to bring about such positive feelings in others without engaging with their feelings themselves often get the opposite reactions, such as mistrust and disappointment. Thus, emotional competence is key to integrating analytics and intuition and making effective decisions.

4.2.5 Somatic marker hypothesis as explanation approach for intuition

In the rational-analytical understanding of personnel selection, a higher rationality concept of decision-making is assumed, which attempts to exclude feelings (Damasio, 1995; de Sousa, 1987). This becomes particularly clear in the dictum "Cogito, ergo sum" ("I think, therefore I am"), coined by the French philosopher René Descartes in his "Discourse on Method (1637), and the uneasiness against feelings resonates. But taking the significance of emotions for human decision-making into consideration, Damasio's sentence: "I feel, therefore I am" is very understandable. He is fascinated that feelings are not just the shady side of reason but also help humans make meaningful judgments and decisions. Moreover, he shows that feelings should not be dismissed as unwanted opponents of rational thinking and that feeling and thinking interact and cannot be clearly separated (Damasio, 1995).

For António R. Damasio, emotion is an unconscious reaction to any internal or external stimulus that activates the brain's neural patterns. Thus, emotions and thinking are mutually influencing each other. There is no thinking and deciding without emotions. "Thinking is inconceivable without feeling," says Damásio in his book *Descartes' Error – Emotion, Reason and the Human Brain* (1995, p. 204).

Damasio is convinced that emotions help people evaluate whether options for action can develop into success or failure. This applies particularly to difficult decisions to calculate in advance, such as personnel selection. Emotions work like unconscious evaluation frameworks and steer human decisions. Especially in personnel selection situations, the participants unconsciously register very quickly how other people affect them, what they trigger in them, and so on. Patterns are unconsciously recognized, and thus positive or negative feelings are activated (e.g., whether someone seems trusting and authentic, and likable).

To integrate his thoughts and ideas into a theoretical approach, Damasio developed the "theory of somatic markers." The somatic marker hypothesis is based on the idea that emotional processes can consciously or unconsciously impact decision-making by creating biomarkers.

A somatic marker refers to a biological evaluation system that arises from the genetic system heritage in the interaction with the individual experiences of people and the associated, often unconscious, emotional evaluation of a stimulus. For example, collected experiences and the human reaction to positive- or negative-perceived stimuli, accompanied by certain body feelings, are stored as somatic markers (Damasio, 1997, p. 237). Thus, decision-making is a process that is influenced by somatic (bodily) markers (e.g., the association of rapid heartbeat or sweating with anxiety or nausea and vomit with disgust) that arise in bio-regulatory processes, including those that express themselves in emotions and feelings. and which act as an unconscious signaling mechanism in decision-making under risk and uncertainty (Bechara & Damasio, 2005, p. 336).

Therefore, somatic markers can influence a decision or action through body signals and accompanying emotions (Treufetter, 2009, p. 65) and, thus, help make appropriate decisions.

This theory can serve as an explanatory approach for intuitions. Damasio shows that people react to significant events, physically and somatically ('soma,' a word of ancient Greek origin meaning 'body'). The body reactions are emotional finger points of the unconscious and are interpreted by the person concerned as an intuitive signal (Damasio, 1995, pp. 237–238; Treufetter, 2009, pp. 64–71; Holtfort, 2013, pp. 35–36).

People are usually not aware of most of these emotional messages until they show up as physical symptoms in the body. This somatic manifestation supports the ability to make appropriate decisions and can inform humans which path to take in their decision-making process. Somatic markers are available as a body signal or "alarm bell," in the sense of good or bad feelings, helping people evaluate situations and make decisions very quickly.

When people encounter a new situation that evokes previous emotional experiences, or when emotional memories are recovered, the physiological states associated with the recalled event are automatically reactivated. For example, listening to a particular piece of music that people heard when they first kissed a boy-/girlfriend can evoke the same somatic reactions and emotions, as it did then. The somatic marker can be seen as "body knowledge," which can be retrieved intuitively. And, Damasio's theory confirms that the body and mind interact permanently.

The "somatic marker" theory shows that the success of human evolution is not only a consequence of human reason and rationality but also of the ability to act on "somatic markers." Thus, they support humans in their judgment and decision-making; and the stronger the (subjective) experience of somatic markers, the faster people realize how to decide and act.

Nevertheless, somatic markers, such as "emotional experiential memory," alone cannot explain specific human decision-making, and are often completed by rational thoughts (Damasio, 1997, p. 238). The hypothesis of somatic markers thus shows that rational analytics and emotions interact and influence each other and cannot clearly be separated in human decision-making processes.

4.2.6 Mirror neurons and intuition

As emotions are influential and essential for human decisions, evolution must have developed this sensor system for good reasons. Obviously, the brain decodes the emotional content of sensory impressions, for example, when meeting other people or presenting products in advertising (Treufetter, 2009, pp. 75–84).

Research shows that the ability to be empathetic, put oneself in someone else's shoes, and take on other perspectives is relevant for intuitive decision-making. Rizzolatti (Rizzolatti & Sinigalia, 2007) developed an explanatory approach for putting oneself in other people's shoes. This approach refers to the so-called mirror neurons. Mirror neurons are nerve cells that show the same activity pattern in the observer's brain, simply by observing a process as if the observer executes the observed situation. They were discovered in the context of doing basic research on motor control, trying to figure out how Macaque monkeys and, by generalization, humans may code movement plans in terms of object-based coordinates (Hickok, 2015b, p. 1).

We all have experienced this scenario ourselves: Our counterpart yawns, and we have to yawn automatically; someone smiles at us, and we smile back without thinking. Or, we simply cannot suppress our tears when we see a sad film. According to this explanatory approach, humans can feel what others feel, no matter whether it is compassion, sadness, or joy. And according to the assumptions of Rizzolatti, this process is based on specific neurons in our brain – the mirror neurons. Research shows that mirror neurons can be seen as a neuronal equivalent of empathy and a prerequisite for empathy (Mukamel et al., 2010, pp. 753–755). Mirror neurons are a resonance system in the brain that makes other people's feelings and moods, sound in their counterparts. The unique thing about these nerve cells is that they already emit signals when someone only observes an action. Thus, the mirror neurons react exactly as if one had performed what s/he has only seen.

Consequently, the concept of mirror neurons helps to understand intuitive decision-making because they can indicate why people show empathy and put themselves in other people's shoes, why it is possible to feel with others, and why body language signals can be evaluated in the right way (Holtfort, 2013, pp. 37–38).

However, there are also criticisms of this approach. On the one hand, it is doubted whether such mirror neurons exist since the brain links impressions in the brain neuronally in a variety of ways. In addition, it is not made clear how strong the ability to empathize is socially conveyed (Hickok, 2015a).

Other research shows that there does not seem to be a specific group of neurons or a distinct brain area where emotional resonance is produced. Instead, producing emotional resonance and empathy is a general ability of the entire brain and its networked parts. The pattern recognition process is also not a mirroring process, like the term mirror neurons suggest, but rather an activation of the observer's patterns of experience, which react because they are similar to what the observer sees (Plassmann, 2019, p. 46).

Even if the theory of mirror neurons reveals many weak points, there is still a need for research to determine exactly how empathy is made possible and mapped in the brain. However, one thing is for sure: There must be a neuronal equivalent in the brain or body for empathy and an intuitive understanding of people.

Related to the concept of somatic markers, Hatfield et al. (1994) show that people's emotions are influenced by the demonstrated emotions of their companions or counterparts, and call it "emotional contagion." This emotional contagion also takes place, for example, in personnel selection interviews.

4.2.7 The enteric nervous system and intuition

The (possible) significance of the enteric nervous system for intuition is already clear from the popular description of intuition as "gut feeling." There is a saying: "In gut, we trust." Thus it is worth examining its contribution to the explanation of intuition.

The enteric nervous system is the intrinsic nervous system of the gastrointestinal tract, colloquially called the "abdominal brain." The idea of investigating the abdominal brain as a biological origin for human abdominal feelings is already being pursued in literature (Mayer, 2011, pp. 453–464).

The enteric nervous system is located primarily in the muscle walls of the intestine, with more than 100 million nerve cells (Gershon, 2001, quoted from Holtfort, 2013, pp. 38–40); the plexus of nerves in the abdominal region, therefore, contains more or less the same number of neurotransmitters as in the brain. This enteric nervous system is a relevant part of the human nervous system and influences our health as a microbiome. In addition, the intestine is the largest immune organ in the body and organizes large parts of our immune defense. Thus, the enteric nervous system perceives specific alarm signals of the body very quickly and unconsciously transports the corresponding signals to the brain. For example, if toxins enter the body, the intestinal brain "feels" the danger first and immediately sends alarm signals to the central nervous system. And thus, it also affects human emotions and decisions. Therefore, the enteric nervous system is also seen as the "window to the brain."

The nervous system is a complex network of nerves and cells that carry messages to and from the central nervous system (brain), spinal cord, and intestine to various body parts. Thus, the central nervous system in the brain affects the "abdominal brain" and vice versa; we speak, for example, of "butterflies in the stomach" when we fall in love. And stress, which is primarily caused by our thoughts, can cause irritable bowel syndrome (Schemann & Neulist, 2004).

Although the enteric system interacts with the central nervous system, it also works largely autonomously and independently. Ninety percent of the information exchange takes place from the enteric nervous system in the abdomen to the central nervous system in the brain. The gut and the brain are closely connected, and the "abdominal brain" supports the interaction between abdominal feelings and intuition (Holtfort, 2013, pp. 38–39; Mayer, 2011, pp. 453–454).

Mayer (2011, Box 2) also refers to Damasio and his hypothesis of somatic markers that memories of body states are associated with previous feeling states. Positive or negative feelings are associated with visceral and other bodily responses (body loops) to certain contextual situations. According to this theory, these body loops, or their meta-representations in the orbitofrontal cortex, and thus the interaction between the enteric nervous system and the brain, play a vital role in influencing feelings and intuitive decision-making (Mayer, 2011, p. 453).

For Fuchs (2020), not only the gut but the whole body is closely connected to the human brain. Regarding "embodied cognitive neuroscience," consciousness results from ongoing vital regulatory processes that involve the whole organism. Without the inclusion of the body, consciousness could not be explained. Consciousness is not a localizable object, to point like a stone or an apple. It is a self-organizational process of the whole biological system of human beings. Fuchs calls this view "embodied anthropology."

Research shows a close connection between the enteric nervous system and intuitive decision-making. But, here too, it is essential to await future research results.

4.2.8 Neuroscientific findings and intuition

What distinguishes humans and sets them apart from most other creatures is their ability to think reflectively and thus to proceed and plan systematically, analytically, and rationally. The prefrontal cortex, which is – for example – responsible for cognitive control and systematic analysis and planning, is large in size, compared to monkeys, and shows much of a difference between humans and their primate cousins. In addition, the human brain has evolved over the millennia, enabling people to make themselves an emotionally, intuitively, and analytically intelligent species. Thus, this ability to self-reflect and demonstrate rational-analytical problem-solving capability distinguishes humans from other "animals" (Levitin, 2020, p. 57).

Neuroscience shows that cognitive processes such as rational-analytical procedures require effort; they are experienced as strenuous. The more cognitive resources are used, the more effort is required. The cognitive effort associated with decision-making depends on whether decision-relevant information is already mentally available or must be sought, structured, and thus consciously processed. Due to the limited cognitive resources, our brain wants to avoid cognitive effort (Pfister et al., 2017, p. 26).

To save energy, the human brain is a pattern-seeking "machine." It receives a vast amount of sensory inputs every second, making sense of the enormous quantity of stimuli it receives by detecting patterns. Pattern recognition is an evolutionary strategy for the survival of humans that allows them to detect threats and find resources in a noisy world. By combining complex details into simpler groups, this strategy reduces the amount of information to be processed (Chen, 2002, p. 28; Robertson, 2019, p. 19).

Neuroscientific research illustrates that many decision processes are not accompanied by consciousness. In addition, consciousness has only limited access to all decision-relevant knowledge (Miller, 1956, p. 96; Dijksterhuis & Nordgren, 2006, pp. 96–97).

Related to the influence of intuitions and related emotions on human decisions, a brief look at the human brain should be taken. First, it should be noted that intuitive decisions are primarily made in the human limbic system; although there is no single emotional or limbic system in the human brain (Plassmann, 2019, pp. 64–65), many researchers call the limbic system the "emotional brain" (LeDoux, 2003).

> We can think of the history of the brain in three general parts: The oldest and most primitive structure, the brainstem and cerebellum, is sometimes called the reptilian brain. The reptilian brain controls automatic functions such as respiration and heartbeat, and roughly classifies everything as food, sex, or danger. The limbic brain emerged later in the first mammals and is responsible for what we call emotions. The most recent to develop is the neocortex or rational brain. . . . Thus, our brains have two parallel processing systems, in addition to the automatic processes of the reptilian brain. The newest system of the brain operates through the cortex and is analytical and logical; it can collect and interpret facts and is capable of abstract reasoning and planning. The other is older, operates through the limbic system including the amygdala, and is emotional. That system was developed as a tool for assessing benefits and threats. It presents us with immediate information about the world and is capable of responding rapidly. Neuroscientists call these two systems cognitive and affective, or analytic and experiential, or rational and emotional, or System 1 and System 2 (Robertson, 2019, p. 17).

Impulses from the limbic system, especially emotional impulses, are emitted about 200 times faster than impulses from the rational-analytically oriented neocortex (Roth, 2009, pp. 301–302; 549–550).

Neuroscience research also shows a complex picture of the relation between cognition and emotion. This applies, for example, to the subcortical parts of the limbic system, where human affects and emotions arise. The limbic system is located in different parts of the brain, for example, limbic parts of the cerebral cortex, the hippocampus formation, the amygdala, basal ganglia, the mesolimbic system, or the neuromodulatory system, which have different functions and, as limbic centers, form the central evaluation system of the human brain. In addition, although the amygdala and cognition can work independently, they also influence each other; the amygdala, a significant part of the emotional memory, can, for example, modulate perception and attention by increasing the likelihood that emotional information will break through to cognition and reflection (Phelps, 2005, p. 73).

Human behavior is controlled by a network of interacting brain regions (and other body regions such as the enteric system), making it difficult to assign a behavior to a specific brain or body region (Elger, 2013, pp. 130–131). Thus, the construction of meaning or knowledge and thus, decision-making processes, depend on many factors, most of which are mediated by the limbic system. The limbic system, for example, mediates intuitions, feelings, and motivation and is thus the most crucial controller of behavior and the learner's success. This limbic system emotionally evaluates all impressions and perceptions of humans, even when facts and logical and rational-analytical arguments are available. This evaluation takes place largely unconsciously in the emotional experience memory. The limbic system checks in every situation whether the situation and the associated experiences and emotions are known or similar to earlier ones (Roth, 2004, p. 498).

As part of the limbic system, the amygdala shows the emotional significance of impressions, communicates with the visual cortex, and stimulates its activity, so that impressions can be perceived more actively (Robertson, 2019, p. 17).

To be effective, communication needs to go beyond analytical facts and be expressed in forms that can reach the emotional system. This includes social meaning, metaphors, and stories (Robertson, 2019, p. 18). From this perspective, convincing people to decide and act in a specific way needs more than purely rational-analytical procedures; more important is to reach people on the emotional level (Tyng et al., 2017, p. 17).

When weighing up in a decision process, the messenger substance, especially the hormone dopamine, plays a vital role in generating positive feelings. If the decision has positive consequences, dopamine is released, and anticipation is created. When making a decision, the brain simulates which emotions may occur after the decision is made. Thus, the limbic system opts for the emotionally most attractive option.

Research, mainly in the 1970s, held "split-brain" or "two brain hemispheres" discussion with the assumption that intuition is created on the right side and rationality on the left side of the brain (Mintzberg, 1976), which is from today's point of view, oversimplifying; not only do millions of nerve fibers connect the two hemispheres, but also the amygdala, one of the most important emotional centers, is located in both hemispheres of the brain (Scheier & Held, 2018, pp. 26–27; Zeibig, 2014). Thus, the assumption of Allinson & Hayes, when creating their cognitive-style index (1996, p. 122), that intuition is only a characteristic of the right brain and analysis of the left brain, is outdated. Referring to the dual-process theories of thinking (rational-analytical and intuitive thinking), Evans (2003, p. 454) speaks of two minds in one brain. The supposed right-brain functions are more associated with creativity, imagination, holistic thinking, insight, and intuition; it is more intimately connected to the limbic system and thus to emotions and feelings. And the left-brain functions are supposed to be more analytical, rational, and linear thinking, logic, reasoning, science, math, language, and so on.

Also, Satpute and Lieberman (2006, p. 86) state that the brain cannot be simply divided into right and left, intuitive and rational-analytical information processing. As the brain is "an interacting network of neural structures and subsystems" (Sadler-Smith, 2019, p. 21), intuitive information processing emanates not only in the right brain hemisphere but in both hemispheres. Moreover, intuitive processing is a complex interaction of neural systems, including the ventro-medial prefrontal cortex and the amygdala (Satpute & Lieberman, 2006, p. 86). Neuroscientific research has also not provided clear evidence of whether phenotypic differences exist in the strength of left-dominant or right-dominant networks. Brain scans demonstrate that activity is similar on both sides of the brain (Nielsen et al., 2013) and that intuitive processes co-occur on the right side and on the left side of the brain (Agor 1984 and

1989; Lieberman 2000 and 2009; Evans & Stanovich, 2013, p. 227; Sadler-Smith, 2019, p. 9).

Hiring managers experience their limbic processes when intuitive and emotional impulses reach the cerebral cortex or the prefrontal cortex or if these impulses influence the enteric nervous system. However, due to unconscious processes, why hiring managers feel in a specific way or want to do something special often remains a mystery.

Although people make various speedy, unconscious, and intuitive decisions every day, personnel selection and hiring decisions go through a more interactive process. How the unconscious affects an applicant or a selection manager and how they feel expresses itself less through the content of what is said but rather on the physical level, by symptoms in facial expressions, gestures, voice, eye movements, posture, and vegetative reactions. This is hardly, or not at all, subject to conscious control, and accordingly, people often do not know what is happening in their limbic system and body. Often, the unconscious excitations are only experienced when they express themselves, for example, through trembling, sweating, or blushing (Ryba & Roth, 2019, 2021).

However, this does not mean that hiring managers are completely at the mercy of such unconscious processes because they can try to consciously reflect and possibly reject the feelings or thoughts that emerge from the unconscious. Instead of reacting affectively in the heat of the moment, reflective thinking and systematic weighing of the pros and cons can lead humans to better solutions (Roth, 2010, pp. 13–15).

And neuroscience research results confirm that decision-making, such as hiring decisions, is based on a complex network of central and enteric nervous systems processes. Emotional memory enhancement appears to involve the integration of cognitive and emotional neural networks. Recent neuroimaging findings have indicated that the amygdala and the prefrontal cortex cooperate with the medial temporal lobe in an integrated manner (Tyng et al., 2017, p. 17).

Neuroscientific research verifies that people do not act solely on rational-analytical clues or scientific facts. Simply delivering scientific facts to hiring managers is not convincing to most of them. For information to be meaningful to hiring managers, it must relate to something already encoded in their nervous system; people take in new information by connecting it to what they already know or think they know. This has implications on how to communicate new information to people. Ideas or knowledge of quality in selection tend to be stored in long-term memory when connected to the experience, personal meaning, and emotions (Robertson, 2019, pp. 19–20).

Tyng et al. (2017, p. 17) show that emotionally charged information is remembered more clearly, accurately, and longer than neutral events. Thus, frame issues are needed that resonate emotionally with them. Learning strategies that emphasize emotional factors are more likely to result in long-term knowledge retention (Tyng et al., 2017, p. 16).

Thus, applying psychometric findings in personnel selection is more likely practiced in the long term, if applying these findings in practice generates a positive emotional response in hiring managers (Robertson, 2019, p. 21).

From these neuroscientific research results, intuitive and rational-analytical processes run parallel in different parts of the brain (and maybe also the enteric system) and influence each other. Thus, for example, decision-making in selection processes is regularly an interaction of rational-analytical and intuitive thinking from a neuroscientific perspective.

Because, from a neuroscientific perspective, people cannot simply turn off their intuitions and emotions, and because these impulses influence human decisions much more quickly than analytical considerations, they determine most human decisions more than conscious rational-analytical considerations (Ryba & Roth, 2021).

4.2.9 Cognitive style and rational-analytical and intuitive decision-making

4.2.9.1 The intuitive and rational-analytical cognitive style

There is a considerable array of dimensions on which cognitive styles can be differentiated. Hayes and Allinson (1994) have extended the list to 29. Nevertheless, the view that there are two qualitatively different types of thinking and decision-making is widely shared (see, e.g., the System 1 ("intuitive style") and System 2 ("Rational-analytical style") approach of Kahneman, Section 4.2.2.4).

According to some researchers, the rational-analytical and intuitive decision-making processes are based on different cognitive styles. For example, there is evidence that some people tend to use feelings as their preferred mode of reception and rely more on their intuitions in decision-making than others. Thus, the rather head-influenced decision-makers decide more thoroughly, create pro and con lists, and so on. And there are the more emotionally oriented decision-makers who pay much attention to their intuitions, feelings, and moods. And there are the insecure decision-makers who trust neither their intuition nor the facts they have gathered and who have to back them up constantly (Sinclair 2005; Sinclair & Ashkanasy, 2005, p. 358).

C.G. Jung (1948) says that the "intuitive type" acts less based on rational judgment than intuitive impulses.

According to Kleebaur (2007, p. 62), the extent to which selection managers use and apply an intuitive or rational-analytical style depends strongly on their personalities and their experiences with these styles. The personality traits of the decision-makers and the confidence in their intuition have a decisive influence on whether decisions are made rational-analytically or intuitively.

For example, suppose decision-makers have experienced that rational-analytical methods support reducing poor judgments of intuitive impulses in the past, this experience influences the recruiter's thinking and behavior. It can also be assumed that risk-averse individuals do not rely exclusively on their intuition but use valid measuring instruments to back up their personnel selection decisions.

Allinson & Hayes (1996, p. 122) assume that people seem to have a relatively permanent stylistic orientation to using intuition or analytics.

> Intuitivists . . . tend to be relatively nonconformist, prefer an open-ended approach to problem-solving, rely on random methods of exploration, remember spatial images most easily, and work best with ideas requiring overall assessment. On the other hand, analysts . . . tend to be more compliant, favor a structured approach to problem-solving, depend on systematic methods of investigation, recall verbal material most readily, and are especially comfortable with ideas requiring step-by-step analysis.

Hayes and Allinson (1994) refer to the evidence of rational-analytical procedures in personnel selection and prefer the cognitive style.

> Cognitive style has been defined as "consistent individual differences in preferred ways of organizing and processing information and experience" (Messick, 1976, p.5). Thus, its relevance to organizational behavior is clear. As Schweiger (1983, p. 143) points out: "If research indicates . . . that particular cognitive styles are more appropriate than others for the conduct of particular managerial activities, then normative recommendations concerning the selection and placement of individuals for these activities may be warranted" (Allinson & Hayes, 1996, p. 119).

EI Othman et al. (2020; see also Rahaman 2014) found in a study among students that a higher extraversion was associated with a lower rational decision-making style, whereas higher agreeableness and conscientiousness were significantly associated with a higher rational decision-making style. More extraversion and openness to experience were significantly associated with a higher intuitive style, whereas higher agreeableness and conscientiousness were significantly associated with a lower intuitive style. More agreeableness, conscientiousness, and neuroticism were significantly associated with less spontaneous decision-making. Jung thought that extraverted intuitive types were likely to be, for example, entrepreneurs (Jung, 1948; to the topic "role of intuition in entrepreneurship" see, e.g., Allinson et al., 2000; Akinci, 2015 or Sadler-Smith, 2015).

Raiz et al. (2012) also found that personality affects decision-making style, but Jalajas & Pularo (2018) state that it didn't affect actual decisions in the way they predicted.

Thus, there may be certain tendencies, but the general assumption that conscientiousness would be a good predictor of slow (and rational) decision-making and extraversion a good predictor for intuitive decision-making must be critically reflected.

Lodato et al. (2011, pp. 357–358) investigated which factors lead to a preference for intuition-based selection practices. Their results showed that intuitive decisions are strongly associated with an experiential thinking style. Miles & Sadler Smith (2014, p. 621) also state that using intuitions depends on the subjective "faith in intuition" and that "managers who preferred intuition-based hiring are likely to be 'experiential' (i.e. feelings based) thinkers." The experiential thinking style is investigated, for example, for the Cognitive-experiential self-theory (CEST) by Seymour Epstein (1990). This approach proposes that rational and experiential thinking styles, as original personality constructs, are not fully explainable by the Big Five personality model of Costa and McCrae. By definition, the experimental thinking style is associated with intuitions, emotions, or imagination, and is used primarily when imagination, creativity, empathy, holistic-integrative perspectives, and so on are required.

Researchers from the Max Planck Institute for Human Development in Berlin and the University of Basel show that whether people make everyday decisions based on their gut feeling or reason has little to do with their kind of decision-maker. Instead, the content of the decision plays a significant role and so does the question of familiarity with the respective topic. For example, the questioned students tended to decide on clothing, restaurants, and choice of partners intuitively. In contrast, their decisions in areas such as medicine, electronics, and holidays are apt to be knowledge-based. For that reason, it should be critically questioned to speak of rational or intuitive types of decision-makers, as is often done (Pachur & Spaar, 2015).

Research results of Elbanna (2015) indicate that the context and thus the characteristics specific to the firm and the environment appear to be more significant to intuition than the type of the decision-maker or the problem to solve. In particular, the contextual circumstances in which SMEs operate and the companies' specifics significantly influence whether more rational-analytical or – as predominant in SMEs – more intuitive decisions are made.

Also, Sinclair & Ashkanasy (2005, p. 360) determine whether people use a more intuitive or rational-analytical decision-making style is

> determined by personal disposition and decision-making context. . . . For example, Burke and Miller (1999) highlighted the importance of situational influences related to the type of decision and problem. Epstein et al. (1996) stressed the role of personal factors, including emotional involvement. Mintzberg et al. (1998) . . . argued that organizational context is paramount. . . . we conclude that intuitive decision-making is affected by four broad categories of factors: (1) problem characteristics, (2) decision characteristics, (3) personal disposition, and (4) decision-making context.

(These four context-specific factors influencing human decisions will be discussed in more detail in Section 5.6.)

Selection managers are well-advised to recognize their decision-making patterns and preferred thinking style in specific decision situations. Thus, decision-makers should know their personality structure well and reflect on the situations in which they tend to be more intuitive and when they tend to be more rational.

Nevertheless, the available research results show tendencies in how personality and contexts affect cognitive styles, especially more rational-analytical or intuitive decision-making. However, further research is needed to get more reliable results.

Nevertheless, one conclusion is that decision-making is a much more complex process involving more influencing factors than personality (see "factors affecting the interplay of rational-analytics and intuition" in Section 5.6 and "multidimensional framework of decision-making in the selection" in Section 10.6.2).

4.2.9.2 Gender and cognitive style

Personality or personal dispositions can also be influenced by gender. For example, Sinclair and Ashkanasy (2005, pp. 361–362) refer to research results that support the commonly held belief that women are more intuitive than men (Agor, 1986; Pacini & Epstein, 1999; Parikh et al., 1994) and have better access to their emotions and intuitions. Gigerenzer et al. (2013) show that both men and women in Germany believe that women have more access to their intuition, while this may not be the case in Spain.

Judith Hall's evaluation of a total of 75 studies shows that females have advantages in intuitively interpreting interpersonal and predominantly nonverbal signals and correctly interpreting the expressive behavior of others. In addition, she concludes that women have learned to pay more attention to emotions and intuitions than men due to their cultural backgrounds and socialization history, role expectations, and biological influences. Women show more interpersonal sensitivity and better nonverbal judgment accuracy than men (Hall, 1978; Hall et al., 2000; Hall et al., 2017. For "Interpersonal Sensitivity: Theory and Measurement," see Hall and Bernieri (Eds., 2001).

Other studies suggest that men may be more intuitive than women, for example, in specific business decisions (e.g., Kirton, 1989; Allinson & Hayes, 1996, p. 128), or have not identified any significant differences between women and men.

Burke & Miller (1999, p. 94) state:

> Although many writers have reported women to be more intuitive, nearly 80 percent of our interviewees did not cite gender when listing people they had witnessed using intuition. Women in male-dominated workplaces may wish to appear analytical rather than emotional in their decision-making, or they may tend to employ their intuition less at work than in non-professional situations. Nevertheless, our findings may call into question traditional gender-based assumptions about decision-making styles in the workplace.

Studies show varying results, some confirming the social attribution of "female intuition" mainly when intuition is associated with empathy and access to their emotions (e.g., Agor, 1986). Thus, although the research results are somewhat contradictory, the premise that there is a tendency for males to be more analytical than females held for almost all samples in our current research. Kirton (1989), however, has warned that findings on gender differences may vary from culture to culture. Moreover, Gigerenzer et al. (2013) point out that these assumptions on intuition lead to stereotypes, which can result, among other things, in fewer women in leadership positions.

4.2.10 The personality–systems–interactions (PSI) theory by Julius Kuhl

Julius Kuhl (1990; see also Bolte et al., 2003), a German psychologist, shows in his research that analytical intelligence and intuition can merge cooperatively into a holistic basis of human experience. The theory of personality–systems–interactions (PSI) provides new perspectives on human decision-making. The core of PSI is the "action control model." It explains individual behavior through the interaction of different psycho-physiological processes. The PSI theory integrates a variety of research findings from, for example, personality and experimental psychology or neuroscience. According to this approach, human behavior essentially results from the integrative interaction of four different functional systems. However, in specific situations, one dominant functional system primarily controls people's behavior. Kuhl's theory is based on the assumption that humans have access to these four functional systems and can even determine for themselves which functional system should be given primary attention.

Two of these functional systems are the "intention memory" and the "intuitive behavior control." While the "intention memory system" controls rational-analytical thinking and behavior, the "intuitive behavioral control system" helps make fast and automatic decisions. In a third system, the "extension memory," all personal experiences are stored and linked with affective evaluations. The fourth system is the "object recognition system." This specializes in detaching individual objects from their context and examining them closely, for example, to find errors or investigate inconsistencies.

PSI is based on the central assumption that positive feelings influence motivation to do particular things. Positive feelings are thus indispensable for action; especially, the "intuitive behavioral control system" is a functional system associated with positive feelings.

Similar to the two process approaches presented in Section 4.2.2, the PSI theory explains the immediate first reactions to situations and stimuli. It gives recommendations for action to "replace" unpleasant or thoughtless first reactions (e.g., caused by intuitions and associated emotions) by learning a helpful second reaction.

This ability of not blindly following one's spontaneous inspirations (e.g., intuitions, emotions) but consciously controlling one's concrete behavior using "second reactions" is a self-control competence that characterizes human beings. Genetics and life experience make people specialists in one of the four systems. The challenge now is to strengthen and try to apply those systems more that have been "neglected" so far, for example, through feedback, self-reflections, anticipation of success, external encouragement, training, or/and critical evaluation of one's decisions and behaviors. Kuhl also emphasizes that a positive benefit, especially on the emotional side, must be recognizable if a behavior is to be exhibited in the longer term.

Hiring managers should clarify for themselves based on which dominant system, for example, the "intuitive behavior control system," they most likely act in specific decision situations. They should strengthen specific behaviors triggered by the other system, for example, the more rational-analytical system of the "intention memory." If certain behaviors are to be exhibited for the long-term, they should be linked with positive feelings. The learning field of managers acting more based on an "intuitive behavioral control system" is thus the rational-analytical controlled behavior based on the "intention memory." And those who act more based on the rational-analytical "intention memory" should develop their functional field of the "intuitive behavioral control system."

Thus Kuhl is convinced that humans should use both systems, analytics and intuition, as sources of knowledge. Both sources of knowledge would have to result in a dialogue in which neither analytic thinking nor holistic intuition should dominate. There would be no one-sided focus on one of the two cognitive systems. The focus would be on the in-between, their relationship, the interaction, and communication between the two knowledge systems. By linking both systems of knowledge and using the holistic experience network of the human being, the human being can grasp the reality of life holistically and, in this way, do justice to holism as a human being. Kuhl imagines the cooperation of both systems in such a way that both knowledge systems compare their results with each other. Then, both could continue to work with the result of the other and take it as feedback to optimize their procedure. For this purpose, one does not have to understand both cognitive systems exactly or even explain them. Instead, it is enough to feel into oneself, dive into one's body perception, perceive a particular word, an impression, a feeling, or even intuition, name it, and then communicate it. And through conscious looking, naming, and subsequent reflection, it can come to a renewed specification and more valid naming of what intuition and the corresponding feelings are perceived and experienced. The "heaven of cognition and human understanding" lies in the judgment-free dialogue between rational-analytical results and intuitive feelings, and linking intuitive understanding and analytical penetration and explication. Through this dialogue, each side can exist as it is, and from the united and reflected interaction, the extraordinary power of intuitive and analytical intelligence can emerge (PSI Impulse, 2020).

4.3 Intuition in selected fields of practice

4.3.1 Intuition of firefighters

Kahneman and Klein (2009, p. 516) and Klein et al. (2010) point out that fire ground commanders make very successful intuitive decisions under conditions of uncertainty and time pressure; they draw on their repertoire of patterns and the tacit knowledge compiled during many years of experience and stored in the subconscious mind.

For example, foreground commanders can interpret a fire's sounds in an emergency and give the correct instructions to the firefighters, taking into account the safety aspects. Under time pressure, they need to assess the specific contextual conditions at lightning speed and make decisions in fractions of a second that the rational mind cannot make under these conditions. And after years of experience, these intuitive decisions can be trusted (Kahneman & Klein, 2009, p. 520).

4.3.2 Intuition in sports

In sports, many decisions have to be made very quickly and spontaneously. Athletes must adjust to the opponent in a fraction of a second and correctly assess complex situations. To do so, they don't have time to think rationally and consciously; instead, they make their decisions intuitively. Intuition, as felt knowledge, enters the consciousness quickly and gives the athlete an impulse to act, such as pass and shoot. According to Gigerenzer, particularly internalized rules of thumb, so-called heuristics, help athletes act correctly.

In a study, cognitive researchers Susan Beilock et al. (2002, 2004) show that experienced athletes actually respond better under time pressure. In their laboratory, they conducted experiments with laypeople and golf experts. The amateurs did better when they had more time, but the pros' stroke was more accurate when they had only three seconds. The experts do better when they have less time. Thus, too much time to think tends to interfere with successful athletes. This is because conscious thinking can lead to slowed and disrupted execution of unconscious body movements (Beilock et al., 2002; Beilock et al., 2004; Gigerenzer, 2007, pp. 42–43).

Another study with handball players proves that the first option coming to a player's mind is usually the best. Through reflection and more thorough analysis, the other moves that come up later are worse options. Accordingly, experienced players should listen to their first intuition and make quick decisions. However, this does not necessarily apply to inexperienced players. For them, more time and reflection can be helpful, if necessary (Gigerenzer, 2007, pp. 43–45; Gigerenzer & Gaissmaier, 2012, pp. 16–17; Johnson & Raab, 2003, p. 215).

Or, in soccer or tennis, good players more often have the correct intuition and know, for example, where to run to get the ball without a conscious analytical intervention. Without thinking too much, intuition does its job and helps athletes know how to hit a ball or where to run. And the athletes are not able to describe how this happens: "If a footballer has scored a brilliant goal, nobody says, 'Give me a reason for that!'" (Gigerenzer, quoted in Kaudela-Baum & Brasser, 2015, p. 117).

The most successful German goal scorer in soccer, Gerd Müller, knew: "When you think, it's too late anyway." The sentence reveals how athletes act successfully in complex situations where fast decisions are necessary: intuitively.

Coaches or managers also have intuitions, for example, about which players they want to put in the starting lineup or substitute. In the opinion of mental coaches of various German national teams and top athletes (football/soccer, ice hockey, etc.), this kind of intuition can be improved by observing systemic and contextual factors. Probably one of the most effective ways to improve intuition is – according to Hermann and Mayer (2020) – to conscientiously analyze the social situation and the interaction of the different forces (factors) the leader/coach or manager of athletes are facing. A leader's competence is to recognize what the team and the individual need from the leader and intervene only if necessary. Managers, coaches, and so on should anticipate and recognize the context and causes of possible disturbances. They must listen to their intuition and ensure they do not succumb to cognitive deception (Hermann & Mayer, 2020, p. 161).

Simon and Chase (1973; see also Simon, 1998) illustrate intuitive decisions with chess. Chess is usually believed to require a high level of intellect as well as a highly analytical approach, with players systematically working out the consequences of moves and countermoves such that a single move can take a substantial amount of time. However, the chess expert takes much less time for each move in simultaneous games as there is no time for careful analysis. Evidence shows that in this rapid play, a large part of the chess master's expertise lies in intuitive capabilities based on a large amount of stored and indexed knowledge derived from training and experience (Akinci, 2011, p. 17; Simon, 1992).

Thus, it can be stated that intuitively made decisions are widely needed and accepted in games and sports.

Excursion: Intuition in selecting athletes in ball sports

Research results and surveys of talent scouts and coaches in team sports clearly show that there are currently no reliable and valid criteria for predicting the future success of young talents (under 18 years) in sports. Apart from the fact that later success depends on many external factors in the environment of the young talent such as parents, trainers, training opportunities and workload, friends of the talent, health/injury susceptibility and freedom (Larkin & O'Connor, 2017, p. 3), the later success is influenced, in particular, by the competencies inherent in the body and the personality of the talent (Achouri, 2014, p. 52).

In particular, personality characteristics such as stamina, seeking success, having (real) "bite" and ambition, learning ability and the desire to develop and improve, self-reflection and critical ability, determination, self-confidence, and the willingness to perform and to succeed, willingness to put other private interests aside, enjoyment of the sport and the ability to adapt, but also intellectual qualities (intelligence/cognitive abilities; understanding of games and tactics; quick thinking and implementation in behavior) and intuition play an important role on the playground (e.g., the ability to think and act quickly, to anticipate where the ball goes or how the opponent will move). These characteristics are more critical for future success than the athletic and physical prerequisites such as the feeling for the ball, technique, dribbling or shooting skill, movement sequences, and size (Radicchi & Mozzachiodi, 2016, p. 28; Larkin & O'Connor, 2017, p. 10; Lobinger, B. H., & Musculus, L., 2018). This does not mean that these athletic and physical factors are unnecessary; thus, they will be tested as a basis for selection by the scouts. And, it is not only essential to adapt to specific environments and look for circumstances and surroundings that best fit one's personality and goals, needs, and interests (Achouri, 2014, p. 60).

Interviews with talent scouts (Michelsen, 2019; Klimach, 2020) and research results (Larkin & O'Connor, 2017) show that athletic and physical skills form the basis for a talent's success.

However, the extent to which talented players become successful athletes and exploit their potential depends primarily on personality competencies.

Therefore, the talent scouts and coaches attach great importance to their intuition when analyzing candidates' potential and personalities. A study by Bradbury and Forsyth (2012) on athlete selection by coaches shows that although coaches have objective criteria, they utilize some form of gut feeling when making selection decisions (Buekers et al., 2015, pp. 1–2).

This intuition, primarily to assess the personality of the potential talent, is based on experience as a player, coach, or talent scout, having accompanied players in their development. In the interviews, they, therefore, repeatedly cite their knowledge of human nature, their empathy, and their ability to communicate and network very well (e.g., to convince and win over talent, parents, and former coaches) as success factors in their work (Michelsen, 2019, pp. 26–27). A successful scout must look at many players and document their physical and mental strengths and weaknesses well.

The benefits of a rational-analytical approach to athlete selection are very impressively shown in the movie *Moneyball. Moneyball*, released in September 2011, is based on a true story about the Oakland Athletics professional baseball team, where players were analyzed using objective, empirically based data and evidence (mathematical, statistical, and criterion-oriented surveys of past performance). Using those data, the selection manager and the baseball team achieved a high degree of success.

Rational-analytical potential analysis and data-based selection procedures are becoming more and more critical. Various test procedures assess physiological, cognitive, psychological, and personality competencies and characteristics (Hottenrott & Seidel, 2017, pp. 126–127; Dodd & Evans, 2018, pp. 8–9). However, all scouts interviewed by Klimach (2020) agree that it is not enough to collect evidence-based data. More critical is interpreting the data correctly and what conclusions are drawn from it. And drawing the correct conclusions is impossible without intuition (Klimach, 2020, p. 28).

However, the surveys by Michelsen (2019) and Klimach (2020) and other study results by Bradbury & Forsyth (2012) show that scouts and coaches do not want to give up relying on their intuition and experiences and their associated emotions. Especially when assessing whether players fit into a team based on their personalities, scouts and coaches also want to use their intuition in the selection process.

4.3.3 Intuition in arts (music, painting, sculpting, etc.)

Because it is challenging to express intuitions or emotions in verbal languages, intuitions and emotions are often manifested in the behavior of people (love, dancing, escape, aggression, etc.) or in their translation into works of painting, sculpting, music, and so on. Music, for example, is an expression of intuitions and the sound of feelings. This removal or uncoupling of the intuitive process from language is discussed by Kant (1990, pp. 94–95), for whom intuitive knowledge belongs to the field of the pre-linguistic and pre-logical, a preliminary phase of the process of knowing. Therefore, for Kant, intuition is a preliminary stage of conceptual knowledge (Thaliath 2012, pp. 4 and 14–15; Vogler, 2012, p. 76).

Artists often report that their creations arise from a deep intuition. Intuition is regarded as a form of cognition and felt knowledge. Chefs intuitively put together their new creations and intuitively know which ingredients go together. Accessing it can require silence and a focused concentration on oneself and the world. "Intuition for me is immediacy, speed of access to an idea; all this in the field of inspiration. It's the moment when the idea you carry around with you is given a certain twist, the intuition: it will work! The visibility of the idea is crucial in artistic work. Intuition plays an important role here" (Heil, 2013, p. 23).

The Art Biennale in Venice dedicated a special exhibition to intuition in 2017. The idea of this exhibition was to reflect on intuition as an inspiration and a basic impulse of human activity, using the example of works of art (Iden, 2017).

Kandel (2012, p. 583) writes that artists and creative projects contribute in their specific way to an increasingly comprehensive understanding of the human mind. Art is best understood as the distillation of pure experience. Therefore, it is a necessary and desirable enrichment of the human mind.

In summary, art is considered a translation of intuitive perception and inspiration and is called the language of intuition (Hinrichs, 2019).

4.3.4 Intuition in medicine

Many medical publications show the influence of intuition, especially in medical diagnostics. Despite all the advances in medical technology, it is essential for physicians to see, talk to, and examine patients in person. Sometimes, just talking to patients in person can develop healing power. Especially in emergencies, where decisions have to be made very quickly and appropriate interventions initiated without deliberated analysis, physicians often act intuitively and rely on stored empirical knowledge and heuristics (such as decision trees and algorithms), which they have very often applied successfully (Gigerenzer, 2007, pp. 46–48; Harteis et al., 2011, pp. 154–155; Possehl & Meyer-Grashorn, 2015, p. 64).

Rothmund & Lorenz (1990) show the meaning of intuition in decisions for a specific surgery, such as an intraoperative procedure, especially if something unforeseen happens during surgery. Sidler (2014) shows how osteopaths draw on their tacit knowledge, heuristics, and, thus, intuitions when treating patients.

Based on the diagnosis, medicals make decisions (e.g., about treatment) that affect clients' well-being and healthcare costs.

Since diagnosing mental disorders is a very complex process, it needs a lot of experience. De Vries et al. (2010) found that doctors increase their reliance on intuitive processes with increasing experience levels, especially when diagnosing mental disorders. Furthermore, their empirical research results indicate that the information relevant for defining and classifying mental disorders in the DSM- (Diagnostic and Statistical Manual of Mental Disorders), processed at an unconscious level, results in more accurate classifications than consciously thinking (De Vries et al., 2010, p. 580).

"An important conclusion . . . is that it is essential to be aware of the existence of moderator conditions under which either conscious or unconscious thinking is likely to result in the best outcomes. For example, the complexity of the decision task appears to moderate the effects of unconscious thought" (De Vries et al., 2010, p. 580). They also state:

> Recent findings in psychology speak to the role of conscious and unconscious processing in judgment and decision-making. Conscious processing does not always increase the quality of judgments and decisions. When decision tasks are complex – that is, involve a large amount of information – people do not always have enough cognitive resources to consciously analyze all relevant pros and cons. Moreover, people often find it rather hard to explicitly know which aspects are most important. In such cases, unconscious processing and reliance on intuition can result in better decisions than conscious, deliberative processing (De Vries et al., 2010, pp. 578–579).

Psychotherapists also emphasize how important their intuition is for their success. Although in the early days of psychoanalysis, intuition was still dismissed as an illusion and excluded as a source of insight, today, the ability of therapists to intuitively perceive and assess patients is considered essential. In addition, intuitive references can be made to subconsciously occurring processes, dreams, and so on. This can also be seen, for example, in the often intuitively performed system or family constellations by clients. Therapists also learn to reflect on their intuitions during their supervision (with other therapists) and thus develop new potentials for their individual therapeutic approaches (Ahel, 2020, pp. 57–63).

Self-awareness and self-reflection play an essential role in training to become a psychotherapist. This involves developing and promoting specific personal and interpersonal competencies, for example, the ability to empathize. In this context, learning objectives also consist of perceiving the intuitions and emotions that the client triggers in one, verbalizing them, communicating them to others, and reflecting on them with others (Wyatt, 1948; Laireiter, 2005, pp. 50–52; Alred, 2012).

As the nurse Karen Schultz (2014) reports:

> What excites me is the realization that I possess a gut reaction . . . . Listening to . . . that little voice inside me, . . . fuels my practice and energizes my drive. It's the feeling I get when looking at a fetal heart monitoring strip when there's no rhyme or reason that the heart rate of the precious life swimming in safety is deteriorating. It's based not just on what I *see*, but also on what I *feel*. . . . In my practice, I try not to focus solely on tasks, numbers, and times. My connection to the human element is what drives my practice and enables me to listen to the voice inside that's telling me something, rather than focusing just on the numbers. As important as it is to teach nurses to use evidence to drive their practice, I believe it's also important to teach nurses to listen to their gut.

On the other hand, technological support in medical diagnostics has increased, improving examination results, medical treatments, and so on. However, it can also be observed that sometimes examinations are carried out that make sense from an economic hospital's point of view, but are, nevertheless, superfluous. Physicians use technological support to reduce the risks of misjudgments, increase confidence in their personal diagnostics, and justify their decisions out of self-protection, for example, to avoid being sued (Gigerenzer & Gaissmaier, 2012, p. 11).

Uncertainty among medical students about becoming family physicians can be traced partly to the associated need to rely on intuition. "Fear of uncertainty correlates with higher diagnostic activities. The attitude towards uncertainty correlates with the medical specialty choice by vocational trainees or medical students. An intolerance of uncertainty, which still increases as medicine is making steady progress, might partly explain the growing shortage of general practitioners" (Wübken et al., 2013).

Despite all the technological advances in medicine, the intuitive-emotional factor of empathizing with people is of utmost importance in the medical care of people.

4.3.5 Intuition of judges

People are not perfect and are, therefore, fallible. This also applies to judges because their judgments can be wrong or they judge differently on the same issue. They are subject to rationality weaknesses and cognitive distortions, bias, or "noise" (Kahneman et al., 2021), such as lack of sleep or concentration.

A judge's decision is based on subjective perceptions of presented allegations, submitted documents, alleged facts, and so on. In principle, a judge should be able to empathize with the people or the accused and understand what drove them to commit the deed or act. However, a judge's purely subjective and intuitive decision on whether a defendant is guilty or innocent is unacceptable and not provided by law. Concrete details and facts are relevant to legal judgment. The judge must analyze these objectively without any emotional influence, including intuition (Possehl & Meyer-Grashorn, 2015, p. 64).

But is that possible and desirable? Research shows that judges rely partially on intuition in practice and that legal intuition is essential for making judgments (Glöckner & Ebert, 2011, p. 159). First, judges must be personally convinced of the guilt of the accused; they must be convinced rationally of the arguments and emotionally of the credibility or incredibility of the accused. Second, judges should not simply be guided in their decisions by a legal dogma; they also need ethical guidelines and should always consider what results they produce using this dogma. For example, in which (political) system do we dispense justice? Finally, judges have to consider their holistic impression of the trial. They must decide based on their discretion, see the specific individual case, and show social competencies such as empathy. This is hardly possible without emotions and intuitions, and Guthrie et al. (2007) show that judges do indeed rely heavily on their intuition.

In the end, judges must critically reflect upon their intuitions and emotions, including bias, stereotypes, and prejudices, re-check their convictions thoroughly and deliberately, and reveal the underlying argumentation (Glöckner & Ebert, 2011, p. 160).

4.3.6 Intuition in management

Management decisions are regularly characterized by uncertainty, incomplete and ambiguous data, and time pressure. Therefore, the effective use of intuition is crucial for the success of management decisions due to the limited capacities for rational analysis (Akinci & Sadler-Smith, 2019, p. 559).

Intuition in management, especially among executives, has been the subject of research for many years; a historical review of the progress in intuition research over the last eight decades until 2012 is given by Akinci & Sadler-Smith (2012; see also Sadler-Smith, 2019 and Klein, 2003).

4.3.6.1 Criticism of the rational model and bounded rationality

The first milestone in managerial research on intuition in management is Chester Barnard‘s book *The Functions of the Executive* (Barnard, 1938). In this book, he articulates the limits of rational approaches in a dynamic and uncertain world and the role and significance of logical (conscious thinking which can be expressed in words or other symbols) and non-logical processes (intuitive mental processes that are not capable of being expressed in words or as reasoning) in managerial work. Barnard (1938, pp. 302, 311, 319–321) sees intuition as essential for sound judgments, grounded in knowledge and experience (Sadler-Smith, 2019, pp. 1–3).

Barnard's thinking profoundly impacted Herbert Simon‘s concept of bounded rationality. As a result, Herbert Simon (1955) was one of the earliest authors to provide a comprehensive critique of the limitations of the rational economic model.

Simon (1987) shows how managerial decision-making is accomplished using emotions, intuitions, and analysis in real-world settings. He demonstrates that managers regularly do not decide according to the classical theory of economic decision-making, where individuals act as maximizing individuals who have complete knowledge of all alternatives that are open to choice, the consequences that will follow on each of the alternatives, and so on (Akinci, 2011, pp. 10–11). Instead, because of limited time, limited available information, limited cognitive capabilities, and so on, most managers make satisfactory decisions, but maybe not the best possible.

Edmund Burke, the Anglo-Irish philosopher, a contemporary of the founders of classical economic theory, speaks out against an image of man that assumed an always perfect and rational human being. Instead, he sees humans as imperfect beings, characterized by both reason and emotional nature. Moreover, Burke sees reason and emotions as interconnected phenomena. At the same time, the ability to reason is very limited and varies significantly between individuals (Hall, 2011, p. 609).

Chester Barnard and Herbert Simon were the pioneers in looking at the non-rational side of managerial decision-making and intuition as a vital force in managerial life (Sadler-Smith, 2019, pp. 1–3).

For Simon, intuition is the capacity for rapid response through recognition. He suggested that "intuition is nothing more and nothing less than recognition" (Simon, 1992, p. 155). In other words, intuition enables the expert's rapid recognition of and response to situations that are marked by familiar cues and thereby gives access to large bodies of knowledge assembled through training and experience (Simon, 1987, p. 63; Simon, 1992, p. 155; see also Simon, 1955 and 1957; Akinci, 2011, p. 13).

Harry Mintzberg's *Harvard Business Review* article "Planning on the Left-Side, Managing on the Right" (1976), influenced by Robert Ornstein's book *The Psychology of Consciousness*, picked up on the assumptions that the left side of the brain is responsible for logic, abstract and analytical thinking, reasoning, numbers, science, mathematics, language, planning, and so on, and the right side of the brain for creativity and imagination, art, music, nonverbal communication, holistic thinking, emotions, and intuition. According to today's understanding, assuming managerial intuition resides on the right side and rational-analytical processes on the left side of the brain is too simple (see Section 4.2.8). But it should be emphasized that Mintzberg already recognized that American psychologists and business schools focus too much on the analytic, verbal, and logical considerations and neglect the intuitive side. And managing calls for intuition, especially when the environment is unstable. Mintzberg does not deny the value of measurement, planning, or rational and statistical analysis, but he also argues for recognizing their limitations and seeing the value of intuition. "To my mind, organizational effectiveness does not lie in that narrow-minded concept called 'rationality'; it lies in a blend of clear-headed logic and powerful intuition" (Mintzberg, 1989, p. 54).

Also, research on emotions in economic decision-making (e.g., Loewenstein & Lerner, 2003; Virlics, 2013) shows that classical and neoclassical economics are based on a simplifying model of decision-makers. "Evidences from behavioural economics, psychology, and neuroeconomics show the importance and necessity of emotions in the economic decision making process" (Virlics, 2013, p. 1011). Thus, concepts of behavioral economics or neuroeconomics integrate emotions experienced in the decision-making theory (Kahneman, 2003a; Loewenstein & Lerner, 2003; Rick & Loewenstein, 2008).

Even if corporate practice and thus also management theory would like to use control methods and tools as in physics or mathematics, the reality is completely different. Practitioners are deciding under conditions of uncertainty and complexity.

Personnel economics, a subdiscipline of economics, business administration, and human resource management, applies (micro)economic methodology and insights to the functioning of companies. This theoretical approach uses human capital theory and new institutional economics, namely principal-agent theory, transaction costs economics, and property rights theory (Dilger, 2011). The principal-agent theory (Jensen &

Meckling, 1976; Eisenhardt, 1989a), a theoretical approach in new institutional economics, assumes decision-makers who are restricted in their decision-making, for example, by asymmetric information distribution, having only incomplete information and different interests and goals. In practice, externally postulated goals and intentions can differ from goals and intentions actually pursued, both by the applicants and the selection managers

From the perspective of the principal-agent theory, there is information asymmetry in personnel selection. Applicants (agents) naturally know better than the employer/hiring manager (principal) how well their competencies are developed and what quality and motivation they can provide. The candidates know their KSAOs, how motivated they usually are at work, and which individual needs, interests, and goals they pursue. The employer can only obtain this knowledge after the applicant has been hired. There is, therefore, an information deficit on the part of the principal. This is reflected in the concept of "hidden characteristics" – the so-called unobservable characteristics of the agent. In this context, if there is already an asymmetric distribution of information ex-ante, i.e., when the employment contract is concluded, this is referred to as adverse selection. This is the result of an unequal distribution of information. This asymmetric distribution in the availability of information can now result in a matching decision in personnel selection that has not been made optimally. This means that the principal may have chosen the wrong agent (applicant) due to the lack of knowledge about their actual competencies. After all, less qualified, i.e., less productive, applicants might try to get this job. Due to the information deficit, the employer risks systematically attracting an unfavorable agent. The constellation can also exist in reverse: Potential employees (agents) are less informed about the future job or how the company is positioned for the future than the principal (Lazear, 1995, 1998, 1999; Backes-Gellner, Lazear, & Wolf, 2001, pp. 395–396; Backes-Gellner, 2004).

According to this principal-agent theory, the unequal distribution of information is a core problem of good personnel selection, both from the perspective of the company and the applicant. Therefore, this newer approach to economic theory no longer assumes that complete information is available.

But even when information is available, recent research shows that people avoid information even though it could be instrumental to their choices and might help them make better decisions (Exley & Kessler, 2021, p. 1, with references to a variety of literature, e g., Dana et al., 2006). A common hypothesis posits that individuals strategically avoid information to hold onto particular individual beliefs or take specific actions such as behaving selfishly. Examples are information about one's consumption behavior (e.g., nutritional facts that might encourage healthier eating), medical tests that might encourage lifestyle changes, environmental consequences of behaviors, investment outcomes, thorough reviews of job applications that might discourage discrimination, and so on. The economists Christine Exley and Judd Kessler found, among other things, that this could be related to people's self-image. They want to be prudently responsible and enlightened, both in the eyes of others and in their own eyes, and the fewer people know, the easier it is to do that. Suppose a person does not retrieve the available further information, this can help avoid cognitive dissonance. At the same time, the researchers find evidence that convenience and inattention may play a role when people are not seeking additional information (Exley & Kessler, 2021).

Therefore, it can be stated that the classical economic principles and assumptions are unrealistic standards for managerial decision-making processes (see also Section 3.7.2).

The concept of bounded rationality or the principal-agent theory can certainly explain and predict human decision-making behavior in organizations better than traditional economic theory. However, highly influential researchers such as Kahneman and Tversky also point out criticisms of an intuitive or heuristics-based approach. The *behavioral decision theory* by Kahneman and Tversky (1974) is a milestone in intuition research in management (Akinci & Sadler-Smith, 2012, p. 108; Sadler-Smith, 2019, p. 4). These two scientists explored the systematic biases resulting from intuition errors in choices and judgments. These errors arise, for example, from fallacies and miscalculations in human information processing (Tversky & Kahneman, 1974, p. 1124). Tversky and Kahneman (1974, p. 1131) explored three heuristics (representativeness, availability, and adjustment and anchoring; see Section 4.2.3) that arise when judging under uncertainty. The authors conclude that these heuristics are, to a great extent, economical and usually effective but can lead to foreseeable and systematic errors. Consequently, people must understand the limited validity of their judgments and be aware of the heuristics and biases (Tversky & Kahneman, 1974, p. 1131).

Thus, intuitions and heuristics do not automatically lead to good decisions. And the managers should also know in which situation which heuristic should be applied (Gigerenzer & Gaissmaier, 2012, p. 23).

4.3.6.2 Intuitive decisions in management

That managers use their intuition when making complex and non-routine decisions, i.e., strategic decisions, has been confirmed by a large number of research results (e.g., Kahneman & Klein, 2009, Akinci & Sadler-Smith, 2019; Eisenhardt, 1999 or Simon, 1987), and these results highlight the benefits of intuition used in strategic decision-making, such as faster decisions, improved performance, and other enhanced decision-making outcomes under conditions of unknowable risks (Samba et al., 2019, p. 1).

Daniel Idenbergs' study (1984, p. 81) of senior managers found that their decisions were highly intuitive:

> Most successful senior managers do not closely follow the classical rational model of first clarifying goals, assessing the situation, formulating options, estimating likelihoods of success, making their decision, and only then taking action to implement the decision. Nor do top

> managers select one problem at a time to solve, as the rational model implies. Instead of having precise goals and objectives, successful senior executives have general overriding concerns and think more often about how to do things than about what is being accomplished. In addition to depending on their ability to analyze, they also rely heavily on a mix of intuition and disciplined analysis in their decision-making and incorporate their action on a problem into their diagnosis of it.

In 1986, he claimed that one of the reasons for this is the complexity of strategic decisions and the information uncertainty.

It is emphasized repeatedly that years of leadership experience cannot be put into words or justified with rational reasons; executives simply feel the right decision. One example is a decision made by Steve Jobs. He introduced the iPod to the market in 2001. Market analyses, marketing surveys, and consultants estimated that the time was wrong. First of all, the device was considered too expensive, and the best times of the New Economy were over. But Jobs had a different gut feeling, prevailed, and was right with his decision (Treufetter, 2006, p. 167). Severin Schwan, CEO of Roche, states: "Without intuition, I would be lost as head of a research-based pharmaceutical company" (Quoted in Fröse et al., 2015, p. 6). Thomas Sattelberger (2019), a former member of the Board of Management for Human Resources at Daimler and Deutsche Telekom, also writes that entrepreneurial plans should be steered by gut feeling, as the economic ratio is not sufficient.

Thus, Dane and Pratt (2007) argue that intuition will be more likely to function as an effective component of decision-making in performance domains that require significant experience and complex domain-relevant schema, a description that fits the world of executives. Therefore, executives use specific rules or heuristics on which they unconsciously and intuitively rely to make decisions regarding people, strategies, and investments. Every executive has a personal toolbox consisting of different intuitive decision rules and heuristics that have emerged from their experiences (Gigerenzer & Gaissmaier, 2016, pp. 34; Maidique, 2011).

Another study by Gigerenzer & Gaissmaier (2012, p. 20) shows that experienced managers often have a gut feeling about the best solution. These managers consider a few significant reasons relevant to a decision and regularly one good reason rather than many in their decision-making because "less time and less information (can) lead to better decisions" (Gigerenzer, 2007, p. 46; see also Dawes, 1979; Gigerenzer & Gaissmaier, 2012, p. 15).

In a survey, Gigerenzer & Gaissmaier (2012, p. 20) found that 100% of respondents from all hierarchical levels answered that they make about 50% of their professional decisions based on their gut feeling. Another survey of 50 top managers and board members from the automotive industry determines how many of the last ten professional decisions were gut decisions. 76% of those surveyed say that they make most of their decisions based on intuition. Even 10% admit that they always listen to their gut feeling. Nobody replies that they had never or only sometimes relied on their gut feeling.

And Julmi et al. (2016, p. 200) found that the more independent the managers and the more often they are in the final decision-making position, they rely on their intuition (Paprika, 2008). The higher the managers are ranked in hierarchy (which is often accompanied by more extraordinary experience), the more likely managers acknowledge their intuition and make intuitive decisions (Gigerenzer & Gaissmaier, 2012, p. 21). Buchanan et al. (2006) found a positive effect on the perception of intuition that arises when good decisions are made based on gut feelings. As a result, managers who have made the right decisions in complex situations based on their intuition are admired and spread optimism.

Harper (1988) examines the differences in competencies between the top- and mid-level managers. He concludes that intuitive skills, in particular, distinguish top managers from mid-level managers. Among other things, they must extract the most critical information for the company from a multitude of data, be visionaries and strategists, and see the big picture. Intuitive skills

> help executives see things that other people don't see and incorporate factors computers still cannot handle. This quality, more than any other, may be what separates the true executive from the hundreds of thousands of managers . . . . They capitalized on their intuitive skills and changed the way people live and work today. . . . It is an interesting paradox that in the middle of the computer revolution, the intuitive skill to sift through all the information – to see the forest through the trees – may be as important as the information itself (Harper, 1988, pp. 13, 15, 16).

Malewska (2015, p. 104) found that top-level managers rely more on their intuition, and middle and lower-management levels rely more on analytics or a mixture of analytics and intuition.

> This can be explained by the fact that at lower levels of management decision problems are often predictable, repeatable and have a clear and complete structure. This promotes the use of the rational approach that requires fuller information, and is often based on previously tested solutions. The study results also allowed for a positive verification of the assumption that styles which integrate the intuitive and rational approaches are dominant in the decision-making practice. On the other hand, decision-makers do not use extreme styles, i.e., "pure" intuitive or "pure" rational. . . . It may be noted that managers more often treat the intuitive and rational approaches as complementary, rather than exclusive styles. This is presumably a growing trend. This stems largely from the environment in which modern enterprises operate. It is characterized by strong competition, unpredictability, volatility and complexity. As the traditional decision support techniques become less useful, managers look for new ways to enhance the effectiveness of decisions. Therefore, they resort to intuition which enables them to acquire and synthesize a large amount of information necessary to make the right decision.

Our empirical research also confirms that the higher the decision-makers are in the company hierarchy, the higher the acceptance of their intuitive decisions (Reichelt, 2020, p. 62). In addition, a majority of the 72% admit to denying intuitive decisions to third parties and using obfuscation strategies. Most respondents state that intuition is often a taboo subject in their company and is not openly discussed (see

Section 5.3 for the topic "rationalization of intuitive decisions"). For the organizational context, intuition is more likely to be accepted in selecting personnel, but less in departments such as accounting and finance (Gigerenzer & Gaissmaier, 2012, p. 21).

Lisa Burke and Monica Miller (1999, pp. 91–94) interviewed 60 experienced professionals holding significant positions in major organizations across various industries in the United States (39 men and 21 women). They found that 56% of the interviewed managers understand intuitive decisions as being based on previous experiences and emotional input. For them, intuition is beneficial and can be trusted in specific scenarios: 49% of respondents say they use intuition often in the workplace; 40% use intuition in personnel or people-related tasks such as interviewing, hiring, or performance appraisals. And almost all respondents (91.5%) say to combine intuition with data analysis. Burke and Miller (1999, p. 94) also state that older or experienced employees in managerial positions tend to use their intuition more than others. And they quote a manager:

> Intuition is not some mystical or magical thing. Instead, it takes advantage of how our brains are designed to think about things subconsciously and bring those things to the forefront when needed. A smart organization will recognize employees who have this skill.

The research of Samba et al. (2019, pp. 2–4) suggests that the benefits of using intuition in decision-making also accrue to teams. The team or collective intuition results from intense team interactions, the richness of interpretations of recognized patterns, or generating a more holistic picture of the decision-making context.

Researchers such as Eisenhardt (1989b, 1999), Okhuysen and Bechky (2009), Salas et al. (2010), Dayan and Elbanna (2011), Dayan and Di Benedetto (2011), Elbanna (2015), or Akinci and Sadler-Smith (2019) conclude that team or collective intuition enhances the ability to identify strategic issues, such as threats and opportunities faster, helps teams to work faster and more effectively, and increases creativity. In addition, team intuition is positively related to the market success and the speed to markets of new products, and higher levels of environmental turbulence increase this impact.

Decision theory and game theory findings also show that human decisions are shaped considerably, not by rationality or the principles of game theory but by subjective assessments and intuitions (Leitl, 2006, pp. 22–25; see Coyne & Horn, 2009).

Intuitive concepts such as "system constellations" are also used by consultants. System constellation can be used, for example, to deal with complex change projects and management situations and to overcome organizational defensive routines of the participants. This intervention tool can also be used to detect relationship structures and related mechanisms of action in organizations, establish or improve relationships, or uncover a hidden truth. Employees participating in these system constellations act as "resonating bodies" to make implicit knowledge about the organization, tangible through mental or physical perceptions, talking about their intuitions, emotions, and so on (Gehlert, 2020; Birkenkrahe, 2008).

Gigerenzer's research (2007) showed that we should trust our intuition when we think about things that are challenging to predict. A rational analysis pays off when it is necessary to explain the past, when the future is highly predictable, or when abundant information is available. But the future is not entirely predictable despite possible advances in AI. Therefore, successful change management should not only be based on rational control but also include intuitive empathy and emotional reflections with the affected employees.

In strategic management, intuitive competencies are necessary to imagine the future, develop imaginations, and draw the correct conclusions from the perception of complex, incomplete, ill-structured, and often contradictory information. Furthermore, it is about assessing the significance of this information for the company and especially for the future. Calabretta et al. (2017) show that both intuition and rationality play essential roles in strategic decision-making. However, a framework that accounts explicitly for the interplay between intuition and rationality is still missing. Their study addressed this gap by using a paradox lens and conceptualizing the intuition–rational-analytical duality as a paradoxical tension. They found that the management of the tension and thus the integration of intuitive and rational practices starts with preparing the ground for paradoxical thinking by creating managerial acceptance of the contradictory elements of rational and intuitive approaches to decision-making.

Huang and & Pearce (2015) found that angel investors' decisions are based on a combination of expertise-based intuition and formal analysis, in which intuition trumps analysis, contrary to reports in other investment contexts. They also found that their reported emphasis on assessments of the entrepreneur accurately predicts extraordinarily profitable venture success four years later.

The research results of Tabesh & Vera (2020) show that managers must understand the value of improvisational decision-making, particularly in the context of crisis, for example, the Covid-19 pandemic or in other uncertain environments (Lloyd-Smith, 2020), and the balanced combination of intuitive and comprehensive decision-making processes.

> Intuition involves deep situational awareness, coupled with experience. While the subconscious mind runs in the background, processing information, intuitive decision-making relies on the ability to listen to these messages (e. g., images or abstractions) and decipher them. . . . By recombining the cognitive or affective elements of prior intuitions with the realities of the crisis at hand, TMTs (top management teams) can find more effective solutions to unanticipated situations than they do with a lack of, or a limited pool of expertise in using intuition . . . (W)e argue that simultaneous attention to both comprehensive and intuitive decision processes enables decision-makers to better handle the tensions inherent in improvisation and the discomfort that accompany paradoxical situations. . . . (T)he highest quality decisions during crisis can be achieved through balanced combination of comprehensive, intuitive, and improvisational approaches to decision-making. Balanced combination of these processes requires paradoxical

> thinking, which in turn, depends on acceptance of the differences and tensions among them (e. g., Calabretta et al., 2017), and recognition that quick analyses and intuitive ability to identify similar patterns in past experienced events are resources that enrich improvisational processes. Organizations can offer executive development training and retention programs to foster expertise in comprehensive and intuitive approaches, as well as paradoxical thinking skills for effective combination of various decision-making tools (Tabesh & Vera, 2020, pp. 16, 19, 28–29).

Despite skepticism from many, especially Western business leaders, who tend to see intuition as mysterious, unexplainable, or overly emotional, and although there is a risk of managers not being taken seriously when talking about their intuitions and (gut) feelings until they can operationalize them – in recent years intuition has become a central topic in research on innovation or strategic management. One main reason for this can be seen in the development that "(m)anagement's overreliance on careful planning, established procedures, and authoritarian lines of hierarchy (is) no longer sufficient in the competitive, complex, and ever-changing business climate of the late twentieth century" (Lussier, 2016, p. 709).

In the rational business world, many managers don't dare rely on their intuitions or those of their employees. In an interview, Gigerenzer (2008c) says that, especially in large companies, managers and decision-makers often rely neither on the intuitions of experienced employees nor on their own intuitions but prefer to hire a consulting firm. Then, if something goes wrong, they are not responsible themselves. For Gigerenzer (2008c), such defensive decision-making processes are the enemy of healthy intuition and error culture. Instead, he advocates using the expertise of experienced employees. Good managers use the skills and experience of other experts at all company levels. In his experience, family businesses, in particular, have the fewest problems with intuition; here, one can say much more openly: I feel that it's better not to do that now.

It becomes apparent that using mental models and patterns and perceiving intuitive impulses are valuable steps in complex decision-making. Tacit knowledge gained through intuition plays a prominent role in management decisions, but specific circumstances, such as a learning-oriented error culture, are also needed to make constructive use of the existing intuitive competencies.

4.3.7 Intuition and entrepreneurship

Duggan (2013) shows that strategic decisions are often based on the intuitions of entrepreneurs and other decision-makers. Anticipating the future, analyzing the market, potentially value-creating business opportunities, or obtaining the necessary resources are significant for successful companies. Business acumen and imagination are thus of particular importance among entrepreneurs and in entrepreneurial thinking. This sense of the market and customer needs is often based on intuitions and the related "flashes of insight." Moreover, the decision-making situations of entrepreneurs are often new and unique, whether it is about entering a new business or buying a company, and so on. Here, the imaginations and visions and the entrepreneurs' intuition play a significant role. Therefore, a rational-analytical approach can solve many entrepreneurial problems and decisions only to a limited extent; they also require the intuitive judgment of individual entrepreneurs.

Miller and Ireland (2005) note that intuition is indispensable for entrepreneurs. The economic reality of constantly changing market conditions, limited knowledge and time, the high complexity of the world, the fast pace of life, and the expectation of quick decisions make intuition especially important for entrepreneurs. Intuition makes it possible to respond quickly to constantly changing circumstances. Additionally, intuition is linked to innovation and leads to more unconventional, creative ideas and, thus, competitive advantages (Miller & Ireland, 2005, pp. 19–20).

Akinci (2015) shows how intuitive decision-making helps entrepreneurs learn. Adopting the dual-process view of thinking and reasoning (System 1 and System 2), she highlights the dynamic interplay of intuition and analysis, for example, in the entrepreneurs' identification and discovery of market opportunities through recognition of cues, drawing from their extensive experience and learning base. Based on her research, she developed a 4 I model (intuiting, interpreting, integrating, and institutionalizing) as a conceptual framework for intuitive entrepreneurial decision-making (Akinci, 2015).

Sadler-Smith speaks of the subjective experience of entrepreneurial intuition and defines this as "affectively charged recognition and evaluation of a business venturing opportunity arising as a result of involuntary, rapid, non-conscious, associative processing" (2016a, p. 212). From his perspective, entrepreneurial intuition is a potentially fruitful but under-researched line of inquiry. Sadler-Smith developed a model of entrepreneurial intuition and drew some practical implications for his research:

> First, intuition should be given greater recognition in the design of management training, entrepreneurship development, and business education programmes, and such programmes should assist novice entrepreneurs in acquiring expert entrepreneurial prototypes, schemas, and scripts and help them build intuitive expertise; second, individual differences in expertise and preferences for intuitive and analytical processing are relevant in the entrepreneurial process and therefore should be taken into account in the selection of teams for business venturing projects, new product development, or business start-ups; third, developing better understanding of intuitive judgment is important self reflexively since knowing when/when not to discount intuitive signals has implications for how entrepreneurs can make optimal choices at crucial life junctures (Sadler-Smith, 2016a, p. 221).

Entrepreneurs of small companies also often make decisions based on the rules of thumb (heuristics) when they prepare and submit a tender, for example, for construction projects (e.g., carpentry work, painting, and plumbing work). However, primarily due to lack of time, they often do not read through every detail of the call for tender and make decisions based on heuristics. Thus, they submit tenders that are not perfect but satisfactory.

Those entrepreneurs decide more intuitively than members of the general population and middle and junior managers (Allinson et al., 2000).

But the research results of Groves & Vance (2008, pp. 149–150)

> do not support the popular notion that successful entrepreneurs favor creative, intuitive, imaginative, and emotion-driven thinking styles over careful analysis, reason, and logic. Rather, successful entrepreneurs appear to employ linear and nonlinear balance in their attention to sources of information (e.g., internal vs. external) and information processing. These exploratory results potentially provide greater insight into the thinking style of successful entrepreneurs and suggest that programs in entrepreneurship education that overemphasize the role of nonlinear modes of thought over linear approaches may risk developing entrepreneurs who are out of balance.

Thus, research on entrepreneurship confirms that entrepreneurs need and use a balance of intuitions and analytics.

4.3.8 Intuition in marketing

In marketing, it has been known for many years that people's buying behavior is controlled not only rationally and consciously but also by unconscious intuitive processes. The importance of implicit processes for purchase decisions is not only acknowledged in literature but is also studied with scientific guidance. However, the relative importance of implicit and explicit processes for judgment formation and how these two processes influence each other is controversial,. The controversy ranges from "predominantly explicit" to "predominantly implicit" to an interplay of both decision patterns. However, current research results show one thing above all: The importance of implicit and explicit processes and their interplay appears to be highly variable or is influenced by various conditions. If the consequences of a wrong decision are low, consumers tend to decide implicitly, typical for decisions at low product involvement. When product involvement is high, consumers tend to make explicit decisions. The more complex the decisions, the more likely intuitive processes enable a conflict-free decision (Naderer & Frank, 2015) and heuristics are used. When companies must decide which customers still belong to the current clientele, experienced marketing or sales managers often apply a simple rule. The hiatus heuristic: If customers have not purchased within the last months, they are no longer customers. The value of this heuristic varies by industry, but the simple rule is often as good as complicated optimization models (Wübben & Wangenheim, 2008).

Marketing managers' decisions are increasingly based on the analysis of data and using specific tools and methods. Assuming the data situation is secure and reasonably complete, decisions are made based on the analyses, and the subsequent marketing measures are implemented and evaluated. Thus, rational-analytical procedures and facts and figures are used in particular to prepare and secure decisions or to negotiate contract terms.

However, evaluating concepts, ideas, and strategies is almost always carried out using intuitions and associated feelings. When it comes to assessing trends and forecasts for the future, empathizing with specific target groups, and which specific measures to consider to address certain target groups on an emotional level, deciding which agencies to work with, which marketing strategy to choose, and so on, the marketing manager's intuition and related experience also play a significant role (Patterson et al., 2012, p. 36). When making new product ideas decisions, Eling et al. (2015) show in an experiment that only one combination, starting with intuitively analyzing the ideas and then rationally considering the results, leads to the highest quality of decisions.

On the other hand, the measurement of success is based mainly on analytics; the evaluation essentially looks at the extent to which the objectives of the measures are achieved and substantiated with figures.

4.3.9 Intuition in accounting, auditing, due diligence, and so on

Especially in number-oriented accounting or auditing, which strongly follows the approach that you can only manage what you can measure, rationally unjustifiable decisions and, thus, intuitions still have a legitimacy problem.

But even in auditing, accounting, or company valuations, it becomes obvious that auditors, accountants, and so on do not only rely on figures but that social skills and intuition are also helpful there. A prerequisite for a high-quality task fulfillment as an auditor is not only the technical expertise but also the competency to judge circumstances or risks, along with the credibility of statements accurately, for example, of employees of the accounting department in an organization. A behavioral audit theory was developed over decades (Egner 1980), and Schreiber (2000) dedicates a whole chapter to the information behavior of auditors and highlights the importance of intuition for their success. In particular, since the amount of information to be processed, legal regulations, various interpretations of professional law, and so on overstrain the conscious human information processing capacity, intuition, and feelings also used in such complex situations (Schmiele, 2012).

The research field of behavioral finance, which builds heavily on the "Prospect Theory: An Analysis of Decisions Under Risk" by Kahneman and Tversky (1979), deals in detail with the often not very rational investment decisions of capital investors. Another study of the banking, industrial, service, and public administration sectors concludes that 66% of all private and professional decisions are intuitive (Kahneman & Riepe, 1998; Thaler, 2016).

For due diligence, Siepe (2002, p. 64) sees a necessity for the experience-based "feelings" of the evaluators to critically question the appropriateness of valuations and supplement rational-analytical valuation systems.

Research shows that professional skepticism and critical thinking (Wolfe et al., 2020) can improve the quality of judgments in auditing, accounting, finance, and so on. The authors examined intuitive versus analytical thinking and found that auditors thinking intuitively were more skeptical. They conclude that auditors tend to become less skeptical when ignoring their intuition. Intuition can be a crucial element stimulating auditor skepticism, whereas overreliance on analytical processing can overwhelm auditors' intuition, thereby reducing skepticism. But whether professional skepticism is a reliable predictor of judgment quality is also critically evaluated because too much skepticism can lead to inefficient and expensive audits (Grohnert et al., 2018a, 2018b). Professionals such as auditors who had not only routine but also critical experience (such as discovering an error, struggling with a client, or finding cues of fraud), combined with the opportunity to learn from these experiences in a supportive learning climate, with valuable feedback and reflection, were found to make significantly higher-quality judgments than auditors who lacked any of the previous factors. Auditors should base their judgments on an objective and systematic approach and related evidence, and listen to their intuition critically. Intuition can give hints that have not yet been substantiated by facts but should be investigated and critically reflected upon.

4.3.10 Intuition in philosophy

Dealing with intuition has a centuries-long tradition in philosophy, and thus there are many approaches and considerations. However, describing these different approaches goes beyond this book's scope. For this reason, only selected aspects are considered here.

Already Plato (428/427 or 424/423 – 348/347 BC) and Aristotle (384–322 BC) advanced the idea that the grasp of facts of the non-sensual kind should be distinguished from reasoning based on sensory perceptions. Other schools of ancient Greek philosophy see intuition as an act of transcendence, by which new realizations about the nature of reality can be won (Ahel, 2020, pp. 39–40).

Duns Scotus (1266–1308) attempted to reconcile the dualism between intuition and rationality in the late Middle Ages. He differentiated between "cognitio intuitive" and "cognitio abstractive" and saw these two forms of cognition as somewhat correlative and complementary, and not contrary. The former form of knowledge occurs in the domain of sensuality before the recognizing object is given to the abstracting intellect (Koßler, 1998).

Also, the Dutch philosopher Spinoza (1632–1677) examined the interplay between intuition and rationality. He distinguishes three levels of knowledge or cognition. The knowledge of the first level is emotional-intuitive; he judges this knowledge as typically confused and false. The second level of knowledge is intellectual knowledge, based on a deliberate mechanism. According to Spinoza, this is based on clear concepts and well-considered universal notions. The third and highest level of knowledge is a combination of intuition, emotion, and intellect. Intuitive reasoning of level three combines the instantaneous mechanism of emotional intuition with the broad perspective and validity of conscious thinking (Ben-Zeèv & Krebs, 2016, p. 45).

In his book *The Righteous Mind*, the contemporary philosopher Jonathan Haidt (2012) addresses the question: What makes human beings moral? Haidt provides the metaphor of the rider and the elephant. The rider is the conscious mind with its rational-analytical functions and volitional power. But the elephant is everything else, especially intuitions and emotions (and all other internal presuppositions, genetic inclinations, subconscious motives, or experiences). Haidt considers the elephant is bigger and more powerful than the rider. His "first rule of moral psychology" is: "Intuitions come first, strategic reasoning second" (Haidt, 2012, p. 367). Human morality is primarily the result of internal predispositions, which Haidt calls intuitions. These intuitions predict how we lean on various issues, questions, or decisions. The rational mind has far less control over our moral frameworks than we might think. Intuition is much more essential and determinative than reasoning. It is the interplay of intuition and rationality that makes up human intelligence.

4.3.11 Intuition in pedagogy and social work

Intuition is a significant element in pedagogical work. Eggenberger shows that pedagogically active persons let their actions be guided by intuition. Pedagogues and social workers report that when they are in a relationship with others, they perceive their intuitions as simply happening, bringing about ideas based on their evident subjective experiences. Intuition provides critical psychological data to identify motives in people's behavior as well as in their interpersonal relationships (Eggenberger, 1998, pp. 7, 202–204, and 500).

The professional behaviors of not just pedagogues and social workers, but also parents' behavior, are based on interaction processes. In addition, pedagogical behaviors often require very fast decisions, so only intuitive understanding, reaction, or action is possible.

In pedagogy, there are essentially two different approaches to dealing with intuition. One is how intuition can be learned (see Chapter 9). The second approach is how intuition is used in pedagogical action and social work.

Intuitions and emotions play a significant role in human learning. For example, the well-known phrase "You learn how you feel!" shows that those who have fun and enjoy learning learn better. And the relationship between the pedagogue/educator and the learner plays a crucial role in this learning process. If the relationship is perceived positively by the parties involved and if the pedagogue succeeds in arousing positive and activating emotions such as enthusiasm and joy of learning, motivation to learn is created. To arouse these positive emotions toward each other, intuitive-empathic skills are required.

Intuition helps to perceive and interpret the affective reactions (expressed, for example, in gestures or facial expressions) of the other person, whereby the interpretation in the perceiver does not necessarily have to correspond to the internal content or the subjective experience of this emotion in the other person (Huber, 2017, p. 452).

To be successful in pedagogical contexts, social work, and counseling, people rely on their unconscious, implicit experiential knowledge.

But intuition serves not only as a source of empathy with others but also of self-organization and self-control. Intuition can also function as an impetus for an educational or therapeutic intervention that asks specific questions and can support other person's insights and lead to changes in behavior.

Intuition is thus essential for the professional building of relationships. This intuitively controlled engagement with another, knowing how to face the other person in a given situation, and intuitively recognizing what the other person is willing to do or not willing to do, are examples of the importance of intuitively grasping the other (Martell, 2018, pp. 21–24).

5 Intuition in personnel selection processes

In the first sentence of their groundbreaking publication, "With recruitment I always feel I need to listen to my gut," Miles and Sadler-Smith (2014, p. 624) illustrate that the use of intuitions is always person- and context-specific and that managers need to use their intuition, especially in employee hiring decisions. Although further research on the topic of intuition in management studies is indicated, especially concerning using intuition in personnel selection, Miles and Sadler-Smith (2014, p. 622) conclude that "(I)ntuition is . . . an important element of the hiring process so long as human judges are involved."

And, this has many reasons and advantages.

5.1 Advantages of intuition in personnel selection

5.1.1 Intuitions are an inner knowledge

Human beings do not function like machines because they are, by nature, endowed with feelings and intuitive abilities. These emotional and intuitive competencies are an evolutionary achievement and show that humans cannot survive without intuitions and emotions.

Intuition is a natural process, just like seeing and hearing. Therefore, it's an essential provider of information. Moreover, humans can rely on this intuitive information in everyday life and trust it in many situations, for example, recognizing dangers and risks or distinguishing a friend from a foe (and undertaking a fight or flight response). Thus, getting messages quickly and unconsciously by intuition is a survival advantage.

The behavioral response to a perceived threat must be translated directly into actions, without intellectual or conscious categorization. From this perspective, it becomes clear that intuition can lead directly to action and that coupling it with consciousness and language is only secondary (Schmid et al., 1999, p. 5). Also, from an evolutionary perspective, too much reflection and differentiated recognition, although necessary, can lead to people not acting quickly enough..

Humans have developed quasi-automated mechanisms and do not consciously perceive most decisions, based on intuition. However, intuitive processes, in which individuals' thoughts, feelings, and actions are subject to a certain automatism, make it possible that internalized ways of thinking, feeling, and behaving can be called up, without any processing effort and be applied without further focusing on them.

Intuition is based on patterns that human beings have developed in their past experiences, such as perceiving and evaluating exhibited behaviors of other people,

https://doi.org/10.1515/9783110980967-005

in a specific way. Intuition arises from one's own experience. That means intuition is based on data. From the time human beings are born, they constantly seek out patterns in their environment; and by unconsciously using these patterns, humans compare information from a stimulus with past experiences and information stored in their memory. The human brain (or body) sorts experienced behaviors and decisions into "successful" and "unsuccessful" categories. If a situation is similar to one the person already knows, human intuition kicks in and guides humans in a particular direction. It ensures that a behavior pattern perceived as successful is unconsciously repeated. Experienced selection managers have developed and internalized these automated selection systems, over time. Essential components of the intuitive information processing system are the visual system and the associative memory (Kahneman et al., 2011, p. 52).

Intuitions as inner knowledge are based on human experience and can provide important information and support people in making coherent decisions. By subconsciously using implicit or tacit knowledge and specific memory patterns, humans have access to the inner treasure trove of intuitive wisdom. Thus, people know more than they are consciously aware of and can verbally communicate.

Based on interviews with hiring managers, Küpers (2015, pp. 71–77) recognizes intuitions and emotions as internal predictors for the quality of the information received. Intuitions help managers match the logic and results of a rational analysis with their experience. Thus, intuition can provide a sense of evidence that leads to security in decision-making.

Intuition is considered a gift of nature to help humans cope with the world's challenges. Thus, Treufetter (2009, p. 13) describes intuition as a valuable human intelligence and inner wisdom.

Ferguson (1999, p. XI) states it as follows:

> I maintain that intuition is a sleeping giant of a capability within every one of us, a wonderful phenomenon of nature that we experience constantly, and a readily available tool for building a better future for humanity.

And Treufetter (2009, p. 7) quotes the US immunologist Jonas Balk:

> It is always exciting to wake up in the morning and wonder what intuition, like gifts from the sea, has brought me. I work with my intuition; I trust it. Intuition is my partner.

Eberle (2017, p. 83) and Lehrer (2009, pp. 319–320) emphasize that intuition brings together all the "wisdom of our experience." If intuition is ignored, the use of the entire "treasure of knowledge" stored in the brain is prevented.

Intuition can broaden perspective and draw on information that cannot be accessed by purely analytical thinking. Thus, intuition can be a valuable source of information, especially in complex decision-making in which people feel uncertain and many influential factors are included – as in personnel selection.

That is why, it is desirable to listen to the inner voice of intuition and have confidence in what it tells, but, at the same time, reflect on it critically, before making important decisions.

5.1.2 Intuition helps cope with complexity

Decision-makers in companies are confronted with the demands of a VUCA world (Bennett & Lemoine, 2014, p. 27; for managing the human dynamics in a VUCA context, see Baran & Wozny, 2021), particularly in fast-changing industries or in quickly evolving markets, where decisions have many interrelations. In particular, when selecting talent, organizations and selection managers act in an interconnected world, with high ambiguity, instability, and, thus, complexity.

Highly complex situations are challenging to manage by only conscious cognitive processing. Thus, the complexity of the modern VUCA world overwhelms people's rational-analytical thinking and capacity. C.G. Jung (1972) states that there is usually no accurate understanding of human life from a rational-analytical perspective alone. Therefore, intuition is indispensable to cope constructively with the world's complexity.

Research, for example, in neuroscience, shows that the capacity of the conscious working memory is limited. However, to make effective selection decisions in these highly complex situations, hiring managers need input from all parts of the brain or body.

Intuitions as context-specific automatic inspirations are based on unconscious processes of associative perception, processing, and information integration. Furthermore, the brain is a "pure self-organization" (Zeuch, 2008, p. 59), enabling humans to unconsciously perceive, store, and process significantly more data than can consciously be called up. Due to the unconscious parallel processing of information, the human brain can simultaneously process a multitude of data and coordinate cognitive schemata. Thus, intuition helps people solve problems, be associative and creative, and develop new things without consciously drawing on the resources in humans' brains.

Intuition allows fast decision-making, with reduced complexity. While the conscious human mind has clear limits to perform in complex situations, the subconscious mind can process several million pieces of information per second (up to 11 million bits per second); the conscious mind only manages 0.1 percent of that maximum capacity of 50–60 bits per second (Markowsky, 2021; Holtfort, 2011, p. 507). Zeuch (2008, p. 59) concludes that this is proof of subconscious resources that serve as the basis for intuition.

According to Dijksterhuis and Nordgren (2006), conscious thought (attention) needs more processing capacity than unconscious thought. This is because the conscious can only think about one subject at a time and remember about seven stimuli for a short period.

> Try to think (consciously!) about where to spend your next summer holiday, about the next paper you want to write, and about what to eat tonight – all at exactly the same time, please. Of course, you cannot do this. Conscious capacity is limited, and generally, consciousness cannot do more than one thing at a time. . . . Depending on the context, consciousness can process between 10 and 60 bits per second. For example, if you read, you process about 45 bits per second, which corresponds to a fairly short sentence. The entire human system combined, however, can process about 11,200,000 bits per second. The visual system alone processes about 10 million bits per second. This interesting early research very clearly points out that conscious processing capacity is very low compared with the processing capacity of the entire human system (Dijksterhuis & Nordgren, 2006, pp. 96–97).

Dijksterhuis (2010) and Dijksterhuis and Nordgren (2006) emphasize the superiority of unconscious information processing (deliberation-without-attention) in complex decisions.

> Unconscious thought and conscious thought have different characteristics, and these different characteristics make each mode preferable under different circumstances. For instance, contrary to popular belief, decisions about simple issues can be better tackled by conscious thought, whereas decisions about complex matters can be better approached with unconscious thought (Dijksterhuis & Nordgren, 2006, p. 95).

In summary, intuition calls up relevant memory patterns and other unconscious information for deciding in complex situations, leading to an experience-based reduction of complexity and effective decision-making (Dane and Pratt, 2007, p. 43). However, intuition is based not only on recognizing and reproducing past experiences, but also on making holistic associations and combining complex elements in the shortest possible time, thus, deciphering a situation. Moreover, associative decision-making is based on connections between different parts of the human brain or – maybe – other parts of the body; it allows for connections (associations) to be formed between seemingly unrelated ideas, and so on. Thus, it allows combining analytical and intuitive cognitive processing.

Hence, before making important decisions about things such as partnership/marriage, career, or hiring, people should not only rely on factual-rational considerations or the help of pro and con lists, but also primarily ask their "inner voice" and listen to their intuition and related feelings.

5.1.3 Intuitive decisions can be time- and cost-effective

Another advantage of using intuition in decision-making is that it can be a resource-saving method (e.g., time, personnel capacities, and money). This aspect is documented in the literature, which states that the time-consuming and cost-intensive implementation of psychometrically valid rational-analytical methods often exceeds the possibilities of an organization or overestimates the economic benefit of analytical personnel selection, especially in SMEs (Miles & Sandler-Smith, 2014, p. 624; Kanning, 2012, pp. 21–22).

Dane et al. (2012, p. 15) identified three main factors for intuition effectiveness: *level of expertise*, *task type*, and *time pressure*. Intuition is relatively more accurate when decision-makers have acquired high domain-specific expertise. This requires managers to gain many years of experience through practice and training (Khatri & Ng, 2000, p. 58). Besides expertise, the relative accuracy of intuitive decision-making differs, according to the task type. For example, analytical decision-making is superior for a structured task with objective success criteria.

In contrast, intuition is superior in decisions that do not involve objective criteria or in solving unstructured problems, such as ethical or political judgments. Finally, time pressure is the last factor that positively influences intuition effectiveness (Dane et al., 2012, p. 15).

As neuroscientific research results show (see Section 4.2.8), although the rational-analytical and intuitive information processing systems are continuously active, the intuitive system usually dominates and is much faster than rational-analytical thinking and decision-making.

In computer simulations, it can be shown that "unconscious" decisions correspond, in the vast majority of cases, to the probabilistic solution of a rational model and, thus, enable people to make very good decisions, very quickly. The unconscious, and, thus, intuition, enables individuals at least potentially to decide and act in the sense of the rational decision model (Jekel et al., 2012, pp. 147–148; Glöckner & Towfigh, 2015, p. 272).

Gigerenzer & Gaissmaier (2015, p. 31) show that accurate intuitive decisions increase with expertise and experience. Schmidt et al. (2016) show that unstructured or semi-structured job interviews can have relatively high validity, if the selection managers are experienced. Thus, intuition based on the experience and expertise of managers should not only be seen as a possible source of error but rather an efficient way of making decisions that leads to equally exact and, under certain circumstances, such as uncertainty, accurate judgments (Hertwig & Todd, 2003, p. 213).

An intuitive decision based on valid experience and correct data can, thus, help identify talent at a relatively low cost. On the other hand, the rational-analytic approach cannot connect (verbal and nonverbal) information needed to make a good decision and weigh and combine them, as quickly.

Therefore, Gigerenzer (2007, p. 19) speaks of intuition as the unconscious intelligence of humans; intuition is not inferior to logic and the rational-analytical approach but should be regarded as its companion.

5.1.4 Intuitions as initial impressions to pick up essential information about the candidate

Intuitions and associated emotions help hiring managers form an initial impression of candidates, although the opinion of many hiring managers to rely on their first or initial impression must be viewed critically, for example, because of possible biases.

But research also shows that essential personality indicators can be perceived correctly, and the perception of only a few non-verbal cues can be a good indicator of the accuracy of personality judgment (Breil & Back, 2019; Breil et al., 2020).

Nachtwei et al. (2013, p. 35) point out that social psychology has provided evidence that only by observing a few behavioral sequences, people are very quickly and intuitively able to predict the future performance of other people (applicants) at work (Eisenkraft, 2013).

Oosterhof & Todorov (2008) state that, based on a quick, automatic, and unconscious evaluation, the first impression of an unknown person tells people whether the unknown person is trustworthy or hostile. This immediate evaluation is perceived as (subjectively) valid. Only in the case of emerging contradictory evidence do people question their initial impression (Pfister et al., 2017, p. 348). These initial impressions by selection managers are based on an interaction of intuitions and emotions and, possibly, also rationally supported selection processes.

In cognitively complex and demanding situations such as assessment centers, intuitive judgments are influential for dimension ratings and evaluation outcomes, such as predicting the performance of candidates (Kleinmann & Ingold, 2019). The assessors' initial impression can serve as a first general anchor that affects their dimension ratings; this might also explain why assessors typically fail to distinguish between the various dimensions. Thus, Ingold et al. (2018) use a dual-process theory perspective to produce a more complete understanding of judgments in assessment centers. They developed and tested a model that integrates dimension ratings in a deliberate, systematic, slow, and controlled mode (System 2) with the initial impressions in an intuitive, fast, automatic processing mode (System1).

> As such, this model offers a much-needed integration between the two modes of judgment that have been too often examined separately in research. . . . Through testing this model, we provide insights on (a) whether and how initial impressions are related to dimension ratings (e.g., analytical skills, cooperation, persuasiveness, presentation skills, organizing and planning); and (b) whether initial impressions introduce potentially biasing (i.e., perceptions of liking and attractiveness) or valid (i.e., perceptions of expressed personality) information into dimension ratings that may hinder or help the prediction of performance (Ingold et al., 2018, p. 2).

Ingold et al. (2018) also consider, according to Kahneman (2003, p. 716), that "highly accessible impressions produced by System 1 control judgments and preferences, unless modified or overridden by the deliberate operations of System 2." The key findings of their research are:

> As a first key conclusion, assessors' initial impressions displayed a considerable positive relationship with dimension ratings. Thus, they seem to serve as an anchor for these subsequent dimension ratings. Initial impressions were also similarly related to all dimension ratings, which helps explain why these ratings are often undifferentiated within an exercise . . . Second, various analyses suggest that assessors' initial impressions captured some accurate and valid information and did not appear to open up the door for biases and stereotypes. This is because the criterion-related validities of dimensions did not increase when controlling for initial impressions, and the mediation model indicates that the personality-related information captured by initial impressions is criterion-relevant. We found evidence that in the first two minutes, assessors pick up personality traits (conscientiousness, emotional stability) that assessees expressed and that converged with their personality self-reports. Although appearance and liking judgments are quickly available at the start of an exercise, these two aspects did not influence assessors' initial impressions. Moreover, initial impressions did not exhibit larger gender differences than AC dimension ratings. These more positive effects of initial impressions run contrary to common thinking in ACs . . . .
>
> Third, our conclusion that initial impression ratings reflect some accurate information should be qualified, because it is based on the average initial impression ratings of five raters . . . . Thus, it should be acknowledged that an *individual* initial impression rating also captures rater idiosyncrasies and shows low interrater reliability . . . . One implication is that multiple raters are needed for initial impressions to show acceptable interrater reliability (Ingold et al., 2018, p. 7).

Thus, this research confirms particular influence and importance of intuitions in assessing candidates. At the same time, it also becomes clear that extensive training of hiring managers and intensive exchange and critical reflection on the initial impressions can increase interrater reliability and reduce negative influences of initial impressions, in selection processes.

5.1.5 Intuition helps assess candidate-manager/supervisor, candidate-team, and candidate-organization fit

Personnel selection refers to the systematic process of assessing and predicting the Person-Job, Person-Team, and Person-Organization fit (Ziegler & Bühner, 2012).

Intuitions create the feeling of knowing for sure whether a candidate fits in terms of personality, values, attitudes, and so on, as also with the selection manager or supervisor, the team, the organizational culture, values, and so on (Nachtwei et al., 2013, p. 38).

Hiring managers experience something that pops into their minds and body, the source and significance of which are not immediately apparent. This may be called a sudden insight, a gut feeling, or a hunch (as synonyms for intuition). For the managers, it's hard to describe it, because they are unaware of the steps that led to that specific emotion and intuition.

This intuition occurs involuntarily and is exposed as positive or negative attitudes towards candidates, and its effectiveness is seen differently, according to the organizational context. For example, when there is a lack of data on which decisions can be made rationally and when hard facts are missing or considered insufficient, intuition is seen as a valuable and effective source of information, particularly in SMEs. For hiring managers, intuitions are an appropriate indicator of a candidate's overall impression and the candidate-manager/supervisor, candidate-team, and candidate-organization fit (Miles & Sadler-Smith, 2014, pp. 615–616).

Companies regularly do not want employees who only meet formal requirements. They also try to assess candidates' attitudes and values, communication and relationship-building skills, emotional competencies, and so on, and if they would like to work with this applicant. People meet other people not only with their ability to think but also with their emotions and their heart. Human perceptions and decisions are always connected with emotions (Nachtwei et al., 2013, p. 34). Also, humans perceive emotions primarily on the non-verbal level.

Social judgments and decisions can not only be explicit and conscious but also implicit and unconscious. Social judgments based on perceiving body language and facial expressions tend to be more implicit and unconscious.

Using the example of recruitment consultants, Kinnunen & Parviainen (2016, pp. 5–7) show that in selection processes, the perception of applicants' body language has a central role. Recruitment is a process of affective decision-making, where hiring managers use their intuitions and feelings to secure the optimal organization-person fit. The authors quote a recruitment consultant with the following sentence:

> It's the feeling when you interview someone, how they behave, what kind of personality they are, how they go down with you . . . It's the impression that you get of the person . . . How they would fit the team, how you could work with them . . . . Quite often the first impression – when you shake hands with them if something prickles in the back of your head because there's something strange – quite often it's better to follow that (Kinnunen & Parviainen (2016, p. 5).

Kinnunen & Parviainen applied, in particular, Dane and Pratt's (2007) conception of intuition as a non-conscious process that involves rapidly produced holistic associations that result in affectively charged judgments. Relying on feelings, the decision-making of the recruitment consultant can be seen as a form of an intuitive process. And it becomes clear that consultants' judgments about candidates' social skills, professional competencies, or how their personalities fit into the working environments are justified by affective resonances in the consultants' bodies. The candidates' body language generates different feelings, such as "good vibrations" or "strange feelings" in the recruitment consultants. Thus, it's not surprising that the recruitment consultants describe their intuition as the core of their professional skills.

Since body language can't lie, in the long run, it is an excellent supplementary source of information to judge people holistically. Alice Miller (2005), who experienced the importance of discovering and accepting emotions for mental health as a psychoanalyst, pointed out: "The body never lies."

According to Kinnunen & Parviainen (2016, p. 12), three main factors influence intuition and, thus, intuitive decision-making in personnel diagnostics.

1. The first factor by which an intuitive assessment and, thus, a prediction of the fit can be made is the body language, for example, the gestures of the applicants. Examples are a firm handshake or a positive way of making eye contact.
2. The second main factor is the appearance of the candidate. Personnel selection decisions are influenced by how the outward appearance is perceived, for example, by the applicant's physical charisma, dress, makeup, visible tattoos, piercings, body shape, for example, overweight, hairstyle, or appearance of fitness, as a predictor of sick leave and resilience (Kinnunen & Parviainen, 2016, p. 13).
3. The third factor that Kinnunen and Parviainen (2016, p. 15) emphasize is the authenticity of an applicant's personality. The intuition of the personnel diagnostician is, therefore, also influenced by the impression of whether the candidate's presentation seems authentic and whether they appear friendly and trustworthy.

The three main factors presented above lead, in particular, to intuitive social assessments and predictions concerning soft skills and personality of the applicant (Kleebaur, 2007, pp. 49, 100) as well as team fit and job performance (Miles & Sadler-Smith, 2014, p. 615).

Hiring managers we interviewed confirm that their intuition helps judge whether applicants' behaviors are perceived as authentic or not. Through the interview statements of the practitioners, the study results of Kinnunen & Parviainen (2016) confirm that in addition to gestures and appearance, authenticity is a significant factor judged intuitively in personnel diagnostics (Deters, 2019, p. 127).

To demonstrate the importance of intuition for personnel selection in practice, two further practical examples are shown below. Gigerenzer & Gaissmaier (2012, p. 4) illustrate how a "headhunter" (recruitment consultant), who has placed more than one thousand top executives in Germany in their positions, experienced the conflict between intuition and analytics in his daily work. On the one hand, he felt threatened by the testing procedures used by young and inexperienced people, especially psychologists. On the other hand, he believed that these tests would be used only to maintain the appearance of objectivity. In practice, however, one could not rely on the results of, for example, personality tests. If a manager is hired, and it turns out that s/he does not perform, the responsible selection managers might say: "we couldn't have known that beforehand. The tests didn't predict that." So, they protect themselves when they use an analytical procedure. The method of that headhunter is to interview candidates and then intuitively feel whether there is a fit between the candidate and the role and the team. He estimates that only about five percent of placements made by relying on his intuition have been unsuccessful over the years. An essential prerequisite for his hiring success is intuition and knowing the specific company, its prevailing culture, and the job requirements.

The team fit can be systematically observed, interpreted, and evaluated. Against the background of the various team situations with individual characters, such a design in the practical corporate context is associated with challenges and considerable effort. One approach could be using company values, which are the basis for company-wide cooperation and form the basis for behavioral anchors in the interpersonal sphere. On the one hand, it is conceivable and possible to use psychometric valid test procedures for a team fit; however, very many companies do not have the resources and knowledge to use such test procedures, adequately. Thus, whether people fit together is decided primarily at the emotional level of the relationship. On this emotional level, both applicants and managers sense whether they fit together and whether there is a match between the company, team, and candidate (Carpender, 2013; Kootz, 2014, pp. 89 and 143; Athanas & Wald, 2014, pp. 14; McCarthy et al., 2017; Miles & McCamey, 2018). Therefore, selection managers usually rely on their intuitive and emotional competencies to test the applicants' team fit and cultural match, and vice versa for the candidates.

As described in more detail in Section 4.2.8, neuroscientific studies show that human survival depends on accurate social judgments, for example, correct interpretation of vocal stimuli such as voice pitch, body language signals, or facial expressions. In addition, in many situations, individuals must decide whether another person is someone to trust or distrust, to approach or avoid. To assess something like that, intuitive-emotional competencies are needed.

Miles & Sadler-Smith (2014, pp. 608–609) describe situations in which selection managers use intuition. Accordingly, intuition helps recruit some employee groups for which no suitable test procedures exist. Examples include software designers and developers who, for example, can be suitable candidates for vacant positions despite striking personality profiles. Furthermore, personnel diagnostic procedures are accompanied by a flood of information and enormous time pressure. Here, too, intuition is deliberately used to benefit from the described reduction in complexity.

According to Miles and Sadler-Smith (2014, p. 622), and this is also confirmed by the selection managers we interviewed, intuition is particularly used for the final personnel decision-making, for example, with equally well-qualified and suitable applicants. And, precisely in such a final selection, the human fit is the decisive decision-making factor

5.1.6 Intuition helps create good relationships and positive candidate experiences in selection processes

Selection, especially a selection interview, is a social exchange (Kanning, 2004, p. 409). Thus, selection interviews are conducted not only to share information but also to build rapport. Intuition and emotions allow hiring managers to unlock more contextual dialogue options that help build positive relationships.

Positive relationships are built, in particular, through consistent, authentic behaviors and appearances in which verbal and non-verbal signals match.

Non-verbal behaviors, such as facial or emotional expressions, are mainly universal social signals (e.g., a friendly smile as an expression of joy) and influence social interactions and emotional exchanges through informative, evocative, and incentive functions (Keltner & Kring, 1998). Thus, gestures, facial expressions, tone of voice, manner of speaking, posture, and other nonverbal expressions give information to hiring managers about the applicant's emotional state, relational status, behavioral intention, and so on. These emotional expressions of the applicants evoke specific responses in the hiring managers and vice versa.

If hiring managers want to win people for a company, a task, or a change, they cannot try to convince with rational arguments alone. They have to win people's hearts. Convincing people, therefore, requires particularly well-developed social-communicative and emotional skills. This includes building a positive and sustainable relationship with the candidate, which is not possible without empathy and the intuitive and authentic expression of positive feelings, especially at the non-verbal level. Also, empathy and intuition are very closely related. Moreover, empathy can be shown at verbal and non-verbal levels. When managers are in good contact with themselves and the candidates, and, at the same time, can sense their own and the candidates' emotional needs, they will be successful.

In a study on the relationship between transformational leadership and performance, Ng (2017) was able to show, among other things, the importance of affective, motivational, and social exchange mechanisms that lead to performance outcomes. Applied to the field of personnel selection, this means that selection managers must positively create the social exchange between themselves and the applicant. To do this, they have to interact with the candidates emotionally. This requires intuitive and emotional competencies.

A psychometrically valid standardized interview with pre-defined questions, strict adherence to the order of the questions, and without the possibility of follow-up questions carries the risk that questions may appear out of place and give the interview the character of an inquiry. Such an interview moves from social exchange and dialogue to an interrogation (Schmidt-Atzert & Amelang, 2012, p. 337).

A selection interview is not only an exchange of questions and answers but also a social process in which the participants influence each other (Kanning, 2004, p. 409). Thus, the formulation of questions or the interviewers' behavior affects their counterparts. For example, if the interview situation is characterized by politeness, respect, appreciation, and concentration, or if the interviewer seems somewhat disinterested and mentally absent, the result of the interview may be very different (Kanning, 2004. p. 409). These different behaviors trigger different feelings in applicants to decide against or for an organization (Kanning, 2004. p. 409).

Research on candidate experiences shows that the competition for the best talent is about recruiting in an applicant-oriented manner (Miles & McCarney, 2018). This goes beyond the mere selection process and attempts to integrate the applicant's perspective. Companies pursue their endeavor of giving candidates a positive experience and overall impression of the company throughout the entire recruiting process, since a positive candidate experience plays a decisive role in whether a candidate decides for or against a job offer (Verhoeven, 2016, p. 14).

Klaffke (2014) and Verhoeven (2016) show that applicants and employees are looking for social and emotional support, security, and purpose in their jobs, especially in the Western world.

Surveys show that the impression from the interviews regarding employer attractiveness is crucial for applicants (85.6%). This shows that, especially in Western cultures, emotional, competent, and transparent communication at eye level and a benevolent attitude that expresses respect and appreciation are crucial to applicants (Athanas & Wald, 2014, pp. 17–18).

A study by Uggerslev et al. (2012, pp. 631–632) determined that, among other things, the behaviors of the selection managers and the relationship with the recruiter significantly influence the employer's attractiveness.

> (O)rganizational characteristics, such as image and reputation, were the strongest predictors of "maintaining the applicant status" stage, the job characteristics, such as compensation, autonomy, and commute, were the strongest predictors of "job choice decision" stage. The recruitment process characteristics, such as message credibility and employee endorsements, became more relevant as the applicants progressed through different stages of the recruitment process. Finally, the recruiter behaviors, such as trustworthiness, informativeness and competence, were important in the first two recruitment stages of generating applications and maintaining the applicant status. The role of trustworthiness in different stages of recruitment process was further unpacked in the narrative review by Klotz et al., (2013). Defining trustworthiness as the perceptions of benevolence, integrity and ability of each party to the other, their findings suggest that establishing perceptions of trustworthiness between applicants and recruiting organizations is key for achieving positive recruitment outcomes (Potočnik, 2021, p. 167).

To establish trustworthiness, applicants want to feel that they are seen and appreciated as individuals, not only in terms of their technical competencies but also concerning their personality, values, goals, personal background, and so on. Even though candidates know that a job application is a situation where people don't always openly and honestly reveal everything about themselves, they are interested in being as open and authentic as possible. In order to be convincing, people's behaviors must be authentic (verbal and non-verbal). This includes showing emotion. The decision for or against hiring an applicant or for or against accepting an offered position is always partly about feeling comfortable with the selection situation. It's about well-being; subjectively, people want to feel good about their decisions.

To activate positive emotions and build a positive relationship with candidates, selection managers need intuition to accurately perceive and assess the candidates' emotions, authenticity, and so on. When people feel accepted and understood by their counterparts, trust is built; and trust is the basis for any good human relationship (Livingstone et al., 2020)

McAllister et al. (2019) show that subordinates tend to rate leaders, based on their personal liking rather than their actual behavior.

> If subordinates like their leaders, they will also say that their leaders are transformational, ethical, authentic, not abusive and that they have strong leader-employee relations. . . . employees will be more satisfied and perform better if their leader is well-liked. . . . The results are very clear – there is no harm in being liked by your subordinates, and our research certainly suggests that it is part of being viewed as an effective leader. This means that well-liked leaders can expect subordinates to consider them as authentic, transformational, ethical, and not abusive. Likewise, teams who like their leaders will be happier at work, go above and beyond what is required of them, experience greater well-being, and perform at a higher level (McAllister et al., 2019, pp. 1–3).

Considering these results, it is understandable that managers of potential employees try to leave a likable and positive impression on the candidate during the application process, especially in selection interviews.

This is why selection managers need well-developed relationship management skills and intuitive-emotional competencies. In addition, it is known from research on communication psychology that people communicate successfully at the factual level, when the relationship between the communication partners is positive. Thus, it is about linking the factual content of the message with a respectful and empathetic relationship message (Schulz von Thun, 2008, pp. 41–44).

It is also conceivable that the applicant's appearance (clothing, body language, sophistication, habits, etc.) causes verbal and non-verbal reactions in the selection manager, such as sympathy/likability or other specific biases and refusals (Kanning, 2004, p. 409).

Interviewers who associate positive characteristics with a candidate will, probably, create a benevolent situation. On the other hand, negative associations may create an unpleasant atmosphere, where the candidate receives little help and, therefore, becomes more stressed (Kanning 2004, p. 409). The interviewer is involved both in collecting the data and in its evaluation (Kanning, 2004, p. 410). This can result in two possible sources of error: first, the interviewers may trigger, through their behavior, more positive or more negative feelings in a candidate; on the other hand, there is great temptation to evaluate the obtained data (possibly the mirrored behavior by the candidates) accordingly, in the same distorted way (Kanning, 2004, p. 410).

A problem that may arise during a standardized interview is that not every candidate is very talkative or hesitant to provide information and, therefore, needs to be motivated to talk. It can help inform the candidate about the purpose of the questions and the interest behind the question. Not being satisfied with initial answers and asking specific questions allow the candidates to show more of themselves. Active listening and sending non-verbal signals can also express listening attentively (Schmidt-Atzert & Amelang, 2012, p. 339). This is social influence, which from a rational-analytical perspective, should be avoided.

Furthermore, social relationships within the team and the relationship with the superior are essential for success, in most roles. Therefore, for each selection decision, team representatives should be involved in the personnel decision. The reference to the team must be related to the candidate's overall performance potential (including team and relationship skills) and weighed up in this context. When hiring managers have to decide between two suitable candidates with similar experiences, skills, and so on, the team fit, cultural match, and personality are especially relevant.

The fact that the social side of the selection process must also be considered, particularly in tight labor markets or internal personnel selection, can be seen, among other things, in the fact that a positive feeling should be left with all applicants, even if they are not suitable for the position to be filled.

In a qualitative study (24 interviews were conducted with personnel decision-makers from mainly large, internationally operating companies in various sectors), Kleebaur (2007) shows that the reason for the limited use of scientifically guided personnel selection procedures is not the stubbornness of personnel managers or inadequate professionalization, but the "nature of the matter" (Böhle, 2007, p. XI). According to Kleebaur, this "nature of the matter" is that experience-based intuitive personnel selection cannot be prevented and is even necessary and helpful, especially to build positive relationships, create positive candidate experience, and convince applicants about the company. Carolina Kleebaur, therefore, advocates more courage for intuition and intuitive decision-making (Kleebaur, 2007, p. 191).

It remains that personnel selection processes are always acquisition processes and that establishing a positive relationship is, therefore, elementary. In order to create a relationship that is perceived as positive on both sides, emotional and intuitive competencies are required.

Thus, intuition is a prerequisite for dealing with other human beings. Whether someone understands a situation in its specific context and can solve a problem by insight into other people is mainly dependent on intuition. According to this view, people cannot understand interpersonal relationships or their counterparts, without intuition (Eggenberger, 1998, p 1).

If managers want to win people for themselves and their organization, they must reach the candidates emotionally. This means that a selection manager must positively respond to the candidates to connect emotionally, because they want to feel valued and appreciated. That means adapting to the respective candidate, considering their cultural imprint and the associated expectations. This can mean, for example, holding back on body language in certain cultures but showing much more body language and expressing emotions in others. When people feel accepted in their specific personality, they can get the impression of being seen as humans and individuals.

5.1.7 Intuition sends essential messages and helps recognize candidates holistically

Hiring managers know the situation: They have absolutely no objective facts or arguments against a candidate. The scores also clearly speak for a specific applicant, yet they feel something wrong with that candidate.

If selectors do not rely on rational-analytics but on their intuition, it is, often, not because they are ignorant of rational-analytical processes. On the contrary, many selection managers want to use them but are not trained as, for example, psychologists, to implement rational-analytical procedures. Even when they do conduct an interview in a rational-analytic way, they are often insecure about recognizing and interpreting applicants' verbal and non-verbal language correctly, from a psychometric perspective ; they often do not know how to analyze what constitutes, for example, authenticity, empathy, narcissism, openness, or emotional stability, scientifically and accurately. Thus, they are dependent on their intuitions and feelings. Intuitions help people perceive inconsistencies in the counterpart's behavior, whether someone appears consistent and authentic in their appearance, and so on.

These intuitions and feelings are not automatically wrong. For example, de Vries et al. (2010) show, in a clinical context, that unconscious information processing led to more correct diagnoses than conscious information processing. Moreover, especially when people find it rather hard to know which aspects are most important, unconscious processing and reliance on intuition can result in better decisions than conscious, deliberative processing (De Vries et al., 2010, p. 579; see also Koppers, 2013, pp. 59–60).

Gassner (2006, p. 22) shows that empathy is needed to perceive complex emotional factors holistically and capture a person's emotional state (e.g., whether a candidate feels comfortable in the interview) multifactorially. These perceptions then express themselves in intuitions and feelings.

Kleebaur (2007, p. 62) confirms in her Ph.D. thesis that intuition helps selection managers make more accurate selection decisions, by holistically grasping applicants' personalities. Intuition means feeling what is good for me and who fits me, my team, and so on. It expresses itself through our body or our well-being. People sense something is wrong but can hardly describe it or put it in words. Thus, this intuition manifests, for instance, in negative feelings or belly rumblings and indicates: Something is not right here. For example, one can perceive discomfort with a candidate. Then, hiring managers are recommended to trace this discomfort and ask themselves what this discomfort is trying to tell them.

Therefore, one must be aware of one's intuitions and feelings and consider them. According to Carl Gustav Jung (2019), intuition is one of four basic psychological functions that enable people to consider future developments with all their options and potential. To use the potential of intuition, people need to make the unconscious, conscious.

Awareness of one's intuition means being aware of one's feelings and consciously giving them the space they deserve. Our body sends signals through feelings; it talks to us.

Antoine Saint-Exupery expresses this idea in his book *The Little Prince*:

> It is only with the heart that one sees rightly; what is essential is invisible to the eye.

Just as intuitions and feelings may signal impending danger in specific situations (De Becker, 1999), they can also help protect against poor selection decisions.

This is especially desirable, for example, in the case of essential selection decisions (choice of partner, choice of studies or training, career planning, choosing a particular company or candidate). Thus, selection managers should consider that intuitions and accompanied feelings carry important messages that shouldn't be suppressed or ignored.

Intuition and related emotions help recognize when something in an applicant's behavior or statements does not seem coherent. This allows selection managers to openly address these intuitive impulses with applicants or colleagues, reflect on them, and ask critical questions.

Thus: Listen to your heart and its messages!

5.1.8 Intuition encourages creativity and improvisation skills

Creative processes are, on the one hand, controlled and conscious and, on the other hand, uncontrolled and spontaneous. Factors such as openness, interest in a task and the problem to be solved, specialist skills, and mastery of appropriate techniques also play a role in creative processes. However, holistic information processing, association skills, or the interplay between conscious and unconscious processes also play a significant role. Therefore, intuition is a part of the creative process (Ahel, 2020, pp. 84–95; see, for example, Section 4.3.3).

According to Dijksterhuis (2010, pp. 153–174), the subconscious mind enables more creative solutions than conscious processes. He gives examples such as Leonardo da Vinci, Newton, Einstein, Mozart, or Picasso, whose products or solutions are essentially the result of unconscious mental activities. Scientists make new discoveries if they are motivated and have appropriate knowledge acquired with the help of consciousness, such as reading. The actual creative discovery, however, arises from the unconscious. Moreover, these unconscious creative processes cannot be forced but are generated spontaneously and situationally.

Spontaneous action is also required when improvisation is needed in specific selection situations. In these situations, intuitions help fully grasp a new or unexpected situation, make adjustments, and make hiring managers (but also candidates) improvise. With increasing experience and many variations of similar situations, the intuitive competency of managers can improve, and, thus, intuition can support the ability to improvise and act creatively, in unforeseen selection situations (Leybourne & Sadler-Smith, 2006).

5.2 Disadvantages and risks of intuitions in selection processes

5.2.1 Overconfidence of selection managers as a risk for ineffective judgments

Research by Kahneman (Kahneman & Klein, 2009, pp. 515; Kahneman, 2011) or Kanning (2015, p. 138) sees overestimating one's expertise and experience as the most significant risk for a professional personnel selection. As long as intuition is based only on subjective experience, it's not a reliable indicator of judgment accuracy. Overconfidence leads to an illusion of control and a misleading feeling of knowing the best decision. This is because the personal intuitive impression and subjective confidence in the accuracy of an intuition-based judgment are no longer questioned. Practitioners blindly trust their intuitions and emotions and no longer question them critically, but justify them with their experiences. The unshakable belief in one's intuitive correctness of judgment can also lead to no evaluation studies being conducted, and no need is seen to change one's behavior or learn something new.

5.2.2 Intuitions lead to no valid complexity reduction

In complex situations like selecting candidates, managers remain capable of acting only if they can reduce complexity, appropriately. However, due to limited cognitive abilities or even resources such as personnel, money, or time in an organization, people are blinded by initial impressions, do not take in all available information, and come to judgments based on simplifying strategies and, thus, inappropriate reductions.

Also, technological developments may help to cope with complexity more accurately. Sahm and von Weizsäcker (2016, pp. 195–196, 202) identified three factors influencing intuitive decision-making effectiveness: the complexity of the problem or task (influenced by the complexity of the environment), cognitive abilities, and previous knowledge and expertise of the decision-maker. They show that rational decision-making is more precise in complex situations if based on the correct data but comes with higher costs, for example, time spent, cognitive capacity, and physical cost of collecting data. These costs decrease, over time, with the increasing expertise of the decision-maker (Soffner, 2021, pp. 26–27). However, technological developments in digitization, AI, and so on, are expected to base decisions on more valid data and make data analytics cheaper and less time-consuming; thus, these developments can support rational-analytical decisions.

5.2.3 Intuitions lead to biases and discrimination

Effective personnel selection is, by no means, a question of subjective "knowledge of human nature," "gut feeling," "intuition," or "life experience," because hiring managers perceive candidates in a systematically distorted way (Dane & Pratt, 2007, p. 42; Miles & Sadler-Smith, 2014, p. 618; Küpers, 2015, p. 82; Kanning, 2017b, p. 90).

Selective perceptions and biases such as confirmation bias, self-serving bias, attribution error, or the halo effect can lead to stereotyping, prejudices, and, thus, discrimination against certain people. At the same time, this can potentially result in the loss of advantages that could arise from a diversely composed workforce.

5.2.4 Intuitive decisions are not transparent and objectively verifiable

Since intuitive judgments occur fast and unconsciously, they are difficult to describe and operationalize. In particular, intuitive personnel selection is associated with positive or negative feelings that are difficult to verbalize. For this reason, intuitive judgments are often not transparent and, thus, not objectively comprehensible (Kanning (2015, pp. 138–139).

As intuitive decisions are considered highly subjective and difficult to justify in retrospect, they are often substantiated by evasive strategies such as post hoc rationalization (Gigerenzer & Gaissmaier, 2012, pp. 10–11; Küpers, 2015, p. 83; see Section 5.3).

5.2.5 Intuitive decisions are not as accurate and effective as rational-analytical ones

Intuitive decisions are inferior to rational-analytical selection procedures in quality and effectiveness and regularly lead to less accurate personnel selection decisions (see Sections 3.2 and 3.6; Schmidt & Hunter, 1998; Highhouse, 2008; Schmidt et al., 2016).

5.3 Rationalization of intuitive judgment and decision-making

Gigerenzer and Gaissmaier (2012, p. 20) show, in their studies, that managers rely about 50% on their gut when making decisions. But 72% of those surveyed say they deny their intuition and justify decisions to third parties with rationally comprehensible reasons.

The reason for this rationalization is that intuitions and emotions are considered suspicious and subjective in many cultures and different areas of our society. Thus, intuitive or emotional knowledge is not generally accepted as a basis for judgment. Moreover, it is considered unprofessional to show emotions, especially in business; thus, it is essential to carefully control emotions and express feelings only in specific contexts (Caruso & Salovey, 2007, introduction). Therefore, it is not surprising that managers in the rational-analytically oriented business world, and due to psychometric demands, try to eliminate intuitions and emotions in personnel selection, as far as possible. Thus, selection managers learn to construct their arguments in order to be accepted (Dreyfus & Dreyfus, 1991, p. 266) and rationally justify their intuitively influenced selection decisions, afterward. The use of intuition in personnel diagnostics, thus, often, leads to a rational justification of intuitive decisions; Miles and Sadler-Smith call this a post hoc rationalization (2014, p. 620).

People often make decisions and do not even know why they have judged and decided that way. Moreover, intuitive decisions based on automatic, unconscious processes are hard to communicate and justify. Thus, it is often difficult to explain the real reasons for intuitive judgments (Gigerenzer & Gaissmaier, 2015, pp. 24–25).

Whether people openly admit to their intuition is influenced both individually-personally and culturally-socially. For example, the (self-) image of the "people of action," which is widespread among top managers such as CEOs and entrepreneurs, is often associated with the ability to deal competently with the future, its uncertainty, and incomplete information and to assess situations, strategies, and so on by intuition (Patterson et al., 2012, pp. 39–42). On the other hand, top executives regularly expect decisions made by subordinate managers to be transparent and backed up with figures.

(Patterson et al., 2012, pp. 41–42) also state those decision-makers use a post hoc rationalization process to justify decisions that were, in fact, of an intuitive nature and aim to satisfy the sender and the receiver of that rationalization. Rationalization means to "consciously select evidence, which will support their intuitive argument."

The more economically significant a decision, the more it should be substantiated and validated by transparent, objective facts, data, figures, and so on, and rational comprehensible reasons. But, managers interviewed in our empirical research confirm that the feeling of having to back up one's intuitive decisions with rational arguments depends on the culture or even the hierarchical position of the decision-maker. The higher the hierarchical position, the lower the subjective obligation to rationalize. Several top managers interviewed also state that they make their perceived intuitions and emotions transparent and justify them, discussing and reflecting on them with other managers (Reichelt, 2020, pp. 64 and 78).

Rationalization is a procedure in which decisions, behaviors, or feelings are justified and explained in a seemingly rational manner, to avoid the true explanation. For example, in personnel selection decisions, rationalization serves to substantiate hiring decisions afterward in the eyes of oneself and others, with understandable reasons and, thus, make the decisions consciously tolerable.

According to Gigerenzer & Gaissmaier (2012, pp. 10–12), different evasive strategies of ex-post rationalization can be distinguished.

5.3.1 Disguising strategy

The first evasion strategy is the obfuscation strategy, in which decision-makers, after making intuitive decisions, invent objective reasons to explain their intuitively made decisions, analytically. Research shows that managers often tend to disguise or hide the fact that a decision was made intuitively and back it up with rational arguments (Agor, 1989; Kline, 2005). In particular, subjective motives and intuitive reasons or feelings for decisions that they are reluctant to admit publicly are often rationalized retrospectively, with objective and acceptable reasons.

Rationalizing decisions, thus, also serves to reduce one's uncertainties and, possibly, anxieties about one's supervisor, so that rational-analytically-based decisions give the decision-maker, security.

To gain acceptance for their decisions and behaviors, especially in management, people have learned not to use words such as hunch, gut feeling, or intuition

(Gigerenzer 2007, 15). Another motivator is the fear of taking responsibility for these intuitive decisions. One can better protect oneself by referring to analytical procedures and rational reasons. Also, reasons and motives are volatile and can change very quickly, from situation to situation. Therefore, people tend to hide that their decision was based on intuition, especially if something goes wrong.

This strategy, also known as "post hoc rationalization," means that decision-makers must invent rational comprehensible reasons to justify their decision. In Gigerenzer & Gaissmaier's (2012, pp. 10–12) perspective, this wastes time, money, and resources, especially for companies.

This human tendency to rationalize reflects the brain's attempt to understand, classify, and deal with decisions and actions, retrospectively. Thus, rationalization can reduce discomfort with decisions (see cognitive dissonance theory by Festinger, 1957, and Section 2.2).

Therefore, people and institutions provide rationalizations that make decisions easier to communicate and facilitate an increase in the acceptance of the decision.

5.3.2 Defensive decision-making

The second strategy is called defensive decision-making, in which the better option is not chosen in favor of the one that can be better justified. This makes decision-makers unassailable, and they avoid taking responsibility for poor decisions. However, this evasion strategy has the same negative consequences as the cover-up strategy, as only the second best option is chosen (Gigerenzer & Gaissmaier, 2012, p. 11).

This can also occur in personnel selection decisions, by choosing the candidate with the highest score at the end of an assessment center, even though the hiring managers have a bad feeling about that candidate. But, this makes intuition as expert knowledge useless, because it is not considered in decision-making (Gigerenzer & Gaissmaier, 2012, p. 11).

Power relations can also influence the degree of acceptance and recognition of intuition, in an organization. For example, executives in higher management positions name intuition as the basis of their decision more often than managers in the middle management, who feel more pressure to make rationally grounded decisions (Sadler-Smith & Shefy, 2004, p. 80) to protect themselves against criticism (Niederhäusern, 2015, p. 184).

5.3.3 Figures, data, and facts are decisive

Many Western entrepreneurs and managers make decisions based on intuition. Nevertheless, they often conduct comprehensive analyses and hire management consultants, because they must justify their decisions with figures and objective data towards themselves and others. After all, they do not want to get in front of their shareholders or employees and say: I listened to my gut feeling.

That intuition has little or no place in business and that numbers, data, and facts have a much higher acceptance and argumentative power than feelings and intuitions, is the experience of many hiring managers. If, for example, in an assessment center, observers perceive applicants intuitively as likable and good fits – from their subjective perspective – they evaluate them, accordingly, with a high score. The same applies to assessments in selection interviews. Although not made transparent, intuitive impressions are backed up by facts and figures and, thus, indirectly justified.

In this context, an interviewed manager from Germany says that his selection decisions are very much based on his intuition and that they have much to do with his experience. And then, he looks primarily for the facts that confirm his intuition. Thus, his rational-analytical procedures and rationalizing reasons confirm what he perceives intuitively (Bublitz, 2021, p. 77).

5.3.4 Intuitive decisions as a taboo subject or a defense mechanism?

Gigerenzer and Gaissmaier (2012, p. 21) state that intuition is often taboo in organizations and is not discussed, at least, not openly.

From a psychoanalytic perspective, rationalization can be a defense mechanism (Freud, 1937), in which emotions and intuitions involved in decisions are denied or suppressed. Defense mechanisms are automated psychological operations and unconscious solution strategies that protect a person from anxiety-producing thoughts and feelings related to internal conflicts or conflicts with others. Those who rationalize show others and themselves that their actions and decisions are rational, logical, and coherent. And unpleasant or unacceptable emotions are kept out of consciousness for the decision-maker. According to Anna Freud, defense mechanisms mean the ego's resistance to embarrassing and unbearable ideas and effects. Thus, these defense mechanisms protect the decision-maker from possible conflicts with the conscious internal or external world (Freud, 1937; König, 2007). According to Mertens (1997), there can even be institutionalized defense mechanisms by implementing structures, norms, and standards or also by shaping (organizational) cultures (Mucha & Rauchhaus, 2021, pp. 35 and 64).

Our empirical research shows that inexperienced selection managers often feel they are not allowed to argue with their intuition and, therefore, try to back up their decisions with objective reason and by referring to rational-analytical procedures.

Research shows that women often do not want to conform to the stereotype of deciding on their "intuitive intelligence" (Proximea, 2011). Therefore, they tend to justify decisions based on intuition with facts and figures. In a Proximea study (2011), 50.7 percent of women state that they are more likely to rely on their gut feeling, when making decisions. Nevertheless, 66.7 percent say that they justify their decisions with rational reasons.

A study on the importance of intuition in strategic management (Vogler (2012) shows that most respondents had a great awareness of the connection between intuitive and deliberative processes. It becomes clear how much managers are influenced by concepts (such as dualistic nature) and other mechanisms (such as the specific recognition of intuition in a culture or organization and the associated feeling of being obliged to rationalize intuition). Vogler describes that the freedom to rely openly on one's intuition rises with the responsibility and power level of the managers. In addition, relying on intuition or feeling obliged to rationalize depends on the social acceptance of intuition in society, culture (e.g., error culture and openness to feelings), and organization (Vogler, 2012, p. 77).

Our surveys also show that intuitive judgments by experienced managers are more accepted than by younger ones. This corresponds with the findings of Gigerenzer and Gaissmaier (2012, p. 20).

Entrepreneurs and managers higher ranked in the hierarchy are more likely to trust their feelings and are also more likely to admit their intuitions.

Nevertheless, it takes courage to stand by one's intuition and gut feeling, in business. Board member Timm Richter (2016) observes that it requires courage to listen to the inner voice and intuitions and emotions. He allows himself to be mindful at the moment and to feel his intuitions and emotions. He is convinced that his intuitions and feelings give him a clear message, when things are difficult and complex.

5.3.5 Rationalization of the feedback given to candidates

It is challenging to admit using feelings and intuitions when candidates have to be accepted or rejected.

Should recruiters honestly explain why an application failed, for example, that they feel for sure that someone would not fit into the team or that they found an applicant unlikable because of his personality? Or do they prefer or resort to a standard refusal?

In many countries, especially in Western cultures, rejections based on intuition or emotions are not accepted. Therefore, especially for employer branding reasons and to maintain a positive employer image, refusals should – in addition to due courtesy – only be formulated with socially accepted reasons.

Experience shows that one cannot always and everywhere deal honestly with others in human relationships. People do not always say what they think or feel not to hurt or humiliate others and not endanger interpersonal relationships, whether private or professional. Ruth Cohn has chosen "selective authenticity" for this kind of communication.

In countries like Germany, where labor law and jurisprudence strongly influence HR/People management, managers are advised to conduct personnel selection based purely on facts, leaving out personal intuitions or emotions, as far as possible. Thus, it is crucial to avoid discrimination and especially accusations of discrimination. In this context, if an applicant is given positive feedback, for example, that they have understood each other during the selection process very well on an interpersonal level and that the applicant fits in very well with the team and the company on a human level, the feedback will usually be completely different if the applicant is rejected.

In Germany, for example, there is no obligation, from a legal point of view, to give reasons for a refusal and no obligation to justify rejecting a candidate. However, this is not the case for candidates with disabilities. Here, a company must give verifiable reasons for the rejection that can be operationalized, as far as possible. Moreover, since disabled people have the right to check the decision by a court, general justifications such as the better suitability of other candidates are insufficient.

Therefore, rejection feedback to applicants should be formulated in terms of facts and based on objectively and transparently verifiable requirements. In practice, this means that reasons for rejection or even reasons for hiring (e.g., to employee representatives such as works councils) are not based on a personal impression or personal fit or positive or negative feelings or intuitions about an applicant, but only on the facts (Apelojg, 2010, pp. 28–30). To avoid complaints or even lawsuits, it is not advisable to mention all decisive reasons for rejections for legal reasons, even if applicants wish to get honest feedback. Since reasons that, at first glance, appear to be purely qualification-related can also conceal an indication of discrimination, this legal risk should not be overlooked (Oechslen, 2019).

However, suppose you want applicants (internal, for example) to learn to present themselves better in future selection processes, they also depend on feedback at the interpersonal level and what feelings they trigger in the other person. This also means that when giving feedback, selection managers should not only rely on presenting quantitative results, but also approach internal applicants with a positive emotional tone. For example, research by Steffens et al. (2018) shows that feedback on leadership potential impacts applicants' ambition, organizational commitment, and performance. When (internal) candidates receive feedback that they have shown low leadership potential, this often leads to lower ambition, lower organizational commitment, and lower performance.

Thus, selection managers should focus individually on each applicant, considering cultural and individual differences, when giving and accepting feedback.

5.4 Conclusions regarding advantages and disadvantages of intuition

If you don't accept what you feel, you can't control what you do afterward. (Graf, 2018, p. 19)

Intuitions, emotions, and rationality are complementary forms of cognition. It corresponds to our occidental tradition of thinking to see reason and intuition, rationality and emotionality as opposites (for the definition of rationality, see Section 3.7.1).

Intuitions and emotions, as also rational-analytics, are undoubtedly human strengths, but they are also potential weaknesses. They have advantages and benefits but also potential disadvantages. Where there are strengths, there are also weaknesses; where there is light, there is also a shadow.

The supposed contradiction between rational-analytics and intuition and the associated ambiguity can lead to a dilemma, when managers have to choose one or the other. However, our research shows that it is not a matter of either-or, but both. Rationality and intuition in decision-making are two sides of the same coin and can complement each other excellently, if they are reflected constructively in their specific strengths and weaknesses.

Since rational-analytically-oriented personnel diagnostics is critical of intuitive decisions, it is vital to recognize, from the neurosciences, that the influence of intuition on decisions cannot be eliminated; and that intuitive impulses are much faster than rational-analytical considerations. Especially in the case of humanly and economically essential decisions such as personnel selection, these quick impulses should not be followed unreflectively.

According to Kahneman & Klein (2009) or Glöckner & Witteman (2010a), people should stick to analysis, when tasks are analytically simple. If a decision is very complex or there is no obvious analytical model to which decision-makers can appeal, intuition is often the only recourse. Consider, for example, certain kinds of aesthetic judgments or even a business person evaluating opportunities for an entirely novel product. These findings provide for a rational-analytical procedure and delay decisions by "sleeping on them," thereby allowing unconscious thought (intuition) to inform them (Hogarth, 2010, p. 345).

We know that the preference of hiring managers for relying on their intuition changes with experience and that intuitive-emotional processes help people use unconscious knowledge and make fast decisions, without the need for conscious effort. Thus, if hiring managers choose immediately what they prefer ("like"), it may be a good strategy in the sense of satisfying one's "true" preferences. But, using one's individual preferences can, in our experience, be seen from two perspectives. One is that of cognitive efficiency. The other is that, in many contexts, our preferences are formed by our idiosyncratic experiences and, thus, might not be consistent with those we would choose after reflection (Hogarth, 2010, pp. 346–347).

People can trust their intuition when their experience represents the situation relevant to the decision and is supported by much valid feedback; if not, care is called for (Kahneman & Klein, 2009). Unfortunately, in many cases, especially in selection situations, it is unclear how representative the situation is or whether the environmental predictability is low or high. Thus, in (analytically) complex situations (and selection situations are always complex, because human beings are complex), and depending, among other things, on the base rate among applicants, selection managers should never rely solely on their intuition.

Instead, intuition and well-founded rational-analytics with evident empirical data should be used in complex tasks. Since most decisions involve both analytic and intuitive elements, the debate is better framed by asking how to bring both to bear on the issues, for example, by explicitly verifying intuitive reactions by analytical consideration (Hogarth, 2010, pp. 343–346).

Miles and Sadler Smith (2014, pp. 620–621) state that in their research, the respondents agree that the best judgments are obtained when analytical procedures are combined with intuitive methods, in personnel selection processes. "For example, in situations where objective methods are proven to work well on a stand-alone basis (e.g. in the assessment of cognitive abilities), intuitions are not required and should not be accorded any role whatsoever in the process, for example, 'she had an intelligent look in her eyes' is not a valid assessment of intelligence (Kahneman, 2011, p. 233)" (Miles & Sadler-Smith, 2014, p. 622). In addition, intuition seems helpful when intuitive judgments of multiple selection managers are reflected upon collaboratively and then combined to "pooled" impressions, and when a distinction has to be made between equally suitable candidates and no other decision bases are available.

As shown in Section 4.2.1.1, decision-makers should only consider trusting their intuitions when past experience is representative of the situation relevant to the decision and supported by valid evaluations of decision results (Miles & Sadler-Smith (2014, p. 622; Hogarth, 2010).

Intuition has a credibility problem, especially in a business setting. However, very many managers noted that their final decisions are often based on their intuitions or are a combining of facts and feelings; they often do not dare to stand by their intuitions and emotions alone. Therefore, intuitions and emotions must come out of the dirty corner of the unspeakable and supposed irrationality.

It is essential to consider that a purely rational-analytical approach is insufficient in personnel selection; it's about the successful interaction of rational-analytical and intuitive procedures.

Resolving the paradoxical tension between rational-analytical and intuitive decision-making is easy if managers, decision-makers, and people generally accept that intuition is always there when human judgments are made. Moreover, the integration into a conscious decision-making process makes intuition a valuable and irreplaceable component in a selection-decision process. Also, because time is always scarce, especially in business, they should consciously take the time to reflect on it (Graf, 2018, pp. 191 and 196).

From an evolutionary point of view, it is inherent in humans that intuitive and emotional information flows very quickly and unconsciously into human decision-making behavior. Both are part of human intelligence (Lehrer, 2009, p. 39). Personnel selection decisions made only rational-analytically can lead to poor decisions. Likewise, decisions made only intuitively can also be wrong. Therefore, intuition and emotion must be combined constructively into an "analytical-intuitive" decision-making procedure to reduce the risk of poor decisions.

In addition, decisions positively affecting the intuitive-emotional level also feel better than decisions made purely analytically, that is, when the head and the gut are equally convinced.

It is helpful to use these evolutionary advantages and let rational-analytics and intuition work together to better grasp the complexity of reality, especially in selecting personnel. This way, managers can draw on their entire conscious and unconscious knowledge base.

5.5 Meaning and implementation of intuitive and emotional decisions in the practice of personnel selection

5.5.1 Understanding of intuition in practice

Surveys of global executives and HR managers conducted as part of research projects at Leuphana University, Lueneburg (Germany) show that they broadly share a common understanding of the term intuition (Deters, 2019, pp. 124–132; Hallerberg, 2019, pp. 52–54). Intuition is perceived as hard to explain, based on experience, and manifests as a feeling that emerges rapidly and involuntarily. Most aspects of intuition agree with this book's definition of intuition (see Section 4.1.1).

Practitioners mentioned synonyms such as "gut feeling," "instinct," or a "chemistry that develops between people." Other selection managers interviewed associate intuition with an "automated competence," an impression formed "immediately," "at the first moment":

> Intuition . . . is when you meet someone (and) within ten seconds the decision is made (Deters, 2019, p. 125).

> For me, intuition is linked to my previous experience, so you look at what the applicants trigger in you when they make certain statements or gestures and facial expressions (Hallerberg, 2019, p. 52).

Intuitive judgment is "poorly supported by measurable criteria" and therefore "subjective" and "not fact-based" or "rational." This summarizes the following statements:

> I understand intuition in personnel selection that you make an applicant, and his aura impacts you, that you register the way he communicates, but it's not so much about the facts and the content (Deters, 2019, p. 125).

Another interviewed expert says:

> Intuition is the sum of all my past experiences and impressions that I have gathered in selection processes and that give me a hint, a mental impulse, although it can also be emotionally colored (Deters, 2019, p. 125).

And, intuition is associated with feelings:

> I feel my intuition as a felt likeability. What do I feel for the person? What kind of connection do we have with each other? And when this positive feeling is there, a completely different flow of conversation and dynamic develops (Hallerberg, 2019, p. 53).

Thus, our empirical research confirms that intuition has regularly been defined as a kind of experience. However, only very few managers interviewed reflect on how stable the environment is in building their experiences (Deters, 2019, pp. 127–128). Moreover, for most hiring managers interviewed, intuition as experience is not used to prove a certain expert status but rather to ask specific questions: What does my intuition tell me? What is the message? Should I follow these messages? Thus, in practice, especially in larger organizations, a combination of intuitive and more or less rational-analytical procedures can be seen.

5.5.2 Perceived advantages of intuitions in practice

Also, several experts emphasize that their intuitions and related emotions are essential clues to be cautious or even suspicious and ask questions, when something incongruous or inappropriate is experienced in the applicant's behavior. Intuitions or intuitive impulses and the associated emotions are considered particularly important, when identifying inconsistencies in application documents or behavior, during an interview. Managers, then, use these intuitive impulses to ask specific questions, elaborate on specific points, or name the perceived inconsistencies and reflect on them, with the applicant. Therefore, intuitions that arise are used to spark more specific questions (Hallerberg, 2019, p. 67).

However, other interviewers indicate that they are well aware of the risks of using intuitions associated with emotions, for example, if the applicant does not deliver in the interview what was expected based on the application documents.

> Sometimes, I can tell very quickly whether an applicant is a good fit or not. And then such a job interview drags on, and it's so embarrassing. So I no longer want to talk to my counterpart. (. . .) That's not very professional, but it's the truth (Hallerberg, 2019, p. 54).

> My experiences give me a feeling of knowing, . . . it is a deep certainty, to decide correctly. . . . My feeling of knowing serves as a navigator and tells me the right direction. . . . My intuition develops in relation to other persons, based on verbal and nonverbal behaviors such as facial expressions, gestures, etc v.

> The intuitions you have learned about your experiences are a good guide (Soffner, 2021, p. 77).

The surveys conducted at Leuphana University also show that experienced selection experts are more likely to rely on and trust their intuition, and endorse this intuitive competence as particularly important.

And, the more experienced the hiring managers are, the more they – in the perspective of the majority of the managers interviewed – can rely on their intuitive judgments. "I'm really back to following my intuition. I have to say, as I get older, I listen to myself more, I really do" (Deters, 2019, pp. 127–128).

Almost all selection managers interviewed by Flörke (2020) admitted to considering their intuitions and emotions, when selecting personnel.

> Despite using scientifically guided procedures and having transparent and precise selection criteria, the final decision is based on my subjective feeling. A 100% objective decision is not possible in personnel diagnostics. Intuition is always a significant factor in decision-making (Deters, 2019, pp. 125–126).

> When it comes . . . to the fit with the company or team, I would say that there is a relatively large amount of subjective gut feeling (Deters, 2019, p. 126).

One interviewee, who had studied psychology, sums it up as follows:

> In my studies at university, I learned to reduce relying on intuition and emotion as much as possible. But having worked in personnel selection for several years, I know how important my intuition is (Flörke, 2020, p. 53).

The experts interviewed largely agree that intuitions cannot be and should not be switched off.

> I think it's unnecessary to think you should ignore your intuitions or gut feelings because, from my point of view, you cannot switch it off. . . . However, I think it's important to pay attention to intuition and use it because, ultimately, you have to work with these people later. Yes, and if my intuition tells me that I don't really like an applicant, the collaboration will never be good. And that's why I think it's important to register this intuition and stand by it (Deters, 2019, p. 129).

An HR specialist from South Africa emphasizes her positive attitude toward intuition as experience increases:

> As a young HR manager, I was still insecure and needed a clear procedure and tools that gave me confidence" (Deters 2019, p. 124). Or: So, the more experienced I am, the more candidates I have interviewed, the more my intuition has developed and grown, and generally you can pick up certain characteristics in terms of body language, tone of voice, you know, those type of things that support that intuition (Hallerberg, 2019, p. 53).

Empirical research by Brauner (2019, p. 95) shows that interpersonal factors are regularly intuitively captured, regardless of analytical methods. Against this background, creating an awareness of this fact and taking it into account when forming a judgment is opportune. One of the interviewed selection managers says:

> When I go into an interview, I try to create a good atmosphere and relationship so that the candidate feels comfortable and gets a good impression of our company. . . . the assessment of whether I would like to work with the candidate and vice versa, and how both sides assess the matching, is an essential component of the personnel selection decision. And this requires precisely this social factor (Flörke, 2020, p. 52).

These interview results agree with research findings from the literature (e.g., Dreyfus & Dreyfus, 1980; Salas et al., 2010; Gigerenzer & Gaissmaier, 2012, p. 181; Possehl & Meyer-Grashorn, 2015, p. 65; see Section 5.1).

Several selection managers interviewed told us that intuitions and emotions play a significant role in selecting personnel, mainly to evaluate the Person-Team or Person-Organization/Culture fit, or when it comes to assessing leadership potential. For example, one reason that is often mentioned is that their team members are like a second family, as more time is spent with them than with their actual families; when I think about the fact that I might have to spend most of my waking time with this candidate, it's obvious that I have to like this person and that I have to have a desire to work with them (Deters, 2019; Hallerberg, 2019; Bublitz, 2021, p. 81).

A Dutch hiring manager emphasizes the importance of a positive emotional connection between team members (Bublitz, 2021, p. 81):

> I believe a company must be seen as a group of people. So, whether it's a sports team or a company or whatever group of people that needs to work together, it must also work at an emotional level. So, if you just put people together who may be theoretically, based on their resume and education, can work together, but there is no [. . .] click between the people, there's no connection, you're never going to get the best out of it. So, I definitely believe that emotions should have a significant role in that process.

A Japanese selection manager interviewed for our projects says:

> But once we choose the people, we have the responsibility to assess candidates fit to my organization. This is a big responsibility, and an important point between human beings (Bublitz, 2021, p. 79).

And German managers state:

> For me, the CV and the facts are virtually the ticket to check minimum requirements. But the decisive factor is the human side. And only with my intuition and at the emotional level can I determine whether we are a good fit for each other and whether the applicant fits into the team (Soffner, 2021, p. 71).

> In personnel layoffs, I decide on a rational-analytical basis. . . . But in the final personnel selection and hiring decision, I rely on my gut feelings. . . . Purely rational-analytical decisions in recruitment are not successful. It should always be a mixture of rational-analytics, intuitions, and emotions (Soffner, 2021, pp. 73–74).

Most interviewed managers assert that despite the scientifically proven superiority of evidence-based methods, they are not willing and not able to eliminate intuitions and emotions from their judgment process (Brauner, 2019, p. 94; see also Sadler-Smith & Shefy, 2004, p. 87; Salas et al., 2010, p. 966).

The interviewed selection managers emphasize that a central strategy for using intuition in personnel selection in a goal-oriented manner is to consciously pay attention to intuitive impulses and make them visible to self and others. Most selection managers we interviewed emphasize that an analytical preselection is first carried out, based on predefined criteria. Several respondents indicate that they challenge and critically examine their intuitions and emotions through data-based analytic processes. However, in the interview, they could not clearly separate analytics and intuition. If the analytical data speaks against a candidate, but the intuition favors the candidate, most interviewees do not decide against their intuition. Most hiring managers rely on their intuition when making the final decision, especially when it has to be made between two equally qualified applicants (Deters 2019, pp. 124–125, 134; Soffner, 2021, p. 79).

None of the managers we interviewed attempted to make intuition precisely measurable. However, they try to make their intuitions visible, and thus, to a certain extent, operationalizable, by consciously perceiving them and then communicating and discussing the intuitive impulses with others involved. They report that selection decisions are usually not made alone and that the impressions, intuitions, and emotions are exchanged with other selection managers.

Mutual trust is vital for openly and honestly exchanging impressions and intuitions. Moreover, discussing intuitions in the organizational context helps to question one's intuitions critically and reduce possible distortions of perception (Riedel, 2015, p. 188).

> I get a second, third or fourth opinion, so I can check whether my initial impressions are correct, and of course, there is an exchange with the other assessors . . . there is also constructive discussion, where one describes one's impressions and intuitions, and compares one's intuitions with those of the others, seeing whether there is a difference (Deters, 2019, p. 131).

Even though, from a psychometric perspective, selection managers should avoid their intuitions and emotions, as much as possible, in personnel selection, none of the managers we interviewed indicates that intuitions and emotions are often taboo in practice. Instead, they state that intuitions should be openly communicated and reflected upon:

> Well, it should not and is not a taboo. It is quite important to me because every person has a gut feeling; I can't take that away from them at all (Deters 2019, p. 131).

The surveys we conducted at Leuphana University show, on the one hand, that there are respondents who –from their perspective – rely purely on their intuitive judgments. On the other hand, only very few (and these mostly had a degree in psychology) state that they are convinced about selecting applicants exclusively in a rational-analytical way. Most respondents, however, rely on interplay of intuition and analytics. This becomes clear in the following quote:

> Yes, I like to use a combination of both aspects. So, especially in the face-to-face interview [. . .]. And I then try . . . to say, okay, that's my first intuitive impression and then based on the further rational and databased procedures . . . I question and challenge my intuitive hypotheses about an applicant (Deters, 2019, p. 135).

Most hiring managers interviewed are convinced of the benefits of their intuition, primarily to assess candidates' soft skills or cultural and team fit. Particularly because emotions and intuition come into play, these competencies are – from their perspective – hard to measure via questionnaires. They state that HR professionals can only identify the best-fitting talents from an integrative perspective and combine scientifically valid instruments with reflection on their intuitions and emotions (Brauner, 2019, p. 94). Most hiring managers state that they use their intuitions in interaction with a more or less structured analytical approach (e.g., using job requirements as criteria to assess application forms or CVs).

Most hiring managers say that reflecting and talking about intuitions and emotions is fundamental for successful hiring decisions. Thus, there must be a structure to provide time and place for reflection on intuitions and emotions individually and with other hiring managers. Most hiring managers who were interviewed do this by discussing their impressions and feelings with their hiring colleagues.

Selection managers interviewed in our projects also state that individual and organizational learning processes occur through the conscious perception of decisions made and the reflection on intuitive and emotional impulses. At the same time, they are convinced that the need for justifying intuitions decreases and the ratio of correct selection decisions increases, by using rational-analytical procedures and consciously reflecting on intuitions and emotions (Reichelt, 2020, p. 86).

However, most of the hiring managers interviewed also stress that despite using intuition and – to a certain degree – a rational-analytical approach, there is always a degree of uncertainty. That is why organizations should have a probationary period after hiring. The probationary period is a safeguard against wrong decisions. During this period, decisions made incorrectly by intuitive or rational-analytical findings can be reversed (Deters, 2019, p. 129).

Although advocates of the psychometric approach in personnel diagnostics recommend eliminating intuition as far as possible, our research suggests that using intuitions and emotions is perceived and used to enrich the analytical process.

5.5.3 Intuition and diagnosing leadership talent

Research shows that human cognitive abilities, specific personality traits, and learning agility are critical predictors of leadership potential and talent (Bouland-van Dam et al., 2020). Scientists and practitioners have developed different competency models for leadership talent (Bartram, 2005; Deters, 2017).

The interviewed hiring managers referred less to these competence models known from the literature than to the following four competence fields, as indicators for leadership potential. It should be noted that most of the selection managers interviewed are from Europe and the U.S. Their construction of leadership is, accordingly, culturally colored. The following results must be viewed against the background of this context.

The selection managers interviewed in our research pay particular attention to the following four leadership competencies: Achieving followership, the motivation to lead, well-developed communication skills, and learning ability and self-reflection. In addition, candidates' attitudes, mindsets, and value awareness play a significant role in identifying leadership talent. These practitioners are convinced that these soft skills cannot only be assessed by using analytical methods but also require intuitive competencies of the selection managers.

1. **Followership and making employees successful:** Achieving followership requires a leader, who stands for something and has a clear point of view, can convey meaning and purpose and stands up for organizational goals and concerns. They deploy employees according to their strengths and support their development. In this way, leaders contribute to employees' success. They inspire and create enthusiasm among their employees. As a result, the employees stand behind and trust the executive and are motivated by the company's vision, mission, and goals.
2. **Well-developed communication skills:** The ability to communicate openly, empathetically, and respectfully is a prerequisite to inspiring and influencing others and developing strong relationships with other people. It's about active listening and eliciting desired information by good questioning.
3. **Self-reflection and openness to learning: The ability and motivation to learn are core requirements** of (global) leaders. A global leader or leadership

talent is open to feedback and can use this feedback to modify behavior. S/he can reflect critically and knows how s/he affects other people. One hiring manager says in this context:

> A manager who does not reflect upon his intuitions and decisions cannot learn from mistakes. Therefore, a manager who cannot question himself and his decisions is not a good manager (Reichelt, 2020, p. 63).

4. **Creative drive, the will to shape, and create something:** Someone who wants to drive a business forward, make a difference and implement something new shows leadership potential. These are people who have demonstrated excellent skills in effecting change.

The managers interviewed stated that they pay attention, above all, to candidates' attitudes, values, and mindsets in selection processes. They assess whether candidates show potential in the four leadership competence fields (verbally and nonverbally). It is about recognizing how applicants affect and inspire the recruiters, whether the recruiters have the impression that a candidate is accepted and respected by followers (with different cultural backgrounds), has the necessary drive to create something, can question and critically reflect on oneself, is open to feedback, learning, and change, and can inspire other people.

Leadership talent should have the flexibility to adapt to the specific circumstances and cultural environments, organizations, or employees and candidates, with their particular backgrounds, needs, and goals. These competencies can best be identified, not only through a rational-analytical procedure but, rather, through observing how applicants show themselves on the emotional level, how they communicate verbally and nonverbally, whether they act congruently and authentically, and how credible and trustworthy they appear, or how they inspire the interviewers.

In this context, the interviewees also clarified that leadership and leadership success are understood differently, in different countries. In addition, understanding the manager's role and the personal exchange between manager and employees varies from culture to culture.

That is why leadership talent is needed to behave in line with different expectations in specific cultural, political, or legal contexts. For example, this could mean that things should be arranged and specified in certain countries like India or China, unlike in countries like Germany, where a participatory process is more usual.

Most Western interviewees say that identifying potential up to the final decision should be about consistently measuring the candidate against the job requirements. Therefore, interviewers should try not to interpret or evaluate behaviors, while observing a candidate. At the same time, however, it was clear that subjectivity, emotions, and intuitions can never be excluded entirely.

Most managers agree that intuition plays an essential role in identifying leadership talent or potential. They say that leadership potential can be identified, to a certain degree, from past experience or even from leadership simulating exercises, in an assessment center. However, a rational-analytical process with a systematic data analysis and based on facts plays an important role. Therefore, the development and implementation of the interviews and assessment centers should be carried out according to rational-analytical aspects, as far as possible, but when it comes to evaluating demonstrated behavior, the intuition of the selection managers is called for.

Nearly all interviewed hiring managers (more than 90 percent) – no matter from which country or culture - say they can only identify leadership potential and talent in an interview or assessment center, using their emotional and intuitive competencies. They emphasize that hiring managers should exchange their impressions, feelings, and intuitions with the other decision-makers about how they assess a candidate's potential for a (global) leadership position: They should use observed behavioral examples to explain their impressions and enable others to discuss and understand the individual intuitions and feelings. This way, emotions and intuitions can be communicated and made transparent and understandable.

Overall, almost without exception, the interviewed hiring managers agree that identifying (global) leadership potential and talent is always the result of a combination of analytical processes and the intuitive experiences of hiring managers.

Thus, they clarify that it is not enough to implement a rational-analytical selection process and check formal criteria, facts, or functional competencies to identify leadership potential.

Intuition helps an interviewer recognize whether applicants are authentic and fulfill the required leadership competencies, whether they are personally convincing, communicate convincingly, achieve followership, build positive relationships, inspire and motivate others, and so on.

The hiring managers admit that their emotions and intuitions have benefits and potential disadvantages. At the same time, it's about making these emotions and intuitions transparent, visible, and, thus, discussable.

However, several interviewees also say they would only be willing to share their intuitions, if they have absolute trust in their counterparts. "I don't do that when I have someone sitting at the table two levels higher or someone I do not really trust" (Deters, 2019, p. 124).

Leadership is a human issue, and the vast majority of hiring managers interviewed in our research projects are convinced that intuition is the best way to determine whether someone has leadership potential and talent or not. Leadership is, first and foremost, people management. No matter how much you do right analytically, if the candidate does not possess the human qualities, then, all the analytics in the world won't help.

5.5.4 Intuition and rationalization in practice

Many hiring managers interviewed also feel the pressure to subsequently back up intuitively influenced selection decisions with rational criteria and supposed facts (Deters, 2019, p. 130). This is also confirmed by an expert interviewed by Hallerberg (2019), p. 56):

> If I have to justify to a third party, for example, my boss, why I want to hire someone, it is not enough to say that I like that applicant and that I think or feel he would fit into my team. He doesn't want to hear that. In this respect, rationality must once again be used in selection processes.

But our research also shows that intuition is less taboo in personnel selection. In our empirical studies (Deters, 2019, p. 130; see also Lindemann, 2020, pp. 62–63), no company explicitly banned talking about intuition.

> Well, intuition is not taboo. On the contrary, it is essential to me because every human being has a gut feeling; I cannot take that away from them.

The majority of the interviewed hiring managers argue as follows:

> Why should we make intuition taboo? It doesn't make sense, it's universal. We can't ban intuition. It's better to name intuitions, reflect on them, and discuss them with colleagues.

We received other exciting feedback from some of our interviewees. Several interviewees say they prefer to talk about their experience rather than intuition and emotion, as this meets with a more positive reaction. As they have had the experience that terms like intuition and emotion are viewed critically, they avoid these terms and prefer to speak of experience-based decisions. Interestingly, a few women interviewed mentioned that intuition and emotion tend to be associated with femininity in business. They, therefore, avoid talking of intuition and prefer the word experiences.

> It has been my experience that my decisions meet with greater acceptance if I do not say they are based on my intuition or emotion. Intuition and especially emotion are seen as primarily female attributes. However, when I say I have made a specific decision based on my experience, it is well accepted and seen positively (Deters, 2019, p. 130).

5.5.5 Perceived limits of intuitive judgments

With very few exceptions, managers interviewed in our empirical research are aware of the limits, the potential for bias, and the difficulties in justifying the use of intuitions.

Most hiring managers who were interviewed use their intuitions at least at the end of the diagnostic process, when analytical methods with standardized performance, evaluation, and interpretation have identified sufficient candidates. And some – but not most – hiring managers interviewed state that the use of intuition should be limited to this final decision when hiring managers – or in many cases, the line manager – have to choose between, for example, two or three equally suitable candidates, or when a decision between several equally strong candidates based on analytical data is not clear or distinct (Brauner, 2019, p. 94).

Hiring managers from large companies, in particular, emphasize the value of feedback and evaluations. This is mirrored in findings by Miles & Sadler-Smith (2014, p. 621), who highlight that "in the absence of meaningful feedback . . . managers are unlikely to develop good hiring-based intuition." In other words, feedback is recognized as an essential part of improving one's intuition.

Most hiring managers interviewed know that their intuitions and emotions could lead to distortions of perception, biases, and so on. Nevertheless, they perceive and listen to their intuitions. Thus, they discuss and reflect on their individual intuitions or emotions triggered by applicants with other selection managers. They, then, try to reach a consensus and compare intuitive impressions with results from analytics. In this way, the "intersubjectivity" demanded in the literature (Laske & Weiskopf, 1996, p. 300; Miles & Sadler-Smith, 2014, p. 623) is also applied in practice (Deters 2019, pp. 122–129).

In our empirical research, different ways of communicating and reflecting on intuition in selection processes are identified and formulated as recommendations for action (Deters, 2019, pp. 133–134; Hallerberg, 2019, pp. 64–65):

1. There needs to be awareness that intuitions and related emotions influence human selection decisions. It makes no sense to deny these intuitions and emotions. On the contrary, the more humans try to suppress them, the more they influence human behavior. Thus, addressing them openly and reflecting transparently on the possible disadvantages and advantages of using intuitions and emotions is crucial.
2. Make intuition visible through communication and try to substantiate the intuitions, by discussing your impressions and emotions and trying to connect these impressions and emotions concretely with observed behaviors. For example, interviewed hiring managers state that it was challenging for them to separate observation and evaluation in the interview, because already during the selection process, they perceive their intuitions and emotions. Thus, it is recommended to reflect on intuitions and emotions in training and consciously write down what the intuition is, what the feeling tells, which behaviors triggered the intuition and emotion, and then, ultimately, make it transparent to others, such as involved hiring managers, or even applicants. Or the corresponding reflection process takes place directly after the interview, and each manager

notes their individual intuitions and then reflects on them, with the other managers.

In addition, some managers interviewed recommend reflecting on one's impressions, intuitions, and emotions with the applicant (or in training sessions with colleagues who play applicants); this can help understand whether an intuition has arisen based on an incorrect subjective interpretation of the observed behavior of candidates. Therefore, the selection manager needs to describe exactly where a specific impression comes from. The candidate is, thus, given a chance to respond to the feedback based on intuition. Communication with the candidate can subsequently help dispel the intuition, if it is a misinterpretation of observed behaviors.

Several interviewed experts point out that the exchange of intuitions should only occur in the final decision meeting, to exclude any prior influence on others.

In addition, the open exchange about intuitions helps verbalize individual intuitions and enables a fruitful debate and discussion. It fosters insights about oneself and why one interprets certain behaviors, in a specific way. Last but not the least, initial intuitive judgments can be corrected through this open exchange, and erroneous decisions may be avoided. In this context, several interviewees also experienced the exchange with other selection managers as a process to rationalize their intuition.

3. Interviewed HR managers could imagine implementing a measuring instrument of intuition, which works on a scale of 0 to 10 that measures likability. Every hiring manager has to scale the likeability of a candidate. For this purpose, questions can measure how likable a candidate is, whether one can imagine the person working in their team, or whether one can imagine being led by that applicant.

In summary, identifying talent in practice is regularly a constructive interplay of analytics and intuition (Deters, 2019, p. 123; Hallerberg, 2019, pp. 69–70). Thus, from most respondents' perspectives, suitability of candidates should be assessed by rational-analytical procedures, supplemented by critical reflection and conscious use of intuitions and emotions.

5.6 Factors influencing the use of intuition in decision-making

In human decision behavior, analytics and intuition operate together to a greater or lesser extent. However, both intuition and analytics can be exaggerated. Calibration and mixing require knowledge, experience, and sensitivity (e.g., Agor, 1989, p. 37; Mintzberg, 1998; Klein, 2004; Sinclair & Ashkanasy, 2005, p. 360). The mixture of both and whether a more intuitive or rational-analytical decision-making style predominates is determined by four moderators or influencing factors. "It is important to acknowledge . . . that managerial and organizational decision-making is an inherently complex, multilevel process, influenced variously by a host of contingent . . . factors" (Hodgkinson & Sadler-Smith, 2018, p. 474). The main four contingent factors influencing the decision-making process in personnel selection are 1) decision-making context; 2) problem characteristics; 3) decision characteristics; and 4) personal dispositions of the decision-maker (Figure 15).

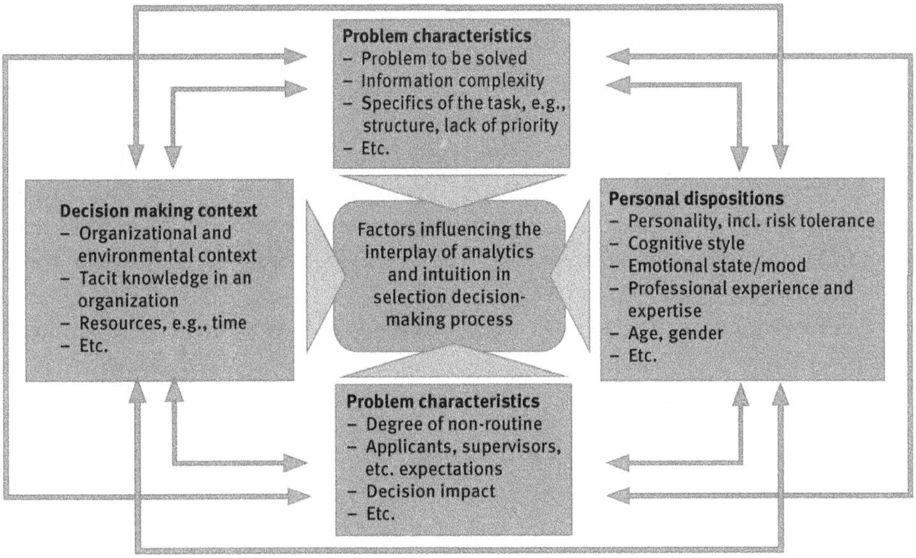

Figure 15: Factors influencing the interplay of analytics and intuition in selection decision-making processes (based on Sinclair & Ashkanasy, 2005, p. 360).

Decision-making context:

- Organizational context resources available, for example, money, time, technology, educated people, tacit knowledge (e.g., psychometric knowledge) in an organization regarding selection procedures. Example: When decisions have to be made very quickly, and there is pressure to come up with the right decision, well-founded rational-analytical processes may be too time-consuming, and then, people rely on their intuitions. Primarily due to available resources, the company's size (Allinson & Hayes, 1996, p. 129) plays a decisive role. Also, the organizational culture and, thus, the acceptance and the development of intuitive and emotional competencies influence the decision-making process.
- Environmental conditions such as national cultures, institutional contexts such as legal and political systems, infrastructure, technology standards in a country/city, industry category, acceptance of specific personnel selection tools, or cultural acceptance of intuitive decisions.

Problem characteristics:
- Information complexity, ambiguity, and level of uncertainty: Problem complexity can overstrain the conscious mind. Thus, the more complex, volatile, unstable, and contradictory the environmental conditions, the more uncertain, incomplete, and imperfect the data situation (e.g., the results of a decision are less scientifically predictable), and the more a problem is ill-defined or lacks clarity, the more people rely on their intuitive abilities.
- Problem to be solved and structure of the problem or task: Shapiro and Spence (1997, p. 63) emphasize the structured nature of the task.

Well-structured problems lend themselves to automation, as evidenced by the explosive growth of management information systems. Ill-defined goals or poorly structured problems, inherently fuzzier, are not conducive to automation. They are the types of problems that gravitate toward senior management, where expert judgment can be used. Unstructured tasks should mostly be handled by experienced employees at higher levels, while structured tasks would be more suitable for inexperienced employees at lower levels.

Less structured problems or tasks such as mergers & acquisition decisions, new product planning, corporate strategy, or research and development typically use – besides data-based analytics – intuition (Shapiro & Spence, 1997, p. 67; see Figure 16).

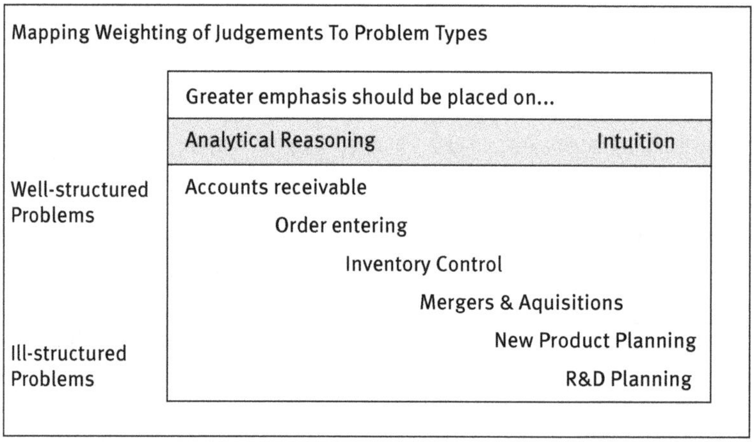

Figure 16: Mapping weighting of judgments to problem types (Shapiro & Spence, 1997, p. 67).

Dane and Pratt (2007, pp. 41 and 45) also state that the more unstructured a problem, the more intuitive judgments occur due to the absence of well-accepted decision-making rules.

Bechtler (1986, pp. 23 and 27–28) shows that different tasks and problems require different approaches. For example, intuition is appropriate for tasks where the problem is not clearly structured, where individual discretion plays a role, and so on. He points out different task areas where intuition is helpful for a goal-oriented completion: 1) personnel management, leadership, and personnel selection; 2) strategic decisions; 3) decisions made under great uncertainty; and 4) tasks where creativity and innovation are required.

Decision characteristics:

- Degree of (non) routine: Isenberg (1984, p. 86) shows that executives use their intuition during all phases of the problem-solving process: problem finding and definition (e.g., use of intuition to detect or anticipate problems, intuition as a provider of insights and solution ideas; intuition as a navigator for recognizing patterns and triggers of quick or routine reactions in everyday situations; intuitions for activating behavioral patterns and standard reactions; intuition as a controller for rational analysis). People also rely more on their intuition to make innovative decisions. Thus, both for familiar and routine tasks, and also to be innovative, intuition is helpful.
- Justification: The more the decisions have to be justified to others (for example, for economic or legal reasons), the more rational-analytical procedures are used, and intuitive decisions are rationalized.
- Available data and materials such as requirement profiles and interview guidelines.
- Equivalent decision alternatives: If there is a choice between several plausible alternative solutions, for example, between two candidates, who are equivalent from a rational-analytical perspective, decision-makers prefer to rely on their intuition
- Behavior and expectations of the candidates
- Expectations and role models of others, for example, supervisors and other managers
- Thinking, behaviors, expectations, resources, competencies, and so on of the co-selection managers

Personal dispositions:

- Personality, and thus, traits such as conscientiousness or extraversion, and other characteristics such as attitudes, habits, cognitive style, and risk tolerance influence individual decision-making. But often, situational influence factors determine the decisions and behaviors; so, for example, although people may be open-minded, when cognitively overloaded with other tasks or problems, they may be more open to intuitive impulses.
- Cognitive ability (e.g., ability to process a variety of complex and interdependent information analytically or not).
- Unconscious bias, stereotypes, prejudices, and other distortions of perception of the selection manager.
- Emotional state or mood.

- "Noise factors" such as being hungry and tired (Kahneman et al., 2021).
- Age/experience, seniority, and gender: Allinson and Hayes (1996, p. 131; see also Mintzberg, 1976) confirm in their research the assumption that there is a positive relationship between high intuitive orientation and age/experience. The older and more experienced the decision-makers, the more they rely on their intuition. Other research shows that an organization's status and hierarchical position also play a role, due to the associated attribution of power and authority. Mintzberg's (1976) hypothesis is that intuition increases with seniority, especially because complexity, uncertainty, and time pressures associated with higher hierarchical management positions call for an intuitive, experience-based approach, rather than detailed analysis. Also, in owner-run companies, the owner entrepreneurs are more likely to stand by and rely on their intuitions. Agor's (1989) survey of American managers provides empirical support for the hypothesis that senior managers in organizations score higher on intuition than their subordinates.
- Tacit knowledge and experience/expertise, competencies: Is the selection manager familiar with scientifically recommended selection procedures and tools, quality standards and their advantages, evaluation procedures, and so on? If the decision-makers have little conscious knowledge to solve a problem, or if they have no or very little previous experience in comparable situations, or when little previous precedent exists, or if the experience and existing knowledge are based on outdated situations, the more they rely on their intuition.

The more experienced the decision-makers with specific problems and the more routine they have developed, the more likely they will proceed intuitively.
- Self-management and social competencies such as emotional regulations and empathy. Empathy helps perceive and assess behaviors (e.g., authenticity) of others accurately.
- Memory and recollection of tacit and implicit information/knowledge/patterns.
- The values, ethics, and goals of hiring managers and their personal involvement may have an impact on whether personnel is selected more intuitively or based on a rational-analytical approach (individual significance of the selection decision, personal/emotional involvement, motivation; or if selection managers are desperate to have a particular candidate or if they are not aware of their ethical standards in personnel selection and their biases, stereotypes, and so on, this may result in a less rational-analytical approach).
- Research also shows that personnel managers make more intuitive decisions than production or financial managers; Kirton (1989) concludes that personnel managers tend to have a relatively intuitive orientation, and Agro's study (1989) revealed that personnel managers working in organizational development decide significantly more intuitively than financial managers (Allinson & Hayes, 1996, p. 129; Allinson et al., 2000).

6 How to measure and operationalize intuition

Chapters 4 and 5 of this book describe the complex construct of intuition from different scientific approaches and viewpoints. They explain how intuition is constructed, and the ontological quality of the construct intuition becomes more explicit even if the phenomenon does not seem to be clearly distinguishable epistemologically from other terms and thus analyzable (Müller-Christ, 2020, p. VIII). But researchers have to struggle with a lack of agreement on what constitutes intuition and its definition.

But despite the linguistic or definitional and conceptual ambiguity surrounding intuition, three commonalities can be identified (Sinclair, 2005). First, most researchers acknowledge that (1) intuitive impulses originate beyond consciousness, (2) information is processed holistically, and (3) intuitive perceptions are frequently accompanied by emotion.

Many researchers do not accept contemplative approaches to measuring intuition by introspection, self-reporting, or in-depth qualitative interviews as valid methods of investigation. Therefore, Sinclair (2005) states that intuition as a construct, operating mostly beyond consciousness through feelings and images, seems immune to scientific inquiry for centuries.

This statement shows there are a lot of methodological challenges in measuring and operationalizing intuition. But "intuition can be defined and theorized about, intuition is open to scientific methods of inquiry, and training, developing, and cultivating managers' intuition is eminently achievable" (Sadler-Smith, 2019, p. 22).

According to the definition of intuition formulated in this book (see Section 4.1.1), intuition has unconscious, cognitive, and (regularly) emotional elements. Thus, it seems appropriate to measure intuitions on these different levels.

Measuring intuition and intuitive competencies is also essential in selecting talent, managers, or employees for research and development departments because intuition is an indicator of creativity and innovation and, thus, appears to be related to organizational success (Andersen, 2000). Therefore, methods and procedures that could assist in measuring intuitive competencies would be helpful.

A possible operationalization also means that intuition can be taught and learned. To answer this question according to the current state of research, an overview of the survey methods in the context of intuition measurement is given further. According to Sadler-Smith (2019), we can differentiate between self-report and non-self-report methods.

https://doi.org/10.1515/9783110980967-006

6.1 Non-self-report methods

6.1.1 Quantitative non-self-report methods

Similar to marketing and market research, it is also evident in human resource management that human behavior can only be adequately researched if implicit and explicit research methods complement each other: System 1 meets System 2!

For example, neuroscience tries to find by brain scanning where intuitive or rational-analytical processes occur in the brain or body.

Scientists and practitioners, for example, psychologists, have developed a broad portfolio of methods that allow access to implicit processes without complex equipment and help understand the interactions between implicit and explicit thought and information processing. For example, the bodily effects of emotions can be measured objectively, for example, by pupil dilation (eye-tracking), skin conductance responses, neuro-imaging, and brain activity (e.g., fMRI functional magnetic resonance imaging, or NIRS Near-infrared spectroscopy, or EEG electroencephalography), heart rate, and facial expressions. Other implicit methods are, for example, "reaction time measurement" or "paper-pencil methods," such as projective questioning or measuring sensitivity to social desirability in response behavior (Naderer & Frank, 2015; Sadler-Smith, 2019, p. 20).

Another quantitative method to operationalize intuition is brain stimulation techniques. In this context, Iannello et al. (2014, pp. 130–131) present and critically review Transcranial Magnetic Stimulation (TMS) and Transcranial Direct Current Stimulation (TDCS). However, according to their statement, such investigations of cortical activities currently cannot be directly related to intuition. Nevertheless, researchers see this as a future field of research to support the constructive application of intuitions and emotions.

Other studies by Lieberman (2007) show that reflexive (intuitive) processing is not correlated to the "right brain," as claimed for many years, but rather a complex interacting network of systems are involved, including the ventro-medial prefrontal cortex (VMPC) and amygdala (Sadler-Smith, 2019, p. 21; on the criticism of the assumption of a right and a left hemisphere of the brain to which specific processes can be directly assigned, see Section 4.2.8 and Satpute & Lieberman, 2006).

Or some studies examine, for example, hormones or other somatic markers in the blood to measure emotional processes. An example is the somatic marker approach by Damasio (1995) and Damasio et al. (1991), in which decision-making is a process that is influenced by somatic (bodily) markers that arise in bio-regulatory processes and express themselves in emotions and feelings (Sadler-Smith, 2019, p. 20).

But the intuitive, implicit processes of System 1 or the interplay of System 1 and System 2 processes can by no means be validly recorded only by measuring neurophysiological processes in the brain or the body.

Although we all know situations where an unexplainable or uneasy feeling creeps upon us that we can't precisely describe (like a hunch), the conscious nature of feelings makes it relatively easy to measure them using self-reporting tools such as interviews, questionnaires, and personality tests, including rating scales and self-assessment procedures. For example, the Self-Assessment Manikin (SAM) of Margaret Bradley and Peter Lang (1994) is a nonverbal pictorial assessment technique that directly measures feelings (pleasure–displeasure) and arousal levels (low–high) of respondents when confronted with various emotional stimuli.

6.1.2 Qualitative non-self-report methods (examples)

6.1.2.1 Measuring intuition using observation

This method is a way of collecting data on decision-making through observation. It involves observing selection managers studying (e.g., taking notes or recording) their spontaneous behavior (verbal and nonverbal) in realistic situations such as an assessment center, an interview, and so on. This type of research aims to gather more reliable insights because researchers can capture data on what participants do instead of what they may say they do.

6.1.2.2 Protocol analysis

According to Baldacchino et al. (2014, pp. 160–161), protocol analysis is another approach, besides interviewing or observation. Here, people are asked to speak their entire thoughts aloud during their decision-making process, allowing for a recording to be made. The basic idea behind this method is to capture intuition through thinking aloud in real-time, thus bypassing the retrospective approach already critically highlighted. Accordingly, protocol analysis attempts to gain insight into thought processes and, thus, the use of intuition.

6.1.2.3 Dialogical inquiry

According to Coget (2014, pp. 176–177), a dialogical inquiry is another qualitative method that attempts to prevent bias and post hoc rationalization through its procedure. The research is divided into four steps and was developed specifically to study intuition in practice. In the first step, an interview is conducted with people to identify their critical psychological characteristics in the organizational and private context. The second step is shadowing and filming active subjects in their working environment. The third step selects sections relevant to the research field from the video material of step two. Then, this material is used as the basis for a discussion in the fourth and most crucial step, the dialogical investigation. Accordingly, the video excerpts are examined more closely in a trusting environment and dialogical form and explained by the respondent. Finally, the facilitator encourages the respondents to describe the situation in their own words and address how they experienced it, what feelings prevailed, and what they thought or why they acted in a specific way. This procedure aims to ascertain and analyze the reasons for the subjects' behavior in practice.

6.2 Measuring intuition using self-reports

Self-reports could be used to investigate the interaction of intuition and rational-analysis decisions in specific episodes such as selection decisions (Hodgkinson & Sadler-Smith, 2014). These reports use the retrospective assessment of individuals on their past decision-making processes. The extent to which someone has access to their feelings and thus to their intuition also plays a role here, to be able to reflect on the decision accordingly (Smerek, 2014, p. 9).

6.2.1 Qualitative methods and self-reports

6.2.1.1 Interviews

Self-reports can be conducted based on qualitative interviews. According to Kleebaur (2007, p. 6), the interview is particularly suitable for operationalization because intuition has been little explored to date. In its context, specifically selected persons can be interviewed about applying intuition. Furthermore, the interview method raises subjective impressions and sensations, which can be seen critically from a quantitative scientific perspective.

Our empirical research is based on qualitative interviews with selection managers from different companies, hierarchical levels, and countries.

The aim is to make people (selection managers) as subjects, the starting point and, simultaneously, the target of the investigation and research, and to capture the subjective experience and the associated subjective constructions of decision-making processes.

Through personal communication and interaction, one can ask follow-up questions, clarify ambiguities, and reflect on backgrounds and possible causes for concrete decision-making behavior, and thus better understand them.

6.2.1.2 Critical incident technique

According to Akinci (2014, pp. 142–143), the second qualitative method also uses the interview technique. However, the interview is semi-structured and asks the interviewees about the so-called critical incidents, for example, how to handle the conflict between intuition and feelings and the results of a rational-analytical process. Thus, critical situations and behaviors are specifically queried, and the focus is placed on the interviewees' reactions described in the retrospective. One advantage of this method is that it allows for questioning in an organizational context (Akinci, 2014, p. 148). However, the possibility of subjectivity and post hoc rationalization described in Section 5.3 cannot be excluded. There is also a risk that factors such as the self-serving bias or contrast effects may significantly influence the interview results (Akinci, 2014, p. 151).

6.2.2 Quantitative methods and self-reports

6.2.2.1 Cognitive style index (CSI)

The CSI, developed by Allinson and Hayes (1996), is designed to assess preferences between two cognitive styles, the intuitive and the analytical. Thus, the CSI is an example of the "continuum approach," where intuition and analytics are the two poles on a continuum. They developed this self-report measure for application in large-scale organizational settings, especially management and business. The authors use the word "intuition" to describe immediate judgments based on feelings and the term "analysis" for judgments based on mental reasoning and a step-by-step approach focusing on details.

The test consists of 38 items using a three-point rating system (true, uncertain, false) and is based on the theoretical understanding that one superordinate, unitary construct of cognitive style exists between the two poles of intuitive and analytical thinking. Thus, the CSI evaluates a unidimensional construct where analysis and intuition are viewed as bipolar opposites on a single continuum on which different degrees of a thinking style are possible. And the prediction or hypothesis is that the higher the rational-analysis orientation, the higher the individual's preference for a rational-analytical procedure.

Coefficients for internal consistency are reported, with alphas ranging from .84 to .92, and temporal stability is suggested by a test-retest coefficient of .90 for a subgroup of the sample who completed the questionnaire on a second occasion after four weeks. Even though Allinson and Hayes (1996) originally used a Likert scale from false to uncertain and true, the response format was a 5-point Likert scale, from 1 = strongly disagree to 5 = strongly agree. This scale was applied to generate more differentiated results and increase comparability with the other measures (Burmeister, 2010, pp. 17–18).

Although the CSI was very well rated in a review of cognitive and learning styles conducted by Coffield et al. (2004), there is a debate about whether a unidimensional continuum is appropriate to position the intuitive and rational-analytical cognitive styles along which all degrees of style and a combination of both styles are possible (Allinson & Hayes, 1996, p. 123, Hammond et al., 1987, p. 754; see Section 4.2.2.7. For cross-national differences in cognitive style, see Allinson & Hayes, 2000).

Sadler-Smith (2019, pp. 17–18) "questions the construct validity of the CSI and argues, from a dual-process standpoint, that its single-factor structure does stand up to empirical scrutiny. Hodgkinson and Sadler-Smith's (2003) empirical evidence based on exploratory and confirmatory factor analyses on data from over 1,000 participants indicated that the CSI should be scored as two independent scales. Subsequent studies supported this interpretation (see Hodgkinson et al., 2009b), although Armstrong and Qi (2016) challenged this view recently."

6.2.2.2 Cognitive style indicator (CoSI)

The Cognitive Style Indicator (CoSI), developed by Cool, Van Den Broeck, and Bouckenooghe (2006), is an 18-item self-report instrument for the rather general measurement of cognitive style. Participants answer on a five-point Likert scale, from 1 = strongly disagree to 5 = strongly agree. Eva Cools and Herman Van den Broeck (2007) describe the development and validation of the Cognitive Style Indicator (CoSI) using three diverse samples (N = 5,924; N = 1,580; and N = 635). Reliability, item, and factor analyses demonstrate the internal consistency and homogeneity of three cognitive styles: knowing, planning, and creating. They state substantial support for the instrument's convergent and discriminant validity by including other cognitive style instruments and personality and academic performance measures in the validation process. Criterion-related validity was confirmed by examining the relation between these cognitive styles and work-related characteristics. The main contributions of this study are the (a) further refinement of the analytic-intuitive cognitive style dimension by splitting the analytic pole into a knowing and a planning style and (b) development of a valid and reliable cognitive style instrument for use in organizations. Concretely, they report internal consistency scores, with α ranging from .73 to .85, and a clear three-factor structure based on the developed subscales, knowing (4 items), planning (7 items), and creating (7 items) style. Knowing the style is similar to conceptualizations of the analytic pole, whereas the creating style shows theoretical resemblance to conceptualizations of the intuitive pool (Cools & Van de Broeck, 2007). Likewise, engagement in sequential planning is understood as a part of deliberate processing because it shows similarity to the analytic pole (Burmeister, 2010, pp. 17–18).

6.2.2.3 General decision-making style (GDMS)

The GDMS, designed by Scott and Bruce (1995), assesses how individuals approach decision situations. The GDMS aims to measure decision-making styles broader than just intuition and deliberation, and distinguishes between five decision-making styles.

- A rational style emphasizes a thorough search for and logical evaluation of alternatives.
- An avoidant style emphasizes postponing and avoiding decisions.
- A dependent style emphasizes a search for advice and direction from others.

- An intuitive style emphasizes reliance on hunches and feelings.
- A spontaneous style emphasizes a sense of immediacy and a desire to get through the decision-making process as soon as possible.

This method is based on the definition that decision-making style is the "learned, habitual response pattern exhibited by an individual when confronted with a decision situation" (Scott & Bruce, 1995, p. 820). The final version of the General Decision-making Style measure consists of 25 items with five-point ratings for each subscale (1 = strongly disagree to 5 = strongly agree). Five subscales, named *rational, intuitive, dependent, spontaneous,* and *avoidant*, are postulated. The coefficients for internal consistency for rational style ranged between α = .77 to .85 and for intuitive style between α = .78 and .84 in a study that included four different samples. The subscale *spontaneous thinking* is related to intuitive decisions (Burmeister, 2010, pp. 17–18).

6.2.2.4 Rational experiential inventory (REI) as a dual-process approach

The Rational Experiential Inventory (REI) is an example of the "dual-process approach," where intuition and analytics are two distinct and independent interacting processes.

The REI is based on Epstein and colleagues' Cognitive-Experiential Self-Theory (CEST) (Epstein et al., 1996), which is a parallel-competitive variant of dual-processing (Sadler-Smith, 2019, p. 18). The approach by Epstein posits that rational (analytical) and experiential (intuitive) processes are interacting but independent systems (Epstein, 1990), a view supported by the research of Lieberman (2007) that suggests that these systems derive from separate neural pathways.

The REI exists in various forms and is a self-reported measure of individual differences in intuitive-experiential and analytical-rational thinking. The measure comprises 31 items assessing two unipolar subscales: Rational thinking is measured by a shortened version of the Need for Cognition scale (NFC) with 19 extracted items (Cacioppo & Petty, 1982), and intuitive thinking is assessed through a Faith in Intuition scale (FI) with 12 items, designed to assess "confidence in one's feelings and immediate impressions as a basis for decisions and actions" (Epstein et al., 1996, p. 394). Internal consistency of the subscales has been reported with α = .87 for NFC and α = .77 for FI (Epstein et al., 1996). The German translation by Keller et al. 2000 shows similar scores for internal consistency (NFC α = .82 and FI α = .86). The response format was a five-point Likert scale, ranging from 1 = strong disagreement to 5 = strong agreement (Burmeister, 2010, p. 27).

Sinclair and Ashkanasy (2005, pp. 363–364) prefer the REI because this test conforms to the two independent dimensions of intuition and rationality, and it is consistent with their definition of intuition.

6.2.2.5 Myers-Briggs type indicator (MBTI)

The MBTI, developed by Isabel Briggs Myers, and her mother, Katharine Briggs (the first MBTI manual was published in 1962), is a self-reporting personality test (questionnaire) based on C. G. Jung, whose psychological types described intuition as a form of unconscious perception of the realm of images, symbols, ideas, and abstractions. The MBTI uses four preference pairs and assigns each individual a "type," based on four categories or scales: extraversion/introversion, thinking/feeling, judging/perceiving, and intuition/sensing. Thus it shows – among other things – if someone has a preference for "sensing" or "intuition" in information processing and also "thinking" and "feeling" in decision-making.

The MBTI frames "intuition" or "thinking" and "feeling" as basic preferences and relatively stable individual personality types. Thus, the MBTI sorts for preferences and does not measure traits, abilities, or character. Instead, the preferences give information about people's perceptions and how they come to conclusions.

The preference pair "thinking" and "feeling" describes how people like to make decisions. For example, do they primarily like to weigh objective principles and impersonal facts (thinking), or do they weigh more personal concerns and the people involved (feeling)? And the preference pair "intuition" and "sensing" is about information processing: Does someone prefer to focus on the basic information s/he takes in through the five senses (sensing), or do they pay more attention to the patterns and possibilities in the information received, and prefer to interpret and add meaning to this information (intuition). In contrast to "sensors," "intuitive people" prefer abstract ideas over concrete facts, potentialities over actualities, future over the present, and holistic over sequential decision-making. According to this theory, everyone has a dominant mode of perception, intuition or sensing, which is their most comfortable and natural way of perceiving the world (Lussier, 2016, pp. 710–711).

When people decide on their preference in each category, they have their specific personality type, which can be expressed as a code with four preferences. Thus, there are 16 personality types identified by the MBTI. For example, it is possible to be an "Intuitive Thinker," for example, the INTP personality type (**I**ntroverted, i**N**tuitive, **T**hinking, **P**erceiving), or an "Intuitive Feeler," for example, the INFJ personality type (**I**ntroverted, i**N**tuitive, **F**eeling, and **J**udging).

The MBTI is an example of the "continuum approach," using four different scales. The main criticism is about the poor validity and reliability, and that the categories measured are not independent, for example, intuition, and feeling (Thyer & Pignotti, 2015, pp. 77–78).

6.2.2.6 Intuitive management survey (AIM)

The main objective of the AIM (**Agor, 1989; A**gor **I**ntuitive **M**anagement Survey**)** is to measure predispositions and further developments of the ability to make successful management decisions based on feelings. The AIM is based on the "intuition-sensing-items" of the MBTI (Myers-Briggs-Indicator), which assesses intuition and analytics as opposite poles on the same continuum. A criticism of this instrument is that intuitive (affective) and analytical components (e.g., tacit knowledge) cannot be clearly separated (Sinclair & Ashkanasy, 2005, pp. 363–364).

AIM is an example of the "continuum approach," where intuition and analytics are the opposite two poles on a continuum.

6.2.2.7 International survey on intuition (ISI)

The ISI (Parikh et al., 1994) was developed for a cross-cultural study to explore how people interpret intuition. This test sees intuition as a multilevel and multi-contextual phenomenon. Similar to the AIM, the ISI views intuition and rationality as mutually exclusive. And the quantitative elements of this test focus less on emotional elements of decision-making than on knowledge-based aspects (Sinclair 2015; Sinclair & Ashkanasy, 2005, p. 363).

The ISI is an example of the "continuum approach" where feelings and analytics are the opposite two poles on a continuum.

6.2.2.8 Linear–nonlinear thinking style profile (LNTSP)

Vance et al. (2004, 2007) developed this self-reporting diagnostic instrument (linear–nonlinear thinking style profile or LNTSP) for measuring an individual's linear and nonlinear thinking style profile. They use this instrument to empirically examine the relationships between managers' and entrepreneurs' nonlinear and linear thinking styles, and the consequences for entrepreneurial success. They examine, for example, whether successful entrepreneurs possess a highly nonlinear (e.g., creative, intuitive) thinking style, as some researchers and popular stereotypes of entrepreneurs would suggest, or a more balanced nonlinear and linear (e.g., rational, logical, and analytic) thinking style. They emphasize that successful entrepreneurs balance linear and nonlinear thinking styles. In addition, their findings show that balanced managerial thinking is also associated with organizational commitment in jobs characterized by high emotional labor (Groves et al., 2008) and that a linear thinking style is positively associated with understanding and regulating emotions (Groves & Vance, 2009).

The LNTSP is an example of the "continuum approach" where intuition and analytics are the opposite two poles on a continuum.

6.2.2.9 Preference for intuition and deliberation (PID)

The preference for intuition and deliberation (PID) was developed by Cornelia Betsch (2004). This test is constructed to quantify individual preferences for intuition and deliberation on two independent scales. Intuition is understood as a purely affective mode, whereas deliberation is a reflective, cognition-based mode. Both styles are independent of the ability to think logically.

Three studies using this test comprising more than 2,500 participants show that a preference for intuition correlates positively with fast decision-making, extraversion, and agreeableness, whereas a preference for deliberation correlates with conscientiousness, perfectionism, and need for structure. Wang et al. (2017, online version 2015, p. 8) confirm these results: "For the Big Five personality traits, intuition tended to have a stronger relation with extraversion, whereas analysis tended to have a stronger relation with conscientiousness and openness to experience."

The PID is an example of the "dual-process approach" where intuition and analytics are two distinct and independent types of processes that interact.

6.2.2.10 Intuitive profile (IQ2 Intuition Quotient Test or Cappon intuition profile)

This nonverbal method to measure intuition was developed by Cappon (1993) and comprises a visual test of information processing, and does not include emotional elements. It assesses, for example, knowledge-based pattern recognition, problem-solving speed under time pressure, and the ability to deal with complex and incomplete information. "The visual nature of the instrument allows for intuition to be tested separately from rational thinking, which implies access to direct knowing without conscious processing" (Sinclair & Ashkanasy, 2005, p. 364).

6.3 Experiments as methods to measure intuition

According to Harteis (2014, pp. 121–127), experiment is another approach to making intuition measurable. An experiment is based on self and external assessment, and follows the exploratory approach. First, the participants are provided with information on which they have to decide. The situational conditions under which the decision is made are varied. For example, time pressure can be created or the participants can be asked to justify their decision in writing. Subsequently, the intuitive and analytically decisions are evaluated according to their quality, considering the experimental conditions. The hypothesis is that intuitive decisions are made under time pressure, whereas decisions without limited time and a required written justification are analytical. The criticism of this method of operationalization is that it is not intuition that is measured, but performance under conditions in which intuition will likely be applied (Harteis, 2014, p. 127).

6.4 Challenges and limitations of the methods to measure intuition

According to Akinci (2014, p. 156), many presented methods have challenges and limitations. For example, Akinci highlights that the self-reporting methods used to operationalize intuition do not go beyond the individual level. However, she maintains that it is necessary to go beyond this level to prevent bias and thus be able to achieve more meaningful research results. According to her, it is necessary to capture the specific field of where and how intuition is used as a whole and include the group/team and organizational levels.

A second point emphasized by Akinci (2014, p. 156) is the need to go beyond cases where intuition leads to a successful and, thus, an effective decision. Instead, there should also be a focus on cases where intuition causes failures and, thus, poor decisions. Answering this question is particularly interesting as intuitive decisions entail serious consequences and risks.

However, it must be emphasized that the self-assessment method can be problematic due to the risk of subjectivity, biases, and so on (Harteis, 2014, p. 120).

Hodgkinson and Sadler-Smith (2014, p. 111), along with Wang et al. (2017), think that the continuum approach (with two opposite ends of a bipolar continuum) and the dual-process approach are conflicting and incompatible perspectives on the relation between intuition and analysis. They are convinced that the dual-process approach is more appropriate and, thus, the preferred way to measure intuition.

For example, Allinson and Hayes' 1996 Cognitive Style Index (CSI), which intends to measure preference according to intuitive and analytic processes, and Vance et al.'s LNTSP, which intends to measure different thinking styles, are considered problematic by Hodgkinson and Sadler-Smith (2014), because the CSI and LNTSP use a continuum perspective and not a dual-process approach. And the other methods to measure intuition imply that the existence of three or more factors that determine a cognitive style is likewise seen as problematic. In contrast, they recommend to prefer tests that are based on and are consistent with the dual-process approach, for example, the REI by Epstein et al. (1996) (Hodgkinson and Sadler-Smith, 2014, p. 111; Sadler-Smith, 2019, p. 19) and the PID by Betsch from 2004. From a psychometric perspective, the REI has several advantages over the CSI. First, it accurately reflects the overall construct definition as Epstein et al. (1996) intended. Second, to measure intuition and analytics separately, the analytic and intuitive scales of the REI or the PID are independent, while the analytical and intuitive factors of the CSI overlap (Hodgkinson and Sadler-Smith, 2014).

According to Sinclair and Ashkanasy (2005, p. 364), an appropriate questionnaire would require that intuitive and analytical decision-making be measured separately and that the design of the test capture all facets of the construct "intuition," such as unconscious information processing or experienced-based pattern recognition. And because the complex construct "intuition" is challenging to measure by a single tool, they recommend a combination of measures, each tapping into the different facets of intuition.

> In this respect, we have identified three alternative approaches that may counterbalance some shortcomings of questionnaire measures: (1) a description of the decision-making process provided by the participant; (2) a word-count of the description (verbalization); and (3) a measure

> of the time needed to make the decision (latency). As a minimum precaution, we suggest that intuition researchers compare questionnaire results with a record of the study participants' descriptions of how they approached a particular decision. Although still reliant on self-report, such a reflective measure may provide additional insights. Furthermore, using content analysis . . . the description can be coded to generate a quantitative score that might be used to verify the questionnaire results. Our research indicates, however, that respondents find it difficult to isolate their verbal assessment of intuitive use from references to rational thinking . . . . As mentioned earlier, this may be caused by the lack of appropriate vocabulary . . . This limitation extends to questionnaires as well as self-description. Nevertheless, content analysis of the description makes it easier to evaluate the use of intuition more accurately (Sinclair & Ashkanasy, 2005, p. 365).

Hodgkinson and Sadler-Smith (2018, p. 486) also prefer a multi-method approach and conclude that the

> self-reporting of analytical and intuitive thinking (cognitive) styles has been a mainstay of much intuition research . . . . However, we advocate supplementing such self-reports of individual differences with research methods that can objectively assess intuitive expertise (e.g., cognitive task analysis, tacit knowledge tests), recover decision episodes to study close up the co-action of intuition and analysis (e.g., the aforementioned phenomenological approaches), and observe intuition and analysis in situ (sic!) (e.g., ethnographic approaches, eye-tracking software), as well as mapping the physiological and neural correlates of intuitive and analytical processing.

7 Acceptance of analytics and intuition in the process of diagnosing talent in different cultures

When selecting talent globally or talent from different cultural backgrounds, it is crucial to understand how and under which circumstances a selection procedure can be applied to culturally diverse candidates. Furthermore, to ensure the success of personnel selection, the acceptance of a selection procedure must be considered. Ma and Allen (2009, pp. 343–344) show that it is essential that selection managers take cultural differences into account when communicating and interacting with candidates. Adapting selection procedures to cultural circumstances is a question of a positive candidate experience and acceptance by the selection managers. Recruitment and selection activities aim to attract applicants with the required qualifications, avoid unwanted withdrawal, and keep them sufficiently interested in the organization, to accept a selection procedure or a job offer. Adapting selection activities to the requirements of a specific cultural context is key to successful global talent recruitment (Ma & Allen, 2009, pp. 343–344). To support a positive candidate experience, the candidates' cultural background and culture-specific expectations should be recognized. Selection managers should have the appropriate intercultural competencies to successfully implement such tasks and understand applicants from different cultures (Jokinen, 2004). This includes knowledge of a specific culture and the culture-specific acceptance of selection procedures. In addition, appropriate intercultural communication and social skills, such as empathy or relationship management, are necessary, including flexible, context-specific behaviors.

Due to globalization, cross-national cooperation between companies and workforces, and teamwork becoming more interculturally diverse, research on the relationship between culture and decision-making has gained considerable importance. Research shows that several cultural factors influence decisions (Chu et al., 1999, p. 148; Minkov & Hofstede, 2011, p. 10; Schwartz, 2014, p. 550).

7.1 Culture and talent selection procedures

Different cultures appreciate different behaviors, communication styles, and competencies in specific situations. What is considered important in a society is strongly determined by its culture. Culture, as a set of learned and shared beliefs, values, social practices, political and legal systems, and so on, determines the values, rules, and norms of individuals, and is at the same time an expression of individual behaviors. Cultural factors serve to maintain a specific social order in a particular culture. Culturally mediated values, social norms, and so on determine the importance and control of intuitions and emotions. Even the perception of emotions, for example, in music, is subject to cultural influences (Thompson & Balkwill, 2010). Consequently,

https://doi.org/10.1515/9783110980967-007

cultural background influences how intuitions and emotions are dealt with in private and professional environments (Eid & Diener, 2001, pp. 869–871), and particularly, which types of feelings are openly displayed and how feelings are perceived and communicated (Matsumoto, 1989, pp. 92–94).

But it is important to consider culture as something dynamic that changes continuously, and people are regularly affected by more than one culture at a time (Gullestrup, 2002, p. 1).

Ryan and Tippins (2009; see also Manroop et al., 2013, p. 3512; Ma & Allen, 2009, pp. 343–344) argue that cultural differences and values are most likely to influence personnel selection processes in different parts of the world, even though these interrelationships have been little researched so far.

Huo et al. (2002, p. 42) note that there will be differences in personnel practice as long as cultural differences exist between countries. For this reason, hiring managers should be aware of the acceptance of specific personnel recruiting procedures in different cultures and among people from different cultural backgrounds.

In this context, Shackleton and Newell (1994, p. 91) put forward the hypothesis that habit, tradition, and culture determine the choice of selection method much more than the relative predictive validities of the techniques.

Aycan (2005, pp. 1086–1087) presents the state of research on the influence of cultural and institutional values on personnel selection in 2005. The author draws on cultural dimensions from various models, including Hofstede and Trompenaars. Results show that the criteria used to select new employees are culture-dependent.

In addition to cultural differences, economic circumstances and differences in education and legal systems influence the procedures used in personnel selection (Krause, 2011, pp. 11–25). Krause (2017, p. 244) explains that organizations must weigh the need for culture-specific design of personnel selection procedures, as against standardization across cultures. To implement a successful global selection process, cultural differences must be considered, both from the applicants' and the hiring managers' points of view.

Therefore, the question is, to what extent can scientific results and, thus, psychometric procedures be implemented in different cultures, how are rational-analytical procedures accepted by people with diverse cultural backgrounds, and what role does intuition play in selecting personnel.

However, Diana Krause (2017, p. 265) found in her research that in most countries, worldwide, the most commonly used personnel selection procedures are from a psychometric perspective and by no means are they regarded as very effective and valid.

For example, due to cultural differences, there are situations where certain recruitment activities are effective when interacting with candidates of one specific culture and are counterproductive when interacting with applicants of another culture.

Manroop et al. (2013, p. 3515) show how cultural misunderstandings lead to cross-cultural differences in interview outcomes. According to them, the applicant's verbal, nonverbal, and self-promotion behaviors influence interview judgments. Interviewers tend to judge candidates based on their own culture and communication style. Therefore, candidates with different verbal or nonverbal communication styles are likely be judged negatively by the interviewer. In addition, if job applicants respond to questions contrary to cultural expectations, it can also lead to an adverse judgment. Further, the authors confirm that the interviewer's final judgment and hiring recommendation depends on the initial impression that is influenced by culturally specific behavior expectations. And, primarily, the nonverbal behaviors of applicants affect the first impression and, therefore, the hiring recommendation.

In addition, the authors find that candidates who perceive low levels of behavioral mirroring will infer a lack of rapport, which leads to psychological stress, which in turn affects their performance. Behavioral mirroring reflects one person's behavior and occurs when people experience a social connection. Finally, cultural differences also moderate how candidates promote themselves in a job interview, impacting the hiring decision.

7.2 Influences on the cultural acceptance of analytical and intuitive selection procedures

Human experiences and behaviors that are influenced by cultural factors are important reasons why human resource management and thus, processes and procedures of personnel diagnostics often have a low degree of harmonization and standardization across different countries as compared to other procedures such as production, accounting, or IT (Bouzguenda, 2013, p. 25; Pudelko, 2006, p. 132). In addition, there are different points of view and diverging interests and expectations, both from a practical (hiring managers and applicants) and a scientific perspective (Lindemann, 2020, p. 3).

Although certain emotions expressed in body language can be universally recognized (Ekman, 1994), cultural differences exist in the experience and expression of intuitions and emotions (Brandstätter et al., 2018, p. 260). Krause (2017, p. 245) notes that the acceptance of intuitions and emotions in personnel selection and the implementation of scientifically based rational-analytical selection procedures vary by country and thus cultural, legal, political, educational, and other circumstances.

7.2.1 Political influence on selection procedures

Countries' political system influences what people expect from a personnel selection system and how they want to be treated in a selection process. Expectations regarding selection procedures in democratic states differ from those in more autocratic systems. For example, in democratic states, expectations include transparency and involvement.

Concerning the influence of politics on selection processes, a country's corruption perceptions index (CPI) is critical (the CPI currently ranks 180 countries on a scale from 100 [very clean] to 0 [highly corrupt]). These corruption indices indicate willingness to corrupt everyday life and are also reflected in personnel selection processes.

In countries and cultures with a very low degree of corruption, selection decisions are often based on valid and rational-analytical methods, for example, transparent decision rules and similar treatment of all applicants (Arvey & Renz, 1992, p. 332). Countries such as Somalia (CPI 12), Sudan (CPI 16), Russia (CPI 30), Brazil (CPI 38), India (CPI 40), or China (CPI 42) are ranked low on the corruption index, which means that corruption is relatively high. On the other hand, countries such as Denmark (CPI 88), Switzerland (CPI 85), or Germany (CPI 80) have some of the highest indices worldwide (Transparency International, 2020).

These research results suggest, for example, that less objective and rational-analytical personnel selection decisions are more commonplace and more accepted in Somalia, Sudan, Russia, or Brazil than in Denmark or Germany. In countries like Germany, the procedures are more based on analytics, as corruption has little influence on the personnel selection process. Conversely, Arvey & Renz (1992, p. 332) show that countries with a high propensity to corruption tend to use more nonrational-analytical procedures, and personnel selection decisions are based less on valid, objective criteria, than on personal preferences.

In connection with the political framework conditions, shedding light on the willingness of individual countries to engage in corruption requires statements about their attitude toward quality standards.

However, since quality standards focus on rational-analytical personnel selection procedures (Ackerschott et al., 2016, pp. 13–14; Braun et al., 2015, pp. 100–101), resistance from Brazil, China, and India to use psychometric standards that may not fit their country-specific political contexts is to be expected.

7.2.2 Legal influences

In addition to general political conditions, legal factors must also be considered since a personnel selection system always goes hand in hand with specific legal regulations in the respective country (Ryan & Tippins, 2009, p. 91). Thus, one possible reason rational-analytical and psychometric procedures are used in countries such as the United States or Germany is the legal regulation, for example, concerning discrimination, data protection, or influence of employee representatives.

A specific country's political and legal system also influences procedural and distributive justice rules and thus the perceived fairness of a selection process. It directly impacts the use of particular personnel selection processes because they reflect social norms and prescribe what can be regarded as legitimate in the context of personnel selection.

Among other things, discrimination laws, co-determination by employee representatives, and data protection influence the procedures used in personnel selection.

Expectations concerning protecting privacy differ among countries (Harris et al., 2003, p. 231). Since data protection is regarded as a fundamental human right in the European Union, for example, in Germany, the Basic Data Protection Regulation lays down principles for the protection of natural persons in relation to the processing of personal data and the circulation of such data (§ 1 Art. 1 EU-DSGVO; European Data Protection Regulation). In other countries, for example, China, data protection rights are less pronounced (Hessler & Freerks, 1995, p. 35). However, for German candidates to feel comfortable in a personnel selection process, their data protection must be ensured, for example, by applying psychometric quality standards such as DIN 33430 or ISO 10667.

At the national level, personnel selection can be determined by many laws. Although the various national laws overlap, they differ in the extent of data protection. Concerning discrimination laws, the variation in protection can be seen particularly well in China, Germany, and the United States. People are legally protected from skin color, religion, race/ethnicity, sexual orientation, disability, age, and gender discrimination. Laws also stipulate that the personnel selection process must be valid, error-free, and systematic (Ryan & Tippins, 2009, p. 92).

Above all, regulations and laws such as the "Equal Employment Opportunity Law," the "Civil Rights Acts," the "Americans with Disabilities Act" (ADA), the "Age Discrimination in Employment Act" are intended to prevent discrimination. However, these regulations engender many court cases in the United States. This leads, among other things, for example, to unstructured interviews being rarely used because this procedure is often judged to be discriminatory. There can also be a conflict of objectives, as the pressure on companies to hire people with specific backgrounds or characteristics and not discriminate is often so intense that they may hire a candidate who is not the most suitable. Thus, a conflict between legal requirements and predictive validity in the United States can occur). As a result, personnel selection processes in the United States are relatively firmly based on analytics due to the legal framework (Krause, 2011, pp. 22–23).

In Germany, the General Equal Treatment Act (AGG) protects not only against discrimination on aspects such as age, but also a person's worldview. Due to the Works Constitution Act and protection against dismissal, personnel selection decisions have a long-term effect on an organization. The works council also significantly influences personnel selection through its co-determination rights (Krause, 2011, p. 19). In Germany, data protection also plays a vital role for applicants. In general, privacy is a fundamental human right in Europe (Harris et al., 2003, p. 231). Candidates, therefore, expect their data to be processed and stored only for a specific purpose (Krause, 2011, p. 24). If companies don't respect their privacy, they may stop the application process or not apply at all. For this reason, they also attach importance to being informed about the process (Krause, 2011, p. 24). Analytical procedures, such as (semi-)structured interviews, are also increasingly used in Germany.

In comparison, sexuality is excluded from the prohibitions of discrimination in China. Moreover, discrimination based on ethnicity, race, gender, religion, and physical limitations is inadmissible (HR Diagnostics, 2018). Hlásny (2017, pp. 457–461) notes that applicants' personal characteristics are openly asked about in Chinese companies, even if this violates officially existing anti-discrimination regulations. These are, for example, marital status, ethnic origin, appearance, or even health data and blood type. But of course, even in other countries and cultures, the possibility of hiring managers violating legally prescribed rules can never be completely ruled out.

The analysis suggests that structured psychometric processes are less used in China, Brazil, and Arab or African countries as the legal framework is often very vague compared to other countries such as the United States or Germany, and Scandinavian countries. As a result, hiring managers in China have more freedom and flexibility in making personnel selection, as there are no or only a few fixed selection procedures.

In summary, it can be stated that psychometric quality standards and regulations to prevent discrimination and corruption are regarded more positively in countries such as Germany, the United States, or Sweden. However, many hiring managers in Western countries, especially SMEs, feel restricted by these laws, rules, standards, or guidelines and try to circumvent them (see Section 2.3).

7.2.3 Economic, technological, and educational influences

The economy, the technological environment (infrastructure), and the educational system (quality of schools, universities, etc.) of a country influence the acceptance and the options of specific selection procedures.

The economic situation in a country influences its technological infrastructure, education system, and the general level of knowledge. These factors influence the possibilities for using rational-analytical methods or technologies, such as the Internet, cloud computing, Big Data, algorithms, and AI, in selecting personnel.

Generally, it can be assumed that in countries with a weak economy and a high unemployment rate, many applicants do not attach too much importance to the fairness of the personnel selection process (Krause, 2011, p.19). However, if there is a high unemployment rate, for example, in Brazil with 11.5% (International Monetary Fund, 2019), applicants may be more willing to accept less valid selection procedures (Deters, 2017, p. 122; Ryan & Tippins, 2009, p. 88). Additionally, in weak economies, it is more likely that resource-intensive selection procedures (time, money, etc.) and methodologically demanding will be less used (Centre for Monitoring Economy, 2019; International Monetary Fund, 2019; Ryan & Tippins, 2009, p. 88). An example of this is the assessment center. This is cost-, time- and personnel-intensive and is rarely used in economically weak countries and companies. This absence increases the risk that the personnel selection processes will have low validity (Krause, 2011, pp.19–20). By contrast, in economically solid countries or countries with a shortage of qualified candidates, potential applicants may not submit their applications if the process seems too complex or does not correspond to their expectations and values (Krause, 2011, p.19).

Therefore, it can be assumed that resource-intensive psychometric selection procedures will be more frequently applied in countries with strong economies and low unemployment rates.

7.2.4 Cultural influences on the acceptance of analytical and intuitive selection procedures

There is a jungle of cultural-theoretical models (Nardon & Steers, 2009, p. 3) and concepts that compare cultures.

Although cultural models, for example, models by Hofstede, have been criticized (McSweeney, 2002; Kirkman et al., 2006), they offer a framework for classification to cope with the complexity of cultural differences and better understand the behavioral preferences of people in different cultures. In addition, it should be seen that there is a wide range of individual differences in every culture. Therefore, it is essential to ensure that these cultural dimensions do not lead to stereotyping (see Section 3.5.2.9).

A cultural model should not intend to map countries' cultures completely but to find a structured way through the complexity by reducing it to essential characteristics. For most researchers, there is an agreement that the proposed dimensions should withstand a review (Ryan et al., 1999, p. 362). And yet cultures, with their values, attitudes, and behaviors, are subject to permanent change. Thus, these changes must also be reflected in the theoretical concepts of culture.

Culture-specific value orientations are classified in literature by well-known models from Hofstede, Hall and Hall, Trompenaars, Gelfand, and so on (Krause, 2011, p. 12). Against the background of the respective cultural dimensions, we can draw conclusions about the acceptance of rational-analytical procedures and the related quality standards and intuitive decisions.

However, it is essential to emphasize that the findings cannot be generalized to the respective countries and cultures, as these are only some possible influencing factors based on the analysis of cultural models. They only give possible hints for the preference of analytical or intuitive procedures.

The results are, however, supplemented by information obtained from interviews. Hogarth (2010, p. 347) considers intuition as cultural capital. He states,

> that, across life, people acquire stocks of intuitions or *cultural capital* that are predominantly the product of tacit learning that has taught us how to survive in our particular cultural niches. Thus, people reared in different environments react differently to the same stimulus, depending on their experiences. . . . The point about cultural capital is similar to preferences. People do not set out to choose their cultural capital in some objective manner. Instead, it represents the idiosyncratic nature of their experiences with life that were not all actively chosen. Thus, attitudes (including prejudices), reactions in social environments, and even religious beliefs are all largely the fruit of tacit learning. Interestingly, whereas individuals may not be aware of the extent to which they have been formed to 'think' in this way, many organizations in society are aware of the power of tacit learning . . . Moral intuitions are .. necessarily culturally and time-specific. . . . But the cultural capital of our moral intuitions is not immutable because, across generations, rationally derived arguments can affect morality and, by influencing behavior, eventually change the moral intuitions of succeeding generations.

7.2.4.1 Acceptance of intuitions and emotions according to Hofstede's cultural dimension

7.2.4.1.1 Intuitions and emotions in high and low power distance cultures

A study by Ryan et al. (1999) examines the relationship between personnel selection methods and the cultural dimensions of uncertainty avoidance and power distance (Hofstede et al., 2010, pp. 76 and 216–217).

Power distance means the extent to which the less powerful members of countries, institutions, and organizations expect and accept that power is distributed unequally (Hofstede-Insights, 2019).

The relationship between applicants and hiring managers is less distant in more egalitarian cultures with low power distance, such as in Scandinavian countries, Germany, or the Netherlands. In low power distance cultures, applicants want to talk to the hiring managers on equal terms and tend to express their own opinions (McFarlin & Sweeney, 2001, p. 72). Thus, in an assessment center, group discussions tend to occur without predefined leadership roles, and in contrast, with predefined functions, such as leader and team members, if the power distance is high (Krause & Thornton III, 2007, p. 226).

Applicants from countries with low power distance expect to communicate on an equal basis with selection managers and influence selection and decision-making procedures (McFarlin & Sweeny, 2001, p. 79). In contrast, hierarchical decisions are more likely to be accepted in countries with a high power distance. Moreover, in cultures with a pronounced power distance, peers are less often involved in personnel selection (Lievens, 2007, p.5). In addition, educational attainments and degrees have greater importance in cultures with a high power distance (Ryan et al., 1999, pp. 372–374). There is also a connection between power distance and concerns about the misuse of private information. Applicants, in a culture with a high power distance, tend to assume the employer's right to collect very personal information, whereas applicants in cultures with a low power distance are more likely to critically question this right (Phillipps & Gully, 2002, p. 82; Lindemann, 2020, p. 31).

In a low power distance country, individuals are prepared to argue with leaders, who must justify their decisions, for example, their selection decisions, with rational and transparent arguments. Candidates in cultures with low power distance expect sufficient information about the desired position or a future employer to feel fairly treated (Schuler & Stehle, 1985, p. 136). For this reason, selection procedures in which information about the procedure, selection criteria, and so on is provided openly are considered more fairly.

Furthermore, a participatory approach to personnel selection is desirable in low power distance cultures. The preference for participative decisions (Rinne et al., 2012, p. 101) may be realized by involving team members in interviews or hiring decisions (Ryan et al., 1999, pp. 363 and 383; Ryan & Tippins, 2009, p. 74). In addition, due to the lower distance in the relationship between hiring manager and applicant, increased exchange of information and greater importance is attached to interpersonal sensitivity and positive relationship building (Steiner & Gilliland, 2001, p. 132).

Germany can be described as a culture with a lower power distance (Hofstede et al., 2010, p. 59). Accepting rational-analytical standards means that people are more open to criticism in the German culture if they oppose specific selection procedures.

In cultures with a high degree of power distance, the opinions of higher-ranked managers are regularly accepted and respected without a contradiction (Hofstede, 2001, p. 98).

Due to the respect for persons in authority and the reputation of the assessors involved, implementation of specific selection standards will likely not be contradicted if a respected manager favors it. Thus, due to their organizational importance and authority, these managers can strongly influence the acceptance of specific selection standards. This aspect is strongly promoted by the manager's good reputation and high status (McFarlin & Sweeney, 2001, p. 72; Stone et al., 2007, p. 157).

For example, in cultures with high power distance, HR managers are less likely to be used as interviewers; instead, interviews are often conducted exclusively by the supervisors (of the new hire) and line managers (Krause, 2011, p. 17). A selection method used by these line managers is more likely to be accepted because this higher-ranked person uses or requests this procedure. On the other hand, candidates may find it inappropriate to provide open and honest feedback or communication directly (Ryan & Tippins, 2009, p. 74), as criticism and questions to higher placed individuals are more uncommon in cultures with pronounced power distance.

A high power distance is typical of Arab countries, Brazil, Mexico, India, Nigeria, Southeast Asian countries, China, or Japan (Ryan & Tippins, 2009, p. 74). These cultures have distinct hierarchical structures, with noticeable gaps between boss and employees or hiring managers and applicants. In these structures, bosses are leaders and usually make the selection decisions. They are also expected to make the decisions. Thus, involving subordinates in the decision-making process can quickly be interpreted as a weakness in leadership.

Husted (1999) states a strong correlation between a country's power distance scores and corruption rates. He attributes this relationship to the idea that high power distance countries facilitate 'paternalism,' in which, subordinates are rewarded by their superiors based on loyalty and are less likely to question unethical or corrupt business practices. In addition, Husted found that collectivism was related to corruption rates, based on his hypothesis that individuals of collectivistic societies are more willing to violate national laws in the interest of their in-group loyalties. Based on these relationships, it is logical that individuals from high power distance and/or collectivistic cultures may more easily justify corrupt behaviors (Fine, 2010, p. 253).

Sinha and Kanungo (1997, p. 97) found in their research that in India, applicants from the same social group as the decision-maker are preferred, especially with otherwise equal competencies.

Regarding the use of emotions in personnel selection, research shows that cultures with high power distance are less likely to value feelings in selection interviews and instead demand the control of emotions at the individual level. However, Matsumoto (1990, pp. 205–210; Matsumoto et al., 2008, p. 931) also shows that the expression of emotions in social interactions depends on the perceived status of the individuals involved. People with higher social status may show negative emotions. At the same time, lower-status individuals may suppress negative emotions but may show pleasure in the interaction in a culture- and context-specific way.

7.2.4.1.2 Intuitions and emotions in individualistic and collectivistic cultures

Individualism is the degree of interdependence a society maintains among its members. Individualism has to do with whether people´s self-image is defined as "I" or "We." In individualist societies, people are supposed to only look after themselves and their direct family. On the other hand, in collectivist cultures, people belong to "in-groups" that care for them in exchange for loyalty (Hofstede-Insights, 2019).

Individualistic cultures, such as the United States and Western Europe, emphasize personal achievement and success, and encourage individual opinions and decision-making. Independence, initiative, self-reliance, and so on are valued (Hofstede-Insights, 2019). In addition, there is a pragmatic and proportional relationship between managers and employees, and they desire mutual feedback (Hofstede et al., 2010, p. 109). Thus, it is more common to base the acceptance of selection procedures on the participants' feedback than in collectivistic cultures (Krause & Thornton III, 2007, p. 227).

Members of individualistic cultures tend to use a direct communication style. Language is precise and straightforward, and emphasizes the speaker's ability to express her/his intentions. Categorical words, such as "absolutely" and "certainly," are often used as well as "no" to give a negative answer. In contrast, members of collectivistic cultures prefer to use the indirect verbal style. People of such cultures often use imprecise and ambiguous words to communicate their message (Gudykunst & Ting-Toomey, 1996, pp. 3–18; Gudykunst & Ting-Toomey, 1988, p. 41).

Collectivistic cultures, such as China, Korea, or Japan, emphasize communities, families, and workgroup goals above individual needs or desires. Collective goals supersede those of the individuals. Rules promote unity, brotherhood, and selflessness.

Collectivist cultures are stricter in what behaviors are found to be acceptable, and they place a big emphasis on obedience. In addition, a desire for social harmony characterizes collectivist cultures; therefore, direct confrontation in communication is considered impolite, for example, using the word "no." Likewise, direct feedback is undesirable so as to maintain harmony in the relationship (Hofstede et al., 2010, p. 109).

People from collectivist cultures are characterized by a high degree of harmony and loyalty, especially to members of the social in-groups. Therefore, both selection managers and candidates find it acceptable to hire candidates based on social considerations. This loyalty or sometimes nepotism can even lead so far that national laws, for example, equal treatment laws or even rules set by the company (e.g., the headquarters in the United States or Europe) are violated in the interest of the in-group (Latukha, 2016, p. 37; Stone et al., 2007, pp. 155–158; Fine, 2010, p. 253; Steiner & Gilliland, 2001, p. 131).

This is illustrated by the Chinese concept of *guanxi*, a network of personal relationships. *Guanxi* describes the phenomenon that personal relationships influence all agreements and contracts. For example, an agreement between candidates and hiring managers needs *guanxi*; so, hiring managers try to establish positive relationships (Xin & Pearce, 1996, p. 1642). A Chinese proverb says: "The more friends you have, the more opportunities arise, and the more paths open up" (Wei & Kotte, 2007, p. 37).

Behind the word *guanxi* is a mutual obligation and not necessarily a close personal relationship. According to the principle of reciprocity, a person is in debt to the person who did her/him a favor. Thus, the focus is not on the person per se but on the benefit that one person can give to another (Fink & Meierewert, 2001, pp. 206–207), and there are hardly any areas not influenced by *guanxi* (Xin & Pearce, 1996, p. 1.642). For this reason, resistance to rational-analytical procedures can be expected from collectivist cultures (Hofstede-Insights, 2019) since quality standards focus, in particular, on aspects such as justice and performance, and disallow the recruitment of applicants solely based on social considerations. Therefore, it can be assumed that collectivist cultures are more willing to violate psychometric quality standards to select in-group people.

If Western applicants or selection managers try to build trust in China, it takes time, shared personal experiences, and effort to establish a positive emotional connection. People can create trust with people of unfamiliar cultures by identifying commonalities; hiring managers and applicants should be open to discussing more personal topics such as family or music. Sharing these commonalities shows interest in the other person, and not just in the business or the job. Because of China's high power distance culture, Chinese applicants are unlikely to speak up during a job interview. That tendency is not due to shyness or lack of self-confidence, but due to respect. If a hiring manager wants answers from candidates, they'll need to ask for them directly (Meyer, 2016).

In individualistic cultures, personnel selection procedures are considered fair if they are transparent, based on objective selection criteria, and have a rational-analytical approach. The focus is on the candidate's performance (Steiner & Gilliland, 2001, p. 131). In individualistic societies, applicants prefer to demonstrate their skills and experience (Ryan & Tippins, 2009, p. 71; Stone et al., 2007, p. 158) and report past successes. Acceptance is, thus, influenced by the possibility of self-expression and by fairness. Therefore, candidates in individualistic cultures find exercises in an assessment center to show their unique abilities crucial (Schuler & Stehle, 1985, p. 136). In addition, there is a pragmatic and rational manager-employee relationship in which both parties seek feedback (Hofstede et al., 2010, p. 109). Therefore, (semi-) structured interviews or assessment centers are more accepted and highly regarded as appropriate tools (Ryan & Tippins, 2009, p. 72; Stone et al., 2007, p. 158). LeFebvre & Franke (2013, p. 138) confirmed these connections between individualism and a rational decision-making style.

While applicants from individualistic cultures like to talk about their successes and achievements and take this for granted, candidates from collectivist countries are more inclined to speak of group successes. In addition, collectivistic candidates tend to find it uncomfortable to take an active leading role in group discussions, role plays, or openly criticize others (Ryan & Tippins, 2009, p. 74).

Another cultural aspect is the consideration of equal rights. Thus, in individualistic cultures, selecting the best-suited applicant is more important than hiring a social in-group member (Steiner & Gilliland, 2001, p. 131).

Rational-analytical selection standards promote transparency and equal rights in personnel selection procedures since different applicants are easily comparable based on job requirements (Ackerschott et al., 2016, p. 13). This corresponds to the values of individualistic cultures and suggests that members of individualistic cultures tend to speak out in favor of rational-analytical standards and accept them.

Thus, acceptance is influenced by the possibility of self-expression and the individual perception of fairness (Schuler & Stehle, 1985, p. 136).

These results lead to the following assumptions: In individualistic cultures, a rational-analytical approach, based on objectively assessing an individual's competencies and skills and how a candidate fulfills the job requirements, is more accepted than an intuitive one, often regarded as subjective and arbitrary. And in individualistic cultures, semi-structured selection procedures are implemented more frequently. This is because individualistic cultures prefer selection processes where applicants can express their achievements and personal strengths (McFarin & Sweeney, 2001, p. 78). But hiring managers in individualistic cultures also rely on their intuitions but, simultaneously, tend to rationalize these intuitions in business.

What is considered fair in personnel selection is culture-dependent. For example, in collectivist cultures, referring to employee recommendations, networking at job fairs, and face-to-face contacts are suitable because they are personal and relationship-oriented (Stone et al., 2007, p. 155, 158). But this also applies to most individualistic countries.

How HR managers reveal their emotions in selection situations can convey different messages to applicants from other cultures (Matsumoto, 1989, p. 98; Gunkel et al., 2013, p. 5). A meta-study by Van Hemert et al. (2007, p. 932) shows that the expression of emotions is seen more positively in individualistic cultures than in collectivistic cultures. As a tendency, it can be assumed that in individualistic cultures, emotions, especially positive ones, are more likely to be expressed in job interviews than in collectivistic cultures (Bublitz, 2021, pp. 20–22).

Other research results show that managers in higher positions, especially in collectivistic cultures, are more allowed to follow their emotions and intuitions than hierarchically less powerful people (Mondillon et al., 2005, p. 1114).

In collectivist cultures, there is a tendency toward less rational-analytical and more informal selection processes and unstructured interviews, including questions about family, childhood, and personal interests (Aycan, 2005, p. 574). An intuitive approach in personnel selection is more accepted than a rational-analytical approach. According to the need principle, collectivist cultures favor group harmony, equality, and distribution (Chen et al., 1998, p. 285; Steiner & Gilliland, 2001, p. 130). Due to the high importance of the collective or group, personnel selection is regarded primarily as a social process.

7.2.4.1.3 Intuitions and emotions in masculine and feminine cultures

A high score on masculinity indicates that a society will be driven by competition, achievement, material success, and different role expectations for men and women. Masculine cultures have a relatively rigid understanding of roles, and tasks are divided based strongly on gender.

Masculinity stands for a society in which social gender roles are clearly distinct: Men are supposed to be assertive, tough, and focused on material success (with success being defined by being the winner/best in the field – a value system that starts in school and continues throughout organizational life. On the other hand, women are supposed to be more modest, tender, and concerned with life quality (Hofstede et al., 2010, p. 141).

Masculine societies are, for example, China, Germany, India, Japan, or the United States (Hofstede-Insights, 2019).

Femininity stands for a society in which social gender roles overlap and are more fluid: Both men and women are supposed to be socially nurturing, modest, tender, and concerned with the quality of life (Hofstede, 2001, p 297). A low score on the feminine dimension means that an essential value in society is caring for others. In a feminine society, the quality of life is a sign of success, and standing out from the crowd is less admirable. Such societies emphasize the importance of consistency and equality in executing procedures. Feminine cultures strive for group harmony and focus on equality, interpersonal relationships, and positive communication (Steiner & Gilliland, 2001, p. 133). Group performance and cooperation are more critical than task-oriented work, so group tasks are better suited to personnel selection. Soft criteria, such as social skills, social class, or age, are the focus. And nonstandardized methods based on personal interaction are preferred (Aycan, 2005, pp. 1088–1089). The Netherlands, Costa Rica, and Scandinavian countries such as Sweden or Norway are considered highly feminine; India and Brazil tend toward a feminine culture (Hofstede et al., 2010, p. 142; Hofstede-Insights, 2019), but with both feminine and masculine traits, they cannot be clearly called one or the other.

According to Hofstede (2001, pp. 298–299), negative emotions, in particular, are not as tightly controlled as in feminine cultures. This is attributed to the fact that masculinity is positively associated with their expression and negatively associated with regulating emotions. However, Gunkel et al. (2013, p. 5) have found limited confirmation of this assumption. On the other hand, Basabe et al. (2000, p. 6) show that feminine cultures tend to promote more emotional stability and encourage the expression of more positive than negative emotions (Bublitz, 2021, p. 23).

As in individualistic cultures, in masculine cultures, great value is placed on hard selection criteria such as work-related knowledge and experience, skills, and technical abilities (Spence & Petrick, 2000, p. 81; McFarlin & Sweeny, 2001, p. 78; Aycan, 2005, p. 1088). Thus, it can be assumed that masculine cultures tend to favor personnel selection procedures that select the most suitable candidate by rational-analytical methods that are based on merit and performance.

The perception of fairness is a top priority and increases the acceptance of selection procedures in a specific culture. Justice's perception can be promoted by using performance characteristics (Ackerschott et al., 2016, pp. 13–14.; Braun et al., 2015, p. 100; Hofstede, 2001, p. 299). In masculine cultures, aspects such as transparency are crucial to a feeling of being treated fairly (Steiner & Gilliland, 2001, pp. 131–132). A high degree of job requirement orientation and the opportunity to show one's competencies in the selection process increase the acceptance of selection procedures in masculine cultures. Also, the degree of standardization of selection methods tends to be higher in masculine cultures. Rational-analytical selection standards such as (semi-) structured interviews with interview guidelines and less personal interaction are more likely to be accepted in masculine cultures (Aycan, 2005, p. 1088). For this reason, parallels can be drawn with the cultural dimension of individualism.

It is fundamentally complicated to draw clear conclusions about accepting rational-analytical standards since the values of a feminine culture are difficult to apply to psychometric selection standards. Moreover, against the background that, for example, a country such as China can be seen as masculine and a culture with a high power distance, no clear conclusions can be derived regarding the acceptance of rational-analytical selection procedures. Rather, the results are contradictory and indicate a need for further research.

Nevertheless, because rational-analytical standards put less emphasis on interpersonal aspects, it can be assumed that masculine cultures accept rational-analytical standards more. However, due to the importance of emotions and group harmony, it can be supposed that in feminine cultures, the acceptance of intuitive decisions and less standardized selection procedures is much higher than in masculine cultures. Dane and Pratt (2007, p. 48) stated that the meaning of feelings is emphasized in feminine cultures. Therefore, a decision-making process connected with affect, emotion, and intuition is favored. This is supported by Hofstede's statement (2001, p. 318) that leaders in feminine cultures are expected to use intuition and deal with feelings.

But Hofstede's descriptions reflect a certain degree of gender stereotyping. Therefore, much is in flux and subject to continual change.

7.2.4.1.4 Intuitions and emotions in cultures of uncertainty avoidance

Uncertainty avoidance is the extent to which the members of a culture feel threatened by ambiguous or unknown situations and have beliefs and institutions that serve to avoid these (Hofstede-Insights, 2019).

To minimize or reduce the level of uncertainty, strict rules, clear instructions, laws, policies, norms, rituals, and regulations are expected and implemented. Thus, an essential goal of uncertainty-reducing cultures is to minimize risks, control situations, eliminate or avoid the unexpected, and make the future as predictable as possible (House et al., 2001, p. 495).

In cultures with a high degree of uncertainty avoidance, a strong rule orientation and thus law and order, have relatively high importance. Especially when people do not yet know each other so well, such as in selection situations, emotions tend to be regulated or concealed in cultures with high uncertainty avoidance. Gunkel et al. (2013, p. 14) show that people from cultures of high uncertainty avoidance observe the emotions of others more carefully to reduce possible risks or disturbances in harmony.

Information about the selection process is crucial to applicants in cultures with high uncertainty avoidance (Ryan & Tippins, 2009, p. 75) because it reduces uncertainty and stress (Schuler et al., 1993, p. 23). And applicants prefer detailed feedback after the personnel selection process (Ryan & Tippins, 2009, p. 75). But in a country such as Thailand, with a relatively high score in uncertainty avoidance, an open feedback culture is not very common.

In cultures with high uncertainty avoidance, security may be felt to be achieved by firmly structured processes. Therefore, strict rules and regulations are needed, even if they are perceived as bureaucratic, and experts with specific knowledge are highly regarded. In decisions, the focus is on content and less on the process (Hofstede-Insights, 2019; Hofstede et al., 2010, pp. 216–217; Dipboye & Johnson, 2007, p. 65).

Levels of uncertainty avoidance are very high in Japan or Brazil, but Germany and Thailand are also regarded as countries that share this attribute (Hofstede-Insights, 2019).

However, it must be seen that cultural behavior is not determined by only one dimension; there is always an interplay of different dimensions, and certain dimensions have a higher or lower significance in specific contexts. For example, although the scores of Brazil and Thailand are comparatively high concerning the urge to follow rules and regulations, the standards of selection procedures are weak, as the dimension of collectivism influences selection behaviors. Loyalty to the group is more valuable than compliance with selection standards or rules (Fine, 2010, p. 253; Hipsher, 2008, pp. 140–141).

Candidates with a high degree of uncertainty avoidance want to know exactly what the selection process involves and its duration. They may also prefer selection procedures with clear questions or answers (Ryan & Tippins, 2009, p. 75). The desire for detailed feedback may also be stronger in cultures with high uncertainty avoidance (Ryan & Tippins, 2009, p. 75).

Based on psychometric criteria, selection standards provide a predefined framework for action through defined rules and regulations, significantly enhancing the feeling of certainty in the personnel selection process. Therefore, selection procedures with closed questions, several components, and extensive background knowledge (Ryan et al., 1999, p. 363; Ryan & Tippins, 2009, p. 75), as well as procedures with a lot of information about the company and the position, are preferred (Schuler et al., 1993, p. 16). In addition, suitable methods are work samples or assessment centers that allow an increased exchange of information (Schuler et al., 1993, p. 16).

Also, relatively objective selection procedures such as (semi-)structured interviews are often carried out in countries with high uncertainty avoidance, as this can reduce the number of poor decisions (Ryan et al., 1999, pp. 363 and 383). And systematic processes of reviewing and evaluating hiring success are more common

(Ryan & Tippins, 2009, p. 80). At the same time, there is less variation between selection methods in these cultures. Therefore, the authors conclude that in cultures with high uncertainty avoidance, there is more need for objective data on which to base the selection decision (Ryan & Tippins, 2009, pp. 386–387).

For cultures with low uncertainty avoidance, a flexible approach, including intuitions and emotions, is more acceptable than predefined guidelines. In these cultures, it is more common to use less standardized selection procedures, and evaluations of selection decisions are made less systematically (Krause, 2011, p. 17). Countries with a relatively low level of uncertainty avoidance are the United States, South Africa, India, and China.

In China, it is argued that based on a single interview, the personal suitability of an applicant can only be assessed to a rudimentary extent. Thus, rather than risk uncertainty about an applicant's fit and loyalty to the company, applicants from established in-groups, such as the family, are selected more frequently than in Western countries (Huo & Von Glinow, 1995, p. 5; Huo et al., 2002).

For Chinese people, the truth may be relative. They are more comfortable with ambiguity than people from Western cultures; the Chinese language is full of ambiguous meanings that can be difficult for Western people to follow (Hofstede-Insight, 2019). And adherence to rules or standards may be flexible to suit the specific situation; thus, pragmatism is a fact of life.

People from cultures with low uncertainty avoidance do not want more rules in selection processes than necessary because they believe in common sense. Therefore, ambiguity and unstructured procedures are more likely to be tolerated. For this reason, in these cultures, deviations from regulations and strictly prescribed selection guidelines are made more quickly, and intuitive-emotional judgments are more accepted (Hofstede, 2001, p. 161). As a result, the focus is not on the content but on the decision-making process itself (Hofstede et al., 2010, p. 217).

Based on these findings, the following assumptions can be formulated: Cultures of high uncertainty avoidance accept the implementation of rational-analytical standards more quickly, and thus psychometric selection procedures. In these countries, selection managers try to reduce intuitions and emotions in selection decisions because they prefer to adhere to fixed rules and scientific quality criteria such as objectivity, and thus selection standards. In addition, the selection process is more likely to be accepted if it gives the candidate a sense of security and predictability.

In low uncertainty avoidance cultures, candidates feel more comfortable with ambiguity and are less risk-averse than people with high uncertainty avoidance.

Since selection standards aim to minimize intuitive and emotional judgments, it can be assumed that rational-analytical selection standards are less implemented in cultures with low uncertainty avoidance, and intuitive judgments are more likely to be accepted in personnel selection. Here, people trust their common sense for cultural reasons and tolerate deviations from selection guidelines (Hofstede et al., 2010, p. 161; Ryan et al., 1999, pp. 363 and 383). Thus, there is a tendency toward unstructured interviews and fewer "objective" tests in personnel selection procedures (Ryan & Tippins, 2009, p. 75).

Concerning the selection of personnel, previous research results on the importance of uncertainty avoidance are contradictory to a certain degree. On the one hand, Aycan (2005, p. 1089) shows that structured interviews are preferred to unstructured ones in countries with high uncertainty avoidance. On the other hand, Ryan et al. (1999, p. 383) show that extensive processes using numerous standardized selection methods are used less frequently in countries with high uncertainty avoidance (Dipboye & Johnson, 2008, p. 61; Lindemann, 2020, pp. 31–32).

One conceivable explanation is that in cultures with high uncertainty avoidance, intuition and emotions are highly trusted in practice. Thus, in cultures with high uncertainty avoidance, selection managers tend to rely more on structured selection procedures and trust their intuitions and emotions in selection processes.

Concerning implementing new selection procedures, including AI, it can be assumed that due to maintaining the status quo, cultures with a high degree of uncertainty avoidance are somewhat critical of new personnel selection methods (Thielsch et al., 2012, p. 60).

In summary, rational-analytical standards correspond particularly with high uncertainty avoidance, since aspects such as justice, equality, and performance are in focus. For low uncertainty-oriented countries such as Brazil, China, India, and Thailand, on the other hand, it can be assumed that, in general, flexible and less structured selection procedures, including judgments based on intuition and emotions, are more accepted. However, a clear conclusion is not possible since contradictions remain within the research of cultural influences on the acceptance of selection procedures.

In addition, selection behavior in specific cultures is not determined by only one cultural dimension, but always by an interplay of the various dimensions, with certain dimensions having a higher or lower significance in specific contexts.

7.2.4.2 Acceptance of intuitions and emotions according to the cultural dimensions of Hall and Hall, Trompenaars, and Gelfand

7.2.4.2.1 Intuitions and emotions in high- and low-context cultures

Hall and Hall distinguish four essential cultural dimensions: Context orientation (high- and low-context cultures), space (distance people need for the protection of their privacy), time orientation (monochronic time/monochronic culture, polychronic time/polychronic culture. Monochronic cultures prefer focusing on one thing at a time, value a certain orderliness, and do not appreciate interruptions; polychronic cultures like to do multiple things simultaneously) and information speed (slow or fast flow of information). This chapter examines the dimension of context orientation in more detail since this is particularly relevant in interactions and decision-making situations such as personnel selection procedures (Hall & Hall, 1987, p. 9).

The dimension of context orientation deals with how explicitly and directly people communicate a message and how important the context is to understand the messages. Hall speaks of so-called high- and low-context cultures (Hall, 1976, p. 105–116).

In low-context cultures such as the United States, Australia, Switzerland, Scandinavian countries, or Germany, people communicate directly and precisely with explicit verbal or very clear nonverbal messages. People try to be as specific as possible and take the time to explain themselves clearly. Thus, to send or understand a message correctly, people need skills to explicitly communicate the verbal and the nonverbal.

In contrast, high-context cultures such as China, Japan, Thailand, or Korea often exhibit less direct verbal and nonverbal communication. Along with most East Asian and Arabic countries, Brazil or India can also be classified as high-context cultures (Hall, 1976, pp. 105–116), and countries such as Spain or Italy to a certain degree. Very little information is contained in the explicit part of the transmitted message because crucial information is conveyed via context; thus, people draw their message from the implicit part of the communication, for example, reading nonverbal cues such as gestures and implied content. The listener's responsibility is to understand the meaning by understanding the context and read between the lines. Too much verbal information can lead to impatience and dissatisfaction with the process (Hall & Hall, 1987, p. 6).

Low-context cultures require additional information to understand the message. Therefore, most information is conveyed explicitly and verbally, and written words are preferred to deliver a message. An elaborate style is characterized by a rich, expressive language, with many adjectives, exaggerations, idiomatic expressions, metaphors, and proverbs. Here, the speaker is responsible for delivering a clear message to the listener. In addition, especially in decision-making situations, much information (education, vocational experience, etc.) is desired and needed (Hall & Hall, 1987, pp. 7–8).

In low-context cultures, the feedback should be precise, direct, and clear to avoid misinterpretation; however, careful attention must also be paid to avoid offending or hurting the recipient.

With feedback in high-context cultures, managers should be careful and not be offensive and direct so that the feedback receiver does not lose face.

It isn't easy for Western people from low-context cultures to understand counterparts from high-context cultures because they need to read between the lines and understand the context. Thus, for example, if Western people have to communicate with Japanese, they should consider what the Japanese call "kuuki yomenai," meaning someone who "cannot read the air."

Why do different countries have different contexts? The answers can be found in history. High-context cultures like Japan have mainly had a homogenous population.

Therefore, people become tuned in to subtle nuances in communication and develop skills in "reading the air." On the other hand, American history is much shorter and has been strongly influenced by immigrants from different cultures and countries, requiring their communication to be more explicit to avoid misunderstandings (Meyer, 2016).

Nonverbal communication plays a central role in human social behavior. Nonverbal signals include facial expressions, gaze (and pupil dilation), gestures and other bodily movements, posture, bodily contact, spatial behavior, clothes and other aspects of appearance, nonverbal vocalizations, and smell. Each of these can be further subdivided. For example, gaze can be subdivided into different variables, for example, looking while listening, looking while talking, and mutual gaze. Nonverbal communication may be intentional, but it can also be unconscious and not intentional (Argyle, 2010, pp. 1–3).

Nonverbal communication can be differentiated into five different functions: (1) expressing emotions, mainly by face and voice, (2) communicating interpersonal attitudes, using spatial behavior, tone of voice, touch, gaze, and facial expression, (3) accompanying and supporting speech, with head nods, glances, and nonverbal vocalizations, (4) self-presentation, which is achieved mainly by appearance and voice; and (5) rituals such as greetings (Argyle, 2010, p. 5).

The main difference between cultures in expressing emotions is the degree of expressiveness. For example, Latin Americans, Africans, Arabs, and Southern Europeans are perceived as expressive and clearly show their feelings. On the other hand, the Japanese are less expressive and hide negative emotions like sadness and anger, due to cultural ideals. Thus, expressive cultures can find nonexpressive cultures inscrutable, and nonexpressive cultures may find people from expressive cultures disturbing because of their readiness to express emotions (Argyle, 2010, pp. 49–52, 66, and 69).

Concerning rational-analytical procedures, it can be assumed that in cultures that place great importance on showing emotions when communicating with others, individuals may see these processes very critically since they require reducing feelings as much as possible.

In the communication of interpersonal attitudes, closeness is the central dimension of variation. This corresponds to the distinction between contact and low-contact cultures. For example, Chinese or Japanese are referred to as low-contact cultures. They don't use many gestures and tend to refrain from touching each other often, maintain more distance, and avoid eye contact. In contrast, examples of contact cultures are Arabs, Africans, Latin Americans, or Southern Europeans; they use a lot of gestures to underline speech and touch each other very often while communicating (Argyle, 2010, pp. 58–60, and 67; Andersen et al., 2003, pp. 74–75). This is explained in the literature by the fact that people in colder regions must adapt to climatic changes to survive, requiring a solid task orientation that induces interpersonal remoteness (Andersen et al., 2003, p. 75). One problem resulting from these differences can be that people from low-contact cultures find behaviors of those from high-contact cultures physically too close, and thus disturbing, and vice versa. As a result, it is often difficult to establish a comfortable personal distance at international meetings or selection interviews (Argyle, 2010, p. 68).

Greeting rituals and rules of etiquette also differ between cultures. Likewise, listening behavior varies a lot between cultures. While, for example, the Japanese frequently nod and use nonverbal vocalizations while listening, people of some other cultures don't look much at their counterparts while listening and may not show any reaction. This lack of response while listening is often a source of annoyance for other cultures (Argyle, 2010, pp. 67 and 69). A further problem can be offense through gestures that people may regard as obscene since some gestures are interpreted differently in different cultures (Argyle, 2010, p. 52).

Selection managers from low-context cultures usually need detailed information to understand the message of their counterparts correctly. Therefore, emotions have a concrete communication function in selection situations since emotions are additional information to better understand the candidate's message. As a result, emotion is generally expressed more frequently in low-context cultures like the United States or Germany than in high-context cultures like Japan or China.

In high context collectivistic cultures, quality in personnel selection can be understood differently than in the psychometric paradigm. Nisbett et al. (2001, p. 293) have examined the extent to which scientific standards of the Western world, for example, standards of personnel selection, are compatible with patterns of thought in collectivist countries such as China. Research shows that Western cultures (e.g., the United States, Canada, and Germany) favor an analytical style, focusing on a single object and internal attributes, while East Asian cultures (e.g., China, Korea, and Japan) favor a holistic style, paying attention to the context and the whole system (Liang & Cherian, 2014, p. 74).

Analytic thinking is characterized by Nisbett et al. (2001, p. 293) as follows:

> We define analytic thought as involving detachment of the object from its context, a tendency to focus on attributes of the object in order to assign it to categories, and a preference for using rules about the categories to explain and predict the object's behavior. Inferences rest in part on the practice of decontextualizing structure from content, the use of formal logic, and avoidance of contradiction.

And they

> define holistic thought as involving an orientation to the context or field as a whole, including attention to relationships between a focal object and the field, and a preference for explaining and predicting events on the basis of such relationships. Holistic approaches rely on experience-based knowledge rather than on abstract logic and are dialectical, meaning that there is an emphasis on change, a recognition of contradiction and of the need for multiple perspectives, and a search for the 'Middle Way' between opposing propositions. (Nisbett et al., 2001, p. 293)

Studies by Masuda and Nisbett (2001) or Masuda et al. (2012) also confirm the contextual influences of collectivist thinking. Although the psychometric paradigm sees candidates as isolable objects, more or less without reference to the context (Nisbett, 2003, p. 100), the Chinese perspective does not allow observing an object and, thus, assessing a candidate regardless of the context. Therefore, the concept of objectivity in the psychometric paradigm is challenging to apply in these Chinese contexts. In fact, the context-specific approach means selecting a candidate can never be seen independent of the context and thus of the selection manager and the overall framework of the selection process. It must be assumed that the selection manager's intuitions are an integral part of their decision-making behavior and thus also have an accepted influence on the selection decision. It is also critical to reflect on how the construct of validity might be viewed in personnel selection in China (Masuda et al., 2012; Hsu & Chiu, 2008, p. 71; Ji et al., 2008; Spina, 2010). Studies by Kunda & Nisbett and Oliveira & Nisbett show that predicting future behavior is only possible if the characteristics supposed to provide information about a candidate's behavior remain stable (Thiedemann, 2021, pp. 33–37).

The low-context communication style in selection interviews in Western cultures means that primarily what can be expressed verbally and made measurable really counts from the psychometric perspective. Therefore, it is not surprising that according to this psychometric paradigm, intuitions and emotions are seen as something to be avoided. In highly context-specific cultures, context must always be considered in the communication process. This means that much of the meaning is conveyed, not through words but symbols, nonverbal behavior, and other context-specific features. Since many things are not put into words but are understood context-specific, intuition is more likely to be accepted in personnel selection in collectivistic cultures such as China. Because of this positive view of intuitions, it is also expected that less justification of intuitions, and thus fewer obfuscation and rationalization strategies, will need to be employed. It can even be seen that analytical thinking incorporates less information into the decision-making process than the context-specific approach of holistic thinking allows (Thiedemann, 2021, pp. 40–43).

Riedel (2016, p. 13) notes that the limitations of highly structured interviews become obvious when dealing with candidates from different cultures in international personnel selection. A highly structured interview takes the psychometric standard and measures the applicant against it. However, applicants from another cultural area may have a completely different concept of correct, reasonable, and socially adequate behavior in the interview. This perspective, which is foreign to Western psychometrics, has nothing to do with the characteristics or competencies of the applicants; it describes differences in social techniques and how applicants communicate their characteristics and competencies in the interview. For example, the self-concept of applicants from East Asian cultural areas can lead them to put their personality on the back burner in the interview, adapt their behavior flexibly to the context, not express their opinions clearly, or generally talk less or more slowly.

From a Western perspective, it would be a fallacy to conclude that applicants are less assertive and self-confident. Thus, for selection managers, who have their own patterns and culturally influenced thinking styles, it is challenging to correctly understand and evaluate candidates' behavior from other cultures.

Nevertheless, a highly structured interview that consistently aligns the interview questions with the job requirements and evaluates the answers accordingly, especially in global talent selection, does not prevent the selection managers from adapting to the situation and the candidate and meeting the applicant in a curious, relationship-oriented, open, trusting and flexible manner.

Even if global companies want to make their global HR policy ethnocentric and carry out selection procedures according to the parent company's standards, they are well-advised to take individual backgrounds into account when interviewing candidates from different cultural backgrounds, even though culture and the associated behaviors are challenging to understand from the outside perspective.

Since the author has no concrete research results about the compatibility of Chinese personnel selection with Western scientific standards, the presented correlations have a hypothetical character that should be investigated in further research. In addition, due to globalization, there are observations of homogenization of cultures and, at the same time, limits of cultural adaptation. Thus, cultures are changing, and it is necessary to wait and explore how these developments affect standards in personnel selection.

Concerning rational-analytical standards of personnel selection, one should consider what kind of communication is required to carry out a selection process. Rational-analytical standards provide direct, explicit, and detailed information. It can be hypothesized that hiring managers in low-context cultures tend to look for direct, fully coded information in the selection process. The possibility that too much information may lead to dissatisfaction in high-context cultures speaks against the acceptance of rational-analytical standards for selection processes.

In summary, it can be assumed that people in low-context cultures such as Germany or the United States accept and expect rational-analytical selection standards. And high-context cultures such as China, Brazil, or India may tend to formally or superficially accept them (if corresponding procedures are required by their Western parent companies) to a certain degree. Still, they tend not to use them strictly in practice because the hiring process is seen more as a social process. Therefore, rational-analytical selection procedures are more accepted in low-context cultures than in high-context cultures. But, most selection managers don't want to make selection decisions entirely without using their intuitions and emotions, whether in high- or low-context cultures.

7.2.4.2.2 Intuitions and emotions in universalistic and particularistic cultures

Fons Trompenaars (1993) and Charles Hampden-Turner (Trompenaars & Hampden-Turner 1998) developed a cultural model that differentiates seven dimensions. This model is based on a large-scale survey of 8,841 managers and employees from 43 countries. The seven dimensions are universalism vs. particularism, individualism vs. communitarianism, specific vs. diffuse, neutral vs. affective, achievement vs. ascription, sequential time vs. synchronous time, and internal direction vs. external direction.

In the following, we refer only to two dimensions: universalism and particularism and neutral versus emotional cultures, as these dimensions are very pertinent to show differences in personnel selection practices.

Trompenaars' research found high universalism in countries like the United States, Canada, the UK, Australia, Germany, or Sweden (Trompenaars & Hampden-Turner, 1998, pp. 41–50). People in cultures with high universalism see one reality, focus on formal rules and prefer standardized procedures, relatively independent of the given situation. Moreover, universalism assumes that ideas and practices such as standardized selection methods can be applied everywhere without modification. Thus, rational-analytical selection standards are more accepted in universalistic than in particularistic cultures.

In particularistic cultures such as Russia, China, India, Venezuela, Indonesia, South Korea, or Thailand, and also in Greece, France, or Italy (Krause, 2017, p. 247), on the other hand, a reaction or decision is only appropriate when consistent with the context and the given situation. Particularism is the belief that specific circumstances dictate how to behave and how ideas and practices should be applied. Thus, particularists consider the situation, relationships, and personal backgrounds when making decisions and are willing to break rules according to the situation to avoid endangering relationships (Kutschker & Schmid, 2011, pp. 738–740; Krause, 2011, p. 18).

Cultures with high particularism see reality as more subjective and emphasize social relationships and context. Recruiting channels in such cultures are set up more informally and are network-oriented (Aycan, 2005, p. 1088). In a particularistic environment, it is crucial to know and see the candidates and consider them individually, against their social and family backgrounds.

It can be followed that unstructured interviews are more frequently used in particularistic cultures, and personal information about an applicant tends to be more decisive than task-related information.

In contrast, formal and structured recruitment channels are preferred in cultures with high universalism, and standardized and job-specific selection methods are (officially) favored.

Universalist cultures try to select people based on objective, verifiable, valid data and rationally comprehensible information (Krause, 2011, p. 21). Personnel selection in universalistic cultures focuses on candidates whose skills and characteristics best match the job requirements. If this person-job fit is identified, personal characteristics such as status, relationship to the interviewer, gender, or ethnic background are less critical or even forbidden to consider (Dipboye & Johnson, 2008, p. 67).

These explanations indicate that rational-analytical selection procedures are more accepted and implemented in universalistic cultures than in particularistic cultures.

7.2.4.2.3 Intuitions and emotions in neutral and affective cultures

Affective or neutral describes how openly people express their emotions. In affective cultures such as Latin and Middle Eastern countries, the Philippines or the United States, Spain, or Italy, showing emotions in conversation is more valued and promoted than in neutral cultures such as in many East Asian collectivistic cultures like Japan or Korea, Russia, and, to a certain degree, Germany. Moreover, most East Asian cultures experience and prefer relatively low arousal emotions and control their feelings carefully (Lim, 2016). Individuals from such neutral cultures tend to emphasize social cohesion and are more likely to suppress their emotional reactions at first, to evaluate the most appropriate response in a specific situation (Matsumoto et al., 2008).

In personnel selection decisions, emotions are of great importance in affective cultures. In these cultures, it is typical for hiring managers and applicants to show their feelings and weigh the affective content of a selection interview very strongly (relationship, body language, gestures, facial expressions, etc.) (Krause, 2011, p. 18). And an emotional-intuitive judgment is preferred.

It can be assumed that in neutral cultures, hiring managers and candidates try to be more influenced by their rationality than by their feelings, and carefully observe and interpret other people's emotional reactions (Trompenaars & Hampden-Turner, 1998, p. 70). For this reason, in neutral cultures, hiring managers try to reduce their emotional influence on the candidate. Furthermore, it can be assumed that in interviews in these cultures, the focus is on diagnosing the applicant's skills rather than the social impression. Thus, candidates from neutral cultures may not accept a selection procedure that does not primarily test their skills and cognitive abilities, and depends on the personal feelings of the interviewers. However, whether this leads, as might be assumed, to managers in neutral cultures being trained in psychometric selection procedures and (theoretically) knowing about their perception distortions, biases, and so on is – with some exceptions – not to be expected and should be investigated by further research.

Concerning acceptance of rational-analytical selection procedures, it can be concluded that hiring managers and applicants in some neutral cultures, such as Germany, regard rational-analytical selection standards as somewhat positive. On the other hand, many affective cultures (Aswathappa, 2008, p. 188) see rational-analytical selection procedures more critically since psychometrics and standardized interviews give little room for the open integration of emotions. This is in line with previous findings of Hofstede and Hall & Hall regarding cultural dimensions.

7.2.4.2.4 Intuitions and emotions in tight and loose cultures

Gelfand et al. (2011) have introduced a further cultural dimension: Tight and loose cultures. While tight or narrow cultures such as China, Japan, Korea, Singapore, Germany, and Sweden have strong social norms and a low tolerance for deviations, loose cultures such as Russia, Brazil, India, or Israel are highly permissive and highly tolerant to deviations, mainly because they are characterized by weaker social norms (Gelfand et al., 2011, p. 1100). In tight cultures, people's thinking and behaviors are more uniform, coordinated, and regulated; thus, these tight cultures prefer an ethnocentric approach, for example, in selecting applicants.

People who have grown up or live in a tight culture feel conformity pressure and tend to adapt their thinking and behavior to a predefined framework. In contrast, people from loose cultures tend to behave almost without social restriction in their thinking and behavior (Gelfand et al., 2011, pp. 1100–1101). Thus, the behaviors of people of loose cultures are comparatively more disorganized and may lack self-control. Loose cultures are more open to new people, ideas, procedures, and change.

In tight cultures, rational-analytical selection standards make unwanted deviations difficult and provide an accepted framework for personnel selection. Accordingly, it can be supposed that tight cultures regard rational-analytical selection standards as relatively positive (Gelfand et al., 2011, p. 1103).

In contrast, loose cultures may feel somewhat restricted by personnel selection standards. Therefore, they tend to not accept the implementation of rational-analytical selection procedures (Gelfand et al., 2011, p. 1103).

In summary, it can be said that within Gelfand's cultural model, Germany positions itself more in favor of quality standards and accepts them. On this point, the same applies to India and China. On the other hand, resistance to quality standards can be expected from Russia or Brazil.

However, these results should be taken with caution, as contradictions and inconsistencies exist between the cultural models and their related results. But it can be assumed that rational-analytical psychometric selection procedures are less implemented and accepted in loose cultures such as Russia, India, or Brazil.

7.2.4.2.5 Intuitions and emotions in linear-active, multi-active, and reactive cultures

Lewis (2006, pp. 29–43) distinguishes between linear-active, multi-active and reactive cultures.

People from multi-active cultures such as Latin Americans, Angola, Nigeria, Saudi Arabia, Spain, or Italy are more talkative, impulsive, and attach great importance to feelings and relationships. They are more people- and dialog-oriented, and like to speak, listen, and do many things simultaneously. Interruptions are frequent, and pauses in conversation are few. They tend to feel confined by fixed agendas and rules. Thus, showing emotions and intuitions in interpersonal communication is more accepted in multi-active cultures. Recruiting managers often use informal sources such as other people's recommendations when interacting with people from multi-active cultures.

In such cultures, it is recommended not to communicate a fixed recruitment process or have a clear interview structure, but rather be flexible, leave space for small talk during the interview, and be relaxed about time and interruptions. Building personal relationships with the applicants and socializing with them is essential. Social invitations associated with eating and drinking during the recruiting process are common to create a personal relationship with applicants and increase their acceptance and interest in the organization. Regarding nonverbal communication, physical closeness and intense eye contact are essential to building trust (Lewis, 2006, pp. 34, 273, and 539).

People from linear-active cultures such as Germany, Switzerland, Scandinavian countries, Britain, Netherlands, Czech Republic, or Australia are highly organized and tend to be task-oriented and do one thing at a time. In linear-active cultures, it is important to communicate an agenda at the beginning of the selection process and be punctual, organized, and prepared. For instance, it is crucial to have a clear structure during the interview, have prepared interview questions in advance, and give guidance. Further, staying professional is recommended, sticking to facts and figures and business-related topics, not overdoing small talk during the interview, and being direct and honest. Regarding nonverbal communication, it is essential to keep spatial distance, not touch the other person, and use subtle body language to underline speech. To build trust and increase the applicant's acceptance, it is important to keep the applicant informed about the application's status and the recruitment process's next steps, meet promised deadlines and be honest (Lewis, 2006, pp. 34 and 233).

Applicants from reactive or listening cultures such as Japan, Vietnam, Korea, or China rarely initiate action or discussion in an interview, preferring to listen to and recognize, accept and react to the other's position. Therefore, job interviews should be formal and follow a circular schedule, with a seating order reflecting hierarchy, experience, and seniority. Further, in many listening cultures, exchanging business cards at the beginning of the interview is essential. The most crucial aspect when dealing with reactive cultures during the selection process is showing respect and being very polite at all times. This includes often standing up, perhaps bowing, and apologizing several times during the interview.

Further, avoiding being too direct is essential to prevent any face loss. Therefore, for example, stress questions in interviews designed to test the resilience and responsiveness of applicants are not appropriate when dealing with reactive cultures. In addition, it is essential to avoid confrontation and interruptions and not to ask about gaps in curricula vitae directly or express any criticism concerning past events (Lewis, 2006, pp. 34 and 519).

7.3 Culture, bias, and other perception distortions

Due to socialization in different countries and cultures, people have different experiences and develop culturally influenced ways of thinking and behaving. As a result, there are cultural differences, biases, and other distortions of perception in human information processing. However, studies dealing with the cultural influence on perception distortions are hardly found so far. Most studies in this research area have been published in Western countries and, above all, in the United States. However, the question remains to what extent the various distortions of perception may differ from culture to culture.

In the following, an attempt will be made to analyze how cultural differences affect various distortions of perception.

Due to the existing shortage of skilled workers, it is essential to address unconscious biases and their impact on the (internal and external global) labor market. Companies regularly tend to recruit candidates who correspond to a well-known and often uniform type of employee and resemble the existing workforce. This usually happens to select "cultural-fit" candidates and leads to a culturally homogeneous workforce. However, the potential of applicants who do not match these "cultural" types, because of their ethnic origin, age, gender, or other characteristics, are often overlooked. If this potential remains undiscovered due to unconscious bias, companies often do not take competitive advantages by using a diverse workforce (Kersting & Ott, 2016, p. 1; Cocchiara et al., 2016, p. 464).

7.3.1 Bias, perception distortions, and individualism-collectivism

In collectivist cultures, where the social origin and social ties are more important than individual performance, experiences and achievements, people tend to be preferred because of social background and membership in specific social groups (e.g., in-groups such as relatives) (Sinha & Kanungo, 1997, p. 99; Dipboye & Johnson, 2007, pp. 63–68; Krause, 2010, p. 17). Thus, it can be assumed that there is a connection between the cultural dimension of individualism-collectivism and the question of preference for a candidate's social group or in-group biases.

It can be concluded that in individualistic cultures, personnel selection is based to a greater extent on decision-making processes that refer to job requirements. In contrast, in collectivist cultures, the hiring decision is more influenced by the social background and status of a candidate, even if this has nothing to do with the qualifications for the vacant position. For this reason, the risk that in-group biases distort perception can be considered higher in collectivist cultures than in individualistic cultures.

7.3.2 Bias, perception distortions, and high- and low-context cultures

A significant bias in individualistic cultures is the fundamental attribution error. Especially in cultures such as the United States or Germany, the fundamental attribution error presented in Section 3.5.2.18 is relatively robust. In East Asian cultures, more attention is paid to situational factors so that the hiring managers' tendency to attribute candidates' behaviors to their personality occurs less frequently (Miyamoto & Kitayama, 2002, p. 1239). This finding can be linked to the dimension of low-context and high context cultures. For example, in a study by Masuda and Nisbett, Japanese and US-American test persons were shown a movie sequence of a fish in an underwater landscape and asked to describe what they saw. The results show that the Japanese attach much greater importance to their background than the Americans (Masuda & Nisbett, 2001, p. 922). These results confirm the high-context dimension of Japanese culture, where a larger amount of situational or context information is collected for evaluation. This suggests that the risk of a fundamental attribution error in personal diagnostics is lower in high-context than in low-context cultures.

7.3.3 Bias, perception distortions, and power distance

In cultures with a high power distance, such as India, applicants belonging to higher or lower castes and having correspondingly higher or lower status are treated differently (Sinha & Kanungo, 1997, p. 99; Dipboye & Johnson, 2007, p. 68; Sinha & Kanungo, 1997, p. 99). Vermeer & Neumann (2008, p. 85) state that it is not uncommon for Indian employers to ask for caste membership as an important information in application forms. This supports the assumption that in specific high power distance cultures, there is a greater risk of perception distortions due to social origin (caste, in-group, etc.), which are more likely to discriminate against applicants from groups other than those of the managers or socially inferior groups.

Hierarchical thinking and hierarchical structures can also lead to not transparently recognizing and reflecting on perceptual distortions and related biases. This can occur particularly in cultures with a high power distance. For example: "It should also be seen that many Asian countries are rather hierarchically structured. Therefore, employees will always wait until they are given the floor. And if the boss is also in the room, they will not contradict him and reflect openly about their personal impressions or feelings" (Deters, 2019, p. 124).

7.3.4 (Gender) bias, perception distortions, and masculinity/femininity

Gender discrimination is another much-studied field of research in personal selection. While in feminine cultures, such as Scandinavia, women and men are treated mainly equally in the corporate context, in masculine cultures, for example, Arab cultures, there is still a strict separation of roles, and women are regularly discriminated against when it comes to filling management positions. Therefore, a more decisive influence of gender-specific stereotypes can generally be assumed in masculine cultures (Dipboye & Johnson, 2007, p. 65).

Research suggests that especially male hiring managers have gender-specific and often unconscious leadership stereotypes that can lead to discrimination against females. For example, women are regarded as more collaborative and are assumed to be friendly, polite, helpful, and caring. On the other hand, men are considered assertive, less emotional, and more confident and self-assured. It can be consequently evaluated as unfavorable if an individual does not behave according to gender-specific expectations (Eagly & Karau, 2002, p. 574).

Like gender roles, there are also expectations in societies about leadership behavior. In a meta-study, three different approaches were used to examine the extent to which a leader's stereotype is male (Koenig et al., 2011, p. 616). All three approaches show that stereotypes of leadership are distinctly masculine. In concrete terms, managers or leaders are perceived as similar to men but not very similar to women. In addition, managers are attributed to masculine characteristics, for example, being more aggressive and competitive than collaborative (Koenig et al., 2011, p. 634).

If a woman behaves as is expected from a manager, she may no longer meet the social expectations of her role as a woman; thus, female applicants are often perceived more negatively in a management position. Since, however, the expectations of behavior in the role of a man are the same as those of a manager, a man, on the other hand, is assessed more positively since he can satisfy both role expectations (Eagly & Karau, 2002, p. 574).

Koch et al. (2015) state that gender biases are more pronounced in masculine cultures, so women are more likely to be discriminated against in a male-dominated environment (Koch et al., 2015, p. 138). In addition, the study shows that male decision-makers tend to prefer men in recruitment, regardless of the gender distribution, within an occupation or society. The finding that men are more responsive to gender congruence than women is consistent with the notion that men are sensitive to changes in the traditional gender hierarchy and are more likely to reject women working in male-dominated, high-level occupations. Since leadership positions in the past were primarily a male domain, many men may still fear that their roles are threatened by women, especially when women seek a male-dominated leadership or expert position (Koch et al., 2015, p. 139).

Research shows that international experience outside the traditional, male-dominated cultures increases the perception of hiring managers that women can successfully fill leadership positions. Thus, hiring managers' international experience can lead to greater job equality between men and women (Biswas et al., 2020, p. 14).

This supports the idea that distortions in personnel selection due to different values and norms differ across cultures. In addition, it shows that biases and stereotypes, even if they seem deeply culturally rooted, are changeable and that interpersonal contact and experience can break down stereotypes and prejudices.

7.3.5 Perception distortions and universalism/particularism

In universalistic cultures such as the United States or Germany, the most critical aim of personnel selection is to find the candidate who best matches the formal requirements of the role to be filled. For this reason, structured rational-analytical methods are recommended in personnel diagnostics.

In particularistic cultures such as China or Brazil, the focus is more on a personal relationship between the candidate and the selection manager. Thus, an interview is more likely to be used as a conversation to get to know each other, in which great emphasis is placed on personal attributes or social background and status. For this reason, rational-analytical procedures are used less in personnel selection, and hiring managers rely more on their intuition and related emotions.

It is thus obvious that in particularistic cultures, the risk of using biases, stereotypes, and other perception distortions in personnel selection decisions is higher than in universalistic cultures (Dipboye & Johnson, 2007, pp. 66–67).

7.3.6 Further cultural factors on distorted perceptions in personnel selection

Personnel selection is people's business. The human side of personnel selection is one of the main reasons personnel selection procedures often have a lower degree of harmonization across different subsidiaries and cultures than in other areas (e.g., production or accounting) in a company.

Before standardizing personnel selection procedures, it is vital to recognize, and critically and constructively reflect on the different perspectives, divergent interests, and expectations of personnel selection from the perspective of applicants and selection managers (Bouzguenda, 2013, p. 25).

The challenge for selection managers is to deal competently with the cultural diversity of different applicants. And at the same time, it must be seen that countries cannot be considered monocultural units and that there may be very different subcultures. This sensitivity to intercultural and subcultural differences is one of the most critical areas of learning and acting for HR managers, especially because insufficient sensitivity to cultural differences is one of the leading causes of poor personnel decisions (Jackson, 2002, p. 455; Anderson & Wivliet, 2008, p. 2; Bianchi & Ostale, 2006, p. 142).

In a study, Kristiina Mäkelä et al. (2010, pp. 138–139) were able to show that talent pool inclusion is determined not only by performance appraisal evaluations but also by several factors that influence decision-making in the second phase of the talent identification process. The greater the cultural and institutional (regional) distance between the selection decision-makers and the candidates, the lower is the probability of selection. The more the similarity in terms of culture and language between a candidate and a selection manager and the more central the position of the candidate, for example, employment at HQ, or in a significant foreign subsidiary or network position, or collaboration in high-level projects or committees, the higher is the probability of being selected.

Other studies show that white people can differentiate between the faces of other white people better than between those of black people and vice versa. Or whites in the United States tend to perceive black faces as angrier than comparable white faces. And white people and nonblack minorities have more problems telling the difference between genuine and fake smiles on black faces than on white faces, a problem black people don't have (American Psychological Association, 2019; Friesen et al., 2019). This can strongly impact, for example, how nonverbal signals are perceived or how accurately emotions are identified.

Culture influences the construction of leadership and behavior as a manager. Thus, a candidate's personality and competencies may be assessed differently, depending on the cultural background of the selection manager. If the same candidate for a global leadership position is evaluated in different cultures or by assessors from different cultures, the result or scoring of the candidate may be very different. For example, Western selection managers may rate candidates from an East Asian culture very negatively if the behavior in an assessment center is assessed based on Western leadership requirements, and not on East Asian leadership requirements.

This leads to a further question: Are people able to observe situations or candidates from different cultural perspectives, or is a cultural imprint too dominant? According to Hong et al. (2000, pp. 709–710), a so-called biculturality is possible. This means that situations can be observed from different cultural perspectives. However, Hong et al. (2000) show that a person should have been exposed to two different social and cultural systems over an extended period. In an experiment, Chinese test persons who completed their studies in the United States and are influenced by Chinese and (to a certain degree) North American culture were chosen. They were asked to describe a film sequence of an underwater scene in a film from a high- and low-context perspective. A symbol of the respective culture signaled the cultural perspective before the scene was played. For example, they described the scene from a low-context perspective when the American flag was shown. On the other hand, seeing the Chinese dragon led to a description from a high-context standpoint.

The experiment suggests that a cultural perspective is learnable. Consequently, this assumption can be made: (Global) selection managers can adapt to different cultural backgrounds in global personnel selection excellent, provided they have lived in a different culture for extended periods. If that doesn't work, intercultural competencies should be developed by training, gaining experience with culturally diverse people, and receiving feedback and systematic evaluations of decisions made and behaviors shown.

7.4 Culture-specific concepts of leadership and consequences for the acceptance of analytics and intuition in personnel selection

Research results show that the ideas of leadership and the leadership requirements differ between cultures and that these differences are primarily due to cultural values (Brodbeck et al., 2016, p. 88). The GLOBE study by House et al. (2004) shows significant differences in leadership behaviors, and thus also in the demands placed on leadership positions in different countries and cultures (Brodbeck et al., 2000; House, 2004; Chhokar et al., 2007; House et al., 2014).

Although Brodbeck (2016, p. 81), with researchers from over 38 countries, has defined a conceptualization of leadership as an individual's ability to influence, motivate, and enable others to contribute to the effectiveness and success of the organization of which they are members, this requires different concrete behaviors in different organizations.

These different behavior expectations affect how applicants for management or leadership positions are perceived in a selection process. For example, if a leader is expected to give clear instructions (such as in India), a participative leadership style or the involvement of employees in decision-making may be seen as a weakness and a negative attribute.

Thus, requirements and demands on leaders can be defined in a context-specific way. Leadership is a social and cultural construction. From a constructionist perspective, the way people create the meaning of leadership is essential because it helps understand how leadership works in different contexts. Leadership's meaning and role expectations differ from culture to culture and may vary from employee to employee. Leadership, as a social construction, is created through dialogue among groups of people in a particular context, including the perceived requirements, responsibilities, and behavior expectations of a leader in a specific organization.

Managers' differing expectations are also related to how leadership success is defined. According to a study by Inceoglu and Bartram (2013, pp. 501–502), leadership success is not defined in the same way in every culture, and selection methods should cover these differences in the requirement profile used. As shown in Section 7.2.4.2.1, people in Germany emphasize clear and direct communication, while in Japan, more verbal restraint is appropriate. According to the classification of Hall and Hall (1990, pp. 6–7), this difference can be traced back to the classification of Germany as a low-context culture and Japan as a high-context culture. Aycan (2005, p. 1089) states that in performance-oriented countries with a high degree of universalism (Trompenaars & Hampden-Turner, 1998, p. 8), great importance is attached to hard and measurable criteria; cultures with a strong performance orientation and universalism prefer formal and structured selection procedures as well as standardized and job-specific methods. No clear results are revealed in the evaluation of culture-dependent applicant acceptance.

In individualist societies, leadership typically refers to a single person who guides and directs the actions of others, often in an obvious way. However, in more collectivistic societies, leadership is often less associated with individuals and more closely aligned with group endeavors (Sanchez-Runde et al., 2012, p. 20).

The role expectations of a manager, for example, concerning employees' involvement in decision-making or giving constructive feedback, vary according to culture. Thus, the concrete behavioral expectations of a manager in India or China are different from those in Germany or the Netherlands because, for example, giving constructive feedback in Germany means something completely different in behavior and communication than providing constructive feedback in China.

And in a (Western) VUCA world with changing demands on leadership toward agility, reduction of hierarchical thinking, empowerment, and the view of leadership as everyone's business, leadership is constructed differently than it was even a few years ago.

While individualistic cultures such as Germany tend to expect a cooperative leadership style, collectivistic cultures like China tend to be characterized by clear hierarchies and patriarchal leadership behavior. This is evident in selection interviews, where selection managers communicate less directly and openly (according to a Western understanding), and meet applicants from a hierarchical position rather than on an equal footing.

The motives for leadership that are expected and assessed in selection processes also vary from culture to culture. Therefore, various scientific concepts of motivation can be used to explain the motivation to lead. A classic approach to understanding leadership motivation was developed by McClelland, who states that every person has one of three primary driving motivators based on culture and life experiences: the need for achievement, affiliation, or power. And the need for power is particularly relevant in leadership selection processes (McClelland, 1988; McClelland & Burnham, 1976). But the work done by McClelland was criticized for being individualistically oriented and neglecting historical, situational, and contextual determinants of human motivation (Maehr, 1974).

Hofer and Chasiotis (2011, pp. 2–3) state that cross-cultural studies on implicit motives (unconsciously represented general dispositions to act in specific ways) are indispensable to understanding differences due to culture-specific variations in individuals' mental processes and behaviors. For example, Ng (2006) reports that Chinese participants in his empirical study were primarily motivated by the status aspect of power, while the US-American students were mainly motivated by the decision-making aspect of power (Hofer & Chasiotis, 2011, pp. 10–11). And research shows that more and more young people in Germany attach less importance to career advancement and are less motivated to achieve a leadership position, as a positively perceived work-life balance is becoming a more central goal (Ernst & Young, 2020, pp. 6–8).

Past and current socio-cultural contexts influence people's personalities and affect forms of expression in selection processes. Inceoglu and Bartram (2013) find that constructs such as personality and cognitive abilities are transferable across cultures; the Big Five model of personality, for example, can be regarded as universal, and thus used in different cultures. However, the specific manifestations of personality traits that characterize successful leaders may vary culturally.

The culture-specific expectations of what leadership means and which requirements leaders should meet, what the primary motivation for leadership should be, and so on influence how a leadership profile is designed, how applicants are interviewed, and whether the selection process is a more rational-analytical review of competencies or more emotional-intuitive engaging with the candidate, or a mixture of both.

Suppose people in a specific culture or hiring managers assume that being authentic, showing emotions, and using intuition are essential for success in a specific role, these factors play a more critical role in selection than in cultures or among hiring managers, where primarily rational-analytical ways of thinking and decision-making are expected.

However, leadership competencies that lead to success in one culture can lead to the exact opposite in another. Therefore, a selection method should recognize the particular context (Inceoglu & Bartram, 2013, pp. 501–502).

The construction of leadership and leadership potential determines the requirements of leaders and leadership talent. And if personality traits, the motivation to lead, the will to create something, to be authentic, and thus specific social and communicative requirements for managers are particularly emphasized (above technical skills), appropriate selection methods and procedures are needed to diagnose and assess these requirements properly. The respective demands on leadership influence how rational-analytical and intuitive ways of selecting personnel are accepted and used.

7.5 Empirical findings on quality standards and intuition in selecting global leadership talent

As mentioned in Section 3.2, a high-quality personnel selection process should meet specific requirements. For example, implementing a psychometric procedure requires that the selection process should be objective and, thus, as far as possible, free of emotions and intuitions. On the other hand, selection managers should act authentically and show emotions to build a positive relationship and thus attract applicants to a company. In practice, this means deciding, on a situational basis, which perspective is most important in a specific context.

In particular, interviewed HR managers from global organizations and those relatively inexperienced in selection confirm research findings from literature that standards as a guideline can lead to more certainty in how personnel selection should be carried out. Also, transparency, objectivity, equality, and fairness can be fostered.

For selecting global leadership talent from all over the world, about 90% of the selection managers interviewed from large global Western enterprises claim to use rational-analytical procedures with uniform requirement criteria (especially a global competency model for global leadership talent), structured interviews, and an interview guideline that leaves room for context-specific questions, and so on. And they also emphasize that their organizations train hiring managers using these rational-analytical procedures (Deters, 2019, p. 111).

These empirical results confirm that for global organizations selecting global leadership talent worldwide, it may not be helpful that every (foreign) branch uniquely defines the process of selecting global leadership talent. Therefore, science and practice recommend harmonizing specific HRM procedures, for example, to implement psychometric quality standards for selecting global leadership talent while ensuring a positive candidate experience (Deters, 2017, p. 37). Here, it must be emphasized that these findings relate to global companies selecting global leaders or global leadership talent (Deters, 2017, p. 12).

Interviewed managers also state that equal rights, comparability of candidates, and measurability are promoted by applying a quality standard that defines how all candidates (for global leadership positions) should be treated and which concrete steps of a selection process they have to go through. They also state that compliance with quality standards makes personnel selection more efficient and realizes specific global organizational values. In addition, organizational structures, processes, or terminology are harmonized through quality standards to make communication precise and easy (Braun et al., 2015, pp. 100–101).

According to the hiring managers interviewed, a rational-analytical approach is already relatively well known in Western countries such as Germany, the Netherlands, Scandinavian countries, Great Britain, or the United States. In addition, they state that Western countries have better access to academic research results, are often more restricted in their entrepreneurial freedom and autonomy, and generally adhere more to prescribed processes to legally secure themselves and to be able to demonstrate a correct and nondiscriminatory selection process. This makes quality standards more acceptable.

On the other hand, the need for or benefit of psychometric quality standards is viewed more critically in countries and organizations with limited access to information, technology, money, qualified personnel, and so on. Especially the lack of expertise and knowledge in specific countries is an obstacle to implementing ISO standards such as 10667 or standards for executing assessment centers.

The statement of one global HR manager is exemplary:

> In the vast majority of our subsidiaries worldwide, there is far too little knowledge on psychometric selection procedures . . . and then . . . any interview is conducted purely intuitively, which is not comparable at all. Thus, we need standards for selecting global leadership talent (Deters, 2019, p. 111).

Since quality standards are associated with high costs and less flexibility, SME interview partners from different countries also see massive resistance to psychometric quality standards.

But there are exceptions: some interviewees who select people for Nigeria or Pakistan experience a higher acceptance of quality standards in their countries because such countries see standards as an opportunity to gain orientation and stabilize or improve their economic conditions.

Nevertheless, standards take very little account of local or cultural contexts and traditions (Tayo Tene et al., 2018, p. 69). Thus, there is resistance in practice to introducing selection standards. Many practitioners fear higher costs and time expenditure, bureaucracy and restrictions in their flexibility, and no room for context-specific adjustments. And hiring managers interviewed note that psychometric quality standards are often viewed as too complex and abstractly formulated, and thus difficult to understand and implement.

On the other hand, people like to hold on to familiar ways of doing things. Thus, a general rejection is often expressed when established, well-known, and subjectively successful procedures should be changed, or the request for change is perceived as personal criticism. Other interviewers confirm the fear that a standardized psychometric procedure will prevent an open "getting to know each other" and prevent intuitive decisions about whether an applicant fits into the team (Kleebaur, 2007, p. 122).

Thus, harmonizing the personnel selection process may work at selecting global leaders or global leadership talent. However, the context-specific cultural, political, technological, and legal factors should be considered for selecting candidates for most other positions. These limits to standardization are emphasized by an interviewed HR manager as follows:

> Standardizing personnel selection procedures, in general, has felt a bit like: We're looking for a food that tastes equally good to everyone in the world. That will not work (Lindemann, 2020, p. 47).

7.5.1 Meaning of positive candidate experience in specific cultures

Many selection managers interviewed say that no matter how valid, objective, and of high psychometric quality a selection procedure may be, if candidates in specific cultures feel uncomfortable in the selection process and therefore do not accept a procedure and possibly do not apply, a selection procedure has to be changed. For most interviewed hiring managers, finding and winning qualified candidates for the relevant positions is more important than meeting psychometric quality criteria. And if, in specific cultures, these candidates find specific selection procedures unsuitable or too elaborate for them, it should be considered to change these methods accordingly. Thus, their organizations implement selection procedures where candidates feel comfortable and can present themselves authentically. This has led some organizations to no longer using, for example, assessment centers for selecting global leadership talent because, for example, candidates from East-Asian cultures may feel uncomfortable with these methods of personnel selection. However, this adaptation to candidates' preferences should not be at the expense of the quality of personnel selection (Deters, 2019, pp. 111–113).

7.5.2 Meaning of intuition and emotions in the practice of different cultures

Although most selection managers interviewed are convinced that rational-analytical procedures lead to more valid results and can help reduce discrimination, the vast majority of the interviewees (HR managers and nearly all line managers) did not want to rely solely on rational-analytical results. Especially the final selection decision is regularly made by listening to messages of emotions and intuitions, especially of what is intuitively felt about who is the best-fit personally and who fits best in the team. Almost all interviewees deliberately rely on their intuition.

Interviewed Global HR managers from Western countries (Germany, Great Britain, the Netherlands, and Scandinavian countries agree that in countries such as China, Arab countries, India, or Spain, selection decisions are made less according to rational-analytical procedures and more based on culture-specific behavioral procedures and particularly intuition.

At the same time, although the acceptance of intuition in selection procedures is strongly influenced by culture, intuition is considered human. For many interviewed practitioners, it is impossible to exclude its use in selection decisions regardless of the culture, as this quotation shows.

> Intuitive decisions are more common in Indian, Chinese, Hispanic, or Arab countries than in Germany, in my experience . . . And in Taiwan, I saw that intuitive decisions are made with a high degree of trust by experienced people in higher positions . . . But intuition is not only a question of culture. It is a factor in every human behavior. . . . It is a global phenomenon. Maybe the Germans are more rational, but they also decide – more or less . . . – based on intuition (Brauner, 2019, pp. 78–80).

Other interviewed managers see Christianity, the Reformation, and the Enlightenment as influencing factors. However, in Western cultures such as Germany, Great Britain, or the United States, what counts first and foremost is what can be measured and proven (Brauner, 2019, p. 80).

Most interviewees clearly emphasize that, especially when selecting at a global level, the psychometric requirement to eliminate emotions and intuition from a selection process is not possible in practice. Despite a given structure or standardization of selection procedures, especially when selecting global leadership talent in various countries, subjective influences, and thus intuition and emotions, can never be switched off, especially in selection interviews. Therefore, most hiring managers state that even standardized personnel selection processes do not eliminate hiring managers from using their feelings and intuition when assessing candidates. These research results are in accordance with Lodato et al. (2011, p. 352) and Miles & Sadler-Smith (2014, p. 606). And the interviewed global selection managers emphasize that decision-makers are more open to their intuitions in many Asian, African, or Central- and South American countries. In contrast, decision-makers often feel pressure to justify their intuitions rationally in Western countries, especially in business. In general, it can be seen that in cultures where intuition is more appreciated, decisions based on intuitions are more accepted.

However, it must also be noted that the line managers surveyed often have little awareness of the possible disadvantages of their intuitively made decisions.

Some global hiring managers interviewed say they need to rely on their judgments. On the other hand, some very experienced hiring managers see limited added value in applying psychometric requirements. While they find standardized procedures beneficial for inexperienced selection managers or young line managers, especially in the pre-selection process, they believe they can do without these standards. They justify this with their experience and intuitive competence, which they confidently emphasize.

The following quote by an executive from England is an example:

> My staff focuses on adherence to scientific standards in the pre-selection process. But when I then conduct interviews with those candidates who have made the shortlist, I use a (semi-) structured interview guideline, but then rely on my experience, and thus also my intuition. . . . Without showing emotions, I can't build a positive relationship in the process. Therefore, I deliberately do not meet all scientific requirements, but this is necessary. And I'm successful in doing it that way (Brauner, 2019, p. 60).

It is emphasized by this global hiring manager that

> candidates should also be aware that, ultimately, we only have this hour to get to know each other. . . . And we try to find out: Do we match? I would try to find out if the candidate actually understands our core values or actually agrees with our core values and fits into our company culture. . . . It's about getting to know each other, in general, and establishing trust and sympathy. And I use the interview to question the analytically collected data (Brauner, 2019, pp. 60–61).

From the perspective of most global selection managers interviewed, particularly when selecting talent for global leadership positions, the focus is on a precise personality assessment. But the interviewed hiring managers agree that no selection decision should be made on the sole basis of a personality test. Rather, the results are used to get information on a candidate's personality from a more objective perspective, learn more about their motivation, and reflect on the test results in the interview. Primarily, the line managers surveyed emphasize using the analytically collected data for quality assurance in the pre-selection process. They expect the HR department or an external HR consultant to present the results of the analytical procedures (e.g., test results) and the pros and cons list of the top three eligible candidates. And for the final decision, they always do an interview and rely on their own assessment using their specific methods, selection criteria, and intuitions (Brauner, 2019, pp. 60–62).

Exemplary for most of those interviewed global hiring managers is the following quote, which shows that, especially in the selection process of leadership talent, intuition plays a significant role:

> I cannot determine whether a candidate is a good fit for my team with standardized procedures, especially a standardized interview guideline with no chance to ask individual questions. . . . To comprehensively assess an applicant . . . I use my gut feeling. . . . To gain a feeling for the candidate and to interview on a personal level . . . to look behind the facade of a candidate . . . to sense whether someone is behaving authentically and I can trust them, I need my intuitions and emotions (Brauner, 2019, p. 74).

And another interviewee, referring to experiences in personnel selection in different countries, thinks:

> An interview process should not be like an arithmetic exercise in which one can analytically sort perceptions into scores and numbers. This does not do justice to the fact that we are dealing with people (Bublitz, 2021, p. 85).

Other global selection managers interviewed emphasized that body language and gestures are more prevalent, specifically in more emotionally oriented cultures such as Portugal, Italy, or South America. And indeed, other countries, such as Thailand, were described by interviewees as "smiling countries." On the other hand, Germans are often perceived as very rational, rule-oriented, and somewhat reserved in body language.

Hiring managers reported that in many African countries, such as Ghana, questions tended to be asked about personal circumstances. For example, the following statement from a Portuguese hiring manager who reported recruiting personnel in ten different countries makes this clear:

> In the UK or Germany, I cannot ask personal questions; I can smile, but I cannot make a joke . . . we need to be very, very careful with our words, . . . feelings and emotions . . . When I have . . . a Portuguese employee . . . or interviewing someone in the UK, I need to tell them, you cannot ask their age, you cannot ask if they are married, you cannot ask if they have kids . . . we don't ask to find out if they will likely work overtime, . . . (but it) gives you information that is important to understand the general profile. But we cannot. . . . But in Portuguese interviews, you discuss where your kids go to school and how you manage weekends with soccer practice . . . . So, it's very different in terms of the human relationship and the emotions that you need to create (Bublitz, 2021, p. 73).

Another interviewed manager from the Netherlands emphasizes that due to his cultural and related linguistic socialization, the selection interview is conducted very differently in the Netherlands and China, especially concerning the topic of language, cultural barriers, and opportunity to build emotional connections and relationships:

> My personnel selection decisions are more emotional here in Holland than in China, which probably has to do with the fact that I can better connect to the people here and get a better feeling of the type of person they are. In China, those interviews were very often with people who spoke limited English, so you don't really get close to each other because there's a language and cultural barrier, so you tend to go more to the rational facts for your decisions. In contrast, there's more emotion involved when you get to know a person better (Bublitz, 2021, p. 96).

Our empirical research results on accepting and using intuitions and rational-analytical procedures in different cultures confirm the findings of Miles & Sadler-Smith (2014, p. 622) and Eisenkraft (2013). Furthermore, they show that, from the perspective of HR practitioners, the most trustworthy judgments in global talent selection processes are made using a combination of analytic and intuitive methods.

7.5.3 How to measure and evaluate the success of hiring global leadership talent

For some interviewed selecting managers responsible for pre-selection, a selection is successful when higher-ranked decision-makers or line managers share their impression about a candidate and are committed to a pre-selected candidate. However, for the vast majority of the selection managers surveyed, "the quality of hire" and "the quality of selection" are the same (for the difference between both, see Sections 3.1 and 3.2). And they agree that the success of personnel selection must ultimately be measured in terms of results or outcomes.

And most interviewees agree that the success of personnel selection is measured across cultures and countries by the subsequent success or performance of the newly hired employees.

But in practice, the success of a hiring decision is measured in different ways. None of the global companies surveyed have a systematic, scientifically guided evaluation process for the quality of selecting their global leadership talent. Moreover, even if some respondents are aware of systematic evaluation procedures and measurement methods, they concede that such practices do not exist in their company or only to a limited extent.

Several selection managers from large global companies referred to measurement and success criteria such as salary growth, promotions, feedback from superiors, the speed with which the new hire becomes visible in the company or receives requests from the board, and so on. The following statement is exemplary for several of those interviewed:

> I have to say that we don't have any systematic evaluation or tracking systems for new hires, neither national nor global (Brauner, 2019, p. 68).

In most cases, the success of a hiring decision is evaluated based on feedback from the superior and the employee's performance assessment in the first annual appraisal. Practitioners consider personnel selection successful if the new employee achieves positive results during or after the probationary period or first six months, shows interest, motivation, and commitment, signals openness to new tasks and the team, and, as a potential global leadership talent has an energetic and inspiring effect on others.

One selection manager interviewed tracked a new hire over two years.

> I do not think this (performance during probation time) is the only way to check. Actually, I feel we need to watch for a long time. . . . So, from time to time, I will ask, 'How is this colleague, how is he performing'? Like that. I always follow new colleagues. . . . But it`s not a systematic evaluation process (Brauner, 2019, p. 68).

7.6 Acceptance of rational-analytical and intuitive selection procedures in a global context

Although Rietiker (2010, p. 218) states that there is no "one and only" global personnel selection procedure for leadership talent and that the process of personnel selection should be adapted to the cultural circumstances and resources of the individual organizations, our qualitative empirical research shows that globally standardized rational-analytical selection processes are implemented in most larger global Western organizations (especially with headquarters in Europe or the United States), when selecting global leaders or global leadership talent. As a rule, these are rational-analytical pre-selection procedures, but intuitions and emotions strongly influence the interview's final decision.

All hiring managers interviewed emphasize the company`s or subsidiary's cultural background and context-specific circumstances for global selection processes. Thus, these organizations adopt personnel selection procedures for specific organizational, cultural, and legal contexts. One selection manager interviewed says that there could be no universal recommendation for a selection procedure due to the different approaches to personnel selection worldwide. The only universal advice is that the match between the position to be filled and the applicant must be suitable (Bublitz, 2021, p. 83).

Several personnel managers emphasized the importance of different cultures accepting intuition and emotions in personnel selection.

According to one hiring manager:

> If you are in a decision-making process with someone in East Asia,
> and the boss of a selection manager is in the room, the selection managers will not talk at all, because that is not possible, they are so polite that they always wait until the boss gives them the floor, which means I have to lead in this interview process differently (Deters, 2019, p. 125).

Furthermore, two ways of dealing with the Asian and Japanese approaches are reported, which are very analytical and based on hard facts and CVs. First, managers tend to keep a low profile because attempting to elicit something "interpersonal" from Asian applicants does not work. In contrast, a human resources manager states that he deliberately relies more on intuition in Japan. Consequently, the selection process must consider the possible effects of the involvement of different hierarchical levels and the cultural imprint of all participants.

And if it turns out after the selection process that someone does not fit into the team, this may show either poor intuition or that too little attention was paid to intuition.

Our empirical research confirms that intuition can primarily rely upon when the decision-making situation is familiar (Gigerenzer & Gaissmaier, 2015, p. 31).

We also know from research that global organizations attach great importance to cultural fit and values as selection criteria; these organizations often made the experience that formal qualifications are not always the best predictors of performance and retention, and that skills are easier to develop than personality traits, attitudes, and values. Therefore, the basis for screening and interviewing are the attitudes and values of applicants (Stahl et al., 2012, p. 28).

For most interviewed global HR experts, recognizing intuitions and emotions is the basis for checking these attitudes, values, and cultural and team fit. In addition, the fit with a specific team is especially considered very important because the same person can perform differently in different teams or cultures.

Finally, on an intercultural level, most global practitioners interviewed see their intuition as a learned and essential skill, and the more they use it, the more reliable it becomes for them.

In our empirical research, we could identify differences between the selection processes of HR managers and line managers or superiors of the potential candidates. For example, while HR managers show a relatively high degree of structuring selection processes in Western cultures, line managers or supervisors worldwide are regularly less analytical, more unstructured, and more intuitive in selecting people.

However, it is also noticeable that specialist competence and technical knowledge are tested much more rigorously by the hiring superior or line manager than by the HR managers; and the HR managers focus more on the social and intercultural competencies or the cultural fit. We also found that selection managers from the HR department were trained much more frequently than line managers to reduce bias or stereotypes, use psychometric procedures, and so on.

Especially for assessing the person-organization or person-team fit, more than 90% of the interviewed global hiring managers confess to relying on their intuition (Brauner, 2019, pp. 35–44, 79–81).

Our interviews with selection managers partly confirm research findings from Ryan and Tippins (2009). Ryan and Tippins conclude that multinational organizations can develop methods for personnel selection that enjoy high acceptance across different cultures, especially for global leadership positions. The managers interviewed confirm this for selecting global leadership talent, and rational-analytical processes are used predominantly for pre-selection candidates. However, the conclusion of Ryan and Tippins that the impact of culture is so small that it should not prevent organizations from using globally consistent selection processes (Ryan & Tippins, 2009, pp. 80–81) cannot be confirmed in this generalizability by our empirical investigations.

Our research shows that despite a move toward global harmonization, selection procedures differ significantly from country to country or national culture to national culture, concerning the acceptance of intuitions and emotions in personnel selection and rational-analytical selection procedures. As a result, understanding, perception, and acceptance of appropriate selection procedures vary. The cultural dimensions of uncertainty avoidance, power distance, individualism-collectivism, and the extent of low- or high-context communication are particularly relevant to the perception of and reaction to selection procedures. At the same time, these differences pose challenges to the cross-cultural standardization of selection procedures that most hiring managers interviewed named as a central success factor to ensure the quality of selecting global leadership talent. Additionally, a high degree of face validity and personal contact positively influence the acceptance of selection procedures (Lindemann, 2020, p. II). If scientifically evident rational-analytic selection procedures are to be implemented on a global scale, not only the minds but also the hearts of people must be won over to such procedures. This can only be achieved if one considers the cultural imprints of the people concerned.

7.7 Implications of culture on the use of intuition and analytics in personnel selection

The specific cultural context always influences the acceptance and implementation of personnel selection standards and the interplay of different cultural dimensions.

Our literature analysis and empirical surveys show that intuition and related emotions are important messages in personnel selection in almost every culture and country.

Our empirical research shows that most global acting hiring managers recommend using a mixture of analytics and intuition. However, they associate an integration of rational-analytics and intuition with two different intentions: While the rational-analytical approach enables reliable and valid assessments of the technical suitability of an applicant, the use of intuition is associated with gaining an overall holistic impression and assessing if a candidate is a good fit personally for the team or the organization.

The HR experts in global companies we interviewed confirm that interpersonal fit tends to be more critical in collective cultures such as East Asian Countries such as China or Japan, or Latin American and Arab countries. To maintain harmony within a team, particular emphasis is placed on the personal fit with the company and team.

Especially in China, *guanxi* is central in personnel selection. Particularly in the pre-selection process, *guanxi* and thus personal connections, social networks, and in-group relationships are an efficient and effective way to reduce the risk of making poor selection decisions (Lindemann, 2020, p. 69). In the Chinese culture, communication is more indirect than, for example, in the United States or Germany. Opinions and emotions are not openly shared. The relatively high power distance, for example, in the Chinese culture, prevents applicants from questioning the selection process; even questioning instructions in an assessment center is regarded as inappropriate and impolite. Building relationships through politeness and social harmony is the focus of any interaction. Thus, *guanxi* is a prerequisite for getting a job in China. This has direct implications for the selection of global leadership talent. HR professionals must respect and be very polite in selection interviews with Chinese candidates. Emotions are to be suppressed and controlled. Anything else is perceived as rude. If Western hiring managers do not understand this principle, they will face severe difficulties when looking for Chinese talent. And European or other foreign selection managers should know that in China, for example, when applicants are asked how successfully they have performed specific tasks in the past, they do not always answer honestly. One reason is that it is more socially acceptable to make up stories about past successes than not answer a question correctly. In addition, Huo et al. (2002) show that in personnel selection in China, less attention is paid to performance in the hiring interview than to work experience or test results (Lievens, 2008, p. 5; Huo et al., 2002, p. 37).

In Latin cultures such as Brazil, emotions are displayed more openly. Hugs are signs of respect, and the communication is familiar and direct. However, this interpersonal closeness requires HR managers to be aware and sensitive to their unconscious biases.

Our interviewed hiring managers state that selection decisions in Brazil are regularly based on emotions and intuitions rather than on rational-analytical selection processes.

Most interviewed experts with personnel selection experience in different cultures recommend combining a scientifically-based approach with a flexible and less standardized intuitive procedure. From the hiring managers' perspective, integrating rational-analytical methods with intuitive impulses can reduce the risk of poor selection decisions. And the use of intuitions and emotions also reduces the risk of distanced relationships with applicants and ensures an empathetic approach and trust building (Lindemann, 2020, p. 70).

The interviewed hiring managers from Western and Northern Europe see rational-analytical diagnostics as the best way of ensuring a scientifically proven objective, reliable and valid procedure in particular for pre-selection. They provide guidelines to avoid falling into any trap and overlooking something important. But in the final decision on who to hire, intuition becomes active. These practitioners state that if the facts of a rational-analytical assessment speak for a specific applicant, but the intuition and related feelings do not, they take these intuitions seriously and reflect on them as essential signals (Lindemann, 2020, pp. 61–62 and 69–70). These results are consistent with those of Riedel (2015, pp. 35 and 188), who states that only understanding and reflecting on one's own intuition and discussing one's intuitions and emotions in a group of international hiring managers can ensure good personnel selection decisions in a global context.

Our interviews show that nearly all interviewed managers from Western and Northern Europe, for example, Germany, England, or Scandinavian cultures, emphasize the importance of critical reflection more strongly than the Chinese, Brazilian, Spanish, or Italian interview partners on their intuitions and emotions. But primarily, interview partners from China, Brazil, or Southern European countries tend to confess to their intuition, emphasize its importance for their personnel selection, and don`t question it (Lindemann, 2020, p. 62).

Our empirical results are also consistent with those of Buchtel & Norenzayan (2008, p. 268), who show that Korean managers, for example, when asked about success factors for work and relationships, classify intuition as more important than logic, while US Americans have no clear preference but a slight tendency toward rational-analytical procedures. East Asian participants rate managers who follow their intuition as more reasonable than those who follow the rules and standards, while participants with a European background make no such distinction.

Norenzayan et al. (2002) also show differences in accepting intuition in different cultures. A study investigating cultural preferences among European, Asian-American, and East Asian participants for formal or intuitive thinking states that Europeans are more willing to put their intuitions aside than East Asians. Europeans tend toward rule-based thinking that emphasizes logical reasoning, with more emphasis on critical thinking and self-reflection. East Asians, on the other hand, prefer the experiential way of thinking that includes the context of experience and ignores rules and logic when they contradict intuition (Norenzayan et al., 2002, p. 678). There are various approaches to explaining this phenomenon. First, decision-making differs fundamentally between the East and the West, with an orientation toward consensus-oriented decision-making in the East, while in the West, the debate is more adversarial.

East Asian and Western cultures differ massively in their philosophical traditions. For example, great Western philosophers attempted to describe the universe with precision and a pronounced distrust of intuition and emotions (e.g., Plato, Kant; see Section 4.3.10), while Chinese philosophers display greater pragmatism and act more intuitively and distrustfully of formal logic and rational differences (Norenzayan et al., 2002, p. 679). An overview of the origins of the more holistic culture in East Asia and the more rational culture in the West, which emerge from two very different social systems and result in other cognitive processes in these cultures, can be found in Nisbett et al. (2001).

Norenzayan et al. (2002, p. 678) indicate a general cultural influence on the tendency toward intuitive decision-making. However, there are significant cultural differences even within West/North and South Europe, for example, concerning compliance with rules. For example, people in Germany or Scandinavian countries are more willing to comply with regulations than in Southern European countries like Greece or Italy. Still, in most cultures, some areas of behaviors are more strictly regulated, and rules and regulations are likely to be followed.

Our research results confirm Norenzayan et al. (2002, p. 678) that people with a Western and Northern European background differentiate from people with an East Asian background in their rule-based thinking and logical reasoning. Whereas in Germany, structures such as the DIN 33430 attempt to standardize personnel selection decisions, intuition is more likely accepted and even requested in countries such as China. For this reason, a universalistic standardization of all personnel selection procedures is difficult to implement (Riedel, 2015, p. 117).

Looking at the personnel selection process in different cultures, it can be roughly stated that Western cultures, particularly, attach great importance to rationality and analytics in the decision-making process. In contrast, in non-Western cultures, decision-makers are more guided by intuition, especially in Latin, East-Asian, or African cultures (Miyamoto & Kitayama, 2002, p. 1239). In general, rational-analytical decision-making processes in personnel selection are implemented primarily in cultures with predominantly high uncertainty avoidance, individualism, masculinity, universalism, neutrality, and cultures that exhibit a low degree of context-orientation (Dipboye & Johnson, 2007, p. 62).

But to what concrete extent cultural differences influence selection procedures remains difficult to answer (Inceoglu & Bartram, 2013, p. 505). This shows that the conclusions regarding the consequences of cultural dimensions for the acceptance of intuition and rational-analytical selection procedures should always be drawn holistically and never based on only one cultural dimension.

However, it must clearly be stated that the research results regarding the influence of culture on personnel selection procedures remain partly contradictory. Research on cultural differences does not produce clear conclusions about the significance of specific cultural dimensions for accepting analytical-rational or intuitive selection methods. Furthermore, since cultures are constantly evolving, regular changes in the acceptance of intuition and analytics in selection procedures can be expected.

No hiring manager can do justice to the diversity and complexity of all applicants in different cultures simply by reading about these cultures. However, it is helpful for selection managers to be generally open to the particularities of other people and cultures, clarify mutual expectations concerning fair selection processes, and critically question their individual perceptions. Adopting different perspectives without detaching oneself from one's own is essential to maintaining authenticity.

A culture-specific design of selection processes helps to accept selection procedures, ensure a positive candidate experience, and communicate an employer's attractiveness. On the other hand, evidence-based research on implementing rational-analytical procedures should be followed to improve selection processes globally. Thus, for example, a semi-structured interview should be conducted using interview guidelines based on a global competency model for global leadership talent, and so on. Therefore, corresponding psychometric procedures are not or only rudimentarily implemented globally.

Interviews with global HR managers show that despite an organizational demand for global standards in selecting global leadership talent, differences remain in how standardized procedures are implemented.

Several selection managers say that global standards are only rudimentarily implemented in their organizations and that there is a resistance to any global standards in personnel selection, especially in specific Asian, African, or South American countries (Deters, 2019, pp. 115–116).

The global HR managers interviewed recommend involving the local selection managers to gain acceptance and support for corresponding procedures globally. Several interviewees emphasize the importance of actively involving those responsible in other countries when implementing standards in personnel selection. This calls for the sensitivity and empathy of hiring managers selecting in a global context. HR managers interviewed explicitly emphasize the importance of intensive communication with local executives and hiring managers in all countries. This is because requirements from headquarters may be acknowledged but not necessarily implemented. In addition, those responsible for personnel selection in a specific country may question their competencies.

In particular, interviewees from Western global organizations who are trying to implement rational-analytical procedures in Asian or South American countries state that some local hiring managers try or verbally support implementing these psychometric standards. But often, they are not really convinced of these standards, and context-specific circumstances (e.g., resources and knowledge) or other decision-making criteria, such as nepotism, are more important than compliance with scientific standards or recommendations from headquarters.

In addition, most interviewees repeatedly say there should be room for context-specific adjustments in implementing selection standards.

> The people should do in Rome as the Romans do. A global standard may not fit with some cultures. A European or American standard may not work with the Asian way, and vice versa (Brauner, 2019, p. 71).

On the other hand, our research shows that hiring managers in those countries which, for example, due to their legal, political, economic, or cultural circumstances, are open to rational-analytical selection procedures, use these predominantly for pre-selection, but continue to rely on their intuition in the final selection.

Our research also shows that selection managers for global leadership talent should be aware of the theories of Hofstede, Hall, Trompenaars, and so on. They should also question these theoretical approaches to culture and thus possibly simplified views may lead to stereotypes. Moreover, such cultural dimensions represent only a tiny part of influencing factors for accepting rational-analytical procedures or intuitions and feelings in personnel selection. Therefore, individual, regional, generational, or even organizational and situational considerations should be supplemented in practice.

Even if studies confirm the validity of Hofstede's dimensions and other cultural differentiating factors (Javidan & Dastmalchian, 2009, pp. 55–56; Javidan et al., 2006), country borders are limited reference systems for differentiating (national) cultures.

Countries are generally not monocultural entities; frequently, there are ethnic or regional subcultures (Deresky, 2008, p. 100). Furthermore, cultural dimensions can only provide information about tendencies at the group level rather than individual attitudes or behaviors. Accordingly, differences in behavior should not be attributed solely to the cultural characteristics of a nation (Schroll-Machl, 2007, p. 31; Scott, 2014, p. 21).

The concept of culture is far too complex to be studied from the viewpoint of one specific approach or one specific group of researchers. And every cross-cultural relationship, for example, in selecting global leadership talent, is not only a complex situation. It is also a unique situation that must be understood individually or context related in each case (Gullestrup, 2002, p. 15).

Moreover, we cannot assume that cultures are stable over time. Instead, studies show that cultural values change according to the socio-economic development of a nation (Beugelsdijk et al., 2015, p. 224; Taras et al., 2009, p. 365; Lindemann, 2020, pp. 23–24).

Therefore, due to dynamic environmental developments, there will be ongoing changes and adjustments in the selection procedures in various countries and cultures to achieve high-quality selection procedures and culturally accepted and context-specific procedures for selecting global leadership talent and to have an efficient and unambiguous exchange of information in the selection process, HR managers in all cultures should actively and creatively move forward and pick up on new developments and knowledge, for example, in global HR/People management, personnel selection, law, and also IT and AI.

Personnel selection is always culture-bound. Even if, for example, the selection of global leadership talent is carried out with global standardized rational-analytical procedures, there is still room for intuition and emotion when evaluating applicants. And the acceptance and use of intuitions and emotions in personnel selection varies significantly from culture to culture.

Most of the selection managers interviewed explicitly emphasize that they do not blindly follow their intuitions and feelings but critically reflect on them (with their colleagues) and compare their intuitions and feelings about a candidate with rational-analytically collected results. In addition, they exchange impressions with other selection managers involved. Thus, the selection decision is a mixture of rational-analytical data and intuitive impulses when selecting global leadership talent. However, most of those interviewed admit that the final decision, particularly if two candidates are equally well suited, is practically never made against the intuitive feeling.

Our research shows that we still know far too little about the influence of rational-analytical and intuitive-emotional processes on selection decisions in different cultures (Kersting, 2009, p. 155). And as a limitation, it must be considered that our interview partners were almost exclusively white men and women from Western European or US (global) companies.

It also became apparent in the interviews we conducted that, due to language barriers (when conducting our research interviews in English), interviewees' answers from non-English-speaking countries were usually shorter and more unspecific than those of interviewees from English-speaking or German-speaking countries. This suggests that in the area of emotions and intuitions, a great deal of information could possibly not be collected in the interviews or was lost (Bublitz, 2021, p. 96).

Following Ryan & Tippins (Ryan & Tippins, 2009), it can be concluded that more scientific research is needed on the relationship between culture and the acceptance and implementation of rational-analytical or intuitive personnel selection processes.

8 Digital technologies and artificial intelligence (AI): implications for using intuition and analytics in personnel selection

Robotics and other combinations will make the world pretty fantastic compared with today. (Bill Gates, 2016)

8.1 Digital technologies and AI in personnel selection

The age of digitalization is bringing about significant changes and new opportunities for' HR practices in companies. New technologies, such as cloud technologies, blockchain, algorithms, artificial intelligence (AI) chapter 8, and other technological innovations, are causing profound changes in HR practices (Michailidis, 2018, p. 169).

Today, online applications and applicant management systems are the standard in many personnel departments, often integrated with an overall HR or people IT system. In addition, digitalization offers new recruitment possibilities to support hiring managers in selecting suitable candidates. This process of digitization was accelerated by the Covid-19 pandemic in 2020–2022.

AI could ultimately have the ability of software and machines, such as robots, to perform specific HR tasks better than humans. The so-called machine learning is of central importance and distinguishes AI from rule-based expert systems such as simple algorithms. Rule-based expert digital systems cannot learn independently.

We, therefore, only speak of AI when, using machine learning, the software autonomously generates rules and knowledge, recognizes patterns, and, thus, becomes a self-learning and self-supervised learning system. Thus, machine learning is "the machine's ability to keep improving its performance without humans having to explain exactly how to accomplish all the tasks it's given" (Brynjolfsson & McAfee, 2017, p. 2).

Like human intelligence or cognitive abilities, which require specific experiences and learning opportunities for its development, AI is also based on experience and learning. Solutions are then derived from machine learning.

AI systems can learn from their own experience. The independently learning networks train themselves to win against human beings in games like GO, chess, or videogames, or when self-propelled vehicles take over human decisions. Open AI, for example, boasts that the new training units go through all past versions of themselves. Each hero in video games is currently controlled by an LSTM (long short-term memory) network that enables the networks to remember earlier experiences.

One subarea of machine learning is the so-called deep learning, in which attempts are made to emulate the learning behavior of the human brain, using artificial neural networks. Machine learning tends to continuous deep learning, based on input and

https://doi.org/10.1515/9783110980967-008

self-generated data or algorithms and improves decision-making through experience growth (Kreutzer & Sirrenberg, 2019, pp. 3–5). Thus, high-quality (training) data should be available to successfully train AI systems (Teetz, 2018, p. 238).

AI, as an approach to simulate the human brain and the cognitive and emotional (or maybe intuitive) abilities of machines, is regarded as the key technology of this century, due to its successes in recent years. AI has enormous potential to solve complex problems independently and improve HR/People management, especially personnel selection. In addition, the supply of information to decision-makers will be expanded and improved, if implemented appropriately.

Although "so much about the brain is still a mystery" (Barrett, 2017a, p. 290), recent developments in AI try to emulate processes of the human brain and reproduce sensitive artificial synapses. For example, computer chips, such as neuromorphic processors or the so-called memristors, try to work the same way as does the human brain, but are somewhat faster than conscious cognitive processes in the human body. Memristive cells and devices are basic units for future nanoelectronic architecture targeting alternative data processing approaches, such as cognitive or neuromorphic computing and alternative logic operations (Lübben et al., 2020). However, further developments will show whether the unconscious processes in the human brain or the use of implicit knowledge and, thus, everything on which human intuition is based can also be mapped accordingly.

AI tools can record, process, and analyze immense volumes of data to learn underlying patterns, enabling computer systems to make complex decisions, predict human behavior (predictive analytics) and employee performance, and recognize images, nonverbal expressions, and human speech, among many other things. Moreover, AI-enabled systems continuously learn and adapt to changing circumstances and requirements. As a result, AI-enabled platforms can help organizations simulate work environments better and create on-demand labor forces. Potential success areas can be those that seamlessly combine and integrate AI with human judgment, (intuitive) experience, and the emotions of HR managers. Thus, a "successful AI-centered operating model needs to integrate human judgment and experience at its core" (Candelon et al., 2020).

In practice, there is need for time- and cost-efficient procedures that nevertheless demonstrate – from a psychometric perspective – compliance with scientific quality criteria such as validity or objectivity. In addition, the perceived professionalism of selection methods and the associated impact on the candidate experience also represent a decisive criterion in the choice of AI-based procedures (Merkle et al., 2009, p. 157).

In personnel selection, the central goal of AI is to make personnel decisions more information-, knowledge- and evidence-based and less based on human intuition or feelings. As a result, AI-based algorithms promise time and cost savings for companies and applicants, increased objectivity, and reduced discrimination (Youyou et al., 2015, p. 1039; Michailidis, 2018, p. 169; Weitzel et al., 2019, p. 17). Thus, AI-based tools are expected to reduce or even eliminate biases and stereotypes from personnel selection processes and minimize the number of wrong or poor hiring decisions and the associated costs (Petry, 2018, pp. 46–47; Petry & Jäger, 2018, p. 44). Thus, digital technologies and AI can create economic added value for the company (Merkle et al., 2009, p. 156).

Due to these advantages, digitally and AI-supported personnel selection procedures are increasingly becoming an integral part of personnel selection. In addition, several study results illustrate that decisions made using algorithm-based data can be superior to those made by human decision-makers (Grove et al., 2000, p. 26; Petry, 2018, p. 49).

However, the challenge is that AI gets trained by using data, and if these data are biased, then the implemented AI (e.g., algorithm) will be biased. Or the data is wrong or outdated and, therefore, not very useful for future decisions. At the same time, data protection, ethical concerns, and user-friendliness must be considered (Bauer et al., 2006, p. 616); and technologically, applicants must be prevented from cheating, when applying it digitally.

In machine learning, rules are created, based on previous data applied to new situations. Therefore, to avoid discrimination, decisions made by AI-supported algorithms should be transparent and monitored by an independent authority. Furthermore, differentiation should be statistically detectable. Finally, the data sets should also be examined to determine whether an algorithm's training is being carried out with data reflecting stereotypes, biases, and so on.

Although the topic of digital technologies and AI in personnel selection has received a great deal of attention in academia and at conferences of practitioners, and despite research showing that digital and AI-supported selection methods are noticeably advantageous for the selection process, AI-based selection procedures have been implemented relatively little in practice, until the beginning of 2020 d. Nevertheless, the use of digital technologies in recruitment, active sourcing, applicant tracking systems, or personnel selection processes is rated positively, overall, by the HR managers and is seen as having great potential for improving HR work; HR/People managers can no longer imagine practice without them (Weitzel et al., 2019, pp. 17 and 23).

The fact that humans increasingly rely on digital technologies can be seen in many examples, such as navigation systems in cars replacing the process of finding a route intuitively or, for example, in partner exchanges that support the preselection of matches, with the help of self-learning AI systems.

In the following, the possibilities of AI-supported personnel selection will be discussed more concretely against the background of rational-analytical and intuitive aspects of the process.

8.2 Algorithm in personnel selection

One possibility of implementing AI in selection processes is using algorithms (Uni Global Union Professionals & Managers, 2020, pp. 6–7). Algorithms can be seen as general digital procedures to screen and evaluate application documents or data on social media. They can be implemented, for example, in:

- Textual analysis algorithms used in designing the wording of job advertisements.
- Targeted placement of job advertisements online.
- Automated background checks on social media to look for appropriate candidates (active sourcing); thus, algorithms play a role before submitting an application. Comparable to social networks such as Facebook, Tinder, or Google search engines, algorithms play a significant role in deciding what content is displayed to users on job boards or career networks ("programmatic advertising").
- Chatbots that are used to guide candidates through the application process.
- CV screening and scanning job applications for keywords and phrases and filtering candidates for the next selection steps. In this preselection process, for example, essential data is automatically read and analyzed from the CV, online profiles, or other application documents (CV parsing). CV screening is a very widespread practice around the world, for example, in large companies with thousands of online applications, where a vast majority of applicants are automatically rejected in an automated screening process before human recruiters assess the remaining candidates.
- Competency-based or other psychometric tests such as cognitive ability tests to provide a further screening filter for candidates.
- Various kinds of automated interview systems (e.g., chatbots) that can ask candidates prerecorded interview questions. without the need for a human interviewer and/or attempt to assess candidates. based on an analysis of their facial expressions, voice, or the answers they provide.

The use of algorithms could, on the one hand, serve as a system for Automated Decision Making (ADM). It can reduce the time expenditure for screening processes and, on the other hand, provide more objectivity and, thus. less arbitrariness or even discrimination in the selection process.

It is possible to distinguish between static and dynamic self-learning algorithms. While a static algorithm constantly evaluates application documents according to the same criteria, a learning algorithm can also learn and develop, on experience. Thus, programming is not only about writing rules into algorithms, but dynamic algorithms are also about learning and applying new rules based on goals.

People can quickly lose track of large amounts of data, and due to limited cognitive processing capacity, it is often difficult for humans to recognize correlations and patterns in the data. Algorithms help generate decision proposals from large amounts of data, quickly.

Dynamic algorithms help analyze, link, and correlate vast quantities of data (big data) in no time, and they can support the fast recognition of patterns or legal requirements, establish correlations, and so on.

These dynamic algorithms represent a form of AI, since they are self-learning systems. By recognizing specific patterns in already evaluated data, they can fall back on these learned patterns in the future, without the need for additional human input. If, for example, the analysis of employee data reveals that other selection criteria than those previously used are required for successfully completing tasks, a dynamic algorithm can recognize this and change the requirement criteria, accordingly. In this way, a dynamic algorithm is a learning system.

While static algorithms are relatively easy to program and implement in practice, dynamic algorithms require vast amounts of high-quality training data. The quality of an AI system depends on the quality of this training data. And, they are mutually dependent: the data and the algorithms improve each other. When past decisions and, thus, used data are affected by prejudices and stereotypes related, for example, to gender, age, skin color, or ethnicity, there is great risk of making wrong or unfair decisions. For instance, in the United States, federal regulations state that a hiring tool can be biased, if it is job-related. Job-related could mean specific characteristics of successful employees. But if all successful employees are white men, then it is almost certain that a job-related hiring assessment will be biased in favor of white men and against women and minorities (Polli, 2019).

Indeed, if correlations between specific candidate characteristics and job performance are identified, they can be helpful for future predictions. Thus, such an approach seems legitimate and logical. If current job holders have specific characteristics (e.g., a certain age or a particular gender), the dynamic algorithm could derive that only applicants of a certain age or gender should be selected. Therefore, such discriminatory possibilities must be excluded, when programming the algorithm.

Thus, contrary to the assumption that an algorithm always processes data in an unbiased and exclusively rational fashion, it can generate biased decisions. Another example is an algorithm that may generate biased decisions if sensitive data are (deliberately) ignored and not captured by the IT system. For example, an algorithm can reduce discrimination by ignoring data that allow social categorization (e.g., gender, age, and ethnicity). Still, it cannot always avoid it, because discrimination can occur even if appropriately sensitive information, such as an applicant's ethnicity or gender, is not explicitly collected (Williams et al., 2018, p. 79; Silva & Kenney, 2018, p. 10). On the other hand, collecting and handling data that allow for social categorization can help make discrimination transparent and, thus, minimize it (Williams et al., 2018, p. 79).

Or, when automated text analysis methods are used, it is not always clear which data and algorithms are used for the analysis. Therefore, there is a risk that the training data used could reflect the biases of a specific society, organization, or even managers and, thus, have an undesirable discriminatory effect. The results of the system, then, can lead to an objectivity illusion.

Thus, rational-analytical personnel selection procedures and instruments, for example, based on standards such as the DIN 33430 or ISO 10667, or ethical principles, legal and diversity requirements should be integrated into the set of rules of an algorithm. In addition, successful heuristics, such as decision trees, can also be translated into algorithms. The data entered into the algorithm should be subject to qualified validation and evaluation.

Transparency of algorithms: Transparent, explainable, and understandable AI is a success factor and quality criterion for accepting selection procedures, namely, by applicants and the selection managers. Thus, recruiters and hiring managers should understand and comprehend from which data the algorithms learn and how they work, for example, in automated personality assessments in video interviews. Combining algorithmic literacy with transparency is, thus, necessary for acceptance (Osoba & Welser, 2017, pp. 23–24; Simbeck et al., 2019, p. 27).

Kuhn (2019) shows that the efficiency of heuristics can be improved by using human intuition. A significant problem is operationalizing the intuitions and feelings that arise during personnel selection and developing measurable indicators. If AI and algorithms try to integrate human intuition into rational heuristics and, then, into algorithms, the underlying indicators for intuition should be transparently shown and, at the same time, justified and explained.

The selection decisions based on algorithms should be made transparent by an evaluation. Feedback loops to self-learning systems are desirable, for example, due to the problem of "shortcut learning," that is, the propensity of an algorithm to seek desired results in the simplest possible way. In doing so, it may take undesirable shortcuts. Therefore, users of test data should not be lulled into a false sense of security (Geirhos et al., 2020; Schramowski et al., 2020). Thus, the quality of an algorithm should not only be evaluated by the results of a decision-making process, but always against the background of the quality of the data, especially when these data reflect indicators of intuitions and feelings.

8.3 Active sourcing and applicant tracking systems

Various procedures can already be used in personnel selection. These procedures range from so-called recommender systems, which automatically bring together applicants and vacancies (Weitzel et al., 2019, p. 13), to techniques that assist in the preselection of applicants, by comparing their skills with the requirements (Weitzel et al., 2019, pp. 13 and 17), to AI-based procedures such as machine learning, (chat-)bots, or video systems (Landers & Schmidt, 2016, p. 3; Weitzel et al. 2019, p. 23).

Specific digital technologies and AI help design and place job advertisements, support recruiting and employer branding, and are used in active sourcing, for example, in professional social networks and addressing fitting candidates, who cannot be reached by passive job advertisements in newspapers or other online job offers. In addition, based on requirement profiles or job descriptions, these digital applications bring together (potential) applicants and jobs with a high degree of matching requirements (Albert, 2019; Verhoeven, 2020, p. 121).

Software-based applicant tracking systems allow companies to track vast amounts of information, for example, cover letters, motivation letters, or resumes/CVs, for specific content such as keywords. If no matches are found, applications are sorted out. However, applicants can adapt their applications to the digital requirements quickly and, thus, improve their chances for the next application. Also, applicants (but also IT systems) learn that, often, it is enough to use phrases and specific keywords from the job advertisement to convince the computer to invite them for an interview.

This may result in inviting less suitable applicants. Here, it is essential to implement systems to avoid such errors, as far as possible. However, it often remains a matter of human competence to recognize, for example, in (telephone or video) interviews, that invited applicants do not have the necessary competencies to fill the position successfully.

8.4 Big data in personnel selection

In HR/People management, larger amounts of data can improve the accuracy of measurements in personnel selection processes and, thus, increase the quality of personnel selection decisions (McAfee & Brynjolfsson, 2012, p. 62; Guilfoyle et al., 2016, p. 128). AI can help better navigate these large amounts of data and the increasing complexity of decisions; a single person may not be able to regularly achieve this, due to limited cognitive capacity. However, it is a matter of processing more and more data, analyzing and weighing it, and ultimately extracting information from it, so that it can be used for decision-making.

Algorithms help analyze data of applicants found in social networks, application forms, or internal company documents such as competence profiles, performance data, appraisals, or completed training (Meißner & Nachtwei, 2017, p. 58). In addition, unstructured personal data such as blog posts, entries in chats, photos, or "likes" on social media can be collected and evaluated (Petry & Jäger, 2018, p.110). Kanning et al. (2019, p. 57) emphasize that data collected in an unstructured and subjective-intuitive way can be analyzed systematically, in this way.

AI can not only be trained with vast amounts of data, but it can also integrate them or apply them to new data, as in CV parsing.

Data-driven recruiting and selection is not only a question of available data. More critical is the quality of data, and hence, finding and assessing the correct and valuable data. Thus, there is a risk of using inaccurate or poor test and training data. In personnel selection, data should not be accepted uncritically. If HR managers want to make good decisions in recruiting and selection with data, they should start from the decision they need to make and then ask which data they need to make a good decision.

8.5 Digital analysis of written words

Specific innovations in AI deal with the analysis of written texts (e.g., choice of words and the structure of the language/sentences), the evaluation of the spoken language or voice of the applicant (Chamorro-Premuzic et al., 2016, p. 627; Fellner, 2019, p. 4). For example, the start-up "100 words" (100 Worte, 2019) analyzes written rather than spoken language and tries to create a personality profile. However, other companies claim that less than 150 words are enough to generate a valid personality profile, according to the Big Five theory or the DISC model and arrive at conclusions about an applicant's maturity level, using machine learning and psychological language processing. They assure to psychometrically analyze all relevant facets of human languages, such as word choice, semantics, speech patterns, syntax, and word contexts (Greple, 2021). This is somewhat reminiscent of the statement of some hiring managers who are very critical of rational-analytical selection procedures and are firmly convinced of their ability to assess applicants correctly, with the help of three questions or in thirty seconds.

Campion et al. (2016, p. 958) analyzed written language in success stories using natural language processing. Natural language processing is "an area of research and application that explores how computers can be used to understand and manipulate natural language text or speech to do useful things" (Chowdhury, 2003, p. 51).

In their study, Campion et al. (2016) asked participants to write success reports of 200 words. From reports describing past performance, conclusions about six defined competencies are drawn (Campion et al., 2016, p. 961). In addition, information on educational background, practical experience, and results of previous tests were included in the evaluation (Campion et al., 2016, p. 961). The reports and scoring of candidates were analyzed using natural language processing by a machine and by qualified and experienced recruiters (Campion et al., 2016, p. 961). In the study, the judgments generated by the machine were very similar to those of human judges. On average, the interrater reliability of the individual human judges attained $r=0.61$, very close to the value of the machine at $r=0.64$ (Campion et al., 2016, pp. 966 and 969). The construct validity of the computer-based scoring was also confirmed (Campion et al., 2016, p. 973). Neither the human evaluation nor the automated analysis disadvantaged people based on gender or origin (Campion et al., 2016, p. 973).

The authors uncovered limitations of the investigation regarding the data used (Campion et al., 2016, p. 974). A large amount of text-based data was available in the study, which provides an ideal database, especially for mechanical evaluation. However, it is doubtful that every company will have similar data sizes, when applying that procedure. Therefore, to provide information on the generalizability of the results, a similar study should be conducted in a different environment (Campion et al., 2016, p. 974). Furthermore, it must be considered that the preparation, especially the software training, requires a great deal of time, although the effort for such a study must always be classified as high (Campion et al., 2016, p. 974). Finally, this procedure might allow applicants, who would otherwise have been excluded by simple keyword queries, to remain in the selection process (Campion et al., 2016, pp. 973–974). All in all, the method can be a good option to preselect large numbers of applications, quickly and cost-effectively (Campion et al., 2016, p. 973).

8.6 Likes in social media and personality

Social media channels are used not only for recruiting and employer branding purposes or to advertise available vacancies; social media analysis also enables organizations to automatically compare job requirements and candidate profiles, such as personality (Guilfoyle et al., 2016, p. 138).

On the one hand, computer-assisted analysis allows conclusions about the personality traits of social media users and, on the other, statements about the accuracy of the results compared to human decision-makers. In various studies, Kosinski et al. use the digital traces of the test persons, more precisely Facebook likes, and relate them to personality traits (Kosinski et al., 2013, p. 5802). Kosinski et al. (2013, pp. 5802–5803) used distinguishing attributes of over 58,000 participants based on their likes, including gender (93% agreement), political orientation (85%), and sexual orientation (88%).

They show that individual traits and attributes, ranging from sexual orientation to intelligence, can be predicted to a high degree of accuracy based on records of users' likes. This also applies to some personality traits, such as openness. The results show that the evaluation of Facebook likes as digital footprints can identify "openness" (as one of the Big Five traits) as accurately as a personality test (Kosinski et al., 2013, p. 5804; Youyou et al., 2015).

Büttner also analyzed social media data. For this purpose, he took information about more than 700 part-time students from the XING platform. Using various algorithmic methods, he examined their predictive validity for the Big Five personality traits. The analysis yielded a predictive validity between $r = 0.31$ and $r = 0.46$ for personality traits (Büttner, 2016; Büttner, 2017, p. 25). This shows that data from the social media platform, XING, allows predictions about users' personalities (Büttner, 2017, p. 25). However, Büttner (2016) criticizes his research design, because the personality profiles were only measured based on the Ten Item Personality Inventory (TIPI). Further personality tests with a more differentiated approach should be included in future studies. Furthermore, considering data protection regulations, the used information could not be extracted directly from XING but by interviewing the participants, which Büttner also considers disadvantageous.

Youyou et al. (2015, pp. 1036 and 1039) compare the results of a personality assessment by close relatives of the test persons with an automated, computer-aided analysis of the corresponding Facebook Likes (the study aims to investigate the accuracy of the measurements concerning the current personality profile of the subjects) (Youyou et al., 2015, p. 1036). A correlation of $r = 0.56$ was found between the automated approach and the assessment of the subjects' personalities by their relatives. Furthermore, the correlation between self-disclosure and the assessment of relatives is $r = 0.49$. Likewise, the interrater reliability of the automated approach ($r = 0.62$) exceeds that of the human decision-makers ($r = 0.38$) (Youyou et al., 2015, p. 1038). The same applies to external validity (Youyou et al., 2015, p. 1039).

The results show that a computer-based assessment can more accurately evaluate a person's personality than humans (Youyou et al., 2015, p. 1039). However, according to the authors, limitations arise from the fact that here, too, only the personality traits of the Big Five model are included, and other personality traits are ignored.

> According to the Realistic Accuracy Model, the accuracy of the personality judgment depends on the availability and the amount of the relevant behavioral information, along with the judges' ability to detect and use it correctly . . . Such conceptualization reveals a couple of major advantages that computers have over humans. First, computers have the capacity to store a tremendous amount of information, which is difficult for humans to retain and access. Second, the way computers use information – through statistical modeling – generates consistent algorithms that optimize the judgmental accuracy, whereas humans are affected by various motivational biases. Nevertheless, human perceptions have the advantage of being flexible and able to capture many subconscious cues unavailable to machines. Because the Big Five personality traits only represent some aspects of human personality, human judgments might still be better at describing other traits that require subtle cognition or that are less evident in digital behavior. Our study is limited in that human judges could only describe the participants using a 10-item-long questionnaire on the Big Five traits. In reality, they might have more knowledge than what was assessed in the questionnaire (Youyou et al., 2015, p.1039).

The benefits of computer-based analysis and deducing personality traits based on social media data can represent a valuable approach for personnel selection (Youyou et al., 2015, p. 1039; Chamorro-Premuzic et al., 2016, p. 629). They represent a chance for personality assessment that is automated, accurate, and cost-effective (Youyou, 2015, p. 1039). The amount of personal information available on the Internet is increasing immensely. Due to further developments in technology and the increasing amount of data, it can be assumed that the significance of this information will increase (Youyou et al., 2015, p. 1039).

8.7 Online test in personnel selection

Digital technologies and AI offer the chance to implement online-based tests. Thus, companies conduct various psychometrically valid tests such as skill tests, knowledge tests, cognitive ability tests, integrity tests, personality tests, and so on. Also, AI helps conduct digital role-plays, case studies, or interactive and multimedia task designs. This increases the simulation capability and, thus, the mapping of tasks (Fellner, 2019, p. 17).

If valid cutoff scores are available in the company, for example, these tests can be used for personnel preselection. Science-based tests used for preselection increase the validity of the selection process and, thus, the probability of inviting only candidates who fit the preselection job requirements to the interview. At the same time, time and costs can be saved, as fewer applicants must be invited to interviews, and selection managers, thus, gain more time for other tasks, such as personal interviews with the shortlisted candidates. In addition, companies can use the results of personality tests to generate specific questions for the interview guideline and/or to reflect on the results, with the candidates in these job interviews.

However, when using test procedures, hiring managers should know which occupational group, country, and so on, a test was designed for, as different competencies or personality traits may be the focus (Danks & London, 2017, p. 4694).

One of the main reasons for the skepticism surrounding AI-based personality tests is that, from a scientific perspective, there are no clear correlations between personality traits and performance on the job. Although some studies show a (moderate) correlation between the personality traits conscientiousness and emotional stability and performance, especially in highly complex jobs (Le et al., 2011), concrete personality test results for personnel selection must be reflected on, critically. As mentioned in other parts of this book, using the results of a personality test as a basis for reflection in interviews can be recommended.

Gamification and recruitainment are also examples of online tests. Using the example of consumer goods manufacturer, Unilever, Feloni (2017; see also Gärtner, 2020) describes a procedure where applicants first have to upload their LinkedIn profile to participate in up to 12 online games, which are then evaluated. Next, the AI-based software compares the results of these computer game players (applicants) obtained with successful employees. Finally, applicants with scores comparable to scores of successful employees are invited to the further selection procedure, for example, a video interview. Research by Gkorezis et al. (2020; see also Nikolaou, 2021) shows that the gamified method has a positive effect on organizational attractiveness, which, in turn, positively predicts recommendation intentions, but only for those who have a high level of video gaming experience (Potočnik, 2021, p. 170).

The company HireVue uses software that analyzes keywords, word choice, intonation, body language, facial expressions, and gestures (Black & van Esch, 2020, p. 7; Feloni, 2017). If candidates also pass this video analysis, they are invited to an on-site applicant day, after which a final decision is made (Feloni, 2017). Unilever sees a positive result from the changeover to this process. According to the company, an increase in diversity in hiring was observed. In addition, the company recorded a doubling of the number of applications received and, at the same time, a reduction in the time-to-hire ratio (time to fill a position) from four months to four weeks. This is primarily due to efficiency improvements. Recruiters spend 75% less time screening resumes and have cumulatively saved 100,000 interview hours globally, since implementation (Feloni, 2017; Gärtner, 2020, p. 76). According to internal data, the organization has cut recruiting costs by $1 million through streamlining (Booth, 2019). A specially conducted survey of 25,000 applicants shows a high level of satisfaction in the process (Gärtner, 2020, p. 76). According to internal evaluations, the acceptance rate of contract offers increased from 64% to 82% (Feloni, 2017).

8.8 Digitally based video or telephone interviews

8.8.1 Analysis of video interviews

For selection purposes in practice, it is possible to record face-to-face interviews or use video interviews. These are either time-shifted or asynchronous, one-way video interviews, where selection managers can put predetermined questions and tasks to candidates, who can answer and solve these on video, without being tied to a specific time and place. Another possibility is conducting a recorded or nonrecorded online interview (synchronous or live interview), for example via telecommunication and video applications such as Skype, WebEx, Teams, or ZOOM, to assess the candidate, including analyzing the facial expression, emotions, authenticity, personality, and so on.

Due to technological improvements and encouraged by the Covid-19 crisis in 2020–2022, selection video interviews have become more popular.

In the case of time-shifted interviews, applicants receive a link. The candidate has a prescribed amount of time to answer standardized questions on various topics. Depending on the company, the time allowed and the number of questions to be answered varies; there are programs where three questions have to be answered within 45 s, and others require recordings that take 30–45 min (Barsch & Trachsel, 2018, p. 83).

Asynchronous videos offer several advantages, such as cost and time savings due to reduced scheduling, global interviewing, and travel, since applicants do not have to be at the interview site. Further advantages are standardization, lower interviewer influences on candidates, and the possibility to replay and review the recording, instead of relying on memory and/or notes. But, where there is light, there must be shadow, and where there is shadow, there must be light. As a result, there is lower information richness due to the inability to ask questions or give feedback and lower media richness through the candidates' limited visibility. In addition, inaccurate conclusions may be drawn due to technical problems or visual cues, such as the design of the visible background (the applicant's home/personal living spaces), and performance in the interview can be compromised by unfamiliarity with technology or a specific selection tool. Also, the lack of personal interaction can lead to relatively low acceptance and skepticism among applicants and hiring managers (Hendrix, 2021, p. 4).

Both forms of interviews can be evaluated by humans or by AI. Video analyzing software or humans can, for instance, evaluate applicants for call centers. Based on data that, for example, successful job holders make frequent eye contact, use specific words and words with more emotional impact, act less fidgety, and show (in Western cultures) positive emotions, for example, through facial expressions, attention is paid to appropriate signals when evaluating an applicant's behavior in the video (Stulle & Thiel, 2018).

Synchronous or live online video interviews are conducted by an interviewer and are designed – as far as possible – like a regular face-to-face interview. However, if the interview is recorded, AI can analyze the candidate. For example, Suen et al. (2020; see also Suen et al., 2019) show that the automated assessment of a candidate's personality based on facial expressions and movements and audio cues in asynchronous video interviews can accurately predict the personality as perceived by experienced observers (Chen et al., 2017). For this purpose, it usually requires many already classified patterns created from (other) video analyses. The evidence base for AI-based video analyses, for example, validity, should be proven (Woods et al., 2020).

The validity of personality judgments can increase if – besides evaluating verbal communication systematically – a structured analysis of visual cues, either by the selection manager alone or with the help of algorithms or other AI support, is included. Judgments, thus, improve when human and computer-based assessments are conducted complementarily (Hendrix, 2021, p. 38). However, for hiring managers, it's often a matter of time and resources, whether they'll watch the video again. Usually, they rely on their impressions during the synchronous interview. Also, an analysis of the applicant performed by AI provides additional information about the candidate.

8.8.2 Analysis of voice

The idea that people's personalities and character could be analyzed via language and that, for example, the Big Five personality traits could be diagnosed via characteristics of the human voice and used words, goes back to the sedimentation or lexical hypothesis, first investigated by Francis Galton in 1884; his approach assumes that differences in characteristics are represented in words used in a society (Fellner, 2019a, p. 4).

Today, such analysis can be conducted via a telephone interview, in which applicants answer standardized questions on various topics (Schaumlöffel et al., 2018, p. 62). To enable a linguistic evaluation, software providers proceed in different ways. Sometimes, the content of what is said is not considered in the assessment. Instead, the speed of speech, the structure of the sentences, the grammar, and the words used are examined closely (Schweizer, 2017, p. 38). In that case, an analysis of the content of the statements is intentionally avoided, because the speaker can easily and consciously control the content.

In such an evaluation, the focus is on the structural analysis of the words used, breaking them down into their parts (Schaumlöffel et al., 2018, pp. 9 and 62–63) and investigating them to uncover linguistic and acoustic peculiarities, with the help of a mechanical procedure (Linnenbürger et al., 2018, p. 23). Other techniques focus on the linguistic content of the applicants' speech (Schossau et al., 2019, p. 30). Finally, the fully automated execution of these methods is carried out to assess the applicant's personality.

Other companies develop speech recognition software to analyze the personality, to evaluate spoken words and expressions, language breaks, and so on. Currently, popular examples of the practice in German-speaking countries are PRECIRE or JobFit (Schaumlöffel et al., 2018; Schmidt-Atzert et al., 2019). Based on language analysis, characteristics, personality traits, or the professional fit of applicants are assessed (Linnenbürger et al., 2018; Bärschneider, 2019). A specific feature of such software is that no questionnaires must be filled out in writing, since the focus is on recording and assessing spoken words (Verhoeven, 2020, pp. 122–124). After checking the application, a potentially suitable candidate gets a phone number and pin code that can be used to submit a language sample. During this automated call, applicants are asked questions to elicit language examples. When enough language examples have been collected, the call is terminated. The software then analyzes the sample and compares the result with a representative comparison group. In addition, a voice check can be performed to test stress and workload capability, or learning areas can be identified.

The analysis of speech or voice is currently also used to assess employee satisfaction in an organization, because the way people speak can tell something about their job happiness and their performance (Marr, 2018, p. 78).

Research in AI-assisted analysis of human speech continues to progress very rapidly. For example, research results have identified a connection between speaking and diseases. Software offered by the company audEERING (2021), for instance, offers algorithm-based software that claims to be able to detect a speaker's level of emotional excitement and to identify over fifty emotional states via analyzing audio data beyond the content of spoken words, for example, vocal timbre, intonation, speech rhythm or pitch, as well as to diagnose health symptoms at an early stage (Köhn, 2021, p. 26).

Example: An applicant converses by phone or video call for about 15 min with a computer voice (bot) and answers questions that have nothing to do with actual job requirements: “What did you do last Sunday?” can be one of them. The responses are recorded and then evaluated by AI-based software. The AI deduces personality traits by analyzing the choice of words, voice pitch, volume, and other language components. In the end, the test persons can read six single-spaced pages, detailing whether they are rather optimistic or pessimistic, neat or chaotic, and so on.

According to Schimansky-Geier (2017, p. 48), such procedures allow filling vacancies, based on objective requirements. Unlike a questionnaire, where people give information about themselves, the software provides more objective results. The result is more objective than what psychologists can measure, because people can hardly consciously control their speech as soon as they speak for more than a few minutes (Hummel, 2015).

Characteristics such as the gender or age of applicants are disregarded by the system, so that subjective distortions of judgment by a human decision-maker are prevented. Thus, selection can be carried out more fairly, and broader diversity can be achieved (Schossau et al., 2019, p. 30).

Although the first software for speech and voice analysis software is already in use, and there is a large branch of research in personnel diagnostics, there is a lack of scientifically valid, evidence-based research on this subject (Fellner, 2019a, p. 4).

8.8.3 Selection support by chatbots or messenger systems

Several companies have implemented the use of chatbots (chat robots or bots). However, non-self-learning chatbots are programmed to respond to specific keywords with a predefined action or response. The risk of such a bot misinterpreting human questions is, accordingly, high. On the other hand, an AI-controlled chatbot can learn to understand the context of the questioner and, by analyzing the reactions of questioners, also recognize their emotions and take corresponding action (Petry & Jäger, 2018, p. 47).

Especially by imitating human speech (and partly emotions), they are used to handle initial contact and arrange appointments with candidates, answer simple and frequently asked questions from applicants, for example, about earnings, hiring requirements, or application procedures.

Research shows that bots can answer about 75% of candidates’ questions. The 25% that remains are often questions that require individual advice (Albert, 2019, p. 218), and the bot forwards these inquiries to the appropriate HR employees. Some chatbots even offer applicants individual tips, such as which job advertisements might be attractive.

Further developments of bots allow for conducting preselection interviews or the so-called prescripted interviews. In this case, all applicants are asked standardized questions, but they do not have the opportunity to ask anything themselves. Both HR managers and applicants repeatedly complain about the lack of interaction, here. It leads to a feeling of lack of appreciation, but this can nevertheless be a first opportunity to make contact at the beginning of a selection process.

At the same time, these systems are constantly improving through self-learning, so that both sides can ask and answer questions individually. A practical example is IBM Watson Candidate Assistant, where applicants have the opportunity to engage with an AI-based chatbot to share information on interests, skills, and potential job fit. The tool analyzes resumes and recommends jobs suited to the applicants' skills and goals. The job seeker can talk with Watson, ask questions, and find out about employment opportunities (IBM, 2017).

Likewise, work is being done on topics of automated communication via messenger systems such as e-mail, WhatsApp, or Signal, which are increasingly individualized and personally tailored to the applicant. In addition, both chatbots and other communication systems are accessible from anywhere in the world (without the applicant needing any special software), are not limited to typical business hours and, can communicate 24 h a day, and can usually answer an unlimited number of queries at the same time (without, as with humans, possibly getting stressed or sick) (Verhoeven, 2020, pp. 106–107; Pasenau, 2021, pp. 65–66).

Chatbots and other digital technologies can have a filtering function by only suggesting jobs to interested parties based on essential criteria such as existing skills and work experience, work location, or working hours, enabling a preselection for applicants.

8.9 AI as an intuitive and emotional system

AI aims to operationalize human intelligence and make it available through IT systems. Human intelligence can be understood as recognizing, making judgments, grasping possibilities, comprehending contexts, and gaining insights (Görz & Wachsmuth, 2003, pp. 1–2). Therefore, AI aims to map not only conscious cognitive abilities but also intuitive and emotional ones.

Intuitions and emotions are human capacities for holistic, associative, and nonlinear thinking. Intuition helps people get inspiration and solve problems in complex and unknown situations. For many years, researchers have advocated a clear division of labor between managers and machines: computers should do what computers could do best – to calculate and process data according to formal logic – while managers should stick to what humans do best, namely to perceive information holistically, seek patterns in data, or in intuitive and emotional impulses. Nowadays, AI research focuses intensely on developing systems and robots that exhibit human intuitions and emotions. In addition, robots with the capacity for emotional expression could be beneficial, because no human being can live without emotional attention.

Dolls that can speak for children, cuddly animals for older people in nursing homes, and social robots in public life or at home or intimate partners such as sex or love dolls that express specific emotions and empathy are just at the beginning of their development. These humanoid machines learn not only to look like humans but also to move like humans, communicate with, and like humans, learn from them, read and understand their emotions, and show specific forms of emotions themselves. For example, in the field of eldercare, Prescott & Caleb-Solly (2017, p. 22) predict that "AI personal assistants and social robots may be able to provide a form of synthetic companionship that people may find engaging, but this will never replace human companionship." Thus, whether these products can replace humans' feelings of closeness and warmth can be questioned, but they are increasingly used.

In this field of AI, the researchers are often not primarily interested in these robots showing real human emotions but rather in what they can do for human beings. For example, robots should convey the feeling of being empathetic by laughing along, rejoicing, looking curiously, mourning, touching, or simply listening, when appropriate. Advancements in Social Signal Interpretation (SSI) help robots recognize and interpret interpersonal interactions' emotional and social dimensions. Such applications can be used in personnel selection and for therapeutic and medical applications (see, e.g., the research and publications of Elisabeth Andre; e.g., Schiller et al., 2020a and 2020b).

It is becoming apparent that whatever is technically feasible and for which there is a market (e.g., sex dolls) will be produced, despite all sorts of ethical debates.

It is essential to wait for further developments and see to what extent such systems, also as humanoid hiring managers (e.g., avatars), can show appropriate intuitions and emotions to job applicants and, thus, shape their behavior.

However, whether machines controlled by AI can think and feel like human beings do, for example, in a holistic and associative way, or can simulate and replicate intuitions and emotions in unconsciously stored experiences can be critically questioned from today's perspective. Currently, AI systems are still far from feeling and showing intuitions and emotions as humans do. And, if possible, which intuitive and emotional capacities could and should be outsourced to machines or which of these remain uniquely human capacities (Lussier, 2018)?

8.10 AI and candidate experience

Since personnel selection aims to acquire and win the best-suited people for an organization, it is essential to consider the applicant's perspective and how AI affects the candidate's experience. Thus, the applicant's perspective on AI in recruiting and selection processes must be discussed more thoroughly.

Employee reactions to technology have become an important research topic in recruiting and selection. For example, Nikolaou (2021) explores new recruiting and selection technologies. He discusses the impact of cybervetting and applicant tracking systems, asynchronous digital interviews, and gamification/games-based assessment on candidates. Also, Langer et al. (2017, 2018, 2019), Wang et al. (2020), or Woods et al. (2020) reviewed applicants' reactions toward digital and internet-based selection methods. For example, a study by Langer et al. (2017) shows no difference in organizational attractiveness levels, but further studies (2018, 2019) state that candidates considered digital interviews less personal, reporting increased privacy concerns. Gamification can be a reliable and valid selection method raising positive reactions among candidates and increasing organizational attractiveness; gamification can promote fun, interaction, and challenge, especially among younger candidates.

Research by Proost et al. (2020) states that reactions to video interviews show that applicants fear having fewer opportunities to show their potential and use their nonverbal behaviors, compared to in-person interviews. Thus, in digital interviews, especially the lack of personal and face-to-face interaction with the interviewer, and the candidates' perception of being unable to influence the outcome of the interview process, maybe a significant drawback of digital interviews, and it will be difficult to change this in the future, despite the apparent advantages they offer (Nikolaou, 2021, pp. 3–4).

A more time-efficient selection of personnel can positively affect the satisfaction of applicants, as they receive feedback on their applications and a decision, more quickly. In addition, an application can be submitted, regardless of time and place. This can be a strategic advantage in the competition for suitable candidates. In addition, applicants may feel they are treated more fairly, as objectivity increases by eliminating bias, stereotypes, and so on, because AI treats all applicants equally, regardless of the individual selection manager.

In addition, chatbots, video, and other AI-based conversations conducted independently of time and location can increase candidates' perception of control. As a result, the selection process can be perceived as more individual, user-friendly, and less time-consuming. Research shows that younger applicants, in particular, are interested in self-determination and want to influence the selection process actively. In addition, digital and AI technologies are considered innovative and modern (Black & van Esch, 2020, p. 7; Hamilton & Davison, 2018, p. 417).

AI allows recruiters to perform routine tasks using machines and focuses on process quality and relationship building with shortlisted candidates (Albert, 2019, p. 217; Lochner & Preuß, 2018, p. 199). Thus, opportunities for appreciation and individuality conducive to a positive candidate experience are seen. However, it must be noted that a more intensive relationship-building only occurs. later in the process. with shortlisted candidates and. thus. not with all applicants. equally.

Thus, the candidate experience can be optimized but also degraded through AI's use. For example, Knobloch & Hustedt (2019, p. 18) speak of dehumanizing the selection process due to the lack of personal relationship building, making it challenging to create trust. In addition, the AI-driven process could be perceived as a black box lacking transparency due to the independent learning of the software and an unclear decision-making process (Fesefeld, 2018, p. 26).

Based on Gilliland's model (1993; see for details Sections 3.2.5.1 and 3.7.9), Dineen et al. (2004, p. 138) examined applicants' perception of fairness in the selection process, depending on whether an algorithm or human experts made the decision. Five criteria of organizational justice were examined (type of decision-maker; availability of information; consistency; possibility to provide feedback; the speed of feedback) to assess the perceived fairness of a computer-based recruiting system. The most significant factor was consistency ($r = 0.45$), followed by the provision of information ($r = 0.27$). However, suppose the selection criteria in an algorithmic assessment are not transparent, applicants experience these evaluations critically, because they cannot identify the assessed requirements and are, thus, not able to adapt their behaviors to requirements (Rahman, 2021).

Overall, participants considered humans more fairly in procedural terms than automated decision-makers. The procedural justice model helps explain this (Lind & Tyler 1988). This model states that fair treatment signals the inclusion or confirmation of group members. Thus, applicants may associate feelings of inclusion or confirmation more with the fairness shown by human recruiters, while automated personnel selection systems are usually unable to communicate these types of signals (Dineen et al., 2004, p. 139).

Although it has been shown that AI can lead to less discrimination regarding personnel selection decisions, human experts are perceived more positively than their digital equivalents. Even if digital systems can better predict a candidate's suitability (Dahm & Dregger, 2019, p. 252; Fortmann & Kolocek, 2018, p. 163), personal contact is expected, especially at management levels (Fellner, 2019, p. 12). Candidates value subjective control and the feeling of influencing the selection results with their behavior, which is possible through personal contact (Fellner, 2019, p. 13).

Applying Davis' (1989) Technology Acceptance Model (TAM) to using AI in personnel selection, research shows that general trust, a willingness to innovate, or even the familiarity with a specific technology promote the acceptance of new technologies; at the same time, perceived risks such as a lack of transparency or privacy concerns reduce acceptance (Lancelot Miltgen et al., 2013, pp. 103 and 110; Black & van Esch, 2020).

On the other hand, younger generations, or digital natives, evaluate the use of AI differently than older applicants or senior managers.

Besides trust in technology and computer playfulness, Dahm & Degger (2019, p. 264) identified five measures that promote the acceptance of AI in personnel selection in Germany (percentage of respondents want):

1. Human contact person (70.6)
2. Detailed explanation of how the system used works (70.2%)
3. Applicants themselves decide which data is made available and stored (63.9%)
4. Detailed explanation of the advantages of the system by the company (50.5%)
5. Shortening of the application process (49.5%)

A further problem is that computer-based systems today are not (yet) capable of capturing moods (Fellner, 2019, p. 12).

Thus, despite the advantages of digitally supported selection procedures, personnel selection procedures carried out and accompanied by people are perceived more positively, by applicants. One of the reasons for this is that machines cannot – although algorithms and robots can reproduce some aspects of human social interaction and despite all the progress made in the development of humanoid robots – replace genuine interpersonal human feelings and recognition of natural human emotions (Frey & Osborne, 2013, p. 26).

In addition, it is questionable whether the current generation of hiring managers will accept these technologies, fearing that the human-empathetic approach to recruiting will fall victim to digital opportunities. However, the possibility of authentically representing human emotions or even responding to the emotional state of applicants using AI tools is seen very critically. Digital technologies cannot recognize the person-organization-fit by intuitive feeling. Thus, human interaction, especially in final selection decisions, particularly interviews, remains critical during a selection process.

To promote a positive candidate experience, companies look at how digitally supported selection procedures meet with applicants' acceptance. However, several interviewed managers argue that the use of language analysis software or the creation of personality profiles based on social media data may deter many applicants: "In the end, it has an impact on the image of our company . . . . That's why I would never rely only on such tools because it could lead to certain people not applying for a job in our company" (Flörke, 2020, p. 60).

While the hard facts in a selection process can be evaluated much faster with the help of AI, as soon as the soft factors, such as the cultural fit between candidate and company or the team fit, are involved, the human element is essential (Mülder, 2018, p. 112). As early as 1976, Schmitt and Coyle (1976, p. 190) showed that personal contact is crucial for candidates and significantly influences their choice of organization. Nothing has changed so far and will probably not change soon.

Although there is currently a lack of valid research on the topic of AI and candidate experience conducted by independent researchers, in summary, critical for the acceptance and, thus, a positive candidate experience with AI are:

1. Trust in the technology: This trust is supported by transparency and comprehensibility concerning the intention of using this AI tool and the process flow, easy comprehensibility and simple operation of the tool, openness of the evaluation

criteria and the decision-making process, and compliance with data protection and ethical standards.
2. A human contact person is available during the recruiting and selection process and should make the final decision.
3. It is essential to clarify the added value, benefits, and goals of using AI-based tools at the beginning of the selection process, such as high speed, more objectivity, fairness, and less discrimination, ensuring high-quality personnel selection.

And to get detailed and constructive feedback is essential for the acceptance of digital selection procedures.

4. Most important: A human being should make the final selection decision based on personal contact, especially in an interview. In addition, applicants want to know how they performed in an interview or specific exercises and their individual scores.

8.11 Limitations of digital and AI-based selection procedures

8.11.1 Data from the past

A problem with using AI or algorithms in management and personnel selection is the quantity and quality of the underlying data. With increasing data quantity and higher data quality, the algorithm's results improve (Tambe et al., 2019, pp. 10–16; Knobloch & Hustedt, 2019, p. 15).

In many organizations, especially SMEs, there is no usable digital data for defining successful employees, or according to which criteria the attribute "successful" can be determined, AI-supported data-driven decisions are based on data that usually reflects the past. Thus, data from the past is subject to the risk of recommending the past, repeatedly, for the future. In this self-reference learning and self-replicating way, algorithms possibly create a future with the past image. However, it is questionable whether the past success principles will also apply to the future because of rapid environmental changes (Klopprogge et al., 2019, p. 208; Klopprogge, 2022, p. 92).

In order to derive a reliable projection for the future, the past-related data would have to be typical for the present and the future. However, this may not be the case. As a result, there is the risk that the algorithm will automatically perpetuate the past and past mistakes, for example, a lack of diversity – in the future.

Suppose the requirements for new employees correspond to the suitability profile of those who were successful in the past, the success principles of the past have a normative character. In this way, the existing practice is repeated in an endless loop, and the "chance of something new, unknown, or disturbing is smothered in the conservative slime of self-referenced entropy" (Klopprogge, 2022, p. 85). Therefore, organizations' ability to change will be jeopardized, if attempts are made to predetermine and clearly define all required criteria for personnel selection by past data.

An algorithm based on past data presents an ethical and business problem, because it may lead to suboptimal selection decisions and not necessarily a desirable future (Diercks, 2021).

Despite all the advances in data analysis, pattern recognition, natural language understanding, and so on, another big problem of AI is still to capture a very complex world to grasp and describe completely what is very fuzzy, contradictory, ambiguous, and constantly changing. Hence, it is about building systems that navigate the hard-to-model real world and learn to make decisions directly, on rich sensor data.

An algorithm is only as good as the data used. Therefore, one of the critical challenges in implementing AI is to provide a large amount of high-quality training data.

An algorithm should not only learn from the past but also be "fed" with data that are particularly important for the future and reflect requirements for future challenges and tasks. This is critical in a rapidly changing world and changes employee requirements.

8.11.2 Huge amount of data and organizational resources

Self-learning systems such as dynamic algorithms must be filled with training data. However, since the quantity of data is constantly growing due to the explosion of machine-generated data and human involvement in social networks, it is questionable which of these data are relevant for personnel selection, to what extent companies have access to this data, or whether they have the resources to generate such data. Large companies have an advantage because they regularly have the resources to use or develop these data; and they process large numbers of applications for specific positions that must be filled repeatedly. Therefore, the development and use of appropriate algorithms are more worthwhile for such companies than SMEs. But, SMEs can be supported by employer associations, consulting companies, or informal cooperation between SMEs to develop appropriate algorithms.

8.11.3 Static algorithms

A deterministic algorithm proceeds according to a predetermined pattern from which it does not deviate, and it does not learn independently. The use of such a tool carries the risk that applicants with atypical CVs but who are certainly interesting for a company (e.g., lateral or "out of the box" thinkers, "colorful applicants") will be sorted out by the algorithm and rejected. The use of algorithms can favor standard profiles and lead to unintentional homogenization of the workforce.

A hiring manager interviewed in our empirical research stated that preprogrammed algorithms could potentially reject highly interesting applicants who fall through the traditional selection grid, because they do not meet the preselection criteria.

> Well, if decisions are only made according to previously defined criteria and programmed algorithms, there is a risk of losing flexibility. Moreover, if one does not also and especially rely on the recruiter as a human being, certain personalities will no longer have a chance to join the company (Flörke, 2020, p. 63).

It is vital that a diverse team of personnel managers, executives, and others should be assembled to discuss and develop criteria for programming the algorithm.

In practice, it is often found in selection procedures that applicants are not eligible for the position to be filled but for other positions. However, if the algorithm rejects such candidates, they are no longer available to the company. Unlike human recruiters, algorithms do not completely view other advertised positions or those that may need to be filled soon.

8.11.4 Biased data

Although algorithms and other digitally supported procedures for personnel selection contribute to greater objectivity, the involvement of humans in programming can lead to the inclusion of personal views, values, and other things, and, thus, to the transfer of stereotypes, prejudices, and other unconscious biases to the algorithm (Petry & Jäger, 2018, p. 112). Thus, training data of the algorithm can be based on information that may not be objective and, therefore, automatically reproduce existing distortions, biases, or even discriminations. "Discriminatory patterns can be reproduced, scaled, and social inequality can be reinforced by all algorithmic systems" (Knobloch & Hustedt, 2019, p. 13).

Flörke (2020, p. 33) notes that independently of the influence of the programmer (Brynjolfsson & McAfee, 2017, p. 16), the algorithm itself can recognize patterns that are anchored in a specific context or society (Langer et al., 2018, p. 35). For example, an algorithm can be based on past decisions, and, therefore, persons who are less strongly represented in the data, possibly members of ethnic minorities, could be overlooked, in future evaluations (Liem et al., 2018, p. 198). The question is: has the machine made an assessment based on a meaningful and also ethically and legally correct correlation of data or based on wrong or impermissible correlations? The more autonomously the system learns and develops new algorithms, the fewer the possibilities for intervention (Diercks, 2021).

An algorithm may be discriminatory by using information such as age, gender, or origin (Buxmann & Schmidt, 2019, p. 16; Stachl & Bühner, 2018, pp. 25–26). Companies could suffer legal consequences if such cases occur and become known (Stachl & Bühner, 2018, p. 26).

Telephone or video interviews, for example, in which the speaking habits of applicants are compared with sample databases, can have discriminatory consequences. Eliminating candidates with a speech impediment or accent or giving them a poor evaluation because the program or the microphone cannot classify speech correctly can mean discrimination based on disability, ethnic origin, gender, or background.

Video and speech analytics by AI can be affected by several factors. The results of speech analysis, in particular, are highly dependent on the task and the situation. For example, the sitting posture of a candidate, a cold, or too much alcohol the night before can lead to a distortion of voice pitch. In addition, nervousness in selection situations can influence the pitch of the voice, the choice of words, or even the speed of speech. Such influencing factors must be considered, particularly against evaluating the reliability of AI-supported selection procedures.

There may also be significant correlations between language characteristics and various personality traits. However, the question is how strong these correlations are. An exclusive (internal) validation of language-analytical procedures by calculating correlations with established personality tests is of only limited value. Even in the case of external validation, in which the language characteristics of applicants are compared with the language characteristics of particularly successful job holders (reference group), it must be critically questioned whether the recorded (language) characteristics of the successful employees are related to their performance. It would have to be demonstrated, beforehand, that language characteristics are directly related to success in a specific job (Schwertfeger, 2015, pp. 33–34). For example, Siegert and Niebuhr (2021) show that during the Covid-19 pandemic in 2020, video conferencing systems have thinned out frequencies of high female voices to save data volume. This could lead to discrimination against women because these female voices were perceived as less expressive, competent, or charismatic.

What data an algorithm is fed with and how it is programmed depends on the respective company and its goals. The nondiscriminatory use of AI is essential; an algorithm must be trained with unbiased, nondiscriminatory data sets, and programming codes and result interpretations should not reproduce possible discrimination. Furthermore, from a legal and ethical point of view, programming must ensure that discrimination based on age, gender, religion, or ethnic origin is avoided. Thus, even if a dynamic algorithm recognizes patterns, for example, that certain positions have only been filled with people of a specific sex or age, it must not select only applicants who correspond to this recognized pattern in terms of age or sex. Therefore, discriminatory criteria such as gender or age should be kept out of the training data. For this reason, the training data should be evaluated and – if necessary – adjusted regularly by diverse and independent teams.

In order to ensure high-quality personnel selection, algorithms should be checked for compliance with scientific quality criteria such as objectivity and reliability.

8.11.5 Limits of (verbal and nonverbal) language analysis

Despite the chances of AI-based language analysis, some scientists have concerns about such methods. There is not yet sufficient research-based evidence of the predictive power of the analysis of personality traits (Schwertfeger, 2015, p. 33). More research is needed to investigate how accurately and validly, automated AI-based video or speech-based assessments can capture a candidate's personality and/or competencies and predict performance on the job to be filled.

Standardized (or semi-structured) job interviews and an automated evaluation of the collected data offer the opportunity to improve the selection process. However, only vague statements concerning reliability or validity can be made, since precise information on the methods used in practice is only available to the public and researchers, to a limited extent. Also, usually, the algorithm is also not transparent to applicants (Buxmann & Schmidt, 2019, p. 16; Stachl & Bühner, 2018, p. 25). Therefore, scientific quality criteria are only partially fulfilled. As long as companies developing and selling AI tools do not subject their data to independent testing, validity statements should be treated critically (Schmidt-Atzert et al., 2019, pp. 19–20). Methods of language analysis can offer advantages, especially concerning objectivity and increased efficiency (Flörke, 2020, pp. 29–32), as shown, for example, in the studies by Campion et al. (2016) or Suen et al. (2019, 2020). On the other hand, scientifically based research is required to make an all-encompassing evaluation of such software.

Practitioners report of recognizing emotions in faces of applicants and using them to form their judgments. However, perceptions and analysis of gestures, facial expressions, voice, and emotions are usually subjective and unstructured. This is where AI and corresponding software-based tools can assist. Research on affective computing is engaged in attempts to detect and measure people's emotions accurately and build AI systems that can recognize and appropriately respond to these emotions.

In AI, there are increasing efforts to develop systems that perceive and accurately assess emotions in other people. This type of special AI-based software claims to be better than humans at recognizing verbal and nonverbal behaviors, including emotions in other humans.

Researchers analyze facial expressions using AI trained on images of faces and develop an algorithm. Using these algorithms, they try to determine the intensity of facial expressions and type of emotion. A research group from the Max Planck Institute of Neurobiology reports in the journal, *Science*, that they have already succeeded in analyzing and developing algorithms for analyzing facial expressions in mice. Particular stimuli, such as drinking water containing sugar or salt, triggered different reactions. Using their algorithms, they could determine the intensity and type of feeling in the facial expressions of the animals, in a fraction of a second. In parallel, the relevant neurons could be identified with two-photon microscopes. In the view of researchers, a significant advantage of discovering mouse mimicry is the possibility of understanding the processes in the brain behind emotions. Unfortunately, this is precisely where the problem has been up to now: without a reliable measurement of emotions, it has hardly been possible to investigate their development in the brain (Dolensek et al., 2020).

Thus, AI-based facial recognition software and software designed to recognize various emotions such as disgust, surprise, anger, joy, sadness, or even fear are constantly being improved (Desoi, 2018, p. 24). Video analysis by face-reading occurs during the interrogation of suspects by the police, during security checks at the airport, and in market research. In addition, the software is used to identify micro expressions that indicate, for example, whether suspects are lying or not (AI as a lie detector). However, these facial and emotion recognition methods are still in their infancy.

Such AI technologies can also be used in personnel selection. As a result, specialist companies see the enormous market potential in this area and promise employers great success in selecting suitable job candidates.

On the other hand, people who know that they are being observed and their emotions analyzed by an AI system may behave differently than when talking to a real person. In addition, the question arises as to what extent applicants experience interaction with a machine as "natural" and authentic.

However, using AI to analyze facial expressions, the tone of voice, and so on to predict certain personality traits accurately can be a helpful tool in selection. On the other hand, skepticism is called for, if AI analyzes body language, clothing, or whether someone wears glasses and pretends to derive personality analyses from this data. However, suppose the results of personality analyses vary depending on whether someone wears glasses, how the visual background of the video is designed, or what clothes someone is wearing, then, there is still considerable potential for improvement in AI development.

Therefore, most of the selection managers surveyed in our empirical research are firmly convinced that correctly perceiving and evaluating applicants' verbal and nonverbal expressions remain one of their core competencies as human beings.

8.11.6 AI and lack of "human eye" and intuition

Practitioners interviewed in our empirical research also point out that the algorithm lacks the human eye for detail and intuition and cannot recognize or depict emotions. The subjective-emotional experiential content of a mental state or a particular human perception is linked to emotionally charged experiences connected to other individual concepts, memories, and experiences. Also, currently, there are limitations to AI being able to replicate that. For example, recruiters often have many years of experience, which allows them to read between the lines and distinguish nuances in application documents and behaviors. However, from the perspective of hiring managers interviewed, these subtleties, or the authenticity and the overall impression, can only be recognized to a limited extent by an algorithm or AI.

HR professionals want to demonstrate their competencies in assessing these human characteristics. Also, they resist thinking and feeling like a machine. Kloprogge et al. (2019, pp. 224–227) even call digital personnel selection inhumane, because it wants to take away from selection managers and treat as a disruptive factor, what human beings are particularly good at and what creates the competitive advantages of companies, in the first place. It's about the human factor in personnel selection and, thus, about deciding which people you want to work with, who you experience as authentic and credible, and, ultimately, who you trust. Trust is the breeding ground and the protective space in which new and additional things can emerge. Trust is an interaction and a resonance, which, in turn, generates trustworthiness. Those who do not trust will never be able to reap the returns of a trusting relationship. Hence, personnel selection is not primarily a decision between two requirements and suitability profiles, but between people.

Harari (2014, pos. 2055) states that computers have trouble understanding how people think, feel, and talk; so humans learn to think, feel and talk in the language of numbers, which computers can understand.

Hence, digital tools in HR or People Management should be designed to support and use the success factors of human decision-making behavior instead of trying to eliminate them as disruptive factors. There is a risk that AI or software will force human decision-making in a particular way or that people have to organize work processes according to software requirements. On the one hand, this can help make good decisions. On the other hand, it can lead to a situation where the focus is more on the correctness of adhering to processes and rules and less on what may be correct from a business perspective. In this way, people's scope for decision-making and, thus, for action and responsibility can be narrowed by AI and software.

For this reason, digital processes and AI should always be critically reflected upon in terms of the extent to which they narrow people's scope for decision-making and responsibility and, thus, possibly prevent people from learning to think independently and assume responsibility. Moreover, as open systems, organizations should be able to cope successfully with the complexity of the demands of their environment, and this requires opening up areas of responsibility for employees and placing decisions, as far as possible, at lower or decentralized levels, following the principle of subsidiarity. Therefore, AI and associated digital processes should always be reflected against the backdrop of the freedom and, thus, responsibilities they leave for people. This is made very clear in the Digital HR Manifesto (Goinger Kreis – Initiative Zukunft Personal und Beschäftigung e.V., 2019).

The Digital HR Manifesto calls for digital tools to support people in thinking about alternatives and allowing for diversity, not to demand a static fit from applicants, and, in particular, not to be an unwilling performer incapable of personal responsibility. Thus, the Digital HR Manifesto calls for increasing the range of options and perspectives rather than reducing them to a single instant solution, and digital instruments should make visible, the full range of different ideas and problems, rather than streamlining behavior. Furthermore, digital tools and AI should encourage active thinking and experimentation at all levels of activity, rather than reducing individuals to mere passive executants; they should allow for individuals to develop, rather than portraying them as consistent and unchanging; they should deliberately allow for exceptions and offer scope for off-piste ideas; they should ensure transparent criteria and methods for evaluating and assessing individuals and their performance, they should encourage the empathetic relationship between people, and strengthen the responsibility of each individual (Goinger Kreis – Initiative Zukunft Personal und Beschäftigung e.V., 2019; Klopprogge et al. 2019, pp. 276–277; Klopprogge, 2022, pp. 489–491; Koenig, 2019).

Thus, algorithms and AI are seen as a support in the decision-making process, which can give a score to applicants, after the first assessment of the application documents or deliver test results, which are then checked and evaluated by the recruiter, for example, in an interview.

"What algorithms . . . do not provide are imaginations and visions. They know neither emotions nor worries, no hope, and no trust. But these are precisely the central resources for decisions that point the way, and thus the entire field of entrepreneurial decision-makers. . . . For entrepreneurial decisions (and personnel selection decisions are one of the most important entrepreneurial decisions, J.D.), in which individual judgment is important, a human decision-maker is still needed" (Hutzschenreuter, 2022).

8.11.7 Ethical particularities of AI

AI tools can significantly support personnel selection but fall short, if not used responsibly. AI, per se, is neither good nor bad: it depends on what it is used for. Technology is usually developed for a specific purpose, for which it is better suited than others, and, therefore, it is not neutral. How digital technologies are used depends not only on programmers, developers, or coders but also on computer science developments and other factors such as law, economics, politics, philosophy, or ethics.

Using AI to analyze candidates' "digital footprint," for example, by examining data on private social media, could limit freedom of expression due to fears that certain information might be interpreted negatively by hiring managers.

Apart from the problem that facial recognition software can be used to monitor certain population groups or people and that AI can be used for "social scoring," it must be critically questioned whether such systems actually identify feelings. AI-based systems may capture someone's behavioral or body-language patterns, classify them, match them with images associated with specific emotions, and infer their emotional state. Specifically, this involves correlating recognized behavioral or body-language patterns to the seven basic feelings of happiness, anger, disgust, fear, contempt, sadness, and surprise. The AI-based systems detect these patterns and micro expressions in the face, but the question remains to what extent emotions can be identified correctly. In addition, the software may have difficulty recognizing signals in certain groups of people, such as people of color. Thus, the risk is that the data used to train the computer programs may reproduce human inadequacies and biases rather than overcome them (Scheer 2021). Barrett et al. (2019, p. 48) conclude: "Efforts to simply 'read out' people's internal states from an analysis of their facial movements alone, without considering various aspects of context, are at best incomplete and at worst entirely lack validity, no matter how sophisticated the computational algorithms. Nevertheless, these technology developments are powerful tools to investigate the expression and perception of emotions . . . Right now, however, it is premature to use this technology to reach conclusions about what people feel based on their facial movements."

AI actively interferes with people's self-image. Therefore, the topic of AI must also be examined from an ethical perspective. There is the question of whether the goal of being objective and less discriminatory by using AI leads to releasing humans from the responsibility of making selection decisions. Or do we want to leave those decisions with humans?

To get a trustworthy and accepted application of AI, many ethical guidelines have been established recently, including in Germany, by the HR Tech Ethics Advisory Board. According to these guidelines, the goal of using digital technologies such as AI must first be defined, before they are used, and the key stakeholders should be involved in this goal-setting process, which should be as transparent as possible. Anyone using AI solutions must ensure that a human has the final personnel decision (Ethikbeirat HR Tech, 2020).

Also, the European Commission has established the High-Level Expert Group on AI. This group has developed an EU-wide framework for using AI that complies with fundamental rights. Among other things, this involves user transparency and also human control. Furthermore, ethics guidelines for trustworthy AI were published. Respect for human autonomy, fairness, transparency, and harm prevention are particularly important. In addition, it is crucial to protect vulnerable people exposed to a particular risk of exclusion in the labor market (e.g., people with disabilities) from discrimination in personnel selection. The guidelines put forward a set of seven key requirements (European Commission, 2019):

1. Human agency and oversight: AI systems should empower human beings to make informed decisions and foster their fundamental rights. At the same time, proper oversight mechanisms need to be ensured, which can be achieved through human-in-the-loop, human-on-the-loop, and human-in-command approaches.
2. Technical robustness and safety: AI systems must be resilient and secure. They need to be safe, ensure a fallback plan if something goes wrong, and be accurate,

reliable, and reproducible. That is the only way to ensure that unintentional harm too can be minimized and prevented.

3. Privacy and data governance: besides ensuring full respect for privacy and data protection, adequate data governance mechanisms must also be guaranteed, taking into account the quality and integrity of the data, and ensuring legitimized access to data.
4. Transparency: the data, system, and AI business models should be transparent. Traceability mechanisms can help achieve this. Moreover, AI systems and their decisions should be explained according to the stakeholder concerned. Finally, humans need to be aware that they interact with an AI system and be informed of its capabilities and limitations.
5. Diversity, nondiscrimination, and fairness: Unfair bias must be avoided, as it could have multiple negative implications, from the marginalization of vulnerable groups to the exacerbation of prejudice and discrimination. Fostering diversity, AI systems should be accessible to all, regardless of any disability, and involve relevant stakeholders through their entire life circle.
6. Societal and environmental well-being: AI systems should benefit all human beings, including future generations. It must, hence, be ensured that they are sustainable and environmentally friendly. Moreover, they should consider the environment, including other living beings, and their social and societal impact.
7. Accountability: Mechanisms should be implemented to ensure responsibility and accountability for AI systems and their outcomes. Auditability, which enables assessing algorithms, data, and design processes, plays a key role, especially in critical applications. Moreover, adequate and accessible redress should be ensured.

These fundamental requirements are prioritized for human action, responsibility and accountability, and human supervision. However, the question remains whether technological systems are accountable from a legal perspective. Therefore, care must be taken to ensure that people remain accountable, that people make (final) decisions, and do not leave them unchecked to machines.

8.11.8 Legal aspects of AI

In many countries, data protection laws apply, especially when generating personality profiles using algorithm-based methods. For example, in Germany, the Federal Data Protection Act states that if assessments of personal characteristics lead to a candidate's rejection, this decision may not be made solely using automated procedures (Büttner, 2017, p. 26).

Big data analysis relies on a vast amount of data; thus, compliance with data minimization principles, storage limitations, or informational self-determination can be challenging (Weitzel et al., 2019, p. 27).

It must be possible to use employee feedback and evaluation data to determine how applicants have performed. Here too, data protection regulation rights must be considered.

Another influencing factor in implementing these digital or AI-based selection procedures in countries like Germany is the codetermination rights of employee representatives such as works councils or social partners. The works council must agree to use technological instruments that can assess the behaviors of employees. One of our interviewed selection managers says: "If (. . .) the social partners have the right of codetermination, it is always a great challenge to incorporate things like algorithms, personality tests, or video interviews into the selection process" (Flörke, 2020, p. 50).

To help employee representatives navigate the complex field of AI in management, recruitment guidelines and critical negotiating demands for unions have been developed. From the UNI Professionals and Managers (2020) perspective, the first step is to understand algorithms, how they are being used properly, and the key risks and opportunities that unions need to bear in mind. Unions must verify the legality of using such tools of data collection. A company that is programming or purchasing management algorithms needs to be adequately aware of the risks of bias and discrimination and take all possible steps to mitigate them. Decisions affecting employees should always be based on transparency. Thus, algorithms should use publicly known criteria, and their decisions should be explainable in clear, understandable language, not technical jargon. Clear records of what decisions have been made and why these decisions have been made should be referred to, in case of future challenges. To avoid biased or discriminatory outcomes, algorithms should also be regularly audited by independent third parties and chosen jointly by employers and unions. The results of such audits should be available to anyone affected by algorithmic decisions, including union representatives. "Human in command" should be the overriding principle. It is never acceptable to pass responsibility for critical decisions to nonhuman agents.

> Algorithms should advise, humans should decide. Algorithms should be used to support managers but never to replace them.

Thus, employers and unions should ensure that selection managers do not use algorithms to avoid taking responsibility for their decisions (Uni Global Union Professionals & Managers, 2020, pp. 22–24).

The ethical topic of the responsibility and imputability of judgments on people is also discussed in jurisprudence, along with the extent to which AI can help process legal cases faster and more competently. AI can learn how judges make decisions in certain situations and specific issues. However, strong voices in the judiciary advocate preserving the human element in decision-making. AI can, if necessary, assist in reducing discriminatory and incorrect judgments. The decision-making process can also be shortened by using AI to help generate data from previous judgments and other decisions, commentaries, and so on, to apply to new cases. Judicial decisions are also about discretion, appreciation of the individual case, and social skills, such as empathy. Therefore, there is great skepticism about automatic judgments by "legal tech" and demands that human judges make judicial decisions. Even though there may be a temptation to allow machine judgments due to time pressure and the large number of cases to be processed, robots as judges, who pass sentences nonstop, are questionable from today's perspective (Nink, D., 2011; Ebers & Navas, 2020).

8.11.9 Limits of using data from social media

Within social media, such as Facebook or LinkedIn, users present information. This means that information can be deliberately withheld from the public or removed from a profile. Therefore, when assessing the quality of data in social media, it should always be considered that making (private) data public may be influenced by factors such as social desirability and deliberate misrepresentation (Kosinski et al., 2015, p. 548). In addition, it is not only that information can be deliberately withheld. It is possible, for example, to falsify a profile by incorporating specific keywords with the help of algorithms (Siemann, 2017). In this way, evaluations of social media data may be based on deliberately falsified data. For example, one of our interviewed managers stated:

> The data on Facebook or other social media are not necessarily more honest and authentic; especially when candidates assume that employers evaluate their statements on social media (Flörke, 2020, p. 56).

Another aspect relates to influencing people in the network within the platform. For example, users can include other users in contributions, leading to a distortion of their profile and its meaningfulness (Landers & Schmidt, 2016, p. 4). It is also essential to recognize that some data give insights into users' privacy (Kosinski et al., 2013, p. 5805). This could lead to findings regarding age, origin, skin color (Landers & Schmidt, 2016, p. 4), sexual orientation, or political views (Youyou et al., 2015, p. 1039), as well as personality (Büttner, 2017, p. 26) of the persons. These criteria can influence the selection decision (Landers & Schmidt, 2016, p. 4) and discriminate against specific persons (Büttner, 2017, p. 26).

Similarly, when using digital social media data, its relevance must be ensured, because it is to be expected that the predicted personality of users will remain relatively stable, but it cannot be assumed that people's likes of specific content, pages, events, pictures, and so on will also remain stable (Stachl & Bühner, 2018, p. 33). Thus, the age, timeliness, and, hence, validity of the evaluated data should be considered. Since the internet does not forget, the sins of youth and posts made at a young age may still be held against the writers in adulthood.

One of the main reasons interviewed selection experts oppose certain social media data is that they attach great importance to separating the private person from the professional person. In particular, data from networks such as Facebook, Instagram, Twitter, or Twitch belong to the private and personal sphere of the candidate:

> I find that it infringes very much on the individual's personal rights, and I would be very, very, very critical. . . . the private must remain private . . . what a person does privately should not be a selection criterion (Flörke, 2020, pp. 56–57).

However, some interviewees state that it is permissible to use data from applicants' social media accounts in professional networks such as LinkedIn, XING, or similar. But they do not rely on more private social media such as Facebook or Instagram (Flörke, 2020, pp. 56–57).

For example, a completely AI-based selection process is currently not legal under German law, so humans must always make the final decision (Fesefeld, 2018, p. 27).

AI methods that use social media data from private networks are ethically problematic, because they process personal data without the applicants' permission and may investigate characteristics that have nothing to do with the job requirements. Thus, many interviewed HR professionals fear that use of social media data by AI could violate the personality and privacy rights of applicants (Berthel & Becker, 2010, p. 341):

> Only when these tools are legally correct and produce results that have been scientifically tested, and a higher level of fairness and objectivity can be achieved, under these conditions I would consider using such tools (Flörke, 2020, p. 61).

Another critical point is that the personality tests based on the evaluation of data from social media should be evaluated scientifically and assessed in terms of their quality (validity, reliability, objectivity, etc.).

8.12 Advantages and disadvantages of AI in personnel selection

Although AI-based software still has several weaknesses in personnel selection (Woods et al., 2020; Tippins et al., 2021; Wall & Schellmann, 2021), AI and algorithms that do not generate one-size-fits-all solutions and recognize the limits of AI and algorithms, as well as the specific characteristics of the situation (individual employee, the particular tasks, team constellation, culture, legal system, etc.), could be very useful in supporting selection decisions. If AI can also identify processes and selection decisions that end discrimination, it can lead to more fairness and objectivity.

AI and algorithms, but also humans, achieve good results, particularly when trained with high-quality and high-value data. Human expertise and human expert experience (and, thus, intuitive and emotional knowledge) can be incorporated into AI. The exchange of information between humans and machines is a critical success factor in that humans tell the machine how they decided and why they decided in the way they did; or they evaluate decision proposals from the AI and report these evaluations back to the AI. On the other hand, AI gives information to humans and makes suggestions. Since human decision-makers, especially in Western cultures, want to know how AI gets specific analysis results and why it judges in a particular way, transparency is essential for accepting AI. In this way, the people and the AI learn through a so-called feedback loop. Woods et al. (2020, pp. 68–73) show evident advantages of digital-based personnel selection, for example, faster, easier, sometimes more vivid, and fun, while expanding the number of applicants by reducing distance, cost, and time barriers. In addition, Algorithms and AI help find possible inconsistencies and judgment errors, and they do not get tired, work 24/7, have no good or bad days, and are not subject to perceptual distortions like noise (see 3.5.2.4). However, their research also highlights significant limitations in understanding the effectiveness of these technologies. In their view, a multi-method scientific research program is necessary because, in some areas, organizations using these new technologies are rather "blind" to their validity, adverse impact, privacy, or impact on applicants.

Main advantages of AI in personnel selection:

1. AI can eliminate or reduce unconscious human bias (Albert, 2019, p. 217).
2. Algorithms and robot recruiting systems should be designed to meet legal and ethical specifications. Thus, the data sets with which AI is trained should be free of bias; furthermore, statistical methods can be used to check whether specific categories are adequately represented. AI should be designed to be audited and evaluated, for example, to find and remove biases. IT technologists, HR specialists, line managers, and legal experts should work together to create the AI software. An AI audit should function just like the safety testing of a new car before someone drives it. If standards are not met, the defective technology must be fixed, before it is allowed into production (Polli, 2019).
3. AI enables much faster assessment, processing more applicants than human recruiters with limited resources and cognitive capacities. AI can check the entire pipeline of candidates, without the risk of time-constrained humans implementing potentially biased processes to shrink the pipeline from the start.

Figure 17 shows a comparison of the old and new selection methods:
However, there are also some risks in using AI. Publications like the anthology "Fake AI," edited by Frederike Kaltheuner (2021), director of the European AI fund, show examples of dubious AI that promises more than it delivers. We can also find collections of such dubious applications of AI on the websites of nongovernmental organizations like Algorithmwatch.

Since people have a deep need for security and can hardly tolerate uncertainty, there is a risk that they will rely on AI in personnel selection, even though it is not yet mature. Delegating tasks to technical systems is called technology-solutionism:

Old methods	New tools	Dimension assessed
Interviews	Digital interviews Voice profiling	Expertise, social skills, motivation, and intelligence
Biodata	Big data (internal)	Past performance
Supervisory ratings		Current performance
IQ		Intelligence, job-related
Situational judgment test **Self-reports**	Gamification	knowledge, and Big Five personality traits or minor traits
Self-reports	Social media analytics	Big Five personality traits and values (identity claims)
Resumés **References**	Professional social networks (LinkedIn)	Experience, past performance, and technical skills and qualifications
360s	Crowdsourced reputation/peer-ratings	Any personality trait, competencies, and reputation

Figure 17: Comparison of old and new personnel selection instruments (Chamorro-Premuzic et al., 2016, p. 627).

People feel overwhelmed and hope that technology will provide a solution that will take the decision away from them. As a result, the overburdened human being relies on the help of at least equally overburdened algorithms and AI that give a decision-making process the appearance of progressiveness, objectivity, and efficiency (Lenzen, 2022).

The evaluation of current literature and our interviews (e.g., Lindemann, 2020, pp. 50–53) clearly show that digital technologies such as software to assess video interviews, chatbots, or digital tests can help make selection processes more efficient, especially in the preselection process by HR-managers. However, AI cannot replace human contact.

Just as people don't only want to experience something digitally but also want to hike, climb, travel, cook and celebrate with others, people also want to meet and interact with real people in personnel selection.

Candidates and hiring managers, worldwide, want to have the opportunity to get to know each other and meet in person, which promotes trust and a sense of belonging. However, getting impressions about a company, the department, and the team via virtual or augmented reality is not enough for applicants. They want to meet personally and see if they like each other, if they fit together, professionally, and especially, humanly and socially. While providing applicants with a positive candidate experience may depend on the specific labor market situation, our literature analysis and empirical research clearly show that this is an important goal of personnel selection, across countries and cultures.

The difficulty with video-based verbal and nonverbal behavior analysis is that face recognition, verbal and nonverbal language, and even other human emotions are very complex. In different contexts, terms and specific body language expressions have different meanings. And, humor, irony, and sarcasm are individual, culture-specific, and complex (Kreutzer & Sirrenberg, 2019, p. 30; Lochner & Preuß, 2018, p. 194). To perceive and evaluate humor or irony accurately, humans draw on implicit knowledge and, thus, on their intuitions and emotions.

AI, currently, has some problems in dealing with ambiguity, irony, humor, or deviations from the expected. In addition, candidates react to the behavior of selection managers and vice versa. They use their experience, background knowledge, values, and interests, anticipate possible behavior and behavioral expectations of the counterpart, and so on. All of this is difficult to capture in rules and, therefore, challenging to map in AI and algorithms. Perhaps, it is not enough to try to imitate the human brain via AI, because there is a complex interplay of brain and body: there is no intelligent mind without the interplay with the human body or gut.

Dahm and Dregger (2019, p. 264) show that the acceptance of AI in personnel selection processes is higher, when human contact is available. In addition, ethical guidelines and legal concerns for AI state that human supervision and human decision-making should take priority (European Commission, 2019)

Despite all the possible advantages of AI-based video interviews, the human element is irreplaceable. The selection managers interviewed in our research rely on face-to-face interviews for the final selection decision. They want to take time for the candidate and directly observe verbal and nonverbal expressions such as facial expressions or gestures. They are convinced that only their intuitions and feelings help assess whether an applicant is empathetic and authentic, can form a positive relationship, and is, all in all, a good fit. AI can help obtain additional information about applicants but will not replace human decision-making.

Indeed, artificial neural networks and material techniques will become more potent in the future, data sets qualitatively and quantitatively better, computing power will be more powerful, and learning algorithms more sophisticated. Yet, some questions remain, for example, how AI can be meaningfully embedded in social, cultural, or even political contexts and developments. Also, some core questions concerning AI remain in personnel selection: How do we get AI to draw the correct conclusions from data? This is where AI continues to develop, including at the level of emotional and intuitive intelligence. But, someday, and no one can predict precisely when, we may have hardware and software to make human decisions as good as or even better than humans do.

However, even if the world will see more progress in AI in the next decade than in the past 100 years, and even if AI achieves increasing success in personnel selection, hiring managers should beware of inflated expectations and promises.

HR managers can and should use algorithms and AI for preselection. But when it comes to deciding whether a candidate is a good fit for a company or a team, line managers (superiors) and possibly team members should be involved. Candidates want to be won over by people. They are willing to work for their company, their managers, and their team, being highly motivated if they feel chosen by them actively (and vice versa) and not by a machine. Thus, humans will remain superior to AI for a long time, especially when it comes to implicit and contextual knowledge, associations, humor, irony, or evaluating and expressing intuitions and emotions.

Most managers we surveyed do not see the threat of recruiters or selection managers being eliminated. Instead, they see that digitalization and AI could upgrade the profession, making the work more exciting and people-oriented. Also, repetitive or routine tasks could be eliminated or reduced, and more time would be left for personal conversations with people (Pasenau, 2021, p. 48).

Thus, it is to be expected that AI will not replace human leadership, and final personnel selection decisions will continue to be made by humans: Recruiters and hiring managers should not hide behind data and AI. They are responsible for selection decisions. Suppose hiring managers concentrate on their human strengths and use their soft skills, intuitions, and emotions to understand people better and build positive relationships, while leaving technical skills or routine tasks to robots. In that case, they will gain the trust of their employees and candidates in their decisions.

Even if the development of human or even superhuman intelligence seems possible to some AI researchers, it remains to be seen as to what extent, for example, corresponding AI can succeed in understanding and mapping human interrelationships, or to what extent it can succeed in creatively developing novel solutions. Therefore, from today's perspective and an ethical standpoint, digital technologies and AI can best realize their strengths in personnel selection, when they complement human capabilities.

There is also the risk that AI as a self-learning system can develop its own intentionality and act autonomously. If these systems act according to their own rules, they, possibly, can no longer be controlled by humans. Therefore, they may make decisions contrary to humans' goals, and such an AI would no longer be humans' servants or partners (Klopprogge, 2022, p. 80). Then, we humans have to answer questions such as: Do we humans want to dominate computers and AI? Or do computers and AI dominate us? What do we want as humans?

HR or people managers and selection managers should never forget that organizations are all about people. People are the problem and also the solution. (Fernandez-Araoz, 2007, S. IX).

9 Learning and developing rational-analytical and intuitive competencies

A decisive success factor for the professionalization of personnel selection is the involvement of trained recruiters. The quality of selection processes rises and falls with the quality of the selection managers (Withelm & Gröben, 2005, p. 181). Thus, an essential step to high-quality selection procedures is to train hiring managers.

This research finding is confirmed in our empirical study. Most of our interviewed selection managers pointed out that HR managers and line managers should be trained to design and carry out effective selection procedures and deal competently with rational-analytical methods, tests results, unconscious bias, emotions, and intuitions.

As shown, especially in Section 5.1, the ability to have intuitions is inherent to every human being. It is not a mysterious gift or an immutable personality trait. Instead, intuition is a human potential that can be fostered and developed (Cohn, 1988, p. 134). With appropriate contexts, practical requirements, and other methods, selection managers can develop this ability.

Training aims to improve the intuitive competencies of selection managers. Therefore, a competence-oriented analysis and personnel development planning for selection of hiring managers should be made, before the training (see Section 10.4.2). The strengths and weaknesses of the (new) selection manager are a suitable basis for developing personnel selection competencies. Training and personnel development can only partially compensate for what is missed when selecting hiring managers.

Since superiors, executives, and other line managers are regularly involved in personnel selections, training is crucial for HR professionals, especially for these line managers. However, when selecting these line managers, less attention is paid to how their competencies for proper personnel selection are pronounced. For this reason, it is essential to conduct comprehensive selection training, with all selection managers involved.

Cognitive, emotional, and environmental influences and prior experience play a particular role in training recruiters and acquiring new knowledge and skills. The first step is acquiring the technical and vocational skills to carry out rational-analytical personnel selection procedures appropriately. Continuous training is crucial to practitioners' ability to break down deeply rooted belief systems (Highhouse, 2008, p. 333), question their own (limited) horizons of experience, and learn how to deal with intuitions, emotions, unconscious bias, stereotypes, or prejudices. A professional application of selection methods should be guided by an in-depth understanding of the advantages and limitations of human intuitions, emotions, and also rational-analytical practices.

https://doi.org/10.1515/9783110980967-009

An essential part of the training can be the presentation and critical reflection on the contents of this book. The effectiveness of learning and training processes can be seen in how the learning goals are achieved and how effectively the learning outcomes can be applied, in everyday work.

Intuitions and emotions are significant components of learning and have a powerful influence on attention, especially modulating the selectivity of attention and motivating action and behavior. Intuitions and emotions influence what people learn, what they assess as interesting and valuable, and how they transfer the learned and personal key takeaways into practice. Therefore, a topic of selection training should reflect the intuitions and emotions that training in high-quality selection sparks in the participants.

Success factors of training and transferring the learning into practice are particularly the motivation to reflect and question one's own thinking and behaviors, the motivation and openness to learn and develop, and participants' willingness to work on their weaknesses and other areas of development. A positive climate in training and in the working area, which is oriented towards the topics and experiences of the participants, is also essential to promote learning. There should be a rotation between knowledge transfer, reflection and feedback processes, and practical exercises such as role-plays, in training (Kirkpatrick & Kirkpatrick, 2006).

9.1 Learning in rational-analytical procedures and behavior

A professional application of rational-analytical selection procedures is regularly accompanied by a better understanding of the limitations of human perception, the advantages of rational-analytical methods (Lodato et al., 2011, p. 359), and an increase in the predictive validity of these methods and, thus, of the performance of the hired candidates (Kanning, 2012, p. 21).

Learning and training can primarily take place in the following ways:

1. On the job – learning personnel selection skills through experience and reflection, coaching and feedback by other hiring or line managers, and evaluation of the selection process and results.
2. Off the job – learning through attending training sessions

Based on research findings, the learning content should address quality in personnel selection from a psychometric perspective, including the legal and ethical issues in different cultures, regions, countries, and organizations. In addition, training participants should be informed about accepting specific selection procedures in differing contexts and how these procedures can contribute to a positive candidate experience.

Without going into detail, the core contents of selection training should be the methodological basics of rational-analytical or psychometric personnel selection and the associated procedures, guidelines, or standards in personnel diagnostics.

This includes communicating and explaining scientific quality criteria such as objectivity, reliability, and validity in selection procedures.

In such training, knowledge is conveyed, reflected upon, deepened, and applied in practical exercises tailored to the specific selection situations in various organizations.

Although the notion of quality and what characterizes high-quality selection processes are understood differently across cultures and between hiring managers, research results, obtained particularly in Western cultures, show that there is overwhelming evidence that a psychometric procedure and, thus, a higher degree of standardization leads to more valid selection results (Kuncel, 2008, p. 343).

Standardizing the personnel selection process by considering the ISO 10667, DIN 33430, or Guidelines for Assessment Centers and using requirement-oriented interview guidelines is recommended. In addition, intensive preparation and training on topics such as observation, evaluation and scoring, biases, and cultural differences are necessary (Ackerschott et al., 2016, pp. 87–103).

Observation and recording can be simulated by an interview report with notes on the (fictive) applicant's answers within this training. If two or more persons conduct an interview, each selection manager should evaluate and score independently and make written observations, based on behaviorally anchored rating scales. Scientifically based scoring scales and behavioral anchors should always be used to assess competencies and potentials (Deters, 2017, p. 178).

Training should be practical and implementation-oriented. The following topics and questions should be addressed. How to:

- carry out a job and requirements analysis, point out successful key behaviors (by using the method of critical incidents), and create a requirements profile (including desired potentials for future challenges);
- formulate legally compliant, non-discriminatory, and motivating job advertisements;
- systematically analyze – based on the job requirements and wanted potentials – application documents, certificates, references, and social media information;
- develop and use appropriate algorithms and digital methods (e.g., AI; see Chapter 8);
- develop an interview guideline with behavioral anchors;
- use the opportunities and know the limits of selection procedures, including cognitive ability tests, personality inventories, job knowledge tests, situational judgment tests, work sample tests, interviews, assessment centers, biodata, reference checks, and so on;
- conduct interviews (face-to-face, telephone, or video) successfully, including interview methods, question techniques, perception and evaluation of behaviors and answers, positive relationship building and attitude towards applicants, successful communication, and so on;

- design and implement assessment centers (e.g., for selecting leadership talent, and if the contextual conditions such as resources, number of applications, etc., support it);
- observe, analyze, and evaluate competencies, motivation, potential, personality, verbal and non-verbal behaviors, and so on;
- reduce unconscious bias (distortions of perception, stereotyping, prejudices, discrimination, culturally influenced perception differences of the observers/selection managers, etc.);
- evaluate an interview or a selection process as a whole.

The following topics should be treated in depth during training, if the participants or their organizations are interested in implementing assessment centers (AC):
- Advantages and disadvantages, how an AC must be designed to meet scientific quality criteria, typical activities, exercises and components, structure, and procedures.
- Explanation of the requirements profile, the structure of observations, using observation sheets, and so on.
- Exercises on perception, biases, and other possible perception distortions and separation (including possible limits) of observation, perception, and evaluation (DIN, 2016, p. 32).
- Familiarity with all activities and exercises planned for the AC, ideally by playing through them, to understand the instructions and exercise goals and develop a feeling for handling the observation and evaluation sheets (Withelm & Gröben, 2005, p. 190).
- Practice feedback discussions, which occur at the end of an assessment center between assessors, and give the candidates feedback about the results (Withelm & Gröben, 2005, p. 190).

International Taskforce on Assessment Center Guidelines (2015, pp. 1250–1251) requires that training:

> must include instruction on the purpose and goals of the assessment center, the behavioral constructs to be assessed and associated behaviors; the assessment center components to be utilized; the materials and rubrics to document, classify, and evaluate behaviors; and the rights and responsibilities of assessees, assessors, and the host organization and affiliated consulting bodies. It must also include instruction on making ratings and calibrating scoring levels associated with specific behaviors and behavioral constructs (often referred to as "frame-of-reference training"). Assessors must be allowed to assess actual assessees only after demonstrating their competence and reliability, both individually and as a group. If assessors also serve as feedback providers, training should address strategies for enhancing feedback acceptance and behavior change.

Companies could offer their selection managers opportunities to participate in appropriate certification courses, for example, according to DIN 33430/ISO 10667. In addition, companies could require corresponding certificates from external personnel consultants, as proof of qualification.

Since emotions and intuitions cannot be avoided in personnel selection processes, training should also deal with how personnel managers should competently deal with their emotions and intuitions, in these settings.

The following describes specific ways to learn the constructive handling of intuitions and emotions.

9.2 Learning intuitive competencies by reflection on intuitions and emotions

Decision-makers, often, do not know how to handle intuitive processes properly, due to a lack of constructive reflection and support. Also, a strong sense of subjective evidence that comes with intuition often makes it difficult to put a relativizing attitude toward these impulses (Weibler & Küpers, 2008, p. 12). To compensate for this deficiency, constructive handling of intuitions should be consciously trained and practiced, both at universities and in companies.

Intuitive competencies should be sharpened, and education and training in recognizing, managing, and using intuition should become a "normal" part of developing managers, recruiters, and especially hiring managers. This argument is not new, but the demands of the twenty-first century make the need for integrating intuition and emotions into the education of HR and leadership students and the training of recruiters, more pressing. Without this, business students will be unprepared for managerial positions, to a certain degree (Sadler-Smith & Burke, 2009, pp. 239–249).

Burke & Sadler-Smith (2006) state that, in general, business educators, for example, at universities, do little to develop this critical capability. Instead, university management education tends to direct students toward a rational–analytic approach. This approach is, likely, appropriate in tightly structured decision-making scenarios involving measurable objective data and clearly defined and measurable outcomes.

Putting analytical thinking first works best when the issue is clear, the data is reliable, and the context is very structured. But there are many managerial situations, especially in an increasingly complex world, where a rational-analytical approach alone is not enough, because it allows only very limited access to the problem to be solved.

To draw attention to the risk of perceptual distortions in intuition in personnel diagnostics, Miles and Sadler-Smith (2014, p. 623) recommend addressing the strengths and limitations of intuition in selection training. Understanding intuition, how it works, and its potential and limitations are crucial to assessing the influence and bias potential of intuitive judgments and weighing them against the scientific evidence for the validity of standardized methods. Increased intuition awareness helps hiring managers recognize whether a decision is based on intuitions, feelings, or rational-analytical processes (or both). Recognizing and critically examining one's intuitions and feelings is, thus, absolutely necessary. Coaching, feedback, and joint reflections with peers can help managers learn how to deal successfully with intuition and emotions in the selection process. Thus, in planning, developing, and evaluating personnel selection instruments and training, it is crucial to talk about the influence of intuition and reflect on it, without condemning it.

In workshops on intuition, Cohn (1988, p. 140) shows that even dealing with the topic of intuition and how it could be trained led to participants making a conscious effort to perceive their intuitions more purposefully.

9.2.1 How to teach and learn intuition?

Whether and how intuition can be taught is difficult to answer. However, in his book *The Intuitive Edge*, Philip Goldberg (1983) shows how to recognize, develop, and use intuition. And the world-renowned intuition researcher Gary A. Klein (2002) shows in his book, *Intuition at Work*, that intuition, far from being an innate "sixth sense," is a learnable skill that can be improved by training.

Based on research on how experts make good decisions, Klein (1998) identified four key ways in which experts learn:
1. engaging in deliberate practice and setting specific goals and evaluation criteria;
2. compiling extensive experience banks;
3. obtaining feedback that is accurate, diagnostic, and reasonably timely; and
4. enriching their experiences by reviewing prior experiences to derive new insights and lessons from mistakes (Phillips et al., 2004, p. 306).

And to learn and develop (specific) intuitive skills (e.g., in selecting people), hiring managers should:
1. enhance their perceptual skills
2. enrich their mental models about the particular domain (e.g., personnel selection)
3. construct an extensive and varied repertoire of patterns
4. provide a larger set of routines
5. provide a more extensive experience base of instances
6. encourage an attitude of responsibility for one's own learning (Phillips et al., 2004, p. 307).

According to Phillips et al. (2004), it is essential to reflect on hiring managers' tacit and implicit knowledge to make decisions, within their job context. They suggest additional learning tactics (Phillips et al., 2004, pp. 308–309). Thus, it is not enough to strengthen intuitive skills by training, more important is practice and feedback. However, feedback should consider the context of decision-making, because received feedback may not be appropriate and could be misleading in some contexts.

Selection managers:

1. should observe, interview, study and/or work together with subject-matter experts to glean insights into why tasks accomplishment were successful for them (e. g., used procedures and tools, decision strategies, handling of heuristics, intuitions, and emotions, etc.)
2. could use case studies to reflect on decisions under particular circumstances, including cases involving critical choices. This could result in developing different patterns to match different situations, boost the experience base, and enrich decision-makers' mental models and mindsets.
3. should employ coaching as an adjunct to practice, get feedback, and question and critically reflect on their emotions and intuitions, subjective mental models, assumptions, recognition patterns, personal goals and needs, biases, stereotypes, prejudices, etc. A coach could be a highly respected hiring manager with many years of experience and success in the field. (Phillips et al., 2004, pp. 308–309)

Guidelines for developing intuition by Hogarth: Hogarth (2010, pp. 348–349) also states that intuition can be learned and taught, because intuition is primarily the result of experience: Thus, if the experience is organized to learn the "right" lessons from people`s interactions with the world, intuition can be taught, and judgments can become more accurate in specific domains. In many ways, teaching intuition is similar to defining the conditions that allow task-specific expertise to emerge.

Also, there is abundant evidence that societies and organizations educate the intuitions of their members. Hogarth calls these kinds of intuition the "cultural capital."

From this perspective, hiring managers can teach intuitions. In his book, *Educating Intuition* (Hogarth 2001; see also 2003), he suggests seven guidelines for teaching intuition. "At the present time, these cannot be considered scientifically validated proposals but more by way of hypotheses garnered from an extensive review of literature" (Hogarth 2001, p. 22).

He considers three of these seven guidelines particularly important. They are (a) seeking feedback; (b) selecting or creating specific environments; and (c) making the scientific method intuitive (Hogarth, 2010, p. 348).

a) Seek evaluation and feedback: Hogarth (2003) states that two

> processes lie at the heart of our automatic, tacit learning: first, is the observation of connections between objects or events. This means to look at the predictive validity of a selection

> procedure. Try to get feedback that reinforces observed connections. Fortunately, this is a system that works very well for many things that we need to do in everyday life (which, presumably, is why evolution led to this system). However, two types of bias can have deleterious effects on the validity of the knowledge generated by the system. The first is bias in sampling connections between events; the second is bias (often absence) of feedback. . . . Deficiencies in feedback are probably the greatest barrier to acquiring effective intuitions. We learn automatically, but we are not necessarily aware of whether experience has been a good teacher (Hogarth, 2003, pp. 13–14).

Thus, a systematic, scientifically guided evaluation of selection decisions and timely and accurate feedback on the effectiveness of intuitive and/or analytical decisions are crucial. Moreover, it's essential to reflect on those decisions that turned out to be successful and those that were not.

b) Deliberately select or create an environment in which people can acquire intuitive skills

This second guideline builds on the environments where people operate and form their intuitions. The potential to develop and use intuition is inherent in every human being. Whether and how this potential is developed and used depends on the circumstances under which the person grows and operates. Therefore, it is essential to create environments to develop the ability to use intuition constructively and positively.

As it is challenging to acquire valid knowledge only through individual experience, intuitions can only be as "good" as the experience they are based on. The quality of the intuitions can be measured by accuracy in making good predictions. If the intuitions have been acquired in an environment that is – among other things – characterized by accurate and timely feedback, they are liable to be valid. However, intuitions gained in a non-stable environment or a context without feedback should be treated with suspicion. Thus, a key to developing "good" intuitions is to be in a decision-making environment that provides accurate and timely feedback and where hiring managers can work with the best experts in this area and observe how these people think, behave, judge, and decide.

Managers need to recognize that feedback on decision-making can be a double-edged sword, because the type of received feedback depends on whether the environment enhances or suppresses intuitions. Thus, the quality of an individual's intuitive capability depends on the kinds of learning contexts. It is possible to distinguish between two types of contexts. First, contexts enhance intuition by valuing it as a message of the unconscious and providing constructive feedback on decisions' consequences. And second, those contexts suppress intuitions and consider them as something whose influence needs to be reduced. For educational purposes, a kind learning culture is one in which there is an awareness of intuition, the opportunity to experiment and learn from mistakes (error culture), role modeling, and open dialogue. Moreover, constructive feedback and acknowledging the role of feelings and intuitions in the decision process pervade such a learning environment (Sadler-Smith & Burke, 2009, pp. 251–252).

Thus, the goal is to create favorable circumstances where intuitions and their integration into personal consciousness can be developed.

In the literature, this process of verbal explication of internal processes by a master of a skill (e.g., experienced and successful hiring managers) and reflecting on their intuitions and emotions with others (apprentices) is referred to as cognitive apprenticeship (Collins et al., 1987). Masters of a skill (e.g., intuitive skill) share their tacit knowledge with the novices. These novices or students can reflect upon their intuitions and emotions with the teacher. This approach to learning about intuition is supported by the "theory of modeling" by Albert Bandura (1997) and learning in the "real-world context." By doing so, the learners understand their intuitions and emotions. Moreover, they know to identify possible problems and handle critical elements, such as biases. In the end, they can handle their intuitions and emotions independently from the teacher.

Thus, a meaningful way to build up expertise is to learn from others (e.g., by mentoring, coaching, extensive job shadowing, structured internships, and apprenticeship), including receiving feedback and systematically evaluating decisions made. Unfortunately, this is still not widespread enough, in practice. Nevertheless, by learning from others, people can acquire a sense of which reactions and decisions are appropriate in a specific situation (Hogarth, 2003, pp. 20–23; 2010, p. 348).

In this context, selection managers' overconfidence could be addressed (Koppers, 2013, p. 53; Kahneman & Klein, 2009, p. 518) (see Sections 2.6 and 3.5.2.29).

Nadja Koppers (2013, pp. 49–50) has dealt intensively with building expertise in personnel selection. She investigates how recruiters learn to make decisions when they receive little or no feedback on the quality of their choices. According to Wottawa & Oenning (2002, p. 50) and Wottawa & Hossiep (1987, p. 61), the learning process of a selection manager can be described as learning by model or learning by imitation (Bandura, 1997). A new hiring manager accompanies the "expert" in the selection and diagnostic procedure and, by imitating the experienced colleague, s/he develops an implicit system of rules in selection decision-making (Wottawa & Oenning, 2002, p. 50).

As a rule, novices will be trained until their decisions are as close as possible to those of the role model. The decision-making system of the role models is usually shaped by their subjective experiences, contextual circumstances such as institutional norms of the company.

If there is no explicit rule system to adopt, the novice must build up an individual and personal decision-making system. Thus, if the evaluative component is lacking, there is a risk that the self-developed rule system is continuously reinforced according to the principle of learning by repetition. This leads to a consolidation of subjective decision rules and an implicit trust in the supposed expert diagnostic knowledge.

However, the validity of subjective decision rules remains doubtful, if the decisions have not been systematically evaluated (Wottawa & Oenning, 2002, p. 50).

By adopting such subjective decision rules, a so-called "expert" may make decisions intuitively and confidently for years, that are objectively wrong from a psychometric perspective (Koppers, 2013, p. 50). Therefore, a recruiter's supposed expert knowledge could also be an unevaluated routine scheme. Routine decisions, like expert decisions, are characterized by low use of cognitive resources. The cognitive effort consists primarily of matching the present decision with remembered decisions made in similar situations. Betsch et al. (2011) were able to show that in this context, contradictory information loses influence in recurring decisions. Also, routine decisions may reinforce the tendency to confirm assumptions and, thus, increase the risk of judgment errors. The inconsistent findings on the positive and negative effects of an interviewer's experience on the validity of the interview also confirm the problematic distinction between expertise and routine.

For this reason, it is necessary to regularly question one's supposed expertise and evaluate one's decisions. Koppers' (2013) findings show that the experience of selection managers can act as an indicator of expertise but also as an indicator of unevaluated routine.

Thus, supposed expertise that is unevaluated can lead to an overestimation of existing competencies. Learning from experience means reflecting on it openly and honestly, sharing these reflections with other hiring managers, getting feedback, and systematically evaluating one's decisions.

Honest reflection on intuitions and emotions should be given space in educational settings.

Aldous Huxley criticizes the overemphasis on rational-analytical thinking in schools and universities. However, people's holistic development also requires the development of the non-verbal humanities and, thus, their intuitive and emotional intelligence.

> In a world where education is predominantly verbal, highly educated people find it all but impossible to pay serious attention to anything but words and notions. There is always money for, there are always doctrines in, the learned foolery of research into what, for scholars, is the all-important problem: Who influenced whom to say what, when? Even in this age of technology, the verbal humanities are honored. The non-verbal humanities, the arts of being directly aware of the given facts of our existence, are almost completely ignored (Huxley, 2021).

Fenkart (2018, p. 6) critically mentions the overall education system that primarily educates persons in reading, writing, and calculating. As a result, the brain is only trained unilaterally, which leads to emotional-intuitive deficits. Thus, Sadler-Smith & Shefy (2007, p. 186) demand that intuition should play a more significant role in management education.

c) Make the scientific method intuitive

The third guideline by Hogarth is that hiring managers should know the “rules” of scientific-based selection procedures.

> The key idea here is to learn these rules so well that you can execute the appropriate steps without having to think what these should be. In other words, you have educated your problem-solving intuition to work according to the best known principles (Hogarth, 2003, p. 26).

It is a matter of implementing selection procedures based on research results so frequently and consistently that they are executed automatically and become second nature.

Suggestions by Burke & Miller: Burke & Miller (1999, pp. 95–96) offer several suggestions for helping managers to develop their intuitive skills. Managers should:
- be more attentive to the overall decision process
- challenge decisions when they feel or sense the need to do so
- reflect on past decisions and the role that intuition played, and attempt to learn from any mistakes
- practice applying intuition in work situations or with hypothetical scenarios, cases, or exercises
- watch and observe when and how others employ their intuition
- become educated about intuitive decision-making by reading books and articles and attending conferences
- learn to take risks when making decisions, without being afraid of the consequences
- practice making decisions, without all the data necessary.

Meditation, journal writing, and mind mapping may also be useful in becoming more knowledgeable about intuition. Executives and managers should pay close attention to how the corporate culture may explicitly or implicitly discourage or encourage intuition to develop employees’ intuitive potential. Research suggests that intuition flourishes if it is valued in an organization. Thus, organizations and, especially, top executives and managers should facilitate and selectively encourage employees to use and reflect on their intuitive skills. Organizational mindsets must be modified to eliminate the myths about intuition and to use it effectively in the workplace (Burke & Miller, 1999, pp. 95–96).

Suggestions by Kleebaur: Caroline Kleebaur’s (2007, p. 65) findings on teaching and learning intuition skills focus on different interlinked types of knowledge. Her research shows that personal experiential knowledge plays a decisive role as a source of judgment and decision-making in personnel selection. This results in a networked use of three forms of knowledge: 1. expert knowledge; 2. explicit experiential knowledge; 3. implicit (experiential) knowledge.

1. **Expert knowledge:** This is primarily declarative expertise on personnel selection acquired through education, studying personnel diagnostics at universities, training, and so on. It includes knowledge about a scientifically based psychometric selection procedure, biases, planning activities, legal and ethical issues, carrying out a systematic selection procedure, learning about the organization, the labor market, candidate experience, and so on.
2. **Explicit knowledge:** The explicit or declarative knowledge is conscious knowing and application of knowledge. For example, it is about professional knowledge recorded in guidelines, standards, manuals, and textbooks. It is knowledge of how to implement specific methods and processes of personnel selection in concrete terms (e.g., rational-analytical procedures), draw conclusions, conduct a selection interview, or integrate observations or ratings of each assessor in a "consensus discussion."

   The repeated application of this knowledge and these methods creates memory patterns that lead to specialist knowledge and – by repeated use – automatic decisions and behaviors. This type of knowledge and its application requires years of experience in problem-solving and both business knowledge and knowledge about the specific organization (Dane & Pratt, 2007, pp. 43–44; Kleebaur, 2007, pp. 65–67; Sadler-Smith & Shefy, 2004, p. 81). The acquisition of explicit knowledge should be supported by constant repetition, regular feedback, and evaluation of decisions. According to Dane and Pratt (2007, pp. 43–44) as well as Küpers (2015, p. 83), this is a very successful way to enable people to conclude from correlations between actions, decisions, and results and, thus, expand their memory patterns and to develop new experiences and intuitions.
3. **Implicit or tacit knowledge:** Implicit or tacit knowledge is also known as experiential knowledge and is based on automatic learning processes and unconscious knowledge acquisition. It differs from explicit knowledge, because it`s unconscious and can hardly be verbalized or explicated. (Dane & Pratt, 2007, pp. 44–45). This explains why it is challenging to justify intuitively made decisions, in retrospect. An example is an implicit conclusion about a candidate's personality traits, based on observing an applicant's behaviors and feelings about that applicant. Here, a selection manager, often, has no explicit knowledge about an applicant's personality, yet s/he forms a judgment and makes decisions, based on tacit knowledge (Kleebaur, 2007, p. 66).

Learning and teaching explicit and implicit knowledge. It is possible to learn and teach declarative or explicit knowledge, consciously. However, declarative and explicit knowledge can also be learned unconsciously, for example, through the unconscious adoption of thought- and behavior patterns from others, for example, from role models.

Selection managers should develop their communication skills and knowledge about how people differ in their linguistic forms (verbal, non-verbal, para-verbal), cultural imprints, knowledge, attitudes, thought patterns, and behaviors. They should know about consciously or unconsciously learned context-relevant schemes and patterns (e.g., corporate values, basic assumptions, and the image of man) and how these should be considered in personnel selection.

Implicit knowledge is learned unconsciously and automatically. People can know something, without being able to put it into words. Since intuition is based primarily on this implicit knowledge, one can learn it, but there are limits to teaching it actively. It is possible to teach the process of connecting with and reflecting upon one's intuition; it's possible to give feedback and evaluate one's own decisions. But, it's not possible to provide a training course in intuition and have everyone in the course transformed into intuitive geniuses.

Thus, teaching intuition requires a more tangential approach. This means that learning intuition can be supported and promoted indirectly. But in the end, intuition must be seen as a natural process of development that can only partially be fostered from outside through supportive environments, role models, repetition, sharing of knowledge and experiences, evaluation of judgments and decisions, reflection on intuitions and emotions, feedback by others, mindfulness, and so on. But, each person must go through these processes individually.

Obermann (2018, chapter 2.7) shows that pure knowledge training to avoid typical appraisal process errors hardly affects appraisal accuracy. Rather, the so-called reference-frame training (Gorman & Rentsch 2009), in which participants write down and compare their observations and evaluations of a specific behavior (for example, using a training video) based on experience, is more effective. The learning effect lies particularly in experiencing possible differences between one's evaluations and those of the other participants in an exemplary manner and, thereby, emotionally and cognitively understanding the distortions to which one's judgment is exposed due to one's frame of reference and the corresponding individual cognitive assignment processes. Thus, training, conscious integration, and critical reflection on one's subjectivity can increase the validity of the selection process (Riedel, 2016, p. 8).

9.2.2 Enhancing intuition through self-awareness

9.2.2.1 Listening to one's intuitions and emotions as important messages

Vaughan (1988, p. 65) shows that intuition can be successfully developed when it is appreciated, wanted, and trusted (Kleebaur, 2007, pp. 182–183). From this perspective, in practice and training, the focus should be on perceiving intuition as a resource. The aim is to familiarize selection managers in-depth with the advantages and disadvantages of intuitions (see Sections 5.1 and 5.2) and to recognize how to deal with them constructively.

For Sadler-Smith & Burke (2009, p. 249), the starting point for fostering a better understanding of intuition is to dispel the myth of intuition as a mystical, magical, or paranormal sixth sense that is always wrong and never to be trusted. The task is to overcome the bad reputation of intuition in science and practice (Burke & Miller, 1999, p. 95).

Sadler-Smith & Shefy (2004, p. 87) formulate guidelines on using intuition, taking its limitations seriously, and exploiting its potential. An overview of these recommendations can be found in Figure 18.

Recommendation	Description
1. Open up the closet	To what extent do you: experience intuition; trust your feelings; count on intuitive judgments; suppress hunches; covertly rely upon gut feel?
2. Don't mix up your I's	Instinct, insight, and intuition are not synonymous; practice distinguishing between your instincts, your insights, and your intuitions.
3. Elicit good feedback	Seek feedback on your intuitive judgments; build confidence in your gut feel; create a learning environment in which you can develop better intuitive awareness.
4. Get a feel for your batting average	Benchmark your intuitions; get a sense for how reliable your hunches are; ask yourself how your intuitive judgment might be improved.
5. Use imagery	Use imagery rather than words; literally visualize potential future scenarios that take your gut feelings into account.
6. Play devil's advocate	Text out intuitive judgments; raise objections to them; generate counter-arguments; probe how robust gut feel is when challenged.
7. Capture and validate your intuitions	Create the inner state to give your intuitive mind the freedom to roam; captureyour creative intuitions; log them before they are censored by rational analysis.

Figure 18: Guidelines for developing an awareness of intuition (Sadler-Smith & Shefy, 2004, p. 88).

Hänsel et al. (2002, pp. 49–51) emphasize that for a successful perception and application of intuitive competencies, a certain degree of trust and, at the same time, professional distance in these intuitive processes is helpful. As with other learning processes, a positive attitude toward the learning content also facilitates implementation in everyday life. For example, if managers are convinced that they can only be good selection managers if they allow their intuitions and feelings to flourish, they can further develop this natural competence (see Sections 9.2, 9.3, 9.6, 10.5.1 and 10.5.2).

There are many things people know long before their rational-analytical mind catches on. Intuitions are readily available 24/7. All day, this intelligent agent sends messages and provides people with information containing knowledge.

This human intuitive and emotional capability has contributed to the survival of humankind. The evolutionary advantage of intuition is why Gigerenzer (2007) talks about intuitions as "the intelligence of the unconscious."

Since the organism never lies (Miller, 2005), people should recognize their body's messages and accept intuitions and feelings (also negative ones) as data and essential information. Hiring managers can develop and improve their intuition by paying attention to their inner voices and emotions; they can learn to perceive and reflect upon intuitions and feelings as messages and expressions of their "unconscious intelligence."

Carl Gustav Jung and Carl Rogers argue that listening to intuition is necessary for mental health. Rogers emphasizes that humans should trust the messages of their intuitions. (Rogers, 1951) and Jung (1948) are convinced that humans with good mental health are open to and listen to the messages coming from the unconscious mind.

Jung (2019) also states that the "unconscious" will direct people`s lives, until they make the unconscious, conscious. This means that the human subconscious carries many positive and negative belief systems, repressed emotions, and so on. Until humans integrate their subconscious and reflect on their intuitions and emotions, they cannot eliminate negative thought patterns and repressed emotions, stereotypes, and other biases. It is not surprising that in a world where the rational-analytical mind is perceived as superior to the intuitive-emotional mind, people may build up inner walls that make it challenging to deal openly with intuition and feelings.

Focusing is also a way to develop intuitive skills in a professional context. This involves exploring feelings and bodily sensations to understand their links with conscious thoughts. The method is based on Rogers' client-centered dialog. Focusing describes perceiving something one feels physically, without knowing precisely what it is and without naming it concretely. Even if focusing and intuition cannot be equated, feeling inside oneself and what the body says can be seen as another possible path to deepening one's intuition (Gendlin & Wiltschko, 2011).

It often takes several years before hiring managers can trust their intuitions and feelings in personnel selection. This means that hiring managers should develop the ability to be aware of and sincerely acknowledge the full range of their intuitions and feelings and those of others, without fear of reprisal (Küpers & Weibler, 2008, p. 268).

Using intuitions and emotions can be especially beneficial when people need to make tough decisions that have far-reaching implications in their lives. This is because their intuition can reveal some aspects of the specific circumstances and experiences that their ability to reason cannot.

When hiring managers begin to self-inquire and reflect on their judgments and decision-making, they learn to trust themselves and their inner voice, which helps develop their skilled intuition.

However, research also shows that intuitions based on experience can lull managers into a false sense of security and self-confidence. Thus, it is equally essential to know intuitions' limits and possible disadvantages (see Section 5.2) and reflect on when to trust intuitions (Kahneman & Klein, 2009, p. 520), for example, by linking various successes and failures in personnel selection with intuitive and emotional experiences.

Hänsel et al. (2002, p. 51) report good success in training the intuitive competencies of consultants by using visualization exercises or exercises for bodily-kinesthetic awareness. Training participants get to know particular forms of expression of their intuition better. The authors emphasize that hiring managers should learn not to control their emotions by suppressing or ignoring them, because this can quickly lead to new problems. Rational-analytics may be appropriate in many decision-making processes. However, people should not forget to listen to their inner voices. They can help to guide people in a way that is difficult to comprehend, but is, nevertheless, often quite correct, especially when it comes to warnings. It is better to perceive, accept, and reflect on intuitions and feelings and examine them with deliberate thinking.

9.2.2.2 Improving intuition by mental relaxation, awareness, and mindfulness training

Strengthening conscious awareness of intuitive and emotional signals can support competent use of intuitions and emotions. Thus, many researchers make a plea for general intuitive awareness training for managers (Sadler-Smith & Shefy, 2004; Sadler-Smith & Burke, 2009, p. 240).

Often, intuitive solutions come to humans after relaxation, or a change of activity, for example, having a shower or going for a walk. Other ways to access intuitions and emotions consciously and, thus, for training intuition are mental relaxation and other meditative, contemplative, or mind-body practices such as breathing techniques, yoga, meditation, Zen training, qigong, or even fighting arts, such as taekwondo. Thus, managers could try to become mentally quiet, remove all noise and voices, and simply observe and center themselves. But, most of these suggestions have met with skepticism for many years, especially in rational-analytical business environments (Sadler-Smith & Burke, 2009, p. 254).

Research on coaching and psychotherapy also shows the meaning and benefit of self-awareness for making good decisions. There is a great deal of research and many established psychotherapeutic approaches to developing somatic awareness and introspection to feel and understand what's happening in the body. This awareness can help self-regulate vital body functions, including coping with stress (e.g., Ogden et al., 2006; Bessel van der Kolk, 2015; see also Section 4.2.5 and the somatic markers hypothesis as explanation approach for intuition).

Mindfulness training is one particularly recommended technique that can improve the ability to perceive, evaluate, develop, or optimize intuition (Sadler-Smith & Shefy, 2004a, 2007).

Mindfulness is a term for focusing on being in the moment. It can be defined as an awareness of all body and mind experiences in an open, non-judgmental, and accepting manner (Kabat-Zinn, 2005, 2013; Kaufmann et al., 2020, p. 1). Mindfulness is a technique to filter out distractions in a specific environment and listen to one's body, emotions, inner voices, and so on. Thus, mindfulness training can be an excellent way to learn to hear the body's messages and listen to one's intuitions and emotions: How do I feel now? What are my thoughts on this?

The success of these focusing techniques is dependent on how people practice introspection and experience self-empathy. The goal is to transform intuitions into conscious thoughts, ideas, and images.

Mindful leaders – besides many other competencies – have mastered three specific ways of processing awareness (Levin, 2018).

1. Taking a meta-position: Mindful hiring managers can observe themselves, their thoughts, intuitions, emotions, and their specific situations from a "meta" or "helicopter perspective." They can take a step back to observe what is happening around them at a distance. Without metacognition, there is no means of escaping our automatic (emotional or intuitive) pilot (Reitz & Chaskalson, 2016a).
2. Allowing non-judgmental awareness: Mindfulness means a non-judgmental perception of the present. Mindful people are open to what is happening at the moment and which thoughts, intuitions, or emotions they have without judging them as something good or bad, instead, accepting them as they are. "Without allowing, our criticism of ourselves and others crushes our ability to observe what is really happening" (Reitz & Chaskalson 2016a).
3. Curiosity: Without curiosity, managers lack the impetus to bring their awareness into the present moment and stay with it. This means taking an interest in one's inner and outer world. Effective leaders have a strong sense of curiosity, and they are open to learning more about their situation, inner world, decision-making processes, and so on.

Mindfulness is attention management. Hiring managers can raise their mindfulness by paying attention to how they engage with others, deciding in selection situations, and influencing their judgments. By a mindful and introspective reflection of their decision-making processes, they can themselves become more effective managers or leaders. In addition, mindfulness increases the likelihood of better communication, because practitioners become more transparent to their colleagues, communicating the reasons for their judgments. Finally, hiring managers can improve cooperation and inspire other managers and co-workers by getting feedback and becoming more open in exchanges, listening actively, and making often difficult topics (emotions, intuition, etc.) discussable.

Arendt et al.'s (2019) findings provide empirical evidence for a positive link between leaders' mindfulness and followers' well-being, and that mindfulness fosters interpersonal skills.

Reitz & Chaskalson (2016b; see also Reitz et al., 2020) show that mindfulness training and sustained practice produces statistically significant improvements in three capacities that are important for successful leadership in the 21st century: resilience, the capacity for collaboration, and the ability to lead in complex situations.

The empirical research of Rupprecht et al. (2019) on the interplay of self-reflection and mindfulness also confirmed the positive impact of mindfulness on relationships between leaders and their followers.

Also, mindfulness is essential to being authentic; only managers who are "with themselves" can behave authentically towards others.

Reitz & Chaskalson (2017) state that mindfulness is effective only if practiced for at least 10 min daily. Through this focused introspection, hiring managers better understand themselves, develop their intuitive competencies, and improve their emotion management.

Remmers et al. (2015) found that mindfulness does not necessarily foster access to intuitive processes; however, they note that future studies investigating the impact of mindfulness on intuition can bring more clarity. Possible explanations for the current findings and limitations are discussed (Remmers et al., 2015, p. 282).

Indeed, neuroscience research results show that after four days of mindfulness training, the activity and interconnectivity of the ventromedial prefrontal cortex increased (Zeidan et al., 2014).

Sometimes the world is noisy, and people aren't even aware that their intuitions or emotions are sending messages. Great ways to carefully give oneself the time and space to refocus and think through a problem are to say: "Just give me a moment to think this through," or "I have to sleep on it." These can be effective ways of integrating intuition and analytical procedures in decision-making.

9.2.3 Developing competencies in reflection on intuition and emotions

The capability for self-reflection is uniquely human; thinking about one's thinking, intuitions, and feelings define the human being (Gigerenzer 2007, p. 6).

Reflection is a thinking practice that can develop reflexivity as competence in professional selection managers. Through reflection, managers can deconstruct their perceptions, convictions, judgments, and decisions, recognizing influencing factors, biases, and so on. They can assess possible consequences of actions, subject their actions to a review against the background of scientific findings and the perceptions of others, and optimize their decision-making behavior in personnel selection (Klempin, 2021, pp. 78–79; Hatton & Smith, 1995).

9.2.3.1 Reflecting on intuition in a context of trust and psychological safety

Intuitive processes work automatically and without conscious control; thus, they cannot easily be accessed by introspection (Betsch & Glöckner, 2010, p. 280).

A conscious introspection process requires awareness of the intuitions. However, Berne (1949) states that what is intuited can differ from what the "intuiter" verbalizes as intuition. Thus, Dane and Pratt (2009) and Sinclair (2014) suggest that retrospective reports can capture the use of intuition, only to a certain degree.

However, managers can develop techniques that may assist in creating the appropriate psychological conditions to encourage intuitions and develop the skills to recognize them.

In an atmosphere of psychological safety, selection managers can learn to perceive and openly articulate their intuitive and emotional inspirations in hiring processes. It, then, becomes possible to constructively reflect on one's own perceived intuitions and emotions with other participants, in a training context (Hänsel et al., 2002, pp. 49–51).

In the protected and trusting atmosphere of psychological safety, training participants can receive open and honest feedback from the trainer and other participants, exchange ideas and perceptions openly, and learn with and from each other. Thus, hiring managers should reflect on their intuitions and emotions with others, preferably experienced colleagues, trainers, coaches, and other experts. By doing this, they can subject intuitions and emotions to rational analysis.

At the same time, it is essential to reflect on the factors that hinder or support the use of intuition, in practice (Nachtwei, 2013, p. 38). Thus, it should be questioned why there is a tendency to discount emotions and intuitions and justify existing intuitions and feelings with rational-analytical arguments (Kleebaur, 2007, pp. 183–184; see Section 5.3).

For a more detailed description of creating a culture of acceptance and reflection of intuition and how the rational-analytical mind (System 2) can monitor intuitive-emotional impulses, see Section 10.5.1.

9.2.3.2 Train and develop emotional competencies

To create positive relationships with candidates, hiring managers must manage and regulate their emotions in interactions with applicants, to fulfill their job requirements. They may display certain emotions for their purposes (e.g., winning a candidate for the company) or change expressive gestures to change feelings. Selection managers must act authentically and empathetically and build and maintain positive relationships, using emotions (Grandey, 2000; Hochschild, 2012; see Sections 2.5, 5.1.6, and 10.3.1 for selection as a social process).

Human resource managers need emotional competencies, especially empathy, to constructively handle emotions in themselves and others and create positive relationships in selection processes. Emotional competencies can be learned by developing self-awareness and sharing experiences about emotions with others, active listening, and self-regulation techniques.

Feelings, as a major expression of intuitions, can give hiring managers crucial clues. As shown in Sections 4.2.4.2 and 4.2.8, the limbic system is an important center of emotions in the human brain. However, this limbic system operates relatively autonomously and is beyond direct cognitive control. Thus, people cannot directly control and influence their emotional reactions. Therefore, blaming oneself or others for spontaneous emotional responses is useless. Instead, it is more interesting to ask what triggered the emotional reactions. More awareness of the trigger helps people understand emotional reactions better and, at the same time, to take a cognitive distance from one`s emotions and, thus, consciously influence the response to them. This process is called emotion regulation.

Emotion regulation is how hiring managers can control or monitor their emotions. In addition, emotion regulation plays a central role in using intuitions and emotions competently, in decision processes (Gross, 2014, gives a good overview of the regulation of emotions).

Awareness and acceptance of feelings are the first steps towards regulating them: rather than being passively influenced by one`s emotions, people can actively shape and control their response to them (Geiselhardt, 2021).

Reflecting on one's feelings and affectively charged judgments can help people check their emotions and consciously use their energy. They can take a step back and become observers of themselves. Sometimes, negative emotions don't stand up to such a reality check; they fizzle out as quickly as they came and a smile at one's overreaction remains.

By observing their emotions, hiring managers can get important insights, namely which messages could be behind the feelings, why they have these feelings, how they affect their behavior, and so on.

Positive psychology shows that positive feelings make people more open in their dealings with other people. Cross-cultural studies prove that test persons recognize more overlaps between themselves and others, when exposed to positive feelings. The feeling of togetherness enables people to have positive relationships and makes people more tolerant of strangers and people of different cultures. Positive feelings allow people to deal positively with other people and, thus, become more socially competent.

Unchecked feelings should not be considered a basis for adequately interpreting and evaluating a situation or an applicant because unconscious bias, stereotypes, and so on, may influence them.

Cohn (1988, pp. 142–144) shows that empathy is needed to recognize people intuitively. In an atmosphere of open interaction, in which one is open to the perceptions, intuitions, emotions, and insights of others, empathy and, thus, also intuition can be developed. When we become aware of our intuitions and feelings, we become more sensitive to the mood and perspectives of other people. People cannot force intuitions, but they can invite and practice them. Thus, intuition grows on the ground of empathy (for oneself and others), self-acceptance, and the ability to self-reflect. It needs awareness and requires calmness, silence, and trusting receptivity. It seeks interaction with others, trust, and openness to understand each other.

A big challenge is to benefit as a manager from experience-based emotion-mediated signals in a complex environment with incomplete information, while avoiding the decision traps of poorly regulated emotions. People, especially hiring managers, should be able to control and regulate their feelings towards others, especially if the feelings against an applicant are negative. At the same time, remaining authentic is a great challenge. Since successful emotion regulation is always dependent on the context, hiring managers should be able to adapt their outwardly shown emotions, flexibly, to the context-specific requirements and be selectively authentic in expressing their feelings.

In training or reflection on their practice with a coach or other managers, hiring managers can develop their competencies in constructively handling their emotions.

Conscious cognitive control represents an essential strategy for regulating emotions. It is particularly crucial to effectively regulate negative emotions that arise in the heat of the moment.

Hiring managers should be able to regulate their emotions so that they can:

(1) maintain appropriate levels of arousal, such that they can respond optimally in dynamic selection situations to every individual applicant;
(2) manage stress;
(3) reflect on and avoid (as far as possible) emotions based on bias or stereotypes;
(4) maintain access to positive and negative emotions that encapsulate experience-based reactions to every single applicant; and
(5) maintain a critical engagement with their emotionally mediated intuitions concerning applicants (Vohra & Fenton- O'Creevyin, 2014, pp. 94–96; these authors refer their recommendations to investment bank traders).

As shown in Section 3.5.2.3 and 3.5.2.4, "mood" and "noise" impact how a hiring manager acts, judges, and decides. Thus, hiring managers should also reflect on their moods and the "noise" in a specific selection situation, and how these moods and "noise" affect their judgments and selection decision-making, and try to meet all applicants with the same, preferably, positive feelings.

9.2.3.3 Training and reflection on perception distortions and biases

People perceive situations selectively and want to avoid emotional discomfort; they pick and choose what they want or expect to see in messages of others and judge people through subjective constructions, based on individual experiences, personal needs, values, attitudes, implicit and explicit knowledge, unconscious bias, and other perception distortions. Also, people often do not recognize their own biases and perceptual distortions influenced by different factors, especially culture, for example, language, values, beliefs, norms and laws, religion, skin color and ethnicity, and expectations concerning behaviors. Cultural biases are learned and, often, come from ignorance of different cultures. For example, people tend to interpret, favor, and recall information to confirm their preexisting beliefs or hypotheses, favor the familiar, and so on (see the different perceptions distortions and biases in Section 3.5.2). When people from Western cultures hear that somebody is Chinese, it is likely that they immediately attach specific characteristics such as shyness to them. Thus, people interpret and judge other people by values, norms, and so on, inherent to their culture.

If people want to reach other people, they should know themselves.

In training, people could learn to regard culture as a lens through which they see the world and other people; there is no right or wrong, just different. Furthermore, they should learn to be aware of their cultural imprints and biases, be consciously honest with themselves, and that (nearly) everyone has some biases and is prejudiced against people of other cultures.

Besides these cultural biases, there are many other perception distortions, biases, and so on. Therefore, to overcome biases, one should know possible biases and be aware of them. And reflecting on where a specific bias originated, what purposes it serves, what negative consequences may result, and so on, is key in constructively handling biases.

During training, the strengths and limits of intuition and rational-analytics should be addressed, to draw attention to the risks of distortions and biases in personnel diagnostics. In addition, from a psychometric perspective, training should provide knowledge about possible biases, stereotypes, and so on, and how they influence human judgments.

Possible distortions of perception should not only be discretized and criticized but also discussed constructively: Where do they come from? What are their purposes and benefits, possible positive and negative consequences, and so on? The aim is to make these perceptions more accessible to the selection managers (Woehr & Huffcutt, 1994 pp. 190–193).

Questioning preconceived opinions, not being deterred by status barriers (e.g., orienting oneself to views of hierarchically higher ranked people), admitting one's own mistakes, and pointing out possible bias, or even errors, to each other in a constructive and trustworthy climate are desirable steps, in this process of reflection.

To reduce biases, for example, the confirmation bias, hiring managers should be sensitized to the great importance of the separation – as far as possible – of their observations and the reporting and scoring of these behavioral observations. The psychometric reason for this is that if assessors evaluate while observing, there is a heightened risk of confirmation bias. Therefore, they should become aware of their subjectivity and tendency to evaluate and score during observations (Achouri, 2010, p. 43). During training, the participants can simulate the separation of observation/recording and evaluation/scoring, and so on (Deters, 2017, p. 178) using the observation sheet and the behaviorally anchored rating scales.

If recruiters experience prejudices or reservations about foreigners, it can be challenging to dismiss them. The term "foreign" means unknown and unfamiliar. Humans may have an evolutionarily fear of the unknown (Carleton, 2016). But, humans can also be curious and interested in strangers and the unknown; people can learn a lot from each other, especially if they have different backgrounds and perspectives. The success of diverse teams and companies clearly shows the positive effect of diversity (McKinsey & Company, 2020). However, becoming aware of one's prejudices against the unknown or foreigners is one thing; overcoming them is quite another – much more complicated, but feasible. Research shows that when people have contact with people of other cultures and ethnicities and experience their fears or prejudices are not justified, the fear of strangers (xenophobia) can be diminished (Carleton, 2016). Therefore, accepting the foreign is a civilizing achievement that global hiring managers should repeatedly appreciate.

To avoid or reduce distortions of perception in practice, a standardization of the personnel selection process, for example, ISO 10,667 or DIN 33,430, could be implemented (Ackerschott et al., 2016, pp. 87–103) since training in implementing rational-analytical processes also requires examining biases and prejudices.

9.2.3.4 Developing and using collective intuition for better decision-making

9.2.3.4.1 The value of collective intuition

Individual reflections are subjective and conscious (re-)constructions, based on memories guided by unconscious or hidden individual interests, motives, and so on. At the same time, reflections can promote identity, for example, the role and self-image as a hiring manager. However, objective and neutral reflections on intuition are not possible, in principle.

Developing awareness of one's intuitions, emotions, and thinking patterns and constantly reflecting on oneself is difficult to learn. Only a few adults succeed in walking this way, alone. The old, familiar patterns and rituals are too tempting. It is easier to strengthen oneself by walking this path with other recruiters.

Eisenkraft (2013) investigates whether individual intuition-based judgments can be trusted in personnel diagnostics. His results show that these individual intuitive impressions should not be used as the exclusive basis for decisions. Concerning personnel diagnostics, Eisenkraft's research (2013) shows that subjective impressions based on individual intuitions tend to be biased, but aggregated intuitive impressions have higher validity. Therefore, initial impressions should only be trusted if it is possible to collect and combine several independent observers' judgments. Unfortunately, intuitive assessments at the individual level are often too burdened by distortions and other cognitive influences to make consistently valid predictions about work performance (Eisenkraft, 2013, p. 278).

He, therefore, recommends reflecting, in open discourse, on the personal intuitive judgments of several persons involved in any decision. In this way, biased measurements can be reduced, and the predictive validity of intuitive decisions can be improved (Eisenkraft, 2013, p. 278; Nachtwei et al., 2013, p. 36).

Akinci & Sadler-Smith (2019) come to similar conclusions. Therefore, it is necessary to collect different perceptions and perspectives, analyze them within a circle of colleagues, compare and explain individual impressions, intuitions, emotions, and interpretations and, then, arrive at a common judgment and selection decision (consensus decision). This does not produce a completely objective picture of the candidate but comprehensible, intersubjectively monitored results.

9.2.3.4.2 Broadening perspectives

If HR managers spend their whole life working in a specific business, they probably have limited experience. These limited perspectives need to be broadened through exchanges with other HR professionals, and by reflecting on individual intuitions and emotions with colleagues and line managers after an interview or in an integration or consensus discussion, at the end of an assessment. Other ways of broadening perspectives are reading research results, attending professional congresses or training, or changing companies.

9.2.3.4.3 Conceptualization of collective intuition

Samba et al. (2019) summarize the current state of research on team or collective intuition in management. Collective or team intuition results from intense team interactions that focus on information (knowledge, observations, beliefs) and intuitions (including feelings). Collective intuition combines information elements holistically and integrates team members' different perspectives and experiences.

Samba et al. (2019) developed a theoretical framework to organize the perspectives on intuition in top management teams. According to their framework, team or collective intuition can be described as the locus of intuition (where it originates: in an individual hiring manager level or at the team level). It can either be conceptualized at the individual level and as the aggregate of team members' intuition by applying and discussing the personal intuitions of every team member, or it can be conceptualized at the team level as integrating intuition and as a holistic and emergent intuition (a newly constructed intuition by and of the team).

This second way of conceptualizing team-/collective intuition is also emphasized by Samba et al. (2019); for them, collective intuition is more than sharing individual intuitions. Team or collective intuition (and cognition) is more than the sum of the individual team members' intuitions (and cognitions). Through coordinated interactions, discussions, and reflections on the applicants, individual impressions, observations, perspectives, intuitions, and emotions, new thoughts, ideas, and interpretations can be generated. The integration of intuitions reflects the synergetic effects of exchanging, imaging, and pooling impressions and intuitions. As a result, a collective intuition emerges (Samba et al., 2019, pp. 4 and 9).

Sinclair and Hamilton (2014) focus on another aspect of collective intuition. They consider that people usually don't catch themselves making intuitive errors. This inability to sense possibly having made a mistake is key to understanding why they generally accept their intuitions at face value. It also explains why they're not excited about eliminating biases, even when they become aware of biases. After all, it's difficult for human beings to fix errors they can't see. Also, knowing we have biases is not enough to overcome them. Thus, hiring managers may accept that they are biased, but they may have problems eliminating – or at least reducing – them, on their own.

But when team members share their mental models in selection decisions, their intuitions, and their emotions with others, they gain the opportunity to reflect critically and question their biases and reduce them. As a result, they can coordinate their decisions more effectively (Hodgkinson & Sadler-Smith, 2018, p. 485). Moreover, this process allows individuals to value and appreciate their intuitions and emotions as helpful messages and, as a result, to use them constructively and collectively.

9.2.3.4.4 Communication of collective intuition in selection processes

The team's communication process should be designed to construct a collective intuition, using their individual perspectives, experiences, emotions, and intuitions. An effective team communication process requires high levels of socio-behavioral integration; this involves three key interrelated and reinforcing elements: (1) level of collaborative behavior; (2) quantity and quality of information exchanged; and (3) emphasis on joint decision-making. In addition, mutual trust, acceptance, appreciation, and positive, fear-free relationships facilitate open exchange within the team (Samba et al., 2019, p. 9).

Akinci & Sadler-Smith (2019) highlight the importance of the interplay of intuition and deliberation in group decisions. By applying the "4 I's" organizational learning framework (Intuiting, Interpreting, Integrating, Institutionalizing), it is possible to develop a deeper understanding of the phenomenon of collective intuition. Expert intuition (e.g., hiring HR experts or line managers) is accepted by other team members in collective decision-making processes, when experts' intuitions are shared and interpreted, collectively. This way, intuitions can be collectivized; and this collective reflection of individual intuitions leads to organizational learning.

Samba et al. (2019, p. 8) also point to the importance of hierarchical structures in these team processes. Collective intuition can be used in discussing interview observations or leadership potential in the integration or consensus discussion, at the end of an assessment.

To identify and evaluate candidates' behavior according to the required competencies, most guidelines for assessment centers stipulate diverse assessors, both in terms of demographics (race, ethnicity, age, sex) and experience (organizational level, functional work area, managers, psychologists). A further fundamental principle is that at least two assessors should observe one candidate, in each exercise. Also, a participant's current supervisor should not be involved in the assessment center (International Taskforce for Assessment Center Guidelines, 2015; Deters, 2017, pp. 182–184).

To encourage team/collective intuition, responsible hiring managers can foster socio-behavioral integration, for example, by reducing hierarchical thinking and acting. The integration and reflection process should be an open and psychologically safe discourse, free of power (formal, professional, and personal) and domination. Thus, hierarchically higher team members and experienced selection managers must hold back their impressions and judgments and let the other team members talk first. In addition, it has proven to be a good idea that all participants record their impressions (including intuitions and emotions) about applicants in writing. The conference moderator reads and visualizes these, at the end of the selection process. This way, it is possible to integrate diverse or opposed perspectives and raise the quality of decisions.

Openness to the intuitions and thought patterns of others and a joint reflection on these topics is a very effective way of developing or expanding the intuitive competencies of recruiters. Thus, reflecting on one's intuitions and emotions in selection processes with other hiring managers and using collective intuition is recommended.

9.2.3.4.5 Developing a high-reliability organization

Using the collective intuition of a team recalls Weick & Sutcliffe's concept of a high-reliability organization (2007); they developed the concept of collective alertness or mindfulness, which enables organizations to avoid errors and failures (no matter how small) and their consequences. Thus, they address building a culture of error, looking at potential errors, constantly seeking information that challenges current and long-held beliefs, creating conditions for openness and feedback, and showing sensitivity to potential failures such as blind spots or bias. This culture of collective alertness can be transferred to personnel selection processes by developing collective intuitions and using rational-analytical selection procedures to reduce errors or failures.

9.2.3.4.6 Reflection on rationalizations of intuition

It is crucial for hiring managers to understand possible rationalizations of intuitions and reflect on and discuss these with other recruiters or professionals. For example, possible reflection questions could be:

- Which intuitions and emotions do I/we have?
- What kind of rationalizations of intuitions do I/ we use?
- What is the function of rationalization? Do rationalizations have more of an explanatory function or a context-specific obfuscation function?
- What are the (positive and negative) consequences of my/our rationalizations?
- Why are decisions based on experience more accepted in practice than judgments based on intuition and emotions?
- How do I/we want to deal with the topic of rationalizing intuitions and emotions in our company?

9.2.3.4.7 Developing intuition through supervision and coaching

Hiring managers can be guided in their decision-making processes by coaching and supervision. Exchanges with other professional coaches or supervisors can help reflect on one`s own frame of reference more clearly and intersubjectively. Kanning recommends using coaches and consultants, who focus on personal decision-making processes and implicit reference systems and question the automated processes constructively with them, also in a team of selection managers (Kanning, 1999, pp. 271–273).

In coaching- and psychotherapy education and extra-occupational personnel development training, reflecting on what the intuitions and emotions of a counterpart or conversation partner provoke in oneself is part of the development program. The intuitive element in judgments can be made conscious through a communicative evaluation of one's judgments and the coach or supervisor. This creates opportunities to examine these intuitions and their ability to support good or bad decisions. Supervising and coaching support managers in articulating their intuitions, reflecting on them constructively, and questioning judgments and decisions can be critical instruments of intuition training.

9.2.3.4.8 Mentalization as a specific approach to reflecting on emotions

The concept of mentalization is an approach to understanding the connection between mental states and behavior. Mentalizing means resonating with someone else's emotions and then reflectively mirroring the feelings. It means tracking one's own emotions, as one feels them. It is about identifying and perceiving one's feelings, naming them, and expressing them to self or others.

The ability to mentalize means to perceive, understand, and respect the perspectives of oneself and others in terms of mental states (e.g., cognitive states such as needs, motives, beliefs, reasons, as well as emotional states) and to interpret behavior as a consequence of these mental states. Thus, mentalizing enables human proximity and understanding.

Human development to a mature personality is supported by reflecting on these relationships and autonomously regulating behavior, based on confidence in one`s ability to perceive oneself and others clearly. Through introspection and reflection on intuitions and emotions, the ability to mentalize is promoted, and with it, the confidence in the ability to perceive and understand human behavior (Fonagy et al., 2002; Kirsch, 2014, pp. 29–30).

A process of mentalization that includes openly admitting and constructive reflecting on one's own needs and motives in a selection process can help clarify one's behaviors and decisions as a recruiter. Mentalizing does not mean simply empathizing with the feelings of another person, but rather understanding and being able to classify the feelings of others as well as one's own. This creates distance and detachment, not to oneself and other people, but the raw feelings themselves (Bergemann, 2020, pp. 24–25).

Mentalizing helps understand one's own and others' feelings and behaviors. It helps selection managers avoid letting emotions overwhelm them, without reflection and protection. Thus, mentalizing is not only of importance for therapists or medical professionals but also helps hiring managers carry out their tasks, more professionally.

9.3 Developing intuition by "brain skill training"

Based on the assumption that the right hemisphere of the brain is the source of intuition, the training tool Herrmann Brain Dominance Instrument (HBDI) was created in the late 1970s (to the criticism of the assumption that specific processes can be directly assigned to the right or left hemisphere of the brain, see Section 4.2.8).

Like the MBTI (see Section 6.2.2.5), the HBDI was based on the notion that everyone has a dominant cognitive style, discernable through the (MBTI) questionnaire, that influences career choices or suitability for a specific goal or job. Since creativity and successful management demand holistic thinking and the ability to tap into different cognitive modes, this theory suggests that managers should train the ability to integrate processes of their "right and left brains" to develop the skills of their weaker hemisphere (Lussier, 2016, p. 715; Herrmann, 1982).

9.4 Journaling intuitions and developing cognitive maps

Sadler-Smith & Burke (2009, pp. 250–251) suggest journaling as a valuable technique for capturing intuitions, before the rational mind censors them. Journaling means regularly reporting in writing (e.g., weekly), an intuitive experience that occurred during the preceding week. In addition, and as part of this intuitive awareness training, students or hiring managers should share their intuitive experiences (messages and information, source, context, distractions, or rationalizations) with other hiring managers or students with fellow students, professors, and so on, to inquire into and reflect on these experiences.

Also, producing visual images or mind maps representing different elements and interrelationships, linking causes to effects, and so on, can help verbalize intuitions and emotions and make judgments and decisions more transparent. The different mind maps can be compared for their similarities and dissimilarities, degree of complexity, and so on.

9.5 Exploring intuition in an intercultural context

In international personnel diagnostics, hiring managers should consider possible cultural biases and stereotypes (see Sections 3.5.2.9, 3.5.2.19, and 9.2.3.3), and specific cultural factors influencing the acceptance and use of rational-analytical procedures or intuitions and emotions (see Sections 3.7.8 and 4.2.4.5, and especially Section 7.2.4).

These specific cultural factors can lead to tensions, such as whether or how standardized selection procedures should be carried out globally, when they do not correspond to cultural values (Naor et al., 2010, p. 202; see Section 7.2.4).

Therefore, during training, selection managers should reflect on how their home culture influences them, and how foreign cultures and other contextual factors affect the acceptance and use of personnel selection procedures. For instance, the acceptance of rational-analytical practices or intuitions in high context cultures compared to low context cultures or the influence of Hofstede's cultural dimensions such as power distance, individualism, or indulgence must be considered.

In East Asian cultures, emotions are less shown in personnel selection procedures than in Western cultures. Nevertheless, personnel managers in these cultures can intuitively understand how applicants affect them and whether they think they fit into the company and the team.

Intuitions are based on personal experiences and, thus, are acquired in a specific cultural context. Therefore, managers, who grew up in different cultures or lived in different countries and cultures for an extended period and gained a wealth of experiences in different cultural contexts, are more likely to develop intuitions and other behaviors appropriate to varied cultural contexts and global applicants.

Learning intuition in an intercultural context takes place, on the one hand, by living in other cultures and the experiences made in other countries, and working with people of different cultural backgrounds. On the other hand, it means carefully observing how people from other cultures act and react and, then, formulating and reformulating hypotheses and cultural explanations for the observed behavior. At the same time, it requires reflecting on one's intuitions and emotions and the related impressions and feelings about applicants with hiring managers from other cultures, giving mutual feedback, and being coached and supported by each other.

Hiring managers, who select in a global context, should not only have intercultural mindsets, intercultural communication skills, and so on (Deters, 2017, pp. 119–121); they should also have intercultural awareness and a comprehensive understanding of situational and environmental aspects of intercultural interactions. This includes training to monitor one's interactions and communication behavior (verbal and non-verbal) in global selection processes and recognizing anything unacceptable to applicants from other cultures. Also, they should have the ability, motivation, and openness to learn from colleagues of different cultures and develop and expand their intercultural intuition.

Osland and Bird (2000, p. 73) recommend learning from others and their experiences and using cultural mentors or former expats and other experienced global managers to correct inaccurate hypotheses (biases, stereotypes) about local cultures and the behavior of local employees or candidates, from other cultures. Maznevski & Distefano (2000) and Mockaitis et al. (2018) show how global leaders can be developed through membership in global teams and working, communicating, and reflecting together.

Osland & Bird also state that one can learn intercultural competencies by reading about other cultures, but cultural assimilation exercises are more recommended. These are critical incidents of cross-cultural encounters, accompanied by alternative explanations of people's behavior from a foreign culture. This can help (global) hiring managers understand the complexity of their own culture and develop the competencies in cultural observation and behavioral flexibility needed to adapt to the specific context and unanticipated situations, for example, by role-playing and videos of cross-cultural interactions (Osland & Bird, 2000, pp. 73–74).

Last but not the least, they can provide a basis for evaluating (global) selection decisions and to reflect on the intuitions and emotions experienced during these global selection processes.

Derous et al. (2021) show that intercultural training for overcoming hiring discrimination against ethnic minority applicants is beneficial, and ". . . discrimination is reduced after .. training interventions. . . . The intercultural effectiveness training leads to improved ability to suppress stereotypes, both immediately after the intervention and after three months" (Potočnik, 2021, p. 170).

Sadler-Smith & Burke (2009, p. 258) claim that it is necessary to reflect in training on questions such as "Do any – and if so – how do possible biases, fears, projections or wishful thinking contaminate the intuition?"

Biases and stereotypes can also be created and passed on by exchange with others. A vicious circle may result: in the desire to combat false assumptions, people may involuntarily implant them in other people. The same risk exists if, for example, one looks, for instance, at Hofstede's cultural dimensions theory, because Hofstede's research findings may be applied stereotypically to everyone in a specific culture.

Thus, Osland and Bird (2000) recommend intercultural training, experience in different cultures, and cultural mentors to combat stereotypes or prejudices. In this intercultural training, managers learn to overcome their assumptions, biases, prejudices, and stereotypes about people of other cultures.

Organizations should provide cross-cultural training to their recruiters to enhance the objectivity, validity, and reliability of personnel selection processes in selecting (global leadership) talent. This training should increase the recruiters' awareness of the influence of culture on their judgment, biases, stereotypes, prejudices, and misunderstandings due to cultural differences. For example, their verbal and non-verbal communication behaviors influence job applicants and their behavior. Further, the training should enable them to differentiate between competencies, skills, personality, and culturally based behavior (Manroop et al., 2013, p. 3526; Lim et al., 2006, p. 267). Organizations can reduce misunderstandings by redesigning how interviews are conducted, for example, by making the purpose of questions explicit and not using vocabulary the applicants are unfamiliar with (Roberts & Campbell, 2006, pp. 166–168).

However, it is recommended that global selection managers have different cultural backgrounds. Then, in training or practice, they can exchange their individual experiences, intuitions, and emotions that applicants trigger and reflect critically and constructively on them. In this way – rooted in their own culture – they can learn with and from each other and expand their intuitive competencies.

9.6 Empirical research results on developing intuition

Reflection on intuitions in practice: Most interviewed hiring managers acknowledge reflecting on and openly discussing their intuitions and emotions regarding certain applicants, with colleagues. However, trust is necessary for this reflecting process and open exchange and discussion (Deters, 2019, p. 124). Thus, many experts ask for impressions from other hiring managers to compare different intuitions. In most cases, they prefer a partnership-based, solution-oriented exchange between hiring managers (Deters, 2019, p. 132).

The managers interviewed in our empirical research confirmed the importance of the interplay of intuition and deliberation and the added value of collectively reflecting on intuitions and rational-analytical results for critical business decisions, especially, selection decisions. Most hiring managers interviewed prefer a collective rather than an individual reflection on intuitions and emotions. Also, they emphasize the need to collectivize hiring decisions, so the responsibility does not rest on one person alone. It is also noted that anyone can be wrong in their judgment (Deters, 2019, p. 133).

> Getting a second, third or fourth opinion, checking whether my initial impressions are correct, of course also in exchange with the other assessors, . . . there is also a constructive discussion where we describe our personal impressions and intuitions and compare our own assessment with that of the others to determine whether there is a gap, and if so, why (Deters, 2019, p. 133).

In addition, interviewed managers emphasize the importance of conscious perception, transparent communication, and reflection on intuitions. In this context, one of the managers says that this could be seen as a collaborative and organizational learning process. They are convinced that shared experiences, intuitions, and emotions increase the proportion of good selection decisions (Reichelt, 2020, pp. 79–80 and 86).

Mutual trust is the basis of this open exchange. Our interviewees have hardly ever experienced problems in an open exchange due to the different hierarchical levels of the hiring managers. Nevertheless, a few interviews show that trust problems can arise, when higher-ranked superiors or executives influence the decision process through their initial statements. Lower ranked or inexperienced hiring managers may hold back possibly differing views (Deters, 2019, p. 125). One manager confirmed that very honest reflection is only possible if there is trust in the relationship with the co-interviewer. He makes it clear:

> I do not openly mention my feelings or intuitions when a much higher-ranked executive has already made it clear that he sees an applicant quite differently than I do (Deters, 2019, p. 124).

Some experts state that they make notes of their intuition about a candidate before deciding. They also recommend this procedure to their colleagues. Other interviewees say they listen to their intuition and question where it comes from; or sleep on it before deciding (Deters, 2019, p. 132).

Only a few interviewed hiring experts state that they do not reflect on their intuition, arguing that reflecting on intuition is not an issue in their company:

> I am not concerned about this, . . . if I make a decision, then I am sure that this decision is the right one . . ., and I do not question it: have I made my decision based on facts, analytical procedures, bias, etc. or did I make a gut decision? I rely on my judgment (Deters, 2019, p. 131).

Only two experts (from a total of about 50 interviewed experts) state that intuition is not a topic of discussion in their company:

> No, I have never talked about intuitions in selection processes. So no, this is actually not an issue. [. . .] I really wouldn't really know how to approach the topic in a conversation in the company either (Deters, 2019, p. 133).

Can intuition be switched off or minimized? According to the psychometric approach, the emotions and intuitions of personnel managers should be avoided or reduced, as far as possible, in a selection process (Schuler, 1996, p. 86). Unfortunately, this is viewed with incomprehension by the vast majority of the experts surveyed.

When asked how to deal with whether intuition can be switched off, most interviewees question why they should want or try intuition to be switched off or why this would be necessary. In any case, the experts largely agree that intuition cannot be switched off.

> Is it necessary . . . ? . . . I think it is unnecessary to think about completely disregarding intuition or gut feeling, because, in my opinion, it is not possible to disregard it (Deters, 2019, p. 131).

This is confirmed by neuroscientific studies (Roth, 2009, pp. 301–302 and 549). The vast majority of interviewed hiring managers, worldwide, do not want to switch off their intuition, as they regard it as an essential message and an individual core competence (Deters, 2019, p. 131):

> Yes, I listen to what my intuition already tells me. However, I think it is important to let intuition tell me whether an applicant fits the team because, ultimately, you have to work with this candidate later on. And if my intuition tells me someone doesn't fit in with my team and me, then I have to consider this. And that's why I think it's important to listen to your intuitions and be open to them (Deters, 2019, p. 131).

Despite the high number of negative examples of intuitively made decisions, a positive tenor towards intuition can be seen. As a strategy for dealing with the fact that intuition cannot be eliminated, interviewees state that intuition should be allowed and that it is essential to become aware of one's intuition. Furthermore, they point out that decision-makers should force themselves to make decisions, based on concrete examples. The interviewees indicate that clearly defined processes, standards, selection criteria, and training can help in this respect (Deters, 2019, p. 136).

The statements from the interviewed hiring managers confirm the active reflection and critical attitude towards intuitions and feelings. Thus, most interviewed managers state that they listen to their intuition, but that rational-analytical procedures, such as detailed requirement profiles and interview guidelines, are also necessary.

Intersubjectivity as part of collective intuition: Intersubjectivity is mentioned by Miles & Sadler-Smith (2014, p. 623) and Laske & Weiskopf (1996, p. 300). Intersubjectivity, in the context of selection, means different hiring managers agree on how they assess an applicant. They share their subjective impressions, reflect on, and interpret these impressions, intuitions, and emotions, and discuss their scoring results and why they assess the applicant as they individually do. At the end of this discussion, they reach a consensus. Our research shows that in most cases, it already seems to be common practice to discuss individual impressions and assessments of the candidates and make personnel selection decisions jointly, by reaching intersubjectivity through aggregating the subjective impressions.

Hiring managers interviewed emphasize that achieving intersubjectivity does not guarantee objectivity. The managers participating in a selection process reach intersubjectivity, but not objectivity, in the sense that a hiring decision is independent of different perceptions, and that involved hiring managers reach the same result and conclusion, independently. From their perspective, it is necessary to involve people in the selection process. Therefore, the goal is to reach intersubjectivity. Intersubjectivity means to reach a consensus and not a poor compromise. Consequently, it is essential to create this discussion process as a discourse that is free of domination and hierarchy and grant all managers the same participation rights.

Empirical research results on intuition and bias: Our empirical research confirms that intuitions and emotions can be biased. From the perspective of the interviewed hiring managers, this demonstrates the importance of dealing with this topic as part of the education and training of hiring managers.

The following deals with negative examples or situations from intuitive personnel selection decisions. For example, one interviewee states that he decided on an applicant, based on his intuitive impression. However, in retrospect, this choice turned out to be a wrong decision, because his judgment was influenced and distorted by the halo effect:

> There are candidates who enter the room and just wow you and take you in, and after a couple of months, you realize it was only hot air (Deters, 2019, p. 129).

The respondents state that the confirmation bias, halo effect, sympathy/ emotional approval, similarity, or stereotyping occur due to their intuitions. In addition, the interviewees say that mainly positive intuitions often make them act too benevolently. It makes them too optimistic and eager to see the positive in the applicant (Deters, 2019, p. 129). Here, the tendency towards leniency (Kleebaur, 2017, p. 108) can be identified as a distortion of judgment.

The managers interviewed state that education and training are more likely to be offered in large or medium-sized enterprises, than in smaller organizations. Therefore, SMEs need some catching up in qualified education and training of selection managers.

At the international level and in intercultural training, the topic of intuitions, emotions, and acceptance of rational-analytical procedures or intuitions and emotions is hardly addressed. Therefore, there is still a considerable need to catch up, here.

Nearly all interviewed personal experts emphasize their intuition as a vital part of the selection process and that attention to intuition should not be abandoned. Intuition and feelings are seen as important signals in deciding whether the candidate fits the values and attitudes of the company and, at the same time, gets along with the team members.

Overall, the interviewed selection experts consider the personal and intuitive components of their work as very valuable and necessary. Also, most of the interviewed selection managers are aware that they can be a source of possible biases in a decision-making situation. Thus, it is necessary to know and reflect on biases.

Practitioners want to use their intuitions as a specific kind of experience and expertise. As experienced selection managers, they can act as mentors and share their experience with new hiring managers. However, all new selection managers must gain their own experience and learn from it. To persuade practitioners to apply scientific findings in personnel diagnostics, they must be made to feel that they can and should continue to use their intuition and the associated experience of competence, in practice. However, they must be prepared to reflect critically and constructively on their intuitions and question their usefulness for responsible personnel selection.

Thus, the interviewed hiring managers confirm the need for training and reflection processes, also at the collective level. Reflective practices may seem time-consuming at the beginning, but they are seen as a good investment that will pay off both in time and in the quality of the decisions.

While joint reflection and learning processes about intuitions and emotions are widespread in practice, training on the topic hardly occurs. It is also confirmed that intuitions or emotions in personnel selection have not been dealt with, comprehensively, during training or studies at university, as they are seen as something negative and to be avoided, especially in science.

Many practitioners complain that scientists don`t recognize that they impose something on managers, from the outside, that doesn't fit. External influences only lead to a change in managerial behavior, if the managers perceive them as relevant. This is why it is essential to speak the language of those researchers who want to connect with the managers' individual experiences, patterns of thought and action, explanation and decision principles, and self-images. This means that researchers must engage with practitioners' constructions of reality.

Sustainable implementation of new learning, for example, learning and implementation of rational-analytical selection procedures and reflected use of intuitions and feelings is possible, if what should be learned is appropriately anchored in people's minds. Due to neuroplasticity, this is possible. People can internalize new thinking or behavior if they are convinced and often repeat it.

Neuroplasticity is an umbrella term referring to the many capabilities of the human brain to reorganize itself throughout life, due to the environment, behavior, and internal experiences. Neuroplasticity, thus, means that the human brain can get used to new things.

The human brain works in neural networks. At the beginning of the learning process, the connections between the nerve cells are still weak. The more often people repeat an activity, the more ingrained the neural pathways become. This means that through practice, for example, mindfulness or reflection, and repetition, people expand their neural network; first, they create a pathway, then a road, and finally, a new data highway in the brain.

Harnessing neuroplasticity in adulthood isn't quite as simple as in specific periods of childhood, but it can be accomplished under particular circumstances. While it is true that the human brain is much more adept at change in the early years, and capacity declines with age, neuroplasticity happens throughout the entire life, from birth until death.

Specific circumstances and a culture of openness, curiosity, and change can foster the individual will and motivation to change behaviors and procedures. At the same time, our research results show that integrating rational-analytics and intuitive-emotional processes in personnel diagnostics can only be implemented consistently, if the practitioners recognize a positive benefit for themselves in this holistic approach. For example, establishing a new behavior should be justified analytically, but the wanted behavior should also be associated with positive emotions. This can be, for example, a positive experience of competence or effective hiring decisions. This also aligns with the research of Ryan and Deci (Ryan, 1995; Ryan & Deci, 2000; Deci & Ryan, 2008), according to which the experiencing of effectiveness and mastery is regarded as one of the most important motivators for human beings.

Human selection decisions in organizations cannot only be traced back to supposedly objective rationalities; intuitive (and emotional) evaluations are always included. De Sousa (2018) states that there is an emotional truth (de Sousa 1987 and 2011). Or, as the French philosopher Pascal (1669) says: "The heart has its reasons which reason knows nothing of. . . . We know the truth not only by reason but also by the heart."

All education and learning – also that of HR managers or HR students – should, according to the German philosopher, Hegel (1803), and many others, include not only professional knowledge but also the education of the heart. This education of the heart requires learning a reflective use of rational-analytics, intuitions, and feelings (Tubbs, 1996; Kaube, 2020).

10 Implementation of a holistic personnel selection approach

A holistic selection approach means integrating rational-analytical procedures and intuitive processes. In the following, these two questions are considered:

- How can the integration and balancing of rational-analytics and intuition be efficiently designed to promote high-quality personnel selection in organizations?
- How can selection managers use analytics and intuitions in a target-oriented and, at the same time, critical and constructive way?

10.1 Consider the organizational context and take a systemic approach

Research shows that specific contexts and fast-changing, unstable, and complex environmental conditions (e.g., influenced by technological change, the intensity of competition in markets, including labor markets, governmental regulations; see Khatri & Ng, 2000, pp. 67–68) favor intuitive decision-making (Sadler-Smith, 2019, p. 2). At the same time, the rational-analytical way of thinking and decision-making is being reinforced by developments in digitization, AI, data availability, and the fast and goal-oriented processing, analysis, and interpretation of this data.

To understand people's decisions and actions, neither theory nor practice should consider individuals detached from their environment. A systemic perspective considers this principle and can thus help integrate intuitive-emotional and rational-analytical procedures in selection decisions. As early as 1966, the American psychologists Katz and Kahn (1966) described organizations as open social systems. Systems theory aims to describe and understand the embeddedness and exchange of organizations with their environment. In this way, the authors show how contextual factors influence individual decisions in organizations. And this perspective can also be applied to personnel selection.

A living system is a cohesive conglomeration of interrelated and interdependent elements that interact with each other. To do justice to the complexity of living systems, interactions, complementary processes, and mutual influences must be considered. Linear models, which explain human behavior based on a single factor or a simple idea of cause and effect, are insufficient to explain and change complex social systems.

Every system is bounded by space and time, influenced by its environment, defined by its structures, processes, and purposes, and expressed through its functioning. A system is more than the sum of its parts, as it represents synergy or emergent behavior.

https://doi.org/10.1515/9783110980967-010

Human and organizational behavior can only be understood if self-dynamics and the ability of a system to self-organize (self-organization is the ability to change one`s function, stabilize oneself, etc.), and thus also consider the complexity of hiring managers as bio-psycho-social systems. Therefore, a systemic approach means, not attributing human and especially hiring decisions to stable personality traits but always considering the decision-making and behavioral context.

In a systemic approach, hiring managers and organizations are regarded as living social systems interacting with their internal and external environments. This interaction with the environment, including other living organisms, such as applicants, is essential for hiring managers and organizations.

Due to external influences, however, open systems repeatedly fall into an imbalance, so they must continuously invest energy to achieve a state of dynamic stability or dynamic balance (equilibrium, homeostasis); thus, hiring managers develop a momentum of their own and try to maintain or reach a state of equilibrium or homeostasis. Due to this inherent dynamic, hiring managers can never be controlled entirely from the outside and thus often elude simple regulation or even guidance from the outside, for example, selection guidelines such as ISO 10667.

To reduce the complexity of selection decisions, hiring managers use patterns of perception based on structural features to see to what extent these patterns fit into existing complex situations such as selection processes in a specific organization.

If a specific pattern does not fit into the situation, living systems as learning systems can adapt their patterns and thus their decision-making behavior.

Learned patterns remain stored in the brain and support fast and good decisions in stable environments. On the other hand, if the environment changes, previously learned patterns may no longer be helpful, and a person must learn to form new patterns.

But our research shows that a constructive interaction of intuitions and analytics successfully supports handling complexities in open and fast-changing environments.

Selection managers cannot be seen as independent and isolated human beings but as open social systems interacting with their environment. Decisions are always embedded in a social system of mutual influence. For example, hiring managers are influenced by other HR managers and line managers, the specific labor market, the legal and technical environment, the financial and time resources, the applicants' behaviors, previous success patterns, mindsets, and so on. Mutual influencing processes are always at work here.

The interplay between the various parts or elements of a system and thus the state of a system can be changed through positive and negative feedback loops. The system itself translates inputs from the environment into its own language and mindsets. In other words, it creates its own informational image of the environment, for example, the requirements of a high-quality selection process.

From a reality-constructing perspective, human beings cannot recognize the outside world objectively because it is created interactively between the observer and the object. The process of how the observers get their image of reality is called "judgment." Therefore, intuition from this constructive perspective is a judgment about reality.

Self-organized systems always perceive environmental influences, and thus the information and knowledge from the environment in terms of their structure and their own experiences, knowledge, and so on, and process them accordingly. Hiring managers, as living systems, decide consciously or unconsciously based on their experiences and learning processes, how they perceive the environment and the corresponding environmental stimuli (e.g., psychometric knowledge about personnel selection), and how they can process them. Such external influences can lead to a change in mindsets and behavior, perceived as relevant to the individual hiring manager.

How selection managers view their reality is subjectively constructed. For example, applicants' perception of selection procedures or knowledge about high-quality personnel selection or intuition is always a product of subjective perceptions. What is perceived and how something is perceived is determined by genetic preconditions and is substantially influenced by previous learning and experiential processes, culture, and so on.

The perception of selection managers is thus based on information that their brains (or bodies) have already stored as important or meaningful in the past. And only what has been anchored as correct or important provides a basis for new perceptions, and thus new behavior. However, it is also known that people rarely question how their stored experiences influence their perceptions and interpretations of behavior or knowledge. Thus, they often rely unreflectingly on their intuitions and emotions (Roth & Menzel, 2001). It is exhausting for the human brain to ignore intuitive assumptions and switch on the rational-analytical mind.

To convince hiring managers, who are self-organized living systems, to use rational-analytical selection procedures and constructively reflect on their intuitions and emotions, it is necessary to speak their language and understand their context. And to achieve a structural linkage of interactions, for example, knowledge about high-quality personnel selection and the implementation of corresponding selection procedures, the selection manager's individual learning experiences and memories should be identified.

A further topic in systemic perspective is the interaction of the elements of an organization. As shown in Sections 2.2 and 2.3, there are many unintended risks associated with using standards (e.g., they can lead to more formalization and bureaucracy, are considered more time-consuming, more expensive, and as restrictions to flexibility).

If the risk of wrong selection decisions can be reduced by using standards, hiring managers are then faced with an increase in other risks. It is a matter of weighing up advantages and possible risks. If HR managers feel no pressure from their management, applicants, and other stakeholders or face no legal requirements to change their selection procedures, why should they change them?

A systemic analysis of this topic means thinking in multiple perspectives and interdependencies rather than in terms of monocausality. From a systemic perspective, not only individual HR managers but also structural, process-related, and cultural context factors determine whether selection decision processes change in organizations or not.

Social reality and decisions made by hiring managers or scientists cannot sufficiently be explained by aggregating individual behavior and related individual intentions. Individual behavior can only be explained within the specific environmental context since specific behavior is part of a greater social context. For example, it is not enough to publish findings about high-quality personnel selection. Such knowledge is embedded in a pattern of individual experiences and expectations, reinterpreted and constructed in people's minds, and at the same time, emotionally charged.

A systemic approach emphasizes structural and institutional elements and argues that behavior in social systems must be analyzed beyond individuals' level. And such institutional elements are, for example, specific patterns of thought and action in organizations (unconscious basic assumptions such as beliefs and values; Schein, 2004, pp. 28–36), regularities in the interaction of employees and managers, formal and informal rules of cooperation, power and hierarchical structures and processes, and so on. From a systemic perspective, this raises the question, to what extent do these elements influence the design of personnel selection systems (e.g., as possible persistence forces). And conversely, the question arises as to what extent a new personnel selection procedure can influence the previous balance and systemic stability of organizations.

10.2 Develop a common understanding of the quality of hiring and personnel selection in theory and practice, and bridge the reference systems of science and practice

Our empirical research shows that, in practice, the decision to use a particular personnel selection procedure is not made solely based on expected validity. Instead, in a holistic approach to the quality of personnel selection, other factors such as individual, organizational or cultural acceptance, conveying a positive candidate experience, cost-effectiveness, and practicability are considered. For this reason, the psychometrical concept, which only accepts a rational-analytical procedure as being of high quality is limited to optimizing personnel selection in organizations.

It turns out that in theory and practice, quality is often defined differently. In practice, recruiters and other managers often define quality as the result, that is, whether someone fits into the company or team and performs well, and has a positive impact on the efficiency and effectiveness of the organization. How the candidate was selected and which hiring methods are used are less interesting. Most important is that the outcome is perceived as positive. As pointed out in Section 3.1, this can be described as the quality of hire.

From a scientific or psychometric point of view, to achieve the quality of hire and the quality of the selection process (see Section 3.2), recruiters should follow specific scientifically proven procedures that are based on evident research results and scientific quality criteria, such as validity. But as long as companies and managers are confident of achieving their hiring goals, even with nonscientifically recommended personnel selection procedures, it is challenging to convince them to use rational-analytical methods.

To deal with each other constructively and learn with and from each other, it is helpful for science and practice to know their respective frames of reference. Thus, a goal is to bridge the fundamental differences in science and practice reference systems. This requires an appreciation and empathy for the other's perspectives.

And it also means – as a first step – knowing and accepting one's own construction of selection quality and one's own internalized truths and thought patterns because this is the first step toward change: "The curious paradox is that when I accept myself just as I am, then I can change. . . . The more I am willing to understand and accept the realities in myself and others, the more change seems to take place" (Rogers, 1994, pp. 33 and 37).

Therefore, besides observing scientific quality criteria, researchers should also aim to solve practical problems. This presupposes a precise knowledge of practical issues and a consideration of practical contexts in developing solutions. If, for example, the implementation of psychometric procedures in SMEs often fails because the required resources are not available or because selection managers see their intuitions as important messages, solutions should be developed that consider this scenario.

Thus, research should be based on a realistic image of selection managers. And research results on effective selection methods should not only be published in scientific journals, but also in publications that are read by practitioners. In addition, open-access publications could contribute to further disseminating scientific findings. Further, practitioners need to know how to implement these procedures in practice.

Researchers often deal with specific questions to publish the results in a high-ranked scientific journal, extend publication lists, and get as many citations as possible. This creates a high level of acceptance and reputation in the scientific community. However, their main interest often lies less in practical impact and translating research results into practice. In the academic world, recognition for practice-oriented research is often lacking; especially in social science, mutual skepticism often marks the cooperation between science and managerial practice.

To bridge the gap between science and practice, scientists in HR or People management, particularly personnel diagnostics, should formulate their research results for potential practitioners.

Even though public relations work, press offices, or "impact managers" at universities have been expanded in recent years, they are currently unable to prepare research results so that practitioners understand. This should be done by the scientists themselves, for example, in cooperation with science journalists. Research results should be communicated via multiple communication channels and be easily readable and implementation-oriented.

From the political side, applied research and thus collaboration between science and practice can be promoted, for example, by funding institutions or innovation agencies such as the Swiss Innosuisse or the Swedish Vinnova.

To have more impact, science in personnel management can move beyond merely counting citations to measure success. Joint research projects between the academia and the managerial practice can be an appropriate starting point for creating more real-world implications.

Science can also support practice in recognizing intuitive evaluation processes, reflecting on them, and critically questioning their strengths and weaknesses. But it is also essential to acknowledge the valuable and positive sides of intuitions and emotions from the scientific side and examine them further in terms of research.

Science can help solve practical problems, for example, how to deal with possible conflicts between intuition and analytics. A further topic is how managers can be convinced of the value of combining intuitive and rational-analytical approaches to decision-making and become more skilled in their joint application. Managers should know these integrating approaches and how intuition and analytics interact, especially when experienced decision-makers are confronted by scenarios that are in their domain of expertise but are sufficiently novel that the requisite knowledge, experiences, patterns, or scripts are inappropriate and hence their expert judgment is confounded (Highhouse, 2008; Klein et al., 2010; Salas et al., 2010; Hodgkinson & Sadler-Smith, 2018, p. 486).

Hiring managers, consultants, or scientists who are personally convinced of the benefits of an integrated and holistic approach can promote a corporate culture that is open to the systematic use of the relevant scientific knowledge.

At universities, evidence-based knowledge and best practices should be taught and put into practice by students when they enter the field as new hires. Likewise, students should be taught different approaches and perspectives to specific problems, and possible ambiguities and paradoxes should be discussed.

Thus, many academics feel an obligation to disseminate evidence-based information. Unfortunately, practitioners have sometimes gathered dubious information with useless selection tools such as graphology or astrology in recruiting. Scientists can create more transparency, communicate with practitioners, and be more strongly represented in social media and internet platforms. For example, scientists can be influencers by publishing in practical journals and newspapers, spreading research results via newsletters or social media such as LinkedIn, Twitter, WebEx-seminars, blogs, or YouTube tutorials, and holding talks at practical events such as conferences, trade fairs, or exhibitions.

Research findings, best practice examples, standards of selection such as the DIN 33430, or guidelines for conducting interviews and implementing assessment centers (e.g., International Taskforce on Assessment Center Guidelines, 2015), using AI and intuitions constructively could be communicated to future practitioners via (video or digital) lectures, seminars, or talks.

But it is not only up to researchers to communicate their findings. Practitioners need to inform themselves about research results. For practitioners, scientific knowledge can be a source of innovative ideas and relevant insights that companies could not develop with their own resources and in the time available. This allows organizations to stand out from competitors and become more successful (Bellmann, 2013, pp. 1042–1043).

Research, practice, and teaching can be well integrated using such opportunities. And research has an impact.

Companies are regularly pleased to support practice-oriented bachelor and master theses and teaching research projects in which company-specific solutions for current problems are developed. Here, the impact of science and students is obvious. However, it is a problem that these results are often not allowed to publish and, thus, are not generally accessible. Here, scientists can reserve the right to use the generated knowledge in an anonymous form and make it available to the general public. Practice-oriented theses and projects with students can also be awarded. The companies receive ideas for solutions tailored to their specific situation that are scientifically substantiated. Practical questions inspire science, possibly providing access to attractive data, and so on.

Thus, to bridge the gap, both managerial practitioners and scientists should become familiar with each other's perspectives and be interested in cooperating and benefiting from each other. Research findings should be neither too specific nor too complex to be valuable and easy to implement. Researchers can engage in solution- and implementation-oriented pragmatism, while practitioners must also accept that scientists need recognition in their scientific community through publishing their findings.

Many people believe recruiting can be done by anyone, and they know how recruiting works well. Nearly everyone believes that they are a good judge of human nature and character. But this is a fallacy.

10.3 Process-oriented and structural integration of rational-analytic and intuitive-emotional processes

> It is true that people are not very predictable,
> but selection decision aids help. (Highhouse, 2008, p. 340)

Chapter 3 describes in detail how a psychometric rational-analytical personnel selection process should be designed. It has become clear how structured rational-analytical procedures contribute to quality assurance in personnel selection, and thus support companies' success. As shown in Section 4.2.1, intuitive decisions made by experts are more accurate than those made by beginners. Therefore, especially newcomers or less experienced recruiters are recommended to use rational-analytical procedures and tools of personnel selection, and systematically apply rational-analytic techniques. At the same time, they need to be supported in using their intuitions and emotions constructively in personnel selection.

From a systemic perspective, supporting managers in implementing a new selection procedure is not only a question of personal knowledge and motivation but also of what is desired and possible in an organizational context. Therefore, the focus must not only be on the individual hiring manager (including line managers and their knowledge, experiences, emotions, and resistance) but on the overall organization, the structures, processes, cultures, mindsets, unconscious basic assumptions, power and micropolitical processes, previous success factors, financial resources, and so on (Mayrhofer, 2004, pp. 189–190). This focus allows identifying interrelationships, dynamics, and behavioral patterns related to implementing new personnel selection procedures.

People often overestimate their competencies and ethical standards, and are convinced to act competently and ethically. However, they may fail, for example, due to biases and so-called ethical "blind spots" (Bazerman & Tenbrunsel, 2013, p. 5). Therefore, to ensure that managers carry out their selection decisions effectively and as nondiscriminatory as possible, it is not enough to reach people on the individual level through information, knowledge transfer, or training. Rather, precise specifications are needed to know how specific selection processes should be carried out; and in addition, these processes need to be structurally anchored. Thus, selection managers should know how to work on a process-oriented level, and thus also at the level of structures, instruments, tools, and methods. By linking structures and processes in personnel selection, selection managers are supported in implementing effective selection procedures, reducing their biases, and thus discrimination.

A practical recommendation by Miles and Sadler-Smith is that a one-size-fits-all approach (2014, p. 623) for implementing a new selection system is not feasible. Therefore, each specific organizational and hiring context, for example, in SMEs, should be considered, and solutions and change processes developed for a particular organization.

A study by Huffcut et al. (2014) concludes that a high degree of structuring selection procedures is superior to a low degree, but that a medium structure (requirements analysis, rough question catalog/interview guideline, evaluation criteria, trained interviewer, ratings to assess responses and behaviors after the interview) has the highest predictive validity for professional success.

Effective personnel selection and integrating rational-analytical with intuitive procedures need structural and process-oriented support. Thus, different approaches and measures will be shown to successfully implement effective selection systems on the process and structure level.

10.3.1 Consider selection and hiring processes as social and acquisition processes

On a process level, it is recommended to understand personnel selection not only as a selection process; other interests such as winning the candidate and the promotion of other business interests could also be pursued, for example, ensuring that even rejected applicants report positively about the company and how they were treated as applicants (Miles & Sadler-Smith, 2014, p. 623). Thus, as shown in Sections 2.5, 3.7.9, and 5.1.6, organizations try to embrace a more candidate-centered approach to hiring processes.

A selection decision is about "interpersonal chemistry," affective positivity, and a feeling of intense connection. Reis et al. (2021, p. 1) state that "the perception of chemistry includes cognitive (i.e., perception of shared identity), affective (i.e., positive affect and attraction), and behavioral (i.e., perceived goal-relevant coordination) components. Thus, practitioners want to use their emotions and intuitions to assess "interpersonal chemistry."

Personnel selection, as a social relationship decision, is always about trust. Trust cannot be achieved by good arguments alone, but rather by positive emotions and experiences. To build trust with candidates in the shortest time possible, selection managers need soft skills. Thus, even standardized personnel selection processes cannot eliminate the need for selection managers to use their intuitions and feelings to build a positive relationship and assess a candidate's organizational, cultural, or team fit, attitudes, credibility, authenticity, social-communicative skills, and so on. Furthermore, applicants need to feel they are in good hands in a company and that it can adequately satisfy their goals and needs. Therefore, they should trust the recruiters.

Considering contextual factors such as the labor market, creating a hiring process as an acquisition is especially true in labor market situations where highly qualified applicants are scarce, and candidates can choose which company they want to work for. The two considerations are summarized in Figure 19. This approach is in line with Highhouse's (2008) view, who, contrary to his frequently expressed preference for standardized rational-analytical procedures, recognizes that the recruitment context must always be considered.

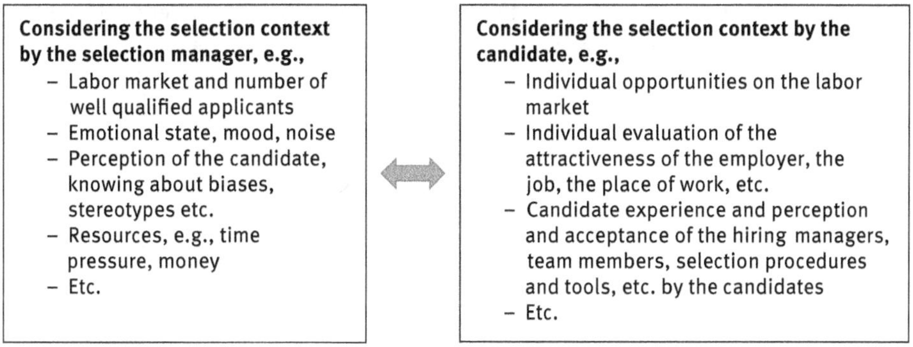

Considering the selection context by the selection manager, e.g.,
– Labor market and number of well qualified applicants
– Emotional state, mood, noise
– Perception of the candidate, knowing about biases, stereotypes etc.
– Resources, e.g., time pressure, money
– Etc.
Considering the selection context by the candidate, e.g.,
– Individual opportunities on the labor market
– Individual evaluation of the attractiveness of the employer, the job, the place of work, etc.
– Candidate experience and perception and acceptance of the hiring managers, team members, selection procedures and tools, etc. by the candidates
– Etc.

Figure 19: Examples of contextual considerations of hiring managers and candidates in a selection process.

Although contextual factors such as available resources should be considered, this should not stop hiring managers from evaluating and critiquing their existing selection processes and looking to improve them.

In selection processes such as interviews, applicants and selection managers interact and influence each other. This process is shaped by individual experiences and selective perceptions, including bias, stereotypes, and prejudices. Example: To get along with a candidate and build a good relationship, managers make small talk before and after the interview. Even if it is desirable to reduce emotions from a psychometric perspective and, in this case, from small talk, this is very questionable for most hiring managers, since they want to win applicants for their organization. Small talk is a simple – but possibly destructive – pitfall. Suppose a candidate and interviewer begin discussing sports, discovering that they both root for the same football, basketball, or soccer team, share a sense of humor, or find that they have the same hobbies or interests, it can unconsciously lead to mutual sympathy. The interviewer may then favor that candidate (see similarity effect, Section 3.5.2.14) when scoring. It may also alienate candidates who dislike sports. The idea that it would be better to choose neutral issues such as the weather is not really helpful, because personnel selection is always about personal connection. Therefore, despite the need to establish a positive emotional relationship with the applicant, selection managers should be aware of these possible biases.

Thus, using intuitions and feelings does not automatically mean assessing applicants as objectively as possible because hiring managers can be aware of possible perceptual distortions and reflect on them transparently in a critical-constructive way for themselves and other hiring managers.

Designing a selection process as a social acquisition process and ensuring positive candidate experiences, a selection process should allow subjectivity by showing individual emotions, and not be depersonalized by ignoring or suppressing intuitions (Klopprogge, 2022, p. 304).

10.3.2 Show understanding for and then critically question the current selection procedures, the experiences, and competencies of practitioners

On the process level, it should be considered that people are more willing to change when they feel appreciated and act in a climate of acceptance; thus, they should not feel devalued in their current competencies and previous professional activities (Rogers, 1994, p. 33).

We also know from research that people are unwilling to use decision aids such as selection standards when they perceive their flexibility and autonomy to be violated (see Section 2.3). From this perspective, it seems unrealistic to expect organizational decision-makers to take their human and intuitive judgment "out of the loop" and leave selection methods entirely to psychometric procedures such as the DIN 33430 or ISO 10667 (Slaughter & Kausel, 2013, pp. 72–73).

Another reason for the resistance of hiring managers to change the current selection procedures is the feeling of being devalued as experts, despite having experience and intuitive knowledge. Hiring managers are often convinced that relying only on rational-analytical generated numbers (scores) is inappropriate, as these only partially reflect human reality. However, they do not want to ignore their feelings and intuitions and see these as sources of competencies that enable establishing personal connection with applicants.

Thus, practitioners' competencies and experiences must be recognized and valued, and the individual constructions that constitute good personnel selection from their point of view should be seen. Researchers will only be able to influence selection managers if they know and respond to their quality constructions in personnel selection. In addition, appreciation of practitioners' previous procedures and experiences will increase their willingness to question previous selection processes critically (Rogers, 1994, p. 33). This also requires establishing a corporate culture where the development of hiring process tools, procedures, and outputs are transparent and they are evaluated critically and constructively.

As research shows, managers can rely relatively well on their intuitions when the experiences they have gained in the past also apply in the future.

Whether intuition leads to good or bad decisions depends on the environment in which intuitive judgments are applied. Was/Is the learning environment suitable for developing good intuition (Gigerenzer, 2008a, p. 48), or might it lead to false intuitions in the future? Does the future environment have similar characteristics to the learning environment in which experiences were acquired, and thus intuitions are formed? Does an intuition that is based on past experience fit future requirements, especially in dynamic environments, times of agility, and when there is considerable pressure for fast and disruptive changes?

Even if the primary issue, namely selecting suitable applicants for a company, remains the same, the answers regarding how to deal with this issue will change. This is because procedures, competencies, and ways of thinking that led to success in the past will not necessarily lead to success in the future. Research shows that the future will likely be more turbulent, complex, and less predictable, so past experience may no longer serve as a good guide. This means that the dynamic changes in our society, whether political, legal, technical, social, ecological, or economic, are calling into question trusted assumptions and successful procedures from the past.

On the other hand, research shows that people should listen to their intuition and use it as a message, especially in unknown and complex situations. Like the best-selling *In Search of Excellence*, a popular management literature, declares that "only the intuitive leap . . . will let us solve problems in the complex world" (Peters & Waterman, 1982, p. 63).

Our surveys of hiring managers show that there is still a great deal of confidence that pattern recognition based on past experience will continue to fit in the future. At the same time, it is recognized that openness and curiosity should be fundamental competencies of managers and that they should learn to enrich and critically question their previous experiences and patterns (Reichelt, 2020, p. 69). But since human brains want to save energy, and thinking and developing new solutions is exhausting, people and thus selection managers tend to stick to the familiar.

However, with this "stick to the well-known" and "we have always done it this way" approach, selection managers will not be successful in the future. In a rapidly changing world, it's important to critically question one's experiences, assumptions, ideas, and opinions. Reliance on previous experiences can lead to failure, because they get out of date. Social psychologists speak of "cognitive entrenchment," when people have so much knowledge in an area that they start to make assumptions that need to be questioned. And they often don't want to rethink and change procedures that they feel comfortable with the way they've always done things. Therefore, the key is to leave personal comfort zones, and doubt what is known and taken for granted. It's more about learning and improving than about proving ourselves. That's a way of showing confident humility (Grant, 2021), staying open to learning, and changing thinking and behavior.

Thus, to use and develop expertise-based intuition, personnel diagnostic experts should critically question previous patterns of success and the environment in which they developed their expertise. They should also evaluate their learning processes by critically reflecting, reviewing, and – if necessary – modifying their decision-making rules and procedures.

Our empirical research clearly shows that practitioners are open to using other, for example, rational-analytical selection procedures, when they recognize the benefits for themselves and their business success (Deters, 2017, pp. 53–54.). Thus, practitioners, especially in SMEs, want to see the benefits and the added value they gain from critically reflecting on their current selection procedures and examining the results of scientific research. In doing so, it is essential to first recognize and value the advantages of the current process. Then, based on the perceived acceptance and appreciation, these critical practitioners will rather be willing to critically question their previous procedures and adopt suggestions based on science.

10.3.3 Demonstrate and communicate the benefits of using effective personnel selection processes

Often, there is resistance to change. Resistance to changing a selection procedure can, among other things, be based on existing beliefs and thought patterns, on loyalties or fears towards other (line) managers and their perspectives, on too few resources, or a preference for recognition and (psychological) safety. When changing a selection procedure, there is always the question of whether the change itself is more threatening than the actual suffering from the current situation. Where there is no suffering associated with the current selection situation or no perceived benefit to changing, hiring managers will probably resist implementing new selection procedures. Thus, the personal benefit of changing a procedure should be demonstrated. This personal profit for the hiring managers must and should not be purely materialistic, for example, saving resources such as time or money. Materialistic rewards accrue quickly and may lead to immediate satisfaction. But social gains (for example, recognition, appreciation, and better selection success) have a more lasting effect.

In many organizations, especially SMEs, informal "rules of the game" can reflect an attitude that anything formal (such as a standard of selection) is bureaucratic and a limitation of flexibility and autonomy. For example, university graduates with knowledge of psychometric personnel selection procedures or intuitions and emotions are working as HR managers in a SME but cannot implement this knowledge because the proposed procedures are seen as bureaucratic, time-consuming, and are thus not accepted. However, this does not mean that individuals are powerless from a systemic perspective; they must convince other managers of the benefits of a new selection procedure.

Practitioners are grateful when concrete hints and practical guidelines are given that don't require many resources.

Since business practices in a profit-oriented context are first and foremost dependent on the perceived economic advantages, the benefits of a rational-analytical selection procedure should be communicated, even if they cannot always be directly expressed in dollars, euros, and so on.

Thus, researchers need to prove that organizations that adhere to selection standards, for example, by using a requirement profile and interview questionnaire, make fewer misjudgments, reduce early turnover, get a higher level of commitment from their employees, and overall and in the long term, reduce their costs for successful personnel selection. Additionally, the applicants' preferences should also be shared, for example, that high-quality selection procedures are perceived as fair by applicants, and therefore appreciated. Furthermore, in cooperation with practitioners, researchers should develop practical guidelines that are easy to understand and explain the procedures, and the benefits of high-quality personnel selection processes to a broad public (Reimann et al., 2009, p. 157).

Practitioners must be shown how to use intuitions and emotions in selection processes, constructively.

Therefore, scientists, science journalists, or practitioners should inform (other) practitioners about the benefits and the added value of rational-analytical procedures and, in particular, support SMEs in implementing minimum selection standards, appropriately. Likewise, the benefit should be shown and recognized when intuitions are not followed blindly, but these are regarded as messages to be used constructively.

Where science is viewed rather suspiciously, there is a need for trusted advocates, for example, from other companies or consultants. For example, if experienced practitioners explain the benefits of using specific selection procedures (e.g., a combination of cognitive ability tests and a structured interview that gives the most reliable prognoses for future professional success; Schmidt et al., 2016) to other selection managers in an SME, and if these selection managers get practical support in implementing these procedures, they are more willing to open up to new ideas and learn and benefit from exchange with others.

To decrease resistance to psychometric procedures or reflect critically on intuitions and emotions, Slaughter and Kausel (2013, pp. 72–74) recommend giving decision support to decision-makers by telling them how to choose selection procedures, rather than which to choose. And it is essential to provide hiring managers with specific decision rules that focus on a limited number of essential cues and rely on the best predictors of job performance.

Slaughter and Kausel (2013) suggest improving selection decision-making to persuade decision-makers using rational-analytical procedures.

1) *Use simple statistics.*

   Although selection researchers obviously have a strong grasp of the meaningfulness of r and $r2$ values (validity, reliability, etc., J.D.), we recommend avoiding their use for trying to convince managers of the usefulness of validated selection tools. In general, managers either do not understand these coefficients, or they use them to criticize selection decision aids (and thus rely exclusively on their intuition, J. D.). . . . A better strategy may be to present validity information in terms of expectancy charts and performance differences between low and high scorers. (Slaughter & Kausel, 2013, p. 69)

2) *Use easily understood utility estimates and causal chain analysis.*

   Most readers are likely to be at least somewhat familiar with utility analysis, which translates the impact of human resource procedures into dollar values. . . . Causal chain analysis demonstrates the linkage of the implementation of HR practices to increases in profits through mediating variables such employee attitudes and customer satisfaction. (Slaughter & Kausel, 2013, p. 70)

3) *Present information to others in terms of narratives. . . .*
Managers are more likely to rely on personnel selection aids – and therefore make better decisions – if they can see the value of the method. One effective way in which a prediction method can gain acceptance is through the use of narratives . . . . People seldom use raw evidence (e.g., numerical information) to make intuitive decisions; rather, they use narrative story structures to organize and interpret evidence . . . . Narratives allow people to mentally simulate situations in which a candidate may behave in certain ways . . . . In employee selection, for example, narratives could allow individuals to imagine situations in which a candidate may behave in certain ways. For example, one could present the information of Candidate A . . . in a narrative format: . . . (S/he) has high general mental abilities, and thus she is likely to process information in an efficient way. This may help her prepare accurate financial reports. (Slaughter & Kausel, 2013, pp. 71–72)

Slaughter and Kausel (2013, pp. 72–73) see that decisions are more likely to be accepted if input comes from human judgment. Thus, it is unrealistic to expect organizational decision-makers do accept that their intuitive judgments should completely be replaced by mechanical combinations of predictors. And they also recommend that managers dare to

> test their intuition . . . by ignoring their gut feelings and choosing based on objective information. For example, they might choose job candidates whose scores on objective assessments are highest but who do not rank first on their intuitive assessment of rapport and fit. They may well find that acting against intuition and relying on validated methods is a pretty good method after all (Slaughter & Kausel 2013, pp. 74–75).

10.3.4 Use boosting and nudging to support effective selection procedures integrating rational-analytical and intuitive-emotional decisions

To steer human behaviors in the desired direction, "boosting" could be used. Boosts are interventions that target people's competencies and try to foster people's competencies through changes in skills, decision tools, or knowledge. "A boost may enlist human cognition (e.g., decision strategies, procedural routines, motivational competences, and strategic use of automatic processes), the environment (e.g., information representation or physical environment), or both. By fostering existing competences or developing new ones, boosts are designed to enable specific behaviors" (Hertwig & Grüne-Yanoff, 2019, p. 8). Thus, fostering selection managers' knowledge and skills, and communicating the benefits of a holistic selection procedure can lead to effective selection decisions.

However, people may not be open to new insights and methods and instead emphasize their nonconformity and subjective knowledge as superior. Whether proven scientific research results and more knowledge can correct such conviction is questionable. But, as also shown, knowledge and information often have minimal effect on changing behavior. People are giants in terms of knowledge – and dwarves regarding implementation.

Thus, procedural and structural support using nudges can help implement an effective selection procedure, integrating rational-analytical and intuitive-emotional procedures. In addition, this decision-making architecture allows default settings or options as pre-set courses of action. And it has nudging elements, provided the decision-makers are also left with some room for (subjective) maneuver. According to Thaler and Sunstein (2008, p. 6), a nudge is "any aspect of the choice architecture that alters people's behavior in a predictable way without forbidding any options" and where this intervention is "easy and cheap to avoid." The integration of rational-analytical and reflected intuitive-emotional selection processes is thus presented as a better alternative and more attractive than other procedures; the decision-maker should voluntarily choose this alternative.

Thus, nudging can complement boosting and support implementing effective selection procedures.

10.3.5 Use a multimodal approach to selection

Feeling internal or external pressure (e.g., from specific stakeholder groups) to look critically at previous selection procedures and seek out ways to improve these procedures will also make practitioners more open to innovations (Deters et al., 2020).

Thus, possible structural support is that different stakeholder groups require a specific rational-analytical procedure like the multimodal or tri-modal approach (Schuler, 2014, pp. 302–315).

Research shows that a structured selection process where hiring managers systematically accumulate information about an applicant's competencies and characteristics is the psychometrically recommended way to make a personnel selection. A scientifically recommended procedure is the multimodal approach, for example, the tri-modal approach by using biography (e.g., interview), simulation-oriented (e.g., tasks-related interviews, assessment center), and construct-oriented methods (cognitive ability tests, personality tests, etc.).

Research shows that the selection procedure' (predictive) validity increases when, for example, interviews are supplemented by valid test procedures such as cognitive ability tests. Therefore, a mix of different selection procedures, such as tests and interviews, should be used, especially for leadership talent or pivotal leadership positions. Furthermore, implementing a multimodal approach increases predictive validity and reduces the risk of falling for faking or impression management professionals and deceptive self-promoters.

Implementing a multimodal interview means satisfying the basic psychometric principles of a rational-analytical selection procedure using a mixture of free and structured parts. At the same time, it meets the goals of providing a positive candidate experience (Schuler, 2002, 2014; see Sections 2.5, 3.2.5, and 10.3.1).

A multimodal interview, oriented on Schuler's framework, can be a suitable instrument for responding to the wish of practitioners to enable critical inquiries and individual responses to the applicant in phases of an interview by simultaneously ensuring a high level of scientific excellence.

The Multimodal Interview (MMI®) consists of a relatively invariant sequence of eight interview components (Schuler, 2014, pp. 302–315):

1. Start of conversation:
   – Short informal conversation, create pleasant and open atmosphere. Introduction and outline of the procedure; This first part of the multimodal interview should be without evaluation (This claim may make sense from a psychometric point of view, but whether it can be implemented in practice is very questionable).
2. Self-introduction of the applicant:
   – Short presentation on personal and professional background, the current situation and expectations for the future; Evaluation according to requirement-oriented judgment dimensions.
3. Professional interests, career, and organization choice: Standardized questions on career choice, job interests, organization choice, the application, and, if appropriate, expertise; assessment is performed on behavior-anchored scales.
4. Free conversation: Continuing the previous two topics; open questions resulting from the self-presentation and the application documents; summarized evaluation.
5. Biography-related questions: derived from the requirements analysis or valid biographical questionnaires, always related to the job to fill; assessing the perceived behaviors on behaviorally anchored grading scales.
6. Realistic role information: Balanced, needs-based information for the candidate by the interviewers about the role, the workplace, the company, and so on; possible critical aspects of the job are not concealed since they are appropriate for self-selection and prevent subsequent disappointment and unwanted staff turnover.
7. Situational questions: Designed to meet the requirements of a specific work role; situational questions on a "critical incident" basis; evaluation on behavior anchored grading scales.
8. Call termination: summarization, answer candidate's questions, next steps, agreements, etc. This eighth part of the multimodal interview is also without evaluation (as for step 1, this claim may make sense from a psychometric point of view, but whether it can be implemented in practice is very questionable).

10.3.6 Use an interview guideline, rating scales for perceived behaviors and intuitions, and decision rules

One of the most consistent findings in the selection interview literature is the importance of structure and standardization. Whereas unstructured interviews leave the content and the evaluation process primarily up to the interviewer's discretion, structured interviews involve a high degree of standardization across applicants regarding the questions asked and the scoring procedures used. The rationale for incorporating structure into the interview process is that it reduces procedural variability across applicants, which results in higher reliability and better predictive validity (Culbertson et al., 2016; Levashina et al., 2014; Schmidt & Hunter, 1998; Kanning, 2015, p. 87). Although a recent study by Schmidt et al. (2016) cannot confirm the general advantage of high structured or standardized interviews, mainly because they show that unstructured or semi-structured job interviews can have relatively high validity if the selection managers are experienced, they confirm a high predictive validity for structured interview forms (see Section 3.2.3.1).

To cope with implementing structured selection procedures, Kahneman and Klein state:

> Naturally, we have somewhat different attitudes toward these problems of implementation, with DK (Daniel Kahneman, J. D.) usually viewing them as obstacles to be overcome and GK (Gary Klein, J.D.) seeing them as reasons to be skeptical about the value of formal methods. Despite our different attitudes toward formal methods, we agree on the potential of semi-formal strategies (Kahneman & Klein, 2009, p. 524).

Thus, a further way of structural support in implementing effective selection procedures is to use a semi-structured interview.

To integrate the advantages of a rational-analytical selection procedure with the benefits of intuitive-emotional insights about a candidate and build a positive relationship with an applicant, a semi-structured procedure with a job requirement-based interview guide is a good compromise.

Huffcut (2010) also formulates some principles for conducting employment interviews:

1. Acknowledge the inherent difficulty of making correct judgments. Try to reflect upon and improve the accuracy of your decisions by applying research results to yourself. Fight the natural tendency to believe that findings from research do not apply to you.
2. Know as little about the candidate as possible. Although this principle may be the most counterintuitive, hiring managers should consider that in selection interviews, there is a tendency to shift from a fact-finding mode into an impression-confirming mode, for example, by unconsciously using confirmation bias resulting from pre-interview impressions.

3. And avoid making judgments early in the interview. Try to separate observation and evaluation of a candidate.
4. Avoid poor questions and use an interview guideline based on job requirements and critical incidents.

Since the future is open, and focusing exclusively on current requirements of existing jobs may jeopardize the ability of organizations to change; the requirements to be assessed must relate to the potential of the candidates for future challenges, and personality aspects, in particular, should also be checked.

It is recommended to use a specific form in which intuitions and emotions about the candidate's fit are recorded in writing. In addition, a rating scale should be developed and used, on which, for example, on a scale of 1–10, hiring managers may mark how they feel about the fit of the candidate (primarily based on observed behaviors, social-communicative skills, authentic appearance, personality, etc.) to the company, to the team, and so on.

Further, selection decisions should be based on agreed decision rules because they allow a more systematic assessment of candidates and lead to more objectivity, fairness, and transparency (see Section 3.2.3.3).

10.3.7 Use digital technologies and AI to support selection decisions

Effective personnel selection processes require top management support, selection managers' knowledge and skills, and an appropriate IT infrastructure and high-quality data. As shown in Chapter 8, digital technologies and AI can give structural support to effective selection procedures, provide important information about applicants, or may make recommendations. Final selection decisions, however, should be left to people.

Campion et al. (2016, p. 958) report that companies often regard methods with high predictive validity as too cost-intensive to be used for all applicants. At the same time, McAbee et al. (2016, p. 281) see technological advances as an opportunity to use more sophisticated methods to analyze large amounts of data for recruitment, written texts, nonverbal and verbal behaviors, and so on. The computer is not subject to any biases, achieves validities and reliabilities similar or better than human evaluators, and the procedure led to significant cost savings (Campion et al., 2016, p. 973; for a critical perspective, see Section 8.12).

Digital selection procedures can use scientifically-based tests with high face and predictive validity (Benit & Söllner, 2013), for example, personality tests based on the Big Five model or high validity cognitive ability tests. If these rational-analytical test procedures are used primarily for a pre-selection, they can be highly effective. Furthermore, if such test procedures are not intended to replace human decisions but support them, they will meet with greater acceptance. Therefore, it is vital to maintain the human side of personnel selection and supplement it with scientifically valid procedures.

Thus, the conviction prevails to carry out personnel selection with digital support (Schuler et al., 2007, p. 68).

The full potential of digital or computer-aided methods and big data is still in its infancy for personnel selection. However, more and more organizations are currently trying to automate processes of matching suitability profiles of (potential) applicants and requirement profiles and use data from social networks to analyze biographical backgrounds, competencies, personalities, and so on. appears that companies will soon no longer have to rely on applicants' applications to collect information but will use data from social media and other digital sources (McAbee et al., 2016, p. 281).

Although AI is capable of autonomous learning and problem solving, it is an instrument that can support recruiters in making accurate and nondiscriminatory decisions. But AI makes the same mistakes as humans when it is based on biased information, inaccurate job descriptions, or other poor data (see Sections 8.11 and 8.12).

When handled correctly, AI and other digital tools can help managers process complex or data-intensive issues quickly and in a goal-oriented manner. Repetitive or tedious tasks can also be supported by AI so that hiring managers make fewer mistakes and instead concentrate on more important things, such as personal interviews.

Data-based analytics, selection procedures, and HR practices that are based on empirically tested findings can lead to better-informed decisions, but not necessarily give insights into whether a candidate fits into the team/organization, culture, and so on. And even if it should be possible to evaluate emotions and authenticity with the help of AI, recruiters and candidates still want to get to know each other personally.

> We agree that the introduction of algorithms and other formal decision aids in organizations will often encounter opposition and unexpected implementation problems. Few people enjoy being replaced by mechanical devices or mathematical algorithms, and many devices and algorithms function less well in the real world than on the planning board (Kahneman & Klein, 2009, p. 524; Yates et al., 2003).

The hiring managers interviewed in our empirical research regard AI and digital procedures for personnel selection merely as supporting instruments. AI assists decision-making, provides information and points out possible errors, consequential costs, or inconsistencies. Practitioners emphasize that optimizing the matching process, exploring the suitable options, and bringing together the right people is the job of pre-selection procedures, algorithms, and AI. But after that, it's about matching people with people, in person, and letting people make the final selection decision. Algorithms and AI may offer important decision-making support in personnel selection, but the final decisions on personnel selection should lie with hiring managers: People should make people decisions. And in many countries, including Germany, this is also a legal requirement.

Hiring managers interviewed don't want to hide behind numbers and data. They want to control decisions; they do not want to be bullied, incapacitated, or patronized by AI or other technologies. They want transparent AI systems that allow them to comprehend on what basis decisions are made. Thus, they want to assess AI-supported selection decisions' trustworthiness, limits, and potential (Ramge, 2020).

Also, the candidates want to know the company and their potential colleagues, managers, and so on. They want to experience personally whether they like their colleagues and managers, enjoy working with them, and fit into the team and the company culture.

The interviewed hiring managers want to use AI to understand and assess candidates better, and get more valid information about them. Since selecting candidates involves inspiring candidates about a company, the emotional level in the selection and hiring process is particularly important. Therefore, hiring managers can use the time saved by using AI to build more intensive emotional relationships with candidates.

In personally conducted interviews, hiring managers, with their specific personality and authenticity, can gather verbal and nonverbal impressions of the candidate. And they can appreciate candidates and emphasize specifics about the company, the team, and the position.

Many decisions are not perfect, not even AI-supported decisions. Thus, hiring managers should be aware that a certain amount of serenity can also be helpful. AI can offer practical support but is never a panacea. Often a solution produces a new problem. Humans often look for the one and only answer and then realize that specific solutions are associated with significant issues they did not anticipate. Knowing that one can never do everything perfectly can be liberating for humans.

While the pre-selection of personnel should be carried out in a consistently analytical manner, intuitions and feelings remain key to the final selection decision.

> AI is at its most powerful only when it is securely integrated into humane, ethical frameworks of scrutiny and regulation. Humans must still act as gatekeepers, and .. still have the last word on decision-making (Gulliford & Parker Dixon, 2019, p. 53).

Systems of AI need to be monitored and steered by humans and not only regulated by voluntary adherence to ethics. And it is precisely in democratically constituted societies that great importance is attached to AI being regulated by laws. Responsibility and accountability for selection decisions must remain with the human being (see Section 10.5.3).

To deal effectively with data and generate usable knowledge, the data should be analyzed, enriched, linked, and compared to other related data. And these other associated data can be specific expert knowledge that is based on intuitions and emotions (Knauf, 2020, pp. 37–38).

AI should not replace humans as selection decision-makers. But it can help balance the rational-analytical approach, creating a positive candidate experience, and the constructive use of intuitions and emotions.

10.3.8 Use intervention techniques to monitor the integrative use of rational-analytical and intuitive selection procedures

Intuitions and associated emotions can make a positive contribution to solving decision problems. However, they can also distort decisions and thus lead to poor ones.

As shown, for example, in Sections 5.1 and 5.5, selection managers tend to follow their intuitions and feelings when selecting candidates. Especially, higher ranked managers or entrepreneurs rely on their intuitions. And precisely, higher-ranked managers or entrepreneurs sometimes present themselves as dominant leaders and want to make the final decision alone. They often see other selection managers involved as advisors, without decision-making power (Bastian, 2018, p. 156).

The subjective feeling of power affects peoples' self-perception, and managers in high leadership or power positions are sometimes perceived as showing a sense of superiority and infallibility, being less self-critical and less open to feedback from others ("manager blindness"), or receiving less honest and constructive feedback, and that they are at risk of turning self-confidence into self-importance, righteousness or self-overestimation (Harris & Jones, 2018).

For personnel selection, relying solely on intuitive judgments or feelings can be disastrous, as one may be subject to certain biases, prejudices, and stereotypes. Thus high-quality personnel selection is not about intuitions first or felt facts or figures, but about linking and matching intuitions and emotions with rational-analytically collected data. Thus, hiring managers should monitor their intuitive impressions and emotional judgments by thinking slowly.

10.3.8.1 Use the rational-analytical mind (or System 2) as a censor

The human unconscious sends intuitive impulses and links them to powerful emotions, and these signals are often stronger than reason. But decisions based on intuitions and feelings can lead to regretted behaviors afterward. Thus, the psychometric approach demands avoiding intuitive and emotional influences on judgments in personnel selection as much as possible (Schuler, 1996, p. 86). But managers cannot simply reduce these impulses. Because intuitions and emotions come naturally and are powerful, selection managers must deal with them competently by consciously perceiving and reflecting on them. This means using the rational mind or System 2 as a censor or advisor for System 1.

To monitor intuitions and emotions,

> little can be achieved without considerable investment in efforts. . . . The way to block errors in System 1 is simple in principle: recognize the signs that you are in a cognitive minefield, slow down, and ask for reinforcement from System 2. . . . (Q)uestioning your intuitions is unpleasant when you face the stress of a big decision. More doubt is the last thing you want when you are in trouble. . . . Organizations are better than individuals when it comes to avoiding errors, because they naturally think more slowly and have the power to impose orderly procedures (Kahneman, 2011, pp. 417–418).

Thus, recruiters are advised to take a moment to pause, observe, and reflect on themselves and their feelings and intuitions. This leads to increased attention to unconscious signals when valuable insight is passed on. This enables bringing the experienced reality of intuitions, feelings, impressions, and so on, into the present, saving it from disappearing, and thus using it more consciously for oneself and possibly others in the future.

Organizations and selection managers should follow Kahneman`s directive to slow down and ask for reinforcement from System 2 by using checklists, guidelines, or standards for selection procedures and implementing reflecting processes to activate System 2.

> The practical implications . . . are that organizational decision-makers, like all decision-makers, should be encouraged to engage in effortful thought in a relatively detailed, structured, and systematic fashion (thereby stimulating Type 2 processes) before selecting a given course of action. To the extent that judgmental biases can be attenuated in this way, practitioners would have at their disposal a readily available intervention technique for enhancing the quality of (their decisions, J.D.) (Hodgkinson & Sadler-Smith, 2018, p. 479).

Using System 2 is crucial in selection processes; thus, before the final selection decision is made, an "intuitive check" is desirable. However, it is important to determine whether intuitive impulses are due to significant implicit knowledge, incorrect assumptions, or an incorrect application, for example, of a heuristic. Personnel selection is too complex that even with a heuristic experience, intuition cannot be guaranteed to lead to a good decision. It should therefore be questioned in any case. When intuitions are not actively made conscious, their influence still persists.

Slow thinking (see System 2) is responsible for rational reflection and information analysis, but this reflective, analytical thinking must be explicitly activated. So, when managers reason about a decision, weigh the advantages and disadvantages, and so on, they primarily use the prefrontal cortex. This is linked to the limbic system and can ensure that people keep their emotions under control and do not follow them blindly. But this process requires conscious reflection, takes time, and is associated with cognitive effort for our brain.

Slow thinking is often far too slow and inefficient to function effectively when making quick decisions. Given the time constraints in management, fast and intuitive decisions are more likely to be made. And since slow thinking is strenuous and costs a lot of energy, managers find it easier to accept their intuitive impulses, and the interpretations constructed by fast thinking (see System 1) are readily adopted. Unfortunately, this can lead to cognitive illusions that are difficult to control since intuitions and emotions cannot be deliberately turned off. But if managers don't want to follow their intuitions and feelings blindly, they have to constantly question them (Hermann & Mayer, 2020, pp. 65–70).

Therefore, hiring managers must, for example, question why they like some people and others not, or which feelings do certain applicants trigger in them. And they must consider that sympathy may have a lot to do with familiarity (see "similarity effect"; Section 3.5.2.14).

Another factor should be recognized: No matter how standardized the personnel selection may be, only a limited amount of information can be consciously processed by recruiters. Also, with the support of requirement analyses, evaluations, and scientifically valid methods, the number of characteristics analyzed is limited. Here, intuitions and emotions can help in making use of the implicit knowledge. And much of this tacit knowledge, which wouldn't turn up in the requirements analysis, can be relevant to making holistic selection decisions (Burke & Sadler-Smith, 2006).

Because humans often act as "cognitive misers" (Evans & Stanovich, 2013, p. 237), it is often not enough to tell oneself, as a selection manager, to use the analytical mind or System 2 to monitor intuitions and feelings (System 1) consciously: systemic, and thus structural support, is also needed. This means implementing intervention techniques and examining intuitive-emotional decision impulses with the help of guidelines, checklists, structured and predefined selection processes such as decision rules or decision trees, and especially with specific questioning techniques.

According to Riedel (2015, p. 188), when questioning one's intuitions, particular attention should be paid to subjectivity and emotionality. Thus, Riedel (2015, p. 69) calls for trained subjectivity. Moreover, Eisenkraft's (2013, p. 278) findings demonstrate that individual intuitive impressions from a candidate can be trustworthy judgments when aggregated and aligned with those of other selection managers.

Thus, hiring managers need room for actively reflecting on their intuitions and emotions. The selection process should provide space before, during, and after an interview to reflect on intuitions and emotions. Before the interview, a short five-minute self-reflection can help identify the current mood and "noise" (see 3.5.2.3 and 3.5.2.4) and try to establish a neutral stance. Through methods like the MBSR (Mindfulness-based stress reduction; Ellis, 2006; Kabat-Zinn, 2013), the organization can offer mindfulness practices to assist their managers in self-reflection (see Section Sections 9.2.2, especially 9.2.2.2).

In addition, there should be room for both parties, selection managers and applicants, to openly address any interpersonal and intuitive or emotional matters during the interview.

Another decisive success factor in using intuition is consciously letting one's intuition and feelings be challenged by psychometric analysis results and performance evaluations on the job. Thus, the selection managers should compare and evaluate the rational-analytical results and their intuitions and feelings about the candidate, and discuss and reflect upon the comparison in an open process among the involved hiring managers.

At the same time, communicating the reasons for a judgment is crucial for accepting decisions. If intuitive or emotional impulses send the signal, "Hey, the person with the best score is strange. It's better to stay away"; hiring managers should definitely pay attention to this feeling and consciously try to identify the reason for their uneasiness.

Concerning emotional intelligence, Goleman (2004, p. 2) claims that without self-awareness, self-regulation, or empathy, managers can have the best training in the world, an analytical mind, and an endless supply of brilliant ideas, but they still won't make great leaders. And these insights can be applied to selection processes and hiring managers. Many other researchers also emphasize the need for emotional intelligence or emotional competencies, and that emotions affect judgments in all aspects of selection processes (Jenkins, 1986, p. 61; Fox & Spector, 2000, p. 204; Robertson & Smith, 2001, p. 454; Askanasy et al., 2017, p. 25), for example, in evaluating potential risks in selecting a specific candidate (Slovic, 1990), assessing the person-job fit (P-J-F), the person-team fit (P-T-F) or the person-organization fit (P-O-F).

10.3.8.2 Reflect on intuition 1 and intuition 2

According to Berner (2017), intuition is not a metaphysical compass needle that mysteriously and infallibly points people in the right direction. Depending on which facts, information, and observations are available to hiring managers, completely different intuitions may arise.

Analytical thinking and individual reflections on intuitions and emotions should integrate into a cohesive whole. Whoever blocks out one of them deprives themselves of an essential part of orientation possibilities. Thus, regardless of whether the selection managers close themselves off to the rational or emotional part, something important is lost in both cases.

This leads to a seemingly paradoxical decision rule that combines reason and intuition in an ingeniously simple way. Therefore, hiring managers should first register their spontaneous feeling or intuition when reading a CV, and so on, which Berner (2017) calls "intuition 1."

Therefore, the initial ideas about a candidate provided by intuition 1 should be registered at the beginning of a decision-making process. This ability of not blindly following these initial intuitions and emotions (initial impression) should consciously control one's concrete behavior through "second reactions"; this self-control competence characterizes human beings (Kuhl, 1990).

It is essential to critically question one's intuitive impulses (intuition 1), make them transparent, discuss them with selection colleagues, and then compare the intuitive-emotional impulses with the results of rational-analytical selection procedures.

And when hiring managers have considered every aspect, they should let it settle – and then – according to Berner – decide finally, intuitively ("intuition 2").

The intuitive evaluation used by managers after a careful analysis of all the facts ("intuition 2") may differ widely from the first "gut feeling" that has developed spontaneously based on possibly incomplete and one-sided information ("intuition 1").

10.3.8.3 Specific questions as intervention techniques to reflect on intuition

When selection managers learn to reflect on selection decisions and how and why they judge applicants specifically, they learn to listen to their inner voice. This can help recognize which thought patterns, self-identities, and so on, influence them and their selection behaviors. In this way, it is possible to conclude retroactively on one's judgments.

Self-reflection and reflection on one's intuitions and emotions with other hiring managers can help contextualize oneself and co-construct knowledge and understanding of perceived behaviors, intuitions, and so on (Etherington, 2016).

> To be reflexive, we need to be aware of our personal responses and to be able to make choices about how to use them. We also need to be mindful of the individual, social, and cultural contexts in which we and others live and work and to understand how this impacts the ways we interpret our world (Etherington, 2004, p. 19).

Sadler-Smith and Burke (2009, p. 258) recommend scrutinizing intuitions by using appropriate inquiry techniques, such as:

- Identify situations where intuition worked and where intuition failed
  a) Intuitions that worked: Think of a selection situation where you relied on your intuition, resulting in a positive outcome. What was the context? What happened, and what were the consequences? Try to identify the assumptions and inferences that led you to follow the intuition. What were they?
  b) Intuitions (and feelings) that failed: Think of a selection situation where you relied on intuitions that resulted in a negative outcome. What was the context? What happened, and what were the consequences? Try to identify the assumptions and inferences that led you to follow the intuition. What were they? (Sadler-Smith and Shefy, 2004, p. 85).
- Raise objections to intuitive judgments
- Challenge underlying assumptions
- Point out alternatives
- Generate counterarguments
- Probe intuitions for inconsistencies, inaccuracies, and irrelevancies

Goleman (1996, 2004) suggests specific steps to incorporate emotional intelligence in the workplace. These steps can also be applied to intuitions and emotions in personnel selection: Showing emotional competencies in selection processes means reflecting on one's intuitions and emotions, and recognizing and understanding their effects on one's judgments and decisions.

Thus, in training or at the end of a selection process, hiring managers can reflect on the following questions:

1. Do you take responsibility for your intuitions and emotions (and other physical impressions) and accept them as messages from your organism? What do these emotions or intuitions want to communicate? What is the key message?

   What are the possible advantages or disadvantages of following this intuition or feeling?
2. How did I feel when interviewing a specific applicant? What specific emotions or intuitions does the candidate trigger in me? Hiring managers should reflect on the applicants' verbal and nonverbal messages, and their impact on the manager`s thinking and behavior in that selection process.

   What are possible reasons for or behind my intuitions and emotions?

   Why does my intuitive-emotional system send me these messages? What are the reasons? In which direction does the intuitive message want to steer my decision and why?

   What about the applicant who causes these intuitions and emotions (Which information in CV, social media, verbal and nonverbal behaviors, and so on, caused my intuitions and feelings)?

   What do the perceived intuitions and emotions have to do with my personality, values, goals, or experiences? Which experiences in my socialization could have caused these intuitions and emotions? Which individual intentions, purposes, and values guide my emotional judgments and pattern recognition? What actually guides me to care about this applicant or not?
3. Reflect on the applicants' emotional and behavioral reactions and responses caused by your behavior. Which behaviors did I show to a specific applicant? How did I influence the applicant's behaviors? For example, be observant of your choice of words, voice modulation, body language, and so on, in a particular selection.
4. Have I discussed and reflected openly on my intuitions and emotions with other managers? Do we have the same intuitions and emotions/feelings? Where are the differences, and why? Can I understand the intuitions and emotions of the other hiring managers and vice versa? Where do our perceptions support and complement each other (or not)?
5. Try to control and question your intuitive and emotional impulses, and reflect on your own and with other involved hiring managers on possible biases, stereotypes, and prejudices, including your initial impressions, halo effects, confirmation

biases, similarity biases, and how these perceptions influence your judgments and decision-making.
6. Can I rely on my emotions and intuitions regarding applicants' perceptions? Are these emotions and intuitions coherent from my point of view?
   Are my emotions and intuitions justified, even after reflection with others, so that I should pay attention to them?
7. Evaluate your "emotional competence" and "intuitive wisdom." When do they support you and help in your decisions? Do they instead, lead to distorted perceptions and poor choices? How likely are these intuitive impulses valid and should therefore be followed? To what extent can they possibly mislead me?
8. What did I learn from following my intuition? What did I learn from going against my intuition?

Sometimes, intuitions are influenced by (unconscious) individual intentions, purposes, or goals. Powerful emotions, and thus strong and unconscious emotional judgments, are difficult to repress through reasoning; this can be intensified by "emotional contagion" when a hiring manager triggers similar emotions in another hiring manager (Hatfield et al., 1993; Schoenewolf 1990). It is challenging to free oneself from this pressure to conform, adapt to colleagues or higher-ranked managers, and think independently.

Studies of managerial decisions have identified three factors that steer the decision-making process in the wrong direction through pattern recognition (Campbell et al., 2009). First, the presence of inappropriate self-interest; second, a personal connection (presence of distorting attachments); and finally, false and misleading memories and biases. Campbell et al. (2009) describe the conditions contributing to biases in people's emotional response to perceived information, thus promoting judgment errors. They developed a monitoring system to discover and reduce these misjudgments. In this system, the managerial decision is checked by a third party. Still, decision-makers can also use it in a shortened form to discover their own biases.

The system contains three main questions. And each individual involved in the decision-making process should answer these three questions to avoid poor decisions:
1. Because decisions are influenced by what people intend and value most, decision-makers should be clear about their values and individual intentions. For example, is there any self-interest or personal sympathy? People should clarify their intention and values and be clear on their purpose because these are filters through which they observe a situation. This requires deep reflection on one's own truth about oneself about where one is headed, and why.
   Thus, hiring managers should openly examine the purposes, intentions, and values that guide their decisions.
2. Are there memories that cause bias to influence the decision? If so, countermeasures must be taken. For example, biases can be counteracted by exposing

the decision-maker to new information and a different view on the problem. Or, ensure that biases, and thus preferences, are confronted explicitly, which works best when the power between the involved selection managers is balanced. Depending on the situation, another point of view can provide new insights or a discussion can help change thought patterns.
3. Is there strong governance and a requirement that a decision be ratified at a higher level?

An exchange with other hiring managers can be enriching and purposeful because it allows them to reflect on the various individual intuitions, and critically and constructively question them.

But many decision-makers find it difficult to adopt a critical attitude towards their judgments and feelings (Küpers, 2015, p. 82). Thus, such exchange can support creating working conditions and organizational cultures where intuition is recognized and accepted.

To achieve this, opportunities should be provided to communicate and reflect openly on emotions and intuitions in the selection and other decision-making processes. It's not about sharing intellectual knowledge, but about sharing experiences, feelings, and intuitions about an applicant and the impact these emotions and intuitions have on every hiring manager.

This collective intuition (see Section 9.2.3.4) helps to get a holistic picture of the decision-making process and reach effective hiring decisions (e.g., Akinci & Sadler-Smith, 2019).

But as long as the communication, acceptance, recognition, and open application of intuition are prevented, the power and wisdom of intuition cannot be used consciously. It can even go so far that executives and hiring managers who suppress their intuition unlearn the ability to interpret it correctly and thus use it constructively. Using intuition to its fullest extent can, in turn, affect individual and collective learning (Sadler-Smith & Shefy, 2004 a, p. C4; 2004, p. 78; McCutcheon & Pincombe, 2001, p. 346).

Organizations can benefit from conceptualizing intuition as valuable by designing a supportive learning environment for their hiring managers. In addition, a culture of openness to intuitions and emotions enables managers to learn from their own and others' experiences (see Sections 10.4 and 10.5). Thus, an open learning climate and a culture where the conscious use of and critical reflection on intuitions and the related emotions is accepted and promoted as positive, is a success factor for organizations.

This culture requires a certain degree of risk and error tolerance (see Section 10.5.2). However, implementing a cultural legitimation of intuition, and a network for exchanging experiences and mutual feedback is desirable. Gathering shared experiences and exchanging ideas is key to acquiring implicit knowledge and intuitive skills. Consequently, temporal spaces for dialogue and discussion should be created, a culture of acceptance of intuitions and emotions can be fostered, and related processes of dealing constructively with intuition can be learned. In this way, organizations can benefit from the advantages of intuitions (Sadler-Smith & Shefy, 2004, p. 82; Niederhäusern 2015, p. 182; Akinci & Sadler-Smith, 2019, p. 560).

To foster this culture of appreciating intuitions and emotions, managers can ask themselves these questions or reflect on them with other managers:

1. What (kind of) decisions have I made today? What criteria do I use to determine whether a decision is good?
2. To what extent do I rely on my intuitions or emotions to make these decisions? How do I know/concretely recognize that intuition/emotion was used?
3. What do my intuitions/emotions tell me concretely?
4. To what extent is my decision based on rational analysis? On which facts is that analysis based?
5. Were there conflicts between intuition and rationality? How does this become concrete? How do I deal with it?
6. In which context (specific situations or types of decisions) do I tend to make analytical-rational decisions, and when intuitive, or both?
7. Do I try to rationalize and justify my intuitive judgment later? How and why do I do that? What are the consequences of my rationalization?
8. Do I consciously reflect on what my intuition (incl. feeling) tells me? Do I also question them? How likely is it that these intuitive impulses are valid and should therefore lead me? To what extent might they mislead me? Is there any self-interest or personal sympathy involved? Are there memories or patterns that make me misjudge the situation? How do I cope with possible biases, prejudices, and stereotypes?
9. Do I reflect on my intuitions (incl. emotions) with other managers? What are their intuitions/emotions? Where and when do we agree, where not, and why?
10. When do I trust my intuition, and when a rational analysis?
11. How do intuitions and analytics work together in my decisions? How do I manage to use my intuition and rational mind simultaneously? How did this manifest itself in my decisions today?

If recruiters do not take conscious stock of their intuitions and emotions, they risk being unconsciously swayed by them. And then it may be that something is attributed to a candidate that has more to do with the recruiter him/herself.

If intuitions are openly reflected upon, and critically and constructively questioned, the risk of a lack of comprehensibility, transparency, and traceability is reduced. And open communication, acceptance, and appreciation of intuitions can also reduce the tendency to rationalize intuitive decisions.

In selection processes in professional sports, Hermann and Mayer (2020) found that many coaches or managers learn not to rely unreflectively on their intuitions. This is evident in the selection of top-level athletes, where rational-analytical methods are increasingly used, and in the decisions of sportsmen and women themselves, for example, a golf caddy may be a good decision advisor before certain shots are taken. Similarly, coaches and managers may consult with their coaching staff on how to proceed tactically or who should be replaced (Hermann & Mayer, 2020, pp. 69–70). Through such an approach, people's conscious and unconscious knowledge can be integrated and used for better decisions.

Balancing reflected intuition and rational-analytical procedures allows people to make better decisions by integrating intuitions (System 1, tacit system, implicit knowledge) and rational-analytical cognitions and results (Miles & Sadler-Smith, 2014, p. 624; Sadler-Smith & Shefy, 2004, p. 76).

Monitoring intuitions and emotions by activating and maintaining analytical thinking (System 2) is mentally exhausting; it requires active willpower to critically reflect on one's intuitions and emotions. Therefore, implementing and maintaining the necessary behavioral patterns means leaving the individual's comfort zone. But it`s a good investment. This support in implementing effective selection procedures also strengthens the intuitive competencies of selection managers.

10.3.9 Evaluate selection processes and hiring decisions

Research by Kanning (2012) and also our own empirical studies show that in practice, an evaluation of personnel selection processes (quality of selection) and results (quality of hire) is rarely made systematically. Instead, a systematic evaluation of the personnel selection process is often replaced by superiors' appraisal of a new hire, whereby lack of achievement is often attributed to the candidate rather than to a flawed selection process. (However, the fact that poor performance of newly hired employees can also be due to specific contextual conditions or incompetent leadership, and therefore has nothing to do with poor personnel selection, is discussed in more detail in Section 3.7.7).

There is a risk that failure to systematically evaluate the selection process could jeopardize the organizational success and deprive the selection managers of developing their competencies in selecting personnel or improving the personnel selection procedures, tools, and so on (Kanning, 2012, pp. 20–21).

Kanning (2012) also recommends a monetary benefit analysis to evaluate personnel selection regarding its cost-effectiveness. The instruments for a systematic evaluation of selection processes and the hiring results are already developed in science, but they are not regularly implemented in practice (Brauner, 2019, pp. 97–98).

However, it must be recognized that systematic evaluation procedures, for example, regarding the measurement of predictive validity, are methodologically challenging to carry out (see Sections 3.7.3 and especially 3.7.7) and require many resources. Therefore, it is not surprising that both larger companies and, in particular, SMEs refrain from carrying out such evaluations.

On the other hand, evaluating selection results through direct feedback to hiring managers (for example, before the completion of the probationary period) and critically questioning hiring decisions can lead hiring managers to examine the chosen selection procedures, and can contribute to the continuous improvement of the selection process and incorporating the latest scientific findings.

And at the end of a selection process, possible questions to facilitate reflection on the process and results of selection decisions are formulated by Niederhäusern (2015, p. 187) as follows:

> To what extent does the hiring decision support the organization in achieving its goals?
>
> How much experience and expertise in high-quality selection procedures were available in the company?
>
> Were key decision-makers and high-ranked and powerful managers involved in this process? How strong were their influence and emotional participation?
>
> Did this participation influence the other hiring managers, and in what respect?

10.3.10 Implement systematic talent management and attract targeted applicants

Personnel planning, attracting, sourcing, identifying, selecting, and employing talent is integral to systematic talent management. To effectively manage talent, specific organizational practices and policies should be implemented to develop, motivate, and retain hired talent.

If the decision about who is considered a talent is primarily based on the intuition of the line managers and the relationship of potential talent to the executive or owner of a company, much potential talent may fall by the wayside and not be identified and selected. Therefore, systematic talent management is required, especially in medium-sized companies.

Research shows no single correct solution to successfully process talent management concerning (global) talent management. And best practices in talent management are only best in the context for which they were designed (Stahl et al., 2012, p. 26). Stahl et al. (2012) identify five guiding principles companies should consider. 1) Internal consistency (of all employer branding and talent acquisition processes, 2) Cultural embeddedness, 3) Alignment with strategy, 4) Management involvement, and 5) Balance of global and local needs (p. 25). Furthermore, according to Deters (2017, p. 28), global IT integration and evaluation are two additional principles that should be included (pp. 29–30). Consequently, seven guiding principles or success factors of the global talent management process should be considered (Figure 20).

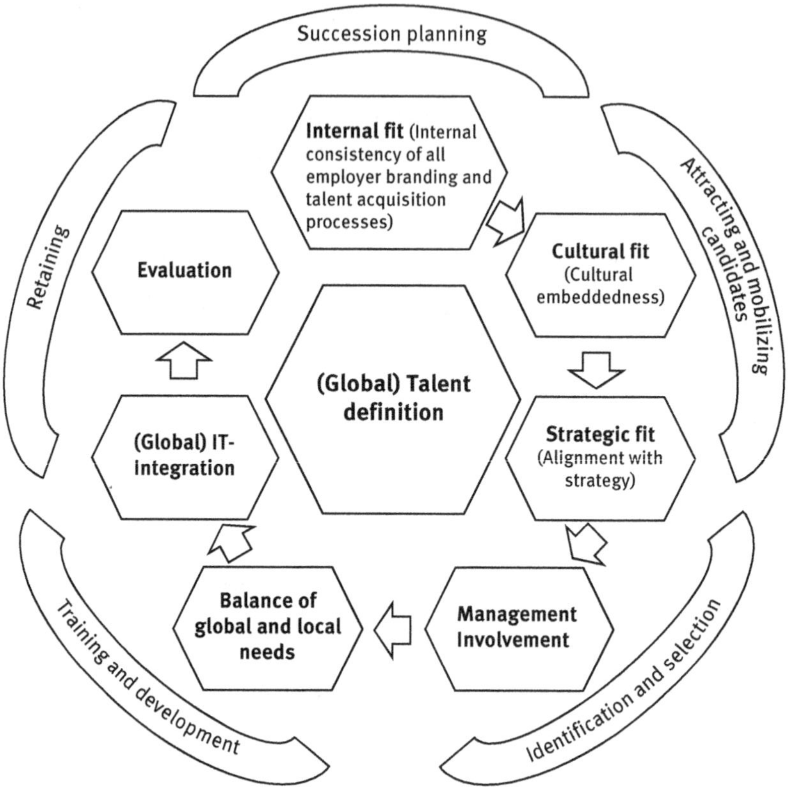

Figure 20: Talent management process (Stahl et al., 2012, p. 27; Deters, 2017, p. 30).

Since all tasks or tools in this talent management process complement each other and are partially interrelated and dependent on each other, they should be viewed as an integrated whole (Mellahi & Collings, 2010; Thunnissen et al., 2013).

In addition, the necessary activities for attracting and sourcing targeted talent, employer branding, and job branding should be implemented to mobilize the best suitable applicants to apply, for example, for a talent pool or leadership positions. This way, the base rate (the share of objectively suitable applicants in the total number of applicants) can be increased, and the entire selection process can be better designed (see Section 3.7.7).

A systematic IT-integrated talent management process can support effective recruitment, selection, and hiring decisions. Therefore, the performance of hired talent is not only a question of high-quality selection processes but also of competent leadership and a systematically designed talent management process.

10.4 Individual integration of rational-analytic and intuitive-emotional processes

10.4.1 Appreciate the interplay of rational-analytical results and intuitive-emotional impulses in personnel selection

Miles and Sadler-Smith (2014, p. 623) speak of a necessary awareness that perfect predictions in personnel selection are not possible. However, they also point to systematic, analytical selection procedures that should be chosen to ensure that performance-related characteristics are assessed. Therefore, selection managers need well-developed rational-analytical competencies.

On the other hand, representatives of the psychometric approach recommend relying exclusively on the rational-analytical data collected and having the courage not to be guided by one's intuition and emotion.

Neuroscientific research shows that the limbic system has the first and last word over the cognitive system (Roth, 2015, p. 175); from this point of view, intuition plays a crucial role, especially in interview situations of personnel selection.

Thus, selection managers need well-developed competencies to handle their intuitions and emotions constructively.

Instead of pitting reason, intuition, or emotion against each other, it makes more sense to think of analytics and intuition as complementary, mutually reinforcing ways to gain knowledge with different advantages and weaknesses. Anyone who wants to get a complete picture of an applicant and make the best possible decisions should not ignore or suppress feelings or the analytical mind.

But Evans and Stanovich (2013, p. 229) state that "perhaps the most persistent fallacy in the perception of dual-process theories is the idea that Type 1 processes (intuitive, heuristic) are responsible for all bad thinking and that Type 2 processes (reflective, analytic) necessarily lead to correct responses."

It is crucial not to focus on the critical aspects of intuitions and emotions but also to acknowledge the positive sides. Making an opposition out of analytics and intuition is about as intelligent as constructing an opposition between seeing and hearing, and then claiming that hearing is the superior way of perceiving or deciding. Like hearing and seeing, rational-analytical understanding and intuitions and feelings are two complementary ways of accessing reality (Berner, 2017).

Some researchers, such as the social psychologist Ap Dijksterhuis (2010), call to leave difficult decisions to the subconscious cannot be agreed to in this apodictic form. This would not be very responsible (Graf, 2018, p. 194). Especially in personnel selection, it is much more important to integrate intuition into a conscious decision-making process.

Intuition and analytics cannot be clearly separated in practicing personnel selection, at least not as long as human beings are involved.

The illusion of unambiguity, the avoidance of networked thinking in interactions, and so-called either-or thinking (Lang, 2016, pp. 28–42) are poor ways of dealing with complexity. Such thinking patterns prevent perceiving holistic solutions. They should be replaced by thinking and deciding by both carrying out rational analyses and listening to emotions and intuitions.

Even though, according to Betsch (2004, pp. 7–8), every person has an individual tendency to proceed more or less intuitively and more or less rationally, the aim of personnel diagnostics should be to clearly recognize the advantages and disadvantages of both procedures and ultimately to produce the best possible synthesis of rational-analytics and intuition.

Personnel selection managers should know how human decision-making systems function and how rationality and intuition interact. With this knowledge, they can competently manage their decision-making processes.

Thus, hiring managers should balance analytics and intuition: The rational-analytical tools of selection should be used to make good decisions as well as the intuitions and emotions of individuals and teams.

10.4.2 Involve well-qualified, trained, and experienced hiring managers

Many research studies show that it is not enough to develop psychometrically valid rating scales, interview guidelines, and so on; instead, qualified and trained hiring managers are needed. A study by Woehr and Huffcut (1994, pp. 198–199) indicates that rater training improves the performance of selection managers. They show that training, especially frame-of-reference training, improves the accuracy of observer judgments (rater and observational accuracy) and reduces the susceptibility to error through biases, and so on.

Sanders et al. (2008, p. 1976) show several possible explanations for why organizations often fail to adopt practices that research has shown to be effective (e.g., Johns 1993). One reason is that HR professionals lack awareness of research findings (Gannon 1983). This could be because HR professionals have or take little time to read research results or publications in relevant professional journals, social media, and so on. Another possible explanation is that professionals are aware of research findings but fail to implement the conclusions (Pfeffer and Sutton 2000) (see Chapter 2).

The studies of Rynes et al. (2002) and Sanders et al. (2008) show that (American and Dutch) practitioners are more likely to agree with research findings when their education level is higher, when they read HRM professional or academic journals more frequently, and when they have a positive attitude towards the applicability and usefulness of research results. And the more they use selection procedures based on HR research results, the more effective they are and the more successful is their organization (Rynes et al., 2002; Huselid, 1995).

A good start would be to check and hire applicants as hiring managers who are aware of research results, best practices, and the interrelation between HR practices and organizational success. And fortunately, the number of students focusing on HR or I/O psychology is increasing. This will enable companies to gradually recruit professionals who are conscious of the newest research findings in personnel selection.

As shown in Chapter 9, it is crucial to train managers involved in selection processes, as well as possibly employee representatives in countries where they are legally involved in personnel selection.

After all, applicants need to exchange information with line managers and get to know them since they will have to work with them later. Therefore, these line managers must be trained specifically in recruiting and personnel selection, and aware of their associated responsibilities.

To get people, and thus also selection managers, to implement specific findings, for example, research results, this application in practice should be individually linked with a positive benefit; and everyday experiences and opportunities should support this new behavior. If hiring managers continue their education and training accordingly, and receive appreciation and support for this from their environment, they can design a high-quality personnel selection process. As neuroscientific research shows, knowledge is implemented sustainably when linked to positive emotions for the individual manager.

Another structural support involves several qualified and diverse selection managers.

A study by Eisenkraft (2013, p. 279) suggests that intuition-based initial impressions should only be trusted when there is an opportunity to collect and combine the judgments of multiple independent raters.

Thus, for example, after an interview, every involved hiring manager should form an independent impression and score separately. Then, they should average the scored impressions, discuss the results with the other involved hiring managers and talk about their intuitions and emotions. This is in accordance with Bernoulli's law of large numbers or Condorcet's jury theorem, which states that the probability of a correct decision between two options increases with the number of decision-makers in the group, provided that the individual probabilities of a correct decision are all greater than chance (Condorcet, 1785), or that according to concepts such as "swarm intelligence," a diverse group can outperform an expert (Krause & Ruxton, 2002; Fific & Gigerenzer 2014, p. 1771).

Thus, intuitions and emotions can be beneficially integrated into personnel selection when corresponding judgments become quasi-collective and are therefore based on open communication and critical reflection upon the intuitions of several hiring managers.

Individual managers are socialized differently, perceive subjectively, process information individually, and have different goals, needs, and personalities. Therefore, the more people, and especially experienced hiring managers participate in a selection decision, and the more open, honest, and trusting they are with each other, the more they can learn from each other, and the less individual personal influencing factors can dominate (Kahle, 2018; Franck & Zellner, 2001, p. 268). Therefore, the inclusion of several selection managers is to be favored.

However, to prevent applicants from sitting in front of too many managers in an interview, interviews should preferably be conducted, or observations in an assessment center be executed by two selection managers.

But research also shows that the best experts in a group sometimes outperform the group's collective score. Several other studies show that the interview validity of some interviewers is better than that of others in selecting the best candidates (Fific & Gigerenzer, 2014, p. 1772). A study by Fific and Gigerenzer (2014) shows that two interviewers are, on average, not superior to the best interviewer. The "best interviewers" were identified by the interviewer's selection validity, measured by the "hit rate." Adding further interviewers will thus necessarily not increase the expected collective hit rate when interviewers are homogeneous (i.e., their hits are nested). The study shows that the quality of the selection decision depends on the number of interviewers, their expertise, and the chance of free riding. Research specifies the conditions when "less is more." This analysis suggests that the best policy is to invest resources into improving the quality of the best interviewers rather than distribute the resources to improve the quality of many interviewers. Using single interviewers also reduces coordination costs, eliminates the costs of sharing information and aggregation, and reduces free riding to a minimum. In general, better recruitment can be achieved by training and grooming the best interviewers, rather than investing equally in all interviewers (Fific & Gigerenzer, 2014, p. 1777). Accordingly, diverse and heterogeneous selection managers, with a high interview validity, should execute the interviews.

Candidates want to see themselves represented within an organization. For example, it can be very intimidating to be the only woman in a room full of men (or vice versa). If a company promotes diversity as a core value, all genders or sexual identities should (if possible) be represented within an interview or selection process. That allows for different perspectives when answering the interviewee's questions and ensures the candidate feels comfortable (or as comfortable as possible in a job interview setting). When doing it that way is not possible, limit the number of people in the interview, with two interviewers to one candidate.

It can be concluded that simply increasing the number of selection managers is not enough. Instead, select the best interviewers, train every selection manager, form a pool of best interviewers, and form diverse pairs of interviewers.

10.4.3 Require intuitive-emotional competencies as selection criteria for selection managers

A core requirement for selection managers is to deal competently with one's own and others' intuitions and emotions. Thus, this competence should not only be trained but also be a selection criterion and job requirement for hiring managers (Hänsel, 2014).

When selecting hiring managers, particular care should be taken to ensure that they exhibit the following competencies as far as possible:

- Knowledge of the requirements of psychometric personnel selection procedures
- Knowledge of employment law, data protection law, ethics, and so on in the field of personnel selection
- Knowledge in the field of digitization and AI to be able to assess and implement its potential properly
- Self-awareness and introspection
- Empathy
- Error tolerance
- Tolerance of ambiguity
- Constructive handling and decision-making ability in the face of complexity and uncertainty
- Situational sense and ability to improvise
- Anticipation of future and aspired developments, including a sense of what is possible and feasible
- Constructive integration of rationality and intuition, including conscious reflection, transparent communication, documentation, and a critical-constructive attitude towards benefits and limits of intuitions and emotions.

10.5 Cultural integration of rational- analytic and intuitive-emotional processes

10.5.1 Create a culture of acceptance and reflection on intuition

In personnel selection processes, even if they are supposedly carried out in an exclusively rational-analytical and psychometric way, it can often not be avoided that recruiters see the scoring results of a selection procedure expressed in numbers and have an intuition or feeling that tells them: "It's not good to select that candidate based on these numerical results; my intuition and feelings tell me not to hire that candidate."

Since intuitive and emotional processes cannot be avoided and intuitions have their possible positive as well as negative aspects, competence in dealing with one's own intuition and the intuitions of teams should be developed. As shown in

Chapter 9, intuitive competencies can be learned and trained by different approaches and measures.

And implementing high-quality personnel selection processes should not only focus on teaching and training psychometric selection procedures, but also on strengthening intuitive competencies. And this is not only knowledge or the connections between intuition and analytics, but also recognizing one's subjective and individual intuitions, questioning them critically and constructively, and reflecting upon them independently and with third parties (Kleebaur, 2007, pp. 181–182). Thus, the intuitive decision-making competencies of hiring managers should be strengthened by critically reflecting on them (see Sections 9.2.3 and 10.4.3).

Intuition is typically unconscious but can be lifted to consciousness (Gigerenzer 2007, p. 47). And in the case of personnel selection, this "lifting" is about consciously perceiving, recognizing, and reflecting on one's intuitions and feelings regarding specific applicants, their backgrounds and behavior, and so on. In this sense, intuition also has its reason, and thus, a culture of acceptance, reflection, and recognition of intuition as a legitimate basis for decisions.

Sadler-Smith and Shefy (2004) emphasize that intuition can guide good decision-making, but only if intuition is recognized, reflected upon, understood, accepted, and actively applied.

> We prefer to argue that executives need to be able to recognize and understand intuition, accept it, establish ways in which they can be comfortable with it, and leverage its potential for success and well-being both for themselves and for those whom they lead (2004, p. 78).

Kahneman (2011, p. 194) emphasizes the importance of questioning the validity of all available information, and also intuitive impulses and emotional information. This means asking oneself and reflecting with others on how valid are perceived intuitions. It also means always critically evaluating and thus validating the decisions made. That is the reason why intuitions and emotions in selection processes need to come to the surface, and be reflected upon (Apelojg, 2010, p. 194).

When analyzing application documents or conducting interviews, both applicants' information and behavior trigger certain intuitions or emotions in the selection manager. Based on previous experience, these intuitions lead selection managers to quickly construct a coherent story about the candidate's suitability. This construction of reality is not based on collecting all possible information but on coherent information from the hiring manager's experience and perspective. As a result, known and familiar clues can be evaluated with high predictive validity, and correct decisions can be made. However, doubts are often left out because this quick construction is usually based on selective perception and suppresses possible contradictions and ambiguities. Suppose the environment in which the acting persons have had the opportunity to develop these intuitions is reasonably stable, intuitive thinking calls upon recognized situations and information, and quickly generates accurate predictions and decisions. But, managers regularly operate in unstable and open environments;

therefore, it should be critically questioned as to what extent the competencies, including intuitions, gained in previous environments can also be used constructively for unstable future situations.

Lanaj et al. (2019, p. 12) emphasize – beyond the subject of analytics and intuition – another remarkable aspect of reflection, and show that managers who participate in a self-reflection intervention focusing on their identity, leadership behaviors, and decisions made, experienced more work engagement and improved prosocial impact on their co-workers. Reflection can also generate new inner resources, and internal resources "as anything perceived by the individual to help attain his or her goals" (Halbesleben et al., 2014, p. 1339) are necessary for self-control (Lanaj et al., 2019, p. 12).

10.5.2 Create flexible learning and error cultures

Errors and wrong decisions can be seen as examples of poor performance and opportunities to learn. Learning from mistakes means not making them twice, if possible. To ensure this possibility, an error management culture is needed. Openness to critically questioning and evaluating one's own decisions is most likely to thrive in a corporate culture where making mistakes is allowed, and errors are seen as chances to learn and improve. Employees do not tend to evaluate their decisions and admit errors when they expect to be punished for them; thus, the feeling of psychological safety (Edmondson, 1999, 2018) is essential to admitting errors and supporting an error management culture. Experienced hiring managers and supervisors or line managers and executives can act as role models by admitting errors, learning from them systematically, or asking for support and feedback (e.g., discovering one's own blind spots).

Research in two European countries (Germany and the Netherlands) shows that a high organizational error management culture (e.g., a system of shared norms and values and a set of common practices, such as communicating openly and transparently about errors, sharing error knowledge, detecting, analyzing, and correcting wrong decisions, evaluating processes such as selection systematically, helping in error situations) is pivotal to the reduction of wrong decisions and the promotion of positive error consequences. Furthermore, organizational error management positively correlates to firm performance (van Dyck et al., 2005, 1228).

Seckler et al. (2021) show that humility is a robust predictor of improving error management and self-efficacy (Bandura, 1977, 1982, 2012). Signs of overconfidence in managers' selection abilities or biases in a selection process (see Sections 2.6 and 3.5.2) can be seen as a signal to support an error management culture that reduces the need to hide behind feigned infallibility and allows showing humility. It should be recognized that humility is not insecurity, but a social skill. Nobody is perfect!

Thus, learning cultures and flexible organizational processes and structures support using intuition as a source of creativity and problem-solving. Intuitive management can be fostered by collaborative, participative, and communicative structures and processes that tolerate complexity, ambiguity, error culture, and even a certain degree of chaos. Diverse teams of experienced selection managers with different perspectives and ways of thinking (for example, more linear and rational-analytically thinking and more intuitive-emotionally thinking managers) could help foster holistic thinking and the capability for synergies within the organization (Herrmann, 1982, p. 82; Lussier, 2016, p. 715).

10.5.3 Demand accountability for selection managers

Etymologically, accountability derives from the Latin accomptare (to account), which stems from computare (to calculate), which, in turn, stems from putare (to reckon). Thus, accountability relates to measurement and answerability. But accountability should not be limited to something that can be measured, for example, by key performance indicators. It is more important that hiring managers feel responsible and account for their decisions. Therefore, accountability must be seen as a multiplication of two words: account × ability (Rao, 2021).

In her research, Koppers (2013, pp. 181–183) confirmed the positive effect of accountability, both at the level of motivation and the quality of the recruiter's judgment and decision-making process. Further, Koppers concluded that implementing and demanding accountability for hiring decisions is an effective contextual framework for monitoring intuitive decisions. Therefore, accountability can improve personnel diagnostics and assessments (Koppers, 2013, pp. 182–183).

Accountability means that selection managers must explain and justify their selection judgments and decisions to colleagues, superiors, or clients in a differentiated manner, and possibly even record them in writing.

Accountability in this context also means outlining the decision-making rules used to select applicants, discussing them with others, and giving sound and understandable reasons.

It is possible to differentiate between accountability for the result of a selection process and the accountability of the process. For example, Brtek and Motowidlo (2002) found that procedure accountability increased interview validity and outcome accountability lowered it. Thus, accountability for the personnel diagnostic process should be ensured. A practical possibility would be – for example – a (semi-)standardized evaluation of the recruitment process. Hiring managers could use a checklist to assess the relevant scientific quality criteria such as objectivity, requirement profile, interview guideline, and so on. This evaluation could be used for consensus discussion or in the context of regular quality circles with other selection managers. This, of course, requires appropriate self-reflection and the willingness of the recruiters to question themselves, discuss the implemented procedures, and be open to feedback and change.

Characteristics such as personal responsibility and commitment, and an unconditional desire to develop and improve are supportive factors in improving a selection process.

Since in many cases, corporate contexts offer only poor evaluation opportunities, responsible selection managers themselves or higher executives in the organization should demand and implement these accountability opportunities. By doing this, selection managers can actively engage with other leaders, colleagues, and so on, and improve selection processes and decisions.

10.6 Holistic approach to personnel selection

10.6.1 Conclusion for theory building

Practice in organizations has a clear interest in and desire for support from science. However, there is also skepticism in practice or even a rejection of research findings; sometimes, researchers are seen as elitist and know-it-all. Yet, scientists often seem to have superior knowledge or insights into decision-making than practitioners. As a result, scientists perceive practitioners as acting irrationally and making foolish errors in personnel selection; and that the scientifically generated knowledge should be implemented in practice in any case since it meets scientific standards of validity or objectivity and could, therefore, be more trusted than subjective experiences (Lopes, 1991, pp. 78–79). Of course, the point that arises is which knowledge can people fundamentally trust more. Knowledge generated on an evidence-based approach that establishes correlations between a particular behavior and outcomes is seen as superior to subjective impressions or feelings. However, the limitations of rational-analytical approaches in science, as presented in Section 3.7, must also be critically examined.

This problem has been spotlighted by the role of science in the Corona crisis of 2020–2022, as well as in the context of climate policy. According to the prevailing scientific opinion, scientific research results should be evidence-based. And in policy practice, it was a matter of listening to the recommendations of scientific experts. And in hindsight, it became apparent to not only listen to the experts of specific scientific disciplines but also to get a holistic picture and involve experts from different scientific disciplines. But it was not the scientists who decided what to implement, but the politicians; they are the ones who are responsible.

And this is similar to the implementation of scientific findings in the practice of organizations. Here, the practitioners are in charge. There is no dogma of factual constraint according to which scientific findings must guide practice. Instead, practice must decide how research results can be implemented. Practitioners decide this against the background of their possibilities and resources, personal benefits, and/

or organizational circumstances (Hirschi, 2021a and 2021b); and they must also bear the consequences of their decisions.

But previous psychometrically focused recommendations for creating selection processes paid too little attention to the fact that – for good reasons – the world of practical decision-making is far from being based on rational-analytics. That´s the reason the science of personnel diagnostics should give intuitions and emotions a new legitimacy. It is both acceptable and necessary to consider feelings and intuitions and express them as legitimate and accepted parts of human decision-making.

Science that ignores and even consciously refutes the obvious need of practitioners to include emotions and intuitions in selection processes is met with skepticism or even rejection. Thus, a personnel selection theory that impacts practice in an organization should break away from the claim that personnel selection, including interviews or assessment centers, can or should be done without intuitions and emotions (Schuler, 1996, p. 86). Instead, the practice should be guided on integrating hiring managers' intuitions and related feelings so as not to endanger the selection process's scientific requirements (especially validity), but to improve selection decisions (Riedel, 2016, pp. 9–10).

To be recognized in the rational world of science and business, scientists try to develop numerically supported, valid knowledge. Most researchers in personnel diagnostics have accepted the concept of evidence and validity by developing rational-analytical procedures. And they are, to a certain degree, right with these scientifically proven procedures. On the other hand, and understandably, the minefield of intuition is threatening to scientists because it is difficult to make the concept of intuition scientifically tangible and measurable.

But awarding the Nobel prizes in economics to Simon in 1978 and to Kahneman in 2002 gives legitimacy to the integrative approach. Both were honored for pointing out that decision-making processes in practice do not take place exclusively in the idealized world of rationality, which does not reflect the reality of human behavior. And encouragingly, there is more and more well-founded research on intuitions and emotions.

Science reveals interrelationships of effects and, in doing so, opens up possibilities for action. But what and how is implemented in practice requires the inclusion of the respective contextual conditions, perspectives, and the risks that may lie outside the framework on which the scientific investigation was based.

One can get the impression that the rational-analytical approach of psychometrics has little to do with hiring managers as holistic human beings because it would like to abolish human striving for autonomy and self-will. However, to conclude that in developing a theoretical approach for personnel selection, the rationally behaving hiring manager, always and everywhere, should be aimed, must be critically questioned. A scientific approach, which could positively influence practice, should not be based on an image of a man who ultimately wants to abolish hiring managers` autonomy and freedom. On the contrary, such a self-abolition of the human being must be consistently counteracted.

The rational-analytical approach in psychometrics wants selection managers to reduce their intuitions and emotions as far as possible. However, this is a limited conception of man (selection managers) that excludes essential sources of knowledge. In addition, selection managers operate in particular contexts and are influenced by these contexts in their decision-making and behavioral patterns. Companies and people are open systems that do not operate in static environments, but have to deal with an open future. For this reason, conceptually, for example, the requirement profiles for applicants should not be formulated too narrowly but rather in a way that is open to the future. Requirement profiles that refer to profiles of jobholders who have been successful in the past should therefore be critically reflected upon, otherwise, there is a risk of repeating the past over and over again, and organizations will not be able to thrive.

Thus, in personnel diagnostics, the aim should be to work with concepts that adequately reflect decision-makers' mental representations and help practitioners solve their problems according to the organizational requirements and possibilities. In addition, the knowledge and the related selection methods and tools recommended for practice should be based on valid, scientifically proven research results and not on concepts that aim selection managers to decide without emotions and intuitions. Thus, the rational-analytical and psychometric approach alone cannot capture practitioners' everyday challenges, and intuitive and emotional competencies.

A holistic and integrated theoretical approach is needed if science in personnel selection wants to do an excellent job of predicting decision-making in personnel diagnostics.

Using a holistic approach, science can describe, explain, and predict why hiring managers behave the way they do. Theory can impact practice by supporting hiring managers in implementing this holistic approach to personnel selection.

Suppose we want economic life to become more human, then science should become more humanized, and subjectivity of researchers should also be allowed, while at the same time seeing the people being studied (in this case, selection managers) as subjects. From this point of view, a realistic science of human beings can be created by people who are aware of their own humanity with all its possibilities and limitations and thus perceive themselves as a whole subject. According to the prevailing (natural) scientific methodology, research should be a desubjectivized process, in which the scientists have to understand themselves like neutrals, data and facts-registering apparatuses. They should abstract from themselves, their interests, needs, goals, and especially, subjective characteristics like emotions. Therefore, the distance of the scientist to themselves as human beings is methodically brought about. It is then not surprising if the people to be examined, like selection managers, should act just as rationally and distanced from themselves as the scientists demand of themselves (Deters, 1990, pp. 36–40).

For Carl Rogers, scientific research and theory building aims to bring significant subjective experiences into an inner order. For him, experience is the highest authority and, at the same time, the most important touchstone for the validity of statements. No idea of other people is as relevant for human decisions as one's own experience (Rogers, 1994, pp. 39–40). Human beings are wiser than only their intellect and rationality; developed human beings have learned to regard their experiences as a reliable instrument to govern their behavior (Rogers, 1985, p. 274. Although Rogers' approach can be criticized for the lack of empirical evidence used in his research, his approach reflects what many practitioners think. They want to rely on their individual experiences and take these into account and, at the same time, be appreciated for them. Just as Simon's criticism of the rational image of man was justified, theory formation in the field of personnel selection can and should no longer assume an ideal image of selection managers as purely rational-analytical beings.

In our increasingly complex world (VUCA world), holistic and networked ways of thinking, deciding, acting, and related theoretical concepts are required, that correspond to the world's complexity, ambiguity, and volatility as far as possible. Thus, rational-analytical and intuitive thinking should develop a constructive dialog in theory-building for personnel selection.

Since, according to Kurt Lewin, nothing is as practical as a good theory, this theory on personnel selection should not be based on ideal decision behavior but on how selection managers actually act in decision-making. Therefore, it is insufficient to consider only the psychometric approach to reach a high-quality selection procedure. Instead, this requires a holistic approach that integrates at least these two different ways of gaining pertinent information in selection processes.

As long as people are directly involved in selecting people, intuitions and related emotions cannot simply be turned off. Rather, the aim must be to consider the disadvantages of purely analytical-rational or intuitive approaches, and instead, in the sense of an integrative and holistic theory formation, to appreciate and integrate their advantages.

Thus, practitioners and scientists must recognize and appreciate the rational-analytical approach and the wisdom of intuitions and emotions. By listening to their intuitions and emotions as well as to the messages of their rational-analytical mind, human beings – and therefore HR managers – can enjoy the benefits of functioning more holistically and take advantage of different sources of wisdom.

Research shows that wide dissemination of a selection procedure promotes its acceptance. Based on the mere-exposure effect, the repeated presentation of an initially neutral stimulus results in a positive evaluation (Zajonc, 1968, p. 1). Thus, the more consistently the rational-analytical approach in personnel selection is integrated and implemented with the critical-constructive use of intuitive procedures, the higher is its acceptance.

At the same time, however, it has become clear that more research is needed to get valid research results, especially on intuitions and emotions in personnel selection. But this requires a research approach that starts from how people are and not how they should be.

10.6.2 Multidimensional framework for decision-making in the personnel selection and hiring processes – a holistic and paradoxical perspective

10.6.2.1 Integrative approach to a scientific analysis of the interplay of analytics and intuition in personnel selection

Since managers operate in complex and fast-changing environments and decision-making behavior is influenced by many factors, a model or framework as a simplified representation of reality can help clarify thoughts and explain behaviors. To do justice to these diverse influencing factors, decision-making processes should be conceptualized as multidimensional and holistic, encompassing bounded rationality, heuristics, intuitions, and emotions (Eisenhardt & Zbaracki, 1992; Sinclair, 2005). Therefore, a holistic and integrated model or a framework of analytical and intuitive decision-making is desirable, where both approaches are used in a complementary and interactive way (Sinclair, 2005).

The following theoretical framework for modeling decision-making is based on identified factors influencing personnel selection decisions presented in this book.

Sadler-Smith explicitly stresses "that managerial intuition will only be understood imperfectly and partially if intuition is considered exclusively and in isolation from its contrastive, or complement, analysis" (Sadler-Smith, 2019, p. 10).

Our research shows that intuition and rational-analytics can be seen as independent but also parallel working systems. As shown in the "parallel (competitive) model," intuitive and analytical processes proceed in parallel. However, the term "competitive" suggests that the two processes virtually act against each other. But it doesn't have to be that way.

Rather, it turns out that people process information by two parallel and concurrently active systems that may interact in a harmonious and supportive but also conflictual manner. However, the two systems operate in different ways (Sinclair & Ashkanasy, 2005), and it is, therefore, more appropriate to speak only of "parallel processes" and not of "parallel competitive processes."

These parallel processes, representing an integrative and holistic approach, rest on three main assumptions (Betsch & Glöckner, 2010, pp. 286–289).

1. Intuitive and analytic processes are distinct, and decision-making in selection and hiring involves these two different processes. Intuitive processes occur quickly, unconsciously, and unintentionally, even if the hiring manager consciously engages in a judgment or decision task. Intuition is based on associative processes of information integration, drawing on knowledge and previous experience,

perceiving and processing nonverbal messages, and so on, that cause preferences for a particular candidate.

On the other hand, analytic methods involve consciously searching for specific information, making sense of given and received data, assessing most valid requirements, enquiring in cases of inconsistencies and ambiguities, anticipating future behavior and fit with the team, or offering an employment contract.

2. Intuitive and analytical processes have different potentials, serve different functions, and suffer from different constraints (see advantages and disadvantages of rational-analytical processes and intuitive processes in Sections 3.6 and 3.7 for rational-analytical procedures, and Sections 5.1 and 5.2 for intuitive processes).

   Developing requirements for applicants and developing a competency model based on the competencies of previous successful job holders can be challenging. For example, suppose circumstances (markets, technology, laws) are stable, and tomorrow is much like yesterday (although this is very unlikely), Gigerenzer recommends using rational-analytical methods, such as statistics. But when it comes to a highly uncertain, complex, and volatile future, Gigerenzer (2021, p. 61) advises using intuition in decision-making.
3. Intuition and analytics are component processes rather than different modes of thinking. A personnel selection decision is usually not made exclusively intuitive or analytical. Instead, intuition and analytics guide different subprocesses (components). Gathering information to evaluate and decide who should be employed in particular jobs is neither an automatic process nor a wholly controlled process, but reflects both approaches, making independent contributions.

When people think analytically about a problem and weigh the pros and cons of a judgment, they use the prefrontal cortex (System 2). This brain area is connected to the limbic system, an important center of emotions, and it can keep emotions under control. However, neuroscientific research knows that the neurological processes that accompany intuitions (and emotions) are much faster than explicit cognitive processes (conscious thinking). Thus, although humans can be so occupied by positive or negative feelings that they can hardly grasp a clear thought, both brain areas work simultaneously. Therefore, for selection decisions in organizations, the idea of parallel processes can be assumed.

This parallel process approach "resonates strongly with how managers actually accomplish decision-making and problem-solving in real-world settings" (Vance et al., 2007; Sadler-Smith, 2019, p. 9). And practical managerial work requires both modes (Simon, 1987).

Also, Sinclair and Ashkanasy (2005, p. 354) assume that analytical and intuitive processes interact and support each other, and that rational-analytical and intuitive processes in selection processes are used complementarily and iteratively (Sinclair & Ashkanasy, 2005, p. 354).

Reason and intuition must not be antagonists; "rather than being set in opposition to each other, intuition and rational analysis are better conceived of as two parallel systems of knowing" (Sadler-Smith & Shefy, 2004, p. 76). Intuitions (and thus also emotions) are not per se threats to rationality. On the contrary, intuitions (and emotions) have the capacity to inform intelligent decisions in complex situations, not to just respond reflexively to threats or affordances of daily life.

De Sousa (2018, p. 13) states that intuitions and emotions can solve

> the "Frame Problem" which is essentially the problem of knowing what to ignore without wasting time examining every possible consequence of a decision to make sure it can be ignored as irrelevant. (Intuitions and, J. D.) (e)motions do this by controlling the salience of information, lines of inquiry, and live practical options. They narrow the focus of attention to ranges of factors that we have "learned", on both the evolutionary and the individual scale, are the most likely to be relevant in any given situation. (Intuitions and, J. D.) (e)motions, therefore, contribute to our capacity for rational decision, even though, as is all too obvious, they sometimes distort judgment and interfere with rational deliberation.

Rationality has – among other things – the function of monitoring intuitions and emotions, and the reverse is also true. In this parallel approach to decision-making, judgments based on rationality are regularly evaluated intuitively and emotionally. Thus, intuitions can also support rational decisions or contradict them.

Thus the "analytical mind' may act, metaphorically, as a mirror, in which quick, automatic evaluations by the 'intuitive mind' may be reflected and scrutinized in the accomplishment of managerial decision-making" (Sadler-Smith & Hodgkinson, 2017, p. 3). This way, rational analytics can monitor intuitions and vice versa.

The rational-analytical approach blocks the use of intuitions, and thus the experience-based expertise of hiring managers in personnel selection (List, 2014); the psychometric approach leaves no room for emotions, except, by implication, disrupters and disturbers of the rational process. The psychometric approach to personnel selection tries to separate rational analytics from intuitions and emotions. But in the practice of decision-making, these processes flow into each other and exert mutual influence. For example, it is understandable that people want security and try to avoid uncertainty. Thus, responsible science in personnel selection decisions considers decision-making's intuitive and emotional side.

We need selection and hiring processes and tools that perform successfully in ambiguous situations. The paradox is that we know from research that a rational-analytical psychometric approach leads to more objective and valid decisions. But, on the other hand, hiring managers will not and cannot neglect their intuitions and emotions; and they want to act authentically.

Judgment and decision-making in selection and hiring processes result from a parallel interplay and collaboration of intuition and analysis.

> Only recognizing the duality and the integrative interplay of intuitive-emotional and rational-analytical approaches to personnel selection will do justice to the complexity of personnel

> selection decisions in practice. Therefore, both the intuitive-emotional and rational-analytical aspects must be considered and examined more closely. The question is not whether an intuitive or rational-analytical approach is better but how the interaction of these approaches can be optimally designed.

This means not neglecting the hiring managers' intuitive-emotional patterns of action, and consciously making them a holistic object of investigation.

In selecting and hiring processes, the selection judgment and hiring decisions interact and flow directly into each other. As a result, selection managers must cope with uncertainty and use probabilistic cues to judge, for example, leadership potential, personality characteristics, or the capacity for teamwork.

Since personnel selection decisions are decisions for the future, selection managers should ensure that the job requirements are developed with the future in mind. With the help of foresight processes and tools such as Scenario-, Delphi-, or creativity techniques, or future workshops, changes in the environment of organizations can be reflected at an early stage and conclusions drawn for today's decisions. In this context, it is essential to anticipate the dynamic interactions between social, political, technological, and economic factors in an open (future) dialog and draw conclusions for the requirements to be met by future employees. In addition, it is crucial to pay particular attention to attitudes, values, mindsets, and personality characteristics, such as flexibility and adaptability, openness, conscientiousness, emotional stability, and so on, which enable people to master future challenges appropriately. And to get support and resources, HR managers need to coordinate these processes with the top management and other key stakeholders.

As shown, a holistic framework of personnel decision-making should be based on the "selection reality" of the selection managers and use the tension and interplay between rational-analytical processes (System 2) and the intuitive processes (System 1).

Since intuitive-emotional impulses are generated much faster in the human organism than using rational-analytical processes, it can be assumed that selection interview judgments are initially made sequentially according to the "default-Interventionist model."

"From the point of view of the two minds model, the intuitive mind may sometimes unconsciously prepare a choice in advance. A big advantage of having two minds is that an intuitive choice can be reversed by the intervention of the analytical mind (or vice versa)" (Soon et al., 2008, 543; quoted in Sadler-Smith, 2010, p. 17). Thus, intuitive and accompanied emotional impulses are first triggered, which can then be consciously reflected on and critically questioned.

But equally, intuitions and emotions can help cope with uncertainties in the selection process, for example, when the rational-analytical approach does not yield clear results or when one has to choose between several equally well-qualified applicants.

When this happens, parallel, interactive processes between intuition and analytics occur. Such reflected personnel selection decisions are thus the result of a combination of intuition and analytics and occur according to the default intervention model and the "parallel (competitive) model."

This is also consistent with our empirical research results. The hiring managers interviewed state that with increasing professional experience, they perceive the selection process as an integrative process of intuition and analytics. As long as they were inexperienced as managers, they tend to look for certainty in analytics and standardized procedures, but with increasing experience, they rely on their intuition. Most of them acknowledge that intuitive-emotional impulses appear first in personnel selection. And these impulses are then subjected to rational-analytical reflection, so that in the end, they talk of a holistic, integrative process of intuition and analytics. The conscious and critical-constructive reflection of the intuitive and emotional impulses – either alone or with other selection managers – and the conscious comparison of the applicant's perceived behavior with the requirements of the position and the fit to the team, ultimately leads to an integration of intuitive and rational-analytical processes (Reichelt, 2020, p. 63).

The interplay between intuition and rational-analytical processes in personnel selection is complex and not yet exhaustively researched. But the capacity of the human brain or body to integrate intuitive and rational-analytical processes allows a holistic interplay of both in human decision-making.

Thus, our empirical research confirms that selection decisions in practice run according to the "default interventionist model" and the "parallel interactive model." In addition, research results have revealed two processes that interact but operate differently ("dual-process-theory"). Some selection managers use both approaches equally, the analytical and intuitive information processing. The approach we propose views analytical and intuitive decision-making as parallel yet interconnected. Both approaches are equally valid, but each can be appropriate in different contexts (Sinclair & Ashkanasy, 2005, pp. 359–360).

Our empirical research results also show that only a few hiring managers base their selection decisions only on objective tests or assessment center results (scores), and not on their intuition or feelings. These very few managers, primarily psychologists, state that if they feel that their intuitions or emotions say no or yes to a specific candidate, they consciously ignore or suppress these intuitive impulses and try to rely on the rational-analytical results; thus, System 2 overrules System 1. But this is rather the exception; the question arises as to what extent this goal is actually realizable or whether they answered according to supposed social acceptability or give the appearance of absolute scientifically recognized professionalism and independence.

Epstein et al. (2003, p. 164) state that people believe that they can make completely rational-analytical decisions mainly because the rational-analytical and intuitive systems are independent of each other. But as the two systems interact and influence each other, every rational decision is likely to be biased by the intuitive system. If rational analysis votes for Jane but the intuitive system says no, we struggle to overcome the intuition. Following our intuitions is more natural and pleasant than acting against them (Kahneman, 2011, p. 194).

Sadler-Smith (2019, p. 19), referring to Wang et al. (2017), assumes that intuition and analytics are uncorrelated, orthogonal, and serve different purposes. Therefore, they should be conceptualized as two unrelated and independent processes from a scientific perspective. And from a scientific perspective, this allows to make both processes operationalizable, and, thus oriented to the methodological ideal of the sciences, clearly separable for investigation.

But it is not always that simple. On the one hand, both processes can act and operate independently; on the other hand, they influence each other and interact. Although it makes sense from a scientific perspective to consider intuition and analytics as two parallel, independent processes, in the practice of decision-making, selection managers cannot clearly divide them. Their bodies, thoughts, and emotions belong inseparably together and interact directly in everyday life. Human beings function only as a whole. For example, our empirical research shows that selection managers in practice cannot clearly separate these two processes. Instead, they experience that both processes interact, mix, and influence their judgments and decision-making concurrently. This confirms Sinclair and Ashkanasy's (2005, p. 365) research results that respondents find it difficult to isolate their verbal assessment of intuitive use from references to rational thinking.

We learned from our interviewed selection managers that System 1 says (unconsciously) while observing a candidate during an assessment center or interview, "I like the candidate, select her/him." And automatically, this candidate will be scored higher by System 2. Thus, the scoring of System 2 is not independent of System 1. Or, if after interviewing all candidates or after getting "objective" test results, System 2 of the selection manager intervenes and says, "Candidate A scores highest, select that candidate." But System 1 produces vague feelings of unease in the hiring manager, although all facts speak for candidate A. And System 1 says, "I have a bad feeling about that candidate. I wouldn't choose him. He doesn't fit the team or the organizational culture." Possible consequence: System 1 has more power (see neuroscientific or Kahneman's research results) and often wins and overrules System 2. At the same time, it becomes obvious that adding up supposedly objective scores only pretends to be objective; it`s an objectivity illusion.

This observation confirms the research results of Barrett et al. (2004, p. 568), who show that individual motivation and goals play a decisive role in how System 2 is used to control System 1 and thus how both systems can interact.

Some researchers place intuition and analytics on a continuum that runs from purely intuitive to purely analytical, where only one score can be registered (see Section 4.2.2.7). But this approach does not allow independent variations in the intensity of use and the relative use of each system (Van Riel et al., 2006). Thus, our empirical research could only partially support the model of intuition and analytics located on a two-pole continuum, with decisions made either more intuitively or more analytically. On the contrary, a "both-and approach" is suggested by our empirical research and also by the research results of Vance et al. (2004, 2007) or Groves et al. (2008).

Selection managers interviewed in our empirical research reported that they based their selection decisions on high intuition (e.g., assessing the team fit) and high analytics (e.g., assessing the cognitive abilities by a test). These managers confirm that these two processes are not mutually exclusive. For them, this dichotomy cannot be clearly mapped onto a continuum, with only one score being registered (see continuum approach, Section 4.2.2.7).

Therefore, we integrate the dual-process model with a new duality approach. We don't use the continuum approach with only one score, but rather a polarity profile. For example, suppose a decision is made with equally very high intuition and very high analytics, the question is how should that be entered on this continuum when only one score can be specified? In addition, it should be transparent what a specific score of intuition or analytics means on a continuum. For example, what does a high degree of intuition or analytics or a strong/weak intuition mean? How is it operationalized – whether a certain degree of intuition is a degree of 6 or 60% or a degree of 3 or 30% on the continuum? A comparable applies to analytics. Therefore, the following attempts to transparently describe what is meant by a specific degree of intuition or analytics.

To describe the degrees of intuition and analytics more clearly, we do not distinguish between degrees of intuition and degrees of analytics in general, but between "Degree of competent implementation of analytical procedures" and "Degree of competent implementation of intuitive procedures." Thus, it`s about the degree of constructively and effectively handling analytics and intuitions as a critical success factor for decision-making.

A score of 10 on the "degree of competent implementation of analytical procedures" means implementing what is described in more detail in Chapter 3, for example,
- a very high degree of compliance with scientific quality criteria such as validity, objectivity, and reliability;
- a very high degree of professional expertise among selection managers regarding scientific quality standards such as ISO 10667, DIN 33430, guidelines for implementation of assessment centers, and so on (e.g., explicit knowledge), and a very high level of implementation of these standards;
- a very high degree of analytical competencies and cognitive abilities;
- and so on.

And a degree of 0 (zero) in "analytics" means deciding without any systematic procedures, without using standards or guidelines, and so on.

A score of 10 on the "degree of competent implementation of intuitive procedures" means, for example,

- a very high degree of reflection on intuition and emotions at the individual level;
- a very high degree of reflection on intuitions and emotions at the collective level;
- a very high degree of reflection on intuition and emotions at the organizational and cultural level, including the status of intuition in a society;
- a very high degree of awareness of perceptual biases such as biases, stereotypes, and so on, and a very well-developed ability to control them;
- a very high degree of intersubjectivity;
- a very high degree of emotional competence, including empathy, authenticity, body awareness, competent relationship building, convincing and attracting candidates, and so on;
- very high imagination skills;
- a very high degree of expertise and experience in personnel selection (e.g., implicit knowledge of personnel selection);
- very highly competent in applying previously learned patterns and experiences to fields of application;
- and so on.

And the degree of 0 (zero) in "intuition" means deciding purely based on intuitions and emotions, and relying blindly on them without critically questioning them, ignoring all other possible information, and evaluating only what is perceived.

No conscious reflection and reduction of perceptual distortions, bias, stereotypes, and so on (see disadvantages of intuitions, Section 5.2).

Using a polarity profile and scaling with two possible scores, on the other hand, makes it possible to enter both a score for a high degree of competent implementation of intuition and a score for a high level of analytics. Thus, although decision-makers rarely represent the pure analytical or intuitive orientation in practice (Malewska, 2015, p. 101), a manager can have a high score in analytics (e.g., on a scale from 1 to 10 with an 8) and, simultaneously, a high score in intuition (e.g., 8), or a high score in analytics (e.g., 8) and a moderate score in intuition (e.g., 4), and so on.

This approach or model is different from the model of Hammond (2000) and Hayes et al. (2003; see Figure 14), where, when one proceeds fully analytically, the intuitive influence goes to zero. Instead, it is possible to proceed simultaneously with a 10 on the "level of competent implementation of intuitive procedures" and with a 10 on the "level of competent implementation of analytical procedures" so that both approaches complement each other (e.g., very analytical in the pre-selection and using a high level of intuitive competencies in the final selection).

This shows that decision-making in specific situations can be located at two different points (see Figure 21) and thus use the information of System1 and System 2 simultaneously. It means overcoming one-dimensional thinking: it's not a matter of "either/or," but of "both/and." It is about using intuition and analytics simultaneously.

Especially when selecting candidates by involving people, System 1 and System 2 interact, and information of System 1 overlaps with information of System 2. Therefore, as experienced by practitioners, Figure 21 depicts the interaction of intuitions and emotions as well as the analytical considerations in overlapping circles.

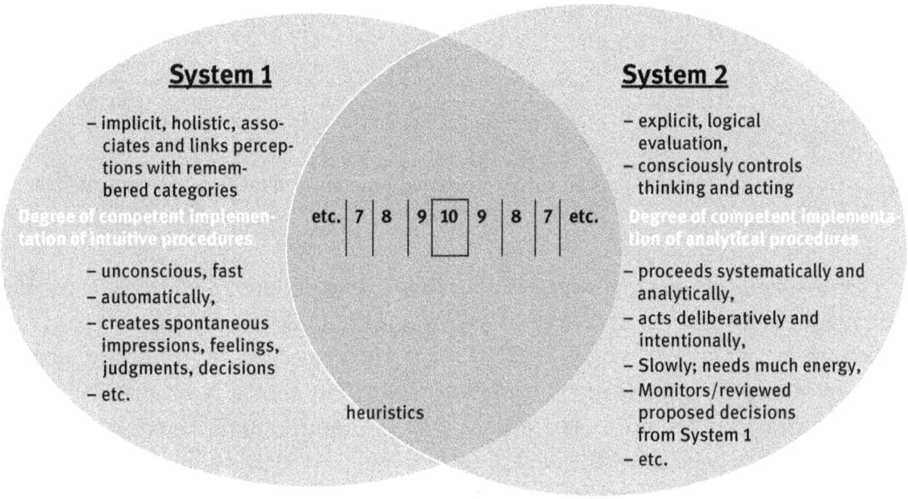
System 1
- implicit, holistic, associates and links perceptions with remembered categories
Degree of competent implementation of intuitive procedures
- unconscious, fast
- automatically,
- creates spontaneous impressions, feelings, judgments, decisions
- etc.
etc. 7 8 9 10 9 8 7 etc.
heuristics
System 2
- explicit, logical evaluation,
- consciously controls thinking and acting
Degree of competent implementation of analytical procedures
- proceeds systematically and analytically,
- acts deliberatively and intentionally,
- Slowly; needs much energy,
- Monitors/reviewed proposed decisions from System 1
- etc.

Figure 21: Overlapping interactions of analytics and intuition.

Goldberg (1983, 1988, p. 31; Landsberg, 2006) vividly illustrates System1 and System 2 in decision-making in the single-hole water faucet model (Figure 22). According to this model, only hot water (information field System 1) or only cold water (information field System 2) can flow, or, depending on the situation (problem to be solved, situational circumstances, etc.), both temperatures can be mixed. Even if this faucet model does not fit 100% for cases where, for example, both a very highly competent implementation of analytics and intuition takes place, it is a comprehensible illustration representing the interplay of analytics and intuitions in the vast majority of cases.

Analytics and intuition are seen as complementary partners that support each other, and sometimes more of System 1, and sometimes more of System 2 is used. The holistic decision-maker balances both ways of gaining insights and information.

Although the managers interviewed perceive analytics and intuition as not clearly separable processes in decision making, Sadler-Smith (2019, p. 19), referring to Wang et al. (2017), states that intuition and analytics are uncorrelated and should be conceptualized as two unrelated and independent processes. Thus, it is possible

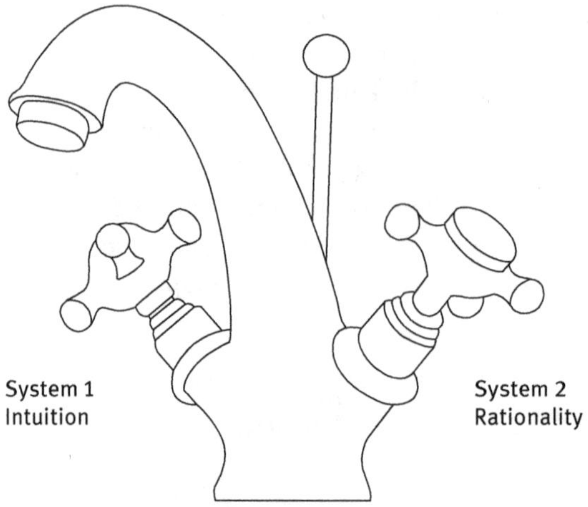

Figure 22: Single hole water faucet model of integrating System 1 and System 2 (according to Goldberg 1983, 1988; Landsberg, 2006).

to perceive and judge something with System 1, independent of System 2, or vice versa. For example, deciding only based on a rational-analytical process (e.g., an algorithm, or results of a cognitive ability test such as GMAT, that decides who to select as a student without involving people), the score on analytics may be 10. On the other hand, and simultaneously, the score in intuition is 0 (zero) because no human manager is directly involved in this selection process. In this case, rational-analytics and intuition should not overlap. But in most cases, they interact, although they work as unrelated and often parallel processes. The following Figure 23 can also illustrate these interacting processes.

In addition, it should be mentioned again that the representation of System 1 (intuitive-emotional processes) and System 2 (analytical processes) and the interaction of intuitive and analytical processes is a representation and metaphor that reduces complexity.

It can be concluded that the higher the competent implementation of rational-analytical and intuitive-emotional processes in personnel selection (carried out by humans), the better are the decisions.

Selection managers should ensure that the perceived information from the rational-analytical and the intuitive-emotional path of knowledge is coherent, and that a decision is made based on a positive signal on both knowledge tracks.

How these paths of knowledge are used and how the parallel interaction, and sometimes the dominance of either the rational-analytical (System 2) or the intuitive approach (System 1) in selection processes, for example, interviews, works, is primarily affected by four broad influencing factors. These four factors are on the left in the following Figure 24 and described in Section 5.6.

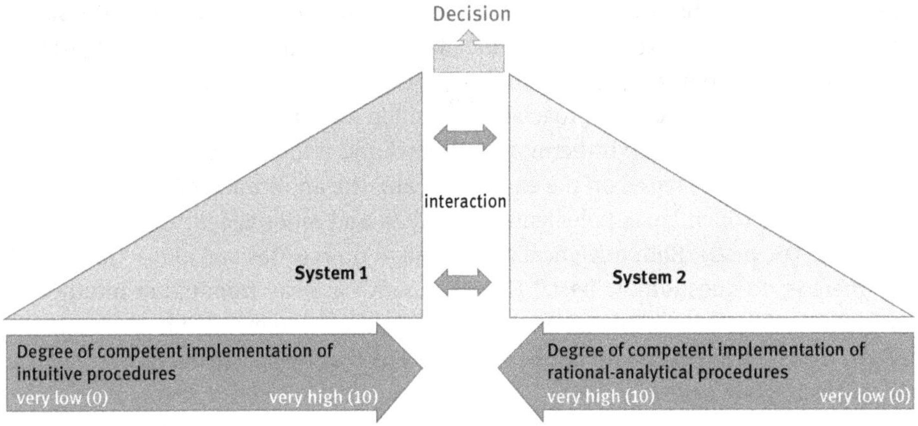

Figure 23: Analytics and intuition as uncorrelated, independent, and simultaneously interacting processes.

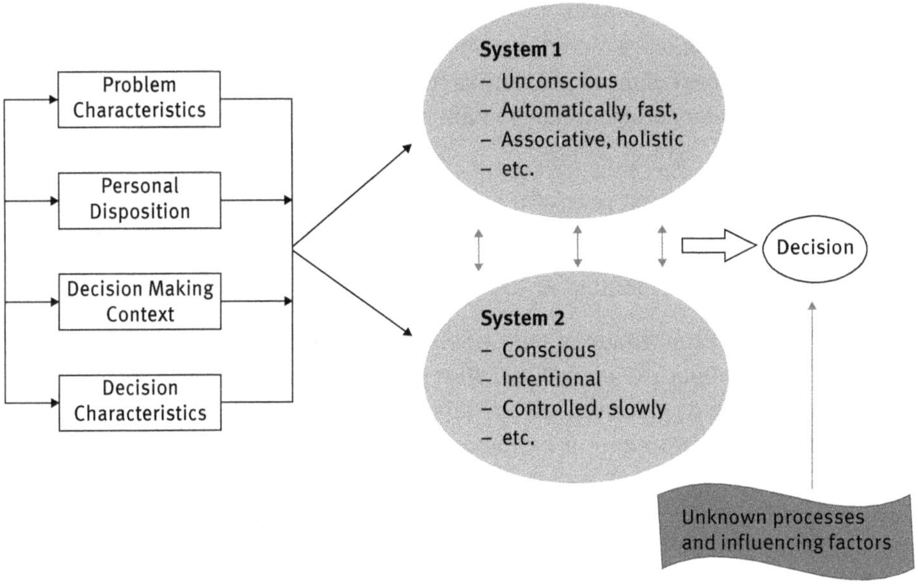

Figure 24: Holistic approach to decision-making (based on Sinclair & Ashkanasy, 2005, p. 360).

10.6.2.2 Duality of intuition and analytics as a paradoxical tension and interplay

The recommended holistic approach to selection decisions accounts explicitly for the interplay and tension between intuition and rationality. According to the dual-process theory, this holistic approach sees intuition and analytics as two independent but interacting processes. Furthermore, reflected and critically questioned intuitions are mental processes based on the experience and the application of known patterns of association, which are supplemented with data and rational deliberation (Miller & Ireland, 2005, p. 21). Both analytical and intuitive procedures and skills are needed, and there is no question of "best." However, moving away from either intuition or analysis to a "both intuition and analysis" mindset is recommended in personnel selection. Thus, intuition should not be conceptualized as opposites but as complementary paths to good decisions.

Miles and Sadler-Smith (2014, p. 622) show that, from the perspective of recruiting practitioners, the most trustworthy judgments are made when a combination of rational-analytic and intuitive methods is used. Accepting feelings or intuition as valid forms of knowledge and reason is not to deny the value of rationality or place it and intuition in opposition to each other: both intuition and rationality have their advantages and limits, and each can sometimes lead to good or bad decisions. For Sadler-Smith and Shefy (2004a), it is important to stress that they are not proposing that intuition is better than rationality or vice versa. Instead, they suggest that a single-minded emphasis on rationality (or intuition) presents a partial view. Managers might achieve a more balanced perspective by considering both rationality and intuition as complementary and mutually reinforcing components of a decision strategy.

> Intuition and rationality are at the heart of an important dynamic in managerial cognition in which both modes have the potential to balance or reinforce each other. . . . *Intuition is not the opposite of rationality:* rationality and intuition are often depicted as opposites, however they could be combined into a 'third, more hybrid powerful style that incorporates the best of both (Sadler-Smith & Shefy, 2004a, pp. C1–C2).

In a holistic conceptualization of personnel selection, rational-analytical and intuitive-emotional approaches are needed. With the rational-analytical approach, it can be ensured that an applicant meets the job requirements on the professional level and that the entire procedure is carried out in a structured and legally compliant manner. On the other hand, integrating the intuitive-emotional approach ensures that the candidate fits in with the company and the team on the social level and that a positive candidate experience is possible (Riedel, 2015, p. 36).

The alternating consideration of analytics and intuition in decision-making is illustrated in the following Figure 25, but especially in personnel selection, the process can start with a rational-analytical evaluation of information about an applicant (e.g. analyzing application documents).

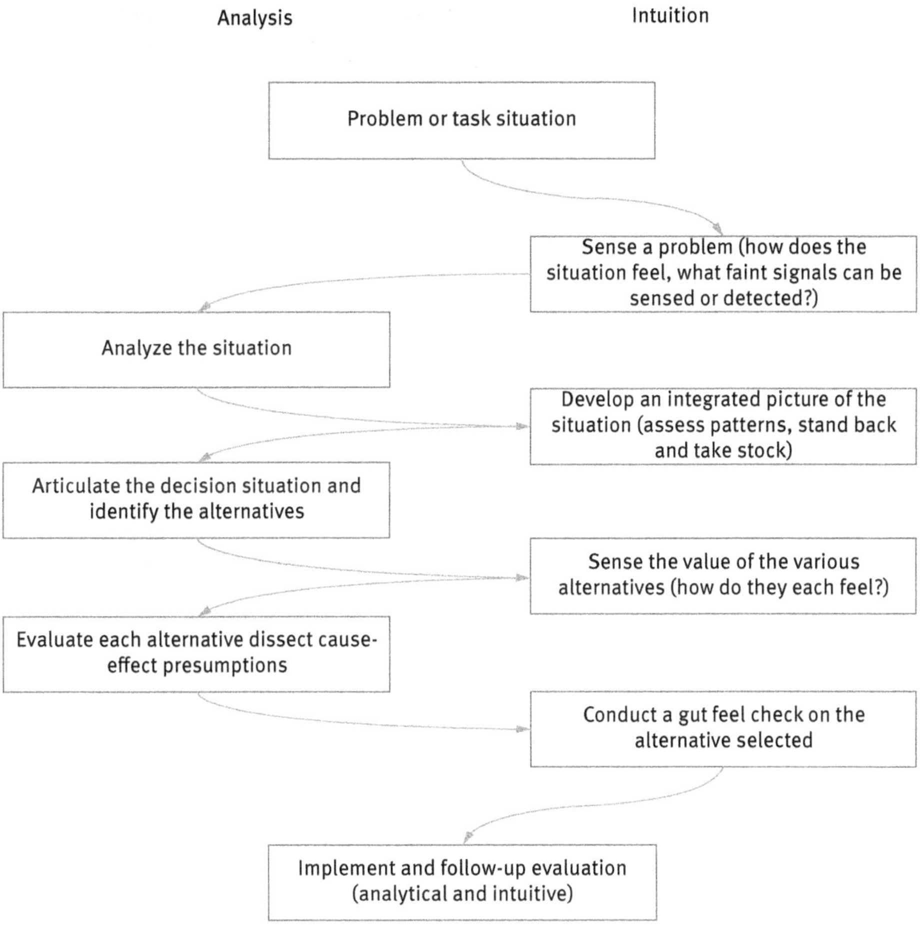
Analysis
Intuition
Problem or task situation
Sense a problem (how does the situation feel, what faint signals can be sensed or detected?)
Analyze the situation
Develop an integrated picture of the situation (assess patterns, stand back and take stock)
Articulate the decision situation and identify the alternatives
Sense the value of the various alternatives (how do they each feel?)
Evaluate each alternative dissect cause-effect presumptions
Conduct a gut feel check on the alternative selected
Implement and follow-up evaluation (analytical and intuitive)

Figure 25: Integration of analytics and intuition in decision making (Sadler-Smith & Burke, 2009, p. 244).

This intuition-analytic duality can be conceptualized as a paradoxical tension and interplay.

Paradox means that supposedly contrary variables (e.g., System 1 and System 2) exist simultaneously.

While dilemmas are decided via weighing pros and cons in terms of an "either-or" decision (since you can't have both at the same time), paradoxes require a balance. As supposedly contradictory but interrelated requirements that occur simultaneously and persist over time, paradoxical elements are complementary and supplement each other.

Each element seems logical when considered individually but in conflict when juxtaposed. Their simultaneity and interplay create tension and can thus generate ambivalence, conflict, and even defensive attitudes. Finding a permanent balance rather than a lasting and clear solution can be experienced as exhausting and demotivating. And it can lead to resistance because people tend to seek unambiguity, particularly in Western countries such as in Germany and the United States.

Schulz von Thun's so-called values-square (2008, pp. 49–76) illustrates this complementary relationship between analytics and intuition. His research shows that a specific value should be "balanced" and supplemented by a complementary sister value to counteract excessive devaluation. Accordingly, analytical personnel selection procedures can only unfold their constructive effect if they are realized in endured tension to a counter value, in this case, intuition. The values and development square describes a tension and complementary field in its possible manifestations and shows development direction. The basic idea of the value square is to see in a particular behavior, value, or approach, first the "positive core" and only in the negative exaggeration, the problem and development direction. Therefore, whoever realizes a specific value in a negative exaggeration has to develop skills toward the opposite positive value. Only the availability of opposing behavioral alternatives allows for flexible and situation-appropriate action. As an example, this is illustrated in Figure 26.

Constructive handling of paradoxes means no longer viewing them as contradictions to be avoided, but as embodying potentially complementary and mutually supporting factors.

This also has to do with tolerance for ambiguity and the competent handling of supposedly opposing forces. It means searching for what unites in what is seemingly contradictory. Instead of thinking in terms of opposites, it is about recognizing and utilizing interactions. It is well known that people often find it challenging to tolerate apparent contradictions. Instead, we strive for unambiguity and explicitness. Ambiguities are irritating, unsettling, and sometimes frightening; thus, we try to avoid ambiguous stimuli.

But in dynamic, interconnected, and complex environments, this desire for unambiguity can quickly prove to be problematic, leading to undesirable exclusions.

Dunja Lang (2016, pp. 28–32) attributes difficulties dealing with paradoxes to rather mechanical, bipolar management training, whose techniques favor a clear, unambiguous solution and see ambiguity per se as a problem.

The experience of a both/and approach and the conscious admission of the apparent contradictions can be enriching. Life retains its agility and dynamism by dealing competently with these supposedly opposing forces. Moreover, paradoxes offer learning and development opportunities for both people and organizations.

It is necessary to recognize and accept paradoxical fields of tension, associated contradictions, complexities, inner conflicts, different perspectives, approaches, and so on, and bring them together. This means integrating the supposed contradictions through cognitive and behavioral processes, such as acceptance and resolution, while maintaining and leveraging their differences.

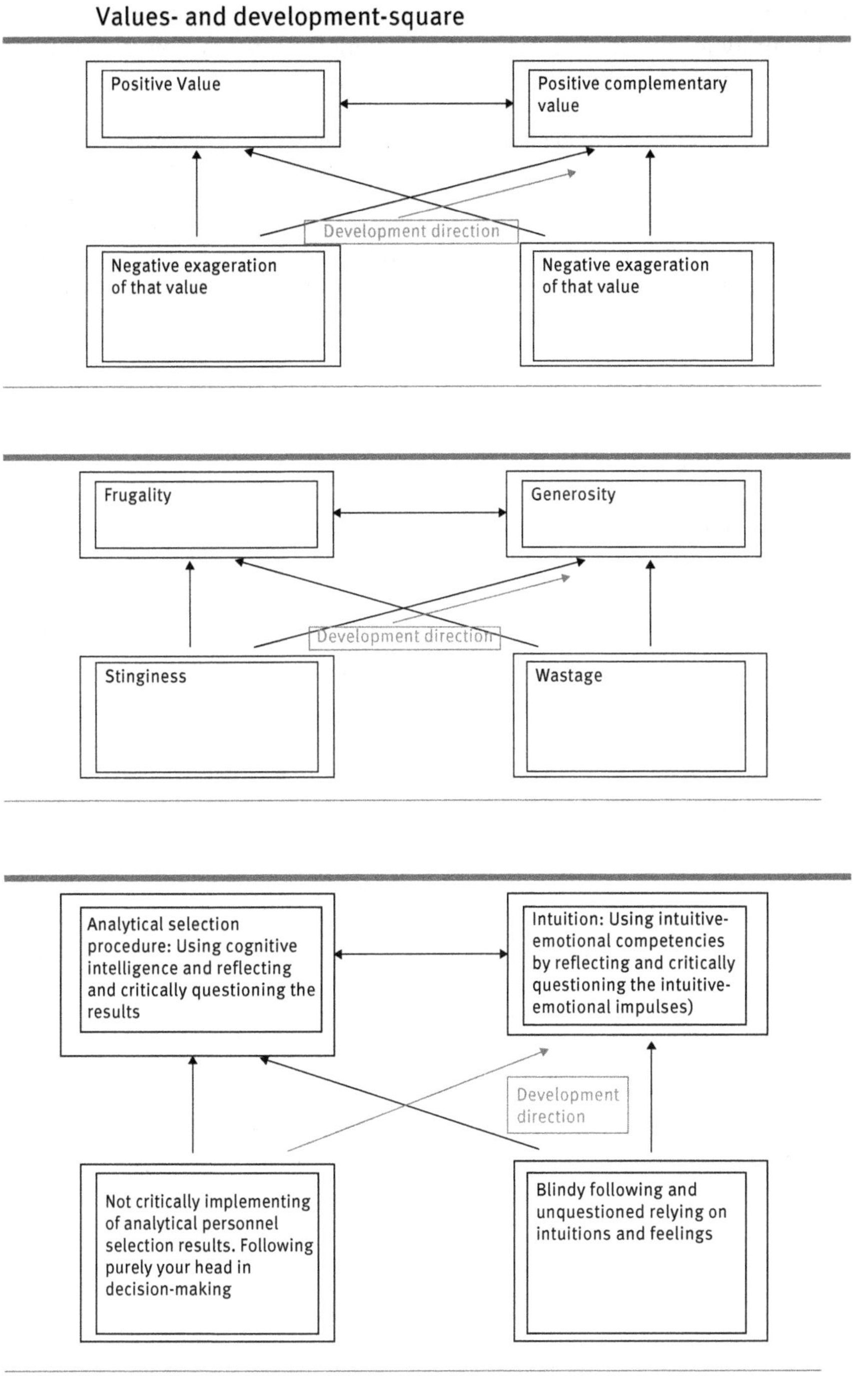

Figure 26: Values- and development-square (based on Schulz von Thun, 2008, pp. 49–76).

And acceptance implies, rather than trying to solve the paradox, embracing it as an opportunity for better outcomes and reframing the tension from an either/or option to a both/and possibility (Calabretta et al., 2017, p. 366).

> Paradoxes imply contradictions that persist over time, require ongoing responses, and are not fully solvable by compromise or by adopting both viewpoints simultaneously . . . . Even though paradoxes cannot be fully solved, prior research suggests that paradoxical tensions can be managed and turned to advantage . . . . Approaches to managing paradoxes include accepting the contradictions and learning to cope with them . . . adopting paradoxical thinking by continuously integrating and differentiating between the alternatives or a combination of the above . . . However, little is known about how to manage the tension between intuition and rationality and whether a paradoxical perspective can enable individuals to combine the benefits of intuition and rationality in strategic decision-making (Calabretta et al., 2017, p. 366).

Step 1: Identifying competing decision-making mechanisms within each case.
Step 2: Identifying paradoxical tensions within each case
Step 3: Identifying categories of tension management practices within each case.
Step 4: Building a theoretical framework

To develop a commitment to paradoxical thinking for conceptualizing personnel selection in theory and practice, the potential of the intuition–rationality tension and interplay could be used by implementing three steps: (1) *preparing* the ground for paradoxical thinking; (2) *developing* outcomes through paradoxical thinking; and (3) *embedding* paradoxical thinking and its outcome in theory and practice.

Adopting the paradoxical perspective can show how selection managers who prefer rational-analytical approaches can integrate intuitive practices into their personnel selection processes, not as an alternative but as a supplement. Similarly, practitioners who prefer intuitive judgments can use this approach to make rational-analytical inputs and methods in decision-making, more attractive and acceptable (Calabretta et al., 2017, p. 396).

This alternative conceptualization of selection processes is a metaphor that provides the complementary dynamics and benefits of System 1 (intuitions) and System 2 (rational-analytics). But it's also about mastering contradictions and conflicts between both systems. Thus, balancing both means creating a dynamic equilibrium; it is not about choosing and opting for analytics or intuition, but seeing that both should be recognized, especially when people are involved in decision-making.

10.6.3 Limitations and further research

The framework proposed in this book is not without its limitations.

Although it is adaptable to different selection situations and cultural contexts, a general application may be challenging because it is grounded in the author's specific Western or German reference system of thinking.

The results presented in this book are based on other researchers' findings and our own qualitatively conducted empirical research at Leuphana University, Lüneburg (Germany). Concerning our research results presented in this publication, some general questions concerning evidence-based research (the current scientific gold standard) remain. For example, when are empirical research results evident? Is empirical evidence given if the observations help understand human decisions and how human behavior works in reality?

We know far too little about how and where thinking or feeling occurs in the human body (head, gut, heart, etc.), how these processes affect each other, how cognitive and emotional processes such as thoughts, intuitions, or feelings are generated, and why there are individual differences. Using various neuroscientific methods to measure what occurs in the body or brain will help better understand these processes. Further research is needed to isolate intuition clearly and make it transparent from other constructs such as emotion, and examine it scientifically from different scientific perspectives and empirical methods.

Even if we are not yet able to measure specific processes according to scientific standards or with scientific methods, this does not mean that nothing is happening in the human brain or body. On the contrary, not being able to yet measure something such as intuition precisely does not mean that it is beyond the reach of empiricism, and that research results are only of scientific quality if quantitative scientific methods are used.

In physics, for example, one could ask whether something can only be regarded as scientific knowledge if there is observable empirical evidence or whether it is sufficient to prove something mathematically. Processes in atoms, for example, can be represented in particles or waveforms. According to the position of many physicists, since the findings of Niels Bohr and Werner Heisenberg, the wave function is a mathematical expression without physical reality; the wave function is – thus far – unobservable. Many physicists accept this view at face value in a conceptual kludge, known as the Copenhagen interpretation. However, Sean Carrol (2019) believes that the wave function is a real entity, not merely a mathematical tool. Even though other physicists criticize Caroll's position, and no matter how this dispute ends, it remains clear that much in the world influences human behavior and is empirically evident without being precisely measurable at the moment. And this also applies to intuitions. Even if something like intuition is not yet clearly measurable and operationalizable, this does not mean that it does not exist or does not affect human decision-making.

We must realize that the world is much more complex than any human picture. All theories, approaches, or categorizations are simplifications, such as dual-process theories. The more insights are gained, the better we understand the interrelationships and the influencing factors of personnel selection decisions. At the same time, however, new questions arise, and we realize how much we do not yet know.

10.6.4 Wise decision

A conception of science underlying psychometrics wants to eliminate the irrational from the world. But intuitions and emotions are not irrational. Irrationality would be to ignore intuitions and emotions. The disregard of intuitions and emotions demanded in psychometrics reduces the selection managers' wholeness and means to control and master themselves and show self-distance. It`s a sign of self-awareness and self-esteem to listen to the messages sent by the organism. Therefore, the holistic selection approach to wise decisions is understood as a possibility to free the selection managers from the clamp of psychometric restrictions and end the paternalism of the individual selection manager by a de-subjectified and de-personalized scientific conception.

It`s inappropriate to see only the negative in intuitions and emotions in personnel selection. This comes close to an act of domination over the individual. Instead, the knowledge, based on rational-analytical procedures and intuitions and emotions, also has its positive sides. Wise deciding people trust their different senses. They can endure ambiguities and turn them positively by seeing the possible chances and risks in the results of analytical procedures and intuitions.

The conscious decision is an iterative process formed in a thought cycle. It`s an interplay between knowing (intuition as expertise) and sensing (intuition as a feeling of knowing). Thus, it is advantageous to welcome intuitions and emotions as something valuable. But humans should not follow them blindly.

The conscious use of both judgment systems integrates the intuitive system with the rational-analytical cognition system. In this way, intuition can be used effectively and intelligently.

Analytical and intuitive-emotional competencies work together as a complex and wise human system. Thus, the wise mind is the field of interaction of high analytical and high intuitive-emotional competence.

Wisdom is about knowing how much people accept, critically examine, and constructively use the results of analytical procedures, their intuitions and emotions, and how well they know their limits.

Wisdom, as a specific form of expert knowledge and a capacity for dealing competently with fundamental life questions, has a cognitive component and an intuitive and emotional one (Figure 27). Therefore, integrating intuition, emotion, and rationality can be considered a form of practiced wisdom (Küpers, 2015, pp. 67–68).

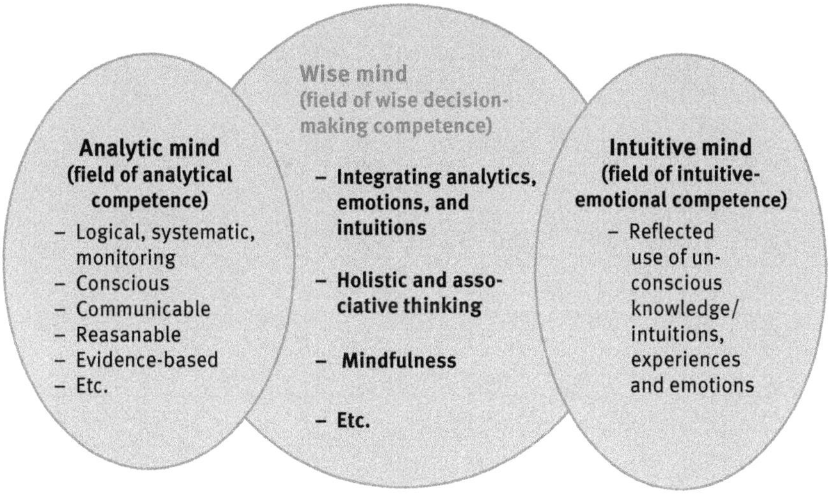

Figure 27: The wise mind.

Wisdom has to do with the ability to perceive and accept one's own intuitions and emotions and use them reflexively, show tolerance for uncertainty and ambiguity, integrate contradictory aspects of challenges in a solution-oriented way, be empathetic and shape relationships positively, and decide issues in a context-specific way. Wisdom manifests itself in a world where not everything is regulated and controlled, where nonscientific laws prevail. Likewise, wisdom can unfold when not everything is arbitrary, random, or unpredictable. Thus, wisdom is the ability to draw the correct conclusions in a world where not everything is entirely foreseeable. It is more about trusting oneself than knowing for sure (Staudinger et al., 1997; Baltes & Staudinger, 2000; Baltes et al., 2002; Baumann & Linden, 2019, pp. 32–40).

Thus, why choose either/or when it is appropriate to choose both/and.

Although a psychometric, analytical approach to personnel selection promises greater certainty in the selection decision, absolute certainty is not possible – mainly because personnel selection procedures make statements about the future.

The human capacity to meet life's challenges is not only based on explicit knowledge, logic, and reason. It also includes the ability to make intuitive decisions and consider emotions. By listening to their intuitions and emotions as well as to the messages of their rational-analytical mind, human beings, especially hiring managers, can enjoy the benefits of functioning more holistically and take advantage of different sources of wisdom (Koffka, 2014; LeBoon, 2018, pp. 74–76).

Wisdom is the balance and harmony of reason, intuition, and emotions. It's the ability to use analytics (including algorithms and AI), intuition, and emotion, to know how to use each and integrate them. The complementary interplay of intuition and analytics makes up human intelligence. As humans, we are not AI, we are holistic beings with analytical, emotional, and intuitive competencies.

References

Achouri, C. (2010). *Recruiting und Placement: Methoden und Instrumente der Personalauswahl und-platzierung [Recruiting and Placement: Methods and Instruments of Personnel Selection and Placement]* (2nd ed.). Gabler.

Achouri, C. (2014). *Talent: Wie entscheidend ist es wirklich für Erfolg? [Talent: How crucial is it really for success?]*. Springer Gabler. https://doi.org/10.1007/9783658058418.

Ackerschott, H. (2020). *HR-Standard Premiere: Video interview* [HR Standard Premiere: Video Interview]. https://eignungsdiagnostik.info/hr-standard-premiere-videointerviews

Ackerschott, H., Gantner, N. S., & Schmitt, G. (2016). *Eignungsdiagnostik: Qualifizierte Personalentscheidungen nach DIN 33430 Mit Checklisten, Planungshilfen, Anwendungsbeispielen [Suitability diagnostics: Qualified personnel decisions according to DIN 33430 with checklists, planning aids, application examples]*. Beuth Verlag GmbH.

Adamsen, B. (2016). *Demystifying talent management: A critical approach to the realities of talent.* Palgrave Macmillan. https://doi.org/10.1057/9781137508676.

Adler, J. E., & Rips, L. J. (Eds.). (2008). *Reasoning. Studies of human inference and its foundations.* Cambridge University Press.

Agerström, J., & Rooth, D.-O. (2011). The role of automatic obesity stereotypes in real hiring discrimination. *Journal of Applied Psychology, 96*(4), 790–805. https://doi.org/10.1037/a0021594

Agor, W. H. (1984). *Intuitive management: Integrating left and right brain management skills.* Prentice Hall.

Agor, W. H. (1989). The logic of intuition: How top executives make important decisions. In W. H. Agor (Ed.), *Intuition in organizations: Leading and managing productively* (pp. 141–153). Sage Publications.

Agor, W. H. (1991). How intuition can be used to enhance creativity in organizations. *The Journal of Creative Behavior, 25*(1), 11–19. https://doi.org/10.1002/j.2162-6057.1991.tb01348.x

Agthe, M., Sporrle, M., & Maner, J. K. (2011). Does being attractive always help? Positive and negative effects of attractiveness on social decision making. *Personality & Social Psychology Bulletin, 37*(8), *1042–1054.*

Ahel, O. (2020). *Intuition im Management Möglichkeitsraum, Spannungsfelder und emergierende Konstellationen [Management possibility space, tension fields and emerging constellations].* Springer Gabler.

Ahlers, F., & Gülke, N. (2016). Personaldiagnostik: Potenziale und Perspektiven [Personnel diagnostics: Potentials and perspectives]. In N. Gülke, & F. Ahlers (Eds.), *Personaldiagnostik: Potenzial- und Perspektivenvielfalt der Eignungsdiagnostik für Unternehmen und Mitarbeiter* (pp. 5–21). Cuvillier Verlag.

Akinci, C. (2011). *Intuition in Decision Making and Learning: Individual and Organisational Perspectives*. Thesis submitted in partial fulfillment of the requirements for the award of Doctor of Philosophy. University of Surrey.

Akinci, C. (2014). Capturing intuitions in decision making: A case for the critical incident technique. In M. Sinclair (Ed.), *Handbook of research methods on intuition* (pp. 147–159). Edward Elgar Publishing. https://doi.org/10.4337/9781782545996

Akinci, C. (2015). Entrepreneurial learning through intuitive decision making. In D. Rae, & C. L. Wang (Eds.), *Entrepreneurial learning: New perspectives in research, education and practice (chapter).* Routledge.

Akinci, C., & Sadler-Smith, E. (2012). Intuition in management research: A historical review. *International Journal of Management Reviews, 14*(1), 104–122. https://doi.org/10.1111/j.1468-2370.2011.00313.x

https://doi.org/10.1515/9783110980967-011

Akinci, C., & Sadler-Smith, E. (2013). Assessing individual differences in experiential (Intuitive) and rational (analytical) cognitive styles. *International Journal of Selection and Assessment, 21*(2), 211–221. https://doi.org/10.1111/ijsa.12030

Akinci, C., & Sadler-Smith, E. (2019). Collective intuition: Implications for improved decision making and organizational learning. *British Journal of Management, 30*(3), 558–577. https://doi.org/10.1111/1467-8551.12269

Albert, E. T. (2019). AI in talent acquisition: A review of AI-applications used in recruitment and selection. *Strategic HR Review, 18*(5), 215–221. https://doi.org/10.1108/SHR-04-2019-0024

Albrecht, A. G., & Deller, J. (2011). Praxisrelevanz – berechnet oder bedacht? Eine Replik auf Maier und Antoni [Practical relevance – calculated or considered? A replica of Maier & Antoni]. *Zeitschrift Für Arbeits- Und Organisationspsychologie, 55*(1), 46–50.

Alder, G. S., & Gilbert, J. (2006). Achieving ethics and fairness in hiring: Going beyond the law. *Journal of Business Ethics, 68*(4), 449–464. https://doi.org/10.1007/s10551-006-9039-z

Aldering, C. (2006). Zur Bedeutung der Potentialanalyse für die Praxis. Was kann unter Potential verstanden werden, und wie lässt sich Potential einschätzen, messen oder bewerten? [On the importance of potential analysis in practice. What can be understood by potential, and how can potential be assessed, measured or evaluated?]. *German Journal of Human Resource Management, 20*(2), 192–196.

Allinson, C. W., & Hayes, J. (1996). The cognitive style index: A measure of intuition-analysis for organizational research. *Journal of Management Studies, 33*(1), 119–135.

Allinson, C. W., & Hayes, J. (2000). Cross-national differences in cognitive style: Implications for management. *International Journal of Human Resource Management, 11*(1), 161–170. doi:10.1080/095851900340042

Allinson, C. W., Chell, E., & Hayes, J. (2000). Intuition and entrepreneurial behaviour. *European Journal of Work and Organizational Psychology, 9*(1), 31–41.

Almlund, M., Duckworth, A. L., Heckman, J., & Kautz, T. (2011). Personality psychology and economics. in Chapter 1. In E. A. Hanushek, S. J. Machin, & L. Woessmann (Eds.), *Handbook of the economics of education* (Vol. 4), 1–181. Elsevier.

Alon, I., & Higgins, J. M. (2005). Global leadership success through emotional and cultural intelligences. *Business Horizons, 48*(6), 501–512. https://doi.org/10.1016/j.bushor.2005.04.003

Alred, G. (2012). *'Where did that come from, what was that about?': an interpretative phenomenological study of intuition in the practice of counselling psychologists* [Unpublished Doctorate Thesis in Counselling Psychology]. University of Teesside.

Alter, A. L., Oppenheimer, D. M., Epley, N., & Eyre, R. N. (2007). Overcoming intuition: Metacognitive difficulty activates analytic reasoning. *Journal of Experimental Psychology. General, 136*(4), 569–576. https://doi.org/10.1037/0096-3445.136.4.569

Ambady, N., & Rosenthal, R. (1993). Half a minute: Predicting teacher evaluations from thin slices of nonverbal behavior and physical attractiveness. *Journal of Personality and Social Psychology, 64*(3), 431–441.

Ambady, N., & Skowronski, J. J. (Eds.). (2008). *First impressions*. Guilford Press.

Amelang, M., & Zielinski, W. (2002). *Psychologische Diagnostik und Intervention [Psychological diagnostics and intervention]* (3rd ed.). Springer-Lehrbuch. Springer.

Andersen, J. A. (2000). Intuition in managers: Are intuitive managers more effective? *Journal of Managerial Psychology, 15*(1), 46–63.

Andersen, P. A., Hecht, M. L., Hoobler, G. D., & Smallwood, M. (2003). Nonverbal communication across cultures. In W. B. Gudykunst (Ed.), *Cross-cultural and intercultural communication* (pp. 73–90). Sage Publications.

Anderson, N. (2017). Das Verhältnis zwischen Praxis und Forschung in der Personalaus-wahl: Weiß die linke Hand, was die rechte tut? [The relationship between practice and research in personnel selection: Does the left hand know what the right hand is doing?]. In D. E. Krause (Ed.), *Personalauswahl* (pp. 1–29). Springer Fachmedien. https://doi.org/10.1007/978-3-658-14567-5_1

Anderson, N., & Shackleton, V. (1990). Decision making in the graduate selection interview: A field study. *Journal of Occupational Psychology, 63*(1), 63–76. https://doi.org/10.1111/j.2044-8325.1990.tb00510.x

Anderson, N., & Witvliet, C. (2008). Fairness reactions to personnel selection methods: An international comparison between the Netherlands, the United States, France, Spain, Portugal, and Singapore. *International Journal of Selection and Assessment, 16*(1), 1–13. https://doi.org/10.1111/j.1468-2389.2008.00404.x

Anderson, N., Herriot, P., & Hodgkinson, G. P. (2001). The practitioner-researcher divide in Industrial, Work and Organizational (IWO) psychology: Where are we now, and where do we go from here? *Journal of Occupational and Organizational Psychology, 74*(4), 391–411. https://doi.org/10.1348/096317901167451

Anderson, N. R., Salgado, J. F., & Hulsheger, U. R. (2010). Applicant reactions in selection: Comprehensive meta-analysis into reaction generalization versus situational specificity. *International Journal of Selection and Assessment, 18*(3), 291–304. https://doi.org/10.1111/j.1468-2389.2010.00512.x

Andriopoulos, C. (2003). Six paradoxes in managing creativity: An embracing act. *Long Range Planning, 36*(4), 375–388. https://doi.org/10.1016/S0024-6301(03)00071-2

Andriopoulos, C. (2018). Strategic agility requires leaders with an ambidextrous mindset. In C. Prange, & L. Haracleous (Eds.), *Agility X: How organizations thrive in unpredictable times* (pp. 32–42). Cambridge University Press.

Andriopoulos, C., & Lewis, M. W. (2010). Managing Innovation Paradoxes: Ambidexterity Lessons from Leading Product Design Companies. *Long Range Planning, 43*(1), 104–122. https://doi.org/10.1016/j.lrp.2009.08.003

Anshel, M. H., & Lidor, R. (2012). Talent detection programs in sport: The questionable use of psychological measures. *Journal of Sport Behavior, 35*(3), 239–266.

Antidiskriminierungsstelle des Bundes (2011). Anonymisierte Bewerbungsverfahren – Das Pilotprojekt [Anonymized application procedures – The pilot project]. https://www.antidiskriminierungsstelle.de/SharedDocs/Downloads/DE/publikationen/AnonymBewerbung/kurzfassung_abschlussbericht_anonymisierte_Bewerbungsverfahren_20120417.pdf?__blob=publicationFile&v=4.

Antonovsky, A. (1979). *Health, stress, and coping: New perspectives on mental and physical well-being*. Jossey-Bass.

Antonovsky, A. (1993). The structure and properties of the sense of coherence scale. *Social Science & Medicine, 36*(6), 725–733.

Apelojg, B. (2009). Personalauswahl: Vom Umgang mit Gefühlen [Personnel selection: Dealing with feelings]. *Zeitschrift Für Human Resource Management, 61*(1), 12–13.

Apelojg, B. (2010). *Emotionen in der Personalauswahl: Wie der Umgang mit den eigenen Gefühlen Entscheidungen beeinflusst [Emotions in personnel selection: How dealing with one's own feelings influences decisions Hochschulschriften zum Personalwesen*. V. T. R. Hummel, H. Knebel, D. Wagner, & E. Zander (hrsg.). Vol. 40, Rainer Hampp Verlag. https://doi.org/10.1688/9783866185692

Apelojg, B. (2012). Recruiting – Lass den Bauch sprechen – Personal auszuwählen ist eine verantwortungsvolle Aufgabe. Dabei ist es eigentlich ganz einfach: Bei der Entscheidung lohnt es sich, seinen Gefühlen zu vertrauen [Recruiting – Let your gut speak – selecting personnel is a responsible task. But it is actually quite simple: When making a decision, it is worth trusting your feelings]. *Magazin Für Human Resources, 39*(5), 59–62.

Arbeitskreis Assessment Center. (2016). *Standards der Assessment Center Methode [Standards of the Assessment Center Method].* https://www.arbeitskreis-ac.de/images/attachments/AkAC-Standards-2016.pdf

Arendt, J. F. W., Pircher Verdorfer, A., & Kugler, K. G. (2019). Mindfulness and Leadership: Communication as a Behavioral Correlate of Leader Mindfulness and Its Effect on Follower Satisfaction. *Frontiers in Psychology, 10*, 667. https://doi.org/10.3389/fpsyg.2019.00667

Argyle, M. (2010). *Bodily Communication.* Taylor & Francis.

Armoneit, C., Schuler, H., & Hell, B. (2020). Nutzung, Validität, Praktikabilität und Akzeptanz psychologischer Personalauswahlverfahren in Deutschland 1985, 1993, 2007, 2020 [Usability, validity, practicability and acceptance of psychological personnel selection procedures in Germany 1985, 1993, 2007, 2020]. *Zeitschrift Für Arbeits- Und Organisationspsychologie A&O, 64*(2), 67–82. https://doi.org/10.1026/0932-4089/a000311

Armstrong, S. J., & Qi, M. (2016). A reassessment of the factor structure of the Allinson-Hayes cognitive style index. *Personality and Individual Differences, 101*, 240–242.

Arvey, R. D., & Renz, G. L. (1992). Fairness in the selection of employees. *Journal of Business Ethics, 11*(5–6), 331–340. https://doi.org/10.1007/BF00870545

Arvey, R. D., & Sackett, P. R. (1993). Fairness in selection: Current developments and perspectives. In N. Schmitt, & W. C. Borman (Eds.), *Personnel selection in organizations* (pp. 171–202). Jossey-Bass.

Arvey, R. D., Renz, G. L., & Watson, T. W. (1998). Emotionality and job performance: Implications for personnel selection. In G. R. Ferris (Ed.), *Research in personnel and human resources management* (pp. 103–147). Elsevier Science/JAI Press.

Asch, S. E. (1946). Forming impressions of personality. *Journal of Abnormal and Social Psychology, 41*, 258–290.

Asendorpf, J. B. (Ed.). (2018). *Persönlichkeit: Was uns ausmacht und warum [Personality: What defines us and why].* Springer. https://doi.org/10.1007/978-3-662-56106-5

Asendorpf, J. B., & Neyer, F. J. (2012). *Psychologie der Persönlichkeit [Psychology of personality]* (5th ed.). Springer. https://doi.org/10.1007/978-3-642-30264-0.

Åslund, O., Hensvik, L., & Skans, O. N. [Oskar Nordström]. (2014). Seeking similarity: How immigrants and natives manage in the labor market. *Journal of Labor Economics, 32*(3), 405–441. https://doi.org/10.1086/674985.

Ashkanasy, N. M., & Dorris, A. D. (2017). Emotions in the workplace. *Annual Review of Organizational Psychology and Organizational Behavior, 4*(1), 67–90. https://doi.org/10.1146/annurev-orgpsych-032516-113231

Ashkanasy, N. M., Troth, A. C., Lawrence, S. A., & Jordan, J. P. (2017). Emotions and emotional regulation in HRM: A multi-level perspective. In M. R. Buckley, A. R. Wheeler, & J. R. B. Halbesleben (Eds.), *Research in personnel and human resources management* (pp. 1–52). Emerald. https://doi.org/10.1108/S0742-730120170000035002

Åslund, O., & Skans, O. N. [Oskar Nordströum]. (2012). Do anonymous job application procedures level the playing field? *ILR Review, 65*(1), 82–107. https://doi.org/10.1177/001979391206500105.

Assary, E., Zavos, H. M. S., Krapohl, E., Keers, R., & Pluess, M. (2020). Genetic architecture of environmental sensitivity reflects multiple heritable components: A twin study with adolescents. *Molecular Psychiatry*, Advance online publication. https://doi.org/10.1038/s41380-020-0783-8.

Assessment Centre Study Group (ACSG) Taskforce on Assessment Centres in South Africa. (2015). *Best Practice Guidelines for the use of the Assessment Centre Method in South Africa.* https://acsg.co.za/sites/default/files/AC-Guidelines-SouthAfrica.pdf

Aswathappa, K. (2008). *International business* (3rd ed.). Tata McGraw Hill Education.

Athanas, C., & Wald, P. M. (2014). Candidate experience – zufriedene Bewerber zahlen sich aus [Candidate experience - satisfied applicants pay off]. Personalwirtschaft, *41*(11),16–18.

audEERING (2021). *Website audEERING.* Intelligent audio engineering for emotion recognition, personal analysis & scene detection. https://www.audeering.com/

Auer, A.-K. (2016). Heuristische Entscheidungen in Gruppen bei der Personalauswahl [Heuristic decisions in groups in personnel selection]. Doctoral thesis Georg-August-Universität Göttingen.

Averill, J. R. (1990). Emotions in relation to systems of behavior. In N. L. Stein, B. Leventhal, & T. Trabasso (Eds.), *Psychological and biological approaches to emotion* (pp. 385–404). LEA.

Aycan, Z. (2005). The interplay between cultural and institutional/structural contingencies in human resource management practices. *The International Journal of Human Resource Management, 16*(7), 1083–1119. https://doi.org/10.1080/09585190500143956

Aycan, Z., Kanungo, R., Mendonca, M., Yu, K., Deller, J., Stahl, G., & Kurshid, A. (2000). Impact of culture on human resource management practices: A 10-country comparison. *Applied Psychology, 49*(1), 192–221. https://doi.org/10.1111/1464-0597.00010

Backes-Gellner, U. (2004). Personnel economics: an economic approach to human resource. *Management. Management Revue, 15*(2), 215–227.

Backes-Gellner, U., Lazear, E. P., & Wolf, B. (2001). *Personalökonomik: Fortgeschrittene Anwendungen für das Management [Personnel economics. Advanced applications to management].* Schäffer-Poeschel.

Bachhiesl, C. (2018a). Intuition und Wissenschaft – eine Einführung [Intuition and Science. An introduction]. In C. Bachhiesl, S. M. Bachhiesl, & S. Köchel (Eds.), *Intuition und Wissenschaft. Interdisziplinäre Perspektiven* (pp. 9–19). Velbrück Wissenschaft.

Bachhiesl, C. (2018b). Erkenntnismodus oder Methode. Wissenschaftshistorische Überlegungen zum epistemischen Stellenwert der Intuition [Mode of cognition or method. Considerations in the history of science on the epistemic significance of intuition]. In C. Bachhiesl, S. M. Bachhiesl, & S. Köchel (Eds.), *Intuition und Wissenschaft. Interdisziplinäre Perspektiven* (pp. 351–394). Velbrück Wissenschaft.

Bachhiesl, C., Bachhiesl, S. M., & Köchel, S. (Eds.). (2018). *Intuition und Wissenschaft. Interdisziplinäre Perspektiven [Intuition and Science. Interdisciplinary perspectives].* Velbrück Wissenschaft.

Bahr, A. (2003). *Vertrauen in Wirtschaftsprüfer [Trust in accountants].* Deutscher Universitätsverlag. https://doi.org/10.1007/978-3-322-81580-4.

Bal, A. C., Reiss, A. E. B., Rudolph, C. W., & Baltes, B. B. (2011). Examining positive and negative perceptions of older workers: A meta-analysis. *Journal of Gerontology: Psychological Sciences, 66*(6), 687–698. 10.1093/geronb/gbr056

Baldacchino, L., Ucbasaran, D., Lockett, A., & Cabantous, L. (2014). Capturing intuition through concurrent protocol analysis. In M. Sinclair (Ed.), *Handbook of research methods on intuition* (pp. 160–175). Edward Elgar Publishing. https://doi.org/10.4337/9781782545996

Baltes, P. B., & Staudinger, U. M. (2000). Wisdom. A metaheuristic (pragmatic) to orchestrate mind and virtue towards excellence. *American Psychologist, 55*(1), 122–136. https://doi.org/10.1037/0003-066X.55.1.122

Baltes, P. B., Glück, J., & Kunzmann, U. (2002). Wisdom. Its structure and function in regulating successful life span development. In C. R. Snyder, & S. J. Lopez (Eds.), *Handbook of positive psychology* (pp. 327–347). Oxford University Press.

Bandura, A. (1977). Self-efficacy: Toward a unifying theory of behavioral change. *Psychological Review, 84*(2), 191–215.

Bandura, A. (1982). Self-efficacy mechanism in human agency. *American Psychologist, 37*(2), 122–147.

Bandura, A. (1997). *Social Learning Theory*. Prentice-Hall.

Bandura, A. (2012). On the functional properties of perceived self-efficacy revisited. *Journal of Management, 38*(1), 9–44.

Bangert, D., Schubert, E., & Dorottya, F. (2014). A spiral model of musical decision-making. *Frontiers of Psychology, 5*(article 320), 1–11. https://doi.org/10.3389/fpsyg.2014.00320

Bar, M., Neta, M., & Linz, H. (2006). Very first impressions. *Emotion, 6*(2), 269–278. doi:10.1037/1528–3542.6.2.269

Baran, B. E., & Woznyj, H. M. (2021). Managing VUCA: The human dynamics of agility. *Organizational Dynamics, 50*(2), 100787. https://www.ncbi.nlm.nih.gov/pmc/articles/PMC7439966/.org/10.1016/j.orgdyn.2020.100787.

Bargh, J. A. (2014). The four horsemen of automaticity: Awareness, intention, efficiency, and control in social cognition. In R. S. Wyer, Jr., & T. K. Srull (Eds.), *Handbook of social cognition* (2nd ed.) (pp. 1–40). Psychology Press.

Barlow, G. (1989). Deficiencies and the perpetuation of power: Latent functions in management appraisal. *Journal of Management Studies, 26*(5), 499–517.

Barnard, C. I. (1938). *The functions of the executive: With an introduction by Kenneth R. Andrews*. Harvard University Press.

Baron-Boldt, J. (1989). *Die Validität von Schulabschlussnoten für die Prognose von Ausbildungs- und Studienerfolg [The validity of school-leaving grades for the prediction of educational and academic success]*. Peter Lang.

Barrantes, L. (2008). Man kann nur managen, was man auch messen kann! Die Messung von Qualität Human resource economics. advanced applications to management. [You can only manage what you can measure! The measurement of quality]. *Controlling & Management, 52*(S3), 10–17. https://doi.org/10.1365/s12176-012-0212-1

Barrett, L. F. (2017a). *How emotions are made. The secret life of the brain*. Houghton Mifflin Harcourt.

Barrett, L. F. (2017b). The theory of constructed emotion: An active inference account of interoception and categorization. *Social Cognitive and Affective Neuroscience, 12*(1), 1–23.

Barrett, L. F., Tugade, M. M., & Engle, R. W. (2004). Individual differences in working memory capacity and dual-process theories of the mind. *Psychological Bulletin, 130*, 553–573.

Barrett, L. F., Adolphs, R., Martinez, A., Marsella, S., & Pollak, S. (2019). Emotional expressions reconsidered: Challenges to inferring emotion in human facial movements. *Psychological Science in the Public Interest, 20*, 1–68.

Barrick, M. R., Mount, M. K., & Judge, T. A. (2001). Personality and Performance at the beginning of the new millennium: What do we know and where do we go next? *International Journal of Selection and Assessment, 9*(1&2), 9–30. https://doi.org/10.1111/1468-2389.00160

Barsch, P., & Trachsel, G. (2018). *Chefsache Fachkräftesicherung [Management issue: Securing skilled workers]*. Springer Gabler.

Barsade, S. G., Brief, A. P., & Spataro, S. E. (2003). The affective revolution in organizational behavior: The emergence of a paradigm. In J. Greenberg (Ed.), *Organizational behavior: A management challenge* (pp. 3–52). Lawrence Erlbaum Assoc.

Bartell, S. (2016). *Qualitätssicherung im Assessment-Center [Quality assurance in the assessment center]*. Springer Fachmedien. https://doi.org/10.1007/9783658152444.

Bartram, D. (2004). Assessment in organisations. *Applied Psychology, 53*(2), 237–259. https://doi.org/10.1111/j.1464-0597.2004.00170.x

Bartram, D. (2005). The great eight competencies: A criterion-centric approach to validation. *The Journal of Applied Psychology*, *90*(6), 1185–1203. https://doi.org/10.1037/0021-9010.90.6.1185

Basabe, N., Páez, D., Valencia, J., Rimé, B., Pennebaker, J., Diener, E., & González, J. L. (2000). Sociocultural factors predicting subjective experience of emotion: A collective level analysis. *Psicothema*, *12*(1), 55–69.

Bastian, V. (2018). *Personalauswahl in der sozialen Arbeit. Eine empirische Studie zum Suchen und Finden pädagogischer Fackräfte [Personnel selection in social work. An Empirical Study on Searching and Finding Pedagogical Experts]*. Springer VS.

Bauer, T. N., Maertz, C. P., JR, Dolen, M. R., & Campion, M. A. (1998). Longitudinal assessment of applicant reactions to employment testing and test outcome feedback. *The Journal of Applied Psychology*, *83*(6), 892–903. https://doi.org/10.1037/0021-9010.83.6.892

Bauer, T. N., Truxillo, D. M., & Paronto, M. E. (2004). The measurement of applicant reactions to selection. In J. C. Thomas (Ed.), *Industrial and organizational assessment. Comprehensive handbook of psychological assessment* (Vol. 4, pp. 482–506). John Wiley & Sons, Inc.

Bauer, T. N., Truxillo, D. M., Paronto, M. E., Weekley, J. A., & Campion, M. A. (2004). Applicant reactions to different selection technology: Face-to-face, interactive voice response, and computer-assisted telephone screening interviews. *International Journal of Selection and Assessment*, *12*(1-2), 135–148. https://doi.org/10.1111/j.0965-075X.2004.00269.x

Bauer, T. N., Truxillo, D. M., Sanchez, R. J., Craig, J. M., Ferrara, P., & Campion, M. A. (2001). Applicant reactions to selection: Development of the selection procedural justice scale (SPJS). *Personnel Psychology*, *54*(2), 387–419. https://doi.org/10.1111/j.1744-6570.2001.tb00097.x

Bauer, T. N., Truxillo, D. M., Tucker, J. S., Weathers, V., Bertolino, M., Erdogan, B., & Campion, M. A. (2006). Selection in the information age: The impact of privacy concerns and computer experience on applicant reactions. *Journal of Management*, *32*(5), 601–621. https://doi.org/10.1177/0149206306289829

Baumann, K., & Linden, M. (2019). *Weisheitskompetenzen und Weisheitstherapie [Wisdom skills and wisdom therapy]. (8. ed.)*. Pabst Science Publishers.

Baumeister, R. F. (1984). Choking under pressure: Self-consciousness and paradoxical effects of incentives on skillful performance. *Journal of Personality and Social Psychology*, *46*, 610–620.

Baumeister, R. F., Dale, K., & Sommer, K. L. (2002). Freudian defense mechanisms and empirical findings in modern social psychology: reaction formation, projection, displacement, undoing, isolation, sublimation, and denial. *Journal of Personality*, *66*(6), 1081–1095. https://doi.org/10.1111/1467-6494.00043

Baumgärtner, S. D., & Borgmann, W. (2012). Psychologische Leistungsdiagnostik – Voraussetzung für die gezielte Talent- und Leistungsentwicklung in Sport und Wirtschaft [Psychological performance diagnostics – a prerequisite for targeted talent and performance development in sports and business]. In P. Wollsching-Strobel, & B. Prinz (Eds.), *Talentmanagement mit system* (pp. 73–87). Springer Fachmedien Wiesbaden. https://doi.org/10.1007/978-3-8349-3780-3_5

Baylor, A. L. (2001). A U-shaped model for the development of intuition by level of expertise. *New Ideas in Psychology*, *19*(3), 237–244. https://doi.org/10.1016/S0732-118X(01)00005-8

Bazerman, M. H., Morgan, K. P., & Loewenstein, G. F. (1997). The impossibility of auditor independence. *Sloan Management Review*, *38*, 89–94. https://www.researchgate.net/profile/Max_Bazerman/publication/247905860_The_Impossibility_of_Auditor_Independence/links/53d1020d0cf25dc05cfe7bfe.pdf

Bazerman, M. H., & Tenbrunsel, A. E. (2013). *Blind Spots – Why we fail to do what's right and what to do about it*. Princetown University Press.

Bärschneider, N. (2019). *Sprachanalysesoftware – das Recruitingtool der Zukunft?* [Speech analytics software – the recruiting tool of the future?]. https://www.humanresourcesmanager.de/news/sprachanalysesoftware-das-recruitingtool-der-zukunft.html.

Bechara, A., Damasio, A. R. (2005). The somatic marker hypothesis: A neural theory of economic decision. *Games and Economic Behavior, 52*(2), 336–372.

Bechara, A., Damasio, H., Damasio, A. R., & Lee, G. P. (1999). Different contributions of the human amygdala and ventromedial prefrontal cortex to decision-making. *The Journal of Neuroscience, 19*(13), 5473–5481. https://doi.org/10.1523/JNEUROSCI.19-13-05473.1999

Bechtler, T. W. (1986). *Management und Intuition*. Verlag Moderne Industrie.

Behaghel, L., Crépon, B., & Le Barbanchon, T. (2015). Unintended effects of anonymous Résumés. *American Economic Journal. Applied Economics, 7*(3), 1–27. https://doi.org/10.1257/app.20140185

Behling, O., & Eckel, N. L. (1991). Making sense out of intuition. *Academy of Management Perspectives, 5*(1), 46–54. https://doi.org/10.5465/ame.1991.4274718

Beilock, S. L. (2011). *Back to school: Dealing with academic stress: Simple psychological interventions can reduce stress and improve academic performance*. American Psychological Association.

Beilock, S. L. (2010). *Choke: What the secrets of the brain reveal about getting it right when you have to*. Simon & Schuster: Free Press.

Beilock, S. L. (2015). *How the body knows its mind: The surprising power of the physical environment to influence how you think and feel*. Simon & Schuster: Atria Books.

Beilock, S. L., & Carr, T. H. (2001). On the fragility of skilled performance: What governs choking under pressure? *Journal of Experimental Psychology. General, 130*, 701–725.

Beilock, S. L., & Carr, T. H. (2005). When high-powered people fail: Working memory and "choking under pressure" in math. *Psychological Science, 16*, 101–105.

Beilock, S. L., Carr, T. H., MacMahon, C., & Starkes, J. L. (2002). When paying attention becomes counterproductive: Impact of divided versus skill-focused attention on novice and experienced performance of sensorimotor skills. *Journal of Experimental Psychology: Applied, 8*, 6–16.

Beilock, S. L., Bertenthal, B. I., McCoy, A. M., & Carr, T. H. (2004). Haste does not always make waste: Expertise, direction of attention, and speed versus accuracy in performing skills. *Psychonomic Bulletin & Review, 11*, 373–379.

Bellmann, M. (2013). Zur mangelnden Rezeption sozialwissenschaftlicher Forschungsbefunde in der management-Praxis [On the lack of reception of social science research findings in management practice]. In W. Sarges (Ed.), *Management-Diagnostik* (4th ed.) (pp. 1039–1044). Hogrefe.

Belmore, S. M., & Hubbard, M. L. (1987). The role of advance expectancies in person memory. *Journal of Personality and Social Psychology, 53*(1), 61–70.

Benit, N., Mojzisch, A., & Soellner, R. (2014). Preselection methods prior to the internal assessment center for personnel selection in German companies. *International Journal of Selection and Assessment, 22*(3), 253–260. https://doi.org/10.1111/ijsa.12074

Benit, N., & Soellner, R. (2013). Scientist-practitioner gap in Deutschland: Eine empirische Studie am Beispiel psychologischer Testverfahren. *Zeitschrift Für Arbeits- Und Organisationspsychologie A&O, 57*(3), 145–153. https://doi.org/10.1026/0932-4089/a000111

Bennett, N., & Lemoine, G. J. (2014). What VUCA really means for you. *Harvard Business Review, 92*(2), 27. https://hbr.org/2014/01/what-vuca-really-means-for-you

Ben-Ze'ev, A. (2009). The Thing Called Emotion. In P. Goldie (Ed.), *The Oxford handbook of philosophy of emotion* (pp. 41–62). Oxford University Press.

Ben-Ze'ev, A., & Krebs, A. (2016). Do only fish swim with the stream? In M. W. Fröse, S. Kaudela-Baum, & F. E. P. Dievernich (Eds.), *Emotion und Intuition in Führung und Organisation (43–64).*

[Emotion and intuition in leadership and organization]. Springer Gabler. https://doi.org/10.13140/2.1.2678.0482
Bergemann, W. (2020). Emotional durchlässig [Emotionally transparent]. *Psychologie Heute*, 16–25.
Berne, E. (1949). The nature of intuition. *The Psychiatric Quarterly*, *23*(2), 203–226. https://doi.org/10.1007/BF01563116
Berner, W. (2017). *Intuition: Rational entscheiden oder „aus dem Bauch heraus"?* [Intuition: Decide rationally or based on your gut feeling?]? https://www.umsetzungsberatung.de/psychologie/intuition.php
Berscheid, E., & Walster, E. H. (1969). Rewards others provide: Similarity. In *Interpersonal attraction* (pp. 69–91). Addison-Wesley.
Berthel, J., & Becker, F. G. (2010). *Personal-Management: Grundzüge für Konzeptionen betrieblicher Personalarbeit [Personnel Management: Basic principles for concepts of operational personnel management]* (9th ed.). Schäffer-Poeschel.
Berthel, J., & Becker, F. G. (2017). *Personal-Management: Grundzüge für Konzeptionen betrieblicher Personalarbeit [Personnel Management: Basic principles for concepts of operational personnel management] (11. ed.)*. Schäffer-Poeschel Verlag.
Berthet, V. (2022). The impact of cognitive biases on professionals' decision-making: A review of four occupational areas. *Frontiers in Psycholgy*, *12*, 802439. doi:10.3389/fpsyg.2021.802439
Bertrand, M., & Mullainathan, S. (2004). Are emily and greg more employable than Lakisha and Jamal? A field experiment on labor market discrimination. *American Economic Review*, *94*(4), 991–1013. https://doi.org/10.1257/0002828042002561
Betsch, C. (2004). Präferenz für Intuition und Deliberation (PID) Inventar zur Erfassung von affekt- und kognitionsbasiertem Entscheiden [Preference for Intuition and Deliberation (PID) Inventory to capture affect- and cognition-based decision making]. *Zeitschrift Für Differentielle Und Diagnostische Psychologie*, *25*(4), 179–197. doi:10.1024/0170-1789.25.4.179
Betsch, T. (2008). The nature of intuition and its neglect in research on judgment and decision making. In H. Plessner, C. Betsch, & T. Betsch (Eds.), *Intuition in judgment and decision making* (pp. 3–22). Lawrence Erlbaum Associates.
Betsch, T., & Haberstroh, S. (2005). *The routines of decision making*. Lawrence Erlbaum.
Betsch, T., & Glöckner, A. (2010). Intuition in judgment and decision making: Extensive thinking without effort. *Psychological Inquiry*, *21*(4), 279–294. https://doi.org/10.1080/1047840X.2010.517737
Betsch, T., Haberstroh, S., & Hohle, C. (2002). Explaining routinized decision making. *Theory & Psychology*, *12*(4), 453–488. https://doi.org/10.1177/0959354302012004294
Betsch, T., Plessner, H., & Schallies, E. (2004). The value-account model of attitude formation. In G. Haddock, & G. R. Maio (Eds.), *Contemporary perspectives on the psychology of attitudes* (pp. 251–273). Psychology Press.
Betsch, T., Funke, J., & Plessner, H. (2011). *Denken – Urteilen, Entscheiden, Problemlösen [Thinking – judging, deciding, problem solving]. 14 Tabellen. Reihe Allgemeine Psychologie für Bachelor*. Springer Medizin.
Bettis, R. A. (2017). Organizationally intractable decision problems and the intellectual virtues of heuristics. *Journal of Management*, *43*(8), 2620–2637.
Beugelsdijk, S., Maseland, R., & van Hoorn, A. (2015). Are scores on hofstede's dimensions of national culture stable over time? A cohort analysis. *Global Strategy Journal*, *5*(3), 223–240. https://doi.org/10.1002/gsj.1098
Bianchi, C. C., & Ostale, E. (2006). Lessons learned from unsuccessful internationalization attempts: Example of multinational retailers in Chile. *Journal of Business Research*, *59*(1), 140–147. 10.1016/j.jbusres.2005.01.002

Biemann, T., & Weckmüller, H. (2016). Mensch gegen maschine: Wie gut sind Algorithmen im HR? [Man versus machine: How good are algorithms in HR?]. *Personal Quarterly, 68*(4), 44–47.
Bierhoff, H. W., & Frey, D. (Eds.). (2006). *Handbuch der Psychologie: Bd. 3. Handbuch der Sozialpsychologie und Kommunikationspsychologie [Handbook of Social Psychology and Communication Psychology]*. Hogrefe.
Birkenkrahe, M. (2008). System constellations as a tool supporting organisational learning and change processes. *International Journal of Learning and Change, 3*(3), 125–144. doi:10.1504/IJLC.2008.023179
Bischoff, S. (2016). Mit Intuition Komplexität bewältigen – Mit Musik intuitive (Management-) Fähigkeiten entwickeln [Managing complexity with intuition – developing intuitive (management) skills with music]. In M. W. Fröse, S. Kaudela-Baum, & F. E. P. Dievernich (Eds.), *Emotion und Intuition in Führung und Organisation* (pp. 211–218). Springer Fachmedien Wiesbaden. https://doi.org/10.1007/978-3-658-12350-5_11
Biswas, K., Boyle, B., & Mitchell, R. (2020). International experience, attitudes toward women and the adoption of supportive HR practices. *Asia Pacific Journal of Human Resources, 58*(1), 66–84. https://doi.org/10.1111/1744-7941.12218
Black, J. S., & van Esch, P. (2020). AI-enabled recruiting: What is it and how should a manager use it? *Business Horizons, 63*(2), 215–226. https://doi.org/10.1016/j.bushor.2019.12.001
Blank, S., & Laatzen, L. (2019). *Personaldiagnostik als sozialer Prozess. Die Bedeutung der positiven Beziehungsgestaltung zur Gewinnung von Kandidaten im Personalauswahlprozess.* [Personnel diagnostics as a social process – the meaning of positive relationship formation for candidate acquisition in the selection process]. Unpublished master thesis, Leuphana University, Lueneburg.
Böhle, F. (2007). Vorwort von Prof. Dr. Fritz Böhle [Foreword by Prof. Dr. Fritz Böhle]. In C. Kleebaur (Ed.), *Personalauswahl zwischen Anspruch und Wirklichkeit: Wissenschaftliche Personaldiagnostik vs. erfahrungsbasiert-intuitive Urteilsfindung* (pp. XI–XII). Hampp.
Bolte, A., Goschke, T., & Kuhl, J. (2003). Emotion and intuition. *Psychological Science, 14*(5), 416–421. https://doi.org/10.1111/1467-9280.01456
Bolz, N. (1997). Theorie der Müdigkeit – Theoriemüdigkeit [Theory of fatigue – theory fatigue] *Teleopolis*. https://www.heise.de/tp/features/Theorie-der-Muedigkeit-Theoriemuedigkeit-3445987.html
Booth, R. (2019). *Unilever saves on recruiters by using AI to assess job interviews*. The Guardian, 25. Oct. https://www.theguardian.com/technology/2019/oct/25/unilever-saves-on-recruiters-by-using-ai-to-assess-job-interviews
Bordalo, P., Gennaioli, N., & Shleifer, A. (2012). Salience theory of choice under risk. *Quarterly Journal of Economics, 127*(3), 1243–1285.
Bordalo, P., Gennaioli, N., & Shleifer, A. (2021). Salience. Working Paper 29274 DOI 10.3386/w29274. Issue Date September 2021
Borst, U., Fischer, H. R., & Schlippe, A. V. (2010). Wieviel Macht der Intuition? Wie viel Intuition ist in der Therapie nützlich? [How much power to intuition? How much intuition is useful in therapy?]. In U. Borst, H. R. Fischer, & A. von Schlippe (Eds.), Übergänge, Identität, Rituale. Familiendynamik *Systemische Praxis und Forschung. 35*(2), 162–164.
Bouland-van Dam, S. I. M., Oostrom, J. K., De Kock, F. S., Schlechter, A. F., & Jansen, P. G. W. (2020). Unravelling leadership potential: Conceptual and measurement issues. *European Journal of Work and Organizational Psychology*, 1–19. https://doi.org/10.1080/1359432X.2020.1787503
Bouzguenda, K. (2013). Towards a global framework of recruitment practices: The effect of culture applied to Tunisian context. *European Journal of Business and Management, 5*(7), 25–37. http://citeseerx.ist.psu.edu/viewdoc/download?doi=10.1.1.904.4112&rep=rep1&type=pdf

Bowen, -C.-C., Swim, J. K., & Jacobs, R. R. (2000). Evaluating gender biases on actual job performance of real people: A meta-analysis. *Journal of Applied Social Psychology*, *30*(10), 2194–2215.

Boyatzis, R., & Boyatzis, R. E. (2008). Competencies in the twenty-first century. *Journal of Management Development*. https://doi.org/10.1108/02621710810840730.

Bozionelos, N. (2005). When the inferior candidate is offered the job: The selection interview as a political and power game. *Human Relations*, *58*(12), 1605–1631. https://doi.org/10.1177/0018726705061437

Böschen, I., Alt, R., Krause, A., Rinne, U., & Zimmermann, K. F. (2012). *Pilotprojekt „Anonymisierte Bewerbungsverfahren" – Abschlussbericht [Pilot project „Anonymous application procedures" – Final report]* (IZA Research Report No. 44). Antidiskriminierungsstelle des Bundes, Institut zur Zukunft der Arbeit, Kooperationsstelle Wissenschaft und Arbeitswelt an der Europa-Universität Viadrina. http://ftp.iza.org/report_pdfs/iza_report_44.pdf

Bradbury, T., & Forsyth, D. (2012). You're in; you're out: Selection practices of coaches. *Sport, Business and Management: An International Journal*, *2*(1), 7–20. https://doi.org/10.1108/20426781211207638

Bradley, M., & Lang, P. J. (1994). Measuring emotion: The self-assessment manikin and the semantic differential. *Journal of Behavior Therapy and Experimental Psychiatry*, *25*(1), 49–59.

Brandstätter, V., Schüler, J., Puca, R. M., & Lozo, L. (2018). *Motivation und Emotion: Allgemeine Psychologie für Bachelor [Motivation and Emotion: Psychology for Bachelor Students]* (2. Ed.). Springer. https://doi.org/10.1007/978-3-662-56685-5

Branson, R. (2021). https://quotefancy.com/quote/899350/Richard-Branson-In-the-same-way-that-I-tend-to-make-up-my-mind-about-people-within-thirty

Braun, C., Dyroff, N., Heinze, J., Klopprogge, A., Kinkel, A., Liebelt, H., Pothmann, H., & Pundt, L. (2015). Globale standards für das human resources management [Global Stanadrads for Human Resource Management]. In Goinger Kreis – Initiative Zukunft Personal und Beschäftigung (Ed.). *Zukunft Personal Beschäftigung* (pp. 93–116). Springer Gabler. https://doi.org/10.1007/978-3-658-09196-5_7.

Brauner, J. (2019). *Entscheidungen in der Auswahl globaler Führungskräfte – Zwischen Rationalität/Analytik und Intuition* [Decisions in the selection of global executives – Between rationality/analytics and intuition]. Unpublished master thesis, Leuphana University, Lueneburg.

Breil, S. M., & Back, M. D. (2019). The perceived and actual relationship between nonverbal cues and personality: An overview of empirical findings. *The Brunswik Society Newsletter*, *34*, 1–3.

Breil, S. M., Osterholz, S., Nestler, S., & Back, M. D. (2020). Contributions of nonverbal cues to the accurate judgment of personality traits In T. D. Letzring, & J. S. Spain (Eds.), *The Oxford handbook of accurate personality judgment*. Oxford University Press. https://doi.org/10.31234/osf.io/mn2je

Breitbach, S., Tug, S., & Simon, P. (2014). Conventional and genetic talent identification in sports: Will recent developments trace talent? *Sports Medicine (Auckland, N.Z.)*, *44*(11), 1489–1503. https://doi.org/10.1007/s40279-014-0221-7

Brewer, M. B., & Caporael, L. R. (2006). An evolutionary perspective on social identity: Revisiting groups. In M. Schaller, J. A. Simpson, & D. T. Kenrick (Eds.), *Evolution and social psychology* (pp. 143–161). Psychosocial Press.

Brewer, P., & Venaik, S. (2012). On the misuse of national culture dimensions. *International Marketing Review*, *29*(6), 673–683. https://doi.org/10.1108/02651331211277991

Brief, A. P., Dietz, J., Cohen, C. C., Pugh, S. D., & Vaslow, J. B. (2000). Just doing business: modern racism and obedience to authority as explanations for employment discrimination.

Organizational Behavior and Human Decision Processes, *81*(1), 72–97. https://doi.org/10.1006/obhd.1999.2867

Brodbeck, F. C. (2016). Führung: Soziale Einflussnahme auf andere [Leadership: Social influence on others]. In F. C. Brodbeck, E. Kirchler, & R. Woschée (Eds.), *Internationale Führung* (pp. 1–32). Springer Gabler. https://doi.org/10.1007/978-3-662-43361-4

Brodbeck, F. C., Frese, M., Akerblom, S., Audia, G., Bakacsi, G., Bendova, H., Bodega, D., Bodur, M., Booth, S., Brenk, K., Castel, P., Den Hartog, D., Donnelly-Cox, G., Gratchev, M. V., Holmberg, I., Jarmuz, S., Jesuino, J. C., Jorbenadse, R., Kabasakal, H. E., & Wunderer, R. (2000). Cultural variation of leadership prototypes across 22 European countries. *Journal of Occupational and Organizational Psychology*, *73*(1), 1–29. https://doi.org/10.1348/096317900166859

Brodbeck, F. C., Kirchler, E., & Woschée, R. (2016). *Internationale Führung: Das GLOBE-Brevier in der Praxis [International leadership: The GLOBE Breviary in practice]*. Springer. https://doi.org/10.1007/978-3-662-43361-4.

Brown, J. D., & Kobayashi, C. (2003). Introduction: Culture and the self-enhancement bias. *Journal of Cross-Cultural Psychology*, *34*(5), 492–495.

Brtek, M. D., & Motowidlo, S. J. (2002). Effects of procedure and outcome accountability on interview validity. *Journal of Applied Psychology*, *87*(1), 185–191. https://doi.org/10.1037/0021-9010.87.1.185

Brynjolfsson, E., & Mcafee, A. (2017). The business of artificial intelligence. *Harvard Business Review*, *95*(7), 1–20.

Bublitz, L. (2021). Emotionen in der globalen Personalauswahl: Inwiefern beeinflussen Emotionen Personalführungsentscheidungen [Emotions in global personnel selection: To what extent do emotions affect personnel leadership decisions? Unpublished master thesis, Leuphana University, Lueneburg

Buchanan, L., & O'Connell, A. (2006). A brief history of decision-making. *Harvard Business Review*, *84*(1), 32–42.

Buchtel, E. E., & Norenzayan, A. (2008). Which should you use, intuition or logic? Cultural differences in injunctive norms about reasoning. *Asian Journal of Social Psychology*, *11*(4), 264–273. https://doi.org/10.1111/j.1467-839X.2008.00266.x

Buckingham, M. (2015). Most HR data is bad data. *Harvard Business Review*, February 09, 2015. https://hbr.org/2015/02/most-hr-data-is-bad-data

Buehl, A.-K., Melchers, K. G., Macan, T., & Kühnel, J. (2019). Tell me sweet little lies: How does faking in interviews affect interview scores and interview validity? *Journal of Business and Psychology*, *34*(1), 107–124. https://doi.org/10.1007/s10869-018-9531-3

Buekers, M., Borry, P., & Rowe, P. M. (2015). Talent in sports. Some reflections about the search for future champions. *Movement & Sport Sciences – Science & Motricité*, *88*, 3–12. https://doi.org/10.1051/sm/2014002

Buijsrogge, A., Derous, E., & Duyck, W. (2016). Often biased but rarely in doubt: How initial reactions to stigmatized applicants affect interviewer confidence. *Human Performance*, *29*(4), 275–290. 10.1080/08959285.2016.1165225

Burke, L. A., & Miller, M. K. (1999). Taking the mystery out of intuitive decision making. *Academy of Management Perspectives*, *13*(4), 91–99. https://doi.org/10.5465/ame.1999.2570557

Burke, L. A., & Sadler-Smith, E. (2006). Instructor Intuition in the Educational Setting. *Academy of Management Learning & Education*, *5*(2), 169–181. https://doi.org/10.5465/amle.2006.21253781

Burks, S. V., Cowgill, B., Hoffman, M., & Housman, M. (2015). The value of hiring through employee referrals. *The Quarterly Journal of Economics*, *130*(2), 805–839.

Burmeister, A. (2010). *Measuring Intuition: A Valid Undertaking? Empirical Construct-Validation of REI, CSI, CoSI and GDMS*. Unpublished bachelor thesis, Leuphana University, Lueneburg.
Bühner, M. (2010). Objektivität von Verhaltensbeobachtungen [Objectivity of behavioral observations]. In K. Westhoff, K., C. Hagemeister, M. Kersting, F. Lang, H. Moosbrugger, G. Reimann, & G. Stemmler (Eds.), *Grundwissen für die berufsbezogene Eignungsbeurteilung nach DIN 33430* (3rd ed.) (pp. 78–81). Pabst Science Publication.
Büssing, A., Herbig, B., & Ewert, T. (1999). *Implizites Wissen und erfahrungsgeleitetes Arbeitshandeln: Konzeptualisierung und Methodenentwicklung [Implicit knowledge and experiential work action: Conceptualization and method development]. Technische Universität München*. Lehrstuhl für Psychologie.
Büter, C. (2010). *Internationale Unternehmensführung: Entscheidungsorientierte Einführung [International corporate governance: Decision-oriented introduction]*. Oldenbourg Wissenschaftsverlag.
Büttner, R. (2016). Personality as a predictor of Business Social Media Usage: An Empirical Investigation of Xing Usage Patterns. *PACIS 2016 Proceedings, 163*. https://aisel.aisnet.org/cgi/viewcontent.cgi?article=1160&context=pacis2016
Büttner, R. (2017). Prädiktive Algorithmen zur Persönlichkeitsprognose auf Basis von Social-Media-Daten [Predictive algorithms for personality prediction based on social media data]. *Personal Quarterly, 3*, 22–27.
Buxmann, P., & Schmidt, H. (2019). Grundlagen der Künstlichen Intelligenz und des Maschinellen Lernens [Basics of artificial intelligence and machine learning]. In P. Buxmann, & H. Schmidt (Eds.), *Künstliche Intelligenz* (pp. 3–19). Springer. https://doi.org/10.1007/978-3-662-57568-0_1
Byrne, D. (1971). *The attraction paradigm*. Academic Press.
Cacioppo, J. T., & Petty, R. E. (1982). The need for cognition. *Journal of Personality and Social Psychology, 42*, 116–131.
Calabretta, G., Gemser, G., & Wijnberg, N. M. (2017). The interplay between intuition and rationality in strategic decision making: A paradox perspective. *Organization Studies, 38*(3-4), 365–401.
Caldwell, C., Thornton, G. C., & Gruys, M. L. (2003). Ten classic assessment center errors: Challenges to selection validity. *Public Personnel Management, 32*, 73–88.
Campbell, W. K., & Sedikides, C. (1999). Self-threat magnifies the self-serving bias: A meta-analytic integration. *Review of General Psychology, 3*(1), 23–43. https://doi.org/10.1037/1089-2680.3.1.23
Campbell, A., Whitehead, J., & Finkelstein, S. (2009). Why good leaders make bad decisions]. *Harvard Business Manager, 87*(02), 1–6. https://www.google.com/search?client=firefox-b-d&q=campbel++Why+good+managers+make+bad+decisions
Campion, M. C., Campion, M. A., Campion, E. D., & Reider, M. H. (2016). Initial investigation into computer scoring of candidate essays for personnel selection. *Journal of Applied Psychology, 101*(7), 958–975. https://doi.org/10.1037/apl0000108
Candelon, F., Reichert, T., Duranton, S., Di Charme Carlo, R., & Bondt, M. D. (2020). *The rise of the AI-powered company in the postcrisis world*. Boston Consulting Group. https://www.bcg.com/de-de/publications/2020/business-applications-artificial-intelligence-post-covid.aspx.
Carleton, R. N. (2016). Fear of the unknown: One fear to rule them all? *Journal of Anxiety Disorders, 41*, 5–21. https://doi.org/10.1016/j.janxdis.2016.03.011
Carpenter, L. (2013). Improving the candidate experience. *Strategic HR Review, 12*(4), 203–208. https://doi.org/10.1108/SHR-03-2013-0017
Carroll, S. (2019). *Something deeply hidden.quantum worlds and the emergence of spacetime*. Oneworld.

Caruso, D. R., & Salovey, P. (2007). *Managen mit emotionaler Kompetenz. Die vier zentralen Skills für Ihren Führungsalltag [Managing with emotional competence. The four central skills for your everyday management]*. Campus Verlag.

Centre for Monitoring Economy. (2019). *CMIE statistics – Unemployment rate*. https://www.cmie.com

Ceschi, A., Sartori, R., & Rubaltelli, E. (2014). Designing a homo psychologicus more psychologicus: Empirical results on value perception in support to a new theoretical organizational-economic agent based model. *Advances in Intelligent Systems and Computing*, *290*(1), 83–89. 10.1007/978-3-319-07593-8_9

Chamorro-Premuzic, T., Akhtar, R., Winsborough, D., & Sherman, R. A. (2017). The datafication of talent: How technology is advancing the science of human potential at work. *Current Opinion in Behavioral Sciences*, *18*, 13–16. https://doi.org/10.1016/j.cobeha.2017.04.007

Chamorro-Premuzic, T., Winsborough, D., Sherman, R. A., & Hogan, R. (2016). New talent signals: Shiny new objects or a brave new world? *Industrial and Organizational Psychology*, *9*(3), 621–640. https://doi.org/10.1017/iop.2016.6

Chan, K.-Y., & Drasgow, F. (2001). Toward a theory of individual differences and leadership: Understanding the motivation to lead. *Journal of Applied Psychology*, *86*(3), 481.

Chan, D., Schmitt, N., DeShon, R. P., Clause, C. S., & Delbridge, K. (1997). Reactions to cognitive ability test: The relationships between race, test performance, face validity perceptions, and test-taking motivation. *Journal of Applied Psychology*, *82*, 300–310.

Chan, D., Schmitt, N., Sacco, J. M., & DeShon, R. P. (1998). Understanding pretest and posttest reactions to cognitive ability and personality tests. *Journal of Applied Psychology*, *83*, 471–485.

Chen, C.C., Chen, X.P., & Meindl, J.R. (1998). How can cooperation be fostered? The cultural effects of individualism-collectivism. *The Academy of Management Review*, *23*(2), 285–304. doi:10.5465/amr.1998.533227

Chen, L., Zhao, R., Leong, C. W., Lehman, B., Feng, G., & Hoque, M. E., (2017). Automated video interview judgment on a large-sized corpus collected online. In *Proceedings of the 7th international conference on affective computing and intelligent interaction* (pp. 504–509). IEEE. https://doi.org/10.1109/acii.2017.8273646

Chhokar, J. S., Brodbeck, F. C., & House, R. J. (Eds.). (2007). *Culture and leadership across the world*. Lawrence Erlbaum Associates.

Chowdhury, G. G. (2003). Natural language processing. *Annual Review of Information Science and Technology*, *37*(1), 51–89.

Chu, P. C., Spires, E. E., & Sueyoshi, T. (1999). Cross-cultural differences in choice behavior and use of decision aids: A comparison of Japan and the United States. *Organizational Behavior and Human Decision Processes*, *77*(2), 147–170. https://doi.org/10.1006/obhd.1998.2817

Church, A. H., Rotolo, C. T., Ginther, N. M., & Levine, R. (2015). How are top companies designing and managing their high-potential programs? A follow-up talent management benchmark study. *Consulting Psychology Journal: Practice and Research*, *67*(1), 17–47. https://doi.org/10.1037/cpb0000030

Ciompi, L. (1997). Zu den affektiven Grundlagen des Denkens [On the affective foundations of thinking]. *System Familie*, *10*(3), 128–134.

Claxton, G. (1998). Investigating without knowing why. *Psychologist*, *11*(5), 217–220.

Claxton, G. (2000). The anatomy of intuition. In T. Atkinson, & G. Claxton (Eds.), *The intuitive practitioner: On the value of not always knowing what one is doing* (pp. 32–52). Open University Press.

Cleeremans, A., & Jiménez, L. (2002). Implicit learning and consciousness: A graded, dynamic perspective. *Implicit Learning and Consciousness*, 1–40.

Cocchiara, F. K., Bell, M. P., & Casper, W. J. (2016). Sounding “Different”: The role of sociolinguistic cues in evaluating job candidates. *Human Resource Management*, *55*(3), 463–477. https://doi.org/10.1002/hrm.21675

Coffield, F., Moseley, D., Hall, E., & Ecclestone, K. (2004). *Learning styles and pedagogy in post-16 learning: A systematic and critical review*. Learning and Skills Research Centre.

Coget, J.-F. (2014). Dialogical inquiry: A qualitative method for studying intuition in the field. In M. Sinclair (Ed.), *Handbook of research methods on intuition* (pp. 176–187). Edward Elgar Publishing. https://doi.org/10.4337/9781782545996

Cohen, D. J. (2007). The very separate worlds of academic and practitioner publications in human resource management: Reasons for the divide and concrete solutions for bridging the gap. *Academy of Management Journal*, *50*(5), 1013–1019. https://doi.org/10.5465/amj.2007.27151946

Cohen, A. R., Stotland, E., & Wolfe, D. M. (1955). An experimental investigation of need for cognition. *The Journal of Abnormal and Social Psychology*, *51*(2), 291–294.

Cohn, R. C. (1988). *Von der Psychoanalyse zur themenzentrierten Interaktion. Von der Behandlung einzelner zu einer Pädagogik für alle [From psychoanalysis to theme-centered interaction. From the treatment of individuals to a pedagogy for all]*. Klett-Cotta.

Colarelli, S. M., & Thompson, M. (2008). Stubborn reliance on human nature in employee selection: statistical decision aids are evolutionarily novel. *Industrial and Organizational Psychology*, *1*(3), 347–351. https://doi.org/10.1111/j.1754-9434.2008.00060.x

Collins, A., Brown, J. S., & Newman, S. E. (1987). *Cognitive apprenticeship: Teaching the craft of reading, writing and mathematics* (Technical Report No. 403). BBN Laboratories, Cambridge, MA. Centre for the Study of Reading, University of Illinois.

Colvin, C. R., & Funder, D. C. (1991). Predicting personality and behavior. A boundary on the acquaintanceship effect. *Journal of Personality and Social Psychology*, *60*(6), 884–894.

Condorcet, M. (1785). *Essai sur l’application de l’analyse à la probabilité des décisions rendues à la pluralité des voix [Essay on the application of analysis to the probability of majority decisions]*. Imprimerie Royale.

Condon, J. W., & Crano, W. D. (1988). Inferred evaluation and the relation between attitude similarity and interpersonal attraction. *Journal of Personality and Social Psychology*, *54*(5), 789.

Conway, J. M., Jako, R. A., & Goodman, D. F. (1995). A meta-analysis of interrater and internal consistency reliability of selection interviews. *The Journal of Applied Psychology*, *80*(5), 565–579. https://doi.org/10.1037/0021-9010.80.5.565

Cools, E., Van den Broeck, H., & Bouckenooghe, D. (2006). “The Cognitive Style Indicator: Development and validation of a new measurement instrument.” Working Papers of Faculty of Economics and Business Administration, Ghent University, Belgium 06/379, Ghent University, Faculty of Economics and Business Administration.

Cools, E., & Van den Broeck, H. (2007). Development and validation of the Cognitive Style Indicator. *The Journal of Psychology*, *141*(4), 359–387.

Costa, P. T., Jr., & McCrae, R. R. (1988). From catalog to classification: Murray’s needs and the Five-Factor Model. *Journal of Personality and Social Psychology*, *55*, 258–265.

Costa, P. T., McCrae, R. R., & Kay, G. G. (1995). Persons, Places, and Personality: Career Assessment Using the Revised NEO Personality Inventory. *Journal of Career Assessment*, *3*(2), 123–139. https://doi.org/10.1177/106907279500300202

Coyne, K. P., & Horn, J. (2009). Wie sie die Aktionen ihrer Konkurrenten vorhersagen [How they predict the actions of their competitors]. *Harvard Business Manager*, May 2009. 34–43.

Cronbach, L. J. (1957). The two disciplines of scientific psychology. *American Psychologist*, *12*(11), 671–684. https://doi.org/10.1037/h0043943

Cronbach, L. J., & Meehl, P. E. (1955). Construct validity in psychological tests. *Psychological Bulletin, 52*(4), 281–302. https://doi.org/10.1037/h0040957

Cropanzano, R. (1994). The justice dilemma in employee selection: Some reflections on the trade-off between fairness and validity. *The Industrial-Organizational Psychologist, 31*(3), 90–93.

Cropanzano, R., & Wright, T. A. (2003). Procedural justice and organizational staffing: A tale of two paradigms. *Human Resource Management Review, 13*(1), 7–39. https://psycnet.apa.org/doi/10.1016/S1053-4822(02)00097-9"https://doi.org/10.1016/S1053-4822(02)00097-9

Cropanzano, R., Bowen, D. E., & Gilliland, S. W. (2007). The management of organizational justice. *Academy of Management Perspectives, 21*(4), 24–48. 10.5465/AMP.2007.27895338

Culbertson, S. S., Weyhrauch, W. S., & Huffcutt, A. I. (2016). A tale of two formats: Direct comparison of matching situational and behavior description interview questions. *Human Resource Management Review, 27*(1), 167–177.

Cyert, R. M., & March, J. G. (1963). *A Behavioral Theory of the Firm*. Prentice Hall.

Czarniawska-Joerges, B. (1994) *The Process of Organizing*. Institute of Economic Research. Working Paper Series Nr. 4. Lund.

Dachler, H. P. (1989). Selection and the organizational context. In P. Herriot (Ed.), *Assessment and selection in organizations: Methods and practice for recruitment and appraisal* (pp. 45–69). Wiley.

Dahlander, L., O'Mahony, S., & Gann, D. M. (2016). One foot in, one foot out: How does individuals' external search breadth affect innovation outcomes? *Strategic Management Journal, 37*(2), 280–302. https://doi.org/10.1002/smj.2342

Dahm, M., & Dregger, A. (2019). Der Einsatz von künstlicher Intelligenz im HR: Die Wirkung und Förderung der Akzeptanz von KI-basierten Recruiting-Tools bei potenziellen Nutzern [The use of artificial intelligence in HR: The effect and promotion of acceptance of AI-based recruiting tools by potential users]. In B. Hermeier, T. Heupel, & S. Fichtner-Rosada (Eds.), *FOM-Edition. Arbeitswelten der Zukunft* (pp. 249–271). Springer Fachmedien. https://doi.org/10.1007/978-3-658-23397-6_14

Damasio, A. R. (1995). *Descartes' error: Emotion, reason and the human brain*. Picador.

Damasio, A. R. (1997). *Descartes' Irrtum: Fühlen, Denken und das menschliche Gehirn [Descartes' error: Feeling, reason and the human brain]. dtv: Vol.* Dteutscher Taschenbuch-Verlag.

Damasio, A. R., Tranel, D., & Damasio, H. (1991). Somatic markers and the guidance of behavior: Theory and preliminary testing. In H. S. Levin, H. M. Eisenberg, & A. L. Benton (Eds.), *Frontal lobe function and dysfunction* (pp. 217–229). Oxford University Press.

Dana, J., Cain, M. D., & Dawes, R. M. (2006). What you don't know won't hurt me: Costly (but quiet) exit in dictator games. *Organizational Behavior and Human Decision Processes, 100*, 193–201.

Dane, E., & Pratt, M. G. (2007). Exploring intuition and its role in managerial decision making. *Academy of Management Review, 32*(1), 33–54. https://doi.org/10.5465/amr.2007.23463682

Dane, E., & Pratt, M. G. (2009). Conceptualizing and measuring intuition: A review of recent trends. In G. P. Hodgkinson, & J. K. Ford (Eds.), *International review of industrial and organizational psychology* (Vol. 24, pp. 1–40). Wiley-Blackwell.

Dane, E., Rockmann, K. W., & Pratt, M. G. (2012). When should I trust my gut? Linking domain expertise to intuitive decision-making effectiveness. *Organizational Behavior and Human Decision Processes, 119*(2), 187–194. https://doi.org/10.1016/j.obhdp.2012.07.009

Danks, D., & London, A. J. (2017). Algorithmic Bias in Autonomous Systems. *Proceedings of the Twenty-Sixth International Joint Conference on Artificial Intelligence*, 4691–4697. https://www.ijcai.org/proceedings/2017/654

Danz, D., Kübler, D., Mechtenberg, L., & Schmid, J. (2015). On the failure of hindsight-biased principals to delegate optimally. *Management Science, 61*(8), 1938–1958. 10.1287/mnsc.2014.2087

Darwin, C. (1872). *The expression of the emotions in man and animals by Charles Darwin*. Murray. https://books.google.de/books?id=1wuJK28YtoOC.
Dastin, J. (2018). *Amazon scraps secret AI recruiting tool that showed bias against women*. https://www.reuters.com/article/us-amazon-com-jobs-automation-insight/amazon-scraps-secret-ai-recruiting-tool-that-showed-bias-against-women-idUSKCN1MK08G
Davis, F. D. (1989). Perceived usefulness, perceived ease of use, and user acceptance of information technology. *MIS Quarterly, 13*(3), 319–340.
Dawes, R. M. (1979). The robust beauty of improper linear models in decision making. *American Psychologist, 34*, 571–582.
Dayan, M., & Di Benedetto, C. A. (2011). Team intuition as a continuum construct and new product creativity: The role of environmental turbulence, team experience, and stress. *Research Policy, 40*(2), 276–286. https://doi.org/10.1016/j.respol.2010.10.002
Dayan, M., & Elbanna, S. (2011). Antecedents of team intuition and its impact on the success of new product development projects. *Journal of Product Innovation Management, 28*(s1), 159–174. https://doi.org/10.1111/j.1540-5885.2011.00868.x
Deci, E. L., & Ryan, R. M. (2008). Self-determination theory: A macrotheory of human motivation, development, and health. *Canadian Psychology/Psychologie Canadienne, 49*(3), 182–185. https://doi.org/10.1037/a0012801
De Becker, G. (1999). *Mut zur Angst. Wie Intuition uns vor Gewalt schützt [Courage to fear. How intuition protects us from violence]*. Wolfgang Krüger Verlag.
Deller, J., & Albrecht, A.-G. (2007). Wie ein Fisch im Trockenen? Zur Praxisrelevanz publizierter Forschungsbeiträge [Like a fish out of water? On the practical relevance of published research articles]. *Zeitschrift Für Personalpsychologie, 6*(4), 150–159. https://doi.org/10.1026/1617-6391.6.4.150
Denes-Raj, V., & Epstein, S. (1994). Conflict between intuitive and rational processing: When people behave against their better judgment. *Journal of Personality and Social Psychology, 66*(5), 819–829. https://doi.org/10.1037/0022-3514.66.5.819
DeNisi, A. S., & Murphy, K. R. (2020). Evaluating job performance measures: Criteria for criteria. In E. F. Stone-Romero (Eds.), *Research methods in human research management: Toward valid research-based inferences* (pp. 107–125). https://doi.org/10.1177/1094428107300342
Deresky, H. (2008). *International management: Managing across borders and cultures text and cases* (6th ed.). Pearson/Prentice Hall.
Derous, E., & Born, M. P. (2005). Impact of face validity and information about the assessment process on test motivation and performance. *Le Travail Humain, 68*(4), 317–336.
Derous, E., & Ryan, A. M. (2019). When your resume is (not) turning you down: Modelling ethnic bias in resume screening. *Human Resource Management Journal, 29*(2), 113–130. https://doi.org/10.1111/1748-8583.12217
Derous, E., Nguyen, H-H D., & Ryan, A. M. (2021). Reducing ethnic discrimination in resumescreening: a test of two training interventions. *European Journal of Work and Organizational Psychology*, 30(2), 225–239. https://doi.org/10.1080/1359432X.2020.1756907
Desrumaux, P., De Bosscher, S., & Léoni, V. (2009). Effects of facial attractiveness, gender, and competence of applicants on job recruitment. *Swiss Journal of Psychology, 68*(1), 33–42. doi:10.1024/1421-0185.68.1.33
Desoi, M. (2018). *Intelligente Videoüberwachung – Rechtliche Bewertung und rechtsgemäße Gestaltung [Intelligent Video Surveillance – Legal Assessment and Legally Compliant Design]*. Springer Fachmedien.
De Sousa, R. (1987). *The rationality of emotion*. MIT Press.
De Sousa, R. (2011). *Emotional truth*. Oxford University Press.

De Sousa, R. (2018). *The rationality of emotion: Biology, ideology and emotional truth*. ISRE Interview (with Carolyn Price) (August 2018, p. 10–19). https://emotionresearcher.com/the-rationality-of-emotion-biology-ideology-and-emotional-truth/

Deters, J. (1990). *Mensch und Betriebswirtschaftslehre. Zur Entwicklung und Kritik der verhaltenstheoretischen Betriebswirtschaftslehre als individualistisches Wissenschaftskonzept [Human Being and Business Administration. On the Development and Critique of Behavioral Business Administration as an Individualistic Concept of Science]*. C.E. Poeschel.

Deters, J. (2017). *Global leadership talent management: Successful selection of global leadership talents as an integrated process*. Emerald Publishing.

Deters, J. (Ed.). (2019). *Einfluss von (Länder-) Kulturen auf die Auswahl globaler Führungskräfte – wissenschaftliche Analytik und erfahrungsbasierte Intuition im internationalen Vergleich. Lehrforschungsprojekt im Master Management & Human Ressourcen [Influence of (country) cultures on the selection of global leaders – scientific analytics and experience-based intuition. An international comparison. Teaching research project. Master Program Management & Human Resources]* (Project manager: Stefanie Blank & Julia Hermann). Unpublished final report. Leuphana University Lueneburg.

Deters, J., Meyer, K., & Schmidt, A. (2020). Vom Wildwuchs zur Norm [From wild growth to the norm]. *Personalmagazin, 22*(7), 68–73.

Deutsch, M. E. (2015). *The myth of the intuitive*. The MIT Press. https://doi.org/10.7551/mitpress/9780262028950.001.0001.

De Vries, M., Witteman, C., Holland, R., & Dijksterhuis, A. (2010). The unconscious thought effect in clinical decision making: An example in diagnosis. *Medical Decision Making*, *30*, 578–581. doi:10.1177/0272989X09360820

Dhami, M., & Ayton, P. (2001). Bailing and Jailing the fast and frugal way. *Journal of Behavioral Decision Making*, *14*, 141–168).

Diagnostik- und Testkuratorium. (2018). *Personalauswahl kompetent gestalten [Competent personnel selection]*. Springer. https://doi.org/10.1007/978-3-662-53772-5.

Diercks, J. (2019). *Studie "Diskriminierungsrisiken durch Verwendung von Algorithmen" mit speziellem Fokus auf die Arbeitswelt [Study "Risks of discrimination through the use of algorithms" with special focus on the world of work]*. https://www.xing.com/news/insiders/articles/studie-diskriminierungsrisiken-durch-verwendung-von-algorithmen-mit-speziellem-fokus-auf-die-arbeitswelt-2859411?ete=15e2f2e01d473347.eyJ0YXJnZXRfaWQiOjI4NTk0MTEsInRhcmdldF90eXBlIjoiYXJ0aWNsZSIsInRhcmdldF91cm4iOiJ1cm46eC14aW5nOmNvbnRlbnQ6aW5zaWRlcl9hcnRpY2xlOjI4NTk0MTEiLCJwYXJlbnRfY29udGFpbmVyX2lkIjoiW1wiNTQ3MTRfMTg1NzQ3NjNcIixcInVybjp4LXhpbmc6Y29udGVudDppbnNpZGVyOjMwOFwiLFsyODU5NDExXSxcInJlY29tbWVuZGVkXCIsXCJlZGl0b3JzX3BpY2tzXCIsudWxsXSIsInBvc2l0aW9uIjowLCJzaXRlX3NlY3Rpb24iOiJlbWFpbCIsImRlbGl2ZXJ5X2lkIjoiNTQ3MTRfMTg1NzQ3NjMiLCJyZWFzb24iOiJyZWNvbW1lbmRlZCIsImFjdG9yIjoidXJuOngteGluZzpjb250ZW50Omluc2lkZXI6MzA4IiwiYWN0b3JfdXJuIjoidXJuOngteGluZzpjb250ZW50Omluc2lkZXI6MzA4IiwidmVyc2lvbiI6IjIuMi4xIn0&link_position=digest&newsletter_id=54714&cce=em5e0cbb4d.%3ASS0g5xlvjOVtKSI6Zz_LBJ

Diercks, J. (2021). Wenn der Roboter rekrutiert: Chance für mehr Menschlichkeit am Arbeitsmarkt? [When the robot recruits: Chance for more humanity in the labor market?]. https://www.xing.com/news/insiders/articles/wenn-der-roboter-rekrutiert-chance-fur-mehr-menschlichkeit-am-arbeitsmarkt-4127216?ete=e38df96667bcd9bc.eyJ0YXJnZXRfaWQiOjQxMzE1MDcsInRhcmdldF90eXBlIjoiYXJ0aWNsZSIsInRhcmdldF91cm4iOiJ1cm46eC14aW5nOmNvbnRlbnQ6cGFnZV9hcnRpY2xlOjQxMzE1MDciLCJwb3NpdGlvbiI6MTEsInNpdGVfc2VjdGlvbiI6ImVtYWlsIiwiZGVsaXZlcnlfaWQiOiI3NzA0MV8zMjY3MjI5MCIsInJlYXNvbiI6InBvcHVsYXJfb3ZlcmFsbCIsImFjdG9yIjoidXJuOngteGluZzpjb250ZW50OnB1Ymxpc2hlcl9wYWdlOjM2NyIsImFjdG9yX3VybiI6InVybjp4LXhpbmc6Y29udGVudDpwdWJsaXNoZXJfcGFnZTozNjciLCJ2ZXJzaW9uIjoiMi4yLjIifQ&link_position=di

gest&newsletter_id=77041&xng_share_origin=email&cce=em5e0cbb4d.%3Aq3F701fDQMns7WGOzYS2BD

Dijksterhuis, A. (2010). *Das kluge Unbewusste*. Denken mit Gefühl und Intuition. *[The wise unconscious.* Thinking with feeling and intuition.*]* Klett-Cotta.

Dijksterhuis, A., & Nordgren, L. F. (2006). A Theory of Unconscious Thought. *Perspectives on Psychological Science: A Journal of the Association for Psychological Science, 1*(2), 95–109. https://doi.org/10.1111/j.1745-6916.2006.00007.x

Dilger, A. (2011). Personnel economics: Strengths, weaknesses and its place in human resource management. *Management Revue, 22*(4), 331–343. 10.1688/1861-9908_mrev_2011_04_Dilger

DIN Deutsches Institut für Normung e. V. (2002). *DIN 33430: Anforderungen an Verfahren und deren Einsatz bei berufsbezogenen Eignungsbeurteilungen [Requirements for procedures and their application in job related proficiency assessment]*. Beuth Verlag.

DIN Deutsches Institut für Normung e. V. (2016). *DIN 33430: Anforderungen an berufsbezogene Eignungsdiagnostik [Job related proficiency assessment]*. Beuth Verlag.

Dineen, B. R., Noe, R. A., & Wang, C. (2004). Perceived fairness of web-based applicant screening procedures: Weighing the rules of justice and the role of individual differences. *Human Resource Management, 43*(2–3), 127–145. https://doi.org/10.1002/hrm.20011

Dipboye, R. L., Arvey, R. D., & Terpstra, D. E. (1977). Sex and physical attractiveness of raters and applicants as determinants of resumé evaluations. *The Journal of Applied Psychology, 62*(3), 288–294. https://doi.org/10.1037/0021-9010.62.3.288

Dipboye, R. L. (1994). Structured and unstructured selection interviews: Beyond the job-fit model. In G. R. Ferris (Eds.), *Research in personnel and human resources management* (Vol. 12, pp. 79–123). JAI Press.

Dipboye, R. L., & Johnson, S. K. (2091). The clash between "Best Practices" for selection and national culture. In D. L. Stone, & E. F. Stone-Romero (Eds.), *The influence of culture on human resource management processes and practices* (pp. 53–84). Psychology Press.

Dolensek, N., Gehrlach, D. A., Klein, A. S., & Gogolla, N. (2020). Facial expressions of emotion states and their neuronal correlates in mice. *Science (New York, N.Y.), 368*(6486), 89–94. https://doi.org/10.1126/science.aaz9468

Doppler, K., & Voigt, B. (2018). *Feel the Change!: Wie erfolgreiche Change Manager Emotionen steuern [How successful change managers manage emotions]*. Campus.

Dorfman, P. W., Hanges, P. J., & Brodbeck, F. C. (2004). Leadership and cultural variation. In R. J. House, P. J. Hanges, M. Javidan, P. W. Dorfman, & V. Gupta (Eds.), *Leadership, culture, and organizations: The GLOBE study of 62 societies (669–719)*. Sage Publications.

Dorfman, P. W., Javidan, M., Hanges, P. J., Dastmalchian, A., & House, R. J. (2012). GLOBE: A twenty year journey into the intriguing world of culture and leadership. *Journal of World Business, 47*(4), 504–518. https://doi.org/10.1016/j.jwb.2012.01.004

Downey, L., Papageorgiou, V., & Stough, C. (2006). Examining the relationship between leadership, emotional intelligence and intuition in senior female managers. *Leadership& Organization Development Journal, 27*(4), 250–264. https://doi.org/10.1108/01437730610666019

Dörfler, V., & Ackermann, F. (2012). Understanding intuition: The case for two forms of intuition. *Management Learning, 43*(5), 545–564. https://doi.org/10.1177/1350507611434686

Dreyfus, S. E., & Dreyfus, H. L. (1980). *A five-stage model of the mental activities involved in directed skill acquisition*. California University Berkeley Operations Research Center. https://apps.dtic.mil/dtic/tr/fulltext/u2/a084551.pdf

Dreyfus, H. L., & Dreyfus, S. E. (1991). *Künstliche Intelligenz: Von den Grenzen der Denkmaschine und dem Wert der Intuition [Artificial intelligence: About the limits of the thinking machine and the value of intuition]*. Rowohlt.

Dreyfus, H. L., Dreyfus, S. E., & Athanasiou, T. (1986). *Mind over machine: The power of human intuition and expertise in the era of the computer*. Free Press.

Duggan, W. (2013). *Strategic intuition: The creative spark in human achievement*. Columbia University Press.

Dunleavy, E. M., Cohen, D. B., Aamodt, M. G., & Schaeffer, P. (2008). A consideration of international differences in the legal context of selection. *Industrial and Organizational Psychology, 1*(2), 247–254.

Eagly, A. H., Ashmore, R. D., Makhijani, M. G., & Longo, L. C. (1991). What is beautiful is good, but. .: A meta-analytic review of research on the physical attractiveness stereotype. *Psychological Bulletin, 110*(1), 109–128. https://doi.org/10.1037/0033-2909.110.1.109

Eagly, A. H., & Karau, S. J. (2002). Role congruity theory of prejudice toward female leaders. *Psychological Review, 109*(3), 573–598. https://doi.org/10.1037//0033-295X.109.3.573

Easterbrook, J. A. (1959). The effect of emotion on cue utilization and the organization of behavior. *Psychological Review, 66*(3), 183–201. https://doi.org/10.1037/h0047707

Eberle, U. (2017). Das Gefühl für die richtige Entscheidung [The feeling for the rigt decision]. In: *GEO kompakt* Nr. 50. Wer bin ich?, 76–85.

Ebers, M., & Navas, S. (Eds.). (2020). *Algorithm and Law*. Cambridge University Press.

Edmondson, A. C. (1999). Psychological safety and learning behavior in work teams. *Administrative Science Quarterly, 44*(2), 350–383.

Edmondson, A. C. (2018). *The fearless organization: Creating psychological safety in the workplace for learning, innovation, and growth*. John Wiley & Sons.

Eggenberger, D. (1994). Überlegungen zur sozialpädagogischen Bedeutung von Intuition. *Sozialarbeit, 13*, 13–22.

Eggenberger, D. (1998). *Grundlagen und Aspekte einer pädagogischen Intuitionstheorie. Die Bedeutung der Intuition für das Ausüben pädagogischer Tätigkeit [Foundations and aspects of a pedagogical theory of intuition. The importance of intuition for the practice of pedagogical activity]*. Haupt.

Egner, H. (1980). *Betriebswirtschaftliche Prüfungslehre*. De Gruyter.

Eid, M., & Diener, E. (2001). Norms for experiencing emotions in different cultures: Inter- and intranational differences. *Journal of Personality and Social Psychology, 81*(5), 869–885. https://doi.org/10.1037/0022-3514.81.5.869

Einhorn, H. J., & Hogarth, R. M. (1978). Confidence in judgment: Persistence of the illusion of validity. *Psychological Review, 85*(5), 395–416. https://doi.org/10.1037/0033-295X.85.5.395

Eisenhardt, K. M. (1989a). Agency theory. An assessment and review. *Academy of Management Review, 14*(1), 57–74.

Eisenhardt, K. M. (1989b). Making fast strategic decisions in high-velocity environments. *Academy of Management Journal, 32*(3), 543–576. https://doi.org/10.5465/256434

Eisenhardt, K. M. (1999). Strategy as strategic decision making. *MIT Sloan Management Review, 40*(3), 65–72.

Eisenhardt, K. M., & Zbaracki, M. J. (1992). Strategic decision making. *Strategic Management Journal, 13*(Special Issue), 17–37.

Eisenkraft, N. (2013). Accurate by way of aggregation. *Journal of Experimental Social Psychology, 49*(2), 277–279. https://doi.org/10.1016/j.jesp.2012.11.005

Ekman, P. (1992). Facial expression and emotion. *American Psychologist, 48*(4), 384–392.

Ekman, P. (1994). Strong evidence for universals in facial expressions: A reply to Russell's mistaken critique. *Psychological Bulletin, 115*(2), 268–287.

Ekman, P., & Friesen, W. V. (1974). Detecting deception from the body or face. *Journal of Personality and Social Psychology, 29*(3), 288–298. 10.1037/h0036006

Ekman, P., & Davidson, R. J. (Eds.). (1994). *Series in affective science. The nature of emotion: Fundamental questions*. Oxford University Press.

Ekman, P., & Keltner, D. (1997). Universal facial expressions of emotion: An old controversy and new findings. In U. C. Segerstråle, & P. Molnár (Eds.), *Nonverbal communication: Where nature meets culture* (pp. 27–46). Lawrence Erlbaum Associates.

Ekuma, K. (2012). The importance of predictive and face validity in employee selection and ways of maximizing them: An assessment of three selection method. *International Journal of Business and Management*, *7*(22), 115–122. doi:10.5539/ijbm.v7n22p115

Elbanna, S. (2015). Intuition in project management and missing links: Analyzing the predicating effects of environment and the mediating role of reflexivity. *International Journal of Project Management*, *33*(6), 1236–1248. https://doi.org/10.1016/j.ijproman.2015.02.004

Elbanna, S., Di Benedetto, C. A., & Gherib, J. (2015). Do environment and intuition matter in the relationship between decision politics and success? *Journal of Management & Organization*, *21*(1), 60–81. https://doi.org/10.1017/jmo.2014.65

Elfenbein, H. A., & Ambady, N. (2002). On the universality and cultural specificity of emotion recognition: A meta-analysis. *Psychological Bulletin*, *128*(2), 203–235. https://doi.org/10.1037/0033-2909.128.2.203

Elger, C. E. (2013). *Neuroleadership: Erkenntnisse der Hirnforschung für die Führung von Mitarbeitern [Neuroleadership: Insights from brain research for the leadership of employees]*. Haufe Lexware.

Eliëns, R., Eling, K., Gelper, S., & Langerak, F. (2018). Rational versus intuitive gatekeeping: Escalation of commitment in the front end of NPD. *Journal of Product Innovation Management*, *35*(6), 890–907. https://doi.org/10.1111/jpim.12452

Eling, K., Langerak, F., & Griffin, A. (2015). The performance effects of combining rationality and intuition in making early new product idea evaluation decisions. *Creativity and innovation management*, *24*(3), 464–477.

Ellis, S., Mendel, R., & Nir, M. (2006). Learning From Successful and Failed Experience: The Moderating Role of Kind of After-Event Review. *Journal of Applied Psychology*, *91*(3), 669–680.

Epstein, S. (1990). Cognitive experiential self-theory. In L. A. Pervin (Ed.), *Handbook of personality: Theory and research* (pp. 165–192). The Guilford Press.

El Othman, R., El Othman, R., Hallit, R., Obeid, S., & Hallit, S. (2020). Personality traits, emotional intelligence and decision-making styles in Lebanese universities medical students. *BMC Psychology*, *8*(46), 2020. https://doi.org/10.1186/s40359-020-00406-4

Engelen, E.-M. (2010). Emotion und Intuition. Zwei ungleiche Geschwister [Emotion and intuition. Two unequal siblings]. In R. Rosenzweig (Ed.), *Geistesblitz und Neuronendonner. Intuition, Kreativität und Phantasie* (pp. 121–137). Mentis.

Epstein, S. (1994). Integration of the cognitive and the psychodynamic unconscious. *American Psychologist*, *49*(8), 709–724. https://doi.org/10.1037/0003-066X.49.8.709

Epstein, S. (2003). Cognitive-experiential self-theory of personality. In I. B. Weiner (Ed.), *Handbook of psychology* (pp. 159–184). John Wiley & Sons, Inc. https://doi.org/10.1002/0471264385.wei0507

Epstein, S. (2008). Intuition from the perspective of cognitive experiential self-theory. In H. Plessner, C. Betsch, & T. Betsch (Eds.), *Intuition in judgment and decision making* (pp. 23–37). Lawrence Erlbaum Associates.

Epstein, S., & Pacini, R. (2000). Some basic issues regarding dual-process theories from the perspective of cognitive-experiential self-theory. In S. Chaiken, & Y. Trope (Eds.), *Dual-process theories in social psychology* (pp. 462–482). Guilford Press.

Epstein, S., Pacini, R., Denes-Raj, V., & Heier., H. (1996). Individual differences in intuitive experiential and analytical-rational thinking styles. *Journal of Personality and Social Psychology, 70*(2), 390–405.

Ernst, H. (2003). Intuition. Können wir unserem Bauchgefühl vertrauen? [Intuition. Can we trust our gut feeling?]. *Psychologie Heute*, 03, 20–27.

Ernst& Young (2020). *EY Studierendenstudie 2020 (EY Student Study 2020)*. https://www.ey.com/de_de/news/2020/10/ey-mehr-als-ein-viertel-der-studierenden-aendert-wegen-corona-plaene-fuer-den-berufseinstieg

Etherington, K. (2004). *Becoming a Reflexive Researcher*. Jessica Kingsley.

Etherington, K. (2016). Personal experience and critical reflexivity in counselling and psychotherapy research. *Counselling and Psychotherapy Research, 17*(2), 1–10. doi:10.1002/capr.12080

Ethikbeirat HR Tech (2020). *Richtlinien für den verantwortungsvollen Einsatz von Künstlicher Intelligenz und weiteren digitalen Technologien in der Personalarbeit [Guidelines for the responsible use of artificial intelligence and other digital technologies in HR work*]. https://www.ethikbeirat-hrtech.de/

European Commission (2019). *Ethics guidelines for trustworthy AI*. https://digital-strategy.ec.europa.eu/en/library/ethics-guidelines-trustworthy-ai

Evans, J. S. B. T. (2008). Dual-processing accounts of reasoning, judgment, and social cognition. *Annual Review of Psychology, 59*, 255–278. https://doi.org/10.1146/annurev.psych.59.103006.093629

Evans, J. S. B. T. (2010a). Intuition and reasoning: A dual-process perspective. *Psychological Inquiry, 21*(4), 313–326. https://doi.org/10.1080/1047840X.2010.521057

Evans, J. S. B. (2010b). *Thinking twice: Two minds in one brain*. Oxford University Press.

Evans, J. S. B. T., & Over, D. E. (2013). *Rationality and reasoning*. Psychology Press.

Evans, J. S. B., & Stanovich, K. E. (2013). Dual-process theories of higher cognition: Advancing the debate. *Perspectives on Psychological Science, 8*(3), 223–241. https://doi.org/10.1177/1745691612460685

Exley, C. L., & Kessler, J. B. (2021). *Information Avoidance and Image Concerns*. NBER Working Paper 28376, January 2021. Revised May 2021. http://www.nber.org/papers/w28376

Eysenck, H. J. (1953). *The structure of human personality*. Methuen.

Fallgatter. (2013). Personalbeurteilung [Personnel appraisal]. In R. Stock-Homburg (Ed.). *Handbuch strategisches personalmanagement* (pp. 171–185). Springer. doi:10.1007/978-3-658-00431-6_10,

Farago, B., Zide, J. S., & Shahani-Denning, C. (2013). Selection interviews: Role of interviewer warmth, interview structure, and interview outcome in applicants' perceptions of organizations. *Consulting Psychology Journal: Practice and Research, 65*(3), 224–239. https://doi.org/10.1037/a0034300

Farr, J. L., & Tippins, N. T. (2010). Handbook of employee selection: An introduction and overview. In J. L. Farr, & N. T. Tippins (Eds.), *Handbook of employee selection* (pp. 1–6). Routledge/Taylor & Francis Group.

Fehrenbacher, D. D. (2019). Subjective performance evaluation – a curse or blessing? *Controlling & Management Review, 63*(3), 30–36. https://doi.org/10.1007/s12176-019-0005-x

Felfe, J., Elprana, G., Gatzka, M., & Stiehl, S. (2012). *FÜMO. Hamburger Führungsmotivationsinventar [Hamburg Motivation to Lead Inventory]*. Hogrefe.

Felfe, J., & Gatzka, M. (2013). Führungsmotivation [Management Motivation]. In W. Sarges (Ed.), *Management-Diagnostik* (4th ed.) (pp. 308–315). Hogrefe.

Fellner, K. (2019). *Moderne Personalauswahl [Modern personnel selection]: Renommierte Experten über Trends, neue Technologien, Chancen und Risiken in der Eignungsdiagnostik*. Springer.

Fellner, K. (2019a). Digitalisierung in der Personalauswahl [Digitization in personnel selection]. In K. Fellner (Ed.). *Moderne Personalauswahl* (pp. 1–16). Springer.

Feloni, R. (2017). *Consumer-goods giant Unilever has been hiring employees using brain games and artificial intelligence – And it's a huge success*. Business Insider. https://www.businessinsider.com/unilever-artificial-intelligence-hiring-process-2017-6?r=DE&IR=T

Fenkart, P. S. (2018). *Chefsache Intuition: Besser managen, beurteilen und entscheiden durch intuitive Kompetenz [Management by intuition: Better management, assessment and decision-making through intuitive competence]*. Springer Fachmedien. https://doi.org/10.1007/978-3-658-14447-0.

Ferguson, G. (1999). *Cracking the intuitive code: Understanding and mastering your intuitive power*. Contemporary Books.

Fernandez-Araoz, C. (2007). *Great people decisions: Why they matter so much, why they are so hard, and how you can master them*. Wiley.

Fesefeld, J. (2018). *Künstliche Intelligenz im Personalmanagement* [Artifical intelligence in human resource management]. (dgp informationen, pp. 6–37). dgp Deutsche Gesellschaft für Personalwesen e. V. https://www.dgp.de/index.php/blogbeitrag-lesen/dgp-informationen-2018.html

Feyerabend, P. K. (1976). On the critique of scientific reason. In R. S. Cohen, P. K. Feyerabend, & M. W. Wartofsky (Eds.), *Essays in Memory of Imre Lakatos. Boston Studies in the Philosophy of Science* (Vol. 39, pp. 109–143). Springer, Dordrecht. https://doi.org/10.1007/978-94-010-1451-9_11

Festinger, L. (1957). *A theory of cognitive dissonance*. Stanford University Press.

Fielden, J. S., & Dulek, R. (1982). What rejection letters say about your company. *Business Horizons*, *25*(5), 40–45. https://doi.org/10.1016/0007-6813(82)90061-1

Fific, M., & Gigerenzer, G. (2014). Are two interviewers better than one? *Journal of Business Research*, *67*(8), 1771–1779.

Fine, S. (2010). Cross-cultural integrity testing as a marker of regional corruption rates. *International Journal of Selection and Assessment*, *18*(3), 251–259. https://doi.org/10.1111/j.1468-2389.2010.00508.x

Fink, G., & Meierewert, S. (2001). *Interkulturelles Management. Österreichische Perspektiven [Intercultural Management. Austrian perspectives]*. Springer.

Finkelstein, L. M., Frautschy Demuth, R. L., & Sweeney, D. L. (2007). Bias against overweight job applicants: Further explorations of when and why. *Human Resource Management*, *46*(2), 203–222. https://doi.org/10.1002/hrm.20157

Finlay, W., & Coverdill, J. E. (1999). The search game: Organizational conflicts and the use of headhunters. *Sociological Quarterly*, *40*(1), 11–30.

Fischhoff, B. (1975). Hindsight is not equal to foresight: The effect of outcome knowledge on judgment under uncertainty. *Journal of Experimental Psychology*, *1*(3), 288–299.

Fischhoff, B., & Beyth, R. (1975). I knew it would happen: Remembered probabilities of once – future things. *Organizational Behavior and Human Performance*, *13*(1), 11–16.

Fiske, S. T., & Taylor, S. E. (2021). *Social cognition: From brains to culture* (4th ed.). Sage Publications.

Flaherty, K. E., & Pappas, J. M. (2004). Job selection among salespeople: A bounded rationality perspective. *Industrial Marketing Management*, *33*, 325–332. doi:10.1016/S0019-8501(03)00082-8

Flörke, I. (2020). *Digitale Transformation – Der Einfluss neuer Auswahlmethoden auf die Personalauswahl* [Digital Transformation – The Influence of New Selection Methods on Personnel Selection]. Unpublished master thesis, Leuphana University, Lueneburg.

Fonagy, P., Gergely, G., Jurist, E. L., & Target, M. (2002). *Affect regulation, mentalization, and the development of the self*. Other Press.

Forgas, J. P. (1995). Mood and judgment: The affect infusion model (AIM). *Psychological Bulletin, 117*(1), 39–66.

Forgas, J. P. (Ed.). (2001). *Studies in emotion and social interaction: Second series. Feeling and thinking: The role of affect in social cognition*. Cambridge University Press.

Fox, S., & Spector, P. E. (2000). Relations of emotional intelligence, practical intelligence, general intelligence, and trait affectivity with interview outcomes: It's not all just 'g'. *Journal of Organizational Behavior, 21*(2), 203–220. https://doi.org/10.1002/(SICI)1099-1379(200003)21:2<203::AID-JOB38>3.0.CO;2-Z

Fortmann, H. R., & Kolocek, B. (2018). *Arbeitswelt der Zukunft [Working world of the future]*. Springer Fachmedien Wiesbaden. https://doi.org/10.1007/978-3-658-20969-8.

Franck, E., & Zellner, J. (2001). Emotionale Grenzen der Vernunft und ihre Konsequenzen für die Neue Institutionenökonomie [Emotional Limits of Reason and their Consequences for the New Institutional Economics]. In G. Schreyögg, & J. Sydow (Eds.), *Emotionen und management* (pp. 249–276). Gabler.

Frank, F., & Kanning, U. P. (2014). Lücken im Lebenslauf. Ein validest Instrument der Personalauswahl? [Gaps in the curriculum vitae. A valid instrument for personnel selection?]. *Zeitschrift Für Arbeits- U. Organisationspsychologie, 58*(3), 155–162.

Franke, M. (2019). *Diese 2 Eigenschaften sind laut Google-CEO bei Bewerbern am wichtigsten [According to Google's CEO, these 2 characteristics are most important for applicants]*. https://arbeits-abc.de/bewerber-muessen-diese-2-eigenschaften-besitzen

Frankl, V. E. (2002). *Der unbewusste Gott – Psychotherapie und Religion* [The unconscious God: psychotherapy and theology]. dtv. (Originally published in 1948).

Frankl, V. E. (2006). *Man's Search for Meaning. An Introduction to Logotherapy*, Beacon Press (Originally published in 1946).

Freud, A. (1937). *The ego and the mechanisms of defence*. Hogarth Press and Institute of Psycho-Analysis.

Frey, C. B., & Osborne, M. A. (2013). *The Future of Employment: How susceptible are jobs to computerisation? Oxford Martin School*. University of Oxford. http://sep4u.gr/wp-content/uploads/The_Future_of_Employment_ox_2013.pdf.

Friesen, J. P., Kawakami, K., Vingilis-Jaremko, L., Caprara, R., Sidhu, D. M., Williams, A., Hugenberg, K., Rodríguez-Bailón, R., Cañadas, E., & Niedenthal, P. (2019). Perceiving happiness in an intergroup context: The role of race and attention to the eyes in differentiating between true and false smiles. *Journal of Personality and Social Psychology, 2019*. doi:10.1037/pspa0000139.

Frijda, N. H. (1986). *The emotions*. Cambridge University Press.

Frijda, N. (1996). *Die Gesetze der Emotionen* ["The laws of emotions"] *Zeitschrift für psychosomatische Medizin und Psychotherapie, 42*, 205–221. https://www.jstor.org/stable/23997755

Fröse, M. W., Kaudela-Baum, S., & Dievernich, F. E. P. (Eds.). (2015). *Emotion und Intuition in Führung und Organisation [Emotion and intuition in leadership and organization]*. Springer Fachmedien. https://doi.org/10.1007/978-3-658-07796-9

Fröse, M. W., Kaudela-Baum, S., & Dievernich, F. E. P. (2015b). *Die Leidenschaften haben die Menschen die Vernunft gelehrt: Eine Annäherung an Intuition und Emotion* [Passions have taught men reason: An approach to intuition and emotion]. In M. W. Fröse, S. Kaudela-Baum, & F. E. P. Dievernich (Eds.), *Emotion und Intuition in Führung und Organisation* (pp. 1–15). Springer Fachmedien. https://doi.org/10.1007/978-3-658-07796-9_1

Fuchs, T. (2020). *Verteidigung des Menschen [Defense of the human being].* Grundfragen einer verkörperten Anthropologie Suhrkamp Taschenbuch Wissenschaft.
Funder, D. C. (2003). Toward a social psychology of person judgments: Implications for person perception accuracy and self-knowledge. In J. P. Forgas, K. D. Williams, W. von Hippel, J. P. Forgas, K. D. Williams, & W. von Hippel (Eds.), *Social judgments: Implicit and explicit processes* (pp. 115–133). Cambridge University Press.
Funder, D. C. (2012). Accurate personality judgment. *Current Directions in Psychological Science, 21*(3), 177–182. doi:10.1177/0963721412445309
Funk, L., Nachtwei, J., & Melchers, K. (2015). Die Kluft zwischen Wissenschaft und Praxis in der Personalauswahl. *Personalquarterly*, 26–31. https://zeitschriften.haufe.de/ePaper/personal-quarterly/2015/E20756CB/files/assets/common/downloads/publication.pdf#page=26.
Gallo, C. (2014). *Talk like TED.* St. Martin's Press.
Gannon, M. J. (1983). Managerial ignorance. *Business Horizons, 26*(3), 26–32. https://doi.org/10.1016/0007-6813(83)90025-3
Garud, R., Tuertscher, P., & van de Ven, A. H. (2013). Perspectives on innovation processes. *Academy of Management Annals, 7*(1), 775–819. https://doi.org/10.5465/19416520.2013.791066
Gassner, B. (2006). *Empathie in der Pädagogik: Theorien, Implikationen, Bedeutung, Umsetzung* [Empathy in pedagogy: theories, implications, meaning, implementation]. Ph.D. thesis Ruprecht-Karls-University Heidelberg, Germany. http://archiv.ub.uniheidelberg.de/volltextserver/id/eprint/7224
Gasteiger, R. M., Kaschube, J., & Rathjen, P. (2016). *Interkulturelle Führung in Organisationen [Intercultural leadership in organisations].* Springer Fachmedien Wiesbaden. https://doi.org/10.1007/978-3-658-12301-7.
Gates, B. (2016). *When Will I Am Met Bill Gates – Inspiring The Future Tech Generation.* https://thesource.com/2016/11/23/when-will-i-am-met-bill-gates-inspiring-the-future-tech-generation/
Gärtner, C. (2020). *Smart HRM: Digitale Tools für die Personalarbeit [Digital tools for HR Management].* Springer Fachmedien. https://doi.org/10.1007/978-3-658-29431-1.
Geffers, G., & Ziegler, M. (2020). Die Zuordnung zu Persönlichkeitstypen ist oft nicht stabil [The assignment to personality types is often not stable]. *Themenzentrierte Interaktion, 34*(1), 64–71. https://doi.org/10.13109/tzin.2020.34.1.64
Gehrlein, T. M., Dipboye, R. L., & Shahani, C. (1993). Nontraditional Validity Calculations and Differential Interviewer Experience: Implications for Selection Interviews. *Educational and Psychological Measurement, 53*(2), 457–469.
Geirhos, R., Jacobsen, J.-H., Michaelis, C., Zemel, R., Brendel, W., Bethge, M., & Wichmann, F. A. (2020). *Shortcut Learning in Deep Neural Networks.* https://arxiv.org/abs/2004.07780v3
Geiselhardt, E. (2021). Was Coaches von den Neuro-Wissenschaften lernen können [What coaches can learn from neuroscience]. *RAUEN Coaching-Newsletter 06/2021* https://www.coaching-magazin.de/prozesse-settings/was-coaches-von-den-neuro-wissenschaften-lernen-koennen
Gelfand, M. J., Raver, J. L., Nishii, L., Leslie, L. M., Lun, J., Lim, B. C., Duan, L., Almaliach, A., Ang, S., Arnadottir, J., Aycan, Z., Boehnke, K., Boski, P., Cabecinhas, R., Chan, D., Chhokar, J., D'Amato, A., Ferrer, M., Fischlmayr, I. C., & Yamaguchi, S. (2011). Differences between tight and loose cultures: A 33-nation study. *Science (New York, N.Y.), 332*(6033), 1100–1104. https://doi.org/10.1126/science.1197754
Gendlin, E. T., & Wiltschko, J. (2011). *Focusing in der Praxis. Eine schulenübergreifende Methode für Psychotherapie und Alltag [Focusing in Practice. A cross-school method for psychotherapy and everyday life].* Klett-Cotta Verlag.

Gendron, M., Roberson, D., van der Vyver, J. M., & Barrett, L. F. (2014). Perceptions of emotion from facial expressions are not culturally universal: Evidence from a remote culture. *Emotion, 14*, 251–262.

Gerrig, R. J. (2015). *Psychologie [Psychology]* (20th ed.). Pearson.

Gigerenzer, G. (2007). *Gut feelings: The intelligence of the unconscious*. Viking.

Gigerenzer, G. (2008a). *Bauchentscheidungen: Die Intelligenz des Unbewussten und die Macht der Intuition [Gut decisions: The intelligence of the unconscious and the power of intuition]*. Goldmann.

Gigerenzer, G. (2008b). Moral Intuition = fast and frugal heuristics? In W. Sinnott-Armstrong (Ed.), *The cognitive science of morality: Intuition and diversity* (pp. 1–26). The MIT Press.

Gigerenzer, G. (2008c). Der Bauch wird unterschätzt [The gut is underestimated]. Interview in *Frankfurter Allgemeine Zeitung*, 18./19.10.2008, p. C5.

Gigerenzer, G. (2013). *Risiko: Wie man die richtigen Entscheidungen trifft [Risk: How to make the right decisions]*. Bertelsmann.

Gigerenzer, G. (2021). Der Meister der klaren Entscheidung [Master of clear decisions]. *Psychologie Heute*, 1, 2021, 58–66.

Gigerenzer, G., & Brighton, H. (2009). Homo heuristicus: Why biased minds make better inferences. *Topics in Cognitive Science, 1*(1), 107–143. https://doi.org/10.1111/j.1756-8765.2008.01006.x

Gigerenzer, G., & Gaissmaier, W. (2011). Heuristic decision making. *Annual Review of Psychology, 62*, 451–482. https://doi.org/10.1146/annurev-psych-120709-145346

Gigerenzer, G., & Gaissmaier, W. (2012). *Intuition und Führung. Wie gute Entscheidungen entstehen [Intuition and leadership. How good decisions are made]*. Bertelsmann Stiftung.

Gigerenzer, G., & Gaissmaier, W. (2015). Intuition und Führung [Intuition and Leadership]. In M. W. Fröse, S. Kaudela-Baum, & F. E. P. Dievernich (Eds.), *Emotion und Intuition in Führung und Organisation* (pp. 19–42). Springer Fachmedien. https://doi.org/10.1007/978-3-658-07796-9_2

Gigerenzer, G., & Selten, R. (Eds.). (2001). *Bounded rationality: The adaptive toolbox*. MIT Press.

Gigerenzer, G., & Todd, P. M. (1999). Fast und frugal heuristics: The adaptive toolbox. In G. Gigerenzer, & P. M. Todd (Eds.), *Simple heuristics that make us smart* (pp. 3–36). Oxford University Press.

Gigerenzer, G., Galesic, M., & Garcia-Retamero, R. (2013). Stereotypes about men's and women's intuitions: A study of two nations. *Journal of Cross-Cultural Psychology, 45*, 62–81. doi:10.1177/0022022113487074

Gigerenzer, G., Hertwig, R., Hoffrage, U., & Sedlmeier, P. (2008). Cognitive illusions reconsidered. In C. R. Plott, & V. L. Smith (Eds.). *Handbook of experimental economics results* (Vol. 1, pp. 1018–1034). Elsevier. doi:10.1016/S1574-0722(07)00109-6

Gilbert, D. T., & Malone, P. S. (1995). The correspondence bias. *Psychological Bulletin, 117*, 21–38.

Gilbert, D. T., Krull, D. S., & Malone, P. S. (1990). Unbelieving the unbelievable: Some problems in the rejection of false information. *Journal of Personality and Social Psychology, 59*(4), 601–613.

Gilliland, S. W. (1993). The perceived fairness of selection systems: An organizational justice perspective. *Academy of Management Review, 18*(4), 694. https://doi.org/10.2307/258595

Gilliland, S. W. (1994). Effects of procedural and distributive justice on reactions to a selection system. *The Journal of Applied Psychology, 79*(5), 691–701. https://doi.org/10.1037/0021-9010.79.5.691

Gilliland, S. W., & Steiner, D. D. (2012). Applicant reactions to testing and selection. In N. Schmitt (Ed.), *Oxford library of psychology: The Oxford handbook of personnel assessment and selection* (pp. 629–666). Oxford University Press.

Gilovich, T., & Griffin, D. (2002). Introduction – heuristics and biases: Then and now. In T. Girovich, D. Griffin, & D. Kahneman (Eds.), *Heuristics and biases: The psychology of intuitive judgment* (pp. 1–18). Cambridge University Press.

Gilovich, T., Griffin, D., & Kahneman, D. (Eds.). (2002). *Heuristics and biases: The psychology of intuitive judgment*. Cambridge University Press.

Gino, F. (2014). *How Data Beats Intuition at Making Selection Decisions: An algorithm beats the experts at hiring*. https://www.scientificamerican.com/article/how-data-beats-intuition-at-making-selection-decisions/

Glaser, B. G., & Strauss, A. L. (1967). *The discovery of grounded theory: Strategies for qualitative research. Observations*. Routledge.

Glöckner, A., & Ebert, I. D. (2011). Legal intuition and expertise. In M. Sinclair (Ed.), *Handbook of intuition research* (pp. 157–167). Edward Elgar.

Glöckner, A., & Engel, C. (2013). Can we trust intuitive jurors? Standards of proof and the probative value of evidence in coherence-based reasoning. *Journal of Empirical Legal Studies*, *10*(2), 230–252. https://doi.org/10.1111/jels.12009

Glöckner, A., & Towight, E. V. (2015). Entscheidungen zwischen "Intuition" und "Rationalität". *Deutsche Richterzeitung*, *15*(07/08), 270–273.

Glöckner, A., & Witteman, C. (Eds.). (2010). *Foundations for tracing intuition: Challenges and methods*. Psychology Press.

Glöckner, A., & Witteman, C. (2010a). Beyond dual-process models: A categorisation of processes underlying intuitive judgment and decision making. *Thinking & Reasoning*, *16*(1), 1–25. https://doi.org/10.1080/13546780903395748

Glöckner, A., & Witteman, C. (2010b). Foundations for Tracing Intuition. In A. Glöckner, & C. Witteman (Eds.), *Foundations for tracing intuition: Challenges and methods* (pp. 1–23). Psychology Press.

Gmür, M., & Schwerdt, B. (2005). Der Beitrag des Personalmanagements zum Unternehmenserfolg: Eine Metaanalyse nach 20 Jahren Erfolgsfaktorenforschung [The contribution of personnel management to the success of the company: A meta analysis after 20 years of success factor research]. *German Journal of Human Resource Management*, *19*(3), 221–251. https://doi.org/10.1177/239700220501900301

Goinger Kreis – Initiative Zukunft Personal und Beschäftigung e.V. (2019). Digital HR Manifesto. https://www.digital-hr-manifesto.org/

Goinger Kreis e.V. (2015). Globale Standards für das Human Resources Management [Global standards for human resources management]. In Goinger Kreis – Initiative Zukunft Personal und Beschäftigung e.V. (Ed.), *Zukunft Personal Beschäftigung* (pp. 93–116). Springer Gabler. https://doi.org/10.1007/978-3-658-09196-5_7

Goldberg, P. (1983). *The intuitive edge. Understanding and developing intuition*. TarcherPerigee.

Goldberg, P. (1989). The many faces of intuition. In W. H. Agor (Ed.), *Intuition in organizations: Leading and managing productively* (pp. 62–77). Sage Publications.

Goldstein, D. G., & Gigerenzer, G. (2002). Models of ecological rationality: The recognition heuristic. *Psychological Review*, *109*(1), 75–90. https://doi.org/10.1037//0033-295X.109.1.75

Goleman, D. (1996). *Emotional intelligence: Why it can matter more than IQ*. Bantam Books.

Goleman, D. (2004). What makes a leader? *Harvard Business Review*, *82*(1), 82–91.

Gore, J., & Sadler-Smith, E. (2011). Unpacking intuition: A process and outcome framework. *Review of General Psychology*, *15*(4), 304–316. https://doi.org/10.1037/a0025069

Gkorezis, P., Georgiou, K., Nikolaou, I., & Kyriazati, A. (2020). Gamified or traditional situational judgement test? A moderated mediation model of recommendation intentions via organizational attractiveness. *European Journal of Work and Organizational Psychology*. https://doi.org/10.1080/1359432X.2020.1746827.

Gorman, C. A., & Rentsch, J. R. (2009). Evaluating frame-of-reference rater training effectiveness using performance schema accuracy. *The Journal of Applied Psychology, 94*, 1336–1344. doi:10.1037/a0016476

Görlich, Y., & Schuler, H. (2014). Personalentscheidung, Nutzen und Fairness [Personnel decisions, benefits and fairness]. In H. Schuler, & U. P. Kanning (Eds.), *Lehrbuch der Personalpsychologie* (3. ed, pp. 1137–1200). Hogrefe.

Görz, G., & Wachsmuth, I. (2003). Einleitung [Introduction]. In G. Görtz, C.-R. Rollinger, & J. Schneeberger (Eds.), *Handbuch der künstlichen Intelligenz [Handbook of Artificial Intelligence* (pp. 1–16). De Gruyter.

Graf, R. (2018). *Die neue Entscheidungskultur. Mit gemeinsam getragenen Entscheidungen zum Erfolg [The new decision-making culture. Success through jointly supported decisions].* Hanser Verlag.

Grandey, A. A. (2000). Emotional regulation in the workplace: A new way to conceptualize emotional labor. *Journal of Occupational Health Psychology, 5*(1), 95–110. https://doi.org/10.1037/1076-8998.5.1.95

Grant, A. (2021). *Think again. The power of knowing what you don't know.* Random House.

Greenberg, J. (1990). Organizational justice: Yesterday, today, and tomorrow. *Journal of Management, 16*(2), 399–432. doi:10.1177/014920639001600208

Greenberg, J., Pyszczynski, T., & Solomon, S. (1982). The self-serving attributional bias: Beyond self-presentation. *Journal of Experimental Social Psychology, 18*(1), 56–67. https://doi.org/10.1016/0022-1031(82)90081-6

Greple (2021). Künstliche Intelligenz in HR [Artifical Intelligence in Human Resource Management). https://greple.de/?cn-reloaded=1

Grohnert, T., Meuwissen, R.H.G., & Gijselaers, W. H. (2018a). Deliberate Practice as a Lever for Professional Judgment: Lessons from Informal Workplace Learning. In G. Messmann, M. Segers, & F. Dochy (Eds.). *Informal learning at work: Triggers, Antecedents, and Consequences*, p. 63–79.

Grohnert, T., Meuwissen, R.H.G. & Gijselaers, W.H. (2018b). Enabling Young Professionals to Learn from Errors - the Role of a Supportive Learning Climate in Crossing Help Network Boundaries. *Vocations and Learning* 12, 217–243 (2019). https://doi.org/10.1007/s12186-018-9206-2

Gross, J. J. (2014). Emotion regulation: Conceptual and empirical foundations. In J. J. Gross (Ed.), *Handbook of emotion regulation* (pp. 3–20). The Guilford Press.

Gross, J. J. (Ed.). (2014). *Handbook of emotion regulation* (2nd ed.). Guilford Press.

Gross, J. J., & Thompson, R. A. (2007). Emotion regulation. In J. J. Gross (Ed.), *Handbook of emotion regulation* (pp. 3–24). The Guilford Press.

Grove, W. M., Zald, D. H., Lebow, B. S., Snitz, B. E., & Nelson, C. (2000). Clinical versus mechanical prediction: A meta-analysis. *Psychological Assessment, 12*(1), 19–30. https://doi.org/10.1037/1040-3590.12.1.19

Groves, K., & Vance, C. (2009). Examining thinking style, EQ, and organizational commitment. *Journal of Managerial Issues, 21*(3), 344–366.

Groves, K. S., Vance, C. M., Choi, D. Y., & Mendez, J. L. (2008). An examination of the nonlinear thinking style profile stereotype of successful entrepreneurs. *Journal of Enterprising Culture, 16*(2), 133–159.

Gudykunst, W. B., & Ting-Toomey, S. (1988). *Culture and interpersonal communication.* Sage Publications.

Gudykunst, W. B., & Ting-Toomey, S. (1996). Communication in personal relationships across cultures: An introduction. In W. B. Gudykunst, S. Ting-Toomey, & T. Nishida (Eds.), *Communication in personal relationships across cultures* (pp. 3–18). Sage Publications.

Guilfoyle, S., Bergman, S. M., Hartwell, C., & Powers, J. (2016). Social media, big data, and employment decisions: Mo' Data, Mo' problems? In R. N. Landers, & G. B. Schmidt (Eds.), *Social media in employee selection and recruitment* (pp. 127–155). Springer International Publishing. https://doi.org/10.1007/978-3-319-29989-1_7

Guion, R. M. (1998). *Assessment, measurement, and prediction for personnel decisions*. Lawrence Erlbaum Associates Publishers.

Guion, R. M. (2011). *Assessment, measurement, and prediction for personnel decisions* (2nd.). Routledge.

Gullestrup, H. (2002). The Complexity of Intercultural Communication in Cross-CulturalManagement. *Journal of Intercultural Communication*, *6*(2002), 1–19.

Gulliford, F., & Parker Dixon, A. (2019). AI: The HR revolution. *Strategic HR Review*, *18*(2), 52–55. doi:10.1108/shr-12-2018-0104

Gunkel, M., Schlägel, C., & Engle, R. L. (2013). Culture's influence on emotional intelligence: An empirical study of nine countries. *Journal of International Management*, *20*(2), 256–274. http://dx.doi.org/10.1016/j.intman.2013.10.002

Guthrie, C., Rachlinski, J. J., & Wistrich, A. J. (2007). Blinking on the bench: How judges decide cases. *Cornell Law Review*, *93*(1), 1–44.

Haarhaus, B., & Ristel, N. (2013). Akzeptanz schriftlicher Testverfahren: Eine empirische Untersuchung auf Basis des DGP A3 [Acceptance of written test procedures: An empirical study based on the DGP A3]. *DGP-Informationen*, *54*(63), https://www.dgp.de/files/dgp/downloads/dgp%20Informationen/DGP%20Informationen%202013.pdf

Hafsi, T., & Turgut, G. (2013). Boardroom diversity and its effect on social performance: Conceptualization and empirical evidence. *Journal of Business Ethics*, *112*, 463–479. doi:10.1007/s10551-012-1272-z

Hagendorff, J., & Keasey, K. (2012). The value of board diversity in banking: Evidence from the market for corporate control. *The European Journal of Finance*, *18*(1), 41–58.

Hahn, D. C., & Dipboye, R. L. (1988). Effects of training and information on the accuracy and reliability of job evaluations. *Journal of Applied Psychology*, *73*(2), 146–153. https://doi.org/10.1037/0021-9010.73.2.146

Haidt, J. (2001). The emotional dog and its rational tail: A social intuitionist approach to moral judgment. *Psychological Review*, *108*(4), 814–834. https://doi.org/10.1037/0033-295X.108.4.814

Haidt, J. (2007). The new synthesis in moral psychology. *Science*, *316*(5827), 998–1002. https://doi.org/10.1126/science.1137651

Haidt, J. (2012). *The righteous mind: Why good people are divided by politics and religion*. Pantheon.

Halbesleben, J. R. B., Neveu, J.-P., Paustian-Underdahl, S. C., & Westman, M. (2014). Getting to the "COR" understanding the role of resources in conservation of resources theory. *Journal of Management*, *40*(5), 1334–1364. https://doi.org/10.1177/0149206314527130

Half, R. (2019). *Job annehmen trotz schlechten Bauchgefühls? Studie zeigt: Mehrheit der Bewerber ist wegen falscher Jobentscheidung unglücklich. Umfrage im Auftrag des Personaldienstleisters Robert Half [Accepting a job despite a bad gut feeling? Study shows: Majority of applicants are unhappy because of wrong job decision. Survey commissioned by the personnel service provider Robert Half]*. https://www.roberthalf.de/presse/job-annehmen-trotz-schlechten-bauchgefuehls

Hall, E. T. (1967). *Beyond culture*. Anchor Books.

Hall, E. T. (1976). *Beyond culture*. Anchor Books.

Hall, E. T., & Hall, M. R. (1987). *Understanding cultural differences: Germans, French and Americans*. Intercultural Press.

Hall, E. T., & Hall, M. R. (1990). *Understanding cultural differences: Germans, French and Americans*. Intercultural Press.

Hall, J. A. (1978). Gender effects in decoding nonverbal cues. *Psychological Bulletin, 85*(4), 845–857.

Hall, J. A., & Bernieri, J. E. (Eds.). (2001). *Interpersonal sensitivity: Theory and measurement.* Lawrence Erlbaum Associates.

Hall, J. A., Carter, J. D., & Horgan, T. G. (2000). Gender differences in nonverbal communication of emotion. In A. H. Fischer (Ed.), *Studies in emotion and social interaction. Second series. Gender and emotion: Social psychological perspectives* (pp. 97–117). Cambridge University Press. https://doi.org/10.1017/CBO9780511628191.006

Hall, J. A., Gunnery, S. D., Letzring, T. D., Carney, D. R., & Colvin, C. R. (2017). Accuracy of judging affect and accuracy of judging personality: How and when are they related? *Journal of Personality, 85*(5), 583–592. https://doi.org/10.1111/jopy.12262

Hall, L. (2011). Rights and the heart: Emotions and rights claims in the political theory of edmund burke. *The Review of Politics, 73*(4), 609–631.

Hallerberg, S. (2019). *Entscheidungen in der Auswahl – zwischen Rationalität und Intuition [Decisions in personnel selection – between rationality and intuition]*. Unpublished maste thesis, Leuphana University, Lueneburg.

Hamilton, R. H., & Davison, H. K. (2018). The search for skills: Knowledge stars and innovation in the hiring process. *Business Horizons, 61*(3), 409–419. https://doi.org/10.1016/j.bushor.2018.01.006

Hammer, C. (2017). *A Look into Lookism: An Evaluation of Discrimination Based on Physical Attractiveness*. Undergraduate Honors Capstone Projects. 207. https://digitalcommons.usu.edu/honors/207

Hammond, K. R. (2000). Intuition, No! . . . Quasirationality, Yes! *Psychological Inquiry, 21*(4), 327–337. https://doi.org/10.1080/1047840X.2010.521483

Hammond, K. R., Hamm, R. M., Grassia, J., & Pearson, T. (1987). Direct comparison of the efficacy of intuitive and analytical cognition in expert judgment. *IEEE Transactions on Systems, Man, and Cybernetics, 17*(5), 753–770. https://doi.org/10.1109/TSMC.1987.6499282

Hanoch, Y., & Vitouch, O. (2004). When less is more: Information, emotional arousal and the ecological reframing of the Yerkes-Dodson law. *Theory & Psychology, 14*(4), 427–452. https://doi.org/10.1177/0959354304044918

Harari, Y. N. (2014). *Sapiens: A brief history of humankind*. Harvill Secker Random House.

Hardy, J. H. I. I. I., Tey, K. S., & Cyrus-Lai, W. (2021). Bias in context: Small biases in hiring evaluations have big consequences. *Journal of Management, January 2021*. doi:10.1177/0149206320982654.

Hargadon, A., & Sutton, R. I. (2000). Building an innovation factory. *Harvard Business Review, 78*(3), 157–166.

Harn, T. J., & Thornton, G. C. (1985). Recruiter counseling behaviours and applicant impressions. *Journal of Occupational Psychology, 58*(1), 57–65. https://doi.org/10.1111/j.2044-8325.1985.tb00180.x

Harper, S. C. (1988). Intuition: What separates executives from managers. *Business Horizons, 31*(5), 13–19.

Harris, A., & Jones, M. (2018). The dark side of leadership and management. *School Leadership & Management, 38*(5), 475–477. 10.1080/13632434.2018.1509276

Harris, M. M., van Hoye, G., & Lievens, F. (2003). Privacy and attitudes towards internet-based selection systems: A cross-cultural comparison. *International Journal of Selection and Assessment, 11*(2–3), 230–236. https://doi.org/10.1111/1468-2389.00246

Harteis, C. (2014). Investigating intuition under the perspective of expertise: Experiences from two experimental studies. In M. Sinclair (Ed.), *Handbook of research methods on intuition* (pp. 116–129). Edward Elgar Publishing. https://doi.org/10.4337/9781782545996.00018

Harteis, C., Morgenthaler, B., Kugler, C., Ittner, K.-P., Roth, G., & Graf, B. (2011). Intuitive decision making in emergency medicine: An explorative study. In M. Sinclair (Ed.), *Handbook of intuition research* (pp. 145–156). Edward Elgar Publishing.

Harter, J. K., Schmidt, F. L., & Hayes, T. L. (2002). Business-unit-level relationship between employee satisfaction, employee engagement, and business outcomes: A meta-analysis. *The Journal of Applied Psychology, 87*(2), 268–279. https://doi.org/10.1037/0021-9010.87.2.268

Hartmann, M. (2010). *Gefühle: Wie die Wissenschaften sie erklären [Feelings: How science explains them]* (2nd ed.). *Campus »Studium«.* Campus Verlag.

Harvey, L., & Green, D. (1993). Defining quality. *Assessment & Evaluation in Higher Education, 18*(1), 9–34. https://doi.org/10.1080/0260293930180102

Hatfield, E., Cacioppo, J. T., & Rapson, R. L. (1993). Emotional Contagion. *Current Directions in Psychological Science, 2*(3), 96–100. https://doi.org/10.1111/1467-8721.ep10770953

Hatton, N., & Smith, D. (1995). Reflection in teacher education: Towards definition and implementation. *Teaching and Teacher Education, 11*(1), 33–49.

Hausknecht, J. P., Day, D. V., & Thomas, S. C. (2004). Applicant reactions to selection procedures: An updated model and meta-analysis. *Personnel Psychology, 57*(3), 639–683. https://doi.org/10.1111/j.1744-6570.2004.00003.x

Hayes, J., & Allinson, C. W. (1994). Cognitive style and its relevance for management practice. *British Journal of Management, 5*(1), 53–71. https://doi.org/10.1111/j.1467-8551.1994.tb00068.x

Hayes, J., Allinson, C. W., Hudson, R. S., & Keasey, K. (2003). Cognitive style index. *Journal of Occupational and Organizational Psychology, 76*(2), 269–278.

Hänsel, M. (2014). Intuition als Schlüsselkompetenz im 21. Jahrhundert. Wissenschaftliche Grundlagen, berufliche Anwendung und transrationale Weiterentwicklung [Intuition as a Key Competence in the twenty-first Century. Scientific foundations, professional application and transrational further development]. *Zeitschrift Für Bewusstseinswissenschaften, 2*, 1–20.

Hänsel, M., Zeuch, A., & Schweitzer, J. (2002). Erfolgsfaktor Intuition [Sucess factor intuition). *OrganisationsEntwicklung, 02*, 40–51.

Hegel, G. W. F. (1803). *Über die Herstellung des gehörigen Verhältnisses der Bildung des Herzes zur Bildung des Kopfes als die dermalige Hauptaufgabe der Erziehung [On the establishment of the proper relationship of the formation of the heart to the formation of the head as the current main task of education].* Bey Joseph Lentner

Heil, A. (2013). *Alle Kunst ist Intuition? [Is all art intuition?].* HAYS. https://www.haysworld.de/ausgaben/2013/01/alle-kunst-ist-intuition

Heinen, E. (1962). Die Zielfunktion der Unternehmung [The goal function of the company]. In H. Koch (Ed.), *Zur Theorie der Unternehmung. Festschrift zum 65. Geburtstag von E. Gutenberg* (pp. 9–71). Gabler.

Heinen, E. (1966). *Das Zielsystem der Unternehmung. Grundlagen betriebswirtschaftlicher Entscheidungen [The goal system of the enterprise. Fundamentals of administaritive decisions].* Springer Fachmedien.

Heinen, E. (1969). Zum Wissenschaftsprogramm der entscheidungsorientierten Betriebswirtschaftslehre [On the scientific program of decision-oriented business administration and management]. *Zeitschrift Für Betriebswirtschaft, 39*(4), 207–220.

Heisenberg, M. (2009). Is free will an illusion? *Nature, 459*(7244), 164–165.

Hendrix, S. (2021). *What Your Visuals Reveal About You: Assessing Personality by Visual Cues in Online Interviews.* Unpublished master thesis, Leuphana University Lueneburg.

Hermann, H.-D., & Mayer, J. (2020). *Make them go!: Was wir vom Coaching der Spitzensportler lernen können [Make them go!: What we can learn from coaching top athletes].* Murmann Verlag.

Herriot, P. (1989). Selection as a social process. In M. Smith, & I. T. Robertson (Eds.), *Advances in selection and assessment* (pp. 171–188). Wiley.

Herriot, P. (1993). A paradigm bursting at the seams. *Journal of Organizational Behavior, 14*(4), 371–375.

Herriot, P., & Anderson, N. (1997). Selecting for change: How will personnel and selection psychology survive. In N. Anderson, & P. Herriot (Eds.), *International handbook for selection* (pp. 1–34). Wiley.

Herrmann, N. (1982). A bulletin special the creative brain. *NASSP Bulletin, 66*(455), 31–46. https://doi.org/10.1177/019263658206645507

Hertwig, R., & Todd, P. M. (2003). More is not always better: The benefits of cognitive limits. In D. Hardman, & L. Macchi (Eds.), *Thinking: Psychological perspectives on reasoning, judgment and decision making* (pp. 213–231). Wiley.

Hertwig, R., & Grüne-Yanoff, T. (2019). Nudging and boosting financial decisions. *Bancaria: Journal of Italian Banking Association, 73*(3), 2–19.

Hesketh, B., & Robertson, I. (1993). Validating personnel selection: A process model for research and practice. *International Journal of Selection and Assessment, 1*(1), 3–17. https://doi.org/10.1111/j.1468-2389.1993.tb00079.x

Hessler, R. M. (1995). Privacy ethics in the age of disclosure: Sweden and America compared. *The American Sociologist, 26*(2), 35–53. https://doi.org/10.1007/BF02692026

Hickok, G. (2015a). *Why we understand what others feel. The myth of mirror neurons.* Hanser Verlag.

Hickok, G. (2015b). The myth of mirror neurons. Interview with Gregory Hickok in *Relational Implicit*, January 2015, 1-8. https://relationalimplicit.com/zug/transcripts/Hickok-2015-01.pdf.

Highhouse, S. (2008). Stubborn reliance on intuition and subjectivity in employee selection. *Industrial and Organizational Psychology, 1*(3), 333–342. https://doi.org/10.1111/j.1754-9434.2008.00058.x

Highhouse, S., Doverspike, D., & Guion, R. M. (2016). *Essentials of personnel assessment and selection* (2nd ed.). Routledge, Taylor & Francis Group.

High-Level Expert Group On Artificial Intelligence. (2019). *Ethics guidelines for trustworthy AI.* European Commission. https://ec.europa.eu/digital-single-market/en/news/ethics-guidelines-trustworthy-ai

Hill, L. A., Brandeau, G., Truelove, E., & Lineback, K. (2014). *Collective genius: The art and practice of leading innovation.* Harvard Business Review Press.

Hinrichs, U. (2019). *Kunst als Sprache der Intuition: Der holografische Ansatz in der Kunsttherapie und kunstanalogen Transformationsprozessen* (1st). Synergia.

Hipsher, S. (2008). *Expatriates in Asia: Breaking Free from the Colonial Paradigm. Chandos Asian Studies Series.* Elsevier Science.

Hirschi, C. (2021a). *Skandalexperten, Expertenskandale: Zur Geschichte eines Gegenwartsproblems [Scandal experts, expert scandals: On the history of a contemporary problem].* Matthes & Seitz.

Hirschi, C. (2021b). Kalkül schägt Kompetenz [Calculation beats competence]. In *Frankfurter Allgemeine Zeitung*, 09.03.2021, p. 9 and 11.

Hirshleifer, D., Levi, Y., Lourie, B., & Teoh, S. H. (2019). Decision fatigue and heuristic analyst forecasts. *Journal of Financial Economics, 133*(1), 83–98. https://doi.org/10.1016/j.jfineco.2019.01.005

Hlásny, V. (2017). Job applicant screening in China and its four pillars. *The Economic and Labour Relations Review, 23*(3), 455–473. http://doi.org/10.1177/103530461770459

Hochschild, A. R. (2012). *The Managed Heart: Commercialization of Human Feeling*. University of California Press.
Hodgkinson, G. P., & Sadler-Smith, E. (2003). Complex or unitary? A critique and empirical re-assessment of the allinson-hayes cognitive style index. *Journal of Occupational and Organizational Psychology, 76*, 243–268.
Hodgkinson, G. P., & Sadler-Smith, E. (2014). Self-report assessment of individual differences in preferences for analytic and intuitive processing: A critical review. In M. Sinclair (Ed.), *Handbook of research methods on intuition* (pp. 101–115). Edward Elgar Publishing. https://doi.org/10.4337/9781782545996.00017
Hodgkinson, G. P., & Sadler-Smith, E. (2018). The dynamics of intuition and analysis in managerial and organizational decision making. *Academy of Management Perspectives, 32*(4), 473–492. https://doi.org/10.5465/amp.2016.0140
Hodgkinson, G. P., Sadler-Smith, E., Burke, L. A., Claxton, G., & Sparrow, P. R. (2009). Intuition in organizations: Implications for strategic management. *Long Range Planning, 42*(3), 277–297. https://doi.org/10.1016/j.lrp.2009.05.003
Hodgkinson, G. P., Sadler-Smith, E., Sinclair, M., & Ashkanasy, N. (2009b). More than meets the eye? Intuition and analysis revisited. *Personality and Individual Differences, 47*, 342–346.
Holodynski, M. (2006). *Emotionen – Entwicklung und Regulation [Emotions – Development and regulation]*. Springer.
Hofer, J., & Chasiotis, A. (2011). Implicit motives across cultures. *Online Readings in Psychology and Culture, 4*(1). https://doi.org/10.9707/2307-0919.1097
Hofstede, G. (1980). *Cultures consequences*. Sage Publications.
Hofstede, G. (2001). *Culture's consequences: Comparing values, behaviors, institutions, and organizations across nations*. Sage Publications.
Hofstede, G., Hofstede, G. J., & Minkov, M. (2010). *Cultures and organizations: Software of the mind: Intercultural cooperation and its importance for survival* (3rd ed.). McGraw-Hill.
Hofstede Insights. (2019). *Compare Countries*. https://www.hofstede-insights.com/product/compare-countries
Hoffman, B., Lance, C. E., Bynam, B., & Gentry, W. (2010). Rater source effects are alive and well after all. *Personnel Psychology, 63*, 119–151.
Hogarth, R. M. (2001). *Educating intuition*. University of Chicago Press.
Hogarth, R. M. (2003). *Educating Intuition: A Challenge for the twenty-first Century*. Published by Centre De Recerca En Economia International (CREI), num. 13. Universitat Pompeu Fabra.
Hogarth, R. M. (2010). Intuition: A challenge for psychological research on decision making. *Psychological Inquiry, 21*, 338–353. doi:10.1080/1047840X.2010.520260
Holtfort, T. (2010). *Emotionsökonomie: Der Faktor Mensch im Finanzdienstleistungssektor [Emotional economy: The human factor in the financial services sector]*. Josef Eul Verlag.
Holtfort, T. (2011). Intuition als Managementfaktor im Finanzdienstleistungssektor [Intuition as a management factor in the financial services sector]. *Versicherungswirtschaft*, (7), 507–511. https://bauchundkopf.de/wp-content/uploads/2016/12/Intuition_als_Managementfaktor_im_Finanzdienstleistungssektor.pdf
Holtfort, T. (2013). *Intuition als effektive Ressource moderner Organisationen: Eine theoretische und empirische Analyse [Intuition as an effective resource of modern organisations: A theoretical and empirical analysis]. FOM-Edition*. Springer Fachmedien.
Holzenkamp, M., et al. (2010). Wie valide sind Assessment Center im deutschsprachigen Raum? Eine Uberblicksstudie mit Empfehlungen fur die AC-Praxis. *Wirtschaftspsychologie Aktuell, 2*, 17–25.

Hong, Y. Y., Morris, M. W., Chiu, C. Y., & Benet-Martínez, V. (2000). Multicultural minds: A dynamic constructivist approach to culture and cognition. *American Psychologist, 55*(7), 709–720. https://doi.org/10.1037/0003-066X.55.7.709

Horak, S. (2017). The informal dimension of Human Resource Management in Korea: Yongo, recruiting practices, and career progression. *International Journal of Human Resource Management, 28*(10), 1409–1432.

Hossiep, R., Paschen, M., & Mühlhaus, O. (2000). *Persönlichkeitstests im Personalmanagement [Personality tests in Human Resource Management]*. Hogrefe.

Hossiep, R., Schecke, J., & Weiß, S. (2015). Zum Einsatz von persönlichkeitsorientierten Fragebogen. Eine Erhebung unter den 580 größten deutschen Unternehmen [On the use of personality-oriented questionnaires. A survey among the 580 largest German companies]. *Psychologische Rundschau 66*(2), 127–129. https://doi.org/10.1026/0033-3042/a000235

Hotho, J., Minbaeva, D., Muratbekova-Touron, M., & Rabbiosi, L. (2020). Coping with favoritism in recruitment and selection: A communal perspective. *Journal of Business Ethics, 165*, 659–679. https://doi.org/10.1007/s10551-018-4094-9

Hottenrott, K., & Seidel, I. (2017). Diagnostik [Diagnostics]. In K. Hottenrott, & I. Seidel (Eds.), *Handbuch Trainingswissenschaft-Trainingslehre* (pp. 120–132). Hofmann.

House, R. J. (2004). Illustrative examples of GLOBE Findings. In R. J. House, P. J. Hanges, M. Javidan, P. W. Dorfman, & V. Gupta (Eds.), *Culture, leadership, and organizations: The GLOBE study of 62 societies* (pp. 3–8). Sage Publications.

House, R. J., Dorfman, P. W., Javidan, M., Hanges, P. J., & Luque, M. F. S. D. (2014). *Strategic leadership across Cultures: The GLOBE Study of CEO leadership behavior and effectiveness in 24 countries*. Sage Publications. https://doi.org/10.4135/9781506374581.

House, R. J., Hanges, P. J., Javidan, M., Dorfman, P. W., & Gupta, V. (Eds.). (2004). *Culture, leadership, and organizations: The GLOBE study of 62 societies*. Sage Publications.

House, R. J., Javidan, M., & Dorfman, P. W. (2001). Project GLOBE: An Introduction. *Applied Psychology, 50*(4), 489–505. https://doi.org/10.1111/1464-0597.00070

Howard, J. A. (2014). Heuristic, intuition, or impulse: How to tell the difference and why it is important to decision makers. In J. Liebowitz (Ed.), *Bursting the big data bubble: The case for intuition based decision making* (pp. 57–68). Taylor & Francis Group. doi:10.1201/b17247-6

Höft, S., & Funke, U. (2006). Simulationsorientierte Verfahren der Personalauswahl [Simulation-oriented personnel selection procedures]. In H. Schuler (Ed.), *Lehrbuch der Personalpsychologie* (2nd ed., pp. 145–187). Hogrefe.

Höft, S., & Kersting, M. (2018). Anforderungsprofil, Verhaltensbeobachtung und Verhaltensbeurteilung [Task profile, behaviour observation and behaviour assessment]. In Diagnostik und Testkuratorium (Ed.), *Personalauswahl kompetent gestalten. Grundlagen und Praxis der Eignungsdiagnostik nach DIN 33430* (pp. 27–63). Springer. https://doi.org/10.1007/978-3-662-53772-5_2

Höft, S., Püttner, I., & Kersting, M. (2018). Anforderungsanalyse, Verfahren der Eignungsbeurteilung sowie rechtliche Rahmenbedingungen [Requirements analysis, suitability assessment procedures and legal framework]. In Diagnostik und Testkuratorium (Ed.), *Personalauswahl kompetent gestalten. Grundlagen und Praxis der Eignungsdiagnostik nach DIN 33430* (pp. 95–153). Springer. https://doi.org/10.1007/978-3-662-53772-5_4

Hösle, V. (2018). *Kritik der verstehenden Vernunft [Critique of Understanding Reason]. Eine Grundlegung der Geisteswissenschaften*. Beck.

Hsu, M. -. L., & Chiu, K. -. Y. (2008). A comparison between I-Ching's early management decision-making model and western management decision-making models. *Chinese Management Studies, 2*(1), 52–75. https://doi.org/10.1108/17506140810866241

Hu, H., Real, E., Takamiya, K., Kang, M.-G., LeDoux, J., Huganir, R. L., & Malinow, R. (2007). Emotion enhances learning via norepinephrine regulation of AMPA-Receptor trafficking. *Cell, 131*(1), 160–173. https://doi.org/10.1016/j.cell.2007.09.017

Huang, L., & Pearce, J. L. (2015). Managing the unknowable: The effectiveness of early-stage investor gut feel in entrepreneurial investment decisions. *Administrative Science Quarterly, 60*(4), 634–670.

Huber, M. (2017). Lernen und Emotion [Learning and emotion]. *Jugendhilfe, 55*(5), 450–457.

Huffcutt, A. I. (2010). From science to practice: Seven principles for conducting employment interviews. *Applied Human Resource Management Research, 12*(1), 121–136.

Huffcutt, A. I., & Culbertson, S. S. (2011). Interviews. In S. Zedeck (Ed.), *APA handbook of industrial and organizational psychology: Volume 2, Selecting and developing members for the organization* (pp. 185–203). American Psychological Association.

Huffcutt, A. I., Culbertson, S. S., & Weyhrauch, W. S. (2013). Employment interview reliability: New meta-analytic estimates by structure and format. *International Journal of Selection and Assessment, 21*(3), 264–276. https://doi.org/10.1111/ijsa.12036

Huffcutt, A. I., Culbertson, S. S., & Weyhrauch, W. S. (2014). Moving forward indirectly: Reanalyzing the validity of employment interviews with indirect range restriction methodology. *International Journal of Selection and Assessment, 22*(3), 297–309. https://doi.org/10.1111/ijsa.12078

Hummel (2015). *Persönlichkeitsanalyse: Deine Sprache verrät dich [Personality analysis: Your language reveals you].* https://www.faz.net/aktuell/gesellschaft/menschen/software-erkennt-persoenlichkeit-mit-sprachanalyse-13596216.html

Hunter, J. E., Schmidt, F. L., & Judiesch, M. K. (1990). Individual differences in output variability as a function of job complexity. *Journal of Applied Psychology, 75*(1), 28–42. 10.1037/0021-9010.75.1.28

Huo, Y. P., & Glinow, M. A. V. (1995). On transplanting human resource practices to China. *International Journal of Manpower, 16*(9), 3–15. https://doi.org/10.1108/01437729510102657

Huo, Y. P., Huang, H. J., & Napier, N. K. (2002). Divergence or convergence: A cross-national comparison of personnel selection practices. *Human Resource Management, 41*(1), 31–44. https://doi.org/10.1002/hrm.10018

Huselid, M. A. (1995). The impact of human resource management practices on turnover, productivity, and corporate financial performance. *Academy of Management Journal, 38*(3), 635–672. https://doi.org/10.5465/256741

Husted, B. W. (1999). Wealth, culture, and corruption. *Journal of International Business Studies, 30*(2), 339–359. https://doi.org/10.1057/palgrave.jibs.8490073

Hutzschenreuter, T. (2022). Künstliche Intelligenz hat Tücke. Algorithmen sind eine Macht, doch wer sich blind auf sie verlässt, kann Scheinmustern zum Opfer fallen [Artificial intelligence has pitfalls. Algorithms are a force, but those who blindly rely on them can fall victim to pseudo-patterns]. In *Frankfurter Allgemeine Zeitung*, 07. 02.2022, p. 16.

Huxley, A. (n.d.). *The Doors of Perception/Heaven and Hell.* Harper Collins Publishers (First edition 1954). https://www.goodreads.com/quotes/849046-in-a-world-where-education-is-predominantly-verbal-highly-educated

Iannello, P., Colombo, B., & Antonietti, A. (2014). Non-invasive brain stimulation techniques in the study of intuition. In M. Sinclair (Ed.), *Handbook of research methods on intuition* (pp. 130–146). https://doi.org/10.4337/9781782545996

IBM. (2017, Juni). IBM Watson Candidate Assistant. Engaging job seekers through an enhanced experience. https://www.ibm.com/downloads/cas/53DOYRVO.

Iden, P. (07.01.19). „Intuition“: Wissen vor dem Wissen [“Intuition“: Knowledge before knowledge]. In *Frankfurter Rundschau.* https://www.fr.de/kultur/kunst/wissen-wissen-11032988.html

ILO (2015). *Women in Business and Management: Gaining Momentum. Global Report.* ILO – Bureau for Employers' Activities (ACT/EMP). https://www.ilo.org/global/publications/ilo-bookstore/order-online/books/WCMS_316450/lang–en/index.htm

Imada, A. S., & Hakel, M. D. (1977). Influence of nonverbal communication and rater proximity on impressions and decisions in simulated employment interviews. *The Journal of Applied Psychology, 62*(3), 295–300. https://doi.org/10.1037/0021-9010.62.3.295

Inceoglu, I., & Bartram, D. (2013). Interkulturalität der Konstrukte und Kompetenzen [Interculturality of constructs and competences]. In W. Sarges (Ed.), *Management-Diagnostik* (4th ed.) (pp. 499–507). Hogrefe.

Ingold, P. V., Kleinmann, M., König, C. J., & Melchers, K. G. (2015a). Shall we continue or stop disapproving of self-presentation? Evidence on impression management and faking in a selection context and their relation to job performance. *European Journal of Work and Organizational Psychology, 24*, 420–432. 10.1080/1359432X.2014.915215

Ingold, P. V., Kleinmann, M., König, C. J., & Melchers, K. G. (2015b). Transparency of assessment centers: Lower criterion-related validity but greater opportunity to perform? *Personnel Psychology, 69*(2), 467–497. doi:10.1111/peps.12105

Ingold, P. V., Dönni, M., & Lievens, F. (2018). A dual-process theory perspective to better understand judgments in assessment centers: The role of initial impressions for dimension ratings and validity. *Journal of Applied Psychology, 103*, 1367–1378. Advance online publication. http://dx.doi.org/10.1037/apl0000333

International Monetary Fund. (2019). *Unemployment rate.* https://www.imf.org/external/datamapper/LUR@WEO/OEMDC/ADVEC/WEOWORLD

International Taskforce on Assessment Center Guidelines. (2015). Guidelines and ethical considerations for assessment center operations. *Journal of Management,* 41(4), 1244–1273. doi: 10.1177/0149206314567780

Isen, A. M., & Means, B. (1983). The influence of positive affect on decision-making strategy. *Social Cognition, 2*(1), 18–31. https://doi.org/10.1521/soco.1983.2.1.18

Isen, A. M., & Daubman, K. A. (1984). The influence of affect on categorization. *Journal of Personality and Social Psychology, 47*(6), 1206–1217. https://doi.org/10.1037/0022-3514.47.6.1206

Isen, A. M., Johnson, M. M., Mertz, E., & Robinson, G. F. (1985). The influence of positive affect on the unusualness of word associations. *Journal of Personality and Social Psychology, 48*(6), 1413–1426.

Isen, A. M., Daubman, K. A., & Nowicki, G. P. (1987). Positive affect facilitates creative problem solving. *Journal of Personality and Social Psychology, 52*(6), 1122–1131. https://doi.org/10.1037/0022-3514.52.6.1122

Isenberg, D. (1984). How managers think. *Harvard Business Review,* November–December 1984, p. 81–90.

Isenberg, D. (1986). *Strategic Opportunism: Managing under uncertainty,* Harvard Graduate School of Business, Working paper 9-786-020, Boston, January 1986

ISO/IEC. (2001). *Rules for the structure and drafting of International Standards.* https://lirics.loria.fr/doc_pub/RulesForTheStructureAndDraftingOfAnInternationalStandard.pdf

ISO. (2011). *Assessment service delivery – Procedures and methods to assess people in work and organizational settings* (ISO 10667-1). International Organization for Standardization. https://www.iso.org/standard/56441.html

ISO. (2020). ISO 10667-1:2020 and ISO 10667-2:2020. Assessment service delivery – Procedures and methods to assess people in work and organizational settings – Part 1: Requirements for the client. Part 2: Part 2: Requirements for service providers. International Organization for Standardization https://www.iso.org/standard/74716.html

Issack, T. S. (1978). Intuition: An ignored dimension of management. *Academy of Management Review, 3*(4), 917–922. https://doi.org/10.5465/amr.1978.4289310

Isson, J. P., & Harriott, J. S. (2016). *People analytics in the era of big data: Changing the way you attract, acquire, develop, and retain talent.* John Wiley & Sons.

Izard, C. E. (2002). Translating emotion theory and research into preventive interventions. *Psychological Bulletin, 128*(5), 796–824.

Jackson, S. E., Schuler, R. S., & Werner, S. (2012). *Managing human resources* (11th ed.). South Western/Cengage Learning, Mason.

Jackson, T. (2002). The management of people across cultures: Valuing people differently. *Human Resource Management, 41*(4), 455–475. doi:10.1002/hrm.10054

Jakšič, M., & Marinč, M. (2019). Relationship banking and information technology: The role of artificial intelligence and FinTech. *Risk Management, 21*(1), 1–18. https://doi.org/10.1057/s41283-018-0039-y

Jalajas, D., & Pullaro, R. (2018). The effect of personality on decision making. *Journal of Organizational Psychology, 18*(5). https://doi.org/10.33423/jop.v18i5.274

James, W. (1890). *The principles of psychology* Vol. 1, CosimoClassics.

Javidan, M., & Dastmalchian, A. (2009). Managerial implications of the GLOBE project: A study of 62 societies. *Asia Pacific Journal of Human Resources, 47*(1), 41–58. https://doi.org/10.1177/1038411108099289

Javidan, M., House, R. J., & Dorfman, P. W. (2004). A nontechnical summary of GLOBE findings. In R. J. House, P. J. Hanges, M. Javidan, P. W. Dorfman, & V. Gupta (Eds.), *Culture, leadership, and organizations: The GLOBE study of 62 societies* (pp. 29–48). Sage Publications.

Javidan, M., House, R. J., Dorfman, P. W., Hanges, P. J., & Sully de Luque, M. (2006). Conceptualizing and measuring cultures and their consequences: A comparative review of GLOBE's and Hofstede's approaches. *Journal of International Business Studies, 37*(6), 897–914. https://doi.org/10.1057/palgrave.jibs.8400234

Jekel, M., Glöckner, A., Fiedler, S., & Bröder, A. (2012). The rationality of different kinds of intuitive decision processes. *Synthese, 189*(S1), 147–160. https://doi.org/10.1007/s11229-012-0126-7

Jenkins, R. (1986). *Racism and recruitment. managers, organisations and equal opportunity in the labour market.* Cambridge University Press.

Jensen, M., & Meckling, W. (1976). Theory of the firm. Managerial behavior, agency costs, and ownership structure. *Journal of Financial Economics, 3*(4), 305–360.

Ji, L.-J., Nisbett, R. E., & Su, Y. (2001). Culture, change, and prediction. *Psychological Science, 12*(6), 450–456. https://doi.org/10.1111/1467-9280.00384

Ji, L.-J., Zhang, Z., & Guo, T. (2008). To buy or to sell: Cultural differences in stock market decisions based on price trends. *Journal of Behavioral Decision Making, 21*(4), 399–413. https://doi.org/10.1002/bdm.595

Johns, G. (1993). Constraints on the adoption of psychology-based personnel practices: Lessons from organizational innovation. *Personnel Psychology, 46*(3), 569–592. https://doi.org/10.1111/j.1744-6570.1993.tb00885.x

Johnson, J. (2014). *Designing with the mind in mind: Simple guide to understanding user interface design guidelines (2. ed.).* Morgan Kaufmann.

Johnson, J. G., & Raab, M. (2003). Take the first: Option-generation and resulting choices. *Organizational Behavior and Human Decision Processes, 91*(2), 215–229. https://doi.org/10.1016/S0749-5978(03)00027-X

Johnston, K., Wattie, N., Schorer, J., & Baker, J. (2018). Talent Identification in Sport: A Systematic Review. *Sports Medicine (Auckland, N.Z.), 48*(1), 97–109. https://doi.org/10.1007/s40279-017-0803-2

Jokinen, T. (2004). Global leadership competencies: A review and discussion. *Journal of European Industrial Training, 29*(3), 199–216. https://doi.org/10.1108/03090590510591085

Jones, E. E., & Goethals, G. R. (1972). Order effects in impression formation: Attribution context and the nature of the entity. In E. E. Jones, D. E. Kanouse, H. H. Kelly, R. E. Nisbett, S. Valins, & B. Weiner (Eds.), *Attribution: Perceiving the causes of behavior* (pp. 27–46). General Learning Press.

Jones, S., & Law, S. F. (2009). A guanxi model of human resources. *Chinese Management Studies, 3*(4), 313–332. doi:10.1108/17506140911007486

Jones, C. A., Mather, D., & Uchill, R. (Eds.). (2016). *Experience: Culture, cognition, and the common sense*. The MIT Press.

Julmi, C., Lindner, F., & Scherm, E. (2016). Intuition sticht Analytik: Wann intuitiv entschieden werden sollte [Intuition Stings Analytics: When to decide intuitively]. *Zeitschrift Führung + Organisation: ZfO, 85*(3), 195–200.

Julmi, C., & Scherm, E. (2013). Intuitives management [Intuitive management]. *WiSt – Wirtschaftswissenschaftliches Studium, 42*(8), 422–427. https://doi.org/10.15358/0340-1650_2013_8_422

Jung, C. G. (1948). *Psychological types*. Harcourt Brace, & Co.

Jung, C. G. (1972). *Typologie: Zur Frage der psychologischen Typen [Typology: On the question of psychological types]*. Allgemeine Beschreibung der Typen; Definitionen; psychologische Typen. Walter.

Jung, C. G. (2019). *Until You Make The Unconscious Conscious It Will Direct Your Life And You'll Call It Fate. Journal 120 Dot Grid/Bullet Pages – 6" x 9" – Planner, Journal, Notebook, Composition Book, Diary for Women, Men, and Kids. Unconscious Conscious Fate Journal*. Independently published.

Jungermann, H. (1983). The two camps on rationality. In R. W. Scholz (Ed.), *Advances in psychology. Decision making under uncertainty – cognitive decision research social interaction development and epistemology* (Vol. 16, pp. 63–86). Elsevier. https://doi.org/10.1016/S0166-4115(08)62194-9.

Jurist, E. (2019). Book review of "How emotions are made: The secret life of the brain". *American Psychological Association, 39*(3), 193–198.

Kabat-Zinn, J. (2005). *Coming to our senses: Healing ourselves and the world through mindfulness*. Piatkus.

Kabat-Zinn, J. (2013). *Full catastrophe living: Using the wisdom of your body and mind to face stress, pain, and illness* (Rev ed.). Bantam Books.

Kahle, E. (1972). Zielplanung durch Anspruchsanpassung [Target planning through entitlement matching]. *Betriebswirtschaftliche Forschung Und Praxis BFuP, 23*(11), 623–643.

Kahle, E. (1973). *Betriebswirtschaftliches Problemlösungsverhalten. Theoretische Überlegungen zum Einfluß von Zielen und Entscheidungsmodellen auf die Lösung betriebswirtschaftlicher Probleme [Business problem solving behavior. Theoretical considerations on the influence of goals and decision models on the solution of business management problems]*. Gabler.

Kahle, E. (1998). System- und evolutionstheoretische Erklärungen [System- and evolutionary theory explanations]. In A. Martin, & W. Nienhüser (Eds.), *Personalpolitik: Wissenschaftliche Erklärung der Personalpraxis* (pp. 351–371). Rainer Hampp.

Kahle, E. (2018). *Betriebliche Entscheidungen [Decisions in Organization] (6., insignificantly modified edition, reprint from 2001)*. De Gruyter Oldenbourg.

Kahneman, D. (2003). A perspective on judgment and choice: Mapping bounded rationality. *American Psychologist, 58*(9), 697–720. https://doi.org/10.1037/0003-066X.58.9.697

Kahneman, D. (2003a). Maps of bounded rationality: Psychology for behavioral economics. *The American Economic Review, 93*(5), 1449–1475.

Kahneman, D. (2011). *Thinking, fast and slow.* Farrar, Straus and Giroux.
Kahneman, D. (2011b). *Thinking, Fast and Slow.* Daniel Kahneman. Talks at Google, https://www.youtube.com/watch?v=CjVQJdIrDJ0
Kahneman, D. (2012). *Schnelles denken, langsames Denken [Thinking, fast and slow].* Siedler Verlag.
Kahneman, D., & Klein, G. (2009). Conditions for intuitive expertise: A failure to disagree. *The American Psychologist, 64*(6), 515–526. https://doi.org/10.1037/a0016755
Kahneman, D., Lovallo, D., & Sibony, O. (2011). Before you make that big decision. *Harvard Business Review, 89*(6), 50–60.
Kahneman, D., Slovic, P., & Tversky, A. (1982). *Judgment under uncertainty: Heuristics and biases.* Cambridge university press.
Kahneman, D., & Tversky, A. (1973). On the psychology of prediction. *Psychological Review, 80*(4), 237–251. 10.1037/h0034747
Kahneman, D., & Tversky, A. (1979). Prospect theory: An analysis of decision under risk. *Econometrica, 47*(2), 263–291.
Kahneman, D., & Tversky, A. (1996). On the reality of cognitive illusions. *Psychological Review, 103*(3), 582–591. https://doi.org/10.1037/0033-295X.103.3.582
Kahnemann, D., & Riepe, M. W. (1998). Aspects of investor psychology: Beliefs, preferences, and biases investment advisors should know about. *Journal of Portfolio Management, 24,* 52-65.
Kahneman, D., Sibony, O., & Sunstein, C. R. (2021). *Noise. A flaw in human judgment.* Little, Brown and Company.
Kalefeld, J. (2021). *Perspectives on Performance Measurement in the Age of Digital Transformation: Potential and Conditions of Digital Technologies for the Enhancement of Validity in Performance Measurement.* Unpublished master thesis, Leuphana University, Lueneburg.
Kaltheuner, F. (Ed.). (2021). *Fake AI.* Meatspace press.
Kandel, E. R. (2012). *Das Zeitalter der Erkenntnis: Die Erforschung des Unbewussten in Kunst, Geist und Gehirn von der Wiener Moderne bis heute [The Age of Insight: The Quest to Understand the Unconscious in Art, Mind, and Brain, from Vienna 1900 to the Present].* (M. Wiese, Trans.) E-Books Random.
Kanning, U. P. (1999). *Die Psychologie der Personenbeurteilung [The psychology of personal assessment].*
Kanning, U. P. (2002). Die Psychologie der Personalbeurteilung [The psychology of personal assessment]. In U. P. Kanning (Ed.), *Handbuch personaldiagnostischer Instrumente.* Hogrefe.
Kanning, U. P. (2004). *Standards der Personaldiagnostik [Standards of personnel diagnostics].* Hogrefe.
Kanning, U. P. (2012). Personalauswahl – Mythen, Fakten, Perspektiven [Personnel selection – myths, facts, perspectives]. In M. T. Thielsch, & T. Brandenburg (Eds.), *MV-Wissenschaft. Praxis der Wirtschaftspsychologie II: Themen und Fallbeispiele für Studium und Anwendung [Practice of Business Psychology II: Topics and case studies for study and application]* (2nd ed., pp. 9–25). Monsenstein und Vannerdat.
Kanning, U. P. (2014). Auswahl von Führungskräften [Selection of managers]. In J. Felfe (Ed.), *Psychologie für das Personalmanagement: [27]. Trends der psychologischen Führungsforschung: [neue Konzepte, Methoden und Erkenntnisse]* (pp. 407–417). Hogrefe.
Kanning, U. P. (2015). *Personalauswahl zwischen Anspruch und Wirklichkeit: Eine wirtschaftspsychologische Analyse [Personnel selection between demand and reality: An economic psychological analysis].* Springer.
Kanning, U. P. (2016a). Über die Sichtung von Bewerbungsunterlagen in der Praxis der Personalauswahl [About the review of application documents in the practice of personnel

selection]. *Zeitschrift Für Arbeits- Und Organisationspsychologie*, *60*(1), 18–32. https://doi.org/10.1026/0932-4089/a000193
Kanning, U. P. (2016b). Wie Bewerberinnen und Bewerber die Praxis der Personalauswahl erleben und bewerten [How applicants experience and evaluate the practice of personnel selection]. *Report Psychologie*, *4*, 56–66.
Kanning, U. P. (2017a). Fairness und Akzeptanz von Personalauswahlmethoden [Fairness and acceptance of personnel selection methods]. In D. E. Krause (Ed.), *Personalauswahl* (pp. 271–299). Springer Fachmedien Wiesbaden. https://doi.org/10.1007/978-3-658-14567-5_12
Kanning, U. P. (2017b). *Personalmarketing, Employer Branding und Mitarbeiterbindung: Forschungsbefunde und Praxistipps aus der Personalpsychologie [Personnel marketing, employer branding and employee retention: Research findings and practical tips from personnel psychology]*. Springer.
Kanning, U. P. (2018). *Diagnostik für Führungspositionen [Diagnostics for management positions]*. Kompendien psychologische Diagnostik Hogrefe.
Kanning, U. P. (2019). *Standards der Personaldiagnostik: Personalauswahl professionell gestalten [Standards of personnel diagnostics: Professional personnel selection]* (2nd ed.). Hogrefe.
Kanning, U. P., Pöttker, J., & Klinge, K. (2008). *Personalauswahl. Leitfaden für die Praxis. [Personnel Selection. A guideline for practice]*. Schäffer-Poeschel.
Kanning, U. P., Kraul, L.-F., & Litz, R. Z. (2019). Einstellungen zu digitalen Methoden der Personalauswahl [Settings for digital methods of personnel selection]. *Journal of Business and Media Psychology*, *10*(1), 57–71.
Kant, I. (1990). *Kritik der reinen Vernunft [Critique of pure reason]*. Meiner.
Kaplan, A. (1964). *The conduct of Inquiry*. Chandler.
Karpinska, K., Henkens, K., & Schippers, J. (2013). Hiring retirees: Impact of age norms and stereotypes. *Journal of Managerial Psychology*, *28*(7/8), 886–906. https://doi.org/10.1108/JMP-07-2013-0223
Kast, B. (2007). *Wie der Bauch dem Kopf beim Denken hilft: Die Kraft der Intuition [How the gut helps the head to think: The power of intuition]*. Fischer.
Katz, D., & Kahn, R. L. (1966). *The social psychology of organizations*. John Wiley & Sons.
Kaube, J. (2020). Hegel, der Erzieher [Hegel, the educator]. Unterwegs zum System. Wie der Philosoph sich als Gymnasialrektor Bildung, Lehre und Lernen vorstellt. In: *Frankfurter Allgemeine Zeitung*, 16.8.2020, p. 33.
Kaudela-Baum, S., & Brasser, M. (2015). Freiräume und Intuition – Gestaltungsaufgabe für die Führung von Innovation [Freedom and intuition – design task for innovation leadership]. In M. W. Fröse, S. Kaudela-Baum, & F. E. P. Dievernich (Eds.), *Emotion und Intuition in Führung und Organisation* (pp. 117–139). Springer Fachmedien. https://doi.org/10.1007/978-3-658-07796-9_1
Kaufmann, M., Rosing, K., & Nicola Baumann, N. (2020). Being mindful does not always benefit everyone: Mindfulness-based practices may promote alienation among psychologically vulnerable people. *Cognition & Emotion*, *35*(2), *241–255*. doi:10.1080/02699931.2020.1825337
Kausel, E. E., Culbertson, S. S., & Madrid, H. P. (2016). Overconfidence in personnel selection: When and why unstructured interview information can hurt hiring decisions. *Organizational Behavior and Human Decision Processes*, *137*, 27–44. https://doi.org/10.1016/j.obhdp.2016.07.005
Kegan, R., & Laskow Lahey, L. (2009). *Immunity to change: How to overcome it and unlock the potential in yourself and your organization. leadership for the common good*. Harvard Business Review Press.

Keinert-Kisin, C. (2016). *Corporate social responsibility and discrimination. Gender bias in personnel selection.* Springer.

Keller, J., Bohner, G., & Erb, H. P. (2000). Intuitive and heuristic judgment – Different processes? Presentation of a German version of the Rational-Experiential Inventory and of new self-report scales of heuristic use. *Zeitschrift Für Sozialpsychologie, 31*(2), 87–101.

Kelly, A. (2017). Think twice: Review of thinking, fast and slow by daniel kahneman (2011). *Numeracy, 10*(2). https://doi.org/10.5038/1936-4660.10.2.15

Keltner, D., & Kring, A. M. (1998). Emotion, social function, and psychopathology. *Review of General Psychology, 2*, 320–342. http://dx.doi.org/10.1037/1089-2680.2.3.320

Kersting, M. (2004). Kosten und Nutzen beruflicher Eignungsbeurteilungen [Costs and benefits of professional qualification assessments]. In L. Hornke, & U. Winterfeld (Eds.), *Eignungsbeurteilungen auf dem Prüfstand: DIN 33430 zur Qualitätssicherung* (pp. 55–77). Spektrum Akad. Verl.

Kersting, M. (2008). Zur Akzeptanz von Intelligenz- und Leiustungstests. *Report Psychologie, 33*, 420–433.

Kersting, M. (2009). DIN 33430: Akzeptanz durch Qualität, Initiative und Geduld [DIN 33430: Acceptance through quality, initiative and patience]. *Zeitschrift Für Personalpsychologie, 8*(3), 154–156. https://doi.org/10.1026/1617-6391.8.3.154

Kersting, M. (2011). Schlaraffenland ist abgebrannt – Warum sich die Bewerberauswahl ändern muss [Candy land has burned down – why the selection of candidates must change]. *Wirtschaftspsychologie Aktuell, 4*, 23–26. http://www.kersting-internet.de/pdf/Kersting_2011_Wirtschaftspsy_23-26.pdf

Kersting, M. (2013). Management-Diagnostik in Zeiten des Personalmangels [Management diagnostics in times of staff shortage]. In W. Sarges (Ed.), *Management-Diagnostik* (4th ed.) (pp. 524–530). Hogrefe. https://www.researchgate.net/profile/Martin_Kersting/publication/297895767_Manage-mentdiagnostik_in_Zeiten_des_Personalmangels/links/56e40f5208ae68afa1105b74/Management-Diagnostik-in-Zeiten-des-Personalmangels.pdf

Kersting, M. (2016). DIN reloaded: Mit Qualität die Zukunft der Personalauswahl gestalten [DIN reloaded: Shaping the future of personnel selection with quality]. *Report Psychologie, 41*, 291–295. http://kersting-internet.de/pdf/Kersting_2016_RP_DIN_33430.pdf

Kersting, M., & Birk, M. (2011). Zur zweifelhaften Validität und Nützlichkeit von Anforderungsanalysen für die Interpretation eignungsdiagnostischer Daten [On the doubtful validity and usefulness of requirements analyses for the interpretation of suitability diagnostic data]. In P. Gelléri, & C. Winter (Eds.), *Potenziale der Personalpsychologie: Einfluss personaldiagnostischer Maßnahmen auf den Berufs- und Unternehmenserfolg* (pp. 83–95). Hogrefe.

Kersting, M., & Hornke, L. (2003). Qualitätssicherung und -optimierung in der Diagnostik: Die DIN 33430 und notwendige Begleit- und Folgeinitiativen [Quality assurance and optimisation in diagnostics: DIN 33430 and necessary accompanying and follow-up initiatives]. *Psychologische Rundschau, 54*(3), 175–178. http://kersting-internet.de/pdf/Kersting_Hornke_PsyRund_2003_175-184.pdf

Kersting, M., & Ott, M. (2016). Diversity-gerechte Personalauswahl [Diversity-oriented personnel selection] In P. Genkova, & T. Ringeisen (Eds.), *Handbuch Diversity Kompetenz: Perspektiven und Anwendungsfelder (1–11)*. Springer Fachmedien. https://doi.org/10.1007/978-3-658-08003-7_8-1

Kersting, M., & Püttner, I. (2018). Einführung in die DIN 33430 [Introduction to DIN 33430]. In Diagnostik und Testkuratorium (Ed.). *Personalauswahl kompetent gestalten. Grundlagen und Praxis der Eignungsdiagnostik nach DIN 33430* (pp. 1–25). Springer. https://doi.org/10.1007/978-3-662-53772-5_1

Kersting, M., & Wottawa, H. (2014). Gegen schlichte Gewohnheiten. Interview/Streitgespräch: Martin Kersting und Heinrich Wottawa zum Thema „Personalauswahl über Schulnoten“ [Against simple habits“. Interview/dispute: Martin Kersting and Heinrich Wottawa on the topic of “Personnel selection via school grades”]. *Personalmagazin*, *10*, 38–39. http://kersting-internet.de/pdf/Personal_Magazin_10_2014_Schulnoten_Wottawa_Kersting.pdf

Khatri, N., & Ng, H. A. (2000). The role of intuition in strategic decision making. *Human Relations*, *53*(1), 57–86. https://doi.org/10.1177/0018726700531004

Kim, D., Pan, Y., & Park, H. S. (1998). High-versus low-Context culture: A comparison of Chinese, Korean, and American cultures. *Psychology and Marketing*, *15*(6), 507–521. https://doi.org/10.1002/(SICI)1520-6793(199809)15:6<507::AID-MAR2>3.0.CO;2-A

Kinnunen, T., & Parviainen, J. (2016). Feeling the right personality. Recruitment consultants' affective decision making in interviews with employee candidates. *Nordic Journal of Working Life Studies*, *6*(3), 5–21.

Kirkman, B. L., Lowe, K. B., & Gibson, C. B. (2006). A quarter century of culture's consequences: A review of empirical research incorporating Hofstede's cultural values framework. *Journal of International Business Studies*, *37*(3), 285–320. https://doi.org/10.1057/palgrave.jibs.8400202

Kirkpatrick, D. L., & Kirkpatrick, J. D. (2006). *Evaluating training programs: The four levels (3. ed.)*. Berrett-Koehler Publisher.

Kirsch, H. (Ed.). (2014). *Das Mentalisierungskonzept in der Sozialen Arbeit [The mentalisation concept in social work]*. Vandenhoeck & Ruprecht.

Kirton, M. J. (1989). *Adaptors and innovators: Styles of creativity and problem-solving*. Routledge.

Klaffke, M. (2014). Erfolgsfaktor Generationen-Management: Handlungsansätze für das Personalmanagement [Success Factor Generation Management: Approaches for Human Resources Management]. In M. Klaffke (Ed.), *Generationen-Management. Konzepte, Instrumente, Good-Practice-Ansätze* (pp. 3–25). Springer Gabler.

Kleebaur, C. (2007). *Personalauswahl zwischen Anspruch und Wirklichkeit: Wissenschaftliche Personaldiagnostik vs. erfahrungsbasiert-intuitive Urteilsfindung [Personnel selection between claim and reality: Scientific personnel diagnostics vs. experience-based intuitive judgment.]*. Hampp.

Klehe, U.-C. (2008). Die DIN 33430 - eine komplexe Norm für eine komplexe Welt. *Zeitschrift für Personalpsychologie*, *7*(4), 183–188. https://doi.org/10.1026/1617-6391.7.4.183" https://doi.org/10.1026/1617-6391.7.4.183

Klein, G. A. (1993). A recognition-primed decision (RPD) model of rapid decision making. In G. A. Klein, J. Orasanu, R. Calderwood & C. E. Zsambok (Eds.), *Decision Making in Action: Models and Methods* (pp. 138–147). Ablex Publishing Corporation

Klein, G. A. (1998). *Sources of power: How people make decisions*. MIT Press.

Klein, G. A. (2002). *Intuition at work: Why developing your gut instincts will make you better at what you do*. Doubleday.

Klein, G. A. (2004). *The power of intuition: How to use your gut feelings to make better decisions at work*. Currency Book Doubleday/Random House.

Klein, G. A. (2008). Naturalistic decision making. *Human Factors*, *50*, 456–460.

Klein, G. A. (2013). *Seeing what others don't: The remarkable ways we gain insights*. Public affairs.

Klein, G. A. (2019). Can you have effective decision making without expertise? *The American Journal of Psychology*, *132*(4), 480–485. 10.5406/amerjpsyc.132.4.0480

Klein, G. A. (2020). The Connection Between Intuition and Expertise. Are they opposites or are they closely related? Psychology Today (posted January 7,2020, reviewed by Jessica Schrader). https://scholar.google.de/scholar?q=klein+learning+intuition&hl=de ≈ sdt=0≈vis=1&oi=scholart#d=gs_qabs&u=%23p%3Dh9B3mKDpFy8J

Klein, G. A., Calderwood, R., & Clinton-Cirocco, A. (2010). Rapid decision making on the fire ground: The original study plus a postscript. *Journal of Cognitive Engineering and Decision Making*, *4*(3), 186–209. https://doi.org/10.1518/155534310X12844000801203

Klein, N., & O'Brien, E. (2018). People use less information than they think to make up their minds. *Proceedings of the National Academy of Sciences of the United States of America*, *115*(52), 13222–13227. https://doi.org/10.1073/pnas.1805327115

Klein, G., Shneiderman, B., Hoffman, R. R., & Ford, K. M. (2019). Why expertise matters: A response to the challenges. *IEEE Intelligent Systems*, *32*(6), 67–73.

Kleinginna, P. R., & Kleinginna, A. M. (1981). A categorized list of emotion definitions, with suggestions for a consensual definition. *Motivation and Emotion*, *5*(4), 345–379. https://doi.org/10.1007/BF00992553

Kleinmann, M., Ingold, P. V., Lievens, F., Jansen, A., Melchers, K. G., & König, C. J. (2011). A different look at why selection procedures work: The role of candidates' ability to identify criteria. *Organizational Psychology Review*, *1*(2) 128–146.

Kleinmann, M., & Ingold, P. V. (2019). Toward a better understanding of assessment centers: A conceptual review. *Annual Review of Organizational Psychology and Organizational Behavior*, *6*, 349–372. 10.1146/annurev-orgpsych-012218–014955

Klempin, C. (2021). Zu Entwicklung und Messung von Reflexionstiefe und -breite von Lehramtsstudierenden [On the development and measurement of student teachers' depth and breadth of reflection] . Eine Mixed Methods Interventionsstudie. *Journal Für lehrerInnenbildung*, *21*(1), 76–85. Focus issue: Mythos Reflexion [Mythos reflection]. https://doi.org/10.35468/jlb-01-2021-07

Klimach, A. (2020). *Talent-und Potenzialdiagnosik im Sport – eine Analyse des Vorgehens von Talentscouts unter Differenzierung von Analytik und Intuition [Talent and potential diagnostics in sport – an analysis of the approach of talent scouts, differentiating between analytics and intuition]. Unpublished bachelor thesis*, Leuphana University, Lueneburg.

Klimoski, R. J., & Strickland, W. J. (1977). Assessment centers – valid or merely prescient. *Personnel Psychology*, *30*(3), 353–361. https://doi.org/10.1111/j.1744-6570.1977.tb00428.x

Kline, D. A. (2005). Intuitive Team decisions. In H. Montgomery, R. Lipshitz, & B. Brehmer (Eds.), *Expertise: Research and applications. How professionals make decisions* (pp. 171–182). Lawrence Erlbaum Associates Publishers.

Klopprogge, A., Burmeister, A., & Braun, M. (2019). Digitalisierung und Personalarbeit im Kernbereich menschlicher Wertschöpfung. Begriffliche Aufräumarbeiten, kritische Analysen und Anforderungen der Personalarbeit an digitale Instrumente. [Digitization and human resources management in the area of human value creation. Conceptual tidying up, critical analyses and requirements of human resources management for digital tools]. In Goinger Kreis – Initiative Zukunft Personal und Beschäftigung e.V (Ed.), *Grenzüberschreitungen zwischen Unternehmen und Gesellschaft. Herausforderungen im System Arbeit gemeinsam bewältigen* (pp. 199–280). Westarp Science – Fachverlage.

Klopprogge, A. (2022). Methode Mensch. Oder die Rückkehr des Handelns. [Human Method. Or the return of action]. Unpublished manuscript.

Klotz, A. C., Da Motta Veiga, S. P., Buckley, M. R., & Gavin, M. B. (2013). The role of trustworthiness in recruitment and selection: A review and guide for future research. *Journal of Organizational Behavior*, *34*(S1), S 104–S 119. https://doi.org/10.1002/job.1891

Knapp, M. L., & Hall, J. A. (2009). *Nonverbal communication in human interaction*. Cengage Learning.

Knauff, M. (2020). Die Mär von der Superintelligenz [The myth of super intelligence]. *Psychologie Heute*, *4*, 36–40. https://www.psychologie-heute.de/gesellschaft/40402-die-maer-von-der-superintelligenz.html

Knobloch, T., & Hustedt, C. (2019). *Der maschinelle Weg zum passenden Personal: Zur Rolle algorithmischer Systeme in der Personalauswahl [The machine route to the right personnel. The role of algorithmic systems in personnel selection]*. https://www.stiftung-nv.de/sites/default/files/snv_robo_recruiting.pdf

Koch, A. J., D'Mello, S. D., & Sackett, P. R. (2015). A meta-analysis of gender stereotypes and bias in experimental simulations of employment decision making. *Journal of Applied Psychology, 100*(1), 128–161. https://doi.org/10.1037/a0036734

Koenig, G. (2019). La fin de l'individu – Voyage d'un philosophe au pays de l'intelligence: Voyage d'un philosophe au pays de l'intelligence artificielle [The end of the individual. A philosopher's journey into the world of Artificial Intelligence]. Editions de l'Observatoire

Koenig, A. M., Eagly, A. H., Mitchell, A. A., & Ristikari, T. (2011). Are leader stereotypes masculine? A meta-analysis of three research paradigms. *Psychological Bulletin, 137*(4), 616–642. https://doi.org/10.1037/a0023557

Koffka, K. (2014). *Principles of Gestalt psychology*. Mimesis International.

Kohn, K. H., & Saar, C. (2006). Makro ist Mikro: Zum Erhalt marktwirtschaftlicher Dynamik durch öffentliche Dienstleistungen am Arbeitsmarkt. Das Beispiel der Arbeitgeberberatung im Bereich der Personalauswahl [Macro is micro: To maintain market economy dynamics through public services in the labour market. The example of employer consulting in the field of personnel selection. In H.-D. Braun, & B.-J. Ertelt (Eds.), *Schriftenreihe der Fachhochschule des Bundes für Öffentliche Verwaltung: Vol. 47. Paradigmenwechsel in der Arbeitsmarkt- und Sozialpolitik?* (pp. 53–70). Fachhochschule des Bundes für Öffentliche Verwaltung. https://core.ac.uk/download/pdf/71728307.pdf#page=55

Kolominski, S. (2009). Der blinde Fleck im Personalauswahlprozess. Identifikation von unbewussten Faktoren im Auswahlprozess am Beispiel von Einstellungsinterviews [The blind spot in the personnel selection process. Identification of unconscious factors in the selection process using the example of recruitment interviews]. Kovač.

Kootz, J. (2014). *Kundenorientiertes Personalrecruiting: Eine empirische Untersuchung unter besonderer Berücksichtigung von Customer Experience Management [Customer-oriented personnel recruiting: An empirical study with special emphasis on Customer Experience Management]* [Dissertation]. Trier University, Trier. https://ubt.opus.hbz-nrw.de/opus45-ubtr/frontdoor/deliver/index/docId/618/file/Kootz_Jochen_Dissertation_Candidate_Experience_022014.pdf

Koppers, N. (2013). *Zu den Determinanten von analytischen und intuitiven Urteils- und Entscheidungsprozessen von Recruitern in Einstellungsinterviews* [On the determinants of analytical and intuitive judgment and decision processes of recruiters in hiring interviews]. PhD thesis, Ruhr University Bochum.

Kosinski, M., Matz, S. C., Gosling, S. D., Popov, V., & Stillwell, D. (2015). Facebook as a research tool for the social sciences: Opportunities, challenges, ethical considerations, and practical guidelines. *The American Psychologist, 70*(6), 543–556. https://doi.org/10.1037/a0039210

Kosinski, M., Stillwell, D., & Graepel, T. (2013). Private traits and attributes are predictable from digital records of human behavior. *Proceedings of the National Academy of Sciences of the United States of America, 110*(15), 5802–5805. https://doi.org/10.1073/pnas.1218772110

Koßler, M. (1998). Der Wandel des Intuitionsbegriffs im Spätmittelalter und seine Bedeutung für das neuzeitliche Denken [The change of the concept of intuition in the late Middle Ages and its significance for modern thinking]. *Zeitschrift Für Philosophische Forschung, 52*(4), 542–567.

Kouzes, J. M., & Posner, B. Z. (2017). *The leadership challenge. How to make extraordinary things happen in organizations* (6th ed.). Wiley.

Köchling, A. C., & Körner, S. (1996). Personalauswahl aus der Sicht der Betroffenen: Zur bewerberorientierten Gestaltung von Beurteilungssituationen [Personnel selection from the point of view of the persons concerned: On the applicant oriented design of assessment situations]. Zeitschrift Für Arbeits- Und Organisationspsychologie, 40(1), 22–37.

Köhn, R. (2021). Was die Stimme über Gesundheit und Gemüt verrät [What the voice reveals about health and state of mind]. In *Frankfurter Allgemeine Zeitung*, 29.5.2021, p. 26.

König, K. (2007). *Abwehrmechanismen [Defense mechanism]*. Vandenhoeck & Ruprecht.

König, C. J., Klehe, U.-C., Berchtold, M., & Kleinmann, M. (2010). Reasons for being selective when choosing personnel selection procedures. *International Journal of Selection and Assessment, 18*(1), 17–27. https://doi.org/10.1111/j.1468-2389.2010.00485.x

König, C. J. & Marcus, B. (2013). TBS-TK-Rezension. Persolog Persönlichkeitsprofil [TBS-TK Review. Persolog Personality Profile]. *Psychologische Rundschau* 64(3),189-191. https://doi:10.1026/0033-3042/a00017

König, C. J., Wong, J., & Cen, G. (2012). How much do Chinese applicants fake. *International Journal of Selection and Assessment, 20*(2), 247–250. https://doi.org/10.1111/j.1468-2389.2012.00596.x

Krause, A., Rinne, U., & Zimmermann, K. F. (2010). *Anonymisierte Bewerbungsverfahren [Anonymous application procedures]* (IZA Research Report No. 27). Institut zur Zukunft der Arbeit.

Krause, D. E. (2011). *Trends in der internationalen Personalauswahl [Trends in international personnel selection]*. Hogrefe.

Krause, D. E. (2017). Anwendung der Personalauswahlverfahren im internationalen Vergleich [Application of personnel selection procedures in an international comparison]. In D. E. Krause (Ed.), *Personalauswahl* (pp. 243–269). Springer Fachmedien. https://doi.org/10.1007/978-3-658-14567-5_11

Krause, D. E., & Thornton III, G. C. (2007). Kulturelle Vielfalt und AC: Handlungsempfehlungen für Theorie und Praxis [Cultural diversity and AC: Recommendations for action in theory and practice]. *Zeitschrift Für Führung Und Organisation, 4*, 223–230.

Krause, J., & Ruxton, G. D. (2002). *Living in groups*. Oxford University Press.

Kreutzer, R., & Sirrenberg, M. (2019). *Künstliche Intelligenz verstehen: Grundlagen, Use-Cases, unternehmenseigene KI-Journey [Understand Artifical Intelligence]*. https://search.ebscohost.com/login.aspx?direct=true&scope=site&db=nlebk&db=nlabk&AN=2110627

Krings, T. (2017). *Erfolgsfaktoren effektiver Personalauswahl [Success factors of effective personnel selection]*. Springer Fachmedien. https://doi.org/10.1007/978-3-658-16456-0.

Kruglanski, A. W., & Gigerenzer, G. (2011). Intuitive and deliberate judgments are based on common principles. *Psychological Review, 118*(1), 97–109. https://doi.org/10.1037/a0020762

Kuhl, J. (1990). Intuition und Logik der Forschung in der Psychologie Intuition and logic of research in psychology. In Max-Planck-Institut für psychologische Forschung (Ed.), *Heinz Heckhausen Erinnerungen, Würdigungen, Wirkungen* (pp. 43–73). Springer.

Kuhn, I. (2019). Heuristische Optimierung durch menschliche Intuition – Das Beste aus zwei Welten [Heuristic optimization through human intuition – The best of both worlds]. In M. Becker (Eds.), *SKILL 2019 – Studierendenkonferenz Informatik* (pp. 97–108). Gesellschaft für Informatik e.V.

Kulik, C. T., Roberson, L., & Perry, E. L. (2007). The Multiple-Category Problem: Category Activation and Inhibition in the Hiring Process. *Academy of Management Review, 32*(2), 529–548. https://doi.org/10.5465/amr.2007.24351855

Kumari, N., & Malhotra, R. (2013). A study of the recruitment and selection process: SMC global. *ZENITH International Journal of Multidisciplinary Research, 3*(2), 244–254.

Kuncel, N. R. (2008). Some new (and Old) Suggestions for improving personnel selection. *Industrial and Organizational Psychology, 1*(3), 343–346. https://doi.org/10.1111/j.1754-9434.2008.00059.x

Kuncel, N. R., Klieger, D. M., Connelly, B. S., & Ones, D. S. (2013). Mechanical versus clinical data combination in selection and admissions decisions: A meta-analysis. *Journal of Applied Psychology, 98*(6), 1060–1072. https://doi.org/10.1037/a0034156

Kuncel, N. R., Kochevar, R. J., & Ones, D. S. (2014). A meta-analysis of letters of recommendation in college and graduate admissions: Reasons for hope. *International Journal of Selection and Assessment, 22*(1), 101–107. https://doi.org/10.1111/ijsa.12060

Kunda, Z., & Nisbett, R. E. (1986). The psychometrics of everyday life. *Cognitive Psychology, 18*(2), 195–224. https://doi.org/10.1016/0010-0285(86)90012-5

Kutschker, M., & Schmid, S. (2011). *Internationales Management* (7th ed.). Oldenbourg.

Küpers, W. (2015). Zur Kunst praktischer Weisheit in Organisation und Führung. In M. W. Fröse, S. Kaudela-Baum, & F. E. P. Dievernich (Hrsg.), *Emotion und Intuition in Führung und Organisation* (pp. 65–100). Springer Gabler. https://doi.org/10.13140/2.1.2678.0482

Küpers, W., & Weibler, J. (2008). Emotions in organization: An integral perspective. *International Journal of Work Organization and Emotion, 2*(3), 256–287.

Laireiter, A.-R. (2005). Selbsterfahrung [Self-experience]. In M. Linden, & M. Hautzinger (Eds.), *Verhaltenstherapiemanual* (pp. 50–55). Springer.

Lammers, C. H. (2011). *Emotionsbezogene Psychotherapie: Grundlagen, Strategien und Techniken [Emotion-based psychotherapy: Principles, strategies, and techniques]*. Schattauer.

Lanaj, K., Foulk, T. A., & Erez, A. (2019). Energizing leaders via self-reflection: A within-person field experiment. *Journal of Applied Psychology, 104*(1), 1–18. https://doi.org/10.1037/apl0000350

Lancelot Miltgen, C., Popovič, A., & Oliveira, T. (2013). Determinants of end-user acceptance of biometrics: Integrating the "Big 3" of technology acceptance with privacy context. *Decision Support Systems, 56*, 103–114. https://doi.org/10.1016/j.dss.2013.05.010

Landers, R. N., & Schmidt, G. B. (2016). Social media in employee selection and recruitment: An overview. In R. N. Landers, & G. B. Schmidt (Eds.), *Social media in employee selection and recruitment* (pp. 3–11). Springer International Publishing. https://doi.org/10.1007/978-3-319-29989-1_1

Landsberg, G. V. (2006). *Intuition at work*. https://studylibde.com/doc/2072833/intuition

Lang, D. (2016). *Gefangen im Komplexitätsdilemma [Caught in the complexity dilemma]*. BoD Books On Demand.

Langdale, J. A., & Weitz, J. (1973). Estimating the influence of job information on interviewer agreement. *Journal of Applied Psychology, 57*(1), 23–27.

Langer, M., König, C. J., & Krause, K. (2017). Examining digital interviews for personnel selection: Applicant reactions and interviewer ratings. *International Journal of Selection and Assessment, 25*(4), 371–382. https://doi.org/doi:10.1111/ijsa.12191

Langer, M., Baum, K., & König, C. J. (2018). *Die (Un-)Nachvollziehbarkeit algorithmen-basierter Entscheidungen: Implikationen und Empfehlungen für die Zukunft [The (in)traceability of algorithm-based decisions: Implications and recommendations for the future]*. https://doi.org/10.22028/D291-31275

Langer, M., König, C. J., & Papathanasiou, M. (2019). Highly automated job interviews: Acceptance under the influence of stakes. *International Journal of Selection and Assessment, 27*(3), 217–234. https://doi.org/10.1111/ijsa.12246

Larkin, P., & O'Connor, D. (2017). Talent identification and recruitment in youth soccer: Recruiter's perceptions of the key attributes for player recruitment. *PLOS ONE, 12*(4), e0175716. https://doi.org/10.1371/journal.pone.0175716

Larrick, R. P., Burson, K. A., & Soll, J. B. (2007). Social comparison and confidence: When thinking you're better than average predicts overconfidence (and when it does not). *Organizational Behavior and Human Decision Processes, 102*(1), 76–94. https://doi.org/10.1016/j.obhdp.2006.10.002

Laske, S., & Weiskopf, R. (1996). Personalauswahl – Was wird denn da gespielt? Ein Plädoyer für einen Perspektivenwechsef [Personnel selection-What is it all about? A plea for a change of perspective]. *German Journal of Human Resource Management, 10*(4), 295–330.

Latukha, M. (2016). *Talent management in emerging market firms*. Palgrave Macmillan UK. https://doi.org/10.1057/978-1-137-50606-1.

Lazear, E. P. (1995). *Personnel economics*. MIT Press.

Lazear, E. P. (1998). *Personnel economics for managers*. John Wiley & Sons.

Lazaer, E. P. (1999). Personnel economics: Past lessons and future directions. *Journal of Labor Economics, 17*(2), 199–236.

Le, H., Oh, I.-S., Robbins, S. B., Ilies, R., Holland, E., & Westrick, P. (2011). Too much of a good thing: Curvilinear relationships between personality traits and job performance. *Journal of Applied Psychology, 96*(1), 113–133. https://doi.org/10.1037/a0021016

LeBoon, R. (2018). *Rethinking intuition: Using the framework of an integrative-brain-assessment for optimal decision-making [Theses]*. University of Pennsylvania. https://repository.upenn.edu/cgi/viewcontent.cgi?article=1013&context=od_theses_mp.

LeDoux, J. E. (1996). *The emotional brain: The mysterious underpinnings of emotional life*. Simon & Schuster.

LeDoux, J. E. (2001). *Das Netz der Gefühle: Wie Emotionen entstehen [The web of emotions: How emotions arise]*. Dtv Deutscher Taschenbuch Verlag.

LeDoux, J. E. (2003). The emotional brain, fear, and the amygdala. *Cellular and Molecular Neurobiology, 23*(4-5), 727–738. https://doi.org/10.1023/A:1025048802629

LeDoux, J. E. (2012). Rethinking the emotional brain. *Neuron, 73*(5), 653–676. https://doi.org/10.1016/j.neuron.2012.02.018

LeDoux, J. E., & Phelps, E. A. (2008). Emotional networks in the brain. In M. Lewis, J. M. Haviland, & L. Feldman Barrett (Eds.), *Handbook of emotions* (pp. 159–179). Guilford.

Lee, A. J. (2005). Unconscious bias theory in employment discrimination litigation. *Harvard Civil Rights-Civil Liberties Law Review, 40*(2), 481–503.

Lee, S. Y., Pitesa, M., Thau, S., & Pillutla, M. M. (2015). Discrimination in selection decisions: Integrating stereotype fit and interdependence theories. *Academy of Management Journal, 58*(3), 789–812. https://doi.org/10.5465/amj.2013.0571

Lehrer, J. (2009). *Wie wir entscheiden: Das erfolgreiche Zusammenspiel von Kopf und Bauch [How we decide: The successful interplay of head and gut]*. Piper.

Leitl, M. (2006). Die Regeln des Spiels verstehen [Understanding the rules of the game]. *Harvard Business Manager*, April 2006, 22-25.

LeFebvre, R., & Franke, V. (2013). Culture matters: Individualism vs. collectivism in conflict decision-making. *Societies, 3*(1), 128–146. https://doi.org/10.3390/soc3010128

Lenzen, M. (2022). KI muss wieder langweiliger werden. In sozialen Lebensbereichen richtet schlechte künstliche Intelligenz viel Schaden an [AI needs to become more boring again. In social areas of life, poor artificial intelligence does a lot of damage. In: Frankurter Allgemeine Zeitung, 06.04.2022,p. N4.

Levashina, J., Hartwell, C. J., Morgeson, F. P., & Campion, M. A. (2014). The structured employment interview: Narrative and quantitative review of the research literature. *Personnel Psychology, 67*(1), 241–293. https://doi.org/10.1111/peps.12052

Levenson, R. W., Soto, J., & Pole, N. (2007). Emotion, biology, and culture. In S. Kitayama, & D. Cohen (Eds.), *Handbook of cultural psychology* (pp. 780–796). The Guilford Press.

Levin, M. (2018). *Harvard Research Reveals How Mindful Leaders Develop Better Companies and Happier Employees*. https://www.inc.com/marissa-levin/harvard-research-reveals-how-mindful-leaders-develop-better-companies-happier-employees.html

Levitin, D. J. (2009). *Der Musik-Instinkt: Die Wissenschaft einer menschlichen Leidenschaft [The musical instinct: The science of a human passion]. Spektrum Akademischer Verlag sachbuch.* Spektrum Akademicher.

Levitin, D. J. (2020). *Successful Aging. A Neuroscientist explores the power and potential of our lives.* Dutton.

Lévy-Leboyer, C. (1994). Selection and assessment in Europe. In H. C. Triandis, M. D. Dunnette, & L. M. Hough (Eds.), *Handbook of industrial and organizational psychology* (pp. 173–190). Consulting Psychologists Press.

Lewis, A. C., & Sherman, S. J. (2003). Hiring you makes me look bad: Social-identity based reversals of the ingroup favoritism effect. *Organizational Behavior and Human Decision Processes, 90*(2), 262–276. https://doi.org/10.1016/S0749-5978(02)00538-1

Lewis, R. D. (2006). *When cultures collide: Managing successfully across cultures* (3rd ed.). N. Brealey Publishing.

Leybourne, S. A., & Sadler-Smith, E. (2006). The role of intuition and improvisation in project management. *International Journal of Project Management, 24, 483–492.* 10.1016/j.ijproman.2006.03.007

Liang, B., & Cherian, J. (2014). American and Chinese thinking styles: Attitude effects on holistic and attribute ads. *Organizations and Markets in Emerging Economies, 5*(1), 74–89. doi:10.15388/omee.2014.5.1.14242

Libbrecht, N., Lievens, F., Carette, B., & Côté, S. (2014). Emotional intelligence predicts success in medical school. *Emotion, 14*(1), 64–73.

Libet, B., Gleason, C. A., Wright, E. W., & Pearl, D. K. (1983). Time of conscious intention to act in relation to onset of cerebral activity (Readiness-Potential)". *Brain, 106*(3), 623–642. 10.1093/brain/106.3.623

Lieberman, M. D. (2000). Intuition: A social cognitive neuroscience approach. *Psychological Bulletin, 126*(1), 109–137. https://doi.org/10.1037/0033-2909.126.1.109

Lieberman, M. D. (2007). Social cognitive neuroscience: A review of core processes. *Annual Review of Psychology, 58*, 259–289.

Lieberman, M. D. (2009). What zombies can't do: A social cognitive neuroscience approach to the irreducibility of reflective consciousness. In J. S. B. T. Evans, & K. Frankish (Eds.), *In two minds: Dual processes and beyond* (pp. 293–316). Oxford University Press. https://doi.org/10.1093/acprof:oso/9780199230167.003.0013

Lieberman, M. D. (In press). The X- and C-systems: The neural basis of reflexive and reflective social cognition. In E. Harmon-Jones, & P. Winkelman (Eds.), *Fundamentals of social neuroscience.* Guilford. http://www.scn.ucla.edu/pdf/X%26C%20(in%20press).pdf

Liem, C. C. S., Langer, M., Demetriou, A., Hiemstra, A. M. F., Sukma Wicaksana, A., Born, M. P., & König, C. J. (2018). Psychology meets machine learning: Interdisciplinary perspectives on algorithmic job candidate screening. In H. J. Escalante, S. Escalera, I. Guyon, X. Baró, Y. Güçlütürk, U. Güçlü, & M. van Gerven (Eds.), *The springer series on challenges in machine learning. explainable and interpretable models in computer vision and machine learning* (pp. 197–253). Springer International Publishing. https://doi.org/10.1007/978-3-319-98131-4_9

Lievens, F. (2001). Assessors and use of assessment centre dimensions. A fresh look at a troubling issue. *Journal of Organizational Behavior, 22*(3), 203–221. 10.1002/job.65

Lievens, F. (2007). Research on selection in an international context: Current status and future directions. In M. M. Harris (Ed.), *Handbook of research in international human resource management* (pp. 107–123). Lawrence Erlbaum Associates.

Lievens, F. (2016). Assessment Centres for Screening and Development of Skill: A Critical Analysis. *Presented at the 1st International Conference on Applied Psychology (2016), Gurgaon, India.* https://www.google.com/url?sa=t&rct=j&q=&esrc=s&source=web&cd=&ved=2ahUKEwi94qLX

luLuAhXOgVwKHYSdCnYQFjAAegQIAxAC&url=https%3A%2F%2Fwww.9links.in%2Fpdf%2Fassessment-centres-for-screening-and-development-of-skill-a-critical-analysis.pdf&usg=AOvVaw2QMWBWa_t62B_BR9sIQ0yH

Lievens, F. (2017). Assessing personality-situation interplay in personnel selection: Toward more integration into personality research. *European Journal of Personality*, *31*(5), 424–440. https://doi.org/10.1002/per.2111

Lievens, F., & Goemaere, H. (1999). A different look at assessment centers: Views of assessment center users. *Journal of Selection and Assessment*, *7*(4), 215–219.

Lievens, F., & Klimoski, R. J. (2001). Understanding the assessment center process: Where are we now? In C. L. Cooper, & I. T. Robertson (Eds.), *International review of industrial and organizational psychology* (Vol. 16, pp. 245–286). John Wiley & Sons.

Lievens, F., & Conway, J. M. (2002). Dimensions and exercise variance in assessment center scores. A large-scale evaluation of multitrait-multimethod studies. *Journal of Applied Psychology*, *86*(6), 1202–1222. doi:10.1037/0021-9010.86.6.1202. https://www.researchgate.net/publication/242078370_Understanding_the_Assessment_Center_Process_Where_Are_We_Now (1-63).

Lievens, F., & Paepe, A. (2004). An empirical investigation of interviewer-related factors that discourage the use of high structure interviews. *Journal of Organizational Behavior*, *25*(1), 29–46. https://doi.org/10.1002/job.246

Lievens, F., Highhouse, S., & Corte, W. (2005). The importance of traits and abilities in supervisors' hirability decisions as a function of method of assessment. *Journal of Occupational and Organizational Psychology*, *78*(3), 453–470. https://doi.org/10.1348/096317905X26093

Lim, C. H., Winter, R., & Chan, C. C. A. (2006). Cross-cultural interviewing in the hiring process: Challenges and strategies. *The Career Development Quarterly*, *54*(2006), 265–268.

Lim, N. (2016). Cultural differences in emotion: Differences in emotional arousal level between the East and the West. *Integrative Medicine Research*, *5*(2), 105–109. https://doi.org/10.1016/j.imr.2016.03.004

Lind, E. A., & Tyler, T. R. (1988). *The social psychology of procedural justice. Critical issues in social justice*. Springer. doi:10.1007/978-1-4899-2115-4_1.

Lindemann, K. (2020). *Die Akzeptanz personaldiagnostischer Verfahren zur Auswahl globaler Führungskräfte – Eine qualitative Vergleichsstudie der Länderkulturen Deutschland und China [The Acceptance of Personnel Diagnostic Procedures for the Selection of Global Managers – A Qualitative Comparative Study of the Country Cultures Germany and China]. Unpublished master thesis*, Leuphana University, Lueneburg.

Lindquist, K. A., Wager, T. D., Kober, H., Bliss-Moreau, E., & Barrett, L. F. (2012). The brain basis of emotion: A meta-analytic review. *Behavioral and Brain Sciences*, *35*, 121–143.

Linkedin. (2019). *How small businesses attract and hire top talent*. https://business.linkedin.com/talent-solutions/resources/talent-strategy/smb-attracting-top-talent

Linnenbürger, A., Greb, C., & Gratzel, D. C. (2018). PRECIRE Technologies. In K. P. Schulle (Ed.), *Psychologische Diagnostik durch Sprachanalyse- Validierung der PRECIRE-Technologie für die Personalarbeit* (pp. 23–56). Springer Gabler.

List, K.-H. (2014). *Bewerberauswahl – Kopf oder Bauch? [Applicant selection – head or gut?]* https://www.perspektive-mittelstand.de/Knackpunkt-Personalauswahl-Bewerberauswahl-Kopf-oder-Bauch/management-wissen/5929.html

Livingstone, A. G., Fernández Rodríguez, L., & Rothers, A. (2020). "They just don't understand us": The role of felt understanding in intergroup relations. *Journal of Personality and Social Psychology*, *119*(3), 633–656. https://doi.org/10.1037/pspi0000221

Lloyd-Smith, M. (2020). The COVID-19 pandemic: Resilient organisational response to a low chance,high-impact event. *BMJ Leader*, 0, 1–4.

Lochner, K., & Preuß, A. (2018). Digitales Recruiting: Die Evolution des Assessments mittels künstlicher Intelligenz [Digital recruiting: The evolution of assessment using artificial intelligence]. *Zeitschrift Für Angewandte Organisationspsychologie*, *49*(3), 193–202. https://doi.org/10.1007/s11612-018-0425-7

Lodato, M. A., Highhouse, S., & Brooks, M. E. (2011). Predicting professional preferences for intuition-based hiring. *Journal of Managerial Psychology*, *26*(5), 352–365. https://doi.org/10.1108/02683941111138985

Loewenstein, G. (1996). Out of control. Visceral influences on behavior. *Organizational Behavior and Human Decision Process*, *65*(3), 272–292.

Loewenstein, G. (2005). Hot-cold empathy gaps and medical decision making. *Health Psychology*, *24*(5 Suppl), S49–S56.

Loewenstein, G., & Lerner, J. (2003). The role of affect in decision making. In R. J. Dawson, K. R. Scherer,&, & H. H. Goldsmith (Eds.), *Handbook of affective science* (pp. 619–642). Oxford University Press.

Lohaus, D., & Habermann, W. (2013). *Personalauswahl im Mittelstand. Nicht die Besten sind die Besten, sondern die Geeignetsten [Personnel selection in medium-sized companies]*. Walter de Gruyter. https://doi.org/10.1026/0932-4089/a000163.

Lopes, L. L. (1991). The rhetoric of irrationality. *Theory Psychology*, (1), 65–82. https://doi.org/10.1177/0959354391011005

Lübben, M., Cüppers, F., Mohr, J., Witzleben, M. V., Breuer, U., Waser, R., Neumann, C., & Valov, I. (2020). Design of defect-chemical properties and device performance in memristive systems. *Science Advances*, *6*(19), eaaz9079. https://doi.org/10.1126/sciadv.aaz9079

Lussier, K. (2016). Managing Intuition. *Business History Review*, *90*(4), 708–718. https://doi.org/10.1017/S0007680517000058

Lussier, K. (2018). From the Intuitive Human to the Intuitive Computer. *Technology's Stories*. Advance online publication. https://doi.org/10.15763/jou.ts.2018.03.16.01

Luxen, M. F., & van de Vijver, F. J. R. (2006). Facial attractiveness, sexual selection, and personnel selection: When evolved preferences matter. *Journal of Organizational Behavior*, *27*(2), 241–255. https://doi.org/10.1002/job.357

Lynch, D. (2007). *Catching the Big Fish. Meditation, Consciousness, and Creativity (10. Anniversary Edition)*. Penguin.

Ma, R., & Allen, D. G. (2009). Recruiting across cultures: A value-based model of recruitment. *Human Resource Management Review*, *19*(4), 334–346.

Macan, T. H., & Dipboye, R. L. (1990). The relationship of interviewers' preinterview impression to selection and recruitment outcomes. *Personnel Psychology*, *43*(4), 745–768. https://doi.org/10.1111/j.1744-6570.1990.tb00681.x

Macan, T. H., Avedon, M. J., Paese, M., & Smith, D. E. (1994). The effects of applicants' reactions to cognitive ability tests and an assessment center. *Personnel Psychology*, *47*(4), 715–738. https://doi.org/10.1111/j.1744-6570.1994.tb01573.x

Mack, O., Khare, A., Krämer, A., & Burgartz, T. (2016). *Managing in a VUCA World*. Springer International Publishing. https://doi.org/10.1007/978-3-319-16889-0.

Maehr, M. L. (1974). Culture and achievement motivation. *American Psychologist*, *29*(12), 887–896. https://doi.org/10.1037/h0037521

Maidique, M. (2011). *Panel of experts presents new research on international leadership*. http://lead.fiu.edu/news/article/the-leaders-toolbox-by-dr-modesto-maidique.html.

Maldei, T., Baumann, N., & Koole, S. L. (2020). The language of intuition: A thematic integration model of intuitive coherence judgments. *Cognition & Emotion*, *34*(6), 1183–1198. https://doi.org/10.1080/02699931.2020.1736005

Malewska, K. (2015). Intuition in decision making – theoretical and empirical aspects. *International Journal of Business and Economic Development, 3*(3), 97–98.
Malewska, K., & Sajdak, M. (2014). The intuitive manager and the concept of strategic leadership. *Management, 18*(2), 44–58. https://doi.org/10.2478/manment-2014-0041
Mamin, C. (2020). Intuition und Erkenntnis: Philosophische Positionen der Neuzeit [Intuition and Knowlege Discovery: Philosophical Positions of the Modern Era]. In Intuition und Erkenntnis, (pp. 9–33). doi: https://doi.org/10.30965/9783957437464_003
Manroop, L., Boekhorst, J. A., & Harrison, J. A. (2013). The influence of cross-cultural differences on job interview selection decisions. *The International Journal of Human Resource Management, 24*(18), 3512–3533.
Marewski, J. N., Gaissmaier, W., & Gigerenzer, G. (2010). Good judgments do not require complex cognition. *Cognitive Processing, 11*(2), 103–121. https://doi.org/10.1007/s10339-009-0337-0
Marewski, J. N., & Gigerenzer, G. (2013). Entscheiden [Deciding]. In W. Sarges (Ed.), *Management-Diagnostik* (4. ed., pp. 228–241). Hogrefe.
Markowsky, G. (2021). Information theory (chapter Physiology). *Encyclopedia Britannica*, https://www.britannica.com/science/information-theory/Physiology
Marlowe, C. M., Schneider, S. L., & Nelson, C. E. (1996). Gender and attractiveness biases in hiring decisions: Are more experienced managers less biased? *Journal of Applied Psychology, 81*(1), 11–21.
Marquard, T. (2017). Der Abschied von individuell-variabler Vergütung. *Changement!, 2*, 12–14.
Marr, B. (2018). *Data-Driven HR: How to Use Analytics and Metrics to Drive Performance.* https://ebookcentral. proquest.com
Martell, K. (2018). *Intuition in der psychosozialen Beratung und ihre Bedeutung für die pro fessionelle Beziehungsgestaltung*. ZKS-Verlag.
Masuda, T., & Nisbett, R. E. (2001). Attending holistically versus analytically: Comparing the context sensitivity of Japanese and Americans. *Journal of Personality and Social Psychology, 81*(5), 922–934. https://doi.org/10.1037/0022-3514.81.5.922
Masuda, T., Wang, H., Ishii, K., & Ito, K. (2012). Do surrounding figures' emotions affect judgment of the target figure's emotion? Comparing the eye-movement patterns of European Canadians, Asian Canadians, Asian international students, and Japanese. *Frontiers in Integrative Neuroscience, 6*(72), 1–9. https://doi.org/10.3389/fnint.2012.00072
Matsumoto, D. (1989). Cultural influences on the perception of emotion. *Journal of Cross-Cultural Psychology, 20*(1), 92–105. https://doi.org/10.1177/0022022189201006
Matsumoto, D. (1990). Cultural similarities and differences in display rules. *Motivation and Emotion, 14*(3), 195–214. https://doi.org/10.1007/BF00995569
Matsumoto, D. (1996). *Unmasking Japan: Myths and realities about the emotions of the Japanese.* Stanford University Press.
Matsumoto, D. (2001). Culture and emotion. In D. Matsumoto (Ed.), *Handbook of culture and psychology* (pp. 171–194). Oxford University Press.
Matsumoto, D., Yoo, S. H., & Nakagawa, S. Multinational Study of Cultural Display Rules. (2008). Culture, emotion regulation, and adjustment. *Journal of Personality and Social Psychology, 94*(6), 925–937. https://doi.org/10.1037/0022-3514.94.6.925.
Mavor, P., Sadler-Smith, E., & Gray, D. E. (2010). Teaching and learning intuition: Some implications for HRD and coaching practice. *Journal of European Industrial Training, 34*(8/9), 822–838. https://doi.org/10.1108/03090591011080995
Mayer, E. A. (2011). Gut feelings: The emerging biology of gut-brain communication. *Nature Reviews. Neuroscience, 12*(8), 453–466. https://doi.org/10.1038/nrn3071
Mayer, J. D., & Salovey, P. (1995). Emotional intelligence and regulation of feelings. **o**. *Applied & Preventive Psychology, 4*(1995), 197–208.

Mayer, J. D., & Salovey, P. (1997). What is emotional intelligence? In P. Salovey, & D. J. Sluyter (Eds.), *Emotional development and emotional intelligence: Educational implications* (pp. 3–31). Basic Books.
Mayer, J. D., Salovey, P., & Caruso, D. R. (2004). Emotional Intelligence: Theory, Findings, and Implications. *Psychological Inquiry*, *15*(3), 197–215.
Mayrhofer, W. (2004). Social systems theory as theoretical framework for human resource management–benediction or curse? *Management Revue*, *15*(2), 178–191.
Maznevski, M. L., & Distefano, J. J. (2000). Global leaders are team players: Developing global leaders through membership on global teams. *Human Resource Management*, *39*(2-3), 195–208.
Mäkelä, K., Björkman, I., & Ehrnrooth, M. (2010). How do MNCs establish their talent pools? Influences on individuals' likelihood of being labeled as talent. *Journal of World Business*, *45*(2), 134–142. doi:10.1016/j.jwb.2009.09.020
McAbee, S. T., Landis, R. S., & Burke, M. I. (2016). Inductive reasoning: The promise of big data. *Human Resource Management Review*, *27*(2), 277–290.DOI: https://doi.org/10.1016/j.hrmr.2016.08.005
McAfee, A., Brynjolfsson, E., Davenport, T. H., Patil, D. J., & Barton, D. (2012). Big data: The management revolution. *Harvard Business Review*, *90*(10), 60–68.
McAllister, C., Moss, S., & Martinko, M. J. (2019). Why likable leaders seem more effective. *Harvard Business Review*, October 29, 2019. https://hbr.org/2019/10/why-likable-leaders-seem-more-effective
McCarthy, J. M., Bauer, T. N., Truxillo, D. M., Anderson, N., Costa, A. C., & Ahmed, S. M. (2017). Applicant perspectives during selection: A review addressing "So What?," "What's New?," and "Where to Next?". *Journal of Management*, *43*(6), 1693–1725. https://doi.org/10.1177/0149206316681846
McClelland, D. (1988). *Human motivation*. Cambridge University Press.
McClelland, D., & Burnham, D. (1976). Power is the great motivator. *Harvard Business Review*, *54*(2), 100–110.
McCutcheon, H., & Pincombe, J. (2001). Intuition: An important tool in the practice of nursing. *Journal of Advanced Nursing*, *35*(3), 342–348.
McDaniel, M. A., Whetzel, D. L., Schmidt, F. L., & Maurer, S. D. (1994). The validity of employment interviews: A comprehensive review and meta-analysis. *The Journal of Applied Psychology*, *79*(4), 599–616. https://doi.org/10.1037/0021-9010.79.4.599
McFarlin, D. B., & Sweeney, P. D. (2001). Cross-cultural applications of organizational justice. In R. Cropanzano (Ed.), *Series in applied psychology. Justice in the workplace* (pp. 67–95). Lawrence Erlbaum Associates.
McGovern, T. V. (1976). The making of a job interviewee: The effect of nonverbal behavior on an interviewer's evaluations during a selection interview. *Dissertation Abstracts Int.*, *37*(9B), 4740–4741.
McKinsey & Company (2020). *Diversity wins. How inclusion matters*. https://www.mckinsey.com/featured-insights/diversity-and-inclusion/diversity-wins-how-inclusion-matters#
McSweeney, B. (2002). Hofstede's model of national cultural differences and their consequences: A triumph of faith – a failure of analysis. *Human Relations*, *55*(1), 89–118. https://doi.org/10.1177/0018726702551004
Medeiros, J. (2018). *Here's Why Steve Jobs Said Intuition is Absolutely More Powerful Than Intellect*. https://www.goalcast.com/2018/06/26/steve-jobs-said-intuition-is-more-powerful-than-intellect/
Meißner, M., & Nachtwei, J. (2017). Bessere Anforderungsprofile – Digitalisierung und HR [Better job profiles – Digitisation and HR]. *Personalführung*, *3*, 56–61.

Mellahi, K., & Collings, D. G. (2010). The barriers to effective global talent management. The example of corporate élites in MNEs. *Journal of World Business*, *45*, 143–149. 10.1016/j.jwb.2009.09.018
Melchers, K. G. (2017). Qualität in der Personalauswahl [Quality in personnel selection]. In D. E. Krause (Ed.), *Personalauswahl* (pp. 57–70). Springer Fachmedien. https://doi.org/10.1007/978-3-658-14567-5_3
Merkle, K. P., Thielsch, M. T., & Holtmeier, S. (2009). HR meets IT: Computergestützte Personalauswahl–zwischen Psychometrie und User Experience [HR meets IT: Computer-aided personnel selection – between psychometrics and user experience]. In *Praxis der Wirtschaftspsychologie*. 156–173. *Mosenstein und Vannerdat*. www.thielsch.org/download/Merkle_2009.pdf
Mertens, W. (1997). Psychotherapie-Repetitorium zum Sammeln und zur Prüfungsvorbereitung. Nr. 2: Psychoanalytische Abwehrlehre (Teil 1) [Psychotherapy Repetitorium for collecting and exam preparation. No. 2: Psychoanalytic Defense Theory (Part 1)]. *Psychotherapie*, *2*(1), 64–69.
Mesmer-Magnus, J. R., & Viswesvaran, C. (2008). Expatriate management: A review and directions for research in expatriate selection, training, and repatriation. In M. M. Harris (Ed.), *Handbook of research in international human resource management* (pp. 183–206). Taylor & Francis Group/Lawrence Erlbaum Associates.
Mesquita, B. (2007). Emotions are culturally situated. *Social Science Information*, *46*(3), 410–415. https://doi.org/10.1177/05390184070460030107
Messick, S. (1976). Personality consistencies in cognition and creativity. In Messick, S.and associates (Eds.), *Individuality in Learning* (4–22). Jossey-Bass.
Messner, C., Wänke, M., & Weibel, C. (2011). Unconscious Personnel Selection. *Social Cognition*, *29*(6), 699–710. https://doi.org/10.1521/soco.2011.29.6.699
Metalbusiness & Proxidea. (2011). *Kreativität und Intuition um Unternehmensalltag [Creativity and intuition about everyday business life]*. http://www.menk.de/download/studie/studie.pdf
Meyer, E. (2016). *The culture map: Decoding how people think, lead, and get things done across cultures*. Public Affairs.
Michailidis, M. P. (2018). The challenges of AI and Blockchain on HR recruiting practices. *Cyprus Review*, *30*(2), 169–180.
Michelsen, L. (2019). *Talent- und Potenzialdiagnostik – ein empirischer Vergleich des Talentmanagements im Sport und im Bereich Global Leadership* [Talent and Potential Identification – An Empirical Comparison between Talent Management in Sports and Talent Management in the Field of Global Leadership]. Unpublished bachelor thesis, Leuphana University, Lueneburg.
Miles, A., & Sadler-Smith, E. (2014). "With recruitment I always feel I need to listen to my gut": The role of intuition in employee selection. *Personnel Review*, *43*(4), 606–627. https://doi.org/10.1108/PR-04-2013-0065
Miles, S. J., & McCamey, R. (2018). The candidate experience: Is it damaging your employer brand? *Business Horizons*, *61*(5), 755–764. https://doi.org/10.1016/j.bushor.2018.05.007
Miller, A. (2005). *The body never lies. The lingering effects of hurtful parenting*. W. W. Norton & Company.
Miller, C. C., & Ireland, R. D. (2005). Intuition in strategic decision making: Friend or foe in the fast-paced twenty-first century? *Academy of Management Perspectives*, *19*(1), 19–30.
Miller, K. I., Considine, J., & Garner, J. (2007). "Let Me Tell You About My Job": Exploring the Terrain of Emotion in the Workplace. *Management Communication Quarterly*, *20*(3), 231–260. https://doi.org/10.1177/0893318906293589
Minkov, M., & Hofstede, G. (2011). The evolution of Hofstede's doctrine. *Cross Cultural Management*, *18*(1), 10–20. https://doi.org/10.1108/13527601111104269

Mintzberg, H. (1976). Planning on the left side and managing on the right. *Harvard Business Review*, *7/8*, 49–57.
Mintzberg, H. (1989). *Mintzberg on management. Inside our strange world of organizations*. Simon & Schuster.
Mintzberg, H., Ahlstrand, B., & Lampel, J. (1998). *Strategy Safari: A guided tour through the wilds of strategic management*. The Free Press.
Miyamoto, Y., & Kitayama, S. (2002). Cultural variation in correspondence bias: The critical role of attitude diagnosticity of socially constrained behavior. *Journal of Personality and Social Psychology*, *83*(5), 1239–1248. https://doi.org/10.1037/0022-3514.83.5.1239
Mockaitis, A. I., Zander, L., & Cieri, H. D. (2018). The benefits of global teams for international organizations: HR implications. *The International Journal of Human Resource Management*, *29*(12), 2137–2158.
Mondillon, L., Niedenthal, P. M., Brauer, M., Rohmann, A., Dalle, N., & Uchida, Y. (2005). Beliefs about power and its relation to emotional experience: A comparison of Japan, France, Germany, and the United States. *Personality & Social Psychology Bulletin*, *31*(8), 1112–1122. https://doi.org/10.1177/0146167205274900
Montel, C. (2006). Multiple Cut-offs zur Ableitung empirisch fundierter Entscheidungsregeln für die Personalauswahl [Multiple cut-offs to derive empirically based decision rules for personnel selection]. In Arbeitsgemeinschaft Betriebliche Weiterbildungsforschung e. V./Projekt Qualifikations-Entwicklungs-Management (Ed.), *Das Graduiertennetzwerk im Programm "Lernkultur Kompetenzentwicklung": Ergebnisse und Erfahrungen. QUEM-report* Vol. 96, 127–152.
Montel, C. (2013). Prädiktorenauswahl und -kombination [Predictor selection and combination]. In W. Sarges (Ed.), *Management-Diagnostik* (4th ed.) (pp. 785–798). Hogrefe.
Montgomery, H. (1983). Decision rules and the search for a dominance structure: Towards a process model of decision making. In A. Vári, P. Humphreys, & O. Svenson (Eds.), *Advances in psychology. Analysing and aiding decision processes* (Vol. 14, pp. 343–369), Elsevier. https://doi.org/10.1016/S0166-4115(08) 62243-8
Morewedge, C. K. & Kahneman, D. (2010). Associative processes in intuitive judment. *Trends in Cognitive Sciences*, 14(10), 435–440.
Morris, S. B., Daisley, R. L., Wheeler, M., & Boyer, P. (2015). A meta-analysis of the relationship between individual assessments and job performance. *Journal of Applied Psychology*, *100*(1), 5–20. https://doi.org/10.1037/a0036938
Motowidlo, S. J., & Kell, H. J. (2012). Job performance. In N. Schmitt, & S. Highhouse (Eds.), *Handbook of Psychology* Volume 12 Industrial and Organizational Psychology (pp. 82–103). Wiley. https://doi.org/10.1002/9781118133880.hop212005
Mount, M. K., Barrick, M. R., & Strauss, P. J. (1994). Validity of observer ratings of the big five personality factors. *Journal of Applied Psychology*, *79*(2), 272–280.
Mount, K. M., Judge, T. A., Scullen, S. E., Sytsma, M. R., & Hezlett, S. A. (1998). Trait, rater and level effect in 360-degree performance ratings. *Personnel Psychology*, *51*, 557–576.
Mucha, A., & Rauchhaus, E. (2021). *Beratung in Organisationen. Umgang mit Widerstand und Abwehrmechanismen [Consulting in organizations. Dealing with resistance and defense mechanisms]*. Vandenhoeck & Ruprecht.
Mueller, A. (2012). *Interkulturelle Eignungsdiagnostik: Auswahl von Mitarbeitern für einen internationalen Führungsnachwuchskreis [Intercultural aptitude diagnostics: Selection of employees for an international management trainee group*]. Unpublished bachelor thesis, Leuphana University, Lueneburg.
Mukamel, R., Ekstrom, A. D., Kaplan, J., Iacoboni, M., & Fried, I. (2010). Single-neuron responses in humans during execution and observation of actions. *Current Biology*, *20*, 750–756.

Murphy, K. R. (2008). Explaining the weak relationship between job performance and ratings of job performance. *Industrial and Organizational Psychology, 1*(2), 148–160. https://doi.org/10.1111/j.1754-9434.2008.00030.x
Musculus, L., & Lobinger, B. H. (2018). Psychological characteristics in talented soccer players – recommendations on how to improve coaches' assessment. *Frontiers in Psychology, 9*, 41. https://doi.org/10.3389/fpsyg.2018.00041
Mülder, W. (2018). Überblick zu Potenzialen neuer Technologien fÜr HR [BOverview over potentials of new technologies for HR]. In T. Petry, & W. Jäger (Hrsg.), *Digital HR: Smarte und agile Systeme, Prozesse und Strukturen im Personalmanagement* (pp. 103–123). Haufe.
Müller-Christ, G. (2020). Geleitwort [Foreword]. In (O. Ahel.), *Intuition im Management Möglichkeitsraum, Spannungsfelder und emergierende Konstellationen [Management possibility space, tension fields and emerging constellations]* (pp. VII–VIII). Springer Gabler.
Müllerschön, A. (2005). *Bewerber professionell auswählen. Handbuch für Personalverantwortliche [Selecting applicants professionally. Handbook for personnel managers]*. Beltz.
Myers, D. G. (2008). *Psychologie [Psychology]* (2nd ed.). Springer-Lehrbuch. Springer.
Myers, D. G. (2015). *Exploring social psychology* (7th ed.). McGraw-Hill Education.
Myors, B., Lievens, F., Schollaert, E., Van Hoye, G., Cronshaw, S. F., Mladinic, A., et al. (2008). International perspectives on the legal environment for selection. *Industrial and Organizational Psychology, 1*(2), 206–246.
Nachtwei, J., Bernstorff, C. V., Uedelhoven, S., & Liebenow, D. (2013). Segen oder Fluch? Intuition bei Personalauswahlentscheidungen [Blessing or curse? Intuition in personnel selection decisions]. *Personalführung, 11*, 34–41.
Nachtwei, J., Uedelhoven, S., Bernstorff, C., & Liebenow, D. (2017). Evidenz statt Voodoo [Evidence instead of voodoo]. *Personalmagazin, 12*, 34–37.
Naderer, G., & Frank, D. (2015). *Den homo heuristicus verstehen: Implizit braucht Explizit – und umgekehrt [Understanding homo heuristicus: Implicit needs explicit – and vice versa]*. https://www.marktforschung.de/dossiers/themendossiers/behavioral-economics/dossier/den-homo-heuristicus-verstehen-implizit-braucht-explizit-und-umgekehrt-teil-1/
Naor, M., Linderman, K., & Schroeder, R. (2010). The globalization of operations in Eastern and Western countries: Unpacking the relationship between national and organizational culture and its impact on manufacturing performance. *Journal of Operations Management, 28*(3), 194–205. https://doi.org/10.1016/j.jom.2009.11.001
Nardon, L., & Steers, R. M. (2009). The culture theory jungle: Divergence and convergence in models of national culture. In R. S. Bhagat, & R. M. Steers (Eds.), *Cambridge handbook of culture, organizations, and work* (pp. 3–22). Cambridge University Press. https://doi.org/10.1017/CBO9780511581151.002
Navarrete, C. D., Kurzban, R., Fessler, D. M. T., & Kirkpatrick, L. A. (2004). Anxiety and intergroup Bias: Terror management or coalitional psychology? *Group Processes & Intergroup Relations, 7*(4), 370–397. https://doi.org/10.1177/1368430204046144
National Council on Measurement in Education (2017). What are the differences between edumetry and psychmetry measurements? http://www.ncme.org/ncme/NCME/Resource_Center/Glossary/NCME/Resource_Center/Glossary1.aspx?hkey=4bb87415-44dc-4088-9ed9-e8515326a061#anchorP Archived 2017- 07-22at the Wayback Machine
National Research Council. (1991). Evaluating the quality of performance measures: criterion-related validity evidence. In *Performance assessment for the workplace: Volume I* (pp. 141–183). The National Academies Press, https://www.nap.edu/read/1862/chapter/10#182. Or: https://doi.org/10.17226/1862

Nelson, M. W. (2009). A model and literature review of professional skepticism in auditing. *AUDITING: A Journal of Practice & Theory, 28*(2), 1–34. https://doi.org/10.2308/aud.2009.28.2.1

Neys, W. D., Vartanian, O., & Goel, V. (2008). Smarter than we think: When our brains detect that we are biased. *Psychological Science, 19*(5), 483–489. https://doi.org/10.1111/j.1467-9280.2008.02113.x

Ng, I. (2006). *A cross-cultural study of power and power motivation in China and the United States.* Unpublished Doctoral Dissertation, University of Michigan, Ann Arbor.

Ng, K. Y., van Dyne, L., & Ang, S. (2009). From experience to experiential learning: cultural intelligence as a learning capability for global leader development. *Academy of Management Learning & Education, 8*(4), 511–526. https://doi.org/10.5465/amle.8.4.zqr511

Ng, T. W. H. (2017). Transformational leadership and performance outcomes: Analyses of multiple mediation pathways. *The Leadership Quarterly, 28*(3), 385–417. https://doi.org/10.1016/j.leaqua.2016.11.008

Nguyen, L. S., Frauendorfer, D., Mast, M. S., & Gatica-Perez, D. (2014). Hire me: Computational inference of hirability in employment interviews based on nonverbal behavior. *IEEE Transactions on Multimedia, 16*(4), 1018–1031. https://doi.org/10.1109/TMM.2014.2307169

Niederhäusern, G. (2015). Intuition als Führungskompetenz anerkennen und reflektieren [Recognize and reflect intuition as a leadership competence]. In M. W. Fröse, S. Kaudela-Baum, & F. E. P. Dievernich (Eds.), *Emotion und Intuition in Führung und Organisation* (pp. 179–192). Springer Fachmedien Wiesbaden. https://doi.org/10.1007/978-3-658-07796-9_9

Nielsen, J. A., Zielinski, B. A., Ferguson, M. A., Lainhart, J. E., & Anderson, J. S. (2013). An evaluation of the left-brain vs. Right-brain hypothesis with resting state functional connectivity magnetic resonance imaging. *PLOS ONE, 8*(8), e71275. https://doi.org/10.1371/journal.pone.0071275

Nikolaou, I. (2021). What is the role of technology in recruitment and selection? *The Spanish Journal of Psychology, 24*(e2), 1–6. doi:10.1017/SJP.2021.6

Nink, D. (2021). *Justiz und algorithm [Judiciary and algorithm].* Duncker & Humblot.

Nisbett, R. E. (2003). *The geography of thought: How Asians and Westerners think differently – and why.* New York Free Press.

Nisbett, R. E., Peng, K., Choi, I., & Norenzayan, A. (2001). Culture and systems of thought: Holistic versus analytic cognition. *Psychological Review, 108*(2), 291–310. https://doi.org/10.1037/0033-295x.108.2.291

Nishii, L., & Wright, P. (2007). Variability Within Organizations: Implications for Strategic Human Resource Management. *CAHRS Working Paper Series.* https://digitalcommons.ilr.cornell.edu/cahrswp/467/

Nolan, K. P., & Highhouse, S. (2014). Need for autonomy and resistance to standardized employee selection practices. *Human Performance, 27*(4), 328–346. https://doi.org/10.1080/08959285.2014.929691

Norenzayan, A. (2002). Cultural preferences for formal versus intuitive reasoning. *Cognitive Science, 26*(5), 653–684. https://doi.org/10.1016/S0364-0213(02)00082-4

Oatley, K. (1993). Social construction in emotions. In M. Lewis, & J. M. Haviland (Eds.), *Handbook of emotions* (pp. 341–352). Guilford Press.

Obermann, C. (2018). *Assessment Center.* Springer Fachmedien. https://doi.org/10.1007/978-3-658-18716-3.

O'Boyle, E., Jr, & Aguinis, H. (2012). The best and the rest: Revisiting the norm of normality of individual performance. *Personnel Psychology, 65*(1), 79–119. https://doi.org/10.1111/j.1744-6570.2011.01239.x

OCEBM. (2011). *Levels of evidence working group: "The Oxford 2011 Levels of Evidence".* Oxford Centre for Evidence-Based Medicine. http://www.cebm.net/index.aspx?o=5653.

Oechslen, V. (2019). Wie man eine rechtssichere Absage erteilt [How to give a legally sound rejection]. *Human Resources Manager*, https://www.humanresourcesmanager.de/news/arbeitsrecht-rechtsichere-absage-erteilen.html.

Ogden, P., Pain, C., & Minton, K. (2006). *Trauma and the body: A sensorimotor approach to psychotherapy*. Norton series on interpersonal neurobiology W.W. Norton.

Oh, I.-S., Wang, G., & Mount, M. K. (2011). Validity of observer ratings of the five-factor model of personality traits: A meta-analysis. *Journal of Applied Psychology, 96*(4), 762–773. https://doi.org/10.1037/a0021832

Oh, I.-S., Postlethwaite, B. E., & Schmidt, F. L. (2013). Rethinking the validity of interviews for employment decision making: Implications of recent developments in meta-analysis. In D. J. Svyantek, & K. Mahoney (Eds.), *Research in organizational science. received wisdom, kernels of truth, and boundary: conditions in organizational studies* (pp. 297–329). Information Age Publishing.

Oh, D., Shafir, E., & Todorov, A. (2020). Economic status cues from clothes affect perceived competence from faces. *Nature Human Behaviour*, *4*(3), 287–293. https://doi.org/10.1038/s41562-019-0782-4

Okhuysen, G. A., & Bechky, B. A. (2009). Making group process work: Harnessing collective intuition, task conflict, and pacing. In E. A. Locke (Ed.), *Handbook of principles of organizational behavior* (pp. 309–325). John Wiley & Sons. https://d1wqtxts1xzle7.cloudfront.net/33042830/Organization-Behavior-Textbook.pdf?1392925647=&response-content-disposition=inline%3B+filename%3DHandbook_of_Principles_of_Organizational.pdf&Expires=1601053886&Signature=Eefdv6vTlXjv5f3YkJ8d0LZOSZZLDIVKnhPedW-GPeVprlOutpO~WoTmk14YbJ4yimTKPT4cpgmjYztefG21EIF7mMnBzB-d5aIcxbx7EfxfkwE97RZzr9UQe0ss0wNNECqnf0AHiuLl8KLknqL3-FmBzleQqYHY0ALEFh9oPu~YTGSWbyfn~VN2gxy6JEioDKXQD1a~ky7n~D1QnLleSd3EsdVf75ivUq9LsvJy7BjBWvMzOX~fIQBBoi6KnxV2hKp4krTUlddFprClXheiDT1pxuhG10hH4zpcg82AXM9NuX9KzAI0smpxieAkhKIpauqgW8j1SaMKRTLyT4-1pA__&Key-Pair-Id=APKAJLOHF5GGSLRBV4ZA#page=341

Oliveira, S. D., & Nisbett, R. E. (2017). Culture changes how we think about thinking: From “Human Inference” to “Geography of Thought”. *Perspectives on Psychological Science*, *12*(5), 782–790. https://doi.org/10.1177/1745691617702718

Olivola, C. Y. & Todorov, A. (20109: Fooled by first impressions? Reexamining the diagnostic value of appearance-based inferences. *Journal of Experimental Social Psychology*, 46(2) 315–324

Ones, D. S., Dilchert, S., & Viswesvaran, C. (2012). Cognitive abilities. In N. Schmitt (Ed.), *Oxford library of psychology: The Oxford handbook of personnel assessment and selection* (pp. 179–224). Oxford University Press.

Oosterhof, N. N., & Todorov, A. (2008). The functional basis of face evaluation. *PNAS 105*(32) 11087-11092; Published by the National Academy of Science of the USA PNAS. https://doi.org/10.1073/pnas.0805664105

Oostrom, J. K., van der Linden, D., Born, M. P., & van der Molen, H. T. (2013). New technology in personnel selection: How recruiter characteristics affect the adoption of new selection technology. *Computers in Human Behavior*, *29*(6), 2404–2415. https://doi.org/10.1016/j.chb.2013.05.025

Oostrom, J. K., Melchers, K. G., Ingold, P. V., & Kleinmann, M. (2016). Why do situational interviews predict performance? Is it saying how you would behave or knowing how you should behave? *Journal of Business Psychology*, *31*(2), *279–291*. doi:10.1007/s10869-015-9410-0

Oracle; Future Workplace. (2019). *From Fear to Enthusiasm: Artificial Intelligence Is Winning More Heads and Minds in the Workplace*. AI@Work Study 2019. https://www.oracle.com/a/ocom/docs/applications/hcm/ai-at-work-ebook.pdf

Orpen, C. (1984). Attitude similarity, attraction, and decision-making in the employment interview. *The Journal of Psychology, 117*(1), 11–120. https://doi.org/10.1080/00223980.1984.9923666"10.1080/00223980.1984.9923666

Orwat, C. (2019). *Diskriminierungsrisiken durch Verwendung von Algorithmen: Eine Studie, erstellt mit einer Zuwendung der Antidiskriminierungsstelle des Bundes [risks of discrimination through the use of algorithms: A study carried out with a grant from the Antidiskriminierungsstelle des Bundes.].* Institut für Technikfolgenabschätzung und Systemanalyse (ITAS); Karlsruher Institut für Technologie (KIT). https://www.antidiskriminierungsstelle.de/SharedDocs/Downloads/DE/publikationen/Expertisen/Studie_Diskriminierungsrisiken_durch_Verwendung_von_Algorithmen.pdf?__blob=publicationFile&v=5

Osman, M. (2004). An evaluation of dual-process theories of reasoning. *Psychonomic Bulletin & Review, 11*(6), 988–1010. 10.3758/bf03196730

Osoba, O., & Welser, W. (2017). *An intelligence in our image. The risks of bias and errors in artificial intelligence (Research report, RR-1744-RC).* Santa Monica, Calif. https://www.semanticscholar.org/paper/An-Intelligence-in-Our-Image%3A-The-Risks-of-Bias-and-Osoba-Welser/bad46479e184639dee73c58445b90ec0f148859e

Osland, J. S., & Bird, A. (2000). Beyond sophisticated stereotyping: Cultural sensemaking in context. *Academy of Management Perspectives, 14*(1), 65–77. https://doi.org/10.5465/ame.2000.2909840

Pachur, T., & Spaar, M. (2015). Domain-specific preferences for intuition and deliberation in decision making. *Journal of Applied Research in Memory and Cognition, 4*(3), *303–311.* 10.1016/j.jarmac.2015.07.006

Pacini, R., & Epstein, S. (1999). The relation of rational and experiential information processing styles to personality, basic beliefs, and the ratio-bias phenomenon. *Journal of Personality and Social Psychology, 76*(6), 972–987.

Palmer, C. & Kersting, M. (2017). Berufliche Eignung und ihre Diagnostik [Professional aptitude and its diagnostics]. In D.E. Krause (Ed.), Personalauswahl (pp.31–56). Springer Fachmedien (DOI 10.1007/978-3-658-14567-5_2

Paprika, Z. Z. (2008). Analysis and intuition in strategic decision making. The Case of California. Budapesti Corvinus Egyetem. In *Encyclopedia of decision making and decision support technologies* (pp. 20–28). Corvinus University of Budapest.

Parikh, J., Neubauer, -F.-F., & Lank, A. G. (1994). *Intuition: The new frontier of management.* Blackwell.

Pascal, B. (1669). Le Pensées (IV, p. 277). https://www.goodreads.com/quotes/559339-the-heart-has-its-reasons-which-reason-knows-nothing-of

Paschen, M., Stöwe, C., Turck, D., & Beenen, A. (2014). *Assessment Center professionell: Worauf es ankommt und wie Sie vorgehen [Assessment Center professional: What is important and how you proceed] (3. ed.).* Hogrefe.

Pasenau, J. (2021). *Robotic Process Automation und Chatbots in der Personalauswahl: Auswirkungen auf die Qualität der Auswahl und die damit verbundene Candidate Experience* [Robotic Process Automation and Chatbots in Recruitment: Impact on the quality of selection and the associated candidate experience. Unpublished master thesis, Leuphana University, Lueneburg.

Patterson, A., Quinn, L., & Baron, S. (2012). The power of intuitive thinking: A devalued heuristic of strategic marketing. *Journal of Strategic Marketing, 20*(1), 35–44. https://doi.org/10.1080/0965254X.2011.628407

Patterson, R. E., & Eggleston, R. G. (2017). Intuitive cognition. *Journal of Cognitive Engineering and Decision Making, 2017*(11) 1, 5–22. 10.1177/1555343416686476

Pendry, L. (2007). Soziale Kognition [Social Cognition]. In K. Jonas, W. Stroebe, & M. Hewstone (Eds.), *Sozialpsychologie* (pp. 111–144). Springer.
Peters, T., & Waterman, R. (1982). *Search of excellence: Lessons from America's Best-Run companies*. Harper & Row.
Petrican, R., Todorov, A., & Grady, C. (2014). Personality at face value. Facial appearance predicts self and other personality judgments among strangers and spouses. *Journal of Nonverbal Behavior, 38*(2), 259–277.
Petry, T. (2018). Digital HR: Veränderung des Personalmanagements durch digitale Medien und Technologien [Digital HR: Changing HR management through digital media and technologies]. In C. Kochhan, & A. Moutchnik (Eds.), *Media Management* (pp. 43–56). Springer Fachmedien. https://doi.org/10.1007/978-3-658-23297-9_3
Petry, T., & Jäger, W. (2018). Digital HR – Ein Überblick [Digital HR – An overview]. In T. Petry & W. Jäger (Eds.), *Digital HR* - Smarte und agile Systeme, Prozesse und Strukturen im Personalmanagement, (pp. 27–99). Haufe.
Pfeffer, J., & Sutton, R. I. (2000). *The knowing-doing gap*. Harvard Business School Press.
Phelps, E. A. (2005). The interaction of emotion and cognition: The relation between the human amygdala and cognitive awareness. In R. R. Hassin, J. S. Uleman, & J. A. Bargh (Eds.), *Oxford series in social cognition and social neuroscience. The new unconscious* (pp. 61–75). Oxford University Press.
Phillips, J. M., & Gully, S. M. (2002). Fairness reactions to personnel selection techniques in Singapore and the United States. *The International Journal of Human Resource Management, 13*(8), 1186–1205. https://doi.org/10.1080/09585190210149475
Phillips, J. K., Klein, G., & Sieck, W. R. (2004). *Expertise in judgment and decision making: A case for training intuitive decision skills*. In D. J. Koehler, & N. Harvey (Eds.), Handbook of Judgment and Decision Making, chapter *15* (pp. 297–315). Blackwell.
Pfister, H.-R., Jungermann, H., & Fischer, K. (2017). Die Psychologie der Entscheidung. Eine Einführung [The Psychology of Decision. An introduction]. Springer.
Plassmann, R. (2019). *Psychotherapie der Emotionen [Psychotherapy of the emotions]*. Psychosozial-Verlag. https://doi.org/10.30820/9783837974881.
Plessner, H. (2006). Die Klugheit der Intuition und ihre Grenzen [The wisdom of intuition and its limits]. In A. Scherzberg (Ed.), *Neue Staatswissenschaften: Vol. 4. Kluges Entscheiden: Disziplinäre Grundlagen und interdisziplinäre Verknüpfungen* (pp. 109–120). Mohr Siebeck.
Plessner, H., Betsch, C., & Betsch, T. (Eds.). (2008a). *Intuition in judgment and decision making*. Lawrence Erlbaum Associates.
Plessner, H., Betsch, C., & Betsch, T. (2008b). Preface. In H. Plessner, C. Betsch, & T. Betsch (Eds.), *Intuition in judgment and decision making* (pp. VII–XV). Lawrence Erlbaum Associates.
Plous, S. (1993). *The psychology of judgment and decision making*. Mcgraw-Hill Book Company.
Ployhart, R. E., & Ryan, A. M. (1997). Toward an explanation of applicant reactions: an examination of organizational justice and attribution frameworks. *Organizational Behavior and Human Decision Processes, 72*(3), 308–335. https://doi.org/10.1006/obhd.1997.2742
Ployhart, R. E., & Ryan, A. M. (1998). Applicants' reactions to the fairness of selection procedures: The effects of positive rule violations and time of measurement. *The Journal of Applied Psychology, 83*(1), 3–16. https://doi.org/10.1037/0021-9010.83.1.3
Ployhart, R. E., Ryan, A. M., & Bennett, M. (1999). Explanations for selection decisions: Applicants' reactions to informational and sensitivity features of explanations. *The Journal of Applied Psychology, 84*(1), 87–106. https://doi.org/10.1037/0021-9010.84.1.87
Polli, F. (2019). *Using AI to Eliminate Bias from Hiring*. https://hbr.org/2019/10/using-ai-to-eliminate-bias-from-hiring?xing_share=news

Pöppel, E. (2008). *Zum Entscheiden geboren: Hirnforschung für Manager [Born to decide: Brain research for managers]*. Hanser.

Potočnik, K., Anderson, N. R., Born, M., Kleinmann, M., & Nikolaou, I. (2021). Paving the way for research in recruitment and selection: Recent developments, challenges and future opportunities. *European Journal of Work and Organizational Psychology, 30*(2), 159–174. 10.1080/1359432X.2021.1904898

Poropat, A. E. (2014). Other-rated personality and academic performance: Evidence and implications. *Learning and Individual Differences, 34*, 24–32. https://doi.org/10.1016/j.lindif.2014.05.013

Porter, L. W., Lawler, E. E., III, & Hackman, J. R. (1975). Choice processes: Individuals and organizations attracting and selecting each other. In L. W. Porter, E. E. Lawler, III, & J. R. Hackman (Eds.), *Behavior in organizations* (pp. 131–159). McGrawHill.

Possehl, G., & Meyer-Grashorn, A. (2015). *Trust yourself: Intuition im Berufsalltag optimalnutzen [Trust yourself: Making the best use of intuition in everyday life]*. Haufe.

Praslova, L. (2008). The legal environment for selection in Russia. Industrial and Organizational Psychology, *1*(2), 264–265.

Premaraja, R. K., Thornton III, G. C., & Padhi, P. K. (2008). Legal Environment for Selection in India. *Industrial and Organizational Psychology, 1*(2), 258–259.

Prescott, T. J., & Caleb-Solly, P. (2017). *Robotics in social care: A connected care EcoSystem for independent living*. EPSRC UK Robotics and Autonomous Systems Network White Papers. http://eprints.whiterose.ac.uk/155146/

Prietula, M. J., & Simon, H. A. (1989). The experts in your midst. *Harvard Business Review, 67*(1), 120–124.

Proost, K., Germeys, F., & Vanderstukken, A. (2020). Applicants' pre-test reactions towards video interviews: The role of expected chances to demonstrate potential and to use nonverbal cues. *European Journal of Work and Organizational Psychology, 30*(2), 265–273. https://doi.org/10.1080/1359432X.2020.1817975

Proximea. (2011). *Studie Kreativität und Intuition [Study creativity and intuition]*. Proximea Unternehmensberatung.

PSI-Impuls 8. (2021). *Vom Nur zum Auch. Wie kann der unbewusste Wille rational und umsichtig sein? [From Only to Also. How can the unconscious will be rational and prudent?*]. https://docplayer.org/199141548-Psi-impuls-8-vom-nur-zum-auch-wie-kann-der-unbewusste-wille-rational-und-umsichtig-sein-version-vom.html

Pudelko, M. (2006). A comparison of HRM systems in the USA, Japan and Germany in their socio-economic context. *Human Resource Management Journal, 16*(2), 123–153. https://doi.org/10.1111/j.1748-8583.2006.00009.x

Pudelko, M., & Harzing, A.-W. (2007). Country-of-origin, localization, or dominance effect? An empirical investigation of HRM practices in foreign subsidiaries. *Human Resource Management, 46*(4), 535–559. https://doi.org/10.1002/hrm.20181

Quinones, M. A., Ford, J. K., & Teachout, M. S. (1995). The relationship between work experience and job performance: A conceptual and meta-analytic review. *Personnel Psychology, 48*, 887–910.

Radicchi, E., & Mozzachiodi, M. (2016). Social talent scouting: A new opportunity for the identification of football players? *Physical Culture and Sport. Studies and Research, 70*(1), 28–43. https://doi.org/10.1515/pcssr-2016-0012

Rahaman, H. M. (2014). Personality and decision making styles of university students. *Journal of the Indian Academy of Applied Psychology, 40*(1), 138–144.

Rahe, C., & Rahe, T. M. (2017). *Nutzung von personaldiagnostischen Instrumenten bei der Auswahl von Führungskräften in deutschen Unternehmen [Use of personnel-diagnostic instruments in*

the selection of executives in German companies]. BDU. https://www.bdu.de/media/296505/rmc-studie_einsatz-von-personaldiagnostischen-verfahren.pdf
Rahman, H. A. (2021). The invisible cage: Workers' reactivity to opaque algorithmic evaluations. *Administrative Science Quarterly*, (4), 1–44. 10.1177/00018392211010118
Raiz, M. N., Raiz, M. A., & Batool, N. (2012). Personality types as predictors of decision making styles. *Journal of Behavioral Sciences, 22*(2), 99–114.
Ramge, T. (2020). *postdigital: Wie wir Künstliche Intelligenz schlauer machen, ohne uns von ihr bevormunden zu lassen [postdigital: How we make artificial intelligence smarter without letting it patronize us].* Murmann.
Rao, H. (2021). Accountability = account x ability. *McKinsey Quarterly*, July 12, 2021. https://www.mckinsey.com/business-functions/organization/our-insights/accountability-equals-account-x-ability
Rath, M. (2019. *Wahrnehmungsverzerrungen und die Konsequenzen für die Rationalität,Analytik und Intuition in der globalen Personalauswahl* [Biases of perception and the consequences for rationality, analytics, and intuition in global recruiting] Unpublished master thesis. Leuphana University, Lueneburg.
Rasmussen, T., & Ulrich, D. (2015). Learning from practice: How HR analytics avoids being a management fad. *Organizational Dynamics, 44*(3), 236–242. https://doi.org/10.1016/j.orgdyn.2015.05.008
Rayasam, R. (2012). *Equal Access: Anonymous Applications Help Immigrants and Women.* https://www.spiegel.de/international/business/test-shows-anonymous-applications-helps-diversify-workforce-a-828322.html
Reckwitz, A. (2020). *The society of singularities.* Polity.
Reichelt, K. (2020). Intuition & Leadership: Inwiefern beeinflusst Intuition Personalführungsentscheidungen [How does intuition influnce leadership decisions]. Unpublished maste thesis, Leuphana University, Lueneburg.
Reid, T. (1764). *An inquiry into the human mind, on the principles of common sense. Cambridge Library Collection. Philosophy.* Cambridge university press.
Reimann, G. (2010). Grundlagen und rechtliche Rahmenbedingungen der DIN 33430 [Basics and legal framework of DIN 33430]. In K. Westhoff, C. Hagemeister, M. Kersting, F. Lang, H. Moosbrugger, G. Reimann, & G. Stemmler T. d. F. D. Psychologenvereinigungen (Eds.), *Grundwissen für die berufsbezogene Eignungsbeurteilung nach DIN 33430* (pp. 15–21). Pabst Science Publishers.
Reimann, G., & Frenzel, T. (2009). *Moderne Eignungsbeurteilung mit der DIN 33430: Mit einer Software zur computergestützten Konformitätsprüfung und einem Originalabdruck mit der DIN 33430 [Modern assessment with DIN 33430: With software for computer-aided conformity testing and an original print of DIN 33430].* VS Verlag für Sozialwissenschaften.
Reimann, G., Frenzel, T., & Michalke, S. (2009). DIN 33430 – Quo vadis? *Zeitschrift Für Personalpsychologie, 8*(3), 156–158. https://doi.org/10.1026/1617-6391.8.3.156
Reimann, G., Frenzel, T., Michalke, S., & Peper, M. (2008). Verbreitung und Akzeptanz der DIN 33430: Eine Stellungnahme [Distribution and acceptance of DIN 33430: A statement]. *Zeitschrift Für Personalpsychologie, 7*(4), 178–180. https://doi.org/10.1026/1617-6391.7.4.178
Reimann, G., Frenzel, T., Michalke, S., & Peper, M. (2009). Verbreitung und Akzeptanz der DIN 33430: Eine zweite Stellungnahme [Distribution and acceptance of DIN 33430: A second statement]. *Zeitschrift Für Personalpsychologie, 8*(1), 35–39. https://doi.org/10.1026/1617-6391.8.1.35
Reis, H. T., Regan, A., & Lyubomirsky, S. (2021). Interpersonal chemistry: What is it, how does it emerge, and how does it operate? *Perspectives on Psychological Science, 1–29.* PMID 34436954. doi:10.1177/1745691621994241.

Reitz, M., & Chaskalson, M. (2016a). Mindfulness works but only if you work at it. *Harvard Business Review*, https://hbr.org/2016/11/mindfulness-works-but-only-if-you-work-at-it.

Reitz, M., & Chaskalson, M. (2016b). How to bring mindfulness to your company's leadership. https://mindleader.org/wp-content/uploads/2017/08/HARVARD-BUSINESS-REVIEW_How-to-bring-Mindfulness-to-your-leadership.pdf

Reitz, M., & Chaskalson, M. (2017). Developing mindful leadership: A reality check. *Positive and Mindful Leader*, *1*(2), 20–23.

Reitz, M., Waller, L., Chaskalson, M., Olivier, S., & Rupprecht, S. (2020). Developing leaders through mindfulness practice. *Journal of Management Development*, *39*(2), 223–239. https://doi.org/10.1108/JMD-09-2018-0264

Remmers, C., Topolinski, S., & Michalak, J. (2015). Mindful(l) intuition: Does mindfulness influence the access to intuitive processes? *The Journal of Positive Psychology*, *10*(3), 282–292. http://dx.doi.org/10.1080/17439760.2014.950179

Reskin, B. (2005). Unconsciousness raising: The pernicious effects of unconscious bias. *Regional Review*, *14*(1), 32–37.

Richter, T. (2016). *Jeder kann führen: Über moderne Führung zwischen Systemdenken und Menschlichkeit [Anyone can lead: On modern leadership between system thinking and humanity]*. Books on Demand.

Rick, S., & Loewenstein, G. (2008). The role of emotion in economic behavior. In M. Lewis, J. M. Haviland-Jones, & L. Feldman Barrett (Eds.), *Handbook of emotions* (3rd ed. Chapter 9 pp. 138–156). The Guilford Press.

Riedel, T. (2015). *Internationale Personalauswahl [International Personnel Selection]*. Vandenhoeck & Ruprecht. https://doi.org/10.13109/9783666491559.

Riedel, T. (2016). Und was, wenn die Praxis doch recht hat? Acht Gründe für eine Neubetrachtung des Themas „Struktur" im Vorstellungsgespräch [.And what if practice is right after all? Eight reasons for reconsidering the topic of "structure" in the interview]. *Interpool*, 1–21. https://www.interpool-hr.com/sites/default/files/19/10/tim_riedel_neubetrachtung_von_struktur_im_vorstellungsgespraech_sep_2016.pdf

Rietiker, J. (2010). Auswahl von personal [Selection of personnel]. In B. Werkmann-Karcher, & J. Rietiker (Eds.), *Angewandte Psychologie für das human resource management* (pp. 215–237). Springer.

Rinne, T., Steel, G. D., & Fairweather, J. (2012). Hofstede and Shane revisited: The role of power distance and individualism in national-level innovation success. *Cross-Cultural Research*, *46*(2), 91–108. doi:10.1177/1069397111423898

Rizzolatti, G., & Sinigaglia, C. (2007). *Mirrors in the Brain. How Our Minds Share Actions and Emotions*. Oxford University Press.

Roberts, C., & Campbell, S. (2006). Talk on Trial: Job interviews, language and ethnicity. In: Research Report No. 344, London: Department of Work and Pensions.

Robertson, I. T., & Smith, M. (2001). Personnel selection. *Journal of Occupational and Organizational Psychology*, *74*(4), 441–472. https://doi.org/10.1348/096317901167479

Robertson, M. (2019). *Communicating sustainability*. Routledge.

Rock, D., & Schwartz, J. (2006). The neuroscience of leadership. *Strategy + Business*, *43*(1–10), https://www.strategy-business.com/article/06207?gko=f1af3

Roese, N. J., & Vos, K. D. (2013). Hindsight Bias. *Perspectives on Psychological Science*, *7*(5), 411–427. doi:10.1177/1745691612454303

Roethlisberger, F. J., Dickson, W. J., & Wright, H. A. (1939). *Management and the worker. An account of a research program conducted by the western electric company*. Hawthorne Works, Chicago. Harvard University Press.

Rogers, C. R. (1951). *Client-centered therapy: Its current practice, implications, and theory. The Houghton Mifflin psychological series*. Houghton Mifflin.

Rogers, C. R. (1985). *Die Kraft des Guten: Ein Appell zur Selbstverwirklichung [The power of good: An appeal for self-realization]*. Fischer-Taschenbuch-Verlag.

Rogers, C. R. (1994). *Entwicklung der Persönlichkeit: Psychotheraphie aus der Sicht eines Therapeuten [Personality development: Psychotherapy from the perspective of a therapist]* (10th ed.). Klett-Cotta.

Rogers, E. M. (2003). *Diffusion of Innovations*. Free Press.

Rolls, E. T. (2014). *Emotion and decision -making explained. Oxford University Press*. https://www.oxcns.org/b11text.html.

Ross, L., & Ward, A. (1996). Naive realism in everyday life: Implications for social conflict and misunderstanding. In T. Brown, E. S. Reed, & E. Turiel (Eds.), *Values and Knowledge* (pp. 103–135). Erlbaum.

Roth, G. (2004). Warum sind Lehren und Lernen so schwierig? [Why is teaching and learning so difficult?]. *Zeitschrift Für Pädagogik, 50*(4), 496–506.

Roth, G. (2009). *Fühlen, Denken, Handeln: Wie das Gehirn unser Verhalten steuert [Feeling, thinking, acting: How the brain controls our behavior]. Suhrkamp-Taschenbuch Wissenschaft: Vol. 1678* Suhrkamp.

Roth, G. (2010). Vorwort [Preface]. In A. Dijksterhuis (Ed.), *Das kluge Unbewusste* (2rd ed.), (pp. 9). Klett-Cotta.

Roth, G. (2015). *Aus Sicht des Gehirns [From the perspective of the brain]*. Suhrkamp.

Roth, G., & Menzel, R. (2001). Neuronale Grundlagen kognitiver Leistungen [Neuronal foundations of cognitive performance]. In J. Dudel, R. Menzel, & R. F. Schmidt (Eds.), *Springer-Lehrbuch. Neurowissenschaft* (pp. 543–563). Springer Berlin Heidelberg. https://doi.org/10.1007/978-3-642-56497-0_25

Roth, G., & Strüber, N. (2020). Emotion, Motivation, Persönlichkeit und ihre neurobiologischen Grundlagen [Emotion, motivation, personality and their neurobiological bases]. In G. Roth, A. Heinz, & H. Walter (Eds.), *Psychoneurowissenschaften* (pp. 147–180). Springer Spektrum.

Rothmund, M., & Lorenz, W. (1990). Einflüsse der Intuition auf Indikationsstellung und intraoperatives Vorgehen [Influence of Intuition on Surgical Indication and Operative Decision-Making]. In E. Ungeheuer (Ed.), *Deutsche Gesellschaft für Chirurgie. Langenbecks Archiv für Chirurgie.* Gegründet 1860 Kongressorgan der Deutschen Gesellschaft für Chirurgie (Supplement II 107. Kongress, 17.–21. April 1990) Vol. 1990. Springer. https://doi.org/10.1007/978-3-642-48163-5_275

Rowe, P. M., Williams, M. C., & Day, A. L. (1994). Selection procedures in North America. *International Journal of Selection and Assessment, 2*(2), 74–79. https://doi.org/10.1111/j.1468-2389.1994.tb00153.x

Röbe-Oltmanns, C. (2020). *Personalauswahl bei kleinen und mittleren Unternehmen – zwischen wissenschaftlichen Anspruch und Einsatz von Emotionen* [Personnel selection in small and medium-sized companies – between scientific demands and the use of emotions]. Unpublished bachelor thesis, Leuphana Universität, Lueneburg.

Rubenstein, H. (2013). *Can anonymous CVs help beat recruitment discrimination?* https://www.theguardian.com/money/work-blog/2013/apr/11/can-anonymous-cvs-help-beat-job-discrimination

Ruffle, B. J., & Shtudiner, Z. (2010). Are good-looking people more employable? *Management Science, 61*(8), 1760–1776. http://dx.doi.org/10.1287/mnsc.2014.1927

Rupp, D. E., Hoffman, B. J., Bischof, D., Byham, W., Collins, L., Gibbons, A., Hirose, S., Kleinmann, M., Kudisch, J. D., Lanik, M., Jackson, D. J. R., Kim, M., Lievens, F., Meiring, D., Melchers, K. G., Pendit, V. G., Putka, D. J., Povah, N., Reynolds, D., & Thornton, G. (2015).

Guidelines and ethical considerations for assessment center operations. *Journal of Management, 41*(4), 1244–1273. https://doi.org/10.1177/0149206314567780

Rupprecht, S., Falke, P., Kohls, N., Tamdjidi, C., Wittmann, M., & Kersemaekers, W. (2019). Mindful leader development: How leaders experience the effects of mindfulness training on leader capabilities. *Frontiers in Psychology, 10*, 1081. https://doi.org/10.3389/fpsyg.2019.01081

Ruthenbeck, F. (2004). *Intuition als Entscheidungsgrundlage in komplexen Situationen [Intui tion as a basis for decision-making in complex situations]*. Monsenstein und Vannerdat.

Ruthmann, A. (2018). Entscheidungen in der Personalauswahl: Zwischen Rationalität und Intuition (Personnel decision making: Between rationality and intuition). Unpublished bachelor thesis, Leuphana University, Lueneburg.

Ryan, A. M., & Sackett, P. R. (1989). Exploratory study of individual assessment practices: Interrater-reliability and judgments of assessor effectiveness. *Journal of Applied Psychology, 74*, 568–579.

Ryan, A. M., McFarland, L., & Baron, H. (1999). An international look at selection practices: Nation and culture as explanations for variability in practice. *Personnel Psychology, 52*(2), 359–392. https://doi.org/10.1111/j.1744-6570.1999.tb00165.x

Ryan, A. M., & Ployhart, R. E. (2000). Applicants' perceptions of selection procedures and decisions: A critical review and agenda for the future. *Journal of Management, 26*(3), 565–606. https://doi.org/10.1016/S0149-2063(00)00041-6

Ryan, A. M., & Ployhart, R. E. (2014). A century of selection. *Annual Review of Psychology, 65*, 693–717. https://doi.org/10.1146/annurev-psych-010213-115134

Ryan, A. M., & Tippins, N. T. (2009). *Designing and implementing global selection systems. TMEZ – Talent Management Essentials*. Wiley-Blackwell.

Ryan, R. M. (1995). Psychological needs and the facilitation of integrative processes. *Journal of Personality, 63*(3), 397–427. doi: https://doi.org/1111/j.1467-6494.1995.tb00501.x

Ryan, R. M., & Deci, E. L. (2000). Intrinsic and extrinsic motivations: Classic definitions and new directions. *Contemporary Educational Psychology, 25*(1), 54–67. doi:10.1006/ceps.1999.1020

Ryba, A., & Roth, G. (Eds.). (2019). *Coaching und Beratung in der Praxis. Ein neurowissenschaftlich fundiertes Integrationsmodel [Coaching and counseling in practice. A neuroscientifically based integration model]*. Klett-Cotta.

Ryba, A., & Roth, G. (2021). Integratives Neuro-Coaching. Coaching mit wissenschaftlicher Fundierung [Integrative Neuro-Coaching. Coaching with a scientific foundation]. *Coaching-Magazin* 2.2021. https://www.coaching-magazin.de/tools-methoden/integratives-neuro-coaching

Rynes, S. L., Colbert, A. E., & Brown, K. G. (2002). HR Professionals' beliefs about effective human resource practices: Correspondence between research and practice. *Human Resource Management, 41*(2), 149–174. https://doi.org/10.1002/hrm.10029

Saarni, C. (2008). The interface of emotional development with social context. In M. Lewis, J. M. Haviland-Jones, & L. F. Barrett (Eds.), *Handbook of emotions* (pp. 332–347). The Guilford Press.

Sacco, J. M., Scheu, C. R., Ryan, A. M., & Schmitt, N. (2003). An investigation of race and sex similarity effects in interviews: A multilevel approach to relational demography. *The Journal of Applied Psychology, 88*(5), 852–865. https://doi.org/10.1037/0021-9010.88.5.852

Sackett, P. R., & Dreher, G. F. (1982). Constructs and assessment center dimensions: Some troubling empirical findings. *Journal of Applied Psychology, 67*(4), 401–410. https://doi.org/10.1037/0021-9010.67.4.401

Sackett, P. R., Shewach, O. R., & Keiser, H. N. (2017). Assessment centers versus cognitive ability tests: Challenging the conventional wisdom on criterion-related validity. *Journal of Applied Psychology, 102*(10), 1435–1447. https://doi.org/10.1037/apl0000236

Sadler-Smith, E. (2007). *Inside Intuition*. Routledge. https://doi.org/10.4324/9780203932070.
Sadler-Smith, E. (2010). *The Intuitive Mind: Profiting from the Power of Your Sixth Sense*. John Wiley & Sons.
Sadler-Smith, E. (2016a). The role of intuition in entrepreneurship and business venturing decisions. *European Journal of Work and Organizational Psychology*, *25*(2), 212–225. doi:10.1080/1359432X.2015.1029046
Sadler-Smith, E. (2016b). What happens when you intuit?: Understanding human resource practitioners' subjective experience of intuition through a novel linguistic method. *Human Relations*, *69*(5), 1069–1093. https://doi.org/10.1177/0018726715602047
Sadler-Smith, E. (2018). *Hubristic leadership*. Sage Publications.
Sadler-Smith, E. (2019). Intuition in management. In E. Sadler-Smith (Ed.), *Oxford research encyclopedia of business and management*, p. 1–34. Oxford University Press. https://doi.org/10.1093/acrefore/9780190224851.013.177
Sadler-Smith, E., & Burke, L. A. (2009). Fostering intuition in management education. *Journal of Management Education*, *33*(2), 239–262. https://doi.org/10.1177/1052562907310640
Sadler-Smith, E., & Hodgkinson, G. P. (2016). An analytic-intervention model of managerial intuition. *Academy of Management Proceedings*, *2016*(1), 11831. https://doi.org/10.5465/ambpp.2016.166
Sadler-Smith, E., & Shefy, E. (2004). The intuitive executive: Understanding and applying 'gut feel' in decision-making. *Academy of Management Perspectives*, *18*(4), 76–91. https://doi.org/10.5465/ame.2004.15268692
Sadler-Smith, E., & Shefy, E. (2004a). Developing Intuition: 'Becoming smarter by thinking.' *Academy of Management Best Conference Paper*, C1–C6.
Sadler-Smith, E., & Shefy, E. (2007). Developing intuitive awareness in management education. *Academy of Management Learning & Education*, *6*(2), 186–205. https://doi.org/10.5465/amle.2007.25223458
Sahm, M., & von Weizsäcker, R. K. (2016). Reason, intuition, and time. *Managerial and Decision Economics*, *37*, 195–207. https://doi.org/10.1002/mde
Salas, E., Rosen, M. A., & DiazGranados, D. (2010). Expertise-based intuition and decision making in organizations. *Journal of Management*, *36*(4), 941–973. https://doi.org/10.1177/0149206309350084
Salgado, J.F. (1997). The five-factor model of personality and job performance in the European Community. *Journal of Applied Psychology*, *82*(1), 30–43.
Samba, C., Williams, D. W., & Fuller, R. M. (2019). The forms and use of intuition in top management teams. *The Leadership Quarterly*, 101349. https://doi.org/10.1016/j.leaqua.2019.101349.
Sanches, M. (2020). Bundespolizei erleichtert Anforderungen für Bewerber [Federal police eases requirements for applicants]. *Hamburger Abendblatt*, January 20, 2020, p. 4. https://www.abendblatt.de/politik/article228185099/Bundespolizei-Was-Bewerber-jetzt-beim-Aufnahmetest-erwartet-Anforderungen-gesenkt.html
Sànchez-Runde, C., Nardon, L., & Steers, R. (2012). Balancing global leadership. *Alumni Magazine IESE*, April-June 2012, No. 125, 18–21.
Sanders, K., van Riemsdijk, M., & Groen, B. (2008). The gap between research and practice: A replication study on the HR professionals' beliefs about effective human resource practices. *The International Journal of Human Resource Management*, *19*(10), 1976–1988. https://doi.org/10.1080/09585190802324304
Sarges, W. (2013). Kritik an der Assessment-Center-Praxis [Criticism of the assessment center practice]. In W. Sarges (Ed.), *Management-Diagnostik* (4th ed.) (pp. 819–824). Hogrefe.

Satpute, A. B., & Lieberman, M. D. (2006). Integrating automatic and controlled processes into neurocognitive models of social cognition. *Brain Research*, *1079*(1), 86–97. https://doi.org/10.1016/j.brainres.2006.01.005

Sauermann, H., & Selten, R. (1962). Anspruchsanmeldungen der Unternehmung [*Zeitschrift für die gesamte Staatswissenschaft. Journal of Institutional and Theoretical Economics*, *118*(4), 577–597. http://www.jstor.org/stable/407486

Sattelberger, T. (2019). Manager ohne Riecher: Große unternehmerische Vorhaben müssen mit Instinkt gesteuert werden – ökonomische Ratio kommt nicht ohne gesellschaftliche Due Diligence aus [Managers without a „nose": Large entrepreneurial ventures must be managed with instinct – economic reason cannot do without social due diligence]. *Manager Magazin* (08/2019). https://heft.manager-magazin.de/MM/2019/8/164930818/index.html

Schaumlöffel, L., Hübner, R., Thiel, S., & Stulle, K. P. (2018). Du bist, was du sprichst–Validierung der Sprachanalysetechnologie PRECIRE® anhand des HEXACO®-Persönlichkeitsmodells [You are what you speak-Validation of the PRECIRE® speech analysis technology based on the HEXACO® personality model]. In K. P. Stulle, & S. Thiel (Eds.), *Psychologische Diagnostik durch Sprachanalyse* (pp. 57–15). Springer Gabler.

Scheer, U. (2021). Ich sehe was, was du nicht fühlst [I see what you don't feel]. In *Frankfurter Allgemeine Zeitung*, 14.4.2021, p. 9.

Scheier, C., & Held, D. (2018). *Wie Werbung wirkt: Erkenntnisse aus dem Neuromarketing [How advertising works: Insights from neuromarketing]*. Haufe-Lexware.

Schein, E. H. (2004). *Organizational culture and leadership* (3rd ed.). The Jossey-Bass business & management series Jossey-Bass.

Schemann, M., & Neunlist, M. (2004). The human enteric nervous system. *Neurogastroenterology and Motility: The Official Journal of the European Gastrointestinal Motility Society*, *16*(Suppl 1), 55–59. https://doi.org/10.1111/j.1743-3150.2004.00476.x

Scherer, K. R. (2004). Feelings integrate the central representation of appraisal-driven response organization in emotion. In A. S. R. Manstead, N. H. Frijda, & A. H. Fischer (Eds.), *Feelings and emotions: The Amsterdam symposium* (pp. 136–157). Cambridge University Press.

Scherer, K. R. (2015). What are emotions? And how can they be measured? *Social Science Information*, *44*(4), 695–792. https://doi.org/10.1177/0539018405058216

Scherer, K. R., & Moors, A. (2019). The emotion process: Event appraisal and component differentiation. *Annual Review of Psychology*, *70*, 719–745. https://doi.org/10.1146/annurev-psych-122216-011854

Scherm, E., Julmi, C., & Lindner, F. (2016). Intuitive versus analytische Entscheidungen [Intuitive versus analytical decisions]. Überlegungen zur situativen Stimmigkeit. In H. Ahn, M. Clermont, & R. Souren (Eds.), *Nachhaltiges Entscheiden: Beiträge zum multiperspektivischen Performancemanagement von Wertschöpfungsprozessen* (pp. 299–318). Springer Gabler. https://doi.org/10.1007/978-3-658-12506-6

Schiller, D., Mertes, S., & André, E. (2020a). Embedded emotions – A data driven approach to learn transferable feature representations from raw speech input for emotion recognition. *Computing Research Repository* CoRR abs/2009.14523. https://arxiv.org/abs/2009.14523

Schiller, D., Huber, T., Dietz, M., & André, E. (2020b). Relevance-based data masking: A model-agnostic transfer learning approach for facial expression recognition. *Frontiers Computer Science*, *2*(6), https://www.frontiersin.org/articles/10.3389/fcomp.2020.00006/full

Schilling, M., Becker, N., Grabenhorst, M. M., & Konig, C. J. (2021). The relationship between cognitive ability and personality scores in selection situations: A meta-analysis. *International Journal of Selection and Assessment*, *29*, 1–18. https://doi.org/10.1111/ijsa.12314

Schimansky-Geier, D. (2017). Fingerabdruck für die Sprache [Fingerprint for the language]. *Human Resources*, E-3 März, 48–49. https://e-3.de/fingerabdruck-fuer-die-sprache/

Schlegel, K., & Wallbott, H. G. (2013). Ausdruck und Eindruck [Expression and impression]. In W. Sarges (Ed.), *Management-Diagnostik* (4th ed.) (pp. 355–362). Hogrefe.

Schlegel, L., Warszta, T., & Kolb, P. (2017). Autonome Bewerbungsanalyse in der Personalrekrutierung [Autonomous application analysis in personnel recruitment]. *Personalwirtschaft*. https://www.personalwirtschaft.de/hr-organisation/hr-software/artikel/autonome-bewerbungsanalyse-in-der-personalrekrutierung.html

Schmid, B., & Gérard, C. (2008). *Intuition und Professionalität: Systemische Transaktionanalyze in Beratung und Therapie [Intuition and professionalism: Systemic transactional analysis in consulting and therapy]*. Carl-Auer-Systeme.

Schmid, B., Hipp, J., & Caspari, S. (1999). Intuition in der professionellen Begegnung [Intuition in the professional encounter]. *Zeitschrift Für Systemische Therapie*, *17*(3), 101–111. https://www.researchgate.net/profile/Joachim_Hipp/publication/237723131_Intuition_in_der_professionellen_Begegnung/links/561df7d208aef097132b2b4c/Intuition-in-der-professionellen-Begegnung.pdf

Schmidt, F. L., & Hunter, J. E. (1998). The validity and utility of selection methods in personnel psychology: Practical and theoretical implications of 85 years of research findings. *Psychological Bulletin*, *124*(2), 262–274. https://doi.org/10.1037/0033-2909.124.2.262

Schmidt, F. L., Oh, I. S., & Shaffer, J. A. (2016). The Validity and Utility of Selection Methods in Personnel Psychology: Practical and Theoretical Implications of 100 Years of Research. Working Paper. *Fox School of Business Research Paper*. https://www.reddit.com/r/IOPsychology/comments/80bmdl/working_paper_schmidt_f_l_oh_i_s_shaffer_j_a_2016/

Schmidt-Atzert, L., & Amelang, M. (2012). *Psychologische Diagnostik [Diagnostic procedures]. Unter Mitarbeit von Thomas Fydrich und Helfried Moosbrugger. (5. ed.)*. Springer. https://doi.org/10.1007/978-3-642-17001-0.

Schmidt-Atzert, L., Krumm, S., & Kersting, M. (2018). Evaluation der Eignungsbeurteilung [Evaluation of the qualification assessment]. In Diagnostik und Testkuratorium (Ed.), *Personalauswahl kompetent gestalten. Grundlagen und Praxis der Eignungsdiagnostik nach DIN 33430* (pp. 189–221). Springer. https://doi.org/10.1007/978-3-662-53772-5_6.

Schmidt-Atzert, L., Künecke, J., & Zimmermann, J. (2019). TBS-DTK Rezension: »PRECIRE JobFit«. *Report Psychologie*, *44*(7/8), 19–21.

Schmiele, C. (2012). *Möglichkeiten und Grenzen der Forderung verantwortlichen Handelns von Wirtschaftsprüfern in moralisch relevanten Situationen [Possibilities and limits of the demand for responsible action by auditors in morally relevant situations]*. Gabler.

Schmitt, N., & Coyle, B. W. (1976). Applicant decisions in the employment interview. *Journal of Applied Psychology*, *61*(2), 184–192. https://doi.org/10.1037/0021-9010.61.2.184

Schmitz-Atzert, L. (2010). Beobachtungsfehler und Beobachtungsverzerrungen [Observation errors and observation biases]. In K. Westhoff, C. Hagemeister, M. Kersting, F. Lang, H. Moosbrugger, G. Reimann, & G. Stemmler T. d. F. D. Psychologenvereinigungen (Eds.), *Grundwissen für die berufsbezogene Eignungsbeurteilung nach DIN 33430* (pp. 74–77). Pabst Science Publishers.

Schneider, K. (2018). Emotionen [Emotions]. In A. Kiesel, & H. Spada (Eds.), *Lehrbuch Allgemeine Psychologie* (4th ed.) (pp. 403–449). Hogrefe.

Schoenewolf, G. (1990). Emotional contagion: Behavioral induction in individuals and groups. *Modern Psychoanalysis*, *15*(1), 49–61.

Schonfeld, I. R., & Mazzola, J. J. (2012). Strengths and limitations of qualitative approaches to research in occupational health psychology. In R. R. Sinclair, M. Wang, & L. E. Tetrick (Eds.), *Research methods in occupational health psychology* (4th ed.) (pp. 268–289). Routledge.

Schossau, H., Winter, N., & Brandt, O. (2019). *KI im HR – Neue Wege für Ihre Talentstrategie [AI in HR – New ways for your talent strategy*]. Webinar-Unterlagen von Cut-e und AON. https://cross

water-job-guide.com/archives/75268/talentpro-muenchen-2019-cut-e-zeigt-neue-wege-im-recruiting-mit-kuenstlicher-intelligenz/
Schrage, M. (2003). *Daniel Kahneman: The thought leader interview.* https://www.strategy-business.com/article/03409?gko=d1233
Schramowski, P., Stammer, W., Teso, S., Brugger, A., Herbert, F., Shao, X., Luigs, H.-G., Mahlein, A.-K., & Kersting, K. (2020). *Making deep neural networks right for the right scientific reasons by interacting with their explanations.* https://arxiv.org/abs/2001.05371
Schreiber, S. M. (2000). *Das Informationsverhalten von Wirtschaftsprüfern: Eine Prozessanalyse aus verhaltenswissenschaftlicher Perspektive [The information behavior of auditors: A process analysis from a behavioral science perspective].* Deutscher Universitätsverlag.
Schroll-Machl, S. (2007). Kurzbeitrag. Interkulturelle Kooperation konkret: Ein Bericht aus der Praxis des interkulturellen Coaching [Short article. Intercultural cooperation in concrete terms: A report from the practice of intercultural coaching]. *Arbeit, 16*(2), 152–157. https://doi.org/10.1515/arbeit-2007-0209
Schuler, H. (1993). Social validity of selection situations: A concept and some empirical results. In H. Schuler, J. L. Farr, & M. Smith (Eds.), *Personnel selection and assessment* (pp. 11–26). Erlbaum.
Schuler, H. (1996). *Psychologische Personalauswahl: Einführung in die Berufseignungsdiagnostik [Psychological personnel selection: Introduction to occupational diagnostics].* Hogrefe.
Schuler, H. (2000). *Psychologische Personalauswahl: Einführung in die Berufseignungsdiagnostik [Psychological personnel selection: Introduction to occupational diagnostics].* Hogrefe.
Schuler, H. (2002). *Das Einstellungsinterview.* Hogrefe.
Schuler, H. (2004). Der Prozess der Urteilsbildung und die Qualität der Beurteilungen [The process of judgement formation and the quality of judgements]. In H. Schuler (Ed.), *Wirtschaftspsychologie. Beurteilung und Förderung beruflicher Leistung* (pp. 33–60). Hogrefe, Verl. für Psychologie.
Schuler, H. (2006). Stand und Perspektiven der Personalpsychologie [Status and perspectives of personnel psychology]. *Zeitschrift Für Arbeits- Und Organisations-psychologie, 50*(4), 176–188. https://doi.org/10.1026/0932-4089.50.4.176
Schuler, H. (2007). Spielwiese für Laien? Weshalb das Assessment-Center seinem Ruf nicht mehr gerecht wird [Playground for laymen? Why the assessment center no longer lives up to its reputation]. *Wirtschaftspsychologie Aktuell, 2,* 27–30.
Schuler, H. (2013). Personalauswahl [Personnel selection]. In R. Stock-Homburg (Ed.), *Handbuch Strategisches Personalmanagement* (2nd ed., pp. 29–58). Springer Fachmedien.
Schuler, H. (2014). *Psychologische Personalauswahl: Eignungsdiagnostik für Personalentscheidungen und Berufsberatung [Psychological personnel selection: Diagnostics for personnel decisions and career advice] (4. ed.).* Hogrefe.
Schuler, H., & Berger, W. (1977). Physische Attraktivität als Determinante von Beurteilung und Einstellungsempfehlung [Physical attractivity as determinant of assessment and hiring recommendations]. *Psychologie Und Praxis, 23,* 59–70.
Schuler, H., Farr, J. L., & Small, M. (Eds.). (1993). *Series in applied psychology. Personnel selection and assessment: Individual and organizational perspectives.* Lawrence Erlbaum Associates, Inc.
Schuler, H., Frier, D., & Kauffmann, M. (1993). *Personalauswahl im europäischen Vergleich [Personnel selection in European comparison]. Beiträge zur Organisationspsychologie: Vol. 13.* VfaP – Verl. für Angewandte Psychologie.
Schuler, H., Hell, B., Trapmann, S., Schaar, H., & Boramir, I. (2007). Die Nutzung psychologischer Verfahren der externen Personalauswahl in deutschen Unternehmen [The use of psychological methods of external personnel selection in German companies]. *Zeitschrift Für Personalpsychologie, 6*(2), 60–70. https://doi.org/10.1026/1617-6391.6.2.60

Schuler, H., & Kanning, U. P. (Eds.). (2014). *Lehrbuch der Personalpsychologie [Textbook of Personal Psychology]* (3rd ed.). Hogrefe.

Schuler, H., & Stehle, W. (1985). Soziale Validität eignungsdiagnostischer Verfahren: Anforderung für die Zukunft [Social validity of diagnostic procedures: Requirements for the future]. In H. Schuler (Ed.), *Beiträge zur Organisationspsychologie: Bd. 1. Organisationspsychologie und Unternehmenspraxis: Perspektiven d. Kooperation* (pp. 133–138). Hogrefe.

Schultz, K. (2014). A Nurse's Six Sense. *Nursing for Women's Health, 18*(3), 259–260. doi: 10.1111/1751-486X.12129

Schulz von Thun, F. (2008). *Miteinander reden: Fragen und Antworten [Talking to each other: Questions and answers]*. Rowohlt.

Schurz, G. (2013) Sind Menschen Vernunftwesen? Zum Zusammenhang von Kognition und Evolution [Are humans rational beings? On the connection between cognition and evolution]. Gekürzt in *Information Philosophie* (5) 16–27. https://www.phil-fak.uni-duesseldorf.de/fileadmin/Redaktion/Institute/Philosophie/Theoretische_Philosophie/Schurz/andere/Sind_Menschen_Vernunftwesen.pdf

Schwantes, M. (2019). *Warren Buffett Says He Won't Even Consider Hiring Someone Who Lacks This 1 Trait: The Oracle of Omaha looks for three things when hiring people. One is non-negotiable.* https://www.inc.com/marcel-schwantes/warren-buffett-says-he-wont-even-consider-hiring-someone-who-lacks-this-1-trait.html?xing_share=news

Schwartz, I. S., & Baer, D. M. (1991). Social validity assessments: Is current practice state of the art? *Journal of Applied Behavior Analysis, 24*(2), 189–204.

Schwartz, S. H. (2014). National culture as value orientations: Consequences of value differences and cultural distance. In V. A. Ginsburgh, & D. Throsby (Eds.), *Handbook of the economics of art and culture* (pp. 547–586). Elsevier. https://doi.org/10.1016/B978-0-444-53776-8.00020-9

Schweiger, D. M. (1983). Measuring managers' minds: A critical reply to Robey and Taggart. *The Academy of Management Review, 8*(1), 143–151. https://psycnet.apa.org/doi/10.2307/257176"https://doi.org/10.2307/257176

Schweizer, M. (2017). Wenn Software Personal auswählt [When software selects personnel]. In: *Computerwoche*, (10–11), 38–40.

Schwertfeger, B. (2015). Personalauswahl per Sprachtest [Personnel selection by language test]. *Personalmagazin, 17*(12), 32–34.

Scott, S. G., & Bruce, R. A. (1995). Decision-making style: The development and assessment of a new measure. *Educational and Psychological Measurement, 55*(5), 818–831. 10.1177/0013164495055005017

Scott, W. R. (2014). *Institutions and organizations: Ideas, interests and identities.* (4th ed.). Sage Publications.

Scullen, S. E., Mount, M. K., & Goff, M. (2000). Understanding the latent structure of job performance ratings. *Journal of Applied Psychology, 85*(6), 956–970.

Sears, G. J., & Rowe, P. M. (2003). A personality-based similar-to-me effect in the employment interview: Conscientiousness, affect-versus competence-mediated interpretations, and the role of job relevance. *Canadian Journal of Behavioural Science / Revue Canadienne Des Sciences Du Comportement, 35*(1), 13–24. https://doi.org/10.1037/h0087182

Seckler, C., Fischer, S., & Rosing, K. (2021). Who Adopts an Error Management Orientation? Discovering the Role of Humility. *Academy of Management Discoveries*. Published online February 2, 2021. https://www.researchgate.net/publication/348986616_Who_Adopts_an_Error_Management_Orientation_Discovering_the_Role_of_Humility. doi: 10.5465/amd.2019.0172

Segrest Purkiss, S. L., Perrewé, P. L., Gillespie, T. L., Mayes, B. T., & Ferris, G. R. (2006). Implicit sources of bias in employment interview judgments and decisions. *Organizational Behavior and Human Decision Processes, 101*(2), 152–167. https://doi.org/10.1016/j.obhdp.2006.06.005

Selten, R. (1999). *Game Theory and Economic Behaviour. Selected Essays* Vol. 1, Edward Elgar.

Seo, M.-G., & Barrett, L. F. (2007). Being emotional during decision making – Good or bad? An empirical investigation. *Academy of Management Journal, 50*(4), 923–940. https://doi.org/10.5465/AMJ.2007.26279217

Shackleton, V., & Newell, S. (1994). European Management Selection Methods: A Comparison of Five Countries. *International Journal of Selection and Assessment, 2*(2), 91–102. https://doi.org/10.1111/j.1468-2389.1994.tb00155.x

Shaffer, J. A., & Postlethwaite, B. E. (2012). A matter of context: A meta-analytic investigation of the relative validity of contextualized and noncontextualized personality measures. *Personnel Psychology, 65*(3), 445–494. https://doi.org/10.1111/j.1744-6570.2012.01250.x

Shaffer, J. A., & Postlethwaite, B. E. (2013). The validity of conscientiousness for predicting job performance: A meta-analytic test of two hypotheses. *International Journal of Selection and Assessment, 21*(2), 183–199. https://doi.org/10.1111/ijsa.12028

Shah, A. K., & Oppenheimer, D. M. (2008). Heuristics made easy: An effort-reduction framework. *Psychological Bulletin, 134*(2), 207–222. https://doi.org/10.1037/0033-2909.134.2.207

Shapiro, S., & Spence, M. T. (1997). Managerial intuition: A conceptual and operational framework. *Business Horizons, 40*(1), 63–69.

Shariatmadari, D. (2021). Daniel Kahneman: "What would I eliminate if I had a magic wand? Overconfidence." *The Guardian*, January, 17, 2021. http://www.theguardian.com/books/2015/jul/18/daniel-kahneman-books-interview

Sherman, R. A., Nave, C. S., & Funder, D. C. (2009). The apparent objectivity of behaviour is illusory. *European Journal of Personality, 23*(5), 430–433.

Sheskin, D. (2007). *Handbook of parametric and nonparametric statistical procedures*. Chapman & Hall/CRC.

Shirley, D. A., & Langan-Fox, J. (1996). Intuition: A review of the literature. *Psychological Reports, 79*(2), 563–584. https://doi.org/10.2466/pr0.1996.79.2.563

Shotland, A., Alliger, G. M., & Sales, T. (2002). *International Journal of Selection and Assessment, 6*(2), 124–130. doi: 10.1111/1468-2389.00081

Sidler, S. (2014). Wie wissen die Finger? Implizites Wissen und Heuristiken als Grundlagen der Intuition [How do fingers know? Implicit knowledge and heuristics as foundations of intuition]. *Osteopathische Medizin, 15*(1), 21–26.

Siegert, I., & Niebuhr, O. (2021). *Speech Signal Compression Deteriorates Acoustic Cues To Perceived Speaker Charisma*. https://www.uni-magdeburg.de/Universit%C3%A4t/Im+Portrait/Profilierungsschwerpunkte/Forschung+_+Transfer/PM+17_2021-p-113520.html

Siemann, C. (2017). *Der Algorithmus ist nur so gut wie die Annahmen, auf denen er basiert [The algorithm is only as good as the assumptions on which it is based]*. https://www.personalwirtschaft.de/recruiting/artikel/der-algorithmus-ist-nur-so-gut-wie-die-annahmen-auf-denen-er-basiert.html

Siepe, G. (2002). Unternehmensbewertung [Company evaluation]. In Institut der Wirtschaftsprüfer in Deutschland e.V (Ed.), *Wirtschaftsprüfer-Handbuch: Handbuch für Rechnungslegung, Prüfung und Beratung Band II* (12th ed.), (pp. 1–149). IDW-Verlag.

Silva, S., & Kenney, M. (2018). Algorithms, platforms, and ethnic bias: An integrative essay. *Phylon: The Clark Atlanta University Review of Race and Culture, Forthcoming, 55*(1–2), 9–37.

Silzer, R., & Church, A. H. (2009). The pearls and perils of identifying potential. *Industrial and Organizational Psychology, 2*(4), 377–412. https://doi.org/10.1111/j.1754-9434.2009.01163.x

Simon, H. A. (1955). A behavioral model of rational choice. *The Quarterly Journal of Economics, 69*(1), 99. https://doi.org/10.2307/1884852
Simon, H. A. (1957). *Models of man: Social and rational*. Wiley.
Simon, H. A. (1959). Theories of decision-making in economics and behavioral sciences. *American Economic Review, 49*(3), 253–283.
Simon, H. A. (1987). Making management decisions: The role of intuition and emotion. *Academy of Management Perspectives, 1*(1), 57–64. https://doi.org/10.5465/ame.1987.4275905
Simon, H. A. (1992). What is an "Explanation" of Behavior? *Psychological Science, 3*(3), 150–161. https://doi.org/10.1111/j.1467-9280.1992.tb00017.x
Simon, H. A. (1998). *The sciences of the artificial* (3rd ed.). MIT Press.
Simon, H. A., & Chase, W. G. (1973). Skill in Chess. *American Scientist, 61*(4), 394–403.
Simbeck, K., Folkerts, F., & Riazy, S. (2019). Automatisierte Textanalyse bei der Personalauswahl – Potenziale und Grenzen [Automated text analysis in personnel selection -potentials and limitations]. *BWP (Berufsbildung in Wissenschaft Und Praxis), 3*, 27–29. https://www.bwp-zeitschrift.de/de/bwp.php/de/bwp/show/10038
Sinclair, M. (2005). Intuition: Myth or a decision-making tool? *Management Learning (2005), 36*(3), 353–370. doi: 10.1177/1350507605055351
Sinclair, M. (Ed.). (2011a). *Handbook of intuition research*. Edward Elgar.
Sinclair, M. (2011b). An integrated framework of intuition. In M. Sinclair (Ed.), *Handbook of intuition research* (pp. 3–16). Edward Elgar.
Sinclair, M. (Ed.). (2014). *Handbook of research methods on intuition*. Edward Elgar Publishing. https://doi.org/10.4337/9781782545996
Sinclair, M., & Ashkanasy, N. M. (2005). Intuition. *Management Learning, 36*(3), 353–370. https://doi.org/10.1177/1350507605055351
Sinclair, M., & Hamilton, A. (2014). Mapping group intuition. In M. Sinclair (Ed.), *Handbook of research methods on intuition* (pp. 199–214). Edward Elgar Publishing.
Sinha, J. B. P., & Kanungo, R. (1997). Context sensitivity and balancing in indian organizational behaviour. *International Journal of Psychology, 32*(2), 93–106. https://doi.org/10.1080/002075997400890
Skvortsova, A., Schulte-Mecklenbeck, M., Jellema, S., Sanfey, A., & Witteman, C. (2016). Deliberative versus intuitive psychodiagnostic decision. *Psychology, 07*(12), 1438–1450. 10.4236/psych.2016.712143
Skrzypinski, C. (2013). *Will Anonymous Job Applications End Hiring Discrimination in Canada?* https://www.shrm.org/resourcesandtools/hr-topics/global-hr/pages/lanonymous-job-applications-canada.aspx
Slaughter, J. E., & Kausel, E. E. (2013). Employee selection decisions. In S. Highhouse, R. S. Dalal, & E. Salas (Eds.), *SIOP organizational frontiers series. Judgment and decision making at work* (pp. 57–79). Taylor and Francis.
Slovic, P. (1990). Perceptions of risk: Reflections on the psychometric paradigm. In S. Krimsky, & D. Golding (Eds.), *Social theories of risk* (pp. *117–152*). Praeger.
Smerek, R. E. (2014). Why people think deeply: Meta-cognitive cues, task characteristics, and thinking dispositions. In M. Sinclair (Ed.), *Handbook of research methods on intuition* (pp. 3–14). Edward Elgar Publishing.
Smith, C. A. (1989). Dimensions of appraisal and physiological response in emotion. *Journal of Personality and Social Psychology, 56*(3), 339–353. https://doi.org/10.1037/0022-3514.56.3.339
Smith, E. E., & Kosslyn, S. M. (2014). *Cognitive psychology: Mind and brain. Always learning.* Pearson Education Limited.

Snyder, J., & Shahani-Denning, C. (2012). Fairness reactions to personnel selection methods: A look at professionals in Mumbai, India. *International Journal of Selection and Assessment, 20*(3), 297–307. https://doi.org/10.1111/j.1468-2389.2012.00601.x

Soffner, L. (2021). *How has the COVID-19 crisis changed what we know about managerial intuition and virtual leadership?* Unpublished master thesis, Leuphana University, Lueneburg.

Soon, C. S., Brass, M., Heinze, H.-J., & Haynes, J.-D. (2008). Unconscious determinants of free decisions in the human brain. *Nature Neuroscience, 11*(5), 543–545. https://doi.org/10.1038/nn.2112

Soyarslan, S. (2013). The distinction between reason and intuitive knowledge in Spinoza's ethics. *European Journal of Philosophy, 24*(1), https://doi.org/10.1111/ejop.12052

Specht, J. (2018). *Charakterfrage: Wer wir sind und wie wir uns verändern [Character question: Who we are and how we change].* Rowohlt Taschenbuch Verlag.

Spence, L. J., & Petrick, J. A. (2000). Multinational interview decisions: Integrity capacity and competing values. *Human Resource Management Journal, 10*(4), 49–67. https://doi.org/10.1111/j.1748-8583.2000.tb00006.x

Spina, R. R., Ji, L.-J., Ross, M., Li, Y., & Zhang, Z. (2010). Why best cannot last: Cultural differences in predicting regression toward the mean. *Asian Journal of Social Psychology, 13*(3), 153–162. https://doi.org/10.1111/j.1467-839x.2010.01310.x

Spinath, F. M., Angleitner, A., Borkenau, P., Riemann, R., & Wolf, H. (2002). German observational study of adult twins (GOSAT): A multimodal investigation of personality, temperament and cognitive ability. *Twin Research, 5*(05), 372–375. https://doi.org/10.1375/twin.5.5.372

Spinath, F. M., & Unz, D. C. (2007). GÜte der diagnostischen Methoden [Quality of the diagnostic methods]. In M. John, & G. W. Maier (Eds.), *Eignungsdiagnostik in der Personalarbeit: Grundlagen, Methoden, Erfahrungen* (pp. 41–58). Symposion.

Spitzer, M. (2004). *Selbstbestimmen: Gehirnforschung und die Frage: Was sollen wir tun? [Self-determination: Brain research and the question: What should we do?].* Spektrum.

Spitzer, N. (2014). Emotionale Welterschließung: Die aktuelle Rolle von Emotionen und die kognitiven Therapien [Emotional access to the world: The current role of emotions and cognitive therapies]. *Zeitschrift Für Rational-Emotive & Kognitive Verhaltenstherapie, 25*, 7–24.

Stachl, C., & Bühner, M. (2018). Maschinelle Lernverfahren kontra Persönlichkeitstests: Big Data und Persönlichkeit [Machine learning methods versus personality tests: Big Data and personality]. *Personalführung, 5*, 22–26.

Stahl, G., Björkman, I., Farndale, E., Morris, S. S., Paauwe, J., Stiles, P., Trevor, J., & Wright, P. (2012). Six principles of effective global talent management. *MIT Sloan Management Review, 53*(2), 25–42.

Stanovich, K. E. (1999). *Who is rational? Studies of individual differences in reasoning.* Psychology Press.

Stanovich, K. E., & West, R. F. (1997). Reasoning Independently of Prior Belief and Individual Differences in Actively Open-Minded Thinking. *Journal of Educational Psychology,* 89(2), 342–357.

Stanovich, K. E., & West, R. F. (2000). Individual differences in reasoning: Implications for the rationality debate? *The Behavioral and Brain Sciences, 23*(5), 645–726. https://doi.org/10.1017/S0140525X00003435

Staub-Bernasconi, S. (20097). *Soziale Arbeit als Handlungswissenschaft. Soziale Arbeit auf dem Weg zu kritischer Professionalität.* UTB Haupt Verlag.

Staudinger, U. M., Lopez, D., & Baltes, P. B. (1997). The psychometric location of wisdom-related performance: Intelligence, personality, and more? *Personality & Social Psychology Bulletin, 23*, 1200–1214.

Steffens, N. K., Fonseca, M. A., Ryan, M. K., Rink, F. A., Stoker, J. I., & Nederveen Pieterse, A. (2018). How feedback about leadership potential impacts ambition, organizational commitment, and performance. *The Leadership Quarterly, 29*(6), 637–647. https://doi.org/10.1016/j.leaqua.2018.06.001

Steiner, D. D., & Gilliland, S. W. (2001). Procedural justice in personnel selection: International and cross-cultural perspectives. *International Journal of Selection and Assessment, 9*(1&2), 124–137. https://doi.org/10.1111/1468-2389.00169

Stierand, M., & Dörfler, V. (2016). The role of intuition in the creative process of expert chefs. *The Journal of Creative Behavior, 50*(3), 178–185. https://doi.org/10.1002/jocb.100

Stone, D. L., Stone-Romero, E. F., & Lukaszewski, K. M. (2007). The impact of cultural values on the acceptance and effectiveness of human resource management policies and practices. *Human Resource Management Review, 17*(2), 152–165. https://doi.org/10.1016/j.hrmr.2007.04.003

Strobel, A., Lammerskitten, E., & Glodek, R. (2010). Die Interview-Standards des Arbeitskreis Assessment Center e.V. – Entwicklung, Inhalte, Nutzen [The Interview Standards of the Working Group Assessment Center e.V. – Development, Contents, Benefits]. *Wirtschaftspsychologie, 2*, 26–31.

Stulle, K. P., & Thiel, S. (2018). Einführung in die psychologische Sprachanalyse [Introduction to psychological language analysis]. In K. P. Stulle (Ed.), *Psychologische Diagnostik durch Sprachanalyse (1–22)*. Springer Fachmedien Wiesbaden. https://doi.org/10.1007/978-3-658-18771-2_1

Suen, H.-Y., Chen, M. Y.-C., & Lu, S.-H. (2019). Does the use of synchrony and artificial intelligence in video interviews affect interview ratings and applicant attitudes? *Computers in Human Behavior, 98*, 93–101. https://doi.org/10.1016/j.chb.2019.04.012

Suen, H.-Y., Hung, K.-E., & Lin, C.-L. (2020). Intelligent video interview agent used to predict communication skill and perceived personality traits. *Human-centric Computing and Information Sciences, 10*(3), 1–12. https://doi.org/10.1186/s13673-020-0208-3

Svenson, O. (1996). Decision making and the search for fundamental psychological regularities. *What Can Be Learned from a Process Perspective? Organizational Behavior and Human Decision Processes, 65, 252–267.*

Tabesh, P., & Vera, D. M. (2020). Top managers' improvisational decision-making in crisis: A paradox perspective. *Management Decision*, 1–39. https://www.researchgate.net/publication/346361487_Top_managers'_improvisational_decision-making_in_crisis_a_paradox_perspective. doi.org/10.1108/MD-08-2020-1060

Tambe, P., Cappelli, P., & Yakubovich, V. (2019). Artificial intelligence in human resources management: Challenges and a path forward. *California Management Review, 61*(4), 1–28. https://doi.org/10.2139/ssrn.3263878

Taras, V., Rowney, J., & Steel, P. (2009). Half a century of measuring culture: Review of approaches, challenges, and limitations based on the analysis of 121 instruments for quantifying culture. *Journal of International Management, 15*(4), 357–373. https://doi.org/10.1016/j.intman.2008.08.005

Taylor, A., & Greve, H. R. (2006). Superman or the fantastic four? Knowledge combination and experience in innovative teams. *Academy of Management Journal, 49*(4), 723–740. https://doi.org/10.5465/amj.2006.22083029

Taylor, S. E., & Brown, J. (1988). Illusion and well-being: A social psychological perspective on mental health. *Psychological Bulletin, 103*(2), 193–210. doi:10.1037/0033-2909.103.2.193

Taylor, S. E., & Gollwitzer, P. M. (1995). Effects of mindset on positive illusions. *Journal of Personality and Social Psychology, 69*(2), 213–226. doi:10.1037/0022-3514.69.2.213

Tayo Tene, C. V., Yuriev, A., & Boiral, O. (2018). Adopting ISO management standards in Africa: Barriers and cultural challenges. In I. Heras-Saizarbitoria (Ed.), *ISO 9001, ISO 14001, and new management standards. measuring operations performance* (pp. 59–82). Springer. https://doi.org/10.1007/978-3-319-65675-5_4

Teetz, I. (2018). Künstliche Intelligenz im Recruiting [Artifical Intelligence in Recruiting]. In T. Petry, & W. Jäger (Eds.), *Digital HR. Smarte und agile Systeme, Prozesse und Strukturen im Personalmanagement* (pp. 225–240). Haufe.

Terpstra, D. E., & Rozell, E. J. (1997). Why some potentially effective staffing practices are seldom used. *Public Personnel Management, 26*(4), 483–495. https://doi.org/10.1177/009102609702600405

Thaler, R. H. (1991). *Quasi rational economics*. Sage.

Thaler, R. H. (Ed.). (1993). *Advances in behavioral finance*. Russell Sage Foundation.

Thaler, R. H. (2016). *Misbehaving: The making of behavioral economics*. W. W. Norton & Company.

Thaler, R., & Sunstein, C. R. (2008). *Nudge: Improving decisions about health, wealth and happiness*. Simon and Schuster.

Thaliath, B. (2012). *Die Strukturelle Intuition [The Structural Intuition]*. Humboldt-Universität zu Berlin. Philosophische Fakultät I.https://doi.org/10.18452/13526

Thiedemann. (2021). *The quality of personnel selection in different countries – Between scientific standards and the use of emotions*. Unpublished bachelor thesis, Leuphana University, Lueneburg.

Thielsch, M. T., Träumer, L., & Pytlik, L. (2012). E-recruiting and fairness: The applicant's point of view. *Information Technology and Management, 13*(2), 59–67. https://doi.org/10.1007/s10799-012-0117-x

Thompson, W. F., & Balkwill, -L.-L. (2010). Cross-cultural similarities and differences. In P. Juslin, & J. Sloboda (Eds.), *Handbook of music and emotion: theory, research, applications* Chapter 27 (pp. 755–788). Oxford University Press.

Thorndike, E. L. (1920). A constant error in psychological ratings. *The Journal of Applied Psychology, 4*(1), 25–29. https://doi.org/10.1037/h0071663

Thornton, G. C., & Gibbons, A. M. (2009). Validity of assessment centers for personnel selection. *Human Resource Management Review, 19*(3), 169–187. https://doi.org/10.1016/j.hrmr.2009.02.002

Thunnissen, M., Boselie, P., & Fruytier, B. (2013). A review of talent management. 'Infancy or adolescence? *The International Journal of Human Resource Management, 24*, 1744–1761. 10.1080/09585192.2013.777543

Thyer, B. A., & Pignotti, M. G. (2015). *Science and pseudoscience in social work practice*. Springer Publishing Company.

Tippins, N., Sackett, P., & Oswald, F. (2018). Principles for the validation and use of personnel selection procedures. *Industrial and Organizational Psychology, 11*(S1), 1–97. https://doi.org/10.1017/iop.2018.195

Tippins, N., Oswald, F., & McPhail, S. M. (2021). Scientific, legal, and ethical concerns about AI-based personnel selection tools: A call to action. *Personnel Assessment and Decisions, 7*(2), 1–22. https://doi.org/10.25035/pad.2021.02.001

Tokarski, K. O. (2008). *Ethik und Entrepreneurship. Eine theoretische sowie empirische Analyse junger Unternehmen im Rahmen einer Unternehmensethikforschung [Ethics and Entrepreneurship. A theoretical and empirical analysis of young companies in the context of business ethics research]*. Gabler Verlag.

Towfigh, E. V., & Glöckner, A. (2015). Entscheidungen zwischen „Intuition" und „Rationalität" [Decisions between „intuition" and „rationality"]. *Deutsche Richterzeitung, 7*(8), 14–17.

Treufetter, G. (2006). Die Stimme aus dem Nichts [Voice from Nowhere]. *Spiegel Heft, 15/2006*, 158–167.

Treufetter, G. (2009). *Intuition: Die Weisheit der Gefühle [Intuition: Die The wisdom of feelings]*. Rowohlt.

Trompenaars, F. (1993). *Riding the waves of culture: Understanding diversity in global business*. Irwin Professional.

Trompenaars, F., & Hampden-Turner, C. (1998). *Riding the waves of culture*. Nicholas Brealey Publishing.

Trope, Y., Liberman, N., & Wakslak, C. (2007). Construal levels and psychological distance: Effects on representation, prediction, evaluation, and behavior. *Journal of Consumer Psychology, 17*(2), 83–95. 10.1016/S1057-7408(07)70013-X

Trope, Y., & Liberman, N. (2010). Construal-level theory of psychological distance. *Psychological Review, 117*(2), 440–463. doi:10.1037/a0018963

Truxillo, D. M., Bauer, T. N., & Sanchez, R. J. (2001). Multiple dimensions of procedural justice: Longitudinal effects on selection system fairness and test-taking self-efficacy. *International Journal of Selection and Assessment, 9*, 336–349. doi:10.1111/1468-2389.00185

Truxillo, D. M., Bauer, T. N., Campion, M. A., & Paronto, M. E. (2002). Selection fairness information and applicant reactions: A longitudinal field study. *Journal of Applied Psychology, 87*, 1020–1031. doi:10.1037/0021-9010.87.6.1020

Tsusaka, M., Greiser, C., Krentz, M., & Reeves, M. (2019). T*he Business Imperative of Diversity*. BCG Henderson Institute. https://www.bcg.com/de-de/publications/2019/winning-the-20s-business-imperative-of-diversity.

Tubbs, N. (1996). Hegel's educational theory and practice. *British Journal of Educational Studies, 44*(2), 181–199. doi:10.2307/3121731

Tversky, A. (1977). Features of similarity. *Psychological Review, 84*(4), 327–352. https://doi.org/10.1037/0033-295X.84.4.327

Tversky, A., & Kahneman, D. (1973). Availability: A heuristic for judging frequency and probability. *Cognitive Psychology, 5*(2), 207–232. https://doi.org/10.1016/0010-0285(73)90033-9

Tversky, A., & Kahneman, D. (1974). Judgment under uncertainty: Heuristics and biases. *Science, 185*(4157), 1124–1131. https://doi.org/10.1126/science.185.4157.1124

Tversky, A., & Kahneman, D. (1981). The framing of decisions and the psychology of choice. *Science, 211*(4481), 453–458. https://doi.org/10.1126/science.7455683

Tversky, A., & Simonson, I. (1993). Context-dependent preferences. *Management Science, 39*(10), 1179–1189.

Tyng, C. M., Amin, H. U., Saad, M. N. M., & Malik, A. S. (2017). The Influences of Emotion on Learning and Memory. *Frontiers in Psychology, 8*, 1454. https://doi.org/10.3389/fpsyg.2017.01454

Uggerslev, K. L., Fassina, N. E., & Kraichy, D. (2012). Recruiting through the stages: A meta-analytic test of predictors of applicant attraction at different stages of the recruiting process. *Personnel Psychology, 65*(3), 597–660.

Ungethüm, J. (2021). Intrapersonal Emotion Regulation of Coaches in the Coaching Process. An Empirical Analysis. Unpublished master thesis, Leuphana University, Lueneburg

Uni Global Union Professionals & Managers. (2020). *Algorithmic Management. A Trade Union Guide*. https://www.google.com/search?client=firefox-b-d&q=uni_pm_algorithmic_management_guide_en

Vance, C. M., Groves, K. S., & Paik, Y. (2004). Measuring and building linear/nonlinear thinking style balance for enhanced performance. *Academy of Management Proceedings*, F1–F6.

Vance, C. M., Groves, K. S., Paik, Y., & Kindler, H. (2007). Understanding and measuring linear/nonlinear thinking style for enhanced management education and professional practice. *Academy of Management Learning and Education, 6*(2), 167–185.

van de Ven, A. H., & Johnson, P. E. (2006). Knowledge for theory and practice. *Academy of Management Review, 31*(4), 802–821. https://doi.org/10.5465/amr.2006.22527385

Van der Kolk, B. A. (2015). *The body keeps the score: Mind, brain and body in the transformation of trauma*. Penguin Books.

Van der Zee, K. I., Bakker, A. B., & Bakker, P. (2002). Why are structured interviews so rarely used in personnel selection? *The Journal of Applied Psychology, 87*(1), 176–184. https://doi.org/10.1037/0021-9010.87.1.176

Van Dyck, K., Frese, M., Baer, M., & Sonnentag, S. (2005). Organizational error management culture and its impact on performance: A two-study replication. *Journal of Applied Psychology Copyright 2005 by the American Psychological Association, 90*(6), 1228–1240.

Van Hemert, D. A., Poortinga, Y. H., & van de Vijver, F. J. R. (2007). Emotion and culture: A meta-analysis. *Cognition & Emotion, 21*(5), 913–943. https://doi.org/10.1080/02699930701339293

Van Riel, A. C., Ouwersloot, H., & Lemmink, J. (2006). Antecedents of effective decision making: A cognitive approach. *The IUP Journal of Managerial Economics, 6*(4), 7–28.

Van Vugt, M., & Schaller, M. (2008). Evolutionary approaches to group dynamics: An introduction. *Group Dynamics: Theory, Research, and Practice, 12*(1), 1–6. https://doi.org/10.1037/1089-2699.12.1.1

Vaughan, F. E. (1988): *Intuitiver leben: wie wir unser inneres Potenzial entwickeln können* [Living more intuitively: how to develop our inner potential]. Kösel. (American original edition 1979: Awakening Intuition. Anchor Press).

Vedder, G. (2019). Lookismus als Unconscious Bias. Der Einfluss des Aussehens auf Personalentscheidungen [Lookism as unconscious bias. The influence of appearance on personnel decisions]. In M. Domsch, D. D. Ladwig, & F. Weber (Eds.), *Vorurteile im Arbeitsleben. Unconscious Bias erkennen, vermeiden und abbauen [Prejudices in working life. Recognizing, avoiding and reducing unconscious bias]* (pp. 103–114). Springer Gabler.

Verhoeven, T. (2016). *Candidate Experience. Ansätze für eine positive erlebte Arbeit-gebermarke im Bewerbungsprozess und darüber hinaus*. Candidate Experience. Approaches for a positive employer brand experience in the application process and beyond Springer.

Verhoeven, T. (2020). Künstliche Intelligenz im Recruiting [Artifical Intelligence in Recruiting]. In T. Verhoeven (Ed.), *Digitalisierung im Recruiting: Wie sich Recruiting durch künstliche Intelligenz, Algorithmen und Bots verändert* (pp. 113–128). Springer Gabler.

Vermeer, M., & Neumann, C. (2008). *Praxishandbuch Indien*. Wie Sie Ihr Indiengeschäft erfolgreich managen. Kultur verstehen, Mitarbeiter führen, Verhandlungen gestalten [Practical Handbook India. How to successfully manage your business in India. Understanding culture, managing employees, shaping negotiations]. Gabler.

Virlics, A. (2013). Emotions in economic decision making: A multidisciplinary approach. *Procedia – Social and Behavioral Sciences, 92*, 1011–1015.

Viswesvaran, C., & Ones, D. S. (2017). Job performance: Assessment issues in personnel selection. In A. Evers, N. Anderson, & O. Voskuijl (Eds.), *The blackwell handbook of personnel selection* (pp. 354–375). Wiley Blackwell. https://doi.org/10.1002/9781405164221.ch16)

Vogler, P. S. (2012). Intuition als Metafähigkeit Interkulturellen Managements–zum Selbstverständnis Interkultureller Manager [Intuition as a meta-ability of intercultural management to the self-image of intercultural managers]. *Interculture Journal: Online Zeitschrift Für Interkulturelle Studien, 11*(19), 67–92. http://www.interculture-journal.com/index.php/icj/issue/view/30

Vohra, S., & Fenton-O'Creevy, M. (2014). Intuition, expertise and emotion in the decision making of investment bank traders. In M. Sinclair (Ed.), *Handbook of research methods on intuition* (pp. 88–98). Edward Elgar Publishing. https://doi.org/10.4337/9781782545996.00015

Vössing, H. (2011). *Emotions-Coaching: Der Einfluss von positiven und negativen Gefühlen auf Lebensqualität und Leistungsfähigkeit [Coaching of emotions:: The influence of positive and negative emotions on quality of life and performance]*. Books on Demand.

Wald, P. M., & Athanas, C. (2017). *Candidate Journey Studie 2017: Good Practices: Vom passenden Kandidaten zum loyalen Mitarbeiter [Candidate Journey Study 2017: Good Practices: From a suitable candidate to a loyal employee]*. https://www.metahr.de/wp-content/uploads/Candidate_Journey_Studie_2017.pdf

Wald, P. M., Athanas, C., & Schimek, T. (2018). Recruiting Experience Studie. Ein aktueller Blick auf die Welt der Recruiter [Recruiting Experience Study. An up-to-date look at the world of recruiters]. Studienreport Recruiting und Recruiter zwischen klassischen und digitalen Herausforderungen. Einblicke in Arbeitsweisen, Selbstverständnis, Tools und Entwicklungsfelder. https://www.metahr.de/studien/Recruiter_Experience_Studie_2018.pdf

Wang, Y., Highhouse, S., Lake, C. J., Petersen, N. L., & Rada, T. B. (2017). Meta-analytic investigations of the relation between intuition and analysis. *Journal of Behavioral Decision Making*, *30*(1), 15–25. First published online 2015 in Wiley Online Library (wileyonlinelibrary.com. 10.1002/bdm.1903

Walter, M. (2016). Grenzen wissenschaftlicher Personaldiagnostik und Einfluss subjektiver Faktoren bei angewandter Personalauswahl [Limits of scientific personnel diagnostics and influence of subjective factors in applied personnel selection]. In N. Gülke, & F. Ahlers (Eds.), *Personaldiagnostik: Potenzial- und Perspektivenvielfalt der Eignungsdiagnostik für Unternehmen und Mitarbeiter* (pp. 103–106). Cuvillier.

Wall, T. D., Michie, J., Patterson, M., Wood, S. J., Sheehan, M., Clegg, C. W., & West, M. (2004). On the validity of subjective measures of company performance. *Personnel Psychology*, *57*(1), 95–118. https://doi.org/10.1111/j.1744-6570.2004.tb02485.x

Wall, S., & Schellmann, H. (2021). *We tested AI interview tools. Here's what we found.* MIT Technology Review. https://www.technologyreview.com/2021/07/07/1027916/we-tested-ai-interview-tools/

Wang, R., Harper, F. M., & Zhu, H. (2020). Factors influencing perceived fairness in algorithmic decision-making: Algorithm outcomes, development procedures, and individual differences. In Proceedings of the 2020 CHI Conference on Human Factors in Computing Systems (pp. 1–14). https://doi.org/10.1145/3313831.3376813

Wason, P. C., & Evans, J. S. B. T. (1974). Dual processes in reasoning? *Cognition*, *3*(2), 141–154.

Watkins, L. M., & Johnston, L. (2000). Screening job applicants: The Impact of physical attractivity and applicants quality. *International Journal of Selection and Assessment*, *8*(2), 76–84. https://doi.org/10.1111/1468-2389.00135

Watson, D. (1989). Strangers' Ratings of the Five Robust Personality Factors. Evidence of a Surprising Convergence With Self-Report. *Journal of Personality and Social Psychology*, *57*(1), 120–128.

Webber, T. A., Critchfield, E. A., & Soble, J. R. (2020). Convergent, discriminant, and concurrent validity of nonmemory-based performance validity tests. *Assessment*, *27*(7), 1399–1415. https://doi.org/10.1177/1073191118804874

Webster, D. M., Richter, L., & Kruglanski, A. W. (1996). On leaping to conclusions when feeling tired: Mental fatigue effects on impressional primacy. *Journal of Experimental Social Psychology*, *32*(2), 181–195.

Wegwarth, O., Gaissmeier, W., & Gigerenzer, G. (2009). Smart strategies for doctors and doctors-in-training: Heuristics in medicine. *Medical Education*, *43*, 721–728. 10.1111/j.1365-2923.2009.03359.x

Weibler, J., & Küpers, W. (2008). Intelligente Entscheidungen in Organisationen – Zum Verhältnis von Kognition, Emotion und Intuition [Intelligent Decisions in Organizations – On the

Relationship between Cognition, Emotion and Intuition]. In A. Bortfeldt, J. Homberger, H. Kopfer, G. Pankratz, & R. Strangmeier (Eds.), *Intelligente Entscheidungsunterstützung – Aktuelle Herausforderungen und Lösungsansätze [Intelligent Decision Support – Current Challenges and Approaches]* (pp. 457–478). Gabler. Festschrift für Hermann Gehring

Weick, K. E., & Sutcliffe, K. M. (2001). *Managing the Unexpected. Assuring High Performance in an Age of Complexity*. Wiley.

Wei, L., & Kotte, J. (2007). *Geschäftlich in China. Verhaltensweisen verstehen und umsetzen [Doing Business in China. Understand and implement behaviors]*. Wissner.

Weiss, H., & Cropanzano, R. (1996). Affective Events Theory: A theoretical discussion of the structure, causes and consequences of affective experiences at work. In B. M. Staw, & L. L. Cummings (Hrsg.), *Research in Organizational Behavior: An annual series of analytical essays and critical reviews (Vol. 18)* (pp. 1–74). Elsevier Science/JAI Press.

Weitzel, T., Maier, C., Oehlhorn, C., Weinert, C., & Wirth, J. (2019). *Digitalisierung und Zukunft der Arbeit: Ausgewählte Ergebnisse der Recruiting Trends 2019 [Digitization and the Future of Work: Selected Results of the Recruiting Trends 2019]*. Otto-Friedrich-Universität Bamberg. https://www.uni-bamberg.de/fileadmin/uni/fakultaeten/wiai_lehrstuehle/isdl/Studien_2018_1_Active_Sourcing_Digital-Version_20180207_ff_A.pdf

Werth, L. (2004). Psychologie für die Wirtschaft. Grundlagen und Anwendungen [Psychology for Business. Fundamentals and Applications]. Spektrum.

Westhoff, K., & Flehmig, H. C. (2013). Empfehlungen zur Eignungsbeurteilung nach der DIN 33430 [Recommendations for assessment according to DIN 33430]. In W. Sarges (Ed.), *Management-Diagnostik* (4. ed., pp. 906–911). Hogrefe.

Weuster, A. (2004). *Personalauswahl: Anforderungsprofil, Bewerbersuche, Vorauswahl und Vorstellungsgespräch [Personnel selection: Task profile, applicant search, pre-selection and interview]*. Gabler. https://doi.org/10.1007/978-3-663-07661-2

Weuster, A. (2012). *Personalauswahl I: Internationale Forschungsergebnisse zu Anforderungsprofil, Bewerbersuche, Vorauswahl, Vorstellungsgespräch und Referenzen [Personnel selection I: International research results on task profile, applicant search, preselection, interview and references]*. Gabler. https://doi.org/10.1007/978-3-8349-3796-4

Wiesner, W. H., & Cronshaw, S. F. (1988). A meta-analytic investigation of the impact of interview format and degree of structure on the validity of the employment interview. *Journal of Occupational Psychology*1988, *61*(4), 275–290. https://doi.org/10.1111/j.2044-8325.1988.tb00467.x

Wild, K. W. (2014). *Intuition*. Cambridge University Press.

Williams, B. A., Brooks, C. F., & Shmargad, Y. (2018). How algorithms discriminate based on data they lack: Challenges, solutions, and policy implications. *Journal of Information Policy*, *8*(1), 78–115.

Winsborough, D., & Chamorro-Premuzic, T. (2016). Talent identification in the digital world: New talent signals and the future of HR assessment. *People and Strategy*, *39*(2), 28–31.

Withelm, P., & Gröben, S. (2005). Beobachtertraining – Ein Beispiel aus der DB GesundheitsService GmbH [Observer training – An example from DB HealthService]. In K. Sünderhauf, S. Stumpf, & S. Höft (Eds.), *Assessment Center: Von der Auftragsklärung bis zur Qualitätssicherung: Ein Handbuch von Praktikern für Praktiker* (pp. 181–195). Pabst Science Publishers.

Woehr, D. J., & Huffcutt, A. I. (1994). Rater training for performance appraisal: A quantitative review. *Journal of Occupational and Organizational Psychology*, 67(3), 189–205.

Wolfe, C. J., Christensen, B. E., & Vandervelde, S. D. (2020). Intuition versus Analytical Thinking and Impairment Testing. *Contemporary Accounting Research*, *37*(3), 1598–1621. https://doi.org/10.1111/1911-3846.12568

Woods, S. A., Ahmed, S., Nikolaou, I., Costa, A. C., & Anderson, N. R. (2020). Personnel selection in the digital age: A review of validity and applicant reactions, and future research challenges. *European Journal of Work and Organizational Psychology, 29*(1), 64–77.

Wottawa, H. (2013). Formalisierung der Urteilsbildung [Formalization of the formation of judgement]. In W. Sarges (Ed.), *Management-Diagnostik* (4. ed., pp. 911–917). Hogrefe.

Wottawa, H., & Hossiep, R. (1987). *Grundlagen psychologischer Diagnostik [Basics of psychological diagnostics]*. Hogrefe.

Wottawa, H., & Oenning, S. (2002). Von der Anforderungsanalyse zur Eignungsbeurteilung: Wie praktikabel ist die neue DIN 33430 bei der Bewerberauswahl? [From the requirement analysis to the suitability evaluation: How practicable is the new DIN 33430 with the applicant selection?]. *Wirtschaftspsychologie, 4*(3), 43–56.

Wübken, M., & Oswald, J. Schneider. (2013). Umgang mit diagnostischer Unsicherheit in der Hausarztpraxis [Dealing with diagnostic uncertainty in general practice]. *Zeitschrift Für Evidenz, Fortbildung Und Qualität Im Gesundheitswesen, 107*(9–10), 632–637.

Wübben, M., & Wangenheim, F. (2008). Instant customer base analysis: Managerial heuristics often "Get it Right". *Journal of Marketing, 72*(3), 82–93. doi:10.1509/jmkg.72.3.082. ISSN 0022–2429.

Wyatt, F. (1948). The self-experience of the psychotherapist. *Journal of Consulting Psychology, 12*(2), 82–87. https://doi.org/10.1037/h0060955

Xin, K. K., & Pearce, J. L. (1996). Guanxi: Connections as substitutes for formal institutional support. *Academy of Management Journal, 39*(6), 1641–1658. https://doi.org/10.5465/257072

Yamagishi, T., Jin, N., & Miller, A. S. (2002). In-group bias and culture of collectivism. *Asian Journal of Social Psychology, 1*(3), 315–328. doi:10.1111/1467-839X.00020

Yates, J. F., Veinott, E. S., & Patalano, A. L. (2003). Hard decisions, bad decisions: On decision quality and decision aiding. In S. L. Schneider & J. C. Shanteau (Eds.), *Emerging perspectives on judgment and decision research* (pp. 13–63). Cambridge University Press.

Yerkes, R. M., & Dodson, J. D. (1908). The relation of strength of stimulus to rapidity of habit-formation. *Journal of Comparative Neurology & Psychology, 18*, 459–482. https://doi.org/10.1002/cne.920180503

Youyou, W., Kosinski, M., & Stillwell, D. (2015). Computer-based personality judgments are more accurate than those made by humans. *Proceedings of the National Academy of Sciences of the United States of America, 112*(4), 1036–1040. https://doi.org/10.1073/pnas.1418680112

Zajonc, R. B. (1968). Attitudinal effects of mere exposure. *Journal of Personality and Social Psychology, 9*(2,Pt.2), 1–27. https://doi.org/10.1037/h0025848.

Zajonc, R. B. (1980). Feeling and thinking: Preferences need no inferences. *American Psychologist, 35*, 151–175.

Zajonc, R. B. & Markus, H. (1982). Affective and Cognitive Factors in Preferences. *Journal of Consumer Research*, 9(2), 123–131, https://doi.org/10.1086/208905

Zárate, M. A., Stoever, C. J., MacLin, M. K., & Arms-Chavez, C. J. (2008). Neurocognitive underpinnings of face perception: Further evidence of distinct person and group perception processes. *Journal of Personality and Social Psychology, 94*(1), 108–115. https://doi.org/10.1037/0022-3514.94.1.108

Zeelenberg, M., Nelissen, R., & Pieters, R. (2008). Emotion, motivation and decision making: A feeling is for doing approach. In H. Plessner, C. Betsch, & T. Betsch (Eds.), *Intuition in judgment and decision making* (pp. 173–189). Lawrence Erlbaum Associates.

Zeidan, F., Martucci, K. T., Kraft, R. A., McHaffie, J. G., & Coghill, R. C. (2014). Neural correlates of mindfulness meditation-related anxiety relief. *Social Cognitive and Affective Neuroscience, 9*(6), 751–759. https://doi.org/10.1093/scan/nst041

Zeuch, A. (2003). *Training professioneller intuitiver Selbstregulation: Theorie, Empirie und Praxis [Training of professional intuitive self-regulation: theory, empiricism and practice]* [Doctoral Dissertation]. Eberhard-Karls-Universität Tübingen.

Zeuch, A. (2006). *Am Rande des Chaos: Intuition als selbstorganisierende Intelligenz [On the edge of chaos: intuition as self-organizing intelligence].* https://web.archive.org/web/20061229123404/http://www.psychophysik.com/html/re-0831-chaos.html

Zeuch, A. (2008). Improvisation, Intuition und Datensurfen [Improvisation, intuition and data surfing]. In A. Ferstl, M. Scholz, & C. Thiesen (Eds.), *Praktische Erlebnispädagogik. Menschen stärken für globale Verantwortung* (pp. 56–63). ZIEL.

Zeuch, A. (2011). Intuition ist viel mehr, als man denkt. Die Grenzen unseres Verstandes sind die Pforten zu mehr nachhaltigem Erfolg [Intuition is much more than you think. The limits of our mind are the gates to more sustainable success]. In F. Narjes, & N. Feltz (Eds.), *Schriftenreihe des Career Center der Universität Hamburg: Vol. 1. Fishing for careers: Karrieremanagement zwischen Planung und Gelegenheiten* (pp. 39–49). Budrich.

Ziegler, M., & Bühner, M. (2012). *Grundlagen der Psychologischen Diagnostik* [*Fundamentals of Psychological Diagnostics*]. Springer.

Zweig, K. (2019). *Ein Algorithmus hat kein Taktgefühl: Wo künstliche Intelligenz sich irrt, warum uns das betrifft und was wir dagegen tun können [An algorithm has no sense of tact: Where artificial intelligence is wrong, why it affects us and what we can do about it].* Heyne.

100 Worte. (2019). 100 Worte {[100 words]. Psychological AI. https://www.100worte.de/.

123test. (2022). IQ test. https://www.123test.com/iq-test/

Index

https://doi.org/10.1515/9783110980967-012

www.ingramcontent.com/pod-product-compliance
Lightning Source LLC
Chambersburg PA
CBHW081212220326
41598CB00037B/6760